SALVATION ARMY
YEAR BOOK
2011

**Dedicated to the glory of God
in whose name and by whose grace
the work described in this volume
has been accomplished**

Annual reports in this edition mostly cover the period 1 May 2009 to 30 April 2010. The staff lists and details of centres of work are generally accurate to 30 September 2010.

Statistics are those for the year ending 31 December 2009.

Officers and lay staff serving in countries other than their own are counted in the statistics of the territory/command in which they are serving.

The 'Biographical Information' section is as accurate as possible at the time of going to press.

THE
SALVATION ARMY
YEAR BOOK

2011

INTERNATIONAL
MISSION STATEMENT

The Salvation Army, an international movement, is an
evangelical part of the universal Christian Church.
Its message is based on the Bible. Its ministry is motivated by
love for God. Its mission is to preach the gospel of Jesus Christ
and meet human needs in his name without discrimination.

THE SALVATION ARMY
INTERNATIONAL HEADQUARTERS
101 QUEEN VICTORIA STREET, LONDON EC4V 4EH, UNITED KINGDOM

First published 2010

Copyright © 2010 The General of The Salvation Army

ISBN 978-0-85412-829-7

Editor: Major Trevor Howes

Assistant Editor: Lieut-Colonel Jayne Roberts

Desktop publishing support: Nathan Sigauke

Cover design: Berni Georges

SALVATION BOOKS

Published by Salvation Books
The Salvation Army International Headquarters
101 Queen Victoria Street, London EC4V 4EH, United Kingdom

Printed in the United Kingdom by Page Bros Ltd, Norwich NR6 6SA
using paper from sustainable sources

Contents

(Continued on next page)

Pressing Onward Valiantly

Foreword by General Shaw Clifton
International Leader of The Salvation Army

IT IS a privilege to introduce and endorse once again another edition of *The Salvation Army Year Book*. My heart is moved as I read the reports and as I scan the statistical data. I am inspired also by the countless names within these pages of faithful Salvationists living and working in 121 countries. They do so, often in lonely places and in unheralded ways, pressing onward valiantly in the cause of Jesus Christ and in the service of humanity.

The human bedrock of The Salvation Army is to be found not so much among the ranks of its senior leaders – though these serve well and tirelessly – but rather among the vast host of Salvation Army soldiers found in innumerable cities, towns and villages in every continent.

General Shaw Clifton and Commissioner Helen Clifton

It is their lives which impact their neighbours, their work colleagues, their fellow students, their wider family circle. It is their service and their prayerfulness which typify those expressions of Salvationism which bring us closest to people.

Becoming a soldier of The Salvation Army is a wonderful thing. It provides an opportunity to take a stand for the things of Christ and to make oneself available for the benefit of others.

The Army senses strongly the ongoing impulse of Almighty God to be at the disposal of the neediest in our communities. Recent months have seen us responding in the name of Christ to many natural disasters, not least to the dreadful earthquake in Haiti and those shortly after in Chile and Indonesia.

Commissioner Helen Clifton and I, with my private secretary Major Richard Gaudion, had visited Port-au-Prince, Haiti, only six weeks before the earthquake struck. We found the Salvationists of Haiti to be gracious and godly in every way. The immense response to their plight, which was seen from every corner of the Salvation Army community, has been a very great blessing and a source of inspiration. We need ongoing funding and personnel for a task that will take years to complete.

It is impossible to work in the field of spiritual endeavour or of social relief without facing up also to issues of social justice. The world continues to contain too many people who experience repression and disadvantage, who continue to be exploited and abused. The Salvation Army's calling under God cannot be understood fully without insight into our heart for justice.

This is typified in the work of our International Social Justice Commission based close to the United Nations headquarters in New York. It is also expressed in countless local initiatives to put right those wrongs that are found in local communities, wrongs such as deprivation of food and water, lack of shelter, inadequate access to education, the sale of pornography, and the exploitation of women and children for sexual purposes. We continue to seek wisdom from God in formulating and giving effect to strategies in these complex matters.

As you read this year book I thank you for your interest and pray that God will bless you in all things. I record my warm thanks to the editor, Major Trevor Howes, and all who have contributed to this latest edition.

International Headquarters,
London

Come Join Our Army

Major Ed Forster* reports on the USA's soldier recruitment campaign

UNDER the leadership of the USA Commissioners Conference, a three-year national soldier recruitment campaign was launched in July 2007 entitled Come Join Our Army. Its basic premise is totally related to the command of Jesus: 'Go into the world and make disciples.'

All four USA territories participated, with events and promotion of the initiative being held in every division and corps.

Additionally, all the territorial newspapers and the Army's national magazine, *The War Cry*, contained major features and news reports on the campaign.

Variety

In his opening statement at the 'Come Join Our Army' launch in Washington, DC, then National Commander Commissioner Israel L. Gaither, said: 'The jewel of America is its people. And the

Some of the senior and junior soldiers enrolled in USA Eastern Territory

Left: These Sudanese sisters were enrolled as junior soldiers at Omaha Citadel, Nebraska (USA Central)

Below right: New soldiers at Oakland, California (USA Western)

history that we share is a tapestry rich in variety. The Salvation Army is indelibly woven into the fabric of our nation, offering a collective "Heart to God and Hand to Man", meeting the most basic of human needs since 1880.

'Every Salvation Army soldier is committed to doing the most good. We are privileged to minister to men, women and children, no matter what their circumstances. And this would not happen if it were not for the absolute commitment of each soldier.

Mission

'As Salvationists, we believe that the one true God, who still speaks through the Bible, has called us to the mission of redemption and reformation of people and places in this nation and around the world. Each

soldier must be strongly committed to God for this grand purpose.'

The commissioner went on to say that more soldiers are needed in this great Army of salvation and that there is a role that committed believers can play in changing conditions and circumstances for people on the margins of society. He urged: 'Come join our Army and make your mark upon the world!'

The campaign added 18,865 senior and junior soldiers to the Army's rolls – and the spirit of the campaign is ongoing.

Majors Steve and Betzann Carroll, the corps officers at Cambridge, Massachusetts, said that when new soldiers got involved in their corps through the campaign, or by other means, they simply 'plugged them into ministry and they let God do the calling'. In recent

4

years, through the Holy Spirit's leading the Carolls have sent eight of their soldiers to officer training.

Spanish language services in Des Plaines, Illinois, and other parts of the country have been effective in reaching many new families. Several other cultural communities are being blessed by the Army's invitation to join.

Some of the gains in soldiership were accomplished through expansion into new places. An example was USA Western Territory's opening in the town of Amo in the Marshall Islands.

Another important tool has been Salvation Army publications telling the stories of how people met the Army. One man reported that he found a book about William Booth at the dump. He took it home and read it. The book inspired him to attend Army meetings and become a soldier; he is now training to be an officer.

Commissioner Max Feener (Territorial Commander, USA Southern) praised God that there were more than 48,000 registered seekers in his territory in a single year. His encouragement for Salvationists everywhere is that they become 'intentional in bringing as many seekers as possible to soldiership in the Army'.

* Major Forster is National Editor-in-Chief and Literary Secretary, USA

Christ Amid the Chaos

by Lieut-Colonel Mike Caffull*

GOD'S promise found in Romans 8:28 has been proved to many people on many occasions: 'We know that in all things God works for the good of those who love him, who have been called according to his purpose' (*NIV*). But in the midst of natural disasters, this truth could be very difficult to believe.

In a few short months at the start of 2010, the international Salvation Army had to deal with several major disasters – typhoons and earthquakes in Taiwan, The Philippines, Indonesia, Chile and Haiti.

With many people perishing and thousands left homeless and without vital needs for basic survival, the devastation was immense.

Spiritual support

Incredibly, within hours of a massive 7.0 Richter earthquake hitting Haiti, the Salvationists at divisional headquarters in Port-au-Prince, despite being made homeless themselves and left without an office, began to serve the people, providing them with physical, emotional and spiritual support.

An estimated 230,000 people died in that earthquake, hundreds of thousands were injured and up to 1.5 million left homeless.

International emergency workers, deployed by International Headquarters and some territories in the United States, were soon on their way to the scene, but due to travel difficulties caused by the earthquake were unable to get there until four days after the event.

Medical aid

This left local Salvationists, themselves traumatically affected by the devastation, to offer the initial assistance of food, water and medical aid to the many people who came to the Salvation Army compound for help.

Since then, many people have travelled to Haiti to assist the massive emergency response. The main task has been to look after 20,000-plus people who have inhabited temporary shelter next to the Army's compound. United Nations representatives gave The Salvation Army the responsibility to manage this facility.

An international strategy conference on the earthquake

Right: A new convert prays during Sunday morning worship, held outdoors five days after the Haiti earthquake hit; more than 1,000 people attended

Below: Temporary homes fill the soccer stadium in Port-au-Prince

disaster, held in London (3-5 March 2010) at the request of General Shaw Clifton, saw 50 international leaders and their teams plan for long-term interventions by The Salvation Army and commit funds to the rebuilding process in Haiti.

A Holy Spirit-filled session given over completely to prayer was powerful as delegates poured out their hearts in prayer for the people of Haiti and those seeking to assist them.

After the Haiti earthquake millions of meals were served, and many thousands of people were given medical treatment and provided with much-needed sheter. But one of the amazing stories to come out of the island concerns Port-au-Prince Central Corps.

Conversions

The Salvation Army hall was badly damaged in the disaster yet, just five days after the earthquake hit, more than 1,000 people attended Sunday morning worship and some 100 conversions were recorded. Many of these were subsequently enrolled as recruits in soldiership classes.

The relief work continues in Haiti, and many wonderful cases of God breaking through and blessing the Army's work are also being reported. Despite the devastation, still God's love is displayed in many sacrificial hours of work carried out by local Salvationists and international responders. Through their continuing and effective ministry, God's Kingdom has grown in Haiti.

Christ is amid the chaos.

* At the time of writing Lieut-Colonel Caffull was Under-Secretary for Programme Resources and Acting International Emergency Services Coordinator, IHQ

Living Right While Righting Wrongs

Commissioner M. Christine MacMillan* writes about the International Social Justice Commission

SINCE the mid-1970s, leaders of the richest nations have met under the umbrella of the G8. In the midst of meeting to address 'common approaches to urgent challenges' facing the world, protestors also gather to chant their dissent. Today, the global resistance movement is the main orchestrator that gathers people from around the world to raise their voices.

The issues on the protestors' agenda are important. They reach out to economic, social and environmental concerns. Regrettably, the demonstrations have tended to be marred by violence.

In The Salvation Army's early days its Founder, William Booth, devised an effective strategy for dealing with issues facing England in his time. His seven principles articulated in the book, *In Darkest England and the Way*

Out, came to the conclusion that whatever remedy was prescribed 'must do good without doing evil at the same time'.

Booth's assertion reflects the biblical mandate to 'overcome evil with good' (Romans 12:21).

As the leader of the International Social Justice Commission, my challenge is to help frame a strategy for these times. How can we combine our collective wisdom with our individual visions to raise our voices in pursuit of social justice? Let me suggest seven principles.

Bend your bias for the poor and vulnerable: Our vision for salvation reaches beyond the personal to the social. Our agenda for holiness includes providing safe water, schools, houses and health care. How then should we dream, work and pray?

Embrace 'social order' as an ally: Government policy and equitable social structures are intended to benefit the people they serve. How can we influence decision-makers to 'seek justice for all'?

Demonstrate global citizenship while surrendering self-interest to the common good: Followers of Jesus belong to God's human worldwide family. We are mandated to love our neighbours –

beyond our own backyard. What does it mean in practice to be global citizens – individually and organisationally?

Protect the right of religious freedom: Dark expressions of injustice lurk in communities and countries where people are not free to examine their beliefs and change their religious convictions. Do we work where the lack of religious freedom restricts our mission?

Distinguish between 'help for the moment' and the 'capacity for sustained living': Alleviating the present-tense pain of poverty is admirable. Implementing strategies that address the causes of poverty creating the pain is transforming. Are we satisfied with the current allocation of our resources – the 'admirable' and 'transforming' mix?

Spend The Salvation Army's social capital to influence public policy: The Salvation Army's strong brand in the market place is our cultural currency in the countries where we serve. The time has come to spend the influence we have worked so hard to establish. Who will lead the way?

Advocate strategically for human rights and equity for all: The vulnerable – the trafficked, the abused, the exploited, the unemployed, the falsely accused, the marginalised – all need advocates. In our different contexts, who will take responsibility to empower the voiceless?

To 'overcome evil with good' while pursing the mission of social justice needs honest evaluation of our present practices and a bold resolve to engage the risks of constructing new pathways – together.

The Salvation Army historically has found its daredevil passion through the prophetic Scriptures. We act not without listening and hear not without contemplation.

The outcries of injustice stimulate a response from within God's people.

However, the foundational platform that gives us a confidence to act is God's love for justice. This attribute of God is an essential, not a thrown-in extra.

The prophetic hope of living within a new world begins with 'living right' principles. The formation of answers through deep penetrating questions explores new possibilities in 'righting wrongs'.

* Commissioner MacMillan is the Director, International Social Justice Commission, IHQ

The daughter of a sex-worker receives a Christmas gift at a Salvation Army drop-in centre in Sangli (India Western) where an anti-trafficking programme is funded by the United Kingdom Territory

WHAT IS THE SALVATION ARMY?

RAISED up by God, The Salvation Army is a worldwide evangelical Christian church with its own distinctive governance and practice. The Army's doctrine follows the mainstream of Christian belief and its articles of faith emphasise God's saving purposes.

Its religious and charitable objects are 'the advancement of the Christian religion ... and, pursuant thereto, the advancement of education, the relief of poverty, and other charitable objects beneficial to society or the community of mankind as a whole'.*

The Army (then known as The Christian Mission) was founded in London, England, in 1865 by William and Catherine Booth and has spread to many parts of the world.

The rapid deployment of the first Salvationists was aided by the adoption of a quasi-military command structure in 1878 when the title 'The Salvation Army' was brought into use. A similarly practical organisation today enables resources to be equally flexible.

Responding to a recurrent theme in Christianity which sees the Church engaged in spiritual warfare, The Salvation Army has used to advantage certain soldierly features such as uniforms, flags and ranks to identify, inspire and regulate its endeavours.

Evangelistic and social enterprises are maintained, under the authority of the General, by full-time officers and employees, as well as soldiers who give service in their free time. The Army also benefits from the support of many adherents and friends, including those who serve on advisory boards.

Leadership in The Salvation Army is provided by commissioned and ordained officers who are recognised as fully accredited ministers of religion.

Salvationists commit to a disciplined life of Christian moral standards, compassion toward others, and witnessing for Christ.

From its earliest days The Salvation Army has accorded women equal opportunities, every rank and service being open to them, and from childhood the young are encouraged to love and serve God.

Raised to evangelise, The Salvation Army spontaneously embarked on schemes for the social betterment of the poor. Such concerns develop, wherever the Army operates, in practical, skilled and cost-effective ways. Evolving social services meet endemic needs and specific crises worldwide. Highly trained staff are employed in up-to-date facilities.

The need for modernisation and longer-term development is under continual review. Increasingly The Salvation Army's policy and its indigenous membership allow it to cooperate with international relief agencies and governments alike.

The Army's partnership with both private and public philanthropy will continue to bring comfort to the needy, while the proclamation of God's redemptive love revealed in Jesus Christ offers individuals and communities the opportunity to know spiritual fulfilment here on earth and a place in Christ's eternal Kingdom.

*Section 3 of the Salvation Army Act 1980

11

THE DOCTRINES OF THE SALVATION ARMY

We believe that the Scriptures of the Old and New Testaments were given by inspiration of God, and that they only constitute the Divine rule of Christian faith and practice.

We believe that there is only one God, who is infinitely perfect, the Creator, Preserver and Governor of all things, and who is the only proper object of religious worship.

We believe that there are three persons in the Godhead – the Father, the Son and the Holy Ghost, undivided in essence and co-equal in power and glory.

We believe that in the person of Jesus Christ the Divine and human natures are united, so that he is truly and properly God and truly and properly man.

We believe that our first parents were created in a state of innocency, but by their disobedience they lost their purity and happiness, and that in consequence of their fall all men have become sinners, totally depraved, and as such are justly exposed to the wrath of God.

We believe that the Lord Jesus Christ has by his suffering and death made an atonement for the whole world so that whosoever will may be saved.

We believe that repentance towards God, faith in our Lord Jesus Christ, and regeneration by the Holy Spirit, are necessary to salvation.

We believe that we are justified by grace through faith in our Lord Jesus Christ and that he that believeth hath the witness in himself.

We believe that continuance in a state of salvation depends upon continued obedient faith in Christ.

We believe that it is the privilege of all believers to be wholly sanctified, and that their whole spirit and soul and body may be preserved blameless unto the coming of our Lord Jesus Christ.

We believe in the immortality of the soul; in the resurrection of the body; in the general judgment at the end of the world; in the eternal happiness of the righteous; and in the endless punishment of the wicked.

FOUNDERS OF THE SALVATION ARMY

William Booth

The Founder of The Salvation Army and its first General was born in Nottingham on 10 April 1829 and promoted to Glory from Hadley Wood on 20 August 1912. He lived to establish Salvation Army work in 58 countries and colonies and travelled extensively, holding salvation meetings. In his later years he was received in audience by emperors, kings and presidents. Among his many books, *In Darkest England and the Way Out* was the most notable; it became the blueprint of all The Salvation Army's social schemes. It was reprinted in 1970.

Catherine Booth

The Army Mother was born in Ashbourne, Derbyshire, on 17 January 1829 and promoted to Glory from Clacton-on-Sea on 4 October 1890. As Catherine Mumford, she married William in 1855. A great teacher and preacher, she addressed large public meetings in Britain with far-reaching results, despite ill health. Her writings include *Female Ministry* and *Aggressive Christianity*.

William Bramwell Booth

The eldest son of the Founder, and his Chief of the Staff from 1880 to 1912, Bramwell (as he was known) was born on 8 March 1856. He was largely responsible for the development of The Salvation Army. His teaching of the doctrine of holiness and his councils with officers and young people were of incalculable value. In 1882 he married Captain Florence Soper (organiser of the Women's Social Work and inaugurator of the Home League), who was promoted to Glory on 10 June 1957. During his time as General (1912-1929), impetus was given to missionary work. Published books include *Echoes and Memories* and *These Fifty Years*. He was appointed a Companion of Honour shortly before his promotion to Glory from Hadley Wood on 16 June 1929.

GLOSSARY OF SALVATION ARMY TERMS

Adherent: A member of The Salvation Army who has not made a commitment to soldiership.

Advisory Board: A group of influential citizens who, believing in the Army's programme of spiritual, moral and physical rehabilitation and amelioration, assist in promoting and supporting Army projects.

'Blood and Fire': The Army's motto; refers to the blood of Jesus Christ and the fire of the Holy Spirit.

Cadet: A Salvationist who is in training for officership.

Candidate: A soldier who has been accepted for officer training.

Chief of the Staff: The officer second in command of the Army throughout the world.

Chief Secretary: The officer second in command of the Army in a territory.

Citadel: A hall used for worship.

Colours: The tricolour flag of the Army. Its colours symbolise the blood of Jesus Christ (red), the fire of the Holy Spirit (yellow) and the purity of God (blue).

Command: A smaller type of territory, directed by an officer commanding.

Command leaders: An officer commanding and spouse in their joint role of sharing spiritual leadership and ministry, providing pastoral care and exemplifying the working partnership of officer couples.

Commission: A document conferring authority upon an officer, or upon an unpaid local officer, eg, secretary, treasurer, bandmaster, etc.

Congress: Central gatherings often held annually and attended by most officers and many soldiers of a territory, command, region or division.

Corps: A Salvation Army unit established for the preaching of the gospel and to provide Christian-motivated service in the community.

Corps Cadet: A young Salvationist who undertakes a course of study and practical training in a corps, with a view to becoming efficient in Salvation Army service.

Corps Sergeant-Major: The chief local officer for public work who assists the corps officer with meetings and usually takes command in his/her absence.

Dedication Service: The public presentation of infants to the Lord. This differs from christening or infant baptism in that the main emphasis is upon specific vows made by the parents concerning the child's upbringing.

Division: A number of corps grouped together under the direction of a divisional commander (may also include social service centres and programmes), operating within a territory or command.

Divisional Commander: The officer in charge of the Army in a division.

Envoy: A Salvationist whose duty it is to visit corps, societies and outposts, for the purpose of conducting meetings. An envoy may be appointed in charge of any such unit.

General: The officer elected to the supreme command of the Army throughout the world. All appointments are made, and all regulations issued, under the General's authority (see under High Council – p 22).

General Secretary: The officer second in charge of the Army in a command (or, in some territories, a large division).

Halfway House: A centre for the rehabilitation of alcoholics or parolees (USA).

Harbour Light Centre: A reclamation centre, usually located in inner city areas.

High Council: See p 22

Home League: See p 34

International Headquarters (IHQ): The offices in which the business connected with the command of the worldwide Army is transacted.

International Secretary: A position at IHQ with responsibility for the oversight and coordination of the work in a specific geographical zone or functional category, and for advising the General on zonal and worldwide issues and policies.

Junior Soldier: A boy or girl who, having accepted Jesus as their saviour, has signed the junior soldier's promise and become a Salvationist.

League of Mercy: Salvationists who visit prisons, hospitals and needy homes, in their own time, bringing the gospel and rendering practical aid (see p 35).

Local Officer: A soldier appointed to a position of responsibility and authority in the corps; carries out the duties of the appointment without being separated from regular employment or receiving remuneration from the Army.

Medical Fellowship: See p 35

Mercy Seat or Penitent Form: A bench provided as a place where people can kneel to pray, seeking salvation or sanctification, or making a special consecration to God's will and service. The mercy seat is usually situated between the platform and main area of Army halls as a focal point to remind all of God's reconciling and redeeming presence.

Officer: A Salvationist who has left secular concerns at God's call and has been trained, commissioned and ordained to service and leadership. An officer is a recognised minister of religion.

Officer Commanding: The officer in charge of the Army in a command.

Order of Distinguished Auxiliary Service: See p 37

Order of the Founder: See p 36

Outpost: A locality in which Army work is carried out and where it is hoped a society or corps will develop.

Pastoral Care Council: Established in each corps for the care of soldiers, etc, and maintenance of the membership rolls. Previously called the census board.

Promotion to Glory: The Army's description of the death of Salvationists.

Ranks of Officers: Lieutenant, captain, major, lieut-colonel, colonel, commissioner, General.

Red Shield: A symbol identifying a wide range of Army social and emergency services.

Red Shield Appeal: A financial appeal to the general public; also known as the Annual Appeal in some countries.

Red Shield Centre: A club for military personnel.

Salvation: The work of grace which God accomplishes in a repentant person whose trust is in Christ as Saviour, forgiving sin, giving meaning and new direction to life, and strength to live as God desires. The deeper experience of this grace, known as holiness or sanctification, is the outcome of wholehearted commitment to God and enables the living of a Christlike life.

Self-Denial Appeal: An annual effort by Salvationists and friends to raise funds for the Army's worldwide operations.

Sergeant: A local officer appointed for specific duty, usually in a corps.

Society: A company of soldiers who work together regularly in a district, without an officer, but with the approval of the divisional commander.

Soldier: A converted person at least 14 years of age who has, with the approval of the pastoral care council, been enrolled as a member of The Salvation Army after signing the Soldier's Covenant.

Soldier's Covenant: The statement of beliefs and promises which every intending soldier is required to sign before enrolment. Previously called 'Articles of War'.

Territorial Commander: The officer in command of the Army in a territory.

Territorial leaders: A territorial commander and spouse in their joint role of sharing spiritual leadership and ministry, providing pastoral care and exemplifying the working partnership of officer couples. The chief secretary is the second-in-command of the territory.

Territory: A country, part of a country or several countries combined, in which Salvation Army work is organised under a territorial commander.

Young People's Sergeant-Major: A local officer responsible for young people's work in a corps, under the commanding officer.

Chronological Table of Important Events in Salvation Army History

1829 Catherine Mumford (later Mrs Booth, 'the Army Mother') born at Ashbourne, Derbyshire (17 Jan); William Booth born at Nottingham (10 Apr).

1844 William Booth converted.

1846 Catherine Mumford converted.

1855 Marriage of William Booth and Catherine Mumford at Stockwell New Chapel, London (16 Jun).

1856 William Bramwell Booth (the Founder's eldest son and second General of the Army) born in Halifax (8 Mar).

1858 William Booth ordained as Methodist minister (27 May). (Accepted on probation 1854.)

1859 *Female Teaching*, Mrs Booth's first pamphlet, published (Dec).

1860 Mrs Booth's first public address (27 May, Whit Sunday).

1865 **Rev William Booth began work in East London** (2 Jul); The Christian Mission, founded; Eveline (Evangeline) Cory Booth (fourth General) born in London (25 Dec).

1867 First Headquarters (Eastern Star) opened in Whitechapel Road, London.

1868 *The East London Evangelist* – later (1870) *The Christian Mission Magazine* and (1879) *The Salvationist* – published (Oct).

1874 Christian Mission work commenced in **Wales** (15 Nov).

1875 *Rules and Doctrines of The Christian Mission* published.

1876 *Revival Music* published (Jan).

1878 First use of the term 'Salvation Army' – in small appeal folder (May); 'The Christian Mission' became **'The Salvation Army'**, and the Rev William Booth became known as the General; deed poll executed, thus establishing the doctrines and principles of The Salvation Army (Aug); first corps flag presented by Mrs Booth at Coventry (28-30 Sep); *Orders and Regulations for The Salvation Army* issued (Oct); brass instruments first used.

1879 First corps in **Scotland** opened (24 Mar) and **Channel Islands** (14 Aug); cadets first trained; introduction of uniform; first corps band formed in Consett; issue No 1 of *The War Cry* published (27 Dec).

1880 First training home opened, at Hackney, London; first contingent of SA officers landed in the **United States of America** (10 Mar); SA work commenced in **Ireland** (7 May); children's meetings commenced at Blyth (30 Jul); SA work extended to **Australia** (5 Sep).

1881 Work began in **France** (13 Mar); *The Little Soldier* (subsequently *The Young Soldier*) issued (27 Aug); *The Doctrines and Disciplines of The Salvation Army* prepared for use at training homes for Salvation Army officers; Headquarters removed to Queen Victoria Street, London (8 Sep).

1882 The Founder's first visit to France (Mar); former London Orphan Asylum opened as Clapton Congress Hall and National Training Barracks (13 May); work began in **Canada** (21 May), **India** (19 Sep), **Switzerland** (22 Dec) and **Sweden** (28 Dec).

1883 Work begun in **Sri Lanka** (26 Jan), **South Africa** (4 Mar), **New Zealand** (1 Apr), **Isle of Man** (17 Jun) and **Pakistan** (then a part of India); first prison-gate home opened in Melbourne, Australia (8 Dec); *The Doctrines and Disciplines of The Salvation Army* published in a public edition.

1884 Women's Social Work inaugurated; *The Soldier's Guide* published (Apr); work began in **St Helena** (5 May); *The Salvation Army Band Journal* issued (Aug); *All the World* issued (Nov).

1885 Commencement of the Family Tracing Service, known as Mrs Booth's Enquiry Bureau; *Orders and Regulations for Divisional Officers* published (10 Jun); *The Doctrines of The Salvation Army* published; Purity Agitation launched; Criminal Law Amendment Act became law on 14 Aug; trial (began 23 Oct) and acquittal of Bramwell Booth – charged, with W. T. Stead, in connection with the 'Maiden Tribute' campaign.

1886 Work begun in **Newfoundland** (1 Feb);

first International Congress in London (28 May-4 Jun); *The Musical Salvationist* issued (Jul); first Self-Denial Week (4-11 Sep); first slum corps opened at Walworth, London, by 'Mother' Webb (20 Sep); work began in **Germany** (14 Nov); *Orders and Regulations for Field Officers* published; the Founder first visited the United States and Canada.

1887 Work began in **Italy** (20 Feb), **Denmark** (8 May), **Netherlands** (8 May) and **Jamaica** (16 Dec); the Founder's first visit to Denmark, Sweden and Norway.

1888 Young people's work organised throughout Great Britain; first food depot opened, in Limehouse, London (Jan); work began in **Norway** (22 Jan); first junior soldiers' brass band (Clapton); the Army Mother's last public address at City Temple, London (21 Jun).

1889 Work begun in **Belgium** (5 May) and **Finland** (8 Nov); *The Deliverer* published (Jul).

1890 Work began in **Argentina** (1 Jan); *Orders and Regulations for Soldiers of The Salvation Army* issued (Aug); the Army Mother promoted to Glory (4 Oct); *In Darkest England and the Way Out*, by the Founder, published (Oct); work began in **Uruguay** (16 Nov); banking department opened (registered as The Salvation Army Bank, 1891; Reliance Bank Ltd, 28 Dec 1900).

1891 The Founder publicly signed 'Darkest England' (now The Salvation Army Social Work) Trust Deed (30 Jan); £108,000 subscribed for 'Darkest England' scheme (Feb); Land and Industrial Colony, Hadleigh, Essex, established (2 May); International Staff Band inaugurated (Oct); work began in **Zimbabwe** (21 Nov) and **Zululand** (22 Nov); the Founder's first visit to South Africa, Australia, New Zealand and India; the charter of The Methodist and General Assurance Society acquired.

1892 Eastbourne (UK) verdict against Salvationists quashed in the High Court of Justice (27 Jan); Band of Love inaugurated; League of Mercy begun in Canada (Dec).

1893 Grace-Before-Meat scheme instituted; *The Officer* issued (Jan).

1894 Second International Congress (Jul); work began in **Hawaiian Islands** (13

Sep) and **Java** (now part of **Indonesia**) (24 Nov); naval and military league (later red shield services) established (Nov); Swiss Supreme Court granted religious rights to SA (Dec).

1895 Work began in **British Guiana** (now **Guyana**) (24 Apr), **Iceland** (12 May), **Japan** (4 Sep) and **Gibraltar** (until 1968).

1896 Young people's legion (Jan) and corps cadet brigades (Feb) inaugurated; work began in **Bermuda** (12 Jan) and **Malta** (25 Jul until 1972); first SA exhibition, Agricultural Hall, London (Aug).

1897 First united young people's meetings (later termed 'councils') (14 Mar); first International Social Council in London (Sep); first SA hospital founded at Nagercoil, India (Dec).

1898 *Orders and Regulations for Social Officers* published; work began in **Barbados** (30 Apr) and **Alaska**; first united corps cadet camp at Hadleigh (Whitsun).

1899 First bandsmen's councils, Clapton (10 Dec).

1901 Work began in **Trinidad** (7 Aug).

1902 Work begun in **St Lucia** (Sep) and **Grenada**.

1903 Migration Department inaugurated (became Reliance World Travel Ltd, 1981; closed 31 May 2001); work began in **Antigua**.

1904 Third International Congress (Jun-Jul); Founder received by King Edward VII at Buckingham Palace (24 Jun); Founder's first motor campaign (Aug); work began in **Panama** (Dec).

1905 The Founder campaigned in the Holy Land, Australia and New Zealand (Mar-Jun); first emigrant ship chartered by SA sailed for Canada (26 Apr); opening of International Staff Lodge (later College, now International College for Officers) (11 May); work began in **St Vincent** (Aug). Freedom of London conferred on the Founder (26 Oct); Freedom of Nottingham conferred on the Founder (6 Nov).

1906 *The YP* (later *The Warrior*, then *Vanguard*) and *The Salvation Army Year Book* issued; Freedom of Kirkcaldy conferred on the Founder (16 Apr).

1907 Anti-Suicide Bureau established (Jan); Home League inaugurated (28 Jan); *The Bandsman and Songster* (later *The*

Musician) issued (6 Apr); honorary degree of DCL, Oxford, conferred on the Founder (26 Jun); work began in **Costa Rica** (5 Jul).

1908 Work began in **Korea** (Oct).

1909 Leprosy work commenced in **Java** (now part of **Indonesia**) (15 Jan); SA work began in **Chile** (Oct).

1910 Work began in **Peru**, **Paraguay** and **Sumatra** (now part of **Indonesia**).

1912 Founder's last public appearance, in Royal Albert Hall, London (9 May); **General William Booth promoted to Glory** (20 Aug); **William Bramwell Booth appointed General** (21 Aug).

1913 Inauguration of life-saving scouts (21 Jul); work began in **Celebes** (now part of **Indonesia**) (15 Sep) and **Russia** (until 1923).

1914 Fourth International Congress (Jun).

1915 Work began in **British Honduras** (now **Belize**) (Jun) and **Burma** (now **Myanmar**); life-saving guards inaugurated (17 Nov).

1916 Work began in **China** (Jan until 1951), in **St Kitts** and in **Portuguese East Africa** (now **Mozambique**) (officially recognised 1923).

1917 Work began in **Virgin Islands** (USA) (Apr); chums inaugurated (23 Jun); Order of the Founder instituted (20 Aug).

1918 Work commenced in **Cuba** (Jul).

1919 Work began in **Czechoslovakia** (19 Sep until 1950).

1920 Work began in **Nigeria** (15 Nov) and **Bolivia** (Dec).

1921 Work began in **Kenya** (Apr); sunbeams inaugurated (3 Nov).

1922 Work began in **Zambia** (1 Feb), **Brazil** (1 Aug) and **Ghana** (Aug); publication of a second *Handbook of Salvation Army Doctrine*.

1923 Work began in **Latvia** (until 1939).

1924 Work began in **Hungary** (24 Apr until 1950), in **Surinam** (10 Oct) and **The Færoes** (23 Oct).

1927 Work began in **Austria** (27 May), **Estonia** (31 Dec until 1940) and **Curacao** (until 1980); first International Young People's Staff Councils (May-Jun).

1928 General Bramwell Booth's last public appearance – the stonelaying of the International (William Booth Memorial) Training College (now William Booth College), Denmark Hill, London (10 May).

1929 First High Council (8 Jan-13 Feb); **Comr Edward J. Higgins elected General**; General Bramwell Booth promoted to Glory (16 Jun); Army work began in **Colombia** (until 1965).

1930 Inception of goodwill league; Order of the Silver Star (now Fellowship of the Silver Star) inaugurated (in USA, extended to other lands in 1936); work began in **Hong Kong**; Commissioners' Conference held in London (Nov).

1931 Work began in **Uganda** and the **Bahamas** (May); The Salvation Army Act 1931 received royal assent (Jul).

1932 Work began in **Namibia** (until 1939).

1933 Work began in **Yugoslavia** (15 Feb until 1948), Devil's Island, **French Guiana** (1 Aug until closing of the penal settlement in 1952) and **Tanzania** (29 Oct).

1934 Work began in **Algeria** (10 Jun until 1970); second High Council elected Commander Evangeline Booth General (3 Sep); work began in **Congo (Kinshasa)** (14 Oct); **General Evangeline Booth took command of The Salvation Army** (11 Nov).

1935 Work began in **Singapore** (28 May).

1936 Work began in **Egypt** (until 1949).

1937 Work began in **Congo (Brazzaville)** (Mar), **The Philippines** (6 Jun) and **Mexico** (Oct).

1938 Torchbearer group movement inaugurated (Jan); *All the World* re-issued (Jan); work spread from Singapore to **Malaysia**.

1939 Third High Council elected Comr George Lyndon Carpenter General (24 Aug); **General George Lyndon Carpenter took command of The Salvation Army** (1 Nov).

1941 Order of Distinguished Auxiliary Service instituted (24 Feb); International Headquarters destroyed in London Blitz (10 May).

1943 Inauguration of The Salvation Army Medical Fellowship (16 Feb) (SA Nurses' Fellowship until 1987).

1944 Service of thanksgiving to mark centenary of conversion of William Booth (in 1844) held in St Paul's Cathedral, London (2 Jun).

1946 Fourth High Council elected Comr Albert Orsborn General (9 May); **General Albert Orsborn took command of The Salvation Army** (21 Jun).

1948 First Army worldwide broadcast (28 Apr).

1950 Work began in **Haiti** (5 Feb); first TV broadcast by a General of The Salvation Army; official constitution of students' fellowship; first International Youth Congress held in London (10-23 Aug); reopening of Staff College (later International College for Officers) (10 Oct).

1954 Fifth High Council elected Comr Wilfred Kitching General (11 May); **General Wilfred Kitching took command of The Salvation Army** (1 Jul).

1956 Work began in Port Moresby, **Papua New Guinea** (31 Aug); first International Corps Cadet Congress (19-31 Jul).

1959 Over-60 clubs inaugurated (Oct).

1962 Work began in **Puerto Rico** (Feb).

1963 Sixth High Council elected Comr Frederick Coutts General (1 Oct); Queen Elizabeth the Queen Mother declared International Headquarters open (13 Nov); **General Frederick Coutts took command of The Salvation Army** (23 Nov).

1965 Queen Elizabeth II attended the International Centenary commencement (24 Jun); Founders' Day Service held in Westminster Abbey, London (2 Jul); work re-established in **Taiwan** (pioneered 1928) (Oct).

1967 Work began in **Malawi** (13 Nov).

1969 Seventh High Council elected Comr Erik Wickberg General (23 Jul); *The Salvation Army Handbook of Doctrine* new edition published (Aug); **General Erik Wickberg took command of The Salvation Army** (21 Sep); work began in **Lesotho.**

1970 Cyclone relief operations in East Pakistan (later **Bangladesh**) (25 Nov) lead to start of work in 1971.

1971 Work began in **Spain** (23 Jul) and **Portugal** (25 Jul).

1972 Work began in **Venezuela** (30 Jun).

1973 Work began in **Fiji** (14 Nov).

1974 Eighth High Council elected Comr Clarence Wiseman General (13 May); **General Clarence Wiseman took com-mand of The Salvation Army** (6 Jul).

1976 Work began in **Guatemala** (Jun); **Mexico and Central America Territory** (now **Latin America North Territory** and **Mexico Territory**) formed (1 Oct).

1977 Ninth High Council elected Comr

Arnold Brown General (5 May); **General Arnold Brown took command of The Salvation Army** (5 Jul).

1978 Fifth International Congress (Jun-Jul), with opening ceremony attended by HRH the Prince of Wales.

1979 The Salvation Army Boys' Adventure Corps (SABAC) launched (21 Jan).

1980 Inauguration of International Staff Songsters (8 Mar); The Salvation Army Act 1980 received royal assent (1 Aug); work began in **French Guiana** (1 Oct).

1981 Tenth High Council elected Comr Jarl Wahlström General (23 Oct); **General Jarl Wahlström took command of The Salvation Army** (14 Dec).

1984 International Conference of Leaders held in Berlin, West Germany (May).

1985 Work began in **Colombia** (21 Apr) and **Marshall Islands** (1 Jun); second International Youth Congress (Jul) held in Macomb, Illinois, USA; work began in **Angola** (4 Oct) and **Ecuador** (30 Oct).

1986 Work began in **Tonga** (9 Jan); *Salvationist* first issued (15 Mar); 11th High Council elected Comr Eva Burrows General (2 May); **General Eva Burrows took command of The Salvation Army** (9 Jul); International Development Conference held at Sunbury Court, London (Sep).

1988 Work began in **Liberia** (1 May); International Conference of Leaders held in Lake Arrowhead, California, USA (Sep).

1989 Work began in **El Salvador** (1 Apr).

1990 Work began in **East Germany** (Mar), **Czechoslovakia** (May), **Hungary** (Jun) and re-established in **Latvia** (Nov); sixth International Congress held in London (Jun-Jul); **United Kingdom Territory** established (1 Nov).

1991 Restructuring of **International Head-quarters** as an entity separate from UK Territory (1 Feb); work reopened in **Russia** (6 Jul); International Conference of Leaders held in London (Jul-Aug).

1992 Opening of new **USA National Headquarters** building in Alexandria, Virginia (3 May).

1993 The 12th High Council elected Comr Bramwell H. Tillsley General (28 Apr); **General Bramwell H. Tillsley took command of The Salvation Army** (9 Jul); work began in **Micronesia**.

1994 First International Literary and Publications Conference held at Alexandria,

Virginia, USA (Apr); General Bramwell H. Tillsley resigned from office (18 May); 13th High Council elected Comr Paul A. Rader General (23 Jul); **General Paul A. Rader took command of The Salvation Army immediately**; work began in **Guam**.

1995 International Conference of Leaders held in Hong Kong (Apr); all married women officers granted rank in their own right (1 May); work began in **Dominican Republic** (1 Jul); work reopened in **Estonia** (14 Aug); following relief and development programmes, work began in **Rwanda** (5 Nov).

1996 Work began in **Sabah (East Malaysia)** (Mar); first meeting of International Spiritual Life Commission (Jul).

1997 International Youth Forum held in Cape Town, South Africa (Jan); first-ever congress held in Russia/CIS; Salvation Army leaders in Southern Africa signed commitment to reconciliation for past stand on apartheid; work began in **Botswana** (20 Nov).

1998 International Conference of Leaders held in Melbourne, Australia (Mar), receives report of International Spiritual Life Commission; publication of a fourth Handbook of Doctrine entitled *Salvation Story* (Mar); International Commission on Officership opened in London (Oct).

1999 International Education Symposium held in London (Mar); work began in **Romania** (May); 14th High Council elected Comr John Gowans General (15 May); **General John Gowans took command of The Salvation Army** (23 Jul).

2000 International Commission on Officership closed and subsequent Officership Survey carried out (Mar-May); work began in **Macau** (25 Mar); The Salvation Army registered as a denomination in **Sweden** (10 Mar); International Conference of Leaders held in Atlanta, Georgia, USA (Jun); seventh International Congress held in Atlanta, Georgia, USA (28 Jun-2 Jul) (first held outside UK); work began in **Honduras** (23 Nov).

2001 International Conference for Training Principals held in London (Mar); International Theology and Ethics Symposium held in Winnipeg, Canada (Jun); International Music Ministries Forum held in London (Jul);

International Poverty Summit held on the Internet and Lotus Notes Intranet (Nov 2001-Feb 2002).

2002 The 15th High Council elected Comr John Larsson General (6 Sep); **General John Larsson took command of The Salvation Army** (13 Nov).

2004 International Conference of Leaders held in New Jersey, USA (29 Apr-7 May); International Music and Other Creative Ministries Forum (MOSAIC) held in Toronto, Canada (Jun); New International Headquarters building at 101 Queen Victoria Street, London, opened by Her Royal Highness, The Princess Royal (9 Nov); IHQ Emergency Services coordinates disaster relief work after Indian Ocean tsunami struck (26 Dec).

2005 Eastern Europe Command redesignated Eastern Europe Territory; Singapore, Malaysia and Myanmar Command redesignated Singapore, Malaysia and Myanmar Territory (both 1 Mar); International Literary and Publications Conference held at Alexandria, Virginia, USA (Apr); European Youth Congress held in Prague, Czech Republic (4-8 Aug); All-Africa Congress held in Harare, Zimbabwe (24-28 Aug); work in **Lithuania** officially recognised by IHQ, and Germany Territory redesignated Germany and Lithuania Territory (Sep); 'Project Warsaw' launched to begin Army's work in **Poland** (23-25 Sep); East Africa Territory redesignated Kenya Territory, with Uganda Region given command status (1 Nov)

2006 The 16th High Council elected Comr Shaw Clifton General (28 Jan); **General Shaw Clifton took command of The Salvation Army** (2 Apr); Salvation Army Scouts and Guides World Jamboree held in Almere, Netherlands (Aug); 2nd International Theology and Ethics Symposium held in Johannesburg, South Africa (Aug)

2007 Website for Office of the General launched (Feb); first of General's pastoral letters to soldiers dispatched electronically (15 Mar); first International Conference of Personnel Secretaries held in London (27 May-3 Jun); International Social Justice Commission established (1 Jul), headed by an International Director for Social

Justice; work began in **Burundi** (5 Aug) and **Greece** (1 Oct)

2008   Work recommenced in **Namibia** (3 Jan); new opening began in **Mali** (7 Feb); ICO renamed International College for Officers and Centre for Spiritual Life Development (Jul); first officers appointed to **Kuwait** (1 Aug); work began in

Mongolia (13 Oct); first International Women Leader Development Programme held at Sunbury Court, UK (18 Nov-6 Dec)

2009   Official opening of work in **Nepal** (15 Apr); largest-ever assembly of SA leaders at International Conference of Leaders held in London, UK (7-13 Jul)

SIGNIFICANT EVENTS 2009-2010

2009
September
IHQ: ICO and CSLD in London hosted first-ever International Prayer Leaders Gathering. (11-18 Sep)

Australia Eastern: 'Brengle Create' – first Brengle Institute for creative Salvationists – held at Collaroy Centre, Sydney (21-25 Sep)

November
South America West: Centenary celebrations in Chile led by the General and Commissioner Helen Clifton (17-23 Nov)

2010
January
Africa Zone: Work began in **Sierra Leone**, under supervision of Liberia (1 Jan)

USA Eastern: Celebrations marking 125th anniversary of Samuel Logan Brengle's experience of sanctification, led by the General in Boston, Massachusetts (9 Jan)

Caribbean Territory: SA emergency services responded to 7.0 magnitude earthquake in Haiti (12 Jan)

February
South America West: Centenary celebrations in Peru (8-12 Feb)

South America West: SA emergency services responded to 8.8 magnitude earthquake and tsunami in Chile (27 Feb)

March
Americas and Caribbean Zone: Salvation Army work expanded to 120 countries as work commenced in **Nicaragua** (1 Mar)

IHQ: International Strategy Conference on

Haiti earthquake disaster held in London (3-5 Mar)

April
IHQ: Retirement salute to first woman Chief of the Staff, Commissioner Robin Dunster (24 Apr)

May
IHQ: Commissioners Barry and Sue Swanson took up office as Chief of the Staff and World Secretary for Women's Ministries (1 May)

May
South Asia Zone: Work begun in **United Arab Emirates**, under IHQ supervision (1 Jun)

July
Sweden and Latvia: Stockholm hosted 'Raised Up' World Youth Convention (15-18 Jul)

Korea: The General opened The Salvation Army Building in Seoul, constructed to celebrate the 2008 centenary of SA work on Korean peninsula (24 Jul)

August
Pakistan: SA emergency teams started relief work after country hit by its worst-ever floods (3 Aug)

September
New Zealand, Fiji and Tonga: SA emergency services in New Zealand mobilised after 7.1 magnitude earthquake struck South Island (4 Sep)

Korea: The Army's first building in Mongolia opened (9 Sep)

THE HIGH COUNCIL

THE High Council was originally established by William Booth in 1904 as a safeguard to allow the removal from office of an incumbent General who had become, for whatever reason, unfit to continue to exercise oversight, direction and control of The Salvation Army. Should such an allegation be made and receive significant support from officers of the rank of commissioner, a High Council would be called to decide upon the matter and to appoint a successor should the General be found unfit.

The Founder intended, however, that the normal method of appointment would be for the General in office to select his or her successor, but only one General – Bramwell Booth in 1912 – was ever selected in this way.

By November 1928, Bramwell Booth had been absent from International Headquarters for seven months on account of illness, and a High Council was called. The 63 members, being all the commissioners on active service and certain territorial commanders, gathered at Sunbury Court near London on 8 January 1929 and eventually voted that the General, then aged 73, was 'unfit on the ground of ill-health' to continue in office. On 13 February 1929 the High Council elected Commissioner Edward Higgins as the Army's third General.

Subsequently, a commissioners' conference agreed to three major constitutional reforms later passed into law by the British Parliament as the Salvation Army Act 1931, namely:

i. the abolition of the General's right to nominate his or her successor, and the substitution of the election of every General by a High Council;

ii. the fixing of an age limit for the retirement of the General;

iii. the creation of a trustee company to hold the properties and other capital assets of the Army, in place of the sole trusteeship of the General.

The High Council is currently constituted under provisions of the Salvation Army Act 1980 as amended by deeds of variation executed in 1995 and 2005.

Since 1929, High Councils have been held in 1934 (electing General Evangeline Booth), 1939 (General Carpenter), 1946 (General Orsborn), 1954 (General Kitching), 1963 (General Coutts), 1969 (General Wickberg), 1974 (General Wiseman), 1977 (General Brown), 1981 (General Wahlström), 1986 (General Burrows), 1993 (General Tillsley), 1994 (General Rader), 1999 (General Gowans), 2002 (General Larsson) and 2006 (General Clifton). The next was scheduled to convene in January 2011.

High Councils are normally called by the Chief of the Staff and have usually met at Sunbury Court but can meet anywhere in the United Kingdom. Since 1995 the High Council has been composed of all active commissioners except the spouse of the General, and all territorial commanders. All TPWMs now attend.

GENERALS ELECTED BY A HIGH COUNCIL

The place and date at the beginning of an entry denote the corps from which the General entered Salvation Army service and the year

Edward J. Higgins

Reading, UK, 1882. General (1929-34). b 26 Nov 1864; pG 14 Dec 1947. Served in corps and divisional work, British Territory; at the International Training Garrison, as CS, USA; as Asst Foreign Secretary, IHQ; Brit Comr (1911-19); Chief of the Staff (1919-29). CBE. Author of *Stewards of God*, *Personal Holiness*, etc. m Capt Catherine Price, 1888; pG 1952.

Evangeline Booth

General (1934-39). b 25 Dec 1865; pG 17 Jul 1950. Fourth daughter of the Founder, at 21 years of age she commanded Marylebone Corps, its Great Western Hall being the centre of spectacular evangelistic work. As Field Commissioner this experience was used to advantage throughout Great Britain (1888-91). The Founder appointed her to train cadets in London (1891-96); then as TC, Canada (1896-1904); Commander of The Salvation Army in the United States of America (1904-34). Author of *Toward a Better World*; *Songs of the Evangel*, etc.

George L. Carpenter

Raymond Terrace, Australia, 1892. General (1939-46). b 20 Jun 1872; pG 9 Apr 1948. Appointments included 18 years in Australia in property, training and literary work; at IHQ (1911-27) for most part with General Bramwell Booth as Literary Secretary; further service in Australia (1927-33), including CS, Australia Eastern; as TC, South America East (1933-37); TC, Canada (1937-39). Author of *Keep the Trumpets Sounding*; *Banners and Adventures*, etc. m Ens Minnie Rowell, 1899; pG 1960. Author of *Notable Officers of The Salvation Army*; *Women of the Flag*, etc.

Albert Orsborn

Clapton, UK, 1905. General (1946-54). b 4 Sep 1886; pG 4 Feb 1967. Served as corps officer and in divisional work in British Territory; as Chief Side Officer at ITC (1925-33); CS, New Zealand (1933-36); TC, Scotland & Ireland (1936-40); Brit Comr (1940-46). CBE, 1943. Writer of many well-known Army songs. Author of *The House of My Pilgrimage*, etc. m Capt Evalina Barker, 1909; pG 1942. m Maj Evelyn Berry, 1944; pG 1945. m Comr Mrs Phillis Taylor (née Higgins), 1947; pG 1986.

Wilfred Kitching

New Barnet, UK, 1914. General (1954-63). b 22 Aug 1893; pG 15 Dec 1977. Served in British Territory corps, divisional and NHQ appointments, then as CS, Australia Southern (1946-48); TC, Sweden (1948-51); Brit Comr (1951-54). Composer of many distinctively Salvationist musical works. Hon LLD (Yonsei, Seoul, Rep of Korea), 1961; CBE, 1964. Author of *Soldier of Salvation* (1963) and *A Goodly Heritage* (autobiography, 1967). m Adjt Kathleen Bristow (Penge, 1916), 1929; pG 1982.

23

Frederick Coutts

Batley, UK, 1920. General (1963-69). b 21 Sep 1899; pG 6 Feb 1986. Served in British Territory in divisional work (1921-25) and as corps officer (1925-35);

for 18 years in Literary Dept, IHQ; writer of *International Company Orders* (1935-46); Editor of *The Officers' Review* (1947-53); Asst to Literary Secretary (1947-52); Literary Secretary (1952-53); Training Principal, ITC (1953-57); TC, Australia Eastern (1957-63). Author of *The Call to Holiness* (1957); *Essentials of Christian Experience* (1969); *The Better Fight* (1973); *No Discharge in this War* (1975), *Bread for My Neighbour* (1978); *The Splendour of Holiness* (1983), etc. Order of Cultural Merit (Rep of Korea), 1966; Hon Litt D (Chung Ang, Rep of Korea), 1966; CBE, 1967; Hon DD (Aberdeen), 1981. m Lt Bessie Lee, BSc, 1925; pG 1967. m Comr Olive Gatrall (Thornton Heath, 1925), 1970, pG 1997.

Erik Wickberg

Bern 2, Switzerland, 1925. General (1969-74). b 6 Jul 1904; pG 26 Apr 1996. Served as corps officer in Scotland; in Germany as Training (Education) Officer, and Private Secretary to CS and TC (1926-34); at IHQ as Private Secretary to IS and Asst to Under Secretary for Europe (1934-39); in Sweden as IHQ Liaison Officer (1939-46) and DC, Uppsala (1946-48); as CS, Switzerland, (1948-53); CS, Sweden (1953-57); TC, Germany (1957-61); Chief of the Staff (1961-69). Commander, Order of Vasa, 1970; Order of Moo Koong Wha (Rep of Korea), 1970; Hon LLD (Rep of Korea), 1970; Grand Cross of Merit, Fed Rep of Germany, 1971; King's Gold Medal (Grand Cross) (Sweden), 1980. Author of *Inkallad* (*God's Conscript*) (autobiography, Sweden, 1978) and *Uppdraget* (*The Charge – My Way to Preaching*) (1990). m Ens Frieda de

Groot (Berne 1, Switz, 1922), 1929; pG 1930. m Capt Margarete Dietrich (Hamburg 3, Ger, 1928), 1932; pG 1976. m Major Eivor Lindberg (Norrköping 1, Swdn, 1946), 1977.

Clarence Wiseman

Guelph, Ont, Canada, 1927. General (1974-77). b 19 Jun 1907; pG 4 May 1985. Served in Canada as corps officer and in editorial work; chaplain with Canadian forces overseas (1940-43); Senior Representative, Canadian Red Shield Services Overseas (1943-45); back in Canada as divisional commander (1945-54), Field Secretary (1954-57) and CS (1957-60); as TC, East Africa (1960-62); Training Principal, ITC (1962-67); TC, Canada & Bermuda (1967-74). Order of Canada, 1976, Hon LLD, Hon DD (Yonsei, Seoul, Rep of Korea). Author of *A Burning in My Bones* (1980) and *The Desert Road to Glory* (1980). m Capt Jane Kelly (Danforth, Ont, Can, 1927), 1932; pG 1993. Author of *Earth's Common Clay*; *Bridging the Year*; *Watching Daily*.

Arnold Brown

Belleville, Canada, 1935. General (1977-81). b 13 Dec 1913; pG 26 Jun 2002. Served in Canada in corps, editorial, public relations and youth work (1935-64); as Secretary for Public Relations at IHQ (1964-69); Chief of the Staff (1969-74); TC, Canada & Bermuda (1974-77). MIPR, Hon LDH (Asbury, USA); Freeman, City of London; Hon DD (Olivet, USA), 1981; Officer, Order of Canada, 1981. Author of *What Hath God Wrought?*; *The Gate and the Light* (1984); *Yin – The Mountain the Wind Blew Here* (1988); *With Christ at the Table* (1991); *Occupied Manger – Unoccupied Tomb* (1994). m Lt Jean Barclay (Montreal Cit, Can, 1938), 1939. Author of *Excursions in Thought* (1981).

Generals of The Salvation Army

Jarl Wahlström

Helsinki 1, Finland, 1938. General (1981-86). b 9 Jul 1918. pG 3 Dec 1999. Served in corps, youth and divisional work in Finland; as Second World War chaplain to Finnish armed forces; in Finland as a divisional commander (1960-63), Training Principal, Secretary of Music Dept (1963-68) and CS (1968-72); as CS, Canada & Bermuda (1972-76); TC, Finland (1976-81); TC, Sweden (1981); Knight, Order of the Lion of Finland, 1964; Order of Civil Merit, Mugunghwa Medal (Rep of Korea), 1983; Hon DHL (W Illinois), 1985; Paul Harris Fellow of Rotary International, 1987; Commander, Order of the White Rose of Finland, 1989. Author of *A Traveller's Song* and *A Pilgrim's Song* (autobiography, Finnish/ Swedish, 1989). m Lt Maire Nyberg (Helsinki 1, 1944).

Eva Burrows

Fortitude Valley, Qld, Australia Eastern, 1951. General (1986-93). b 15 Sep 1929. Appointed to corps in British Territory, before post-graduate studies; served at Howard Institute, Zimbabwe (1952-67); Head of Teacher Training (1965), Vice-Principal (1965-67); as Principal, Usher Institute (1967-70); Asst Principal, ICO (1970-74), Principal (1974-75); Leader, WSS (GBI) (1975-77); TC, Sri Lanka (1977-79); TC, Scotland (1979-82); TC, Australia Southern (1982-86). BA (Qld); M Ed (Sydney); Hon Dr of Liberal Arts (Ehwa Univ, Seoul, Rep of Korea), 1988; Hon LLD (Asbury, USA), 1988; Paul Harris Fellow of Rotary International, 1990; Hon DST (Houghton), 1992; Hon DD (Olivet Nazarene Univ), 1993; Hon Dr Philosophy (Qld), 1993; Hon Dr of University (Griffith Univ), 1994; Companion of Order of Australia, 1994; Living Legacy Award from Women's International Center, USA, 1996.

Bramwell Tillsley

Kitchener, Ont, Canada, with wife née Maude Pitcher, 1956. General (1993-94). b 18 Aug 1931. Served in Canada in corps, youth, training college and divisional appointments, including Training Principal (1974-77), Provincial Commander in Newfoundland (1977-79) and DC, Metro Toronto (1979-81); as Training Principal, ITC (1981-85); CS, USA Southern (1985-89); TC, Australia Southern (1989-91); Chief of the Staff (1991-93). Resigned from the office of General in 1994. BA University of Western Ontario. Has written extensively for SA periodicals. Author of *Life in the Spirit*; *This Mind in You*; *Life More Abundant*; *Manpower for the Master*.

Paul Rader

Cincinnati Cit, USA Eastern, w wife née Frances Kay Fuller, BA (Asbury), Hon DD (Asbury Theol Seminary) 1995, Hon LHD (Greenville) 1997, 1961. General (1994-99). b 14 Mar 1934. Served in corps prior to transfer to Korea in 1962; in Korea in training work (1962-73), as Training Principal (1973), Education Secretary (1974-76), Asst Chief Secretary (1976-77) and CS (1977-84); in USA Eastern as Training Principal (1984-87), DC, Eastern Pennsylvania (1987-89) and CS (1989); as TC, USA Western (1989-94). BA, BD (Asbury); MTh (Southern Baptist Seminary); D Miss (Fuller Theological Seminary); Hon LLD (Asbury); 1984 elected to board of trustees of Asbury College; 1989 elected Paul Harris Fellow of Rotary International; Hon DD (Asbury Theol Seminary), 1995; Hon LHD (Greenville), 1997; Hon DD (Roberts Wesleyan), 1998.

John Gowans

Grangetown, UK, 1955. General (1999-2002). b 13 Nov 1934. Served in British Territory as corps officer, divisional youth secretary, National Stewardship Secretary and divisional commander; as Chief Secretary, France (1977-81); in USA Western as Programme Secretary (1981-85) and DC, Southern California (1985-86); TC, France (1986-93); TC, Australia Eastern & Papua New Guinea (1993-97); TC, UK (1997-99). Paul Harris Fellow of Rotary International; Hon DLitt (Yonsei, Seoul, Rep of Korea); Freedom of the City of London (2000). Songwriter. Author of *O Lord!* series of poetry books and *There's a Boy Here* (autobiography, 2002). Co-author with John Larsson of 10 musicals. m Lt Gisèle Bonhotal (Paris Central, France, 1955) 1957.

John Larsson

Upper Norwood, UK, 1957. General (2002-06). b 2 Apr 38. Served in corps; at ITC; as TYS (Scotland Territory); NYS (British Territory); CS, South America West (1980-84); Principal, ITC (1984-88); Assistant to Chief of the Staff for UK Administrative Planning, IHQ (1988-1990); TC, UK (1990-93); TC, New Zealand & Fiji (1993-96); TC, Sweden & Latvia (1996-99);

Chief of the Staff (1999-2002). BD (London). Author of *Doctrine without Tears* (1964); *Spiritual Breakthrough* (1983); *The Man Perfectly Filled with the Spirit* (1986); *How Your Corps Can Grow* (1989); *Saying Yes to Life* (autobiography, 2007). Composer of music and co-author with John Gowans of 10 musicals. m Capt Freda Turner (Kingston-upon-Thames, UK, 1964) 1969.

Shaw Clifton

Edmonton, UK, with wife née Helen Ashman, 1973. General (2006-present). b 21 Sep 45. Served as corps officer in British Territory; in Literary Department, IHQ (1974); in Zimbabwe as Vice Principal, Mazoe Secondary School (1975-77) and CO, Bulawayo Citadel (1977-79); in further BT corps appointments (1979-82, 1989-92); at IHQ as Legal & Parliamentary Secretary (1982-89); in UK as divisional commander (1992-95); in USA Eastern as DC, Massachusetts (1995-97); as TC, Pakistan (1997-2002); TC, New Zealand, Fiji & Tonga (2002-04); TC, UK (2004-06). LLB (Hons), AKC (Theol), BD (Theol) (Hons), PhD. Freedom of the City of London (2007). Author of *What Does the Salvationist Say?* (1977); *Growing Together* (1984); *Strong Doctrine, Strong Mercy* (1985); *Never the Same Again* (1997); *Who are these Salvationists?* (1999); *New Love – Thinking Aloud About Practical Holiness* (2004), *Selected Writings, vols 1 & 2* (2010).

COUNTRIES WHERE THE SALVATION ARMY IS AT WORK

THE Salvation Army is at work in 121 countries. A country in which the Army serves is defined in two ways:

(i) Politically

(ii) Where the General has given approval to the work, thus officially recognising it, ensuring it has legal identity and a Deed Poll is published to acknowledge this.

As far as political status is concerned, for the Army's purposes, three categories are recognised:

(a) Independent countries, eg USA and New Zealand;

(b) Internally independent political entities which are under the protection of another country in matters of defence and foreign affairs, eg The Færoes, Isle of Man, Puerto Rico;

(c) Colonies and other dependent political units, eg Bermuda, French Guiana, Guernsey, Jersey.

Administrative subdivisions of a country such as Wales and Scotland in the UK are not recognised as separate countries for this purpose. The countries fulfilling the quoted criteria, with the date in brackets on which the work was officially recognised, are as follows:

Angola ....(1985)	Chile....................(1909)	El Salvador ....(1989)
Antigua ....(1903)	China ....(1916)	Estonia ....(1927)
Argentina ....(1890)	Colombia ....(1985)	............(reopened 1995)
Australia..............(1881)	Congo, Republic of	
Austria ....(1927)	(Brazzaville) ....(1937)	Færoes, The ....(1924)
	Congo, Democratic	Fiji ....(1973)
Bahamas..............(1931)	Republic of (Kinshasa)	Finland................(1889)
Bangladesh..........(1971)	............................(1934)	France ....(1881)
Barbados ....(1898)	Costa Rica ....(1907)	French Guiana ....(1980)
Belgium ....(1889)	Cuba....................(1918)	
Belize..................(1915)	Czech Republic ..(1919)	Georgia ....(1993)
Bermuda..............(1896)	............(reopened 1990)	Germany ....(1886)
Bolivia ....(1920)		Ghana..................(1922)
Botswana ....(1997)	Denmark ....(1887)	Greece ....(2007)
Brazil ....(1922)	Dominican Republic	Grenada ....(1902)
Burundi ....(2007)	............................(1995)	Guam ....(1994)
		Guatemala ....(1976)
Canada ....(1882)	Ecuador ....(1985)	Guernsey ....(1879)

27

Countries where The Salvation Army is at work

Guyana................(1895)
Haiti ....(1950)
Honduras ....(2000)
Hong Kong ....(1930)
Hungary ....(1924)
...........(reopened 1990)

Iceland ....(1895)
India....................(1882)
Indonesia ....(1894)
Ireland, Republic of
 (Eire) ....(1880)
Isle of Man..........(1883)
Italy ....(1887)

Jamaica ....(1887)
Japan ....(1895)
Jersey ....(1879)

Kenya..................(1921)
Korea ....(1908)
Kuwait ....(2008)

Latvia..................(1923)
...........(reopened 1990)
Lesotho ....(1969)
Liberia ....(1988)
Lithuania ....(2005)
Macau ....(2000)
Malawi................(1967)
Malaysia..............(1938)
Mali ....(2008)
Marshall Islands..(1985)

Mexico ....(1937)
Micronesia ....(1993)
Moldova..............(1994)
Mozambique ......(1916)
Myanmar ....(1915)

Namibia ....(1932)
...........(reopened 2008)
Netherlands, The (1887)
New Zealand ......(1883)
Nicaragua............(2010)
Nigeria ....(1920)
Norway ....(1888)

Pakistan ....(1883)
Panama................(1904)
Papua New Guinea
...........................(1956)
Paraguay ....(1910)
Peru ....(1910)
Philippines, The ..(1937)
Poland ....(2005)
Portugal ....(1971)
Puerto Rico ....(1962)

Romania..............(1999)
Russia..................(1913)
...........(reopened 1991)
Rwanda ....(1995)

St Christopher Nevis
 (St Kitts) ....(1916)
St Helena ....(1884)

St Lucia ....(1902)
St Maarten ....(1999)
St Vincent ....(1905)
Sierra Leone........(2010)
Singapore............(1935)
South Africa........(1883)
Spain ....(1971)
Sri Lanka ....(1883)
Suriname ....(1924)
Swaziland............(1960)
Sweden................(1882)
Switzerland ....(1882)

Taiwan ....(1965)
Tanzania..............(1933)
Tonga ....(1986)
Trinidad and Tobago
...........................(1901)

Uganda................(1931)
Ukraine ....(1993)
United Arab Emirates
...........................(2010)
United Kingdom (1865)
United States of
 America ....(1880)
Uruguay ....(1890)

Venezuela ....(1972)
Virgin Islands ....(1917)

Zambia................(1922)
Zimbabwe ....(1891)

INTERNATIONAL STATISTICS
(as at 1 January 2010)

Countries and territories where SA serves
(at 30 September 2010, see pp 27-28) 121
Languages used in SA work, including
some tribal languages....................175
Corps, outposts, societies, new
plants and recovery churches....15,422
Goodwill centres..................................279
Officers 26,329
Active..17,145
Retired...9,184
Auxiliary-captains..............................189
Envoys/sergeants/non officer personnel,
full-time.......................................1,361
Cadets 1,162
Employees....................................104,248
Senior soldiers 1,124,760
Adherents......................................181,398
Junior soldiers 375,103
Corps cadets...................................43,121
Senior band musicians..................26,231
Senior songsters.............................96,648
Other senior musical group
members.....................................86,136
Senior and young people's
local officers 145,236
Women's Ministries (all groups) –
members 639,645
League of Mercy – members......124,924
SAMF – members.........................7,802
Over-60 clubs – members.............99,608
Men's fellowships – members......65,615
Young people's bands –
members 12,203
Young people's singing
companies – members..............86,420
Other young people's music
groups – members..................119,463
Sunday schools – members........661,468
Junior youth groups
(scouts, guides, etc, and clubs) –
members...................................226,316

Senior youth groups – members ....
....107,995
Corps-based community development
programmes............................17,347
Beneficiaries/clients 992,733
Thrift stores/charity shops
(corps/territorial) 1,484
Recycling centres 15

Social Programme
Residential
Hostels for homeless and transient....420
Capacity 24,841
Emergency lodges............................379
Capacity 18,830
Children's homes 259
Capacity 10,725
Homes for the elderly.......................115
Capacity 6,207
Homes for the disabled 53
Capacity 2,044
Homes for the blind 9
Capacity 428
Remand and probation homes.............40
Capacity 818
Homes for street children...................29
Capacity 563
Mother and baby homes.....................50
Capacity 1,281
Training centres for families 11
Capacity 98
Care homes for vulnerable people 45
Capacity 1,568
Women's and men's refuge
centres 66
Capacity 1,703
Other residential care
homes/hostels 141
Capacity 8,137

Day Care
Community centres............................598

Early childhood education centres....108
    Capacity 5,282
Day centres for the elderly................100
    Capacity 3,860
Play groups..5
    Capacity 90
Day centres for the hearing
    impaired 5
    Capacity 114
Day centres for street children 16
    Capacity 412
Day nurseries 165
    Capacity 11,175
Drop-in centres for youth....................68
Other day care centres 354
    Capacity 20,709

Addiction Dependency

Non-residential programmes 63
    Capacity 4,103
Residential programmes....................206
    Capacity 13,547
Harbour Light programmes 26
    Capacity 2,409
Other services for those with
    addictions 30
    Capacity 2,425

Service to the Armed Forces

Clubs and canteens...............................41
Mobile units for service personnel......37
Chaplains 41

Emergency Disaster Response

Disaster rehabilitation schemes 177
    Participants 11,679
Refugee programmes –
    host country 59
    Participants 3,933
Refugee rehabilitation programmes......2
    Participants 4,000
Other response programmes..............889
    Participants 66,001

Services to the Community

Prisoners visited 386,933
Prisoners helped on discharge....197,189
Police courts – people helped 249,879
Missing persons – applications......8,098

Number traced............................5,404
Night patrol/anti-suicide –
    number helped........................426,928
Community youth programmes 2,067
    Beneficiaries 279,929
Employment bureaux –
    applications 72,929
    initial referrals..........................83,828
Counselling – people helped......177,660
General relief – people
    helped 3,670,277
Emergency relief (fire, flood,
    etc) – people helped 707,088
Emergency mobile units 768
Feeding centres 77
Restaurants and cafes..........................31
Thrift stores/charity shops
    (social).....................................1,115
Apartments for elderly 887
    Capacity 10,152
Hostels for students, workers, etc......61
    Capacity 1,192
Land settlements (SA villages,
    farms etc) 7
    Capacity 1,823
Social Services summer camps 262
    Participants 22,104
Other services to the community
    (unspecified)...................................241
    Beneficiaries........................8,039,383

Health Programme

General hospitals 21
    Capacity 2,286
Maternity hospitals..............................23
    Capacity 438
Other specialist hospitals 17
Capacity 4,155
Specialist clinics..................................35
    Capacity 5,596
General clinics/health centres 138
    Capacity 2,362
Mobile clinics/community health
    posts 35
Inpatients.....................................264,013
Outpatients 906,637
Doctors/medics 3,759

Non medical staff............................1,599
Invalid/convalescent homes.................20
   Capacity 5,562
Health education programmes
   (HIV/Aids, etc) 59
   Beneficiaries............................707,618
Day care programmes...........................5

Education Programme
Kindergarten/sub primary..................509
Primary schools 1,020
Upper primary and middle schools ..135
Secondary and high schools..............191

Colleges and universities 53
Vocational training schools/centres ...93
Pupils..409,505
Teachers 17,592
Schools for the blind (included in
   above totals).....................................12
Schools for the disabled (included in
   above totals).....................................13
Boarding schools (included in
   above totals).....................................27
Colleges, universities, staff training
   and development study and distance
   learning centres................................19

SALVATION ARMY PERIODICALS
BY TERRITORY/COMMAND

International Headquarters: *All the World*, *Revive*, *The Officer*

Australia National: *Kidzone*, *Warcry*

Australia Eastern: *Creative Ministry*, *Pipeline*, *Venue*, *Women in Touch*

Australia Southern: *On Fire*

Brazil: *O Oficial*, *Rumo* and *Ministério Feminino – Devocionais* (Women's Ministries magazines)

Canada and Bermuda: *Edge for Kids*, *En Avant*, *Faith & Friends*, *Foi & Vie*, *Salvationist*

Caribbean: *The War Cry*

Congo (Brazzaville): *Le Salutiste*

Democratic Republic of Congo: *Echo d'Espoir*

Denmark: *Mennesker & Tro*, *Vision-Mission*

Eastern Europe: *Vestnik Spaseniya* (*The War Cry*), *The Officer* (both Russian)

Finland and Estonia: *Krigsropet* (Swedish), *Nappis*, *Sotahuuto* (both Finnish)

France and Belgium: *Avec Vous*, *Le Bulletin de la Ligue du Foyer*, *Le Fil*, *Le Magazine*, *L'Officier*, *Quand Même*

Germany and Lithuania: *Danke*, *Heilsarmee-Forum*, *Heilsarmee-Magazin*

Ghana: *Salvationist Newsletter*

Hong Kong and Macau: *Army Scene*, *The War Cry*

India National: *The War Cry* (English)

India Central: *Home League Magazine*, *Udyogasthudu*, *Yovana Veerudu*, *Yudha Dwani*

India Eastern: *Sipai Tlangau* (*The War Cry*), *The Officer*, *Young Salvationist*, *Chunnunpar*, *Naupang Sipai* (all Mizo)

India Northern: *Home League Yearly* (Hindi and English), *Mukti Samachar* (Hindi and Punjabi), *The Officer*, *Yuva Sipai* (both Hindi)

India South Eastern: *Chiruveeran*, *Home League Quarterly*, *Poresathan*, *The Officer* (all Tamil)

India South Western: *Home League Quarterly* (Malayalam/English), *The Officer*, *Youdha Shabdan*, *Yuva Veeran* (all Malayalam)

India Western: *Home League Quarterly*, *The Officer*, *The War Cry*, *The Young Soldier* (all Gujarati and Marathi)

Indonesia: *Berita Keselamatan* (*The War Cry*), *Cakrawala* (*Waves of Hope*), *Medical Fellowship Bulletin*, *Oasis Fajar* (Daily Devotions)

Italy: *Il Bollettino del Dipartimento Società e Famiglia, Il Grido di Guerra*

Japan: *Home League Quarterly, The Officer, The Sunday School Guide, Toki-no-Koe, Toki-no-Koe Junior*

Kenya East: *Sauti ya Vita* (English and Kiswahili)

Kenya West: *Sauti ya Vita* (English and Kiswahili)

Korea: *Home League Programme Helps, Loving Hands* (Sponsorship magazine), *The Officer, The War Cry*

Latin America North: *Voz de Salvación* (*Salvation Voice*), *Arco Iris de Ideas* (*Rainbow of Ideas*)

Mexico: *El Grito de Guerra* (*The War Cry*), *El Eslabon* (*The Link*)

Mozambique: *Devocionias para Encontros da Liga do Lar* (Home League resource manual)

The Netherlands and Czech Republic: *Dag in Dag Uit, Heils-en Strijdzangen, InterCom, Strijdkreet* (all Dutch), *Prapor Spásy* (Czech)

New Zealand, Fiji and Tonga: *War Cry*

Nigeria: *Salvationist, The Shepherd, The War Cry*

Norway, Iceland and The Færoes: *Frelsesoffiseren, Krigsropet, Uni-form* (all Norwegian), *Herópid* (Icelandic)

Pakistan: *Home League Annual, The War Cry* (in Urdu)

Papua New Guinea: *Tokaut*

The Philippines: *The War Cry*

Portugal: *O Salvacionista, Ideias e Recursos* (for Women's Ministries)

Rwanda: *Salvationist News*

Singapore, Malaysia and Myanmar: *The War Cry*

South America East: *El Oficial, El Salvacionista*

South America West: *El Grito de Guerra, El Trébol* (for Women's Ministries)

Southern Africa: *Echoes of Mercy, Home League Highlights, Home League Resource Manual, Outer Circle Newsletter, SAMF Newsletter, The Reporter, The War Cry*

Sri Lanka: *Yudha Handa* (*The War Cry*)

Sweden and Latvia: *Stridsropet*

Switzerland, Austria and Hungary: *Espoir, Dialogue, Just 4 U, Trampoline* (all French), *Dialog, Klecks, Trialog* (all German), *IN* (French and German)

Taiwan: *Taiwan Regional News*

United Kingdom with the Republic of Ireland: *Kids Alive!, Salvationist, The War Cry*

USA National: *The War Cry, Women's Ministries Resources, Word & Deed – A Journal of Theology and Ministry, Young Salvationist*

USA Central: *Central Connection*

USA Eastern: *¡Buenas Noticias!, Cristianos en Marcha* (both Spanish), *Good News!* (English and Korean), *Priority!, Ven a Cristo Hoy* (Spanish)

USA Southern: *Southern Spirit*

USA Western: *Caring, New Frontier, Nuevos Fronteras* (Spanish)

Zimbabwe: *Zimbabwe Salvationist, ZEST* (women's magazine)

Books Published during 2009-10

International Headquarters: *Charlie Called and Chosen* (audio CD) by Pat Charlesworth; *The Salvation Army Handbook of Doctrine; The Salvation Army in the Body of Christ – Study Guide* (English, French, Spanish); *The Salvation Army Year Book 2010; What A Hope* by Gilbert Ellis; *Words of Life.*

International Literature Programme: *Adventurers* Junior Soldiers Training Course; *Discovery* Discipling Programme for Young People; *International Bible Lessons for Children*

Australia Eastern: *Salvation Stories Vol 1* edited by Miriam Gluyas and Fay Foster;

Books Published 2009-10

Samuel Logan Brengle – Heart for God edited by Peter Farthing; *50 Ways to Grow a Healthy Corps Vol 1* edited by Miriam Gluyas and Fay Foster

Australia Southern: *Born of the Spirit* by Ian Southwell; *Boston Common* edited by Stephen Court; *Consolations* by John Staite; *Hallmarks of The Salvation Army* edited by Henry Gariepy and Stephen Court; *Holiness Incorporated* by Geoff Webb, Rowan Castle and Stephen Court; *In Her Own Words* edited by Carolyn Knaggs; *Mission Inc* by Robert Watson; *Other Voices* by Christine Faragher; *Prayers in Exile* by Graeme McClimont; *The Pink Mist* by Faye Michelson

Finland and Estonia: *Hän Kulkee Edellä (He precedes)* by Terho Tiainen (Finnish)

Hong Kong and Macau: *The Salvation Army In The Body of Christ – An Ecclesiological Statement; Servant Leadership* by Robert Street

Japan: *The Salvation Army In The Body Of Christ – An Ecclesiological Statement* (Japanese)

Korea: *Creed and Deed* by John D. Waldron; *Expand the Grounds of the Tabernacle* by Commissioner Kim, Hai-duk; *Mustard Seed Notes (3)* by Kang, Sung-hwan; *Never the Same Again;* by Shaw Clifton; *One Thing* by Jim Knaggs and Stephen Court; *Toward a Christian Theology of Social Services in The Salvation Army; Corps Cadet Lessons 2009-10; Corps Cell Group Study Manual 2010; Daily Devotions for Salvationist Families 2010; Home League Resources 2010; Summer Bible School 2010* (handbook and workbooks); *Young People's Company Lessons 2009-10* (manual and workbooks)

Sri Lanka: *Heroes of the Cross* (Sinhala)

United Kingdom: *The Best of Both Worlds* by Brindley Boon

USA National: *Every Sober Day Is A Miracle* by John Cheydleur and Ed Forster; *Hallmarks of The Salvation Army* by Henry Gariepy and Stephen Court; *Quotes of the Past and Present – a compilation*

Published with the assistance of grants from the International Literature Programme, IHQ:

Brazil: *Fé e Obras (Creed and Deed)* by John D.Waldron (Portuguese)

Caribbean: *Adventurers; Discovery; International Bible Lessons for Children*

Congo Brazzaville: *Bible Lessons for Children* (French); *Women's Ministries Manual*

Eastern Europe: *Adventurers Junior Soldier Book 6; Corps Cadet Book 1 and 2; Children's Christmas books; Discovery; Holiness Unwrapped* by Robert Street; *Marvellous In Our Eyes* by Edward H Joy; *More than an Icon;* (all Russian) *Servants Together; The Salvationist and the Sacraments* by Clifford Kew; *Who are these Salvationists* by Shaw Clifton; (all Russian) *The Way of Holiness* by Samuel Logan Brengle (Romanian)

Ghana: *Adventurers; Discovery; International Bible Lessons for Children;*

India National: *Finding a New Hope in Christ* (Women's Ministries booklet)

India Eastern: *YP Sunday Bible Lessons (Senior, Intermediate, Junior, Primary, Beginners); The History of The Salvation Army in India Eastern Territory; We Have An Altar*

India Western: *Marathi Song Book*

Malawi: *Discovery*

Nigeria: *International Bible Lessons for Children*

Papua New Guinea: *Sunday School Manuals*

The Philippines: *Adventurers; International Bible Lessons for Children*

Singapore Malaysia and Myanmar: *Sunday School Lessons* (Mizo)

South America West: *Adventurers; Dear Paul* by Wesley Harris; *Discovery; Sanctified Sanity* by R. David Rightmire; (Spanish)

Sweden and Latvia: *International Bible Lessons for Children; The Salvation Army in the Body of Christ*

Tanzania: *Discovery*

MINISTRIES AND FELLOWSHIPS

WOMEN'S MINISTRIES

THE ideal basic unit of society is the home and family, where women play a vital and definitive role. Furthermore, as natural providers of hope, women play an important part in shaping society. Therefore, any fellowship of women in which Christian influence is exerted and practical help given benefits not only the individual and the family, but also the nation.

Women's Ministries provide a programme of meetings and other activities based on the fourfold aim of the Army's international women's organisation, the Home League, which was inaugurated in 1907. Those aims are worship, education, fellowship, service. The motto of the Home League is: 'I will live a pure life in my house' (Psalm 101:2 *Good News Bible*).

The mission of Women's Ministries is to bring women into a knowledge of Jesus Christ; encourage their full potential in influencing family, friends and community; equip them for growth in personal understanding and life skills; address issues which affect women and their families in the world.

Commissioner Helen Clifton (WPWM) makes a presentation to the Territorial Women's Ministries Queen in Congo Brazzaville. More than 3,500 women attended a rally in Moungali which featured music and a drama item about human trafficking. In response to the commissioner's Bible message 500 people knelt at the mercy seat.

THE LEAGUE OF MERCY AND COMMUNITY CARE MINISTRIES

THE League of Mercy began in 1892 in Canada and is made up of people of all ages whose mission is to engage in a caring ministry. The main objective of the League of Mercy is to respond to the spiritual and social needs of the community. The ministry is adapted according to the local situation, the size of its membership and the skill of its members, and endeavours to follow Christ's injunction, 'Inasmuch as ye have done it unto one of the least of these my brethren, ye have done it unto me' (Matthew 25:40 *Authorised Version*).

THE FELLOWSHIP OF THE SILVER STAR

THE Fellowship of the Silver Star, inaugurated in the USA in 1930 and extended worldwide in 1936, expresses gratitude to parents or other significant life mentors of Salvation Army officers.

THE SALVATION ARMY MEDICAL FELLOWSHIP

THE Salvation Army Medical Fellowship, instituted in 1943 by Mrs General Minnie Carpenter, is an international fellowship of dedicated medical personnel. Physical suffering in our world today challenges both the medical and the physical and emotional resources of medical personnel. The fellowship encourages a Christian witness and application of Christian principles in professional life while at the same time being involved with practical application in hospitals, clinics and various other places of medical care. The motto of the Fellowship is: 'If we walk in the light, as he is in the light, we have fellowship one with another' (1 John 1:7 *Authorised Version*).

THE SALVATION ARMY STUDENTS' FELLOWSHIP

THIS fellowship started in Norway in 1942 and later spread to other countries, receiving an official constitution in 1950. It comes under the world presidency of the General. The aim of the fellowship is to unite Salvationist students and graduates of universities, colleges and other centres of higher education in Christian fellowship and such Salvation Army service as may be appropriate.

THE SALVATION ARMY BLUE SHIELD FELLOWSHIP

IN 1974 the Blue Shield Fellowship was formed by two British Salvationist policemen to provide friendship and support to Christian policemen as they face present-day challenges. Membership is open to both active and retired police officers, and there are members in many countries.

SALVATION ARMY HONOURS

ORDER OF THE FOUNDER

Instituted on 20 August 1917 by General Bramwell Booth, the Order of the Founder is the highest Salvation Army honour for distinguished service

HISTORY OF THE ORDER

IN 1917, five years after the death of William Booth, his son, General Bramwell Booth, inaugurated the Order of the Founder 'to mark outstanding service rendered by officers and soldiers such as would in spirit or achievement have been specially commended by the Founder'.

The first awards were made in 1920 to 15 officers and one soldier. Three years later, seven officers and one local officer were honoured, but since then the awards have been made much more sparingly and, to date, 156 officers and 93 lay Salvationists have been recognised with the Army's highest honour – a total of 249 in 91 years (1920-2010).

The first presentation was to a soldier, Private Herbert Bourne, for outstanding Christian witness and service during military service in the First World War. A few senior leaders such as Commissioner Henry Howard, General Evangeline Booth and Commissioner Catherine Bramwell-Booth have been recipients but, much more commonly, faithful and devoted service by less well-known personalities has been acknowledged.

The honour is rarely given because every nomination is carefully scrutinised by a panel of senior leaders at International Headquarters. Salvationists have every reason to be proud of those who have been awarded this outstanding recognition for meritorious Christian example, witness and service.

Recipients of the Order of the Founder 2009-10

Brigadier Ngurliana (India Eastern Territory). The brigadier's deep faith and courage in the face of adversity enabled The Salvation Army to become established in Mizoram. Through tireless and sacrificial dedication to his calling and unique ministry, many people have been led to the Saviour. He made outstanding literary and musical contributions, and served the Army above and beyond the call of duty. Admitted to the Order of the Founder on 1 January 2010.

Commissioner Mannam Samuel (India Central Territory). During a lifetime of committed Salvation Army service Commissioner Samuel's evangelistic fervour and personal integrity have been evident to all. He gave a compassionate ministry to the

Brigadier Ngurliana is overjoyed to receive his Order of the Founder certificate from Commissioner Lalkiamlova (IS, South Asia) at Ebenezer Corps, Aizawl, just 10 weeks before his 100th birthday

marginalised and unreached people of India. Admitted to the Order of the Founder on 16 January 2010.

CSM (Dr) John Syamkutty (India South Western Teritory). Dr Syamkutty is a devoted Salvationist and loyal corps sergeant-major. For 33 years he has dedicated his considerable medical knowledge and expertise to the Lord's service through Salvation Army medical work. As chief medical officer at the Evangeline Booth Hospital he has addressed the needs of leprosy patients with extraordinary dedication, deep love and compassion. He has enriched community life and his consistent Christian witness has been exemplary. He is an asset to Salvation Army medical services in India and beyond. Admitted to the Order of the Founder on 10 April 2010.

ORDER OF DISTINGUISHED AUXILIARY SERVICE

On 24 February 1941 General George Carpenter instituted this order to mark the Army's appreciation of distinguished service rendered by non-Salvationists who have helped to further its work in a variety of ways

Recipients of the Order of Distinguished Auxiliary Service 2009-10

There were no admissions to the Order of Distinguished Auxiliary Service during the period under review (1 May 2009-30 April 2010).

INTERNATIONAL HEADQUARTERS

The Salvation Army, 101 Queen Victoria Street, London EC4V 4EH, United Kingdom

Main entrance: Peter's Hill, London EC4

Tel: (020) 7332 0101 (national)
[44] (20) 7332 0101 (international);
fax: (020) 7192 3413; email: websa@salvationarmy.org;
website: www.salvationarmy.org

General
SHAW CLIFTON
(2 April 2006)

Chief of the Staff
COMMISSIONER BARRY C. SWANSON
(2 May 2010)

INTERNATIONAL Headquarters exists to support the General as he leads The Salvation Army to accomplish its God-given worldwide mission to preach the gospel of Jesus Christ and meet human need in his name without discrimination. In so doing, it assists the General:

☐ To give spiritual leadership, promote the development of spiritual life within the Army, and emphasise the Army's reliance on God for the achievement of its mission.
☐ To provide overall strategic leadership and set international policies.
☐ To direct and administer the Army's operations and protect its interests – by means of appointments and delegation of authority and responsibility with accountability.
☐ To empower and support the territories and commands, encourage and pastorally care for their leaders, and inspire local vision and initiatives.
☐ To strengthen the internationalism of the Army, preserve its unity, purposes, beliefs and spirit, and maintain its standards.
☐ To promote the development, appropriate deployment and international sharing of personnel.
☐ To promote the development and sharing of financial resources worldwide, and manage the Army's international funds.
☐ To promote the development and international sharing of knowledge, expertise and experience.
☐ To develop the Army's ecumenical and other relationships.

The General directs Salvation Army operations throughout the world through the administrative departments of International Headquarters, which are headed by international secretaries. The Chief of the Staff, a commissioner appointed by the General to be second-in-command, is the Army's chief executive whose function is to implement the General's policy decisions and effect liaison between departments.

The Christian Mission Headquarters, Whitechapel Road, became the Army's first International Headquarters in 1880. However, the Founder soon decided that a move into the City of London would be beneficial and in 1881 IHQ was moved to 101 Queen Victoria Street. Sixty years after this move the IHQ building was destroyed by fire during the Second World War. The rebuilt International Headquarters was opened by Queen Elizabeth, the Queen Mother, in November 1963.

When it was decided to redevelop the Queen Victoria Street site, IHQ took up temporary residence at William Booth College, Denmark Hill, in 2001. Three years later IHQ returned to 101 Queen Victoria Street and the new building was opened by Her Royal Highness The Princess Royal in November 2004.

Website of the Office of the General:
www.salvationarmy.org/thegeneral

INTERNATIONAL MANAGEMENT COUNCIL

The International Management Council (IMC), established in February 1991, sees to the efficiency and effectiveness of the Army's international administration in general. It considers in detail the formation of international policy and mission. It is composed of all London-based IHQ commissioners, and meets monthly with the General taking the chair.

Sec: Lt-Col Rob Garrad
Asst Sec: Maj Richard Gaudion

GENERAL'S CONSULTATIVE COUNCIL

The General's Consultative Council (GCC), established in July 2001, advises the General on broad matters relating to the Army's mission strategy and policy. The GCC is composed of all officers who qualify to attend a High Council, and operates through a Lotus Notes database. Selected members also meet three times a year in London with the General taking the chair.

Sec: Lt-Col Rob Garrad
Asst Sec: Maj Richard Gaudion

ADMINISTRATION DEPARTMENT

The Administration Department is responsible for all matters with which the Chief of the Staff deals; for the effective administration of IHQ; for IHQ personnel; for international external relations; for providing legal advice; and for ensuring that the strategic planning and monitoring process is implemented and used effectively.

International Secretary to the Chief of the Staff

COMR WILLIAM COCHRANE (1 Jun 2009)

Under Sec for Administration (Admin):
tba
Under Sec for Administration (Personnel):
Lt-Col David Shakespeare
Executive Sec to the General/Research and Planning Sec: Lt-Col Rob Garrad
P/S to the General: Maj Richard Gaudion
P/S to the Chief of the Staff: Maj Mark Watts
Sec for International Ecumenical Relations:
Lt-Col Richard Munn
Sec for Spiritual Life Development:
Lt-Col Janet Munn
Director, International Social Justice Commission: Comr M. Christine MacMillan
International Doctrine Council:
Chair: Comr William Francis
International Moral and Social Issues Council: Chair: Comr M. Christine MacMillan
IHQ Chaplain and City of London Liaison Officer: Comr Shona Forsyth
Legal and Constitutional Adviser to the General: Comr Kenneth G. Hodder
Project Coordinator, The Salvation Army Song Book: Maj Christine Clement

WOMEN'S MINISTRIES

World President of Women's Ministries

COMR HELEN CLIFTON (2 Apr 2006)

World Secretary for Women's Ministries and World President,

SA Scouts, Guides and Guards

COMR SUE SWANSON (1 May 2010)

Personal Asst to WPWM and WSWM: Maj Lynn Gibbs

INTERNATIONAL PERSONNEL DEPARTMENT

The International Personnel Department works in the interests of international personnel in support of the Chief of the Staff and the zonal international secretaries. Responsibilities include facilitating the personal and vocational development of all personnel, their pastoral care and physical well-being. The department exists to encourage and facilitate the sharing and appropriate deployment of personnel resources on a global basis; to assist in the identification of officers with potential for future leadership; to monitor training and development; to register and coordinate all offers for international service.

International Secretary for Personnel

COMR KENNETH G. HODDER (1 Jun 2009)

Associate Int Sec for Personnel: Comr Jolene Hodder
Sec for Officer Development and Records: Maj Christine Clement
Medical Sec for Personnel: Lt-Col Wendy Leavey

BUSINESS ADMINISTRATION DEPARTMENT

The Business Administration Department is responsible for international accounting, auditing, banking, property and related matters. The International Secretary for Business Administration has the oversight of the finance functions in territories and commands.

International Secretary for Business Administration

COMR ANN WOODALL (1 Mar 2008)

Finance Sec: Lt-Col Walter Fuge
Chief Accountant: Maj Jeffrey Wills
Chief International Auditor: Lt-Col Edmund Chung
  Auditors: Maj João Paulo Ramos (Asst Chief International Auditor) Maj Samuel Amponsah, Maj Alan Milkins, Maj Francis Nyakusamwa, Capt Emerald Urbien, Miss Karen Dare
Facilities Management Coordinator: Mr Andrew Holden
Information Technology Manager: Mr Mark Calleran

Property Manager: Mr Howard Bowes
Travel Manager: Mr Mark Edwards

PROGRAMME RESOURCES DEPARTMENT

The mission of the Programme Resources Department is to participate with others in envisioning, coordinating, facilitating and raising awareness of programmes that advance the global mission of The Salvation Army.

International Secretary for Programme Resources

COMR ROBIN FORSYTH (1 Jul 2008)

Under Sec: Maj Dean Pallant
International Emergency Services:
  IES Coordinator (Acting): Maj Dean Pallant
International Health Services:
  IHS Coordinators: Majs Dean and (Dr) Eirwen Pallant
International Projects and Development Services:
  IP Coordinator: Maj Richard Welch
Communications Section:
  Communications Sec, Editor-in-Chief and Literary Sec: Lt-Col Laurie Robertson
  Editor *All the World*: Mr Kevin Sims
  Editor *Revive*: Lt-Col Carolynne Chung
  Editor *The Officer*: Maj Sandra Welch
  Editor *The Year Book*: Maj Trevor Howes
  Writer *Words of Life*: Maj Beverly Ivany
  International Literature Programme Officer: Lt-Col Simone Robertson
  Editorial fax: (020) 7332 8079

ZONAL DEPARTMENTS

The zonal departments are the main administrative link with territories and commands. The international secretaries give oversight to and coordinate the Army's work in their respective geographical areas.

AFRICA
International Secretary

COMR AMOS MAKINA (1 Jul 2004)

Under Secs: Lt-Col David Burrows and Lt-Col Margaret Wickings
  fax: (020) 7332 8231
Zonal Sec WM: Comr Rosemary Makina

AMERICAS AND CARIBBEAN
International Secretary

COMR LARRY BOSH (1 Oct 2008)

Under Secs: Lt-Cols F. Bradford and
Heidi Bailey
Zonal Sec WM: Comr Gillian Bosh

Under Sec: Col Ross Gower
fax: (020) 7332 8219
Zonal Sec WM: Comr Lalhlimpuii

EUROPE
International Secretary

COMR ROBERT STREET (1 Nov 2010)

Under Sec: Lt-Col Jonathan Roberts
fax: (020) 7332 8209
Zonal Sec WM: Comr Janet Street
Officer for EU Affairs: Maj Göran Larsson

SOUTH PACIFIC AND EAST ASIA
International Secretary

COMR JAMES CONDON (1 Nov 2010)

Under Sec: Lt-Col Jennifer Groves
fax: (020) 7332 8229
Zonal Sec WM: Comr Jan Condon

STATISTICS

Officers 73 **Employees** 71

SOUTH ASIA
International Secretary

COMR LALKIAMLOVA (1 Jan 2004)

International College for Officers and Centre for Spiritual Life Development

The Cedars, 34 Sydenham Hill, London SE26 6LS, UK

Tel: [44] (020) 8299 8450; fax: [44] (020) 7192 3056; website: www.salvationarmy.org/ico

Principal: Lieut-Colonel Richard Munn (1 Jul 2008)

During the International Congress held at the Crystal Palace, Sydenham, London, in 1904, Commissioner Henry T. Howard voiced what he saw as the young Salvation Army's need for leaders inspired with the aggressive spirit of Salvationism. William Booth took up the idea and the International Staff Training Lodge was opened at Clapton on 11 May 1905.

Following the purchase of The Cedars in Sydenham – formerly used to house orphaned children at the end of the Second World War – the International Staff College started in 1950. Four years later it became the International College for Officers (ICO), with General Albert Orsborn declaring it to be 'an investment in the great intangibles without which our cogs and wheels would soon be rusty and dead'.

In July 2008 the role of the college was broadened to include aspects of spiritual life development that go beyond officers' attendance at the eight-week sessions, and the college was renamed International College for Officers and Centre for Spiritual Life Development (CSLD).

ICO MISSION STATEMENT
The Salvation Army's International College for Officers exists to further develop officers by:
☐ **nurturing personal holiness and spiritual leadership**
☐ **providing opportunity to experience the internationalism of the Army**
☐ **encouraging a renewed sense of mission and purpose as an officer**

CSLD MISSION STATEMENT
The Centre for Spiritual Life Development exists to facilitate the development of the spiritual lives of Salvationists by:
☐ **offering conferences and events that are spiritually enriching and that help form people in Christlikeness**
☐ **providing resources to cultivate spiritual life development**
☐ **encouraging implementation of intentional and systematic opportunities for spiritual growth throughout the international Salvation Army**

DURING 2009-10 the ICO hosted more than 100 officer-leaders from around the world in four sessions (Numbers 204-207). These included Mizo and Indonesian translation sessions. Delegates conducted corps meetings in Peterborough, Poole,

41

Branksome and Chatham; one entire session attended the UK Territorial Congress in Harrogate.

The Centre for Spiritual Life Development continued to sharpen its ministry by ratifying the CSLD Mission Statement (given overleaf) and expanding its resource provision role. On-site events also increased; they included hosting the International Doctrine Council and the 'Come To The Table' International Gathering of Secretaries for Spiritual Life Development.

Of particular note was the two-week 'Time To Be Holy 458' holiness event for young adults that immediately preceded the 2010 World Youth Convention. This was the first time in The Cedars' history that a resident delegation consisted entirely of soldiers.

STATISTICS
Officers 6 **Employees** 5

STAFF
Associate Principal and Secretary for Spiritual Life Development: Lt-Col Janet Munn
Executive Asst to the Secretary for Spiritual Life Development: Lt-Col Karen Shakespeare
Programme Sec: Maj Janet Robson
Business Sec: Maj Peter Forrest
Personnel Sec: Maj Julie Forrest

International Social Justice Commission
221 East 52nd Street, New York, New York 10022, USA
Tel: [1] (212) 758-0763; website: www.salvationarmy.org/isjc
Director: Commissioner Christine MacMillan (1 Jul 2007)

The International Social Justice Commission (ISJC) came into being on 1 July 2007. Its secretariat is in New York, with the commission and its director being attached to the Administration Department of IHQ. The ISJC advises the General and other senior leaders at IHQ in matters of social justice. The director and staff are the Army's principal international advocate and adviser on social, economic and political issues and events giving rise to the perpetuation of social injustice in the world. They assist the Army in addressing social injustice in a systemic, measured, proactive and Christian manner.

The commission has absorbed and extended the current work of the Moral and Social Issues desk at IHQ, reintroducing an International Moral and Social Issues Council (IMASIC).

THE ISJC continues to develop its educational resources: 'Jesus and Justice' is a theological framing of the importance Jesus Christ gave to living and teaching a just way of life; 'The Principles of Justice' provide a theoretical perspective for understanding social justice and testing action.

The 'Speakout' Conference in March 2010 resulted in an ongoing wealth of development and gathered material on the topic of advocacy, which also becomes a resource to the international Salvation Army.

The ISJC seeks to fulfil its mandate through the implementation of a strategic plan to:
☐ Raise strategic voices to advocate with the world's poor and oppressed.
☐ Be a recognised centre of research and critical thinking on issues of global social justice.
☐ Collaborate with like-minded organisations to advance the global cause of social justice.
☐ Exercise leadership in determining social justice policies and practices of The Salvation Army.
☐ Live the principles of justice and compassion and inspire others to do likewise.

STATISTICS
Officers 3 **Employees** 5 (full-time 1 part-time 4)
Policy Interns 4

STAFF
Deputy Director: Lt-Col Geanette Seymour
Personal Asst to Director and UN Rep: Maj Victoria Edmonds (New York)
UN Reps: Maj Elisabeth Frei (Vienna) Maj Sylvette Huguenin (Geneva) Lt-Col Julius Mukonga (Nairobi) Comrs Roy and Arda Frans (SPEA Zone)

The Africa Development Centre

Moi Avenue, Nairobi, Kenya

Postal Address: PO Box 40575, Nairobi 00100 GPO, Kenya

Tel: [254] (020) 221 2217

On 17 April 2009, IHQ gave approval for the relocation of The Salvation Army Leadership Training College (SALT College) of Africa to Nairobi and the establishment of the Africa Development Centre. Each having its individual title and role, the SALT College of Africa, the Africa Programme Development Office and the Zonal Facilitation Resource Office serve as focal points whilst coordinating activities for the Africa Zone on behalf of IHQ, reporting to the International Secretary for Africa. Operations carried out through the Africa Development Centre became effective 1 January 2010.

STATISTICS Officers 6 **Employees** 2

The Salvation Army Leadership Training College (SALT College) of Africa

Prompted by the request of territorial leaders of Africa, The Salvation Army Leadership Training College of Africa was established in 1986. Its purpose is to coordinate officer and local officer in-service training across Africa through distance-learning courses and seminars, monitored by an extension training officer in each territory.

An IHQ-sponsored education and training facility, SALT College offers distance learning in 15 countries across the African continent. Its students include officers, envoys, local officers, candidates and soldiers.

Principal: Maj Kapela Ntoya
Director of Studies: Maj Juliana Musilia
Director of Special Studies: Maj Rose-Nicole Ntoya
Office Administrator: Maj Benjamin Musilia
tel: [254] (020) 221 2217;
email: leadcoll_africa@sal.salvationarmy.org

Africa Programme Development Office

The office is under the leadership of the Programme Development Secretary. Its purpose is to help implement the policies and strategies of African territories, commands and region in relation to community development. Its role includes giving support to senior leadership and project officers in project design, reporting and implementation. Also, in collaboration with IHQ (Africa Zone and International Projects and Development Services) and in conjunction with local headquarters leadership it will pursue external donor potential and the training and development of staff.

The office also helps to implement policies and strategies for developing the skills of potential women leaders, in collaboration with and on behalf of the Zonal Secretary for Women's Ministries (IHQ) and headquarters leadership throughout Africa.

Programme Development Sec: Lt-Col Mary Capsey
email: Mary_Capsey@salvationarmy.org

Zonal Facilitation Resource Office

The office is under the leadership of the Zonal Facilitation Resource Officer who reports to the Under Secretary for Africa (IHQ) and the Programme Development Secretary, and who has a technical relationship to the International Health Services Coordinator.

The office enables territories, commands and regions in Africa to better use facilitation as a way of working both internally and in the wider community. This will help people to respond more faithfully to challenges and result in more sustainable, integrated mission and ministry.

Zonal Facilitation Resource Officer: Capt Lena Wanyonyi

International Administrative Structure

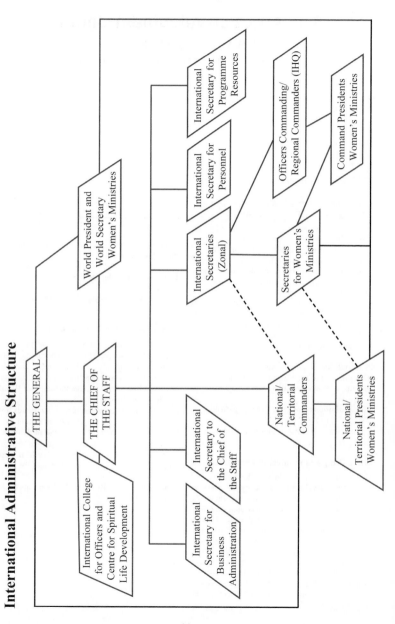

The Salvation Army International Trustee Company

Registered Office: 101 Queen Victoria Street, London EC4V 4EH

Registration No 2538134. Tel: (020) 7332 0101

Company Secretary: Lieut-Colonel Walter Fuge

DIRECTORS: Comr Barry C. Swanson (Chair), Comr Ann Woodall (Managing Director and Vice Chair), Comr Larry Bosh, Comr William Cochrane, Comr James Condon, Comr Robin Forsyth, Comr Kenneth Hodder, Mr Andrew Justice, Mr David Kidd, Comr Lalkiamlova, Comr Amos Makina, Mr Trevor Smith, Comr Robert Street.

The company is registered under the Companies Acts 1985 and 1989 as a company limited by guarantee, not having a share capital. It has no assets or liabilities, but as a trustee of The Salvation Army International Trusts it is the registered holder of Salvation Army property both real and personal including shares in some of the Army's commercial undertakings. The company is a trust corporation.

Reliance Bank Limited

Faith House, 23-24 Lovat Lane, London EC3R 8EB

Tel: (020) 7398 5400; fax: (020) 7398 5401; email: info@reliancebankltd.com;
website: www.reliancebankltd.com

Chairman: Commissioner Ann Woodall
Managing Director: Trevor J. Smith, ACIB

Finance Director: Kevin Dare, BA(Hons), CIMA
Banking Lending Manager and Company Secretary: Paul Underwood, ACIB
Banking Services Manager: Andrew Hunt, ACIB
Business Development Manager: Nichola Keating

DIRECTORS: Comr Ann Woodall (Chairman), Comr William Cochrane, Col Brian Peddle, Lt-Col Walter Fuge, Maj David Hinton, Maj Alan Read, Maj Jeffrey Wills, Mr Trevor Smith, Mr Kevin Dare, Mr Philip Deer, Mr Gerald Birkett, ACIB.

Reliance Bank Ltd is an authorised institution under the Banking Act 1987, regulated by the Financial Services Authority and registered under the Companies and Consumer Credit Acts.

OWNED by The Salvation Army through its controlling shareholders – The Salvation Army International Trustee Company and The Salvation Army Trustee Company – Reliance Bank accepts sterling and foreign currency deposits, carries on general banking business, and provides finance for Salvation Army corporate customers and private and business customers.

The bank can grant mortgages, personal loans and overdrafts, and also provides travel currency, cheques and safe custody facilities. It offers current accounts, together with a Reliance Bank Visa debit card, fixed deposits and savings accounts, and provides money transmission transactions both within the UK and abroad. Internet banking and telephone banking services are also offered.

The bank pays at least 75 per cent of its taxable profits by means of Gift Aid donation to its controlling shareholders.

Brochures are available on request, or visit www.reliancebankltd.com

STATISTICS Employees 22

OVERSEAS SERVICE FUNDS 2009-2010 INCOME

	International Self-Denial Contributions £	International Self-Denial Special £	Special Projects £	Donations via IHQ £	Total £
Australia Eastern	436,047		696,771	726,319	1,859,137
Australia Southern	483,786		1,183,066	597,364	2,264,216
Bangladesh	780				780
Brazil	20,063			1,244	21,307
Canada and Bermuda	1,055,002		1,291,768	74,915	2,421,685
Caribbean	22,954				22,954
Congo (Brazzaville)	73,619				73,619
Democratic Republic of Congo	47,147			628	47,775
Czech Republic	2,106				2,106
Denmark	50,000			44,733	94,733
Eastern Europe	11,896				11,896
Finland	56,383		98,933	69,699	225,015
France and Belgium	20,369			2,877	23,246
Germany and Lithuania	56,666			178,912	235,578
Ghana	9,524				9,524
Hong Kong	67,792		32,347	361,187	461,326
India Central	56,247			639	56,886
India Eastern	29,853			270	30,123
India Northern	16,492			2,876	19,368
India South Eastern	35,851			1,000	36,851
India South Western	23,145			313	23,458
India Western	19,634			1,239	20,873
Indonesia	33,788			1,887	35,675
Italy	12,700				12,700
Japan	78,701		61,583	28,979	169,263
Kenya East	31,323			835	32,158
Kenya West	27,487				27,487
Korea	54,514		1,982	29,117	85,613
Latin America North	8,070			4,390	12,460
Liberia	351				351
Malawi	3,924				3,924
Mexico	17,090			13,892	30,982
Mozambique	1,039				1,039
Myanmar	1,535				1,535
Netherlands	188,349		1,464,411	182,522	1,835,282
New Zealand, Fiji and Tonga	370,670		208,382	80,880	659,932
Nigeria	11,887				11,887
Norway, Iceland and The Færoes	374,986		1,342,396	1,225	1,718,607
Pakistan	1,692				1,692
Papua New Guinea	5,093				5,093
Philippines	4,333			1,355	5,688
Portugal	2,895			2,168	5,063
Rwanda and Burundi	2,343				2,343
Singapore, Malaysia and Myanmar	66,153			78,526	144,679
South America East	10,124				10,124
South America West	20,507			736	21,243
Southern Africa	28,696			16,281	44,977
Spain	4,611			20,496	25,107
Sri Lanka	1,230			122	1,352
Sweden and Latvia	85,144		861,152	118,280	1,064,576
Switzerland, Austria and Hungary	535,613		2,175,429	83,355	2,794,397
Taiwan	3,976	-	-	-	3,976
Tanzania	3,585	-	-	-	3,585
Uganda	1,214	-	-	-	1,214
United Kingdom	1,579,928	-	1,805,705	160,393	3,546,026
USA Central	2,472,802	586,166	1,491,868	191,019	4,741,855
USA Eastern	2,511,143	194,729	2,277,150	219,087	5,202,109
USA Southern	2,790,934	255,011	1,303,182	188,195	4,537,322
USA Western	2,193,390	106,553	2,597,978	205,141	5,103,062
USA SAWSO	-	-	2,001,264	107,410	2,108,674
Zambia	31,378	-		1,860	33,238
Zimbabwe	107,470	-	-	300	107,770
	16,276,024	1,142,459	20,895,367	3,802,666	42,116,516

OVERSEAS SERVICE FUNDS 2009-2010 EXPENDITURE

	Support of Overseas Work	Special Projects	Donations via IHQ	Total
	£	£	£	£
Africa, General	146	80,230		80,376
Americas, General	53,396		6,037	59,433
Angola	45,965	157,056	288	203,309
Austria	30,729			30,729
Australia Southern	-	110,251		110,251
Bangladesh	154,528	316,846	1,906	473,280
Brazil	680,750	948,882	51,223	1,680,855
Burundi	28,265			28,265
Caribbean	726,694	2,164,558	13,780	2,905,032
Congo (Brazzaville)	476,700	217,365	12,507	706,572
Democratic Republic of Congo	523,174	590,670	28,821	1,142,665
Czech Republic	394,223	457,738	241	852,202
Eastern Europe	1,946,723	1,001,995	30,281	2,978,999
Estonia [Finland]	114,433	70,954	12,028	197,415
Europe, General	2,100		13,839	15,939
Fiji & Tonga [New Zealand]	-	14,228	441	14,669
Germany and Lithuania	137,642	56,170		193,812
Ghana	185,946	249,347	21,217	456,510
Hong Kong	17,072	367,205	1,073	385,350
Hungary	75,106	109,531	124	184,761
India National Secretariat	68,130	26,389	742	95,261
India Central	246,433	465,167	6,309	717,909
India Eastern	106,585	300,124	10,380	417,089
India Northern	281,146	423,074	5,550	709,770
India South Eastern	248,971	387,324	9,095	645,390
India South Western	360,536	154,000	22,850	537,386
India Western	253,758	459,598	15,377	728,733
Indonesia	80,676	709,493	134,992	925,161
Italy and Greece	252,666	222,467	632	475,765
Kenya East	375,569	1,033,865	17,798	1,427,232
Kenya West	336,893	297,479	10,251	644,623
Korea	8,611	112,608	4,298	125,517
Kuwait	-	234,029		234,029
Latin America North	673,978	755,375	8,785	1,438,138
Latvia (Sweden)	120,367	81,309	474	202,150
Liberia	181,258	305,540	15,341	502,139
Malawi	111,855	516,385	24,628	652,868
Mali	34,464	64,363	7,033	105,860
Mexico	425,184	152,765	20,616	598,565
Mozambique	152,626	143,181	3,019	298,826
Myanmar	103,938	44,822	10,154	158,914
Nigeria	188,451	305,227	-	493,678
Norway	-	100,257	-	100,257
Pakistan	467,995	371,878	8,402	848,275
Papua New Guinea	401,903	460,232	16,552	878,687
Philippines	404,788	385,626	178,217	968,631
Poland	22,449	14,514	25,000	61,963
Portugal	324,981	160,527	-	485,508
Rwanda	121,120	118,009	4,466	243,595
SALT College	50,471	-	-	50,471
Singapore & Malaysia	38,763	390,444	17,930	447,137
South America East	539,429	457,245	16,117	1,012,791
South America West	474,080	1,620,429	105,177	2,199,686
South Asia, General	53,194	-	-	53,194
Southern Africa	192,891	243,898	19,614	456,403
SPEA, General	53,406	-		53,406
Spain	341,024	195,374	942	537,340
Sri Lanka	98,810	323,094	71,541	493,445
Taiwan	52,058	254,152	15,812	322,022
Tanzania	172,658	312,371	19,426	504,455
Uganda	173,513	209,173	17,622	400,308
Zambia	469,034	458,634	9,440	937,108
Zimbabwe	448,976	711,905	55,592	1,216,473
Crisis Relief	-	-	2,268,937	2,268,937
Central Pension Scheme	-	-	1,253,673	1,253,673
Other International Operations	1,529,741	-	-	1,529,741
	16,636,971	20,895,372	4,626,590	42,158,933

COMMUNITY DEVELOPMENT PROJECTS

THE Salvation Army thanks those listed below who, during 2009, assisted in its ministry to some of the world's most vulnerable people. This was done through community development projects overseen by the International Projects and Development Services (IPDS) at IHQ. These involved:

Combating the HIV/Aids pandemic; developing savings and loans groups; promoting healthy communities; supporting educational services; improving access to safe water and sanitation; supporting social service programmes to the aged, the marginalised and the young; responding to disaster-hit areas

Country	*Donor*	US $*
Australia	Eastern Territory (AusAID)	973,794
Canada	CIDA (Canada)	734,161
Germany	Christoffel Blindenmission	51,447
	Kindernothilfe	634,740
Netherlands	Goossens Trust	37,440
	Government grants	498,043
	New Life Foundation	23,122
Norway	NORAD	1,719,862
Sweden	Dispurse Foundation	222,140
Switzerland	Switzerland, Austria and Hungary Territory	3,475,390
	Bread for All	225,744
	Government grants	383,819
	Government grants in kind: milk products	292,309
	Solidarity Third World	32,262
	Swiss Solidarity	1,149,290
	Various foundations	245,330
United Kingdom	COAP	5,562
	Count Zoltan RM Von Rosenthal Charitable Trust	2,017
	Government grant: Dept for International Development	601,893
	Hope HIV	170,811
	Sloane Robinson Investment	1,552
	Vidi Foundation	3,103
	J. Cooper Legacy	115,001
	A. Jackson Legacy	8,531
	G. Petterson Legacy	139,632
USA	National Headquarters (SAWSO and USAID)	7,524,811
TOTAL		**US$ 19,271,806**

*As per exchange rate at time amounts recorded by the IPDS at IHQ

ANGOLA COMMAND

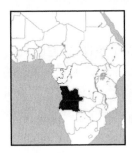

Command leaders:
Lieut-Colonels Ambroise and Alphonsine Zola

Officer Commanding:
Lieut-Colonel Ambroise Zola
(1 Mar 2008)

General Secretary:
Major S. Edward Horwood (1 Jan 2011)

**Command Headquarters: Igreja Exército de Salvação,
Bairo Marçal – Rangel 2 MA n° 15, Luanda, Angola**
Postal address: Caixa Postal 1656-C, Luanda, Angola
Tel: [00244] 928-570867; email: angosalvo@yahoo.com

Salvation Army work in Angola was officially established in 1985. Having been part of the Congo (Kinshasa) and Angola Territory, it became a separate command on 1 March 2008.

In 1974, two officers originally from Angola but trained and serving in Congo (Kinshasa) entered Angola by Uige Province to commence Salvation Army meetings in that part of the country. In 1978, other Salvationists from Kinshasa met in Angola's capital, Luanda, and 'opened fire'. The Salvation Army was officially recognised by the Angola Government on 14 February 1992.

Zone: Africa
Country included in the command: Angola
'The Salvation Army' in Portuguese: Exército de Salvação
Languages in which the gospel is preached: Humbundu, Kikongo, Kimbundu, Lingala, Ngangela,
    Portuguese

GROWTH and development have been evident as the command opened new corps and outposts. In the two Luanda sections, for example, 12 corps are now self-supporting and outposts are ready to be upgraded to corps status.

In Luanda 2 Section, converts were registered as a result of open-air meetings, recruits were prepared for soldiership and a new outpost was opened with 26 soldiers.

Although there is a shortage of officer personnel, three corps have been established in Muxico Section.

A water supply project is greatly benefiting the district.

Uige, Zaire and Cabinda Sections continue to grow. Families in Uige were happy to help the Army build a school for the children of that community.

On the Atlantic coast, people in Benguela erected their own hall with local resources and established an outpost in the maritime port of Lobito. The Army's work at Lubango is developing to include the town of Namibe.

The command was further encour-

Junior soldiers from Palanca join in Angola's 25th anniversary rejoicings

aged when more than 820 people filled the Luanda Central Corps hall to welcome nine cadets of the Ambassadors of Holiness Session. At the close of a God-glorifying event 104 people publicly dedicated their lives to Christ.

With Angola experiencing a time of relative peace and safety after many years of conflict, Salvationists in the command took every opportunity to advance God's Kingdom.

STATISTICS
Officers 34 (active 30 retired 4) **Cadets** 9
Employees 6
Corps 15 **Outposts** 13 **Schools** 2
Senior Soldiers 2,515 **Junior Soldiers** 683

STAFF
Women's Ministries: Lt-Col Alphonsine Zola (CPWM) Maj Deborah Horwood (CSWM) Maj Mamie Makuntima (HL)
Candidates: Maj Isabella Vuanza
Extension Officer: Capt Daniel Diantelo
Finance: Capt Sergio Nsumbu
Property: Capt Daniel Ngonga (pro tem)
Social: tba
Statistics: Capt Daniel Diantelo
Training: Majs Norbert and Isabelle Vuanza (Asst Officers)
Youth: Capt Timothée Lukanu

National BM: Sgt Raimond Nkuansambu
National SL: Sgt Kinavuidi

SECTIONS
Cabinda: Maj Antoine Kupesatel;
    tel: (00244) 924-868087
Luanda 1: Maj Joâo Mpembele;
    tel: (00244) 923-748074
Luanda 2: Maj Domingo Makuntima;
    tel: (00244) 923-742759
Uige: Capt Antonio Nsingi;
    tel: (00244) 924-118717
Zaire: Maj Joâo Batista Ndombele;
    tel: (00244) 934-657978

TRAINING COLLEGE
Rua Capola, Casa no 5/Bis, Q9/SAPU,
    Kilamba Kiaxi; tel: (00244) 926-842134

SECONDARY SCHOOL
Rua da Esquarda Intealao dos Moradores
    (Antigo Empromac), Bairo Hoji ha Yenda,
    Municipio do Cazenga;
    tel: (00244) 928-138191; Mr Paulo Mafuta
    (Director)

SCHOOL NZOANENE
Rua 21 de Janeiro, Bairo Rocha Pinto,
    Municipio de Maianga;
    tel: (00244) 923-607311; Sgt Nsumbu
    Mavug (Director)

SOCIAL SERVICES
Development and Emergencies
Moxico (vaccination programme and water
    supplies); Luena 1 Corps (polio project);
    Luao Corps (polio project and water supplies)

50

AUSTRALIA NATIONAL SECRETARIAT

Offices: 2 Brisbane Ave, Barton, Canberra, ACT 2600

Postal address: PO Box 4256, Manuka, ACT 2603, Australia

Tel: [61] (02) 6273 3055; fax: [61] (02) 6273 1383; email: Kelvin.Alley@aue.salvationarmy.org

Two Christian Mission converts, John Gore and Edward Saunders, pioneered Salvation Army operations on 5 September 1880 in Adelaide. These were officially established on 11 February 1881 by the appointment of Captain and Mrs Thomas Sutherland. In 1921 the work in Australia was organised into Eastern and Southern Territories with headquarters in Sydney and Melbourne.

A National Secretariat serving the whole of Australia and funded jointly by both territories was established in 1987.

Periodicals: *Kidzone, Warcry*

THE National Secretariat represents the views of The Salvation Army's two Australian territories to the Australian Federal Government as required or requested by both territorial commanders. The Secretariat addresses issues of spiritual, moral, ethical and social welfare by means of written submissions, personal dialogue with members of parliament and attendance at open forums.

The Secretariat also engages in dialogue with government departments, the not-for-profit sector, the diplomatic community and the national press.

The National Secretary is responsible for overseeing operations of the Red Shield Defence Services (RSDS), a philanthropic support group within the Australian Defence Force (ADF). RSDS personnel are accredited by the ADF to provide support to members of the ADF.

Twenty-seven officers and soldiers from both Australian territories provide pastoral and welfare support. An ADF brigade commander speaking at the RSDS Biennial Conference paid tribute to the vital role The Salvation Army plays in addressing concerns for his brigade's welfare, morale and general well-being.

RSDS 'Hop In' recreational centres on military bases are supplied with four-wheel-drive vehicles that become mobile 'Hop In' centres, providing hot and cold drinks, light refreshments, Christian reading material and a listening ear while in the field.

From time to time RSDS representatives are appointed to Australian peacekeeping units for a six-month tour of duty, the most recent deployment being to East Timor.

In 2011 Red Shield Defence Services commence operations in Adelaide, South Australia. This will give RSDS a presence in every major Australian city from Darwin in the north, around the eastern states, Victoria and west to Adelaide.

National Sec: Maj Kelvin Alley

Editorial Department: 95-99 Railway Rd, Blackburn, Vic 3130 (PO Box 479); tel: 03 8878 2303; fax: 03 8878 4816

National Editor-in-Chief: Capt Mal Davies

Red Shield Defence Services: PO Box 3246, Manuka, ACT 2603; tel: (02) 6273 2280; fax: (02) 6273 1383

Chief Commissioner: Maj Barry Nancarrow

AUSTRALIA EASTERN TERRITORY

Territorial Commander:
Commissioner Linda Bond
(1 May 2008)

Chief Secretary:
Colonel Wayne Maxwell (1 Nov 2010)

Territorial Headquarters: 140 Elizabeth Street, Sydney, NSW 2000

Postal address: PO Box A435, Sydney South, NSW 1235, Australia

Tel: [61] (02) 9264 1711 (10 lines); fax: [61] (02) 9266 9638; website: www.salvos.org.au

Two Christian Mission converts having pioneered Salvation Army operations in Adelaide in September 1880, the work in Australia was organised into Eastern and Southern Territories in 1921, with headquarters for the Eastern Territory being set up in Sydney.

Zone: South Pacific and East Asia
States included in the territory: New South Wales, Queensland, The Australian Capital Territory (ACT)
Languages in which the gospel is preached: Cantonese, English, Korean, Mandarin
Periodicals: *Creative Ministry, Pipeline, Venue, Women in Touch*

THE territory has focused on communicating its seven mission priorities in every area of ministry, and putting in place processes to ensure that they are actioned throughout the territory. Convinced that the Holy Spirit has spoken through the grassroots, the territory trusts him for the power and grace to see the vision realised.

The vision embodies what the Army will look like when the priorities are taken hold of:

'We will be a Spirit-filled Army of the 21st century, convinced of its calling, moving forward together into the world of hurting, broken, lonely, dispossessed and lost, reaching them by all means with the transforming message of Jesus,

bringing freedom, hope and life.'

A memorable congress entitled 'Uprising' took place, during which a Bible study book was issued, with one study for each of the territory's mission priorities. The seven priorities plus the vision statement shaped the content of the congress.

In keeping with a priority on holiness, the territory held a 'Brengle Create' symposium. Delegates were writers, songwriters, poets, graphic artists, painters and banner-makers from all parts of the territory. Ten international delegates participated.

More than 400 people have pledged to meet at 7.30 on Thursday mornings to pray for the territory and its priorities. They meet in groups in their homes, corps, social services centres, DHQs and at THQ where officers and employees spend 30 minutes in a unified prayer meeting.

An initiative known as 'Salvos Legal' has been formed as part of the 'One Army, One Mission' concept. Realising William Booth's vision in 1890 of a 'Poor Man's Lawyer', it takes a holistic approach to social injustice issues, such as homelessness, poverty, unemployment or a lack of spiritual well-being.

STATISTICS

Officers 1,000 (active 548 retired 452) **Cadets** (1st Yr) 18 (2nd Yr) 12 **Employees** 3,820
Corps 160 **Outposts/Plants/Missions** 37 **Social Centres/Programmes** 265 **Community Welfare Services** 185 **Thrift Stores/Charity Shops** 227
Senior Soldiers 8,652 **Adherents** 2,919 **Junior Soldiers** 525
Personnel serving outside territory Officers 35 Layworkers 5

STAFF

Women's Ministries: Comr Linda Bond (TPWM) Col Robyn Maxwell (TSWM)
Business: Lt-Col Peter Laws
Personnel: Lt-Col Philip Cairns
Programme: Lt-Col Miriam Gluyas
Asst Chief Sec (Governance): Lt-Col Jan Laws
Asst Chief Sec (Projects): Maj Cec Woodward
Territorial Legal Counsel: Mrs Sarah Hogan
Asst Sec for Business (Administration): Capt Stuart Evans
Aged Care Plus: Ms Sharon Callister
Audit: Mr Tim Green
Booth College: Lt-Col John Hodge
Candidates: Capts Craig and Donna Todd
Communications and Public Relations: Maj Glenn Whittaker
Counselling Service: Maj Robyn Smartt
Emergency Services: Mr Norm Archer
Finance: Mr Ian Minnett
Information Technology: Mr Wayne Bajema
Mission and Resource Team:
  Territorial Mission Directors: Majs Neil and Sharon Clanfield
  Territorial Mission Director (Social): Capt Paul Moulds

Territorial Youth Sec: Maj Kevin Unicomb
Music and Creative Arts: Mr Graeme Press
Moral and Social Issues Council: Maj Colin Lingard
Property: Mr Peter Alward
Red Shield Defence Services: Maj Barry Nancarrow
Salvation Army International Development Office (SAID): Lt-Col Pamela Hodge
Salvationist Supplies: Mr Graham Lang
Salvos Stores: Mr Neville Barrett
Sydney Staff Songsters: S/L Graeme Press

DIVISIONS

Australian Capital Territory and South NSW: 2-4 Brisbane Ave, Barton, ACT 2600; PO Box 4224, Kingston, ACT 2604; tel: (02) 6273 2211; fax: (02) 6273 2973; Majs David and Sandra Godkin
Central and North Queensland: 54 Charles St, North Rockhampton, QLD 4701; PO Box 5343, Red Hill, Rockhampton, QLD 4701; tel: (07) 4999 1999; fax: (07) 4999 1915; Majs Rodney and Wendy Walters
Newcastle and Central NSW: cnr of Union and Parry St, PO Box 684, The Junction, NSW 2291; tel: (02) 4926 3466; fax: (02) 4926 2228; Maj Kerry Haggar
North NSW: cnr Taylor and Beardy Sts, PO Box 1180, Armidale NSW 2350; tel: (02) 6771 1632; fax: (02) 6772 3444; Majs Phillip and Nancy McLaren
South Queensland: 342 Upper Roma St, Brisbane QLD 4000; GPO Box 2210, Brisbane, QLD 4001; tel: (07) 3222 6666; fax: (07) 3229 3884; Majs Mark and Julie Campbell
Sydney East and Illawarra: 61-65 Kingsway, Kingsgrove NSW 2208; PO Box 740, Kingsgrove, NSW 1480; tel: (02) 9336 3320; fax: (02) 9336 3359; Majs John and Narelle Rees
The Greater West: 93 Phillip St, Parramatta, NSW 2150; PO Box 66, Parramatta, NSW 2124; tel: (02) 9635 7400; fax: (02) 9689 1692; Majs Gary and Judith Baker

BOOTH COLLEGE

Bexley North, NSW 2207: 32a Barnsbury Grove, PO Box 4063; tel: (02) 9502 0400 fax: (02) 9502 4177

SCHOOL FOR OFFICER TRAINING

Bexley North, NSW 2207: 120 Kingsland Rd, PO Box 4063; tel: (02) 9502 1777; fax: (02) 9554 3298

SCHOOL FOR CHRISTIAN STUDIES
Bexley North, NSW 2207: 32a Barnsbury
Grove, PO Box 4063; tel: (02) 9502 0432;
fax: (02) 9502 0476

SCHOOL FOR LEADERSHIP TRAINING
Stanmore, NSW 2048: 97 Cambridge St;
tel: (02) 9557 1105; fax: (02) 9519 7319

SCHOOL FOR YOUTH LEADERSHIP
Lake Munmorah, NSW 2259: 42 Greenacre Ave;
tel: (02) 4358 8886; fax: (02) 4358 8882

HERITAGE PRESERVATION CENTRE
Bexley North, NSW 2207: 32a Barnsbury Grove,
PO Box 4063; tel: (02) 9502 0424;
fax: (02) 9502 0481;
email: AUEHeritage@aue.salvationarmy.org;
Maj Ken Sanz

EMPLOYMENT PLUS
Director: Maj Ritchie Watson
National Support Office: Level 3, 10 Wesley Ct,
East Burwood, VIC 3151; tel: 136 123
(Australia wide)

TERRITORIAL MISSION AND RESOURCE TEAM – RECOVERY
Sydney: 85 Campbell St, Surry Hills 2010;
Locked Bag 1000, Surry Hills, NSW 2010;
tel: (02) 9212 4000; fax: (02) 9212 4032;
Maj David Pullen

BRIDGE PROGRAMME – ADDICTION RECOVERY
(Alcohol, other drugs and gambling)
Brisbane: Brisbane Recovery Services Centre,
Moonyah, 58 Glenrosa Rd, PO Box 81,
Red Hill QLD 4059; tel: (07) 3369 0922;
fax: (07) 3369 9294 (acc men 84, detox unit 12,
halfway house 9)
Canberra: Canberra Recovery Services Centre,
5-13 Mildura St, Fyshwick ACT 2609,
PO Box 4181, Kingston ACT 2604;
tel: (02) 6295 1256; fax: (02) 6295 3766
(acc men 38, halfway house 3)
Central Coast: Central Coast Recovery Services
Centre, Selah, 60 Berkeley Rd, Berkeley Vale,
PO Box 5019, NSW Chittaway 2261;
tel: (02) 4388 4588; fax: (02) 4389 1490
(acc women 36, halfway house 4)
Fairfield: The Salvation Army Problem Gambling
Service, Fairfield Suite 11, 22 Harris St,
Fairfield, NSW 2165; PO Box 1041, Fairfield,
NSW 1860; tel/fax: 02 9723 8124

Gold Coast: Gold Coast Recovery Services
Centre, Fairhaven, 168 Macdonnell Rd, Eagle
Heights, QLD 4271; tel: (07) 3173 6215;
fax: (07) 5526 3989 (acc men 36, detox unit 11,
women 18)
Hunter Region Recovery Services:
Lake Macquarie Recovery Services Centre,
93 Russell Rd, PO Box 93, Morisset,
NSW 2264; tel: (02) 4973 1495;
fax (manager): (02) 4970 5807
Miracle Haven Bridge Programme (acc 78 men)
Endeavour Duel Diagnosis Bridge Programme
(acc 27 men)
Newcastle Bridge Youth and Family Drug and
Alcohol Support Programme (Bridge House):
100-102 Hannell St, PO Box 125, Wickham,
NSW 2293; tel: (02) 4961 1257 (acc halfway
house 3 males)
Leura: Blue Mountains Recovery Services Centre,
6 Eastview Ave, Leura NSW 2780;
PO Box 284, Wentworth Falls, NSW 2782;
tel: (02) 4782 7392; fax: (02) 4782 9127
(acc men 17, halfway house 3)
Nowra: Shoalhaven Bridge Programme, cnr
Salisbury Rd/St Anns St, Nowra, NSW 2541;
tel: (02) 4422 4604; fax: (02) 4422 4672
Penrith: The Involuntary Treatment After-care,
Penrith, Involuntary Care Trial, After-care
Service and The Salvation Army Problem
Gambling Service, 3/76 Henry St, Penrith,
NSW 2750; PO Box 702, Penrith B/C 2751
Sydney:
William Booth House Recovery Services
Centre, 56-60 Albion St, Surry Hills,
NSW 2010; PO Box 209, Surry Hills,
NSW 2010; tel: (02) 9212 2322;
fax: (02) 9281 9771 (acc men and women 131)
Alf Dawkins Detoxification Unit, 5-19 Mary St,
Surry Hills, NSW 2010; tel: (02) 8218 1209;
fax: (02) 9211 0455 (acc 10 men)
Townsville:
Townsville Recovery Services Centre,
312-340 Walker St; PO Box 803,
Townsville, QLD 4810; tel: (07) 4772 3607;
fax: (07) 4772 3174 (acc men 30)
Townsville Recovery Services Women's
out-Client Service, Grace Cottage

SALVOS STORES
General Manager: Mr Neville Barrett
Head Office: 4 Archbold Rd, Minchinbury, NSW
2770; tel: (02) 9834 9030, fax: (02) 9677 1782
ACT and Monaro Area: 15 Mildura St, Fyshwick,
ACT 2609; PO Box 7034, Canberra BC,
ACT 2610; tel: (02)6239 0117;
fax: (02) 6295 9788 (retail stores 8)

Brisbane Area: 80 Glenrosa Rd, Red Hill,
QLD 4059; tel: (07) 3369 0222;
fax: (07) 3368 6344 (retail stores 18)
Central Coast: 30b Central Coast Hwy,
W Gosford, NSW 2250; tel: 02 4331 5750;
fax: 02 4365 9349 (retail stores 5)
Eastern Sydney Area: 7 Bellevue St, St Peters,
NSW 2044; tel: (02) 9516 5089;
fax: (02) 9519 2924 (retail stores 18)
Gold Coast: 3-9 Precision Drive, Molendinar,
QLD 4214; tel: (07) 5571 5777;
fax: (07) 5574 4893 (retail stores 13)
Illawarra Area: 29-31 Waverley Drive,
Unanderra, NSW 2526; tel: (02) 4228 5644;
fax: (02) 4228 1040 (retail stores 8)
Newcastle Hunter Area: 900 Hunter St,
Newcastle, NSW 2300; tel: (02) 4961 3889;
fax: (02) 4961 2623 (retail stores 11)
Townsville Area: Lot 4, High Range Rd,
Thuringowa, QLD 4817; tel: (07) 4725 7360;
fax: (07) 4725 7370 (retail stores 3)
Western Sydney Area: 4 Archbold Rd,
Minchinbury, NSW 2770; tel: 02 9834 9001;
fax: 02 9625 2253 (retail stores 19)

RURAL CHAPLAINS

ACT and South NSW Div: c/o DHQ Canberra;
tel: (02) 6273 2211; fax: (02) 6273 2973
Longreach, QLD 4730: 149 Eagle St,
PO Box 127; tel: (07) 4658 3590
Newcastle and Central NSW Div: c/o DHQ
Newcastle; tel: (02) 4926 3466;
fax: (02) 4926 2228
North NSW Div: c/o DHQ Armidale;
tel: (02) 6771 1632; fax: (02) 6772 3444
South Queensland Div: c/o DHQ Brisbane;
tel: (07) 3222 6666; fax: (07) 3229 3884

AERIAL SERVICE

Flying Service Base: 10 Steelcon Pde,
Mt Isa, QLD 4825; tel: (07) 4749 3875;
fax: (07) 4749 3870

CONFERENCE AND HOLIDAY HOUSES/UNIT

Collaroy, NSW 2097: The Collaroy Centre,
Homestead Ave, Collaroy Beach,
PO Box 11; tel: (02) 9982 9800 (office),
(02) 9982 6570 AH; fax: (02) 9971 1895;
www.collaroycentre.org.au
Budgewoi, NSW 2262: 129 Sunrise Ave;
bookings through THQ Property Dept;
tel: (02) 9266 9723 (cottage acc 6)
Cairns, QLD 4870: 281-289 Sheridan St;
bookings through DHQ Rockhampton;
tel: (07) 4999 1999 (4 units)

Caloundra, QLD 4551: 4 Michael St, Golden
Beach; bookings through THQ Property Dept;
tel: (02) 9266 9723 (house)
Main Beach, QLD 4217: Unit 23 Ocean Park
Towers, 3494 Main Beach Pde;
bookings through THQ Property Dept;
tel: (02) 9266 9723 (apartment)
Margate, QLD 4019: 2 Duffield Rd;
bookings through THQ Property Dept;
tel: (02) 9266 9723 (3 units)
Monterey, NSW 2217: 1/60 Solander St;
bookings through THQ Property Dept;
tel: (02) 9266 9723
Tugan, QLD 4224: 3/15 Elizabeth St;
bookings through THQ Property Dept;
tel: (02) 9266 9723 (unit)
THQ Property Dept contact: Elaine Whittaker;
mob: +61 4 11222905; email:
Elaine.Whittaker@aue.salvationarmy.org

RED SHIELD DEFENCE SERVICES

RSDS Administration: Canberra ACT;
tel: (02) 6273 2280; fax: (02) 6273 1383;
mob: 0417 794 883
Gallipoli Barracks, Brisbane, QLD:
RSDS representative; mob: 0417 797 785;
fax: (07) 3851 3979
Holsworthy Military Camp, Sydney, NSW:
RSDS representative; mob: 0417 796 973
Lavarack Barracks, Townsville, QLD:
RSDS representative; mob: 0417 614 596
Puckapunyal School of Armoured, VIC: Trucks
& Artillery; mob: 0418 334 778
Royal Military College, Duntroon, ACT:
RSDS representative; mob: 0407 830 488
Singleton Infantry Centre, NSW:
RSDS representative; mob:0419 626 723;
fax: (02) 6573 4512

SOCIAL SERVICES
Residential Aged Care

Arncliffe, NSW 2205: Macquarie Lodge,
171 Wollongong Rd; tel: (02) 9556 6900;
fax: (02) 9567 5043 (acc nursing home 65,
hostel 49)
Balmain, NSW 2041: Montrose, 13 Thames St,
PO Box 2; tel: (02) 9818 2355;
fax: (02) 9818 5062 (acc hostel men 44)
Bass Hill, NSW 2197: Weeroona Village;
14 Trebartha St; tel: (02) 9645 3220;
fax: (02) 9645 1390 (acc hostel 45, nursing
home 60)
Canowindra, NSW 2804: Moyne, 161 Nangar Rd,
PO Box 156; tel: (02) 6344 1475;
fax: (02) 6344 1902 (acc nursing home 29,
hostel 44)

Chelmer, QLD 4068: Warrina Village,
35 Victoria Ave, PO Box 239, Indooroopilly;
tel: (07) 3379 9800; fax: (07) 3379 7839
(acc nursing home 40, hostel 42)

Dee Why, NSW 2099: Pacific Lodge,
15 Fisher Rd, PO Box 109; tel: (02) 9982 8477;
fax: (02) 9982 9174 (acc hostel 51)

Dulwich Hill, NSW 2203: Maybanke,
80 Wardell Rd, PO Box 286;
tel: (02) 9560 4457; fax: (02) 9569 1301
(acc nursing home 25, hostel 38)

Erina, NSW 2250: Woodport Village,
120-140 The Entrance Rd; tel: (02) 4365 2660;
fax: (02) 4365 1812 (acc hostel 73, nursing
home 96)

Goulburn, NSW 2580: Gill Waminda, Mary St,
PO Box 233; tel: (02) 4823 4300;
fax: (02) 4823 4317; (acc hostel 63, nursing
home 40)

Merewether, NSW 2291: Carpenter Court,
46 John Pde, PO Box 246; tel: (02) 4963 4300;
fax: (02) 4963 6489 (acc 42)

Narrabundah, ACT 2604: Mountain View,
Goyder St, PO Box 61; tel: (02) 6295 1044;
fax: (02) 6295 1473 (acc 67)

Parkes, NSW 2870: Rosedurnate, 46 Orange St,
PO Box 100; tel: (02) 6862 2300;
fax: (02) 6862 3756 (acc nursing home 29,
hostel 46)

Port Macquarie, NSW 2444: Bethany,
2-6 Gray St, PO Box 2016;
tel: (02) 6584 1127; fax: (02) 6584 1045
(acc nursing home 50, hostel 40)

Riverview, QLD 4303: Moggill Ferry Rd,
PO Box 6042; tel: (07) 3282 1000;
fax: (07) 3282 6929 (acc nursing home 50,
hostel 143)

Rockhampton, QLD 4700: Bethesda,
58 Talford St, PO Box 375; tel: (07) 4922 3229;
fax: (07) 4922 3455 (acc hostel 50)

Independent Living Retirement Villages

Arncliffe, NSW 2205: Macquarie Lodge,
171 Wollongong Rd; tel: (02) 9556 6900;
fax: (02) 9567 5043 (acc units 82)

Bass Hill, NSW 2197: Weerona Village,
14 Trebartha St, Bass Hill, NSW 2197;
tel: (02) 9645 3220; fax: 9645 1390
(acc units 36)

Burwood, NSW 2134: Shaftesbury Court,
75a Shaftesbury Rd; tel: (02) 9560 4457
(acc units 35)

Chelmer, QLD 4068: Warrina Village,
35 Victoria Ave, PO Box 239;
tel: (07) 3379 9800; fax: (07) 3379 7839
[Indooroopilly, QLD 4068] (acc units 12)

Collaroy, NSW 2097: Warringah Place,
1039 Pittwater Rd, PO Box 395;
tel: (02) 9971 1933; fax: (02) 9971 4155
(acc self-care units 64, serviced apartments 44)

Erina, NSW 2250: Woodport Village,
120-140 The Entrance Rd; tel: (02) 4365 2660;
fax: (02) 4365 1812 (acc units 64)

Narrabundah, ACT 2604: Karingal Court,
11 Boolimba Cresc; tel: (02) 6295 1044;
fax: (02) 6295 1473 (acc 36)

Parkes, NSW 2870: Rosedurnate, 46 Orange St,
PO Box 100; tel: (02) 6862 2300;
fax: (02) 6862 3756 (acc units 17)

Riverview, QLD 4303: Moggill Ferry Rd,
PO Box 6042; tel: (07) 3282 1000;
fax: (07) 3282 6929 (acc units 26)

Aged Care Respite and Day Care

Rivett, ACT 2611: Burrangiri, 1-7 Rivett Place,
PO Box 8065; tel: (02) 6288 1488;
fax: (02) 6288 0321 (acc 15, respite day care 20)

Children's Services
(including Day Care and After School)

Carina, QLD 4152: 202 Gallipoli Rd;
tel: (07) 3395 0744

Gladstone, QLD 4680: Family Day Care,
198 Goondoon St; tel: (07) 4972 2985;
fax: (07) 4972 7835

Macquarie Fields, NSW 2564: Eucalyptus Dr,
PO Box 1; tel: (02) 9605 4749;
fax: (02) 9618 1492

Slacks Creek, QLD 4127: Communities for
Children, 123 Paradise Rd, PO Box 998;
tel: (07) 3290 5200; fax: (07) 3290 5394

Counselling Service

Head Office: Rhodes, NSW 2138: 15 Blaxland Rd,
PO Box 3096; tel: (02) 9743 4535

Batemans Bay, NSW 2536: 25 Old Princes Hwy;
tel: 0431 659 682

Brisbane, QLD 4122: 5/46 Mount Gavatt-
Capalaba Rd, Upper Mount Gravatt,
PO Box 6266, Upper Mt Gravatt;
tel: (07) 3349 5046

Campbelltown, NSW 2560: 27 Rudd Rd,
Leumeah; refer to Penrith Office,
tel: (02) 4731 1554

Canberra ACT 2602: Ste 3, Southwell Park
Offices, Montford Cresc; tel: (02) 6248 5504

Fairfield – refer to Penrith Office

Gosford, NSW 2250: 120 The Entrance Rd, Erina;
refer to Sydney Office; tel: (02) 9743 2831

Penrith, NSW 2751: Ste 15, Lethbridge Ct,
20-24 Castlereagh St, PO Box 588;
tel: (02) 4731 1554

Stafford, QLD 4053: 32 Hayward St; refer to
Brisbane Office
Sydney, NSW 2138: 15 Blaxland Rd,
PO Box 3096, Rhodes; tel: (02) 9743 2831
Tuggeranong, ACT 2900: cnr Anketell and
Reed Sts; refer to North Lyneham Office

Moneycare Financial Counselling Services

Armidale, NSW 2350: 108 Beardy St;
tel: (02) 6771 1632; fax: (02) 6772 3444
Auburn, NSW 2144: Harrow Rd;
tel: 0483 476 514
Brisbane, QLD 4001: 342 Upper Roma St,
PO Box 2210, tel: (07) 3222 6666;
fax: (07) 3229 3884
Caboolture, QLD 4510: 82 Lower King St;
tel: (07) 5495 4627
Campbelltown, NSW 2560: 27-31 Rudd Rd,
PO Box 2041 Leumeah; tel: (02) 4620 7482
Campsie, NSW 2194: 30 Anglo Rd, PO Box 399;
tel: 9787 5375; fax: 9718 6775
Cooma, NSW 2630: 2 Mittagong Rd;
tel: (02) 6452 1798
Central QLD 4701: 54 Charles St, North
Rockhampton, PO Box 5343, CQMC 4702;
tel: (07) 4999 1999; fax: (07) 4999 1915
Dickson, ACT 2602: 4 Hawdon Pl, PO Box 1038;
tel: (02) 6247 1340 (Direct Line),
(02) 6247 3635; fax: (02) 6257 2791
Goulburn, NSW 2580: 6 Hovell St;
tel: (02) 4822 2115
Hurstville, NSW 2220: 23 Dalcassia St;
appointments through Kingsgrove;
tel: (02) 9336 3320; fax: (02) 9336 3359
Kingsgrove, NSW 1480: 61-65 Kingsway,
PO Box 740; tel: 9336 3346; fax: 9336 3359
Lethbridge Park, NSW 2150:
2-6 Bougainville Rd; tel/fax: (02) 9835 2756
Leumeah, NSW 2560: 27 Rudd Rd;
tel: (02) 4620 7482
Newcastle West, NSW 2302: cnr Union and
Parry Sts; tel: (02) 4929 2300;
fax: (02) 4926 2228
Mackay, QLD 4740: 48 Gregory St;
tel: (07) 4911 0929
Maroochydore, QLD 4558: cnr Briadmeadows
and Maroochydore Rds; tel: 5443 1702
North NSW: inland outreach service, 2-6 Gray St,
Port Macquarie; tel: (02) 6583 5963
Parramatta; NSW 2150: Suite 1, 2nd Fl,
95 Phillip St, PO Box 3681;
tel: (02) 9633 5011; fax: (02) 9633 5214
Surry Hills, NSW 2010: 5 Mary St;
tel: (02) 8218 1244
Taree, NSW 2430: Suite 1, 10 Pulteney St;

tel: (02) 6552 6237; fax: (02) 6892 4405
Tuncurry, NSW 2428: 7 South St;
tel: (02) 6554 6101; fax: (02) 6555 3347
Box Hill, VIC 3128: 17 Nelson Rd;
tel: (03) 9890 2993

Crisis and Supported Accommodation (homelessness services)
Adults (singles)

Cairns North, QLD 4870: Centennial Lodge,
281 Sheridan St, PO Box 140N;
tel: (07) 4031 4432; fax: (07) 4031 9473
(acc men 25, women 20, women with
children 6, patient transfer scheme men 5,
women 5)
Campbelltown, NSW 2560: Shekinah,
127b Lindesay St; PO Box 662;
tel: (02) 4625 9022 (acc women and children
4 units)
Carrington, NSW 2294: The Anchor, PO Box 73,
cnr Young and Cowper Sts; tel: (02) 4961 6129;
fax: (02) 4961 4038 (acc men 21)
Griffith, NSW 2680: cnr Binya and Anzac Sts;
tel: (03) 6964 3388 (acc hostel 5, men in
community 6)
Leeton, NSW 2705: 9 Mulga St;
tel: (02) 6953 4941 (acc family units 3)
Mount Isa, QLD 4825: Serenity House,
4 Helen St; PO Box 2900; tel: (07) 4743 3198
(acc women and children 11, patient transfer
scheme 7)
Newcastle, NSW 2293:
Clulow Court, PO Box 414, The Junction,
NSW 2291 (acc single women, crisis hostel
beds 8)
The Ark, 116-120 Hannell St, PO Box 94,
Wickham; tel: (02) 4969 8066;
fax: (02) 4969 8073 (community acc 24)
Southport, QLD 4215: Still Waters,
173 Wardoo St, PO Box 888, Ashmore City
4214; tel: (07) 5591 1776 (acc crisis beds
women 24, women and children 7 units,
single women medium-term 16)
Spring Hill, QLD 4004: Pindari Men's
Programme, 28 Quarry St, PO Box 159;
tel: (07) 3832 1491 (acc hostel 120,
community units 9)
Spring Hill, QLD 4004: Pindari Women's
Programme, 28 Quarry St; tel: (07) 3832 6073
(acc 18)
Surry Hills, NSW 2010:
Foster House, 5-19 Mary St;
tel: (02) 9212 1065; fax: (02) 9218 1248
(acc men's hostel 96 beds; Knudsen Place,
IPU 23 beds; community places 85)
Samaritan House, 348 Elizabeth St,

PO Box 583; tel: (02) 9211 5794;
fax: (02) 9212 5430
(acc women crisis beds 24, medium-term
beds 20, community units 8)

Tewantin, QLD 4565: 26 Donella St, PO Box 671;
tel: (07) 5447 1184; fax: (07) 5447 1854
(acc families, community places 16)

Toowoomba, QLD 4350: 5 Russell St,
PO Box 2527; (acc men's crisis)
tel: (07) 4632 5239; fax: (07) 4639 1821;
(family community places) tel: (07) 4639 1998

Youth Services

Bundaberg QLD 4670: Youth Refuge,
71 Woongarra St, Bundaberg 4670;
tel: (07) 4151 3400; fax: (07) 4152 6044
(acc 16)

Canberra, ACT 2601: Oasis Support Network,
PO Box 435; tel: (02) 6248 7191;
fax: (02) 6249 8116

Canberra, ACT 2601: Oasis Youth Residential
Service, Canberra, PO Box 63;
tel: (02) 6288 6248; fax: (02) 6288 0646
(acc crises 8, medium term 3, community 5)

Canley Vale, NSW 2166: YouthLink,
214 Sackville St, PO Box 188W, Fairfield
West, NSW 2165; tel: (02) 9725 7779;
fax: (02) 9725 7781

Fortitude Valley, QLD 4006: Youth Outreach
Service, 20 Baxter St, PO Box 248;
tel: (07) 3854 1245; fax: (07) 3854 1552

Minchinbury NSW 2770: Joblink, Unit 31b,
40 Sterling Rd; tel: (02) 9675 5972;
Mt Druitt office tel: (02) 9625 8533;
fax: (02) 9625 4933

Newcastle, NSW 2293: Newcastle Youth Crisis
and Training Service; The Ark,
116-120 Hannell St, PO Box 94, Wickham;
tel: (02) 4969 8066; fax: (02) 4969 8073 (acc 24)

Surry Hills, NSW 2010: Oasis Youth Support
Network; 365 Crown St, PO Box 600,
Darlinghurst 1300; tel: (02) 9331 2266
(acc crises 16, medium-term 5, community 12)

Wyong, NSW 2259: Oasis Youth Centre,
5 Hely St, PO Box 57, Wyong;
tel: (02) 4353 9799; fax: (02) 4353 9550

Intellectually Disabled Persons Services

Broken Hill NSW 2880: LISK, 633 Lane St,
PO Box 477; tel: (08) 8088 2044;
fax: (08) 8087 7669

Toowong, QLD 4066: SAILSS (Salvation Army
Individual Lifestyle Support Service),
15 Elizabeth St; tel: (07) 3368 0700;
fax: (07) 3367 1844 (acc home support
services 31 adults)

Toowoomba, QLD 4350: Horton Village,
2 Curtis St, PO Box 289; tel: (07) 4639 4026;
fax: (07) 4638 3248 (acc 28)

Family Tracing Service

Brisbane, QLD 4000: 342 Upper Roma St,
PO Box 2210, Brisbane 4001;
tel: (07) 3222 6661; fax: (07) 3229 3884

Sydney, NSW 2000:
PO Box A435, Sydney South 1235;
tel: (02) 9211 0277; fax: (02) 9211 2044
Special Search, tel: (02) 9211 6491; 1300 667
366 Australia Wide; fax: (02) 9211 2044

Telephone Counselling Service

Five Dock, NSW 2049: Salvo Care Line,
NSW 2046; 1 Barnstaple Rd, PO Box 178;
tel: (02) 8736 3297 (office); fax: (02) 8736 3278

Brisbane, QLD 4001: Salvo Care Line;
QLD 4000; 342 Upper Roma St,
GPO Box 2210; tel: (07) 3222 6666

Domestic Violence Programme*

Chatswood, NSW 2067: cnr Johnson and Archer
Sts; tel: (02) 9411 7728; fax: (02) 9411 7174

Hostel for Students

Toowong, QLD 4066: 15 Jephson St,
PO Box 1124; tel: (07) 3371 1966 (acc 66)

Employment Preparation and Skills Training

Bundaberg, QLD 4670: Tom Quinn Community
Centre; 8 Killer St, Bundaberg 4670;
tel: (07) 4153 3557; fax: (07) 4151 1746

Canley Vale, NSW 2166: YouthLink,
214 Sackville St, PO Box 188W, Fairfield West,
NSW 2165; tel: (02) 9725 7779

Fortitude Valley, QLD 4006: Youth Outreach
Service, 20 Baxter St, PO Box 248;
tel: (07) 3854 1245

Hamilton, NSW 2303: This Way Up Furniture
Company, 3/24 Hudson St, Hamilton North,
PO Box 162; tel: (02) 4969 5695;
fax (02) 4969 5665

Minchinbury, NSW 2770: Job Link,
6 Colyton Rd; PO Box 55, Mt Druitt 2770;
tel: (02) 9625 8533; fax (02) 9625 4933

Riverview, QLD 4304: Canaan Training Centre,
29 Riverview Rd; PO Box 359, Booval,
QLD 4304; tel: (07) 3282 1300;
fax: (07) 3816 2903

Surry Hills, NSW 2010: Oasis Youth Support
Network, 365 Crown St, PO Box 600,
Darlinghurst; tel: (02) 9331 2266;
fax: (02) 9331 2200

Wickham, NSW 2293: Newcastle Youth Crisis
and Training Service, 116-120 Hannell St,
PO Box 94, Wickham; tel: (02) 4969 8066;
fax: (02) 4969 8073

Court and Prison Ministry

ACT and South NSW Div, ACT 2604:
PO Box 4224, Kingston; tel: (02) 6273 2211;
fax: (02) 6273 2973

Central and North Queensland Div, QLD 4702:
PO Box 5343 CQMC, Rockhampton;
tel: (07) 4999 1999; fax: (07) 4999 1915

Greater West Div, NSW 2124: PO Box 66,
Parramatta; tel: (02) 9635 7400;
fax: (02) 9689 1692

Newcastle and Central NSW Div, NSW 2291:
PO Box 684, The Junction; tel: (02) 9426 3466;
fax: (02) 9426 2228

South Queensland Div, QLD 4001:
PO Box 2210, Brisbane; tel: (07) 3222 6670;
fax (07) 3229 3884

Sydney East and Illawarra Div, NSW 1480:
PO Box 740, Kingsgrove; tel: (02) 9336 3320;
fax: (02) 9336 3359

Chaplains to Statutory Authorities

New South Wales Fire Brigades, NSW 2000:
City of Sydney Fire Stn, Level 52
Rosemeath Ave, Kingsgrove, NSW 2208;
tel: (02) 9265 2736; fax: (02) 9718 9837

New South Wales Rural Fire Service, NSW 2142:
15 Carter St, Lidcomb, Locked Mail Bag 17,
Granville NSW 2142; tel: (02) 8741 5555;
fax: (02) 9553 1854

Queensland Fire and Rescue Service, QLD 4005:
Kemp Place Fire Stn, Ivory St, Fortitude
Valley, PO Box 1472, New Farm;
tel: (07) 3635 1985; fax (07) 3406 8328

Community Service

Auburn, NSW 2144: 5-7 Mary St;
tel: (02) 9749 7150

Brisbane, QLD 4003: 97 Turbot St,
PO Box 13688, George St 4003;
tel: (07) 3211 9230; fax: (07) 3211 9234

Broken Hill, NSW 2880: Algate House
Community Centre, 633 Lane St, PO Box 477;
tel: (08) 8088 2044; fax: (08) 8087 7669

Campsie, NSW 2194: 30 Anglo Rd, PO Box 399;
tel: (02) 9787 2333; fax: (02) 9718 6775

Canberra, ACT 2602: 4 Hawdon Pl, Dickson;
PO Box 1038, Dickson; tel: (02) 6247 3635;
fax: (02) 6257 2791

Dee Why, NSW 2099: Northern Beaches Centre,
1 Fisher Rd, PO Box 210; tel: (02) 9981 4472;
fax: (02) 9972 9976

Dulwich Hill: 54 Dulwich St; tel: (02) 9569 4511;
fax: (02) 9569 4677

Greenslopes, QLD 4120: 481 Logan Rd;
PO Box 221, Stones Corner;
tel: (07) 3394 4184; fax: (07) 3324 2409

Hurstville, NSW 2220: St George Centre,
23 Dalcassia St, PO Box 930, Hurstville,
NSW 2220; tel: (02) 9579 3897;
fax: (07) 9579 6094

Inala, QLD 4077: 83 Inala Ave, PO Box 1050;
tel: (07) 3372 1889

Ipswich, QLD 4305: 14 Ellenborough St,
PO Box 227; tel: (07) 3812 2462;
fax: (07) 3812 3818

Logan City, QLD 4114: 8 Blackwood Rd,
Woodridge, PO Box 816; tel: (07) 3808 2564;
fax: (07) 3290 0310

Macquarie Fields, NSW 2564: cnr Eucalyptus
and Peppermint Cresc, PO Box 1;
tel: (02) 9605 4717

Maroubra, NSW 2035: Eastern Beaches Centre,
100 Boyce Rd, PO Box 209; tel: (02) 9314 2166

Nerang, QLD 4211: Shop 5, Dalmar Centre,
43-45 Price St, PO Box 599;
tel: (07) 5596 0764; fax: (07) 5527 4681

Newcastle West, NSW 2302: 96 Parry St,
PO Box 2364, Dangar, NSW 2309;
tel: (02) 4929 2300

North Brisbane, QLD 4018: cnr Roghan and
Handford Rds, PO Box 155, Taigum;
tel: (07) 3865 1416; fax: (07) 3265 5841

Parramatta NSW 2150: 30-32 Smith St;
PO Box 6178, Parramatta BC;
tel: (02) 9891 4526

Southport, QLD 4215: 3/80 Davenport St,
PO Box 1680; tel: (07) 5591 2729;
fax: (07) 5591 1216

Sydney, NSW 2010: Inner City (Streetlevel)
Centre, 339 Crown St, Surry Hills 2010;
tel: (02) 9360 1000; fax: (02) 9331 7276

Townsville, QLD 4810: 54 Charles St,
N Rockhampton, PO Box 5343; CQMC 4702;
tel: (07) 4999 1999; fax: (07) 4999 1915

Wollongong, NSW 2500: Illawarra Centre,
29 Ellen St, PO Box 6102; tel: (02) 4225 1372;
fax (02) 4225 3509

Wynnum, QLD 4178: 107 Akonna St,
PO Box 701; tel: (07) 3393 4713;
fax: (07) 3393 5066

*The territory also has 5 women's refuge centres
which include accommodation for mothers and
children. Addresses and telephone numbers are
confidential.*

AUSTRALIA SOUTHERN TERRITORY

Territorial leaders:
Commissioners Raymond and Aylene Finger

Territorial Commander:
Commissioner Raymond Finger
(1 Jul 2010)

Chief Secretary:
Colonel Peter Walker (1 Jul 2010)

Territorial Headquarters: 95-99 Railway Road, Blackburn 3130, Victoria

Postal address: PO Box 479, Blackburn 3130, Victoria, Australia

Tel: [61] (03) 8878 4500; fax: [61] (03) 8878 4841; email: Salvosaus@aus.salvationarmy.org;
website: www.salvationarmy.org.au

Two Christian Mission converts having pioneered Salvation Army operations in Adelaide in September 1880, the work in Australia was organised into Eastern and Southern Territories in 1921, with headquarters for the Southern Territory being set up in Melbourne.

Zone: South Pacific and East Asia
States included in the territory: Northern Territory, South Australia, Tasmania, Victoria,
    Western Australia
Languages in which the gospel is preached: Arabic and Nuer (Sudanese), Cantonese, English, Korean, Mandarin, local aboriginal
    languages
Periodicals: *On Fire*

IN 2007 the territory had conducted a special congress, conference and commissioning event called 'Connections 07'. After much research of the conference findings, territorial and divisional consultations and prayerful preparation, May 2009 saw the launch of 'Connecting Forward' – an intense focus throughout the territory on The Salvation Army's mission and values, and key areas for the territory to advance in.

Many centres held special 'Connecting Forward' events, used new resources from THQ departments, began study groups and implemented community outreach activities, often under the banner of the 'Salvos Out There' programme.

However, it was not all about new directions – there was also time for celebration of achievements. In June 2009 the Springvale Chinese Corps celebrated its 10th anniversary; also, more than 150 African Salvationists from corps around the territory gathered in Melbourne. Both events helped to highlight the multicultural nature of Salvation Army worship in the territory.

In similar vein, August saw the opening of 'The Couch' – a support programme for international students, based at Melbourne 614 Corps in the heart of the city. After media attention on the plight of students being far from home, it was encouraging to see the Army take such a public and well-accepted stand.

In late November a very special series of events also received public recognition. Retired General Eva Burrows having celebrated her 80th birthday two months earlier, the commissioning weekend included not only the ordination and commissioning of the Prayer Warriors Session and the visit of then Chief of the Staff Commissioner Robin Dunster, but also a tribute to the 'matriarch' of the territory, General Burrows.

Saturday evening's tribute concert saw the presentation of the one-woman show *The Three Bonnets* by Carol Jaudes (USA Eastern). Spoken tributes came from General Shaw Clifton (via a video clip), various officers, family members and friends.

One such friend was General Burrows's biographer, Colonel Henry Gariepy OF, who earlier in the day took part in the launch of a new book, *Hallmarks of The Salvation Army*, co-edited by himself and Major Stephen Court. The book was dedicated to General Burrows and included reflections on Salvation Army ministry by 30 leading Salvationist writers and thinkers.

The year 2010 opened with the 'Insane' Territorial Youth Conference. More than 300 teenagers gathered at Mountain Valley Camp for a week of worship, electives, recreational activities and spiritual challenge. For many it was a life-changing event.

In March, 'iSalvos' was launched. Tapping into the online social networking phenomenon, 'iSalvos' provides online worship, a discussion forum, live streaming, chat forums and podcasts of special Army events at www.isalvos.net

STATISTICS

Officers 921 (active 515 retired 406) **Cadets** (1st Yr) 13 (2nd Yr) 25 (in appointment) 8 **Employees** 5,065

Corps 170 **Outposts** 11 **Social Centres/ Programmes** 256 **Salvos Stores** 210 **Community Support Centres** 123 **Outback Flying Service** 1

Senior Soldiers 8,386 **Adherents** 2,553 **Junior Soldiers** 1,153

Personnel serving outside territory Officers 24 Layworkers 6

STAFF

Women's Ministries: Comr Aylene Finger (TPWM) Col Jennifer Walker (TSWM) Lt-Col Jennifer Barnard (Asst TSWM)

Asst to the CS: Maj Gary Hart

  Executive Support Officer: Capt Kerryn Roberts

  Training Principal: Maj Geoff Webb

  National Editor-in-Chief: Capt Malcolm Davies

Business Administration: Lt-Col Rodney Barnard

  Asst Sec for Business Admin and Overseas Development Secretary: Maj Sandra Maunder

  Asst Sec for Business and Territorial Legal Secretary: Capt Malcolm Roberts

  Audit: Mr Cameron Duck

  Salvos Stores: Mr Allen Dewhirst

Finance: Mr Gregory Stowe
Salvationist Supplies: Mrs Karen Newton
Information Technology: Mr Larry Reed
Property: Mr David Sinden
Public Relations: Maj Neil Venables
Personnel: Lt-Col Frank Daniels
  Asst Sec for Personnel: Maj Winton Knop
  Candidates: Maj Cilla Bone
  Human Resources: Ms Katrina D'Ore
  Leader Development: Maj Carelle Begley
  Overseas Personnel: Maj Lorraine Hart
  Pastoral Care: Maj Graeme Faragher
  Spiritual Development: Maj Christine
    Faragher
Programme: Lt-Col Ian Hamilton
  Asst Sec for Programme: Maj Ray Begley
  Family Tracing: Maj Sophia Gibb
  Melbourne Staff Band: B/M Ken
    Waterworth
  Melbourne Staff Songsters: S/L Brian Hogg
  Social Programme: Maj Robyn Fernihough
  Youth: Capt Rowan Castle

DIVISIONS

Eastern Victoria: 347-349 Mitcham Rd,
  Mitcham, Vic 3132; tel: (03) 8872 6400;
  Maj Winsome Merrett (DC) Lt-Col Marilyn
  Hamilton (DDWM)
Melbourne Central: 1/828 Sydney Rd,
  North Coburg, Vic 3058; tel: (03) 9353 5200;
  Majs Graeme and Karyn Rigley
Northern Victoria: Bramble St, Bendigo,
  Vic 3550; tel: (03) 5443 4288; Majs John and
  Wendy Freind
South Australia: 39 Florence St, Fullarton,
  SA 5063; tel: (08) 8408 6900; Maj Winsome
  Mason
Tasmania: 27 Pirie St, New Town, Tas 7008;
  tel: (03) 6278 7184; Majs Graeme and
  Helen McClimont
Western Australia: 333 William St,
  Northbridge, WA 6003; tel: (08) 9227 7010;
  Majs Dennis and Patricia Rowe
Western Victoria: 102 Eureka St, Ballarat,
  Vic 3350; tel: (03) 5337 1300; Majs Bruce
  and Debra Stevens

REGION

Northern Territory: Level 2 Suite C, Paspalis
  Centre, 48-50 Smith St, Darwin, NT 0800;
  tel: (08) 8944 6000; Majs Gordon and
  Dianne Main

OFFICER TRAINING COLLEGE

Parkville, Vic 3052: 303 Royal Parade;
  tel: (03) 9347 0299

ARCHIVES AND HERITAGE CENTRES

Melbourne, Vic 3000: Territorial Archives and
  Museum, 69 Bourke St, PO Box 18187,
  Collins St E, Melbourne, Vic 8003;
  tel: (03) 9639 3618
Nailsworth, SA 5083: Heritage Centre,
  2a Burwood Ave; tel: (08) 8342 2545
Northbridge, WA 6003: Historical Society
  Display Centre, 3rd Floor, 333 William St;
  tel: (08) 9227 7010

CONFERENCE AND HOLIDAY CENTRES

Bicheno, Tas 7215: Holiday Home,
  11 Banksia St
Busselton, WA 6280: Holiday Unit 2,
  12 Gale St; tel: (08) 9227 7010/7134
Cowes, Vic 3922: Holiday Unit,
  2/28-30 McKenzie Rd; tel: (03) 5952 6497
Daylesford, Vic 3460: Holiday Flat,
  Unit 5/28, Camp St
Geelong, Vic 3219: Conference Centre, Adams
  Court, Eastern Park; tel: (03) 5226 2121
Ocean Grove, Vic 3226: Holiday Home,
  4 Northcote Rd
Victor Harbor, SA 5211: Encounters Conference
  Centre, 22 Bartel Blvd; tel: (08) 8552 2707
  (acc 148)
Weymouth, Tas 7252: Holiday Camp, Walden St;
  tel: (03) 6382 6359 (acc 32)

EMPLOYMENT PLUS

National Office: Level 3, 10 Wesley Court,
  Burwood, Vic 3151; tel: (03) 9847 8700;
  Maj Ritchie Watson
Service Delivery Centres: New South Wales 24;
  Queensland 15; South Australia 7; Tasmania;
  Victoria 27; Western Australia 7
Enquiries: tel: 136 123

FLYING PADRE AND OUTBACK SERVICES

PO Box 43289, Casuarina, NT 0811;
  tel: (08) 8945 0176; Capt David Shrimpton

RED SHIELD DEFENCE SERVICES

Puckapunyal Representative;
  tel: (03) 5793 1294
Robertson Barracks Representative;
  tel: (08) 8935 2526/8981 7663

SOCIAL SERVICES
Aboriginal Ministry
Alice Springs, NT 0870: Aboriginal Programme,
  88 Hartley St; tel: (08) 8951 0207

Retired General Eva Burrows at the Melbourne launch of *Hallmarks of The Salvation Army*, with co-authors Colonel Henry Gariepy and Major Stephen Court

Fullarton, SA 5063: Divisional APY Lands Project, 39 Florence St; tel: (08) 8408 6900

Aged Care Non-Residential Services

Healthlink – Aged Care Day Therapy Services: 138 Reservoir Rd, Modbury SA 5092; tel: (08) 8264 8300

cnr Lindisfarne and Melsetter Rds, Huntfield Heights, SA 5163; tel: (08) 8186 6987

West Melbourne, Vic 3003: Community Aged Care Programme, 9 Roden St; tel: (03) 9329 5777

New Town, Tas 7008: Accommodation and Housing for the Aged, 115 New Town Rd; tel: (03) 6278 3256

Ulverstone, Tas 7315: Community Aged Care, 14 Grove Rd; tel: (03) 6425 6004

Alcohol, Other Drugs and Corrections

Bendigo, Vic 3550: Intensive Rehabilitation Community Programme, 65-71 Mundy St; tel: (03) 5442 7699

Burnie, Tas 7320: Court Mandated Diversion, Drug and Alcohol Day Programme with

Outreach, 24 View St, tel: (03) 6431 6706

Howrah, Tas 7018: Crime Prevention Programme, 135 Clarence St; tel: (03) 6244 4615

Launceston, Tas 7250:

Bridge Outreach Service, 109 Elizabeth St; tel: (03) 6331 6760

Drug and Alcohol Day Programme, 109 Elizabeth St; tel: (03) 63316760

Needle Syringe Programme, 109 Elizabeth St, tel: (03) 6331 6760

New Town, Tas 7008:

Bridge Programme, Creek Rd; tel: (03) 6278 8140

Drug and Alcohol Day Programme with Outreach, Creek Rd; tel: (03) 6278 8140

XCELL Prison Support Service, Creek Rd; tel: (03) 6278 8140

Transitional Housing Support for Prisoner, 117 New Town Rd; tel: (03) 6278 2817

Seymour, Vic 3660: AOD Youth Outreach, 12 Tallarook St; tel: (03) 5735 2055

Stuart Park, NT 0820: Drug and Alcohol Services, Lot 5043 Salonika St, Stuart Park 0820; tel: (08) 8981 4199

Chaplaincy – Police, Fire and Emergency Services

Kununurra, WA 6743: Fire and Emergency Services Chaplain, PO Box 1367, tel: 9169 2344

Perth, WA 6000: FESA chaplain; tel: 0407 294 312

Winnellie, NT 0821: Police, Fire and Emergency Services Chaplain, PO Box 39764; tel: (08) 8999 4154

Child Care and Family Services

Balga, WA 6061: Long Day Care, 10-18 Lavant Way; tel: (08) 9349 7488

Ballarat, Vic 3550: Karinya Occasional Childcare, 6 Crompton St; tel: (03) 5329 1100

Bendigo, Vic 3552: Fairground Family Access Programme, 65-71 Mundy St; tel: (03) 5442 7699

Devonport, Tas 7310: Parenting Partners Programme, 166 William St; tel: (03) 6424 9211

Hobart, Tas 7000: Communities for Children, 250 Liverpool St; tel: (03) 6234 2299

Howrah, Tas 7018: Parenting Partners Programme, 135 Clarence St; tel: (03) 6244 4615

Kingborough, Tas 7052: 3 Opal Dr; tel: (03) 6229 8058

North Coburg, Vic 3031: Crossroads Youth and Family Services, 2/828 Sydney Rd; tel: (03) 9353 1011

Sunshine, Vic 3020: Westcare Child and Adolescent Services, Home-based One-to-One Care, Intensive Case Management Services, 34 Devonshire Rd; tel: (03) 9312 3544

Ulverstone, Tas 7315: Parenting Partners Programme, 21 Victoria St; tel: (03) 6425 5382

Court and Prison Services

Alice Springs, NT 0870: 88 Hartley St; tel: (08) 8951 0200

Ballarat, Vic 3350: cnr Eureka and Main Sts; tel: (03) 5226 6239

Beechworth, Vic 3747: PO Box 130; tel: (03) 5728 3245

Bendigo, Vic 3552: 65-71 Mundy St; tel: (03) 5442 7699

Broadmeadows, Vic 3047: Broadmeadows Court, cnr Pearcedale and Dimboola Rds; tel: (03) 9221 8908

Castlemaine, Vic 3450: Loddon Prison; tel: 0428 176 635

Dandenong, Vic 3175: PO Box 392; tel: (03) 9767 1350

Deer Park, Vic 3023: Dame Phyllis Frost Centre/Tarrengower Prison, Riding Boundary Rd

Frankston, Vic 3199: PO Box 316, tel: (03) 9784 5739

Geelong, Vic 3220: Gordon St; tel: (03) 5225 3353

Heidelberg, Vic 3084: Heidelberg Court, Jika St; tel: (03) 8601 6734

Horsham, Vic 3400: 12 Kalkee Rd; tel: (03) 5382 1770

Latrobe Valley, Vic 3841: PO Box 3430, Gippsland Mail Centre; tel: (03) 5169 1558

Laverton North, Vic 3212: HM Port Phillip/ HM Barwon Prison; tel (03) 9329 6022

Manningham, SA 5086: 109 Hampstead Rd; tel: (08) 8368 6800

Melbourne, Vic 3000:
Children's Court, 477 Little Lonsdale St; tel: (03) 8601 6734
HM Melbourne Assessment Prison, 317 Spencer St; tel: (03) 9321 4111
Melbourne Magistrates Court, 233 William St; tel: (03) 9628 7797

Moorabbin, Vic 3189: PO Box 2042; tel: (03) 9871 4470

Northbridge, WA 6003: 333 William St; tel: (08) 9260 9500

Ringwood, Vic 3174: 139 Ringwood St; tel: (03) 5442 7699

Stuart Park, NT 0820: Lot 5043 Salonika St; tel: (08) 8981 4199

Sunshine, Vic 3020: Sunshine Court, 10 Foundry St; tel: (03) 9300 6263

Swan Hill, Vic 3583: 190 Beveridge St; tel: (03) 5033 1718

Wangaratta, Vic 3677: 13-17 Garnet Ave; tel: (03) 5722 1129

West Melbourne, Vic 3033: Senior Courts and Prisons Chaplain, 9 Roden St; tel: (03) 9329 6022

Yinnar Vic 3869: PO Box 45; tel: (03) 5169 1503

Intensive Living and Learning Environments – ILLE Programmes

St Albans; Taylors Lakes; Sunshine; North Altona; Kealba; Melton: contact through Westcare, 34 Devonshire Rd, Sunshine, Vic 3020; tel: (03) 9312 3544

Children's Homes and Cottages

Sunshine, Vic 3020: Westcare, 34 Devonshire Rd; tel: (03) 9312 3544

Community Programmes

Alice Springs, NT 0890: 88 Hartley St;
tel: (08) 8951 0206

Bendigo, Vic 3552: 65-71 Mundy St;
tel: (03) 5442 7699

Berri, SA 5343: Riverland Community Services,
20 Wilson St; tel: (08) 8582 3182

Brunswick, Vic 3056: 256 Albert St;
tel: (03) 9387 6746

Darwin, NT 0800; Darwin Life Centre,
49 Mitchell St; tel: (08) 8981 5994

Hawthorn, Vic 3122: Hawthorn Project,
Homeless Outreach Project, Community
Connection Project, Equity and Access
Project, 16 Church St; tel: (03) 9851 7800

Kununurra, WA 6743: Community Outreach
Centre, 106 Coolibah Drive;
tel: 0429 802 885

Melbourne, Vic 3000: Melbourne Corps
Project 614 and Life Centre, 69 Bourke St;
tel: (03) 9650 4851

Mornington, Vic 3931: PYFS, Reconnect
Programme, Shop 9, 234 Main St;
tel: (03) 5976 2231

Port Augusta, SA 5700: Flinders and Riverland
Community Service, 35 Flinders Tce;
tel: (08) 8641 1021

Rosebud, Vic 3939: Peninsula Community
Support Programme, 17-19 Ninth Ave;
tel: (03) 5986 7268

Family Violence Services

Adelaide, SA 5000: Central Violence
Intervention Project, Pirie St;
tel: (08) 8100 8155

Ballarat, Vic 3350: Karinya; tel: (03) 5329 1100
(acc 8)

Belmont, Vic 3216: Kardinia Women's Services;
tel: (03) 5241 9149

Darwin, NT 0801: Catherine Booth House,
PO Box 189; tel (08) 8981 5928 (acc 12)

Fullarton, SA 5063: Bramwell House,
PO Box 305; tel: (08) 8379 7223 (acc 5 adults
and children)

Karratha, WA 6714: tel: (08) 9185 2807 (acc 16)

New Town, Tas 7008: McCombe House;
tel: (03) 6228 1099 (acc 12)

North Coburg, Vic 3058: Crossroads (MAFVS),
828 Sydney Rd; tel: (03) 9353 1011

Onslow, WA 6710: tel: (08) 9184 6481

Perth, WA 6000: Graceville Centre,
PO Box 8025, Perth Business Centre 6849;
tel: (08) 9328 8529 (acc 43)

St Kilda, Vic 3182:
Crisis Services, 27 Grey St:
tel: (03) 9536 7730

Inner South Domestic Violence Services,
29 Grey St; tel: (03) 9536 7720,
toll free 1800 627 727

Crisis Services

Balga, WA 6061: Family Accommodation
Programme, 10-18 Lavant Way;
tel: (08) 9349 7488

Croydon, Vic 3136: Gateways Crisis Services,
PO Box 1072; tel: (03) 9725 8455

Frankston, Vic 3199: Peninsula Counselling
Service, Peninsula Crisis Centre,
37 Rossmith Ave East; tel: (03) 9784 5050

Geraldton, WA 6530: Family Crisis
Accommodation, 42 Ainsworth St;
tel: (08) 9965 3627

Ingle Farm Community Services Programme:
Emergency Relief, Family Supported
Accommodation, Youth Outreach Services,
Substance Abuse Support Service ForYouth,
Communities For Children, Community
Work Programme: cnr Bridge and Maxwell
Rds, Ingle Farm 5098; tel: (08) 8397 9333

Burlendi Youth Shelter: 22 Spains Rd,
Salisbury 5108; tel: (08) 8281 6641

Muggy's Accommodation Service Youth
Hostel and Outreach Services:
88 Henderson Ave, Pooraka;
tel: (08) 8260 6617

Muggy's Accommodation (Southern Campus):
Unit 2, 424 Marion Rd, Plympton;
tel: (08) 8371 2080

Leongatha, Vic 3953: GippsCare Domestic
Violence Outreach Service, 51 McCartin St;
tel: (03) 5662 4502

New Town, Tas 7008: SA Supported Housing,
117 New Town Rd; tel: (03) 6278 2817

Rosebud, Vic 3939: Crisis and
Transitional Support, 17-19 Ninth Ave;
tel: (03) 5986 7122

St Kilda, Vic 3182:
Access Health Service, 31 Grey St;
tel: (03) 9536 7780
Crisis Accommodation, 4b Upton Rd;
tel: (03) 9536 7730, toll free 1800 627 727
Health and Information, 29 Grey St;
tel: (03) 9536 7703, toll free 1800 627 727
YWOP, 31 Grey St; tel: (03) 9536 7780

Emergency Accommodation

Alice Springs, NT 0870: 11 Goyder St;
tel: (08) 8952 1434 (acc service, single men,
dual diagnosis)

Ballarat, Vic 3350: Karinya, 6 Crompton St;
tel: (03) 5329 1100 (acc women with
children 8)

Australia Southern Territory

Belmont, Vic 3350: Kardinia Women's
Services; tel: (03) 5241 9149 (acc women
with children 6)

Berri, SA 5343: Riverland Community Services,
20 Wilson St; tel: (08) 8582 3182 (acc 30)

Bunbury, WA 6230: cnr Bussell H'way and
Timperly Rd; tel: (08) 9721 4519 (acc family
units 2)

Burnie, Tas 7320: Oakleigh House, 24 View Rd;
tel: (03) 6431 5791 (acc 61)

Corio, Vic 3214: Kardinia Men's Services;
tel: (08) 5274 9550

Croydon, Vic 3136: Gateways, PO Box 1072;
tel: (03) 9725 8455

Geraldton, WA 6530: Ainsworth St;
tel: (08) 9964 3667 (acc family units 3)

Horsham, Vic 3400: 12 Kalkee Rd;
tel: (03) 5382 1770 (acc family units 3,
single 3)

Jacana, Vic 3047: 23 Sunset Blvd;
tel: (03) 9309 6289 (acc family units 4,
community houses 6)

Kalgoorlie, WA 6430: Oberthur St;
tel: (08) 9021 2255 (acc family units 2)

New Town, Tas 7008: McCombe House,
63 Creek Rd; tel: (03) 6228 1099 (acc 8, exit
houses 4)

Sale, Vic 3850: cnr Cunningham and Marley Sts;
tel: (03) 5144 4564 (acc 6)

Emergency Family Accommodation

Berri SA 5343; Riverland Community Services –
Supported Accommodation for Families and
Personal Support Programme: 20 Wilson St;
tel: (08) 8582 3182

Burnie, Tas 7320: Oakleigh House, 24 View Rd;
tel: (03) 6431 5791 (acc 61)

Horsham, Vic 3400: 12 Kalkee Rd;
tel: (03) 5382 1770 (acc family units 3, single 3)

New Town, Tas 7008: McCombe House,
Swanston St Family Units;
tel: (03) 6229 1099

Port Augusta, SA 5700: 35 Flinders Tce;
tel: (08) 8641 1021 (acc 65)

St Kilda, Vic 3182: Upton Rd;
tel: (03) 9536 7730 (acc 20)

Emergency Services

Darwin, NT 0800: tel (08) 8981 2500/4199

Eltham, Vic 3095: Lower Factory 5,
266 Bolton St; tel: (03) 9439 7786

Hobart, Tas 7000: tel: (03) 6228 8400

Malaga, WA 6944: PO Box 2131;
tel: 0407 611 466

Pooraka, SA 5095: Units 7 & 8, 95 Research Rd;
tel: (08) 8262 7834

Family Outreach (Community Programme)

Jacana, Vic 3047: Wheatsheaf Rd;
tel: (03) 9309 6289

Moonah, Tas 7008: 73 Hopkins St;
tel: (03) 6228 0910

Port Augusta, SA 5700: 35 Flinders Tce;
tel: (08) 8641 1024

Seymour, Vic 3660: Pathways, 6 Tallarook St;
tel: (03) 5799 1581

Shepparton, Vic 3630: Pathways,
43A Wyndham St, tel: (03) 5833 1099

Salvos Stores

Administration: 233-235 Blackburn Rd,
Mt Waverley 3149; tel: (03) 9845 4000

Stores: Northern Territory 6; South Australia 36;
Tasmania 10; Victoria 96; Western Australia 44

Community Support Services (CSS)
Northern Territory Region CSS

Alice Springs, NT 0807: 88 Hartley St, Alice
Springs; tel (08) 8951 0206

Anula NT 0812: cnr Lee Point Rd and Yanyula
Drive; tel (08) 8927 9566

Darwin, NT 0800: 49 Mitchell St,
tel: (08) 8981 5994

Katherine, NT 0850: Community Outreach
Ministry, 3/10 Third St; tel: (08) 8971 2265

Palmerston, NT 0830: cnr Temple Tce and
Woodroffe Ave; tel: (08) 8932 2103

South Australia Division CSS

Aberfoyle Park, SA 5159: The Hub Worship and
Community Complex; tel: (08) 8370 5003

Adelaide, SA 5000: 277 Pirie St;
tel: (08) 8227 0199

Elizabeth East, SA 5112: Kinkaid Rd;
tel (08) 8255 8811

Gawler, SA 5118: 150 Murray St;
tel: (08) 8523 4844

Ingle Farm, SA 5098: cnr Bridge and
Maxwell Rds; tel (08) 8397 9333

Kapunda, SA 5373: Jeffs St; tel: (08) 8566 3388

Kilkenny, SA 5009: 1-7 Gray St;
tel: (08) 8445 2044

Millicent, SA 5280: Bramwell St;
tel: (08) 8733 3642

Modbury, SA 5092: 138 Reservoir Rd;
tel: (08) 8360 6444

Morphett Vale, SA 5162: 186 Elizabeth Rd;
tel: (08) 8384 6014

Mount Gambier, SA 5290: cnr Gray and
Wyatt Sts; tel: (08) 8725 9900

Norwood, SA 5067: 55 George St;
tel: (08) 8332 0283

Peterborough, SA 5422: 139 Main St;
tel: (08) 8651 3426

Port Augusta, SA 5700: 35 Flinders St;
tel: (08) 8641 1021

Port Lincoln, SA 5606: 41 Marine Ave;
tel: (08) 8682 4296

Renmark, SA 5341: 104-109 Renmark Ave;
tel: (08) 8586 4109

Seacombe Gardens, SA 5047: cnr Sturt and
Morphett Rds; tel: (08) 8377 0001

Victor Harbour, SA 5211: Crozier St;
tel: (08) 8552 7474

Whyalla Norrie, SA 5608: 5 Viscount Slim Ave,
Whyalla Norrie; tel: (08) 8645 7101

Wynn Vale, SA 5127: 99 Wynn Vale Dr:
tel: (08) 8289 4784

Tasmania Division CSS ('Doorway Centres')

Burnie, Tas 7320: 99 Wilson St;
tel: (03) 6431 8722

Devonport, Tas 7310: 166 William St;
tel: (03) 6424 9211

Hobart, Tas 7000: 180 Elizabeth St;
tel: (03) 6231 2237

Howrah, Tas 7018: 135 Clarence St;
tel: (03) 6244 4615

Launceston, Tas 7250: 109a Elizabeth St;
tel: (03) 6228 0910

Moonah, Tas 7009: 73 Hopkins St;
tel: (03) 6228 0910

New Norfolk, Tas 7140: 79 Hamilton Rd;
tel: (03) 6261 5996

Victoria – Melbourne Central Division CSS

Altona, Vic 3018: 108 Queen St;
tel (03) 9398 1750

Brunswick, Vic 3056: 256 Albert St;
tel: (03) 9387 6746

Coburg North, Vic 3058: 828 Sydney Rd;
tel: (03) 9353 1089

Craigieburn Vic, 3064: 35 Craigieburn Rd;
tel: (03) 9303 8661

Greensborough, Vic 3088: 2 Flodden Way;
tel: (03) 9434 6990

Melbourne, Vic 3000: 69 Bourke St;
tel: (03) 9653 3249

Mill Park, Vic 3075: cnr Morang Dr and Fred
Hollows Way; tel: (03) 9436 9200

Moonee Ponds, Vic 3040: cnr Mount
Alexander Rd and Buckley St;
tel: (03) 9375 3249

Preston, Vic 3072: 263 Gower St;
tel: (03) 9471 9111

Richmond, Vic 3121: cnr Lennox and
Garfield Sts; tel: (03) 9429 2117

St Kilda, Vic 3182: Crisis Contact Centre,

29 Grey St; tel: (03) 9536 7777,
toll free 1800 627 727

Sunbury, Vic 3429: 27-37 Anderson Rd;
tel: (03) 9744 2095

Sunshine Vic 3020: SASHS Shop 6,
147 Harvester Rd; tel: (03) 9312 5424

Werribee, Vic 3030: 209 Watton St;
tel: (03) 9731 1344

Victoria – Eastern Victoria Division CSS

Bairnsdale, Vic 3875: 63 McLeod St;
tel: (03) 5152 4201

Bentleigh, Vic 3204: 87 Robert St;
tel: (03) 9557 2644

Berwick, Vic 3806: cnr Parkhill Dr and Ernst
Wanke Rd; tel: (03) 9704 1940

Box Hill, Vic 3128: 17-23 Nelson Rd;
tel: (03) 9890 2993

Camberwell, Vic 3124: 7 Bowen St;
tel: (03) 9889 2468

Carrum Downs, Vic 3201: 1265 Frankston-
Dandenong Rd; tel: (03) 9782 0383

Cranbourne, Vic 3977: 1 New Holland Dr;
tel: (03) 5991 1777

Dandenong Vic 3175: 55 James St;
tel: (03) 9793 3933

Dingley Village, Vic 3172: Unit 13-12-16,
Garden Boulevard; tel: (03) 9558 2045

Doncaster, Vic 3109: 37 Taunton St;
tel: (03) 9842 4744

Doveton, Vic 3177: 1a Frawley Rd;
tel: (03) 9793 3933

Ferntree Gully, Vic 3156: 37 Wattletree Rd;
tel: (03) 9752 3604

Frankston, Vic 3200: 15 Forest Dr;
tel: (03) 9776 9155

Glen Waverley, Vic 3150: 958 High St Rd;
tel: (03) 9803 2587

Healesville, Vic 3777: 114 Maroondah Hwy;
tel: (03) 5962 2486

Leongatha, Vic 3953: 52 Anderson St;
tel: (03) 5662 4670

Moe, Vic, 3825:
37 Elizabeth St; tel: (03) 5126 2845
18-22 George St; tel: (03) 5126 1683

Mooroolbark, Vic 3138:
88 Brice Ave; tel: (03) 9727 4777
55 Manchester Rd; tel: (03) 9727 4777

Morwell, Vic 3840:
cnr Bridle Rd and Laurel St;
tel: (03) 5133 9366
160 Commercial Rd; tel: (03) 5133 9366

Noble Park, Vic 3174: 12 Buckley St;
tel: (03) 9548 5022

Oakleigh, Vic 3166: 50 Atherton Rd;
tel: (03) 9563 0786

Pakenham, Vic 3810: 51 Bald Hill Rd;
tel: (030 5941 4906
Ringwood, Vic 3134: 47 Wantirna Rd;
tel: (03) 9879 2894
Sale, Vic 3850: 139 Cunningham St;
tel; (03) 5144 6374
The Basin, Vic 3154: 1 Basin-Olinda Rd;
tel: (03) 9762 3490
Traralgon, Vic 3844: Lot 1 Cross's Rd;
tel: (03) 5174 1998
Warragul, Vic 3820: 120 Burke St;
tel: (03) 5623 1090
Wonthaggi, Vic 3995: McKenzie St;
tel: (03) 5672 1228

Victoria – Western Victoria Division CSS
Ballarat, Vic 3350: 102 Eureka St;
tel: (03) 5337 0600
Colac, Vic 3250: 100 Bloomfield St;
tel: (03) 5231 1178
Geelong, Vic 3220: 26-28 Bellerine St;
tel: (03) 5223 2434
Hamilton Vic 3300: 89 Kennedy St;
tel: (03) 5572 1907
Stawell, Vic 3380: 50 Main St;
tel (03) 5358 2657
Warrnambool, Vic 3280: cnr Lava and
Henna Sts; tel: (03) 5561 6792

Victoria – Northern Victoria Division CSS
Beechworth, Vic 3747: 35 Ford St;
tel: (03) 5728 3245
Benalla, Vic 3672: 72 Fawkner Dr;
tel: (03) 5762 6396
Bendigo, Vic 3550: 65-71 Mundy St;
tel: (03) 5442 7699
Broadford, Vic 3658: 25-27 Powlett St;
tel: (03) 7584 1635
Castlemaine, Vic 3450: 47 Kennedy St;
tel: (03) 5470 5389
Echuca, Vic 3564: 50-52 Sturt St;
tel: (03) 5482 6722
Kyabram, Vic 3620: 24 Unit St;
tel: (03) 5853 2684
Maryborough, Vic 3465: 58 High St;
tel: (03) 5461 2789
Mildura, Vic 3500: 1401-1415 Etiwanda Ave;
tel: (03) 5021 2229
Red Cliffs, Vic 3496: 16 Heath St;
tel: (03) 5024 2110
Rochester, Vic 3561: cnr Elizabeth and
Ramsay Sts; tel: (03) 5484 1364
Seymour, Vic 3660: Victoria St;
tel: (03) 5799 2583
Shepparton, Vic 3630: 43a Wyndham St;
tel: (03) 5831 1551

St Arnaud, Vic 3478: 14 Queens Ave:
tel: (03) 5495 1385
Swan Hill, Vic 3585: 190 Beveridge St;
tel: (03) 5033 1718
Wangaratta, Vic 3677: 13-17 Garnet Ave;
tel: (03) 5722 1129
Wodonga, Vic 3690: 210 Lawrence St;
tel: (03) 6024 2886

Western Australia Division CSS
Albany, WA 6330: 152-160 North Rd;
tel: (08) 9841 1068
Armadale, WA 6997: 57 Braemore St;
tel: (08) 9497 1803
Balga, WA 6024: 10-18 Lavant Way;
tel: (08) 9349 7488
Bentley, WA 6102: Dumond St;
tel: (08) 9458 1855
Busselton, WA 6280: Kent St;
tel: (08) 9754 2733
Ellenbrook, WA 6069: cnr Highpoint and
Woodlake Blvds; tel: (08) 9296 7197
Geraldton, WA 6530: 42 Ainsworth St;
tel: (08) 9964 3627
Heathridge, WA 6919: 36 Christmas Ave;
tel: (08) 9401 3408
Kalgoorlie, WA 6430: Oberthur St;
tel: (08) 9021 2255
Karratha, WA 6714: 2 Bond Pl;
tel: (08) 9185 2148
Kwinana, WA 6167: cnr Medina Ave and
Hoyle Rd; tel: (08) 9439 1585
Mandurah, WA 6210: Lot 5, Lakes Rd;
tel: (08) 9535 4951
Morley, WA 6943: 565 Walter Rd;
tel: (08) 9279 4500
Narrogin, WA 6312: Doney St;
tel: (08) 9881 4004
Northam, WA 6401: Wellington St;
tel: (08) 9622 1228
Northbridge, WA 6003: 333 William St;
tel: (08) 9328 1690
Merriwa, WA 6030: 26 Jenola Way;
tel: (08) 9305 2131
Rivervale, WA 6103: 96 Norwood Rd;
tel: (08) 9355 2799
Swan View, WA 6056: 371-379 Morrison Rd;
tel: (08) 9294 2811

Unit for Intellectually Disabled Persons
Ottoway, SA 5013: Centennial Court,
30-32 Edward St; tel: (08) 8341 0413

Red Shield Housing Network Association
Hobart, Tas 7008: 223 Macquarie St;
tel: (03) 6223 8050

Manningham, SA 5086: 109 Hampstead Rd;
tel: (08) 8368 6800

Family Tracing Service
Adelaide, Fullarton, SA 5063: 39 Florence St;
tel: (08) 8408 6950
Darwin, Anula, NT 0812: cnr Lee Point Rd and
Yanyula Dr; tel: (08) 8927 6499
Hobart, New Town, Tas 7008: 27 Pirie St;
tel: (03) 6228 8404
Perth, Northbridge, WA 6003: 333 William St;
tel: (08) 9260 9500
Victoria and Inter-Territorial enquiries only:
Blackburn, Vic 3130: 95-99 Railway Rd;
tel: (03) 8878 4500

Hostels for Homeless Men
Abbotsford, Vic 3067: Anchorage Hostel,
81 Victoria Cres; tel: (03) 9417 5820
Adelaide, SA 5000: Towards Independence,
277 Pirie St; tel: (08) 8110 8500 (acc 75)
Alice Springs, NT 0870: 11 Goyder St;
tel: (08) 8952 1434 (acc 27)
Darwin, NT 0820: Sunrise Centre, Lot 5344
Salonika St; tel: (08) 8981 4199 (acc 26)
Mount Lawley, WA 6050: Tanderra Hostel,
68 Guildford Rd; tel: (08) 9271 1209
(acc 27)
North Melbourne, Vic 3051: The Open Door,
166 Boundary Rd; tel: (03) 9329 6988
(acc 45)
Perth, WA 6000: Lentara, cnr Short and
Nash Sts; tel: (08) 9328 3102 (acc 55)
St Kilda, Vic 3182: St Kilda Crisis
Accommodation Centre, 4B Upton Rd;
tel: (03) 9536 7730 (acc 20)
West Melbourne, Vic 3003: Flagstaff Crisis
Accommodation, 9 Roden St;
tel: (03) 9329 4800 (acc 64)

Hostels for Homeless Youth
Fitzroy, Vic 3065: 12 Tranmere St;
tel: (03) 9489 1122
Frankston, Vic 3199: 37 Rossmith Ave East;
tel: (03) 9784 5050 (4 houses)
Kalgoorlie, WA 6430: 10 Park St;
tel: (08) 9091 1016 (acc 12)
Karratha, WA 6714: 2 Bond St;
tel: (08) 9144 1881 (acc 8)
Lansdale, WA 6065: Lansdale House,
460 Kingsway; tel: (08) 9302 1433 (acc 8)
Leongatha, Vic 3953: GippsCare Cross-target
Transitional Support, 51 McCartin St;
tel: (03) 5662 4502
Mirrabooka, WA 6061: Oasis House, 68-70
Honeywell Blvd; tel: (08) 9342 6785 (acc 8)

Pooraka, SA 5095: Muggy's, 88 Henderson Ave;
tel: (08) 8260 6617 (acc 10)
Salisbury, SA 5108: Burlendi, 22 Spains Rd;
tel: (08) 8281 6641 (acc 8)
Shepparton, Vic 3630: Brayton Youth and Family
Services, 360 River Rd; tel: (03) 5823 2277
St Kilda, Vic 3182: 4b Upton Rd;
tel: (03) 9536 7730

**Hostels for Intellectually Disabled
Persons**
Manningham, SA 5086: Red Shield Housing
Network Services, 109 Hampstead Rd;
tel: (08) 8368 6800 (properties 310)

Social Housing – SASHS
Alice Springs, NT 0870: Towards Independence,
88 Hartley St; tel: (08) 8951 0203
Anula, NT 0812: Towards Independence Top
End, cnr Lee Point Rd and Yanyula Dr;
tel: (08) 8927 5189
Box Hill, Vic 3128: 31-33 Ellingworth Pde;
tel: (03) 9890 7144
Grovedale, Vic 3216: Barwon South-West
Region, 142 Torquay Rd;
tel: (03) 5244 2500
Hawthorn, Vic 3122: EastCare Housing
Services, 16 Church St; tel: (03) 9851 7800
Leongatha, Vic 3953: Gippsland Region,
51a McCartin St; tel: (03) 5662 4538
Manningham, SA 5086: Red Shield Housing
Network Services, 109 Hampstead Rd;
tel: (08) 8368 6800
New Town, Tas 7008: 117 Main Rd;
tel: (03) 6278 2817
Sunshine, Vic 3020: 6/147 Harvester Rd:
tel: (03) 9312 5424
Warragul, Vic 3820: 64 Queen St;
tel: (03) 5622 0351
Warrnambool, Vic 3280: 70 Henna St;
tel: (03) 5561 6844

Mobile Ministry
Jingili, NT 0810: 5 Murphy St (Flying Padre);
tel: (08) 8945 0176
Karratha, WA 6714: (Mobile Ministry)
1 Nelson Ct, Peggs Creek; tel: (08) 9144 2985

**Independent Units for Intellectually
Handicapped Persons**
Ottoway, SA 5013: Centennial Court,
30-32 Edward St; tel: (08) 8341 0413 (acc 18)

Men's Support Service
Medina, WA 6167: cnr Hoyle Rd and
Medina Ave; tel: (08) 9439 1585

Asylum Seeker Support
Brunswick, Vic 3056: 12-14 Tinning St;
tel: (03) 9384 8334
Doveton, Vic 3177: 1a Frawley Rd;
tel: (03) 9793 3933

Positive Lifestyle Counselling Services
Dandenong, Vic 3175: Shops 6 & 7,
147-151 Foster St; tel: (03) 9794 9533
Ringwood, Vic 3134: Suite 4, Level 1,
23 Ringwood St; tel: (03) 9870 9170

Red Shield Hostels
Alice Springs, NT 0870: 11 Goyder St;
tel: (08) 8952 1434 (acc 27)
Darwin, NT 0800: 49 Mitchell St;
tel: (08) 8981 5994 (acc 64)

Rehabilitation Services
Abbotsford, Vic 3067: Detox Unit,
81 Victoria Cres; tel: (03) 9495 6811
Adelaide, SA 5000:
Bridge Drug and Alcohol Outreach
Programme (inc Police and Drug Court
Diversion initiative), 62 Whitmore Sq;
tel: (08) 8211 8423
'IT' Futures Initiative (computer-based
support programme); tel: (08) 8227 0893
Sobering Up Unit: 62a Whitmore Sqr;
tel: (08) 8110 8546
Supported Accommodation Services,
3/2 Dawkins Pl; tel: (08) 8227 0349
Warrondi Stabilisation Unit, 146 Gilbert St;
tel: (08) 8212 1215 (acc 22)
Warrondi Transitional Support Programme
(inc Warrondi Engage and Link initiative),
146 Gilbert St, Adelaide 5000;
tel: (08) 8212 1251
Bendigo, Vic 3550:
Intensive Rehabilitation Community
Programme, 65-71 Mundy St;
tel: (03) 5442 769
Northern Victoria Drug and Alcohol
Coordinator, 65-67 Mundy St;
tel (03) 5442 7931
Bendigo Bridge Community Outreach,
65-71 Mundy St; tel: (03) 5442 8558
Box Hill, Vic 3128: Aurora Women's
Accommodation Service, 310 Elgar Rd;
tel: (03) 9890 4549
Brunswick, Vic 3056: 256 Albert St;
tel: (03) 9387 6746
Geelong, Vic 3220: Kardinia Alcohol and
Other Drugs (inc Geelong Withdrawal Unit),
Goldsworthy St; tel: (03) 5275 3500

Gosnells, WA 6110: Harry Hunter Adult
Rehabilitation, 2498 Albany H'way;
tel: (08) 9398 2077
Hawthorn, Vic 3122:
Aurora Women's Accommodation Service,
Drug and Alcohol Counselling Programme,
16 Church St; tel: (03) 9851 7800
4 C's D&A Counselling, 16 Church St;
tel: (03) 9851 7800
Highgate, WA 6003: Bridge House, 15 Wright St;
tel: (08) 9227 8086 (acc 27)
New Town, Tas 7008: The Bridge Programme,
Creek Rd; tel: (03) 6278 8140
Preston, Vic 3072: Bridgehaven, 1a Jackman St;
tel: (03) 9480 6488 (acc 15)
Ringwood, Vic 3134: Drug Diversion
Programme, PO Box 333, Vic 3134;
tel: (03) 9871 4470
St Kilda, Vic 3182: The Bridge Centre,
12 Chapel St; tel: (03) 9521 2770
Stuart Park, NT 0820:
Drug and Alcohol Services – Top End,
Lot 5344, Salonika St; tel: (08) 8981 4199
(acc 26)
Sunrise Centre, Lot 5034 Salonika St;
tel: (08) 8981 4199
Swan Hill, Vic 3585: 190 Beveridge St;
tel: (03) 5033 1718
The Basin, Vic 3154: The Basin Centre,
Basin-Olinda Rd; tel: (03) 9762 1166
Warrnambool, Vic 3280: 52-54 Fairy St;
tel: (03) 5561 4453

Rural Outreach and Drought Relief
Bendigo, Vic 3550: Operation Living Waters,
75 Strickland Rd; tel: (03) 5441 7959
Fullarton, SA 5063: Drought Relief,
PO Box 300; tel: (08) 8408 6900
Geraldton, WA 6530: Drought Relief,
PO Box 167; tel: (08) 9964 3627
Hobart, Tas 7000: Drought Relief,
250 Liverpool St; tel: (03) 6236 9933
Horsham, Vic 3440: Drought Relief,
12 Kalkee Rd; tel: (03) 5382 1770
Kaniva, Vic 3419: Drought Relief,
34 Progress St; tel: (03) 5392 2304

Senior Citizens' Residences
Angle Park, SA 5010: Linsell Lodge
Residential Aged Care Facility;
2-16 Cardigan St; tel: (08) 8231 4687
(acc 53)
Clarence Park, SA 5034: Jean McBean Court,
35 Mills St; tel: (08) 8231 4687 (acc single
units 10, double 4)

Footscray, Vic 3011: James Barker House,
78 Ryan St; tel: (03) 9689 7211 (acc 45)
Gosnells, WA 6110: Seaforth Gardens,
2542 Albany H'way; tel: (08) 9398 5228
(acc hostel 53, units 50)
Lenah Valley, Tas 7008: MacFarlane Court,
16-22 Ratho St (acc units single 22,
double 8)
New Town, Tas 7008: Barrington Lodge,
120 Swanston St; tel: (03) 6228 2164
(acc res beds 77)

Soup Runs

Adelaide, SA 5000: 277 Pirie St (c/o Adelaide
Congress Hall); tel: (08) 8223 7776
Northbridge, WA 6003: 108 Beaufort St;
tel: (08) 9227 1780

Telephone Counselling Service

Adelaide, SA 5000: Financial Telephone
Counselling, 277 Pirie St; tel: 1800 025 539
Morley, WA 6943: Salvo Care Line,
PO Box 1, Morley; tel (08) 9442 5777

Youth and Family Services

Alice Springs, NT 0870: Towards Independence,
88 Hartley St; tel: (08) 8951 0203
Box Hill, Vic 3128:
Intensive Case Management Service,
Specialist Consulting and Assessment
Service, Children in Residential Care
Education Support, Work and Recreation
Programme with Education, Residential
Youth Services, Leaving Care,
31-33 Ellingworth Pde; tel: (03) 9890 7144
JJHIP (Juvenile Justice Housing Initiative
Pathways); tel: (03) 9890 7144
Brunswick, Vic 3056: Brunswick Youth Services
Creative Opportunities, 10-18 Tinning St;
tel: (03) 9386 7611
Kew, Vic 3101: The Hawthorn Project,
85 High St; tel: (03) 9851 7800

Leongatha, Vic 3953: GippsCare Adolescent
Community Placement, 51 McCartin St;
tel: (03) 5662 4502
Melbourne, Vic 3000: Melbourne Counselling,
69 Bourke St; tel: (03) 9653 3250
Moonee Ponds, Vic 3039: Crosslink
Employment Services, 33a Taylor St;
tel: (03) 9372 0675
Mornington, Vic 3931:
Peninsula Home-based Care Services, Shop 9,
234 Main St; tel: (03) 5976 2231
Peninsula Adolescent Community Placement,
Peninsula High Risk Adolescent Programme,
Peninsula Reconnect Programme,
Shop 9, 234 Main St; tel: (03) 5976 2747
Northbridge, WA 6003: Crossroads West –
Perth, 333 William St; tel: (08) 9260 9551
North Coburg, Vic 3058: Transitional Support,
Independent Living Programmes
inc Youth Services, Transitional Support
Accommodation for Youth (TSAY), Anger
Management, Reconnect, 2/828 Sydney Rd;
tel: (03) 9353 1011
Salisbury, SA 5108: CHIPS Internet Cafe,
20b John St; tel: (08) 8285 9406
Shepparton, Vic 3630:
Brayton Youth and Family Services,
360 River Rd; tel: (03) 5823 2277
Pathways, 43b Wyndham St; tel: (03) 5833 1099
Seymour, Vic 3660: Pathways 12 Tallarook St;
tel:(03) 5799 1581
Swan Hill, Vic 3585: Y-Space, 5 Campbell St;
tel: (03) 5033 1411

**Youth Centres for Homeless
Unemployed**

Brunswick, Vic 3056: Brunswick Youth Services,
16 Tinning St; tel (03) 9384 8334
Mornington, Vic 3931: Toast Cyber Cafe,
Shop 7, 234 Main St; tel: (03) 5976 5500
North Coburg, Vic 3058: 2/828 Sydney Rd;
tel: (03) 9353 1011

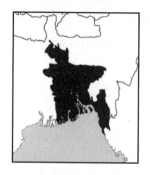

BANGLADESH COMMAND

Officer Commanding:
Lieut-Colonel Ethne Flintoff (1 Jul 2002)

General Secretary:
Major Leopoldo Posadas (1 Aug 2008)

**Command Headquarters: House 365/2, Lane 6 (West),
Baridhara DOHS, Dhaka 1216**
Postal address: GPO Box 985, Dhaka 1000, Bangladesh

Tel: [880] (2) 8411755/6; fax: [880] (2) 8411757; email: banleadership@ban.salvationarmy.org

Work in Bangladesh began immediately after the Liberation War with Pakistan in 1971. Thousands of people moved from refugee camps in Calcutta, where Salvationists had served them, and a team of Salvationists accompanied them. A year earlier, relief operations had been carried out by The Salvation Army in East Pakistan (later Bangladesh) following a severe cyclone. On 21 April 1980, The Salvation Army was incorporated under the Companies Act of 1913. Bangladesh was upgraded to command status on 1 January 1997.

Zone: South Asia
Country included in the command: Bangladesh
'The Salvation Army' in Bengali: Tran Sena
Languages in which the gospel is preached: Bengali, English

PROGRESS with the command's five-year strategic plan that began in 2006 has been reviewed. Meetings held in several centres focused on strategic objectives achievements.

During the year under review the command experienced a series of challenges to The Salvation Army's work in the country, but Salvationists believe God is in control and is leading them in learning patience and endurance as they continue to find ways to move forward.

A successful men's rally in which 100 men from multifaith backgrounds gathered for a day of fellowship and teaching was the first such event to be held in Dhaka District. Discussion groups dealt with family and marriage relationships. These are topics of great importance in Bangladeshi society, where family violence is not uncommon.

A youth camp, the first to be held in the north-west of the country, drew 59 young people from two corps areas.

In a series of seminars arranged by Tearfund UK, several officers and staff received training on such issues as climate change adaptation, disaster risk reduction, disaster preparedness and management. This was timely in developing the command's capacity to address climate change, since the country is at the frontline of vulnerability.

A cyclone at the end of May 2009 washed away coastal embankments (levies), leaving the sea to encroach inland on vast areas of coastal farm-land and villages. Attempts to rebuild the levies following the disaster have largely failed.

STATISTICS
Officers 81 **Cadets** (2nd Yr) 6 **Employees** 319
Corps 31 **Outposts** 12 **Institution** 1 **Schools** 14
  Clinics 8 **HIV/Aids Counselling Centres** 2
Senior Soldiers 1,763 **Adherents** 646 **Junior
  Soldiers** 218

STAFF
Women's Ministries: Lt-Col Ethne Flintoff
  (CPWM) Maj Evelyn Posadas (CSWM)
Director of Finance: Mrs Sarah Biswas
Information Technology Development:
  Mr Palash (Paul) Baidya
Projects: Capt Elizabeth Nelson
Training: Capt Milon Dias
Youth and Candidates: Capt Stephen Baroi

DISTRICTS
Dhaka: House 365/2, Lane 6 (West), Baridhara
  DOHS, Dhaka 1216; tel: (0171) 1546012;
  Maj Alfred Mir
South Western: PO Box 3, By-Pass Rd,
  Karbala, Jessore 7400; tel: (0421) 68759;
  Maj Ganendro Baroi

TRAINING COLLEGE
Genda, Savar, Dhaka; tel: (02) 7712614

COMMUNITY WORK
Disaster Preparedness & Management Training
  Programme: South Western District
HIV/Aids Counselling Centres: Jessore, Old
  Dhaka
Income-generating Cooperatives: Jessore,
  Khulna
Training and Counselling Programme: Kalaroa,
  Satkhira

EDUCATIONAL WORK
Adult Education
Jessore, Khulna

Schools for the Hearing Impaired
Dhaka (acc 30); Jessore (acc 30)

Primary Schools
(pupils 2,122)
Dinajpur: Shahargachchi
Gopalgonj: Bandhabari, Rajapur
Jessore: Arenda, Bagdanga, Fatepur, Ghurulia,
  Kholadanga, Konejpur, Ramnagar,
  Sitarampur, Suro
Joypurhat: Vanuikushalia
Khulna: Andulia, Komrail, Krisnanagar

**Integrated Education for Sighted and
  Visually Impaired**
Savar (pupils 280)

Vocational Training
Dhaka, Jessore, Khulna

MEDICAL AND DEVELOPMENT WORK
**Urban Health and Development Project
(UHDP)**
Dhaka: Mirpur Clinic, with Leprosy and TB
  Control Programmes

**Community Health and Development
  Projects (CHDP)**
Jessore: New Town and Kholadanga Clinics,
  with Leprosy and TB Control Programmes
Khulna: Andulia Clinic
Village Clinics: Fatepur, Ghurulia, Konejpur,
  Ramnagar, Sitarampur

SOCIAL WORK
Integrated Children's Centre (ICC)
Savar (acc 44)

'SALLY ANN' PROGRAMME
'Sally Ann' Bangladesh Ltd (employees 23
  production workers 950)
  Manager: Mr Utpal Halder
  Chair of Board: Maj Leopoldo Posadas
  email: SallyAnn@ban.salvationarmy.com
  website: www.sallyann.com
  Shop: House 365/2, Lane 6 (West),
    Baridhara DOHS, Dhaka 1216; Satu Barua
    (shop manager)

BRAZIL TERRITORY

Territorial leaders:
**Commissioners Oscar and
Ana Rosa Sánchez**

Territorial Commander:
Commissioner Oscar Sánchez
(1 Aug 2010)

Chief Secretary:
Lieut-Colonel Alfred Ward (1 Mar 2008)

**Territorial Headquarters: Rua Juá 264 - Bosque da Saúde,
04138-020 São Paulo-SP**

**Postal address: Exército de Salvação; Caixa Postal 46036, Agência Saúde
04045-970 São Paulo-SP, Brazil**

Tel: [55] (011) 5591 7070; fax: [55] (011) 5591 7075; email: BRA_Leadership@bra.salvationarmy.org;
website: www.exercitodesalvacao.org.br

Pioneer officers Lieut-Colonel and Mrs David Miche unfurled the Army flag in Rio de Janeiro on 1 August 1922. The Salvation Army operates as a national religious entity, Exército de Salvação, having been so registered by Presidential Decree 90.568 of 27 November 1984. All its social activities have been incorporated in APROSES (Assistência e Promoção Social Exército de Salvação) since 1974 and have had Federal Public Utility since 18 February 1991.

Zone: Americas and Caribbean
Country included in the territory: Brazil
'The Salvation Army' in Portuguese: Exército de Salvação
Language in which the gospel is preached: Portuguese
Periodicals: *O Oficial (The Officer)*, *Rumo* and *Ministério Feminino – Devocionais* (Women's Ministries magazines)

'GROWING in Compassion', the territorial theme for 2009, was predominant throughout the territory in inspiring talks, seminars and personal spiritual challenge. An expression of this theme was the *Sorrindo com Cristo* ('Smiling With Christ') programme in which dentist Tercio Obara, a longstanding friend of The Salvation Army, organised professional colleagues to work in deprived urban areas and rural communities. This work is now registered as part of the Army's social services.

During evangelism campaigns dental and medical care was given to children and adults. Many Salvationists took part in the campaigns, demonstrating Christ's compassion among the most neediest people.

The Territorial Women's Congress in May 2009 had a life-changing effect on many of the 550 delegates.

Women came from all parts of the territory, some travelling for up to 36 hours by bus to attend. Each delegate received a copy of *Having a Mary Heart in a Martha World* and this was the theme developed by Lieut-Colonel Martha Jewett (USA Southern). The event, sponsored by USA Southern Territory, was an unforgettable experience especially for those from some of Brazil's remote areas.

The territory responded to national emergencies in two areas in the Amazon basin. Extensive flooding washed away newly planted crops, leaving many communities without food and income.

A cry for help from local Christians was answered and a special grant from USA Southern Territory enabled two Salvationists to travel to Manaus. They helped to organise the distribution of aid and proclaimed the gospel among many communities.

In Rio de Janeiro, many steep hillsides became death traps when exceptionally heavy rains caused numerous mudslides that engulfed houses and people. In the Morro da Bumba *favela* a disused rubbish tip buried 60 houses and 200 people.

The Salvation Army responded immediately and remained for 13 days to support rescue workers as they dug through mud and decomposing waste looking for human remains. Salvationists offered material and spiritual help to the rescue workers and families of missing people.

The territory faces many challenges but continues to proclaim in word and deed the life-transforming message of the risen Saviour and a God of compassion.

STATISTICS

Officers 177 (active 131 retired 46) **Cadets** (1st Yr) 7 (2nd Yr) 3 **Employees** 337
Corps 47 **Outposts** 6 **Social Institutions** 35
Senior Soldiers 1,798 **Adherents** 57 **Junior Soldiers** 463
Personnel serving outside territory Officers 4

STAFF

Women's Ministries: Comr Ana Rosa Sánchez (TPWM) Lt-Col Mary Ward (TSWM) Maj Iolanda Camargo (TSAWM & TSLM)
Personnel: Maj Verônica Jung
Communications: Maj Téofilo Chagas
Editor-in-Chief: Maj Paulo Soares
Education: Maj Wilson Strasse
Finance: Capt Ricardo Iung
Legal/Property: Maj Giani Azevedo
Music: Maj Paulo Soares
National Band: B/M João Carlos Cavalheiro
National Songsters: S/L Vera Sales
Projects: Maj Joan Burton
Social: Mrs Marilene Oliveira
Training: Majs Wilson and Nara Strasse
Youth and Candidates: Maj Elisana Lemos

DIVISIONS

North East: Rua Carlos Gomes 1016, 50751-130 Recife – PE; tel/fax: (81) 3227-7513; Majs Maruilson and Francisca Souza
Paraná and Santa Catarina: Rua Mamoré 1191, 80810-080 Curitiba, PR; tel/fax: (041) 3336-8624; Majs Alberto and Maria José Serem
Rio de Janeiro and Minas Gerais and Centre West: Rua Visconde de Santa Isabel no 20, salas 712/713, 20560-120, Rio de Janeiro – RJ; tel/fax: (21) 3879-5594; Majs Edgar and Sara Chagas
Rio Grande do Sul: Rua Machado de Assis 255, 97050-450, Santa Maria, RS; tel/fax: (55) 3026-1935; Majs Adão and Vilma Gonçalves
São Paulo: Rua Taguá 209, Liberdade 01508-010, São Paulo – SP; tel/fax: (11) 3207-3402; Majs Márcio and Jurema Mendes

TRAINING COLLEGE
Rua Juá 264, Bosque da Saúde, 04138-020,
São Paulo – SP; tel: (11) 5071-5041

SOCIAL WORK
Centre for Street Children
São Paulo: Projeto Três Corações, Rua Taguá 209,
Liberdade, 01508-010, São Paulo – SP;
tel: (11) 3275-0622 (acc 40)

Clinics
Porto Alegre: Integrated Centre Porto Alegre,
Av São Pedro 1116, 90230-123, Porto
Alegre – RS; tel: (51) 3342-4170
THQ: 'Sorrindo com Cristo' Itinerant Dental
Clinic attending needy areas

Community Centres
*These centres have after-school programmes for
children at risk*
Carmo do Rio Claro: 'Recanto da Alegria',
Rua Luiz Améilo Freire 250, 37150-000,
Carmo do Rio Claro – MG; tel: (35) 3561-2175
(acc 40)
Cubatão: 'Vila dos Pescadores', Rua Amaral
Neto 211, 11531-070, Cubatão – SP;
tel: (13) 3363-2111 (acc 300)
Curitiba: Socio-Educacional Support Unit for
Children, Rua Manoel Martins de Abreu 274,
80215-430 Curtiba; tel: (41) 3353-1537
Pelotas: Pelotas Integrated Centre, Av Fernando
Osório, 6745, Três Vendas, 96070-005,
Pelotas – RS; tel: (53) 3273-6909 (acc 45)
Prudente de Moraes: Arco Verde Integrated
Family Centre, Av Antonio Pires 1790,
35715-000, Prudente de Moraes – MG;
tel: (31) 3711 1370 (acc 40)
Recife: Torre Integrated Community Centre,
Rua Conde de Irajá 108, Torre, 50710-310,
Recife – PE; tel: (81) 3228-4740 (acc 250)
Rio de Janeiro:
Socio-educational Centre, Lar do Méier,
Rua Garcia Redondo 103, 20775-170,
Rio de Janeiro – RJ; tel: (21) 2595-5694
(acc 40)
Nova Divinéia Community Centre,
Rua Bambuí 36, 20561-201,
Rio de Janeiro – RJ; tel: (21) 2298-2574
(acc 50)
São Paulo: Projeto Três Corações, Rua Taguá 209,
Liberdade, 01508-010, São Paulo – SP;
tel: (11) 3275-0622 (acc 40)
Uruguaiana: Integrated Centre Uruguaiana,
Rua Gal Câmara 1403, 97500-281,
Uruguaiana – RS; tel: (55) 3412-4930
(acc 65)

Early Childhood Education Centres and Crechés
Carmo do Rio Claro: 'Recanto da Alegria',
Rua Luiz Améilo Freire 250, 37150-000, Carmo
do Rio Claro – MG; tel: (35) 3561-2175 (acc 100)
Guarulhos: Rua NS Aparecida 10, 07191-190,
Guarulhos – SP; tel: (11) 2409-1500 (acc 50)
Itaquaquecetuba: Av Antonio fugas 190,
08215-730, Itaquaquecetuba – SP;
tel: (11) 4640-4304 (acc 30)
Pelotas: Pelotas Integrated Centre, Av Fernando
Osório, 6745, Três Vendas, 96070-005,
Pelotas – RS; tel: (53) 3273-6909 (acc 15)
Recife: Torre Integrated Community Centre,
Rua Conde de Irajá 108, Torre, 50710-310,
Recife – PE; tel: (81) 3228-4740 (acc 50)
São Gonçalo: 'Arca de Noé', Rua Rodrigues da
Fonseca 315, 24440-110, São Gonçalo – RJ;
tel: (21) 2604-9821 (acc 150)
São Paulo: Ranchinho do Senhor, Rua Bertioga
470/480, 04141-100, São Paulo – SP;
tel: (11) 5589-4609 (acc 60)
Suzano: Lar das Flores, Rua Gal Francisco
Glicério 3048, 08665-000, Suzano – SP;
tel: (11) 4747-1098 (acc 245)

Home for Street Children
Curitiba: Rua Bartolomeu Lourenço de
Gusmão 5167, Boqueirão, 81730-040,
Curtiba – PR; tel: (41) 3286-3662 (acc 11)

Mother and Baby Home (adolescent mothers)
São Paulo: Rancho do Senhor, Rua Caramurú 931,
04138-002, São Paulo – SP; tel: (11) 2275-4487
(acc mothers 10, babies 10)

Old People's Home
Campos do Jordão: Lar do Outono, Rua João
Rodrigues Pinheiro 335, 12460-000, Campos
do Jordão – SP; tel: (12) 3662-2154 (acc 24)

Prison Work
Piraí do Sul and Carmo do Rio Claro

Social Services Centres
Cubatão: Vila dos Pescadores Community
Centre, Rua Amaral Neto 211, 11531-070,
Cubatão – SP; tel: (13) 3363-2111
Curitiba: Rua Manoel Martins de Abreu 274,
80215-430 Curtiba; tel: (41) 3353-1537
Guarulhos: Rua NS Aparecida 10, 07191-190,
Guarulhos – SP; tel: (11) 2409-1500
Itaquaquecetuba: Av Antonio fugas 190,
08215-730, Itaquaquecetuba – SP;
tel: (11) 4640-4304

Salvationists offer material and spiritual help to rescuers and families of missing people after heavy rains on the steep hillsides around Rio de Janeiro caused mudslides that engulfed houses and people. Relief teams remained for 13 days to support the rescue workers.

Joinville: Rua 15 de novembro 3165, 89216-201, Joinville – SC; tel: (47) 3453-0588

Paranaguá: Rua Cavalheiro Manoel de Jordão 39, 83212-030, Paranaguá – PR; tel: (41) 3423-6115

Pelotas: Av Fernando Osório, 6745, Três Vendas, 96070-005, Pelotas – RS; tel: (53) 3273-6909

Porto Alegre: Av São Pedro 1116, 90230-123, Porto Alegre – RS; tel: (51) 3342-4170

Prudente de Moraes: Av Antonio Pires 1790, 35715-000, Prudente de Moraes – MG; tel: (31) 3711 1370

Recife: Rua Conde de Irajá 108, Torre, 50710-310, Recife – PE; tel: (81) 3228-4740 (acc 250)

Rio de Janeiro: Rua Bambuí 36, 20561-201, Rio de Janeiro – RJ; tel: (21) 2298-2574

Rio de Janeiro: Rua Garcia Redondo 103, 20775-170, Rio de Janeiro – RJ; tel: (21) 2595-5694

São Paulo: Rua Taguá 209, Liberdade, 01508-010 São Paulo – SP; tel: (11) 3275-0622

Uruguaiana: Rua Gal Câmara 1403, 97500-281, Uruguaiana – RS; tel: (55) 3412-4930

Students' Residences

Brasília: Av L2 Sul, 610B, Lot 69, 70200-700, Brasília – DF; tel: (61) 3443-3332 (acc 14)

Santa Maria: Rua Jerônimo Gomes 74, 97050-350, Santa Maria – RS; tel: (55) 3222-1935 (acc 26)

Territorial Camp

Suzano: Rua Manuel Casanova 1061, 08664-000, Suzano – SP; tel: (11) 4746-3843

Thrift Stores

São Paulo:

Salvashopping I, Av Santa Catarina 1781, 04378-300, São Paulo – SP; tel: (11) 5562-2285

Salvashopping II: Av Cupecê 3254, 04366-000, São Paulo – SP; tel: (11) 5563-9937

Salvashopping V: Rua D Belmira Marin 900, 04846-000, São Paulo – SP; tel: (11) 5925-2327

Rio de Janeiro: Breshopping, Blvd 28 de Setembro 354, 20551-031, Rio de Janeiro – RJ; tel: (21) 3879-9600

Breshopping, Rua Dr Odilon Benévolo, 196, 20911-230, Rio de Janeiro – RJ

Vocational Training – Adolescents and Youth

Arco Verde: 'Arco Verde' Integrated Family Centre, Av Antonio Pires 1790, 35715-000, Prudente de Moraes – MG; tel: (31) 3711 1370 (acc 30)

Joinville: João de Paula Integrated Centre, Rua 15 de novembro 3165, 89216-201, Joinville – SC; tel: (47) 3453-0588 (acc 90)

Paranaguá: Honorina Valente Integrated Centre, Rua Cavalheiro Manoel de Jordão 39, 83212-030, Paranaguá – PR; tel: (41) 3423-6115 (acc 200)

Recife: Torre Integrated Community Centre, Rua Conde de Irajá 108, Torre, 50710-310, Recife – PE; tel: (81) 3228-4740 (acc 120)

CANADA AND BERMUDA TERRITORY

Territorial leaders:
**Commissioners William W. and
Marilyn D. Francis**

Territorial Commander:
Commissioner William W. Francis
(1 Jul 2007)

Chief Secretary:
Colonel Floyd J. Tidd (1 Mar 2010)

**Territorial Headquarters: 2 Overlea Blvd, Toronto,
Ontario M4H 1P4, Canada**

Tel: [1] (416) 425-2111; fax: [1] (416) 422-6201; email: can_leadership@can.salvationarmy.org;
websites: www.salvationarmy.ca; www.salvationist.ca

There are newspaper reports of organised Salvation Army activity in Toronto, Ontario, in January 1882, and five months later the Army was reported holding meetings in London, Ontario. On 15 July the same year, Major Thomas Moore, sent from USA headquarters, established official operations. In 1884 Canada became a separate command. The League of Mercy originated in Canada in 1892. An Act to incorporate the Governing Council of The Salvation Army in Canada received Royal Assent on 19 May 1909.

The work in Newfoundland was begun on 1 February 1886 by Divisional Officer Arthur Young. On 12 January 1896 Adjutant (later Colonel) Lutie Desbrisay and two assistant officers unfurled the flag in Bermuda.

Zone: Americas and Caribbean
Countries included in the territory: Bermuda, Canada
Languages in which the gospel is preached: Creole, English, French, First Nations languages (Gitxsan, Nisga'a, Tsimshian), Korean, Lao, Portuguese, Spanish, Thai
Periodicals: *Edge for Kids*, *Faith & Friends*, *Foi & Vie*, *Salvationist*

IN May 2009 a new state-of-the-art Harbour Light ministries building was opened in Toronto. It encompasses a range of activities – from transitional housing to English as a second language classes for new immigrants – demonstrating how the Harbour Light has diversified from its foundations as a residential addictions treatment centre.

The Gateway of Hope centre in Langley, British Columbia, was opened in November 2009, with 55 beds available to homeless men and women, a food bank and support services for people in need.

The ordination and commissioning of the Witnesses For Christ Session, held in Toronto (19-21 June 2009), resulted in spiritual enrichment and renewal. The territory also celebrated 71 graduates of William and Catherine

Booth College in Winnipeg, almost double the previous year's total. The commissioning events included an 'Among the Nations' concert, featuring testimonies of newcomers to Canada who had been helped by The Salvation Army.

More than 200 students and faculty members gathered at Jackson's Point Conference Centre in Ontario for the National Music and Gospel Arts Camp (August 2009). Guest leaders Colonels Robert and Gwenyth Redhead brought inspiration and challenge. A high level of artistic skill was evident, but the greater emphasis was on fellowship and spiritual growth.

A new National Advisory Board was established in November 2009. Comprised of 13 business and civic leaders, the board will support The Salvation Army with strategic guidance on its national operations and services.

Bermuda's congress, led by Commissioners William and Marilyn Francis in November 2009, was something of a homecoming as former corps officers as well as family and friends of Bermudians returned to the island. The celebration meetings, historical presentations and prayer walks were events for honouring the past and embracing the future.

After the massive earthquake devastated much of Port-au-Prince, Haiti, in January 2010, the territory moved quickly to offer support. In addition to $7 million being raised for relief work, a Canadian team travelled to Haiti immediately after the disaster to assess the situation and provide assistance.

The territory also finalised its development project in Sri Lanka, building 650 homes and 11 community centres in the wake of the 2004 tsunami in South Asia. This was in partnership with the Canadian International Development Agency and The Salvation Army World Service Office.

At the 2010 Winter Olympics in Vancouver, British Columbia, the Army had a substantial impact through its More Than Gold mission teams. Some 2,000 Army volunteers gave out more than 600,000 hot beverages at 22 different sites over 17 days and shared the gospel through personal contact and Christian literature.

Over the past eight years, 85 Salvation Army leaders have participated in the Executive Leadership Development Programme led by Simon Fraser University in British Columbia. This leadership model is focused on self-awareness, trust-building and coaching relationships. A number of key Salvationist coaches have been identified to model and train personnel in this approach.

In June 2010 a World Religions Summit was held at the University of Winnipeg in conjunction with G8 and G20 meetings. The Canadian delegation included Commissioner William Francis, who responded to G8 politicians on behalf of the religious leaders.

Canada and Bermuda Territory

STATISTICS

Officers 1,787 (active 860 retired 927) **Cadets** (1st Yr) 13 (2nd Yr) 20 **Employees** 9,270
Corps 314 **Outposts** 9 **Institutions** 121 **University College** 1
Senior Soldiers 18,582 **Adherents** 41,607 **Junior Soldiers** 2,838
Personnel serving outside territory Officers 49 Layworkers 7

STAFF

Women's Ministries: Comr Marilyn Francis (TPWM) Col Tracey Tidd (TSWM)
Personnel: Lt-Col Sandra Rice
  Officer Personnel Dept: Maj Douglas Hefford
  Leadership Development: Maj Mona Moore
Programme: Lt-Col Junior Hynes
Business: Lt-Col Neil Watt
Asst Chief Sec: Maj Alison Cowling
Corps Ministries: Maj Elizabeth Lewis
Editor-in-Chief and Literary Sec: Maj James Champ
Finance: Mr Paul Goodyear
Music and Gospel Arts/Staff Band: Maj Kevin Metcalf
Information Technology: Mr Robert Plummer
Property: Maj Douglas Lewis
Public Relations and Development: Mr Graham Moore
Recycling Operations: Mr John Kershaw
Social: Mrs Mary Ellen Eberlin
Training: Maj Eric Bond
William and Catherine Booth University College: Dr Donald Burke
Youth: Capt Mark Hall

DIVISIONS

Alberta and Northern Territories:
  9618 101A Ave NW, Edmonton, AB T5H OC7; tel: (780) 423-2111; fax: (780) 425-9081; Majs Frederick and Wendy Waters
Bermuda: PO Box HM 2259, 76 Roberts Ave, Hamilton, HM JX Bermuda; tel: (441) 292-0601; fax: (441) 295-3765; Majs Shawn and Brenda Critch
British Columbia: 103-3833 Henning Dr, Burnaby, BC V5C 6N5; tel: (604) 299-3908; fax: (604) 299-7463; Maj Susan van Duinen
Maritime: 282-7071 Bayers Rd, Halifax, NS B3L 2C2; tel: (902) 455-1201; fax: (902) 455-0055; Majs Larry and Velma Martin
Newfoundland and Labrador: 21 Adams Ave, St John's, NL A1C 4Z1; tel: (709) 579-2022/3; fax: (709) 576-7034; Lt-Cols Alfred and Ethel Richardson

Ontario Central-East: 1645 Warden Ave, Scarborough, ON M1R 5B3; tel: (416) 321-2654; fax: (416) 321-8136; Lt-Cols Wayne and Myra Pritchett
Ontario Great Lakes: 371 King St, London, ON N6B 1S4; tel: (519) 433-6106; fax: (519) 433-0250; Lt-Cols Lee and Deborah Graves
Prairie: 204-290 Vaughan St, Winnipeg, MB R3B 2N8; tel: (204) 946-9101; fax: (204) 946-9169; Majs Wayne and Deborah Bungay
Quebec: 1655 Richardson St, Montreal, QC H3K 3J7; tel: (514) 288-2848; fax: (514) 288-4657; Majs Kester and Kathryn Trim

COLLEGE FOR OFFICER TRAINING

100-290 Vaughan St, Winnipeg, MB R3B 2N8; tel: (204) 924-5606; fax: (204) 924-5603; Maj Eric Bond (Principal)

THE WILLIAM AND CATHERINE BOOTH UNIVERSITY COLLEGE

447 Webb P1, Winnipeg, MB R3B 2P2; tel: (204) 947-6701/6702/6950; fax: (204) 942-3856; Dr Donald Burke (President)

ETHICS CENTRE

447 Webb Pl, Winnipeg, MB R3B 2P2; tel: (204) 957-2412; fax: (204) 957-2418; email: ethics_centre@can.salvationarmy.org; Dr James Read

SALVATION ARMY ARCHIVES

Archives: 26 Howden Rd, Scarborough, ON M1R 3E4
Museum: 2 Overlea Blvd, Toronto, ON M4H 1P4; tel: (416) 285-4344; fax: (416) 285-7763; email: Heritage_Centre@can.salvationarmy.org Col John Carew

NATIONAL RECYCLING OPERATIONS

2 Overlea Blvd, Toronto, ON M4H 1P4; tel: (416) 425-2111; fax: (416) 422-6167
Alberta Region: 37-2355 52nd Ave SE, Calgary, AB T2C 4X7; tel: (604) 944-8747; fax: (604) 944-3158
Atlantic Region: 1127 Champlain St, Dieppe, NB E1A 1P9; tel: (506) 857-8477; fax: (506) 858-0453
British Columbia Region: 2520 Davies Ave, Port Coquitlam, BC V3C 4T7; tel: (604) 944-8747; fax: (604) 944-3158

Bermuda Donquili (Call to Dance) rhythm group performs at the Bermuda Congress. The event was something of a homecoming as family and friends of Bermudians returned to the island for the celebrations.

Montreal Region: 1620 Notre Dame W, Montreal, QC H3J 1M1; tel: (516) 935-7425; fax: (514) 935-6093

Ontario Central Region: 2360 South Service Rd W, Oakville, ON L6L 5M9; tel: (905) 825-9208; fax: (905) 825-8953

Ontario East Region: 6-1280 Leeds Ave, Ottawa, ON K1B 3W3; tel: (613) 247-1435; fax: (613) 247-2243

Prairie Region: 1-111 Inksbrook Dr, Winnipeg, MB R2R 2V7; tel: (204) 953-1508; fax: (204) 953-1505

SOCIAL SERVICES (UNDER THQ)
Hospitals (public)
Rehabilitation
Montreal, QC H4B 2J5, Catherine Booth Hospital, 4375 Montclair Ave; tel: (514) 481-2070

General (B Class)
Windsor, ON N9A 1E1, Hotel-Dieu Grace Hospital, 1030 Ouellette Ave; tel: (519) 973-4444

Complex Continuing Care
Toronto, ON M4Y 2G5, Toronto Grace Health Centre, 650 Church St; tel: (416) 925-2251

Hospital Chaplaincy
Toronto, ON M1W 3W3 Scarborough Hospital, 3030 Birchmount Rd; tel: (416) 495-2536
Winnipeg, MB R3J 3M7 Winnipeg Grace Hospital, 300 Booth Dr; tel: (203) 837-0515

Family Tracing Services
2 Overlea Blvd, Toronto, ON M4H 1P4; tel: (416) 422-6219; fax: (416) 422-6221

SOCIAL SERVICES (UNDER DIVISIONS)
Hospices
Calgary, AB T2N 1B8, Agape Hospice, 1302 8th Ave NW; tel: (403) 282-6588 (acc 20)
Regina, SK S4R 8P6, Wascana Grace Hospice, 50 Angus Rd; tel: (306) 543-0655 (acc 10)
Richmond, BC V6X 2P3, Rotary Hospice, 3111 Shell Rd; tel: (604) 244-8022 (acc 10)

Adult Services to Developmentally Handicapped
Fort McMurray, AB T9H 1S7, 9919 MacDonald Ave; tel: (780) 743-4135
Hamilton, ON L8S 1G1, Lawson Ministries, 1600 Main St W; tel: (905) 527-6212 (acc 21)
Toronto, ON M4K 2S5, Broadview Village, 1132 Broadview Ave (Residential Living for

Developmentally Handicapped Adults);
tel: (416) 425-1052; fax: (416) 425-6579
(acc 160)
Winnipeg, MB R3A 0L5, 324 Logan Ave;
tel: (204) 946-9418

Adult Services Mental Health
St John's, NL A1E 1C1, Wiseman Centre,
714 Water St; tel: (709) 739-8355/8 (acc 30)
Toronto, ON M6K 1Z3, Liberty Housing,
248 Dufferin St; tel: (416) 531-3523 (acc 23)

Sheltered Workshops
Etobicoke, ON M8Z 4P8, Booth Industries,
994 Islington Ave; tel: (905) 255-7070
(acc 160)
Toronto, ON M3A 1A3, 150 Railside Rd;
tel: (416) 693-2116 (acc 44)

Addictions and Rehabilitation Centres (Alcohol/Drug Treatment)
Men
Calgary, AB T2G 0R9, 420 9th Ave SE;
tel: (403) 410-1150 (acc 34)
Edmonton, AB T5H 0E5, 9611 102 Ave NW;
tel: (780) 429-4274 (acc 158)
Glencairn, ON L0M 1K0, PO Box 100;
tel: (705) 466-3435/6 (acc 35)
Hamilton, Bermuda HM JX, PO Box HM 2238;
tel: (441) 292-2586 (acc 10)
Kingston, ON K7L 1C7, 562 Princess St;
tel: (613) 546-2333 (acc 24)
Montreal, QC H3J 1T4, 800 rue Guy;
tel: (514) 932-2214
Sudbury, ON P3E 1C2, 146 Larch St;
tel: (705) 673-1175/6 (acc 45)
Toronto, ON M5B 1E2, 160 Jarvis St;
tel: (416) 363-5496 (acc 85)
Vancouver, BC V6A 1K8, 119 East Cordova St;
tel: (604) 646-6800 (acc 70)
Victoria, BC V8W 1M2, 525 Johnson St;
tel: (250) 384-3396 (acc 109)
Winnipeg, MB R3B 0A1, 72 Martha St;
tel: (204) 946-9401 (acc 32)

Women
Toronto, ON M5R 2L6, The Homestead,
78 Admiral Rd; tel: (416) 921-0953 (acc 18)
Vancouver, BC V6P 1S4, The Homestead, 975
57th Ave W; tel: (604) 266-9696 (acc 32)

Residential Services (Hostels, Emergency Shelters)
Men
Barrie, ON L4M 3A5, Bayside Mission Centre,
16 Bayfield St; tel: (705) 728-3737 (acc 32)

Brampton, ON L6T 4X1, Wilkinson Road
Shelter, 15 Wilkinson Rd; tel: (905) 452-1335
(acc 85)
Brantford, ON N3T 2J6, Booth Centre,
187 Dalhousie St; tel: (519) 753-4193/4
(acc 38)
Calgary, AB T2G 0J8, Booth Centre,
631 7 Ave SE; tel: (403) 262-6188 (acc 276)
Campbell River, BC, 291 McLean St;
tel: (250) 287-3720 (acc 27)
Chilliwack, BC V2P 2N4, 45746 Yale Rd;
tel: (604) 792-0001 (acc 11)
Fort McMurray, AB T9H 1S7, 9919 MacDonald
Ave; tel: (780) 743-4135 (acc 32)
Halifax, NS B3K 3A9, 2044 Gottingen St;
tel: (902) 422-2363 (acc 49)
Hamilton, ON L8R 1R6, Booth Centre,
94 York Blvd; tel: (905) 527-1444 (acc 99)
Langley, BC V3A 0A5, Gateway of Hope,
5787 Langley-By-Pass; tel: (604) 514-7375
(acc 55)
Montreal, QC H3J 1T4, Booth Centre,
880 rue Guy; tel: (514) 932-2214 (acc 195)
Nanaimo, BC V9R 4S6, 19 Nicol St;
tel: (250) 754-2621 (acc 31)
New Westminster, BC V3L 2K1, 32 Elliot St;
tel: (604) 526-4783 (acc 33)
Ottawa, ON K1N 5W5, Booth Centre,
171 George St; tel: (613) 241-1573 (acc 213)
Pembroke, Bermuda HM JX, 5 Marsh Lane;
tel: (441) 295-5310 (acc 83)
Penticton, BC V2A 5J1, 2469 South Main St;
tel: (250) 492-6494 (acc 20)
Prince Rupert, BC V8J 1R3, 25 Grenville Court;
tel: (250) 624-6180 (acc 20)
Quebec City, QC G1R 4H8, Hotellerie,
14 Côte du Palais; tel: (418) 692-3956
(acc 60)
Regina, SK S4P 1W1, 1845 Osler St;
tel: (306) 569-6088 (acc 75)
Regina, SK S4P 1W1, Waterston Centre,
1865 Osler St; tel: (306) 566-6088 (acc 40)
Richmond, BC V6X 2P3, Richmond House
Emergency Shelter, 3111 Shell Rd;
tel: (604) 276-2490 (acc 10)
Saint John, NB E2L 1V3, Booth Centre,
36 St James St; tel: (506) 634-7021 (acc 75)
St Catharine's, ON L2R 3E7, Booth Centre,
184 Church St; tel: (905) 684-7813 (acc 21)
Saskatoon, SK S7M 1N5, 339 Avenue CS;
tel: (306) 244-6280 (acc 50)
Thunder Bay, ON P7A 4S2, CARS,
545 Cumberland St N; tel: (807) 345-7319
(acc 46)
Toronto, ON M5T 1P7, Hope Shelter,
167 College St; tel: (416) 979-7058 (acc 108)

Canada and Bermuda Territory

Toronto, ON M5C 2H4, The Gateway,
107 Jarvis St; tel: (416) 368-0324 (acc 100)

Toronto, ON M5A 2R5, Maxwell Meighen
Centre, 135 Sherbourne St; tel: (416) 366-2733
(acc 378)

Toronto, ON M5B 1E2, 160 Jarvis St;
tel: (416) 363-5496 (acc 98)

Vancouver, BC V6A 1K7, James McCready
Residence, 129 East Cordova St;
tel: (604) 646-6800 (acc 44)

Vancouver, BC V6A 1K7, The Haven,
128 East Cordova St; tel: (604) 646-6800
(acc 40)

Windsor, ON N9A 7G9, 355 Church St;
tel: (519) 253-7473 (acc 111)

Women

Brampton, ON L6X 3C9, The Honeychurch
Family Life Resource Center, 535 Main St N;
tel: (905) 451-4115 (acc 73)

Mississauga, ON L5A 2X3, Cawthra Road Shelter,
2500 Cawthra Rd; tel: (905) 281-1272

Montreal, QC H3J 1M8, L'Abri d'Espoir,
2000 rue Notre-Dame oust;
tel: (514) 934-5615 (acc 36)

Quebec City, QC G1R 4H8, Maison Charlotte,
14 Cote du Palais; tel: (418) 692-3956
(acc 25)

Toronto, ON M6P 1Y5, Evangeline Residence,
2808 Dundas St W; tel: (416) 762-9636
(acc 77)

Toronto, ON M6J 1E6, Florence Booth House,
723 Queen St W; tel: (416) 603-9800
(acc 60)

Vancouver, BC V5Z 4L9, Kate Booth House,
PO Box 38048 King Edward Mall;
tel: (604) 872-0772 (acc 12)

Mixed (male and female)

Abbotsford, BC V2S 2E8, 34081 Gladys Ave;
tel: (604) 852-9305 (acc 34)

Calgary, AB T2G 0R9, Centre of Hope,
420 9th Ave; tel: (403) 410-1111 (acc 295)

Courtney, BC V9N 2S2, 1580 Ftizgerald Ave;
tel: (250) 338-5133 (acc 9)

Fort St John, BC, 10116 100th Ave;
tel: (250) 785-0506 (acc 20)

London, ON N6C 4L8, Centre of Hope,
281 Wellington St; tel: (519) 661-0343
(acc 253)

Maple Ridge, BC V2X 2S8, 22188 Lougheed
Hwy; tel: (604) 463-8296 (acc 43)

Medicine Hat, AB T1A 1M6, 737 8th St SE;
tel: (403) 526-9699 (acc 30)

Oakville, ON L6L 6X7, Lighthouse Shelter,
750 Redwood Sq; tel: (905) 339-2918 (acc 25)

Sudbury, ON P3A 1C2, 146 Larch St;
tel: (705) 363-5496 (acc 91)

Vancouver, BC V6A 4K9, Grace Mansion,
596 East Hastings St; tel: (778) 329-0674
(acc 85)

Vancouver, BC V6B 1K8, Belkin House,
555 Homer St; tel: (604) 681-3405 (acc 257)

Vancouver, BC V6B 1G8, The Crosswalk,
138-140 W Hastings St; tel: (604) 669-4349
(acc 35)

Winnipeg, MB R3B 0J8, Booth Centre,
180 Henry Ave; tel: (204) 946-9460 |
(acc 208)

Family

Mississauga, ON L5R 4J9, Angela's Place,
45 Glen Hawthorne Rd; tel: (905) 791-3887

Montreal, QC H3J 1M8, L'Abri d'Espoir,
2000 rue Notre-Dame oust;
tel: (514) 934-5615 (acc 25)

Youth

Sutton, ON L0E 1R0, 20898 Dalton Rd,
PO Box 1087; tel: (905) 722-9076

Community and Family Services

Alberta: Calgary, Cranbrook, Drumheller,
Edmonton, Fort McMurray, Grande Prairie,
High River, Lethbridge, Lloydminster,
Medicine Hat, Peace River, Red Deer,
St Albert.

Bermuda: Hamilton.

British Columbia: Abbotsford, Campbell River,
Chilliwack, Courtenay, Duncan, Dawson Creek,
Fernie, Fort St John, Gibsons, Kamloops,
Kelowna, Maple Ridge, Nanaimo, Nelson,
New Westminster, North Vancouver, Parksville,
Penticton, Port Alberni, Powell River,
Prince George, Prince Rupert, Quesnel,
Richmond, Salmon Arm, Surrey, Terrace,
Trail, Vancouver, Vernon, Victoria,
White Rock, Williams Lake.

Manitoba: Brandon, Dauphin, Flin Flon,
Portage La Prairie, Thompson, Winnipeg (2).

New Brunswick: Bathurst, Campbelltown,
Fredericton, Miramichi, Moncton, Saint John,
Sussex.

Newfoundland and Labrador: Corner Brook,
Gander, Grand Falls-Windsor, Labrador City/
Wabush, Pasadena, Springdale, St Anthony,
St John's, Stephenville.

Nova Scotia: Bridgewater, Glace Bay, Halifax,
Kentville, New Glasgow, Sydney, Truro,
Westville, Yarmouth.

Ontario: Ajax, Belleville, Bowmanville,
Brampton, Brantford, Brockville, Burlington,

Cambridge, Chatham, Cobourg, Collingwood, Cornwall, Essex, Etobicoke (2), Fenelon Falls, Fort Frances, Gananoque, Georgetown, Goderich, Gravenhurst, Guelph, Hamilton, Huntsville, Ingersoll, Jackson's Point, Kemptville, Kenora, Kingston, Kirkland Lake, Kitchener, Leamington, Lindsay, Listowel, London, Midland, Milton, Mississauga (3), Napanee, New Liskeard, Newmarket, Niagara Falls, North Bay, North York (2), Oakville, Orillia, Oshawa, Ottawa, Owen Sound, Pembroke, Perth, Peterborough, Renfrew, Ridgetown, Sarnia, Sault Ste Marie, Scarborough, Simcoe, Smiths Falls, St Catharines, St Marys, St Thomas, Stratford, Strathroy, Sudbury, Thunder Bay, Tillsonburg, Toronto (3), Trenton, Wallaceburg, Welland, Whitby, Windsor, Woodstock.

Prince Edward Island: Charlottetown, Summerside.

Quebec: Montreal, Quebec City, Sherbrooke, St-Hubert, Trois-Rivieres.

Saskatchewan: Moose Jaw, Prince Albert, Regina.

Yukon Territory: Whitehorse.

Correctional and Justice Services
Community Programme Centres

Barrie, ON L4M 5A1, 400 Bayfield St, Ste 255; tel: (705) 737-4140

Chilliwack, BC V2P 2N4, 45742B Yale Rd; tel: (604) 792-8581

Corner Brook: PO Box 1018 Corner Brook, NL A2H 6J3; tel: (709) 639-1719

Guelph, ON N1L 1H3, 1320 Gordon St; tel: (519) 836-9360

Hamilton, ON L7R 1Y9, 2090 Prospect St; tel (905) 634-7977

Kingston, ON K7K 4B1, 472 Division St; tel: (613) 549-2676

Kitchener, ON N2H 2M2, 151 Frederick St, Ste 502; tel: (519) 742-8521

London, ON N6B 2L4, 281 Wellington St; tel: (519) 432-9553

Medicine Hat, AB T1A 0E7, 874 2 St E; tel: (403) 529-2111

Moncton, NB E1C 1M2, 68 Gordon St; tel: (506) 853-8887

Ottawa, ON K1Y K1N, 171 George St; tel: (613) 725-1733

Peterborough, ON K9H 2H6, 219 Simcoe St; tel: (705) 742-4391

Prince Albert, SK S6V 4V3, 900 Central Ave; tel: (306) 763-6078

Regina, SK S4P 3M7, 2240 13th Ave; tel: (306) 757-4711/2

St Catharines, ON L2R 3E7, 184 Church St; tel: (905) 684-7813

St John's, NL A1C 4Z1, 21 Adams Ave; tel: (709) 726-0393

Thunder Bay, ON P7A 4S2, 268 Pearl St; tel: (807) 344-0683

Toronto, ON M5A 3P1, 77 River St; tel: (416) 304-1974

Trois Rivieres, QC G8Y 3N8, 3885 De Landerneau; tel: (819) 840-3420

Winnipeg, MB R3A 0L5, 324 Logan Ave, 2nd Floor; tel: (204) 949-2100

Windsor, ON N9A 7G9, 355 Church St; tel: (519) 253-7473

Adult/Youth Residential Centres

Brampton, ON L6X 1C1, 44 Nelson St W; tel: (905) 453-0988 (acc 12)

Dartmouth, NS B3A 1H5, 318 Windmill Rd; tel: (902) 465-2690 (acc 20)

Dundas, ON L9H 2E8, 34 Hatt St; tel: (905) 627-1632 (acc 10)

Ilderton, ON N0M 2A0, PO Box 220; tel: (519) 666-0600 (acc 28)

Kitchener, ON N2G 2M4, 657 King St E; tel: (519) 744-4666 (acc 21)

Milton, ON L9P 2X9, 8465 Boston Church Rd; tel: (905) 875-1775 (acc 10)

Moncton, NB E1C 8P6, 64 Gordon St, PO Box 1121; tel: (506) 858-9486 (acc 22)

Regina, SK S4P 1W1, Waterston Centre, 1865 Osler St; tel: (306) 566-6088 (acc 8)

Saskatoon, SK S7M 1N5, 339 Avenue C S; tel: (306) 244-6280 (acc 15)

Sudbury, ON P3A 1C2, 146 Larch St; tel: (705) 363-5496 (acc 4)

Thunder Bay, ON P7A 4S2, 268 Pearl St; tel: (807) 344-0683 (acc 4)

Toronto, ON M4X 1K2, 422 Sherbourne St; tel: (416) 964-6316/967-6618 (acc 53)

Vancouver, BC V6B 1K8, Belkin House, 555 Homer St; tel: (604) 681-3405 (acc 30)

Whitehorse, YT Y1A 6E3, 91678 Alaska Hwy; tel: (867) 667-2741 (acc 16)

Yellowknife, NWT X1A 1P4, 4927 45th St; tel: (867) 920-4673 (acc 33)

Health Services
Long-Term Care/Seniors' Residences

Brandon, MB R7A 3N9, Dinsdale Personal Care Home, 510 6th St; tel: (204) 727-3636 (acc 60)

Calgary, AB T3C 3W7, Jackson/Willan Seniors' Residence, 3015 15 Ave SW; tel: (403) 249-9116 (acc 18)

Salvationist Nancy Turley gets involved in outreach in anticipation of the 2010 Winter Olympics in Vancouver, where 2,000 Army volunteers gave out more than 600,000 hot drinks over 17 days and shared the gospel through personal contact and Christian literature

Edmonton, AB T5X 6C4, Grace Manor,
  12510 140 Ave; tel: (780) 454-5484 (acc 100)
Kitchener, ON N2H 2P1, A. R. Goudie Eventide
  Home, 369 Frederick St; tel: (519) 744-5182
  (acc 80)
Montreal, QC H4B 2J4, Montclair Residence,
  4413 Montclair Ave; tel: (514) 481-5638
  (acc 50)
New Westminster, BC V3L 4A4, Buchanan
  Lodge, 409 Blair Ave; tel: (604) 522-7033
  (acc 112)
Niagara Falls, ON L2E 1K5, The Honourable
  Ray and Helen Lawson Eventide Home,
  5050 Jepson St; tel: (905) 356-1221
  (acc 100)
Ottawa, ON K1Y 2Z3, Ottawa Grace Manor,
  1156 Wellington St; tel: (613) 722-8025
  (acc 128)
Regina, SK S4R 8P6, William Booth Special
  Care Home, 50 Angus Rd; tel: (306) 543-0655
  (acc 81)

Riverview, NB E1B 4K6, Lakeview Manor,
  50 Suffolk St; tel: (506) 387-2012/3/4
  (acc 50)
St John's, NL A1A 2G9, Glenbrook Lodge,
  105 Torbay Rd; tel: (709) 726-1575
  (acc 114)
St John's, NL A1A 2G9, Glenbrook Villa,
  107 Torbay Rd; tel: (709) 726-1575
  (acc 20)
Toronto, ON M4S 1G1, Meighen Retirement
  Residence, 84 Davisville Ave;
  tel: (416) 481-5557 (acc 84)
Toronto, ON M4S 1J6, Meighen Manor,
  155 Millwood Rd; tel: (416) 481-9449
  (acc 168)
Vancouver, BC V5S 3T1, Southview Terrace,
  3131 58th Ave E; tel: (604) 438-3367/8
  (acc 57)
Vancouver, BC V5S 3V2, Southview Heights,
  7252 Kerr St; tel: (604) 438-3367/8
  (acc 47)

Victoria, BC V9A 7J6, Matson Sequoia Residence, 554 Garrett Pl Ste 211; tel: (250) 383-5821 (acc 30)

Victoria, BC V9A 4G7, Sunset Lodge, 952 Arm St; tel: (250) 385-3422 (acc 108)

Winnipeg, MB R2Y 0S8, Golden West Centennial Lodge, 811 School Rd; tel: (204) 888-3311 (acc 116)

Immigrant and Refugee Services

Toronto, ON M5B 1E2, 160 Jarvis St; tel: (416) 360-6036

Women's Multi-Service Programmes (and unmarried mothers)

Hamilton, ON L8P 2H1, Grace Haven, 138 Herkimer St; tel: (905) 522-7336 (acc 12)

London, ON N6J 1A2, Bethesda Centre, 54 Riverview Ave; tel: (519) 438-7371 (acc 14)

Ottawa, ON K1Y 2Z3, Bethany Hope Centre, 1140 Wellington St; tel: (613) 725-1733

Regina, SK S4S 0X5, Gemma House, 3820 Hill Ave; tel: (306) 586-5388 (acc 8)

Regina, SK S4S 7A7, Grace Haven, 2929 26th Ave; tel: (306) 352-1421 (acc 7)

Saskatoon, SK S7K 0N1, Bethany Home, 802 Queen St; tel: (306) 244-6758 (acc 15)

Child Day Care/Pre-schools

Barrie, ON L4V 5X5, Sonlight Child Care Centre, 151 Lillian Cres; tel: (705) 734-9080 (acc 93)

Brampton, ON L6S 4B7, Noah's Ark Day Care Centre, 9395 Bramalea Rd N; tel: (905) 793-5610 (acc 46)

Chilliwack, BC V2P 1C5, Happy Hearts Day Care, 46420 Brooks Ave; tel: (604) 792-5285 (acc 23)

Guelph, ON N1L 1H3, Salvation Army Nursery School, 1320 Gordon St; tel: (519) 836-9360 (acc 121)

London, ON N6J 1A2, Cantara, 54 Riverview Ave; tel: (519) 438-8371 (acc 20)

London, ON N5W 2B6, The Salvation Army Village Day Nursery, 1340 Dundas St E; tel: (519) 455-8155 ext 308 (acc 75)

Medicine Hat, AB T1B 3R3, Rise and Shine Day Care, 164 Stratton Way SE; tel: (403) 529-2003 (acc 58)

Mississauga, ON L5L 1V3, Erin Mills Day Care, 2460 The Collegeway; tel: (905) 820-6500 (acc 32).

Mississauga, ON L5N 4W8, Gentle Guidance Day Care, 3025 Vanderbilt Rd; tel: (905) 785-0522 (acc 24)

Mississauga, ON L5A 2X4, Mississauga Temple Day Care, 3173 Cawthra Rd; tel: (905) 275-8430 (acc 82)

Moncton, NB E1E 4E4, Small Blessings, 20 Centennial Dr; tel: (506) 857-0588 (acc 95)

New Westminster, BC V3L 3A9, Kids Place Day Care, 325 6th St; tel: (604) 521-8223 (acc 20)

Owen Sound, ON N4K 2X9, Salvation Army Day Care, 365 14th St W; tel: (519) 371-9540 (acc 99)

Peace River, AB T8S 1E1, School Readiness, 9710-74 Ave; tel: (780) 624-2370 (acc 43)

Scarborough, ON M1W 3K3, Agincourt Temple Child Care, 3080 Birchmount Rd; tel: (416) 497-0329 (acc 94)

Scarborough, ON M1R 2Z2, Scarborough Citadel Child Care, 2021 Lawrence Ave E; tel: 416-759-5340 (acc 36)

Windsor, ON N8T 2Z7, Learning Corner Day Care Centre, 3199 Lauzon Rd; tel: (519) 944-4051 (acc 111)

Winnipeg, MB R3E 1E6, Weston Child Care, 1390 Roy Ave; tel: (204) 786-5066 (acc 59)

Parent Child Resource Centres

Courtney, BC V9N 2S2, 1580 Fitzgerald Ave; tel: (250) 338-6200

Kitchener, ON N2E 3T1, 75 Tillsley Dr; tel: (519) 745-335

The General on campaign

From top (left to right) **USA EASTERN:** The General kneels to pray in Boston, Massachusetts, during the 125th anniversary celebration of Samuel Logan Brengle's sanctification experience. **CARIBBEAN:** The General and Commissioner Helen Clifton take the salute at a march-past in Port-au-Prince, Haiti. **SOUTH AMERICA WEST:** President Michelle Bachilet Jeria of Chile receives the Army's world leaders in Santiago. **CONGO BRAZZAVILLE:** General Clifton opens a new Army building in Moungali. **USA SOUTHERN:** Staff at Atlanta Kroc Centre are prayed for by the General. **ZAMBIA:** Flags fly during the congress in Lusaka.

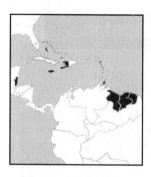

CARIBBEAN TERRITORY

Territorial leaders:
Colonels Onal and Edmane Castor

Territorial Commander:
Colonel Onal Castor (1 May 2009)

Chief Secretary:
Lieut-Colonel Lindsay Rowe (1 May 2009)

Territorial Headquarters: 3 Waterloo Rd, Kingston 10, Jamaica

Postal address: PO Box 378, Kingston 10, Jamaica, WI

Tel: [1876] 929 6190/91/92; fax: [1876] 929 7560; email: car_leadership@car.salvationarmy.org;

website: www.salvationarmycarib.org

In 1887 The Salvation Army 'opened fire' in Kingston, and thence spread throughout the island of Jamaica and to Guyana (1895), Barbados (1898), Trinidad (1901), Grenada (1902), St Lucia (1902), Antigua (1903), St Vincent (1905), Belize (1915), St Kitts (1916), Suriname (1924), the Bahamas (1931), Haiti (1950), French Guiana (1980) and St Maarten (1999). The General of The Salvation Army is a Corporation Sole in Jamaica (1914), Trinidad and Tobago (1915), Barbados (1917), Belize (1928), Guyana (1930), the Bahamas (1936) and Antigua (1981).

Zone: Americas and Caribbean
Countries included in the territory: Antigua, Bahamas, Barbados, Belize, French Guiana, Grenada, Guyana, Haiti, Jamaica, St Kitts, St Lucia, St Maarten, St Vincent, Suriname, Trinidad and Tobago
'The Salvation Army' in Dutch: Leger des Heils; in French: Armée du Salut
Languages in which the gospel is preached: Creole, Dutch, English, French, Surinamese
Periodical: *The War Cry*

AT 16.53 on Tuesday 12 January 2010 a 7.0 magnitude earthquake with its epicentre just south of Port-au-Prince shook Haiti's capital city and surrounding area, causing buildings to crumble and thousands of people to die. By 24 January, at least 52 aftershocks measuring 4.5 or greater had been recorded. An estimated three million people were affected by the quake.

The Haitian Government reported that an estimated 230,000 people had died, 300,000 been injured and

a million made homeless. It was also estimated that 250,000 residences and 30,000 commercial buildings had collapsed or were severely damaged.

Within minutes, victims of the earthquake started arriving at The Salvation Army's facilities in Delmas 2, Port-au-Prince, where they were given medical attention. Salvationists served more than 10 million meals; treated thousands of victims for earthquake related wounds; managed a tent city near its compound housing at least 20,000 victims, providing them with food, clothing, lodging, emotional and spiritual support; built nearly 600 transitional houses, and developed a comprehensive plan for long-term support, recovery and rebuilding.

The territory expresses sincere appreciation to the global Salvation Army family and people of all nations who responded with great generosity and tremendous support for the emergency relief work. Since the earthquake, up to a thousand converts have been recorded by the Army in Haiti.

Characterised by complexity and diversity, with a ministry across 16 countries of the Caribbean, the territory continues to experience growth through new converts and committed discipleship.

A highlight of the year came when General Shaw Clifton and Commissioner Helen Clifton (WPWM) made their first visit to the Caribbean (23-30 November). They inspired Salvationists throughout the territory, particularly in Jamaica and Haiti.

At a Sunday morning march of witness in Port-au-Prince the General took the salute as more than 2,500 Salvationists marched past their international leader.

The year was also one of new approaches to leadership development. The territory held its first Social Justice Conference (24-26 June), under the leadership of Commissioner Christine MacMillan (Director, International Social Justice Commission), and its first Territorial Soldiers College (13-20 July).

Ten cadets of the Witnesses For Christ Session were ordained and commissioned as lieutenants on Sunday 28 June. Eight members of the Prayer Warriors Session received their summer assignments.

Gospel artists from across the territory, supported by musicians from USA Southern, gathered in Kingston for CARIMI (Caribbean Music Institute).

STATISTICS

Officers 299 (active 223 retired 76) **Cadets** (1st Yr) 8 (2nd Yr) 10 **Employees** 1,021
Corps 129 **Outposts** 46 **Institutions** 59 **Schools** 167
Senior Soldiers 9,431 **Adherents** 1,286 **Junior Soldiers** 2,848
Personnel serving outside territory Officers 7

STAFF

Women's Ministries: Col Edmane Castor (TPWM) Lt-Col Lynette Rowe (TSWM) Lt-Col Trypheme McKenzie (TLOMS, TWAS)
Personnel: Lt-Col Sydney McKenzie
Programme: Lt-Col Devon Haughton
Business: Lt-Col Edwin Masih
Coordinator for Disaster Services: Envoy John Williamson
Editor: Maj Molvie Graham
Leader Development: Lt-Col Verona Haughton
Pastoral Care: Maj Keith Graham
Prayer Coordinator: Maj Keith Graham
Projects/Sponsorship: Mr Stephen Williamson
Property: Lt-Col Sydney McKenzie
Spiritual Life Development: Lt-Col Verona Haughton
Training: Maj Ronald Millar
Youth and Candidates: Capt Sherma Evelyn

DIVISIONS

Antigua: PO Box 2, 36 Long St, St John's; tel: [1268] 462-0115; fax: [1268] 462-9134; Maj Rosemarie Brown
Bahamas: PO Box N 205, Nassau, NP; tel: [1242] 393-2340; fax: [1242] 393-2189; Maj Lester and Capt Beverley Ferguson
Barbados: PO Box 57, Reed St, Bridgetown; tel: [1246] 426-2467; fax: [1246] 426-9369; Majs Dewhurst and Vevene Jonas

Guyana: PO Box 10411, 237 Alexander St, Lacytown, Georgetown; tel: [592] 22 72619/54910; fax: [592] (22) 50893; Majs Sinous and Marie Theodore

Haiti: (temporary address) 65 Autoroute de Delmas, Building Valerico Canez, Port-au-Prince; tel: [509] 25 1036 71; Majs Lucien and Marie Lamartiniere

Jamaica Eastern: PO Box 153, Kingston; 153b Orange St, Kingston; tel: [1876] 922-6764/0287; fax: [1876] 967-1553; Majs Stanley and Hazel Griffin

Jamaica Western: PO Box 44, Lot #949 West Green, Montego Bay, St James; tel: [876] 952-3778; Majs Allen and Esther Satterlee

Trinidad and Tobago: 154a Henry St, Port-of-Spain, Trinidad; PO Box 248, Port-of-Spain; tel: [1868] 625-4120; fax: [1868] 625-4179; Majs Darrell and Joan Wilkinson

REGIONS

Belize: PO Box 64, 41 Regent St, Belize City, Belize; tel: [501] 2273 365; fax: (501) 2278 240; email: Belize HQ/BEL/CAR/SArmy; Maj Brenda Greenidge

French Guyana: PO Box 329,97327 Cayenne Cedex, French Guyana; tel: [594] 31-5832; Maj Serge St Aime

Suriname: PO Box 317, Henck Arron Straat 172, Paramaribo; tel: [597] 47-3310; fax: [597] 41-0555; email: Suriname HQ/SUR/CAR/SArmy; Maj Jean Miller and Capt Joan Cantave

COUNTRIES NOT IN DIVISIONAL OR REGIONAL LISTS

Grenada: Grenville St, St George's, Grenada; tel: [1473] 440-3299

St Kitts: PO Box 56, Cayon Rd, Basseterre, St Kitts; tel: [1869] 465-2106

St Lucia: PO Box 6, High St, Castries, St Lucia; tel: [1758] 452-3108; fax: [1758] 451-8569

St Maarten: 59 Union Rd, Cole Bay, PO Box 5184, St Maarten, Netherlands Antilles; tel: [5995] 445424

St Vincent: Hall Melville St, PO Box 498, Kingstown, St Vincent; tel: [1784] 456-1574; fax: [1784] 456-1082

TRAINING COLLEGE

GPO Box 437, 174 Orange St, Kingston, Jamaica; tel: [1876] 922-2027; fax: [1876] 967-7541

CITY WELFARE OFFICES

Bahamas: 31 Mackey St, Nassau NP
Jamaica: 57 Peter's Lane, Kingston

COMMUNITY CENTRES

Bahamas: Meadow and West Sts, Nassau
Barbados: Checker Hall, St Lucy; Wellington St, Bridgetown; Wotton, Christchurch
Jamaica:
Rae Town Goodwill Centre, 24 Tower St, Kingston; tel: [1876] 928-5770/930-0028
Allman Town, 18-20 Prince of Wales St, Kingston 4; tel: [1876] 92-27279

FEEDING CENTRES

Antigua: Meals on wheels
Bahamas: Mackey St and Grantstown, Nassau
Barbados: Reed St, Bridgetown
Belize: 9 Glynn St, Belize City (acc 50)
Guyana:
237 Alexander St, Georgetown;
Third Ave, Bartica;
Rainbow City, Linden
Haiti: Port-au-Prince (Nutrition Centre)
Jamaica: Peter's Lane, Kingston; Jones Town, Kingston; Spanish Town, St Catherine; May Pen, Clarendon; St Ann's Bay, St Ann; Port Antonio, Portland; Montego Bay, St James; Savanna-La-Mar, Westmoreland
St Lucia: High St, Castries
Suriname: Gravenstraat 126, Paramaribo

For Children
Bahamas: Nassau, Mackey St
Grenada: St Georges
Guyana: Georgetown, Bartica, Linden
St Vincent: Kingstown

MEDICAL WORK
Haiti:
Bethel Maternity Home and Dispensary, Fond-des-Negres
Bethesda TB Centre, Fond-des-Negres
Primary Health Care Centre and Nutrition Centre, Port-au-Prince
Jamaica: Rae Town Clinic, 24 Tower St, Kingston; tel: (876) 928-1489/930-0028

PRISON, PROBATION AND AFTERCARE WORK
Antigua; Grenada; Guyana (Georgetown, Bartica, New Amsterdam); Jamaica; St Kitts; Suriname; Tobago; Trinidad

Prison Visitation Services
Belize: directed by Regional Commander

RETIRED OFFICERS' RESIDENCES
Jamaica: Francis Ham Residence,
57 Mannings Hill Rd, Kingston 8;
tel: (876) 924-1308 (acc 7)
Barbados: Long Bay, St Phillip
Guyana: East La Penitence

SOCIAL SERVICES
Blind and Handicapped
Adults
Bahamas: Visually Handicapped Workshop,
Ivanhoe Lane, PO Box N 1980, Nassau NP;
tel: (242) 394-1107 (acc 19)
Jamaica: Francis Ham Residence (Home for
Senior Citizens), 57 Mannings Hill Rd,
Kingston 8; tel: (876) 924-1308 (acc 37)

Children (schools)
Bahamas: School for the Blind,
33 Mackay St, PO Box N 205, Nassau NP;
tel: (242) 394-3197 (acc 15)
Jamaica: School for the Blind and Visually
Impaired, 57 Mannings Hill Rd, PO Box 562,
Kingston 8; tel: (876) 925-1362 (residential
acc 120)

Women (vocational training)
Jamaica: Evangeline Residence, Kingston;
Port Antonio, Portland

SOCIAL SERVICES
Children
Day Care Centres (nurseries)
Barbados:
Wellington St, Bridgetown (acc 50)
Wotton, Christchurch (acc 50)
Grenada: St Georges (acc 25)
Jamaica:
Allman Town, Kingston (acc 40) Havendale,
Kingston (acc 16) Lucea, Hanover (acc 30)
Montego Bay, St James (acc 40)
St Lucia: Castries (acc 50)
St Vincent: Kingstown (acc 20)
Trinidad: San Juan (acc 20)

Homes
Antigua: St John's Sunshine Home (acc 12)
Haiti:
Bethany, Fond-des-Negres (acc 22)
La Maison du Bonheur, Port-au-Prince
(acc 52)
Jamaica:
Hanbury Home, PO Box 2, Shooter's Hill PO,
Manchester; tel: [1876] 603-3507 (acc 90)
The Nest, 57 Mannings Hill Rd, Kingston 8;
tel: [1876] 925-7711 (acc 45)

Windsor Lodge, PO Box 74,
Williamsfield PO, Manchester;
tel: [1876] 963-4222 (acc 80)
Suriname: Ramoth, Henck Arron Straat 172,
PO Box 317, Paramaribo; tel: [597] 47-3191
(acc 62)

Playgrounds
Jamaica: Rae Town, Kingston; Lucea, Hanover;
Montego Bay, St James
Suriname: Henck Arron Straat 126,
Paramaribo

Schools
Basic (kindergartens)
Antigua: St John (acc 150)
Barbados:
Checker Hall (acc 50) Wellington St (acc 10)
Guyana: Bartica (acc 90)
Haiti:
Abraham (acc 63) Aquin (acc 112)
Arcahaie (acc 45) Balan (acc 30)
Bainet (acc 32) Bellamie (acc 35)
Bellegarde (acc 40) Belle Riviere (acc 24)
Bocolomond (acc 47) Bodoin (acc 17)
Brodequin (acc 64) Campeche (acc 43)
Cayot (acc 70) Couyot (acc 65)
Deruisseaux (acc 10) Dessources (acc 30)
Duverger (acc 77) Fond-des-Negres (acc 96)
Fort National (acc 26) Gardon (acc 40)
Gros-Morne (48) Guirand (acc 12)
Jacmel (acc 34) Kamass (acc 12)
L'Azile (acc 51) L'Homond (acc 75)
La Colline (acc 21) Laferonnay (acc 34)
Lafosse (acc 82) Lajovange (acc 35)
Le Blanc (acc 34) Lilette (acc 37)
Limbe (acc 20) Montrouis (30)
Moulin (acc 75) Perigny (acc 25)
Petit Goave (acc 53) Plaisance (acc 15)
Port-de-Paix (acc 14) Puit Laurent (acc 36)
Rossignol (acc 53) St Marc (acc 91)
Verena (acc 211) Vieux Bourg (acc 175)
Violette (acc 42)
Jamaica:
Bath (acc 25) Bluefields (acc 49)
Cave Mountain (acc 30) Cave Valley (acc 75)
Falmouth (acc 86) Great Bay (acc 40)
Kingston Allman Town (acc 150)
Kingston Havendale (acc 90)
Kingston Rae Town (acc 100)
Linstead (acc 65) Lucea (acc 200)
May Pen (acc 60) Montego Bay (acc 240)
Port Antonio (acc 50) St Ann's Bay (acc 36)
Savanna-la-mar (acc 110) Top Hill (acc 93)
St Kitts: Basseterre (acc 80)
St Lucia: Castries (acc 100)

Trinidad and Tobago:
San Fernando (acc 80) Scarborough, Tobago
(acc 70)
Tragarette Rd, Port-of-Spain (acc 20)

Home Science
Barbados: Project Lighthouse (acc 12)
Haiti:
Aquin; Carrefour; Desruisseaux; Duverger;
Fond-des-Negres, Gros Morne; Vieux Bourg

Primary Schools
Belize: 12 Cemetery Road, Belize City;
tel: (501) 227-2156 (acc 250)
Haiti:
Abraham (acc 183) Aquin (acc 305) Arcahaie
(acc 212) Bainet (acc 150) Balan (acc 178)
Bas Fort National (acc 259) Bellamy (acc 215)
Bellegarde (acc 235) Belle Riviere (acc 203)
Boco Lomond (acc 255) Bodoun (acc 76)
Brodequin (acc 141) Campeche (acc 130)
Carrefour/Desruisseaux (acc 250) Cayot
(acc 273) Couyot (acc 375) Dessources
(acc 160) Duverger (acc 265) Fond-des-Negres
(acc 574) Fort National (acc 259) Gardon
(acc 166) Gros Morne (acc 325) Guirand
(acc 206) Jacmel (acc 97) Kamass (acc 21)
L'Azile (acc 174) L'Homond (acc 209)
La Colline (acc 125) La Fosse (acc 367)
La Jovange (acc 255) La Zandier (acc 170)
Laferonnay (acc 215) Lilette (acc 130) Limbe
(acc 55) Luly (acc 182) Montrouis (acc 131)
Moulin (acc 180) Peirigny (acc 205) Petit
Goave (acc 165) Petite Riviere (acc118)
Plaisance (acc 174) College Verena (acc 486)
Port-de-Paix (acc 315) Puits Laurent (acc 195)
Rossignol (acc 239) St Marc (acc 222) Vieux
Bourg (acc 617) Violette (acc 133)

Evening Schools
Guyana: Happy Heart Youth Centre, New
Amsterdam (acc 20)
Haiti: Port-au-Prince (acc 83)

Secondary Schools
Haiti: Port-au-Prince (acc 450) Gros-Morne
(acc 325)

SOCIAL SERVICES
Men and Women
Centre for Homeless
Belize: Raymond A. Parkes Home,
18 Cemetery Rd, Belize City;
tel: [501] 207-4309 (acc 12)

Eventide Home
Trinidad: Senior Citizens' Centre,
34 Duncan St, Port-of-Spain;
tel: [868] 624-5883 (acc 13)

SOCIAL SERVICES
Men
Guyana: MacKenzie Guest House, Rainbow
City, PO Box 67, Linden Co-op MacKenzie,
Guyana; tel: [592] 444-6406 (acc 10)

Hostels and Shelters
Guyana:
Men's Hostel, 6-7 Water St, Kingston,
Georgetown; tel: [592] 226-1235 (acc 40)
Drug Rehabilitation Centre,
6-7 Water St, Kingston, Georgetown;
tel: [592] 226-1235 (acc 18)
Jamaica:
Men's Hostel, 57 Peter's Lane, Kingston;
tel: [1876] 922-4030 (acc 25)
William Chamberlain Rehabilitation Centre,
57 Peter's Lane, Kingston (acc 25)
Suriname: Night Shelter, Ladesmastraat 2-6,
PO Box 317, Paramaribo; tel: [597] 4-75108
(acc 70)

SOCIAL SERVICES
Women
Eventide Homes
Belize: Ganns Rest Home, 60 East Canal St,
Belize City; tel: [501] 227 2973 (acc 12)
Guyana: 69 Bent and Haley Sts, Wortmanville,
Georgetown; tel: [592] 226-8846 (acc 22)
Suriname:
Elim Guest House, Henck Arron
Straat 126, PO Box 317, Paramaribo;
tel: [597] 48-4325 (acc 15)
Emma House, Dr Nassylaan 76, PO Box 2402,
Paramaribo; tel: [597] 47-3890 (acc 22)

Hostels and Shelters
Bahamas: Women and Children's Emergency
Residence, Grantstown, PO Box GT 2216,
Nassau NP; tel: [242] 323-5608 (acc 21)
Jamaica: Evangeline Residence, 153 Orange St,
Kingston; tel: 1 (876) 922-6398 (acc 50)
Trinidad:
Geddes Grant House, 22-24 Duncan St,
Port-of-Spain; tel: 1 (868) 623-5700
(acc 34)
Josephine Shaw House, 131-133 Henry St,
Port-of-Spain; tel: 1 (868) 623623-2547
(acc 106)

CONGO (BRAZZAVILLE) TERRITORY

Territorial leaders:
Colonels Joseph and Angelique Lukau

Territorial Commander:
Colonel Joseph Lukau (1 Dec 2010)

Chief Secretary:
Lieut-Colonel Gerrit Marseille (1 Mar 2008)

Territorial Headquarters: Rue de Reims, Brazzaville, République du Congo

Postal address: BP 20, Brazzaville, République du Congo

Tel: [242] 2811144; email: congo_brazzaville_info@con.salvationarmy.org

In 1937 The Salvation Army spread from Léopoldville to Brazzaville, and in 1953 French Equatorial Africa (now Congo) became a separate command. Commissioner and Mrs Henri Becquet were the pioneers. The command was upgraded to a territory in December 1960.

Zone: Africa
Country included in the territory: The Republic of Congo
'The Salvation Army' in French: Armée du Salut; in Kikongo: Nkangu a Luvulusu; in Lingala: Basolda na Kobikisama; in Vili: Livita li Mavutsula
Languages in which the gospel is preached: French, Kikongo, Kituba, Lingala, Vili
Periodical: *Le Salutiste*

GENERAL elections for the presidency were held in the Congo in July 2009. There was some apprehension in the months leading up to this event because of the experience of previous elections, so the territory organised a spiritual retreat in every division in June as an occasion for Salvationists to pray for the nation.

The Women's Ministries Department arranged a number of camps for its members, also hosting the visit of women officers from across the Congo River, in the Democratic Republic of Congo Territory.

The National Music Camp took place in Pointe Noire and the National Scouts Camp in Nkayi. A corps cadet camp was held in Brazzaville and seven divisional summer holiday camps for young people were also organised.

That these exchanges and camps are again possible is an encouraging indication that people find their situation secure enough to organise such gatherings in the country. Unfortunately, parents do not always have the means to send their children to camp even for a modest fee.

On 1 October 2009 the training

The corps officer at Bilala shows some people from his neighbourhood how to make beehives. This Salvation Army-sponsored project encourages families to take up beekeeping and produce honey so that they can have an income to help feed and clothe their children.

college welcomed a new session as 26 cadets of the Ambassadors Of Sanctification Session started their two-year training under the leadership of a new team of officers.

Also in 2009 two corps building projects were started in the north of the country where The Salvation Army is not yet seen very often. In January 2010 Commissioner Mfon J. Akpan (then TC) opened the hall at Makoua and April saw the opening of the hall in Doungou. Considerable public interest was shown in the towns' newest churches.

General Shaw Clifton and Commissioner Helen Clifton (WPWM) visited the territory in February 2010. During their whirlwind tour, 185 soldiers and 190 junior soldiers were enrolled.

At Nzoko Salvationists were excited to witness the Army's world leader conduct the dedication to God of their new corps hall. A guest house in Moungali was also opened by General Clifton.

One thousand women were enrolled as home league members in a packed Moungali Corps hall. On the Sunday some 7,000 soldiers and friends gathered for a holiness meeting, after an impressive march past of about 3,000 soldiers.

A music festival featuring the Territorial Band, Songsters, Timbrel Group and *sakalas* (bongos) rounded off the international leaders' visit. A well-attended spiritual weekend for 200 members of the territory's music groups was later organised at the rural Boko Corps.

STATISTICS

Officers 323 (active 266 retired 57)
Employees 171
Corps 102 **Outposts** 57 **Maternity Unit** 2
Clinics 6 **Centres** 2 **Schools** 17
Senior Soldiers 22,569 **Adherents** 2,468
Junior Soldiers 6,640
Personnel serving outside territory Officers 6

STAFF

Women's Ministries: Col Angelique Lukau (TPWM) Lt-Col Eva Marseille (TSWM) Lt-Col Monique Bakemba (THLS)
Sec for Personnel: Lt-Col Prosper Bakemba
Sec for Programme: Lt-Col Alexis Sakamesso
Sec for Business Administration: Maj Jean Pierre Sonda
Extension Training: Capt Prosper Komiena
Financial Administrator: Sgt Jean Mayandu
Health Services Coordinators: Majs Sebastien and Martine Diantezulua
Information Technology: M'Passi Loukeba Richard
Music: Wilfrid Milandou
Projects: Sgt Edy Seraphin Kanda
Property: Maj Aristide Samba
Public Relations: Capt Guy Bonaventure Conckot
Social: Capt Blaise Kombo
Territorial Bandmaster: Sgt Sensa Malanda
Territorial Songster Leader: Wilfrid Milandou
Training: Maj Dieudonnee Louzolo
Youth and Candidates: Capt Edith Dibantsa

DIVISIONS

Brazzaville 1: c/o THQ; tel: 21 13 15; Majs Victor and Emma Nzingoula
Brazzaville 2: c/o THQ; tel: 68 95 14; Majs François and Louise Mavouna

Lekoumou: c/o THQ; tel: 58 63 92; Majs Patrick and Clémentine Tadi
Louingui: c/o THQ; Majs Jérôme and Jeanne Nzita
Mbanza-Ndounga: c/o THQ; Majs Gabin and Philomene Mbizi
Niari: BP 85, Dolisie; tel 5364319; Majs Urbain and Judith Loubacky
North: c/o THQ; Majs Antoine and Marianne Massiélé
Pointe Noire: BP 686, Pointe Noire; tel: 94 00 16; Majs Daniel and Angèle Taty
Yangui: BP 10, Kinkala; Majs Philippe and Rose Bonazebi

DISTRICTS

Bouenza: c/o THQ; Maj Alphonse Mayamba
Tchitondi: c/o THQ; Maj Jean-Pierre Douniama

TRAINING COLLEGE

Nzoko: c/o THQ; tel: 56 95 72

SOCIAL AND EDUCATIONAL CENTRES

Day Care Centre
Ouenze Corps, Brazzaville

Guest Houses
Moungali (Brazzaville); Pointe-Noire

Home for the Visually Impaired
Yenge, Nzoko: c/o THQ

Institute for the Blind
c/o THQ

Schools
Nursery School
Véronique Makoumbou Nursery School, Nzoko

Primary School
John Swinfen Primary School, Loua

HEALTH SERVICES

Health Clinic and Eye Treatment Centre
Moukoundji-Ngouaka: c/o THQ

Health Clinics
Loua: BP 20, Brazzaville
Moungali: BP 20, Brazzaville
Nkayi: BP 229, NkayiNkouikou, Pointe Noire

Health Clinics and Maternity Units
Dolisie: BP 235, Dolisie

DEMOCRATIC REPUBLIC OF CONGO TERRITORY

Territorial Commander:
Commissioner Madeleine Ngwanga
(1 Dec 2009)

Chief Secretary:
Lieut-Colonel Barry Schwartz (1 Dec 2009)

Territorial Headquarters: Ave Ebea 23, Kinshasa-Gombe, Democratic Republic of Congo

Postal address: Armée du Salut 8636, Kinshasa 1, Democratic Republic of Congo

Tel: [243] 997-526050; email: kin_leadership@kin.salvationarmy.org

The first Salvation Army corps was established in Kinshasa in 1934 by Adjutant (later Commissioner) and Mrs Henri Becquet. By decree of Léopold III, Armée du Salut was given legal status, with powers set out in a Deed of Constitution, on 21 February 1936. Work spread to Congo in 1937 and 16 years later it became a separate command, later being elevated to territory status. Congo (Kinshasa) and Angola Territory was renamed on 1 March 2008 when Angola became a command, then became Democratic Republic of Congo Territory on 1 June 2008.

Zone: Africa
Countries included in the territory: Democratic Republic of Congo
'The Salvation Army' in French: Armée du Salut; in Kikongo: Nkangu a Luvulusu; in Lingala: Basolda na Kobikisa; in Swahili: Jeshi la Wokovu; in Tshiluba: Tshiluila Tsha Luhandu
Languages in which the gospel is preached: Chokwe, French, Kikongo, Lingala, Swahili, Tshiluba, Umbundu
Periodical: *Echo d'Espoir*

ALTHOUGH the country was relatively peaceful during the year under review, there continued to be political instability in many areas of the Democratic Republic of Congo. The Salvation Army furthered its humanitarian work in many of the troubled areas and is contributing positively towards peace and stability – especially in the eastern part of DRC. The spiritual ministry of The Salvation Army has taken hold in many of these areas.

There are plans to establish education and health facilities in a number of villages in eastern DRC, where agriculture and shelter projects are already in operation. This will provide a more integrated ministry and build on relationships already established.

New schools have been built – five in Bandundu, three in Equateur, two in Bas-Congo. Three schools have been completely renovated in Kinshasa. This work is all part of the territory's determination to ensure that as many children as possible will receive quality Christian-based education.

The Army's medical work continues to expand and improve, with the building of three clinics and the re-roofing of two others. Good-quality medical care is offered through clinics and hospitals in many isolated parts of the country and the Army has been very involved in encouraging the distribution and use of mosquito nets in infected areas.

The Salvation Army increased its help to women and girls caught up in sex-trafficking. Further training facilities are enabling women and girls to learn income-generating skills, giving them the means to turn away from a life of prostitution and abuse. In addition to the training centres, many corps run local classes in their local communities, so increasing the number being rescued.

The spiritual impact of the Army continued to improve with the opening of new corps. 'Share Your Testimony!' – the theme for 2010, which was introduced at the installation of new territorial leaders in December 2009 – resulted in a focus on the teaching and preaching of holiness, with Salvationists realising that the most effective way to share their testimony is to live God-honouring lives.

STATISTICS

Officers 418 (active 335 retired 83) **Cadets** (1st Yr) 17 (2nd Yr) 17 **Employees** 4,350
Corps 180 **Outposts** 101 **Health Centres** 27 **Maternity Hospitals/Clinics** 5 **Other specialist hospitals** 1 **Other specialist clinics** (inc HIV/Aids, dental) 4 **Institutions** 5
Schools: Secondary 127 **Primary** 178
Boarding 2 **Maternal** 6 **University** 1

Senior Soldiers 26,778 **Adherents** 1,943 **Junior Soldiers** 12,382
Personnel serving outside territory Officers 22

STAFF

Women's Ministries: Comr Madeleine Ngwanga (TPWM) Lt-Col Anja Schwartz (TSWM) Maj Bibisky Nzila (THLS) Lt-Col Celestine Ngoy (LOM, Literacy) Maj Marie-Thérèse Mabwidi (Women's Dev/Anti-sex Trafficking) Lt-Col Lydia Matondo (JHLS, Officers' Children) Lt-Col Simone Kiboti (Widowed, Bible Studies, Retired Officers)
Sec for Business Administration: Lt-Col Gracia Matondo
Sec for Personnel: Lt-Col Hubert Ngoy
Sec for Programme: Lt-Col Theophile Kiboti
Development and Emergency Services: Capt Dieudonné Tsilulu
Editorial/Literature: Maj Josué Leka
Extension Training: Maj Norbert Makala
Finance: Maj Barthélemy Nzila
Information Technology: Sgt Mbumu Muba Jean-Marc
Medical: Dr David Nku Imbie
Music and Creative Arts: Maj Philippe Mabwidi
 National Bandmaster: Sgt Jean-Marc Mbumu
 National Songster Leader: Sgt Joseph Nsilulu
 National Timbrel Leader: Sgt Pauline Matanu
Property: Mr Claude Huguenin
Public Relations: Capt Andre
Schools Coordinator: Raymond Luamba Ntolani
Social: Maj Philippe Mabwidi
 HIV/Aids Section: Paul Kunzebiko
 Sponsorship: Capt Philippine Tsilulu
Training: Maj Pierre Mukoko
Youth: Maj Laurent-Barnabas Ibemba
 Candidates: Maj Jeannette Ibemba

DIVISIONS

Bas-Fleuve/Océan: BP 123, Matadi; Majs Isidore and Marthe Matondo (mobile: 0990023962)
Inkisi: Armée du Salut, Kavwaya, BP 45; Majs Esaïe and Marie-José Ntembi (mobile: 0991668909)
Kasaï-Occidental: BP 1404, Kananga; Majs Jean-Jacques and Alice Nsumbu (mobile: 0997811298)
Kasangulu: BP 14, Kasangulu; Majs Norbert and Hélène Nkanu (mobile: 0815261920)
Katanga: BP 2525, Lubumbashi; Majs Denis and Modestine Mafuta (mobile: 0815102424)
Kinshasa Central: BP 8636, Kinshasa; Majs Alphonse and Bernadette Mayasi (mobile: 0998449971)

Kinshasa East: BP 8636, Kinshasa;
Majs Emmanuel and Madeleine Diakanwa
(mobile: 0998336208)

Kinshasa West: Lt-Cols Henri and Josephine
Nangi   (mobile: 0999371303)

Luozi: Armée du Salut, Luozi; Majs Clément
and Béatrice Ilunga (mobile: 0998627937)

Mbanza-Ngungu: BP 160; Majs Emmanuel
and Albertine Mpanzu (mobile: 0995662729)

Orientale (Kisangani): BP 412, Kisangani;
Majs Sebastien and Godette Mbala
(mobile: 0992814124)

DISTRICTS

Bandundu: Armée du Salut, Bandundu;
Maj André Mobubu (mobile: 0811620092)

Isiro: BP 135 (under supervision of THQ)

Plateau: Maj Pascal Matsiona
(mobile: 0998036399)

Tanganyika: (under supervision of Katanga)

SECTIONS

Bukavu: Maj Pierre Masundu
(mobile: 0993187354)

Kwilu: Maj Germain Mbeni
(mobile: 0991302116)

TRAINING COLLEGE

BP 8636, Kinshasa

UNIVERSITY

William Booth University: BP 8636, Kinshasa;
Rector: Dr Mpiutu ne Mbodi Gaston

ATTACHED TO THQ

Conference Centre: Mbanza-Nzundu

MEDICAL WORK
Health Centres

Bas-Congo: Kasangulu, Boko-Mbuba, Kifuma,
Kingantoko, Kingudi, Kinzambi, Kintete,
Nkalama, Shefu, Kavwaya, Kimayala,
Mbanza-Nsundi, Mbanza-Nzundu

Kananga: Moyo

Kinshasa: Amba (Kisenso), Bakidi (Selembao),
Bomoi, Bopeto (Ndjili), Boyambi (Barumbu),
Elonga, Esengo (Masina), Kimia (Kintambo),
Molende (Kingasani)

Kisangani: Libota, Mokela, Dengue

Clinic
Maj Leka (Maluku/Kinshasa)

Dental Clinics
Boyambi (Barumbu), Elonga (Masuna),
Kasangulu (Bas-Congo)

Diabetic Clinic
Kananga

Foot Clinic
Boyambi

Maternity Units
Bomoi Kinshasa (acc 60); Kasangulu,
Bas-Congo (acc 13); Kavwaya, Bas-Congo
maternity and centre (acc 14) Maluku
Kinshasa (acc 12)

EDUCATION
Secondary Schools

Bandundu: Institut Elonga; Institut Kwango;
Institut Mabwidi; Institut Ngampo Maku;
Institut Ngobila; Institut Momwono;
Institut Nsele Mpibiri; Institut Wembe;
Institut Tomokoko; Institut Masamuna;
Institut Ngabidjo; 11 primary schools,
11 secondary schools

Bas-Congo: Institut Boyokani (Matadi);
Institut Diakanwa; Institut Kavwaya (Inkisi);
Institut Beti 1; Institut Beti 2;
Institut Kimbumba-Nord; Institut Bongo-Bongo;
Institut Kingudi; Institut Pédagogique Kasi;
Institut Dikal (Lufuku); ITP Kintete;
Institut Kimayasi; Institut Kinzadi 1;
Institut Kinzadi 2; CS Kimbongo;
Institut Kinzambi 1 (Kasangulu);
Institut Kinzambi 2 (Luozi);
Institut Lemba Diyanika; Institut Ludiazo;
Institut Mampemba; Institut Mikalukidi;
Institut Kitundulu; Institut Kivunda;
Institut Kumba Ndilu; ITS Kumbi; ITC Lovo;
Institut Maduma; Institut Manionzi;
Institut Matanda; Institut Mateso;
Institut Nkundi (Mbanza-Ngungu);
CS Nsanga-Mamba; ITC Mbanza-Nsanda;
ITA Mbanza-Nsundi; Institut Mbanza-Nzundu;
Institut Mwala-Kinsende; ITA Nsongi-Kialelua;
Institut Ndandanga; ITC Ngongolo;
Institut Shefu; Institut Sombala;
Institut Viaza; Institut Buetesa;
Institut Kimbata 1; Institut Landulu;
ITP Lukengo; Institut Mawangu;
Institut Miprosco; Institut Odeco;
Institut Sundi-Mamba;
Collège William Booth (Kasangulu);
64 primary schools, 1 kindergarden

Equateur: ITM Bukaka; Institut Obotela;
Institut Elonga; ITCA Lihau;
Institut Mambune; Institut Masobe;
Institut Mokuta; Institut Yambo;
ITA Yamwenga; Institut Yangola;

Institut Embonga; ITM Armée du Salut;
12 primary schools, 12 secondary schools,
2 kindergardens

Kasaï-Occidental (Kananga): Institut Bena-
Leka 1; Institut Bena-Leka 2;
ITAV Bena-Mbiye; Institut Bobumwe;
Institut Muzemba; Institut Mwanza-Ngoma;
Institut Tshibuayayi; ITC Bobumwe;
Institut Bukole; Institut Butoke;
Institut Kasende; Institut Katshimba;
Institut Kuetu; Institut Mande Muile;
ITAV Mfwamba; Institut Mpoyi;
Institut Mwanza-Ngoma; Institut Muyembe;
Institut Salut; ITAV Salut; Institut Tuelekeja;
Institut Tuende; 21 primary schools,
20 secondary schools

Kinshasa: Institut Bakidi; Collège
Gabriel Becquet (Selembao);
Collège Bimwala;
ITC Bimwala; Institut Dianzenza;
Institut Ilona; ITC Kwamouth;
Institut Lukubama;
Collège John Mabwidi;
Institut Mabwidi; Lycée Matonge;
Lycée Technique de Matonge;
ITS Mbala; ITA Menkao;
Institut Mpiutu; ITC Ndjili-
Kilambu; Institut Ngizulu;
Institut Nsemi; ITC Ntolani;
ITI Ntolani; Institut Rwakadingi;
Institut Wabaluku;
Institut Yanda Mayemba;
Institut Yimbukulu; 24 secondary
schools, 38 primary schools

Province Orientale (Kisangani):
Institut Bonsomi; Institut Elikya;
Institut Ilota; Institut Ketele;
Institut Wagenia; Institut Litoka;
Institut Yataka; Institut Afutami;
Institut Bagwasa; Institut Bakota;
Institut Bambunze;
Institut Kambale; Institut Lisami;
Institut Lohale; Institut Lomongo;
Institut Lotumbe; Institut Lusa;
Institut Yaengala; Institut
Yalokambe; Institut Yasaa;
Institut Yasanga; Institut
Yawenda; 22 secondary schools,
42 primary schools,
2 kindergartens

Sud-Katanga (Lubumbashi): ITC
Wokovu (Katuba); ITC Tujenge;
Institut Flambeau; 3 secondary
schools, 1 kindergarden,
5 primary schools

SOCIAL SERVICES
**Children's Home and Community
Child Care**
Kinshasa (acc 20 and 20)

Development and Emergencies
Impini; Kasungulu; Kavwaya; Mato;
Mbanza-Nzundu

Old People's Home
Kinshasa-Kintambo (acc 20)

Vocational Training Centres
Barumbu Kinshasa (acc 22); Ndjili Kinshasa
(acc 13); Sud-Katanga Lubumbashi (acc 10)

**Cadets from Congo (Brazzaville) Territory take
a dugout canoe to get to campaign meetings**

99

DENMARK TERRITORY

Territorial Commander:
Colonel Birgitte Brekke
(1 Nov 2010)

Chief Secretary:
Lieut-Colonel Aino Muikku
(1 Aug 2009)

**Territorial Headquarters: Frederiksberg Allé 9,
1621 Copenhagen V, Denmark**

Tel: [45] 33 31 41 92; fax: [45] 33 25 30 80; email: Frelsens@den.salvationarmy.org;
website: www.frelsens-haer.dk

The work of The Salvation Army in Denmark commenced in Copenhagen on 8 May 1887, pioneer officers being Major (later Lieut-Colonel) and Mrs Robert Perry.

Zone: Europe
Country included in the territory: Denmark
'The Salvation Army' in Danish: Frelsens Hær
Language in which the gospel is preached: Danish
Periodicals: *Mennesker & Tro*, *Vision-Mission*

AS integrated mission continues to be the main theme and challenge for the territory, The Salvation Army's family work has grown rapidly. There are great opportunities as large numbers of families seek support, advice and practical help from the Army. Good relationships are being built and a number of 'family consultants' now work alongside corps officers around the country. The challenge is how to integrate this successful ministry into more traditional corps work.

Once again a record-breaking number of families received Christmas aid, participated in camps and enjoyed excursions to amusement parks. As people look to the Army, the challenge is for Salvationists to build meaningful relationships with them.

For the first time The Salvation Army in Denmark arranged an art exhibition to which young contemporary artists donated exhibits. The title was *Am I?*, a question people marginalised by society might ask concerning self-worth, and a reminder of the Army's mission of calling such people into its fellowship.

The Danish tradition of confirmation, where young teenagers in the national church confirm their Christian faith, is a growing event in The Salvation Army as well. Preparations for confirmation provide a great opportunity for Salvationists to teach young people about faith, Christian lifestyles and the Army's mission. Eleven young people attended the annual confirmation camp.

The territory's social work having focused on mothers and children in recent years, a new development was launched when the first Fathers and Children's Camp took place in the summer of 2009. Another initiative was Father's Day, when fathers who do not have custody of their children on an everyday basis could take their children to the Army and enjoy time together in a safe environment. This project was also taken up by homeless fathers who never see their children or have only irregular contact with them.

A tour by the Chicago Staff Band (USA Central) in June 2009 was among several visits by Army groups and bands from abroad.

STATISTICS

Officers 82 (active 37 retired 45)
  Employees 284
Corps 32 **Outpost** 1 **Social Institutions** 17
  Welfare Centres 6
Senior Soldiers 926 **Adherents** 287 **Junior Soldiers** 3
Personnel serving outside territory Officers 5

STAFF

Women's Ministries: Col Birgitte Brekke (TPWM) Maj Pia Mogensen (HL)
Sec for Business Administration: Lars Lydholm
  Chief Accountant: Eva Haahr
  Property: Maj Terje Tvedt
  Public Relations and Information Technology: Lars Lydholm
  Recycling: Annie Kristensen
Sec for Personnel: Maj Lisbeth Anderson
  Training: Maj Ingrid Larsen
Sec for Programme: Maj Henrik Andersen
  Development: Maj John Wahl
  Editors: Bent Dahl-Jensen (*Mennesker & Tro*) Capt Levi Giversen (*Vision-Mission*)
  Family: Maj Hanne Wahl
  Home League and Over-60s: Maj Pia Mogensen
  Missing Persons: Col Jørn Lauridsen

Mission: Maj Ingrid Larsen
Missionary and Child Sponsorship: Lt-Col Miriam Frederiksen
Vulnerable Adults: Maj Kurt Pedersen
Youth and Candidates: Maj Joan Munch

SOCIAL INSTITUTIONS AND COMMUNITY CENTRES
Recycling Centres
6705 Esbjerg Ø, Ravnevej 2; tel: 75 14 24 22; fax: 75 14 00 47
5000 Odense C, Roersvej 33; tel: 66 11 25 21; fax: 66 19 05 21
9560 Hadsund, Mariagervej 3; tel: 98 57 42 48; fax: 98 57 38 72
4900 Nakskov, Narviksvej 15; tel: 54 95 12 05; fax: 54 95 12 04

Second-hand shops
Head Office: Frederiksberg Alle 9,1621 Copenhagen V; tel: 33 31 41 92
Shops: Århus, Brønderslev, Copenhagen (3), Esbjerg (2), Falster, Frederikshavn, Grindsted, Haderslev, Hadsund, Helsingør, Herning, Hjørring, Kolding, Nakskov, N Nebel, Nyborg, Nykøbing Odense (2), Randers, Vejle.

Community Centres
1408 Copenhagen K, Wildersgade 66; tel: 32 54 44 10 (acc 80)
1864 Frederiksberg C, Grundtvigsvej 17 st; tel: 33 24 56 67
2200 Copenhagen N, Kalejdoskop, Thorsgade 48 A; tel: 35 85 00 87
2500 Valby, Valby Langgade 83; tel: 36 45 67 67
2700 Brønshøj; tel: 33 31 41 92
3000 Helsingør, Strandgade 60, Regnbuen Community Centre; tel: 49 21 10 06
4800 Nykøbing Falster, Jernbanegade 42, Community Centre and Corps; tel: 54 85 71 89
4900 Nakskov, Niels Nielsengade 6; tel: 54 95 30 06 (acc 60)
5700 Svendborg, Lundevej 2; tel: 62 21 21 63
7100 Vejle, Midtpunktet, Staldgårdsgade 4; tel: 75 82 78 38
9000 Aalborg, Skipper Clementsgade 11; tel: 98 11 50 62
9560 Hadsund, Nørregade 10, Den Åbne Dør Community Centre; tel: 23 26 19 15

Family Work
1661 Copenhagen, Frederiksberg Alle 9; tel: 33 31 41 92
3000 Helsingør, Strandgade 60; tel: 30 17 94 41

Denmark Territory

5220 Odense, Peder Skrams Vej 31;
tel: 30 17 94 40

6700 Esbjerg, Skolegade 55; tel: 30 17 94 42

8000 Århus, Klostergade 54; tel: 30 17 94 32

Day Nurseries

9900 Frederikshavn Humlebien, Knudensvej 1B;
tel: 98 42 33 27 (acc 40)

2000 Frederiksberg, Melita, Mariendalsvej 4;
tel: 38 87 01 48 (acc 58)

2500 Valby, Solsikken, Annexstræde 29;
tel: 36 16 23 11 (acc 22)

2650 Hvidovre, Kastanjehuset, Idrætsvej 65A;
tel: 36 78 40 23 (acc 33)

2650 Hvidovre, Solgården, Catherine Booth vej
22; tel: 36 78 07 71 (acc 100)

7500 Holstebro Solhøj, Skolegade 51;
tel: 97 42 61 21 (acc 30)

Emergency Shelters for Families

2650 Hvidovre, Svendebjerggård, Catherine
Booth vej 20; tel: 36 49 65 77
(acc 25)

1754 Copenhagen V, Hedebygade 30,
Den Åbne Dør; tel: 33 24 91 03
(acc 15)

4700 Næstved, Østergade 13; tel: 55 77 22 70
(acc 6)

Rehabilitation Centre

Hørhuset, 2300 Copenhagen S, Hørhusvej 5;
tel: 32 55 56 22 (acc 64)

Project for Long-term Unemployed

Nørholmlejren, Oldenborrevej 2, 9000 Aalborg;
tel: 98 34 18 10 (acc 10)

Eventide Nursing Centre

2200 Copenhagen N Aftensol, Lundtoftegade 5;
tel: 35 30 55 00 (acc 43)

Students Residence

2100 Copenhagen Ø, Helgesengade 25;
tel: 35 37 74 32 (acc 41)

Summer Camps

9000 Aalborg, Nørholmlejren, Oldenborrevej 2;
tel: 98 34 18 10 (acc 50)

8700 Horsens, Hjarnø; tel: 75 68 32 24
(acc 25)

5450 Otterup, Rømhildsminde, Ferievej 11-13,
Jørgensø; tel: 64 87 13 36

Holiday Home and Conference Centre

2791 Dragør, Baggersminde, Fælledvej 132;
tel: 32 53 70 18; fax: 32 53 70 98
(acc 80)

5500 Middelfart, Lillebælt, Nørre Allé 47, Strib;
tel: 64 40 10 57; fax: 63 40 02 82 (acc 30)

Radio Station (Copenhagen area)

1621 Copenhagen V. Frederiksberg Allé 9;
tel: 33 31 41 25 (studio)

During the 'Time to Serve' campaign in Denmark, a young Salvationist shares the gospel with two girls in Aalborg

EASTERN EUROPE TERRITORY

Territorial leaders:
Colonels Kenneth and Paula Johnson

Territorial Commander:
Colonel Kenneth Johnson (1 Mar 2010)

Chief Secretary:
Lieut-Colonel Alistair Herring (16 Sep 2006)

Territorial Headquarters: Krestiansky Tupik 16/1, Moscow

Postal address: Russian Federation, 109044 Moscow, Krestiansky Tupik 16/1

Tel: [7] (495) 911 2600/2956; fax: [7] (495) 911 2753; email: Russia@eet.salvationarmy.org;
website: www.thesalvationarmy.ru

Work was initiated in Russia in 1910 by Colonel Jens Povlsen of Denmark but circumstances necessitated his withdrawal after 18 months. Army operations then recommenced in St Petersburg in 1913 as an extension to the work in Finland. After the February 1917 revolution the work flourished, Russia became a distinct command and reinforcements arrived from Sweden. As a result of the October revolution they had, however, to be withdrawn at the end of 1918, leaving 40 Russian and Finnish officers to continue the work under extreme hardship until the Army was finally proscribed in 1923.

Salvation Army activities were officially recommenced in July 1991, overseen by the Norway, Iceland and The Færoes Territory with the arrival of Lieut-Colonels John and Bjorg Bjartveit. It became a distinct command in November 1992. Work was extended to Ukraine (1993), Georgia (1993), Moldova (1994) and Romania (1999). On 1 June 2001 the command was redesignated the Eastern Europe Command. It was elevated to territory status on 1 March 2005. The final stage of registering 'the Moscow Branch of The Salvation Army' was completed in April 2009.

Zone: Europe
Countries included in territory: Georgia, Moldova, Romania, Russian Federation, Ukraine
'The Salvation Army' in Georgian: Khsnis Armia; in Moldovan/Romanian: Armata Salvarii; in Russian: Armiya Spaseniya; in Ukrainian: Armiya Spasinnya
Languages in which the gospel is preached: Georgian, Moldovan, Romanian, Russian, Ukrainian
Periodicals: *Vestnik Spaseniya* (*The War Cry*), *The Officer* (both Russian)

AS The Salvation Army celebrated the 10th anniversary of commencing its work in Romania, the four corps of this region continued growing. New soldiers were enrolled and social work was extended. The new plant in Iasi established a laundry project to help meet the needs of gypsy people living in communal housing. Six soldiers have been enrolled here as a direct link with people from this community. The Craiova plant also witnessed the enrolment of soldiers and growth continues.

Other new plants around the territory are beginning to bear fruit: soldiers have been enrolled in the Ukraine city of Dnepropetrovsk, while the corps plant in Murmansk, Russia, continued its outreach to homeless people through feeding schemes and made its first soldiers.

Leadership development continues to remain a prime focus in the territorial mission strategy. Officers councils in 2009 brought together 149 officers from five countries to a retreat in Moldova. The theme 'Growing Together in Faith, Joy, Unity and Love' was explored. Training was organised for officers and local officers in each of the countries, targeting subjects specific to the region.

The bi-annual ordination and commissioning of new officers was held in Moldova in June 2009. Due to the political situation in Georgia, restricted travel between that country and Russia affected three cadets, so the final semester of training was carried out in Moldova prior to the commissioning weekend. A new session of eight cadets was welcomed into training.

Child sponsorship has supported many very needy children through the years. As Eastern European countries recover from the post-Soviet era and services improve, the territory is moving from a system of individual to group sponsorship. Using corps connections, children come for educational support, games, gospel lessons and a healthy meal. Individual support for disabled and sick children will continue.

Property ownership is a growing need as the territory fights the battle of escalating rental costs to its annual operating budgets. Sponsorship for property purchases during the year allowed for the purchase of a new quarters in Batumi, Georgia, and the building of a hall in Cahul, Moldova.

Work commenced to replace the Moldova DHQ building and to erect a hall for the Rainbow of Hope Corps in Chisinau, but this is a lengthy and costly process.

STATISTICS

Officers 143 (active) **Envoys** 5 **Cadets** (1st Yr) 8 **Employees** 232
Corps 55 **Corps Plants** 4 **Outposts** 4 **Rehabilitation Centres** 2
Senior Soldiers 1,832 **Adherents** 816 **Junior Soldiers** 324

STAFF

Women's Ministries: Col Paula Johnson (TPWM)
Sec for Business Administration: Maj Richard Herivel
Sec for Personnel: Col Paula Johnson
Sec for Programme: Lt-Col Astrid Herring
Editorial: Capt Anna Kotrikadze
Mission Training: Capt Alexander Sharov
Training: Capt Svetlana Sharova
Prayer Ambassador: Capt Vadim Kolesnik
Projects Coordinators: Maj Ron Cochrane
Public Relations: Maj Lyn Cochrane
Territorial Sergeant-Major: Envoy Yuri Gulanitsky

DIVISIONS

Russia: 105120 Russia, Moscow, Khlebnikov Pereulok, 7 bld, 2; tel: 495 678 03 51; fax: 495 678 91 60; Capts Anthony and Patricia Kennedy
Moldova: Chisinau, 2012, Armata Salvarii; Postal address: PO Box 412, Petru Movila 41; tel: (37322) 237972; telefax: (37322) 235076; Majors Ian and Vivien Callander
Ukraine: 01023, Ukraine, Kiev, Shota Rustavely St 38, Suite 3 3; tel/fax: (380 44) 287 4598, 287 3705, 246 6689

REGIONS

Georgia: 16 Ikalto St, Tbilisi 0171, Georgia; tel: (995 32) 33 37 85/86; fax: (995 32) 33 02 27; Maj Bradley Caldwell

Salvationists in Ukraine minister to homeless people through a regular feeding programme

Romania: 722212 Bucharest, Sector 2,
Str Pargarilor Nr 2; tel: [10] (4037) 270 51 99;
Capt Valery Lalac

MISSION TRAINING AND EDUCATION CENTRE – INSTITUTE FOR OFFICER TRAINING

Russia, Moscow, 105120 Karl Larson Centre,
Khlebnikov Per 7/2;
tel: (495) 678 55 14, 678 03 51

SOCIAL SERVICES

Georgia
Children's After-school Programmes: Rustavi,
Samgory, Ponichala, Central, Batumi, Lagodeki
Laundry Projects: Samgori, Rustavi, Didi Digomi
Humanitarian Aid; Dry Food Distribution;
Feeding Schemes

Moldova
Mobile Medical Clinic; Rusca Women's Prison
Project; 'Sally Ann' Programme; Shoe Project;
Humanitarian Aid Distribution

Romania
Laundry Projects; After-school Programmes;
Support for Young Families

Russia
Moscow:
Karl Larsson Centre, Unified Homeless
Services, Khlebnikov pereulok 7, bld 2;
tel: (495) 678 03 51
Feeding Programme; Food and Clothing
Distribution; First Aid
Rostov-on-Don:
The Bridge Programme, Lermontovskaya
St 229; tel/fax: (8632) 248-2410;
email: tateosova_valery@mail.ru
HIV+ Crisis Intervention; Group Services
St Petersburg:
Liteini Prospect # 44 B, 191104;
tel: (812) 273-9297
Homeless Feeding Programme; Food and
Clothing Distribution; Seniors' Support Group
Programme; Medical Clinic; HIV/Aids
Outreach and Support Programme; Support
for Orphans with HIV/Aids

Ukraine
Kharkov Corps Social Centre: Ukraine, Kharkov,
Moskovsky prospect 122, 'Kalibr club';
tel: (380-57) 759-42-48;
email: Kharkiv_corps@ukr.net
Kirovograd Corps Social Centre: 25028 Ukraine,
Kirovagrad, Volova St, #15, SPTU #8;
tel: (380-522) 56-45 78;
email: armiyas@rambler.ru
Simferopl Children's Arts Centre: 95000 Ukraine,
Simferopl, ulitsa Nekrasova, 22 office 1;
tel: (380-652) 510-729

FINLAND AND ESTONIA TERRITORY

Territorial leaders:
Commissioners Dick and Vibeke Krommenhoek

Territorial Commander:
Commissioner Dick Krommenhoek
(1 Oct 2008)

Chief Secretary:
Lieut-Colonel Arja Laukkanen (1 Jun 2004)

Territorial Headquarters: Uudenmaankatu 40, 00120 Helsinki

Postal address: Post Box 161, 00121 Helsinki, Finland

Tel: [358] (09) 6812300; fax: [358] (09) 6812 3033; email: finland@pelastusarmeija.fi;

website: www.pelastusarmeija.fi

Work in Finland was commenced on 8 November 1889 in Broholm's Riding School, Helsinki, by four aristocratic Finns – Captain and Mrs Constantin Boije with Lieutenants Hedvig von Haartman and Alva Forsius. Within six months Hedvig von Haartman was appointed leader of the work in the country.

Work in Estonia first commenced in 1927 and continued until 1940 when it was closed due to the Second World War. It recommenced in the autumn of 1995 when three Finnish officers were assigned to start the work in Tallinn.

Zone: Europe
Countries included in the territory: Estonia, Finland
'The Salvation Army' in Estonian: Päästearmee; in Finnish: Pelastusarmeija; in Swedish: Frälsningsarmén
Languages in which the gospel is preached: English, Estonian, Finnish, Russian, Swedish
Periodicals: *Krigsropet* (Swedish), *Nappis* (Finnish), *Sotahuuto* (Finnish)

THE 120th anniversary of The Salvation Army in Finland was celebrated in Helsinki (19-22 November 2009) with thanksgiving meetings, indoors and in the open air. A magnificent concert in the capital's world-famous Church of the Rock featured Zürich Central Band from Switzerland, the popular Finnish singer Jaakko Ryhänen and a specially formed territorial choir.

Most significant was the ordination and commissioning of three new officers as God continues to call people into his service within the Army. The territory also rejoices at having new candidates and cadets preparing for officership.

However, the territory does not only celebrate the past; the Army in Finland and Estonia is facing a bright future. Where during recent years it was unavoidable to close a number of corps, there are now plans to reopen work on the border with Sweden and to establish another corps in Estonia. Salvationists also rejoice in a steady growth in youth work and the enrolment of junior soldiers in Estonia, where work reopened 15 years ago.

The Territorial Roots Congress took place in Kannonkoski, Central Finland, during June 2009. A meeting of the Nordic Leadership Institute was hosted in Helsinki (7-11 September).

February 2010 saw six venues hosting 'A Day Before the Word', an event with a longstanding tradition. Bible messages of God's unfailing and perfect love, given by guest speaker Major Philip Garnham (UK), made a profound impact.

After having a temporary THQ for more than two years, staff moved back into their fully renovated building. The complex also has 28 brand-new flats, which will be let to generate income for the Army. Renovation of the Helsinki Temple Corps premises, also part of the block of buildings, is still in process.

STATISTICS
Officers 158 (active 56 retired 102) Cadets 3 Employees 425
Corps 28 Outposts 8 Goodwill Centres 3 Institutions 25
Senior Soldiers 806 Adherents 91 Junior Soldiers 48

STAFF
Women's Ministries: Comr Vibeke Krommenhoek (TPWM)
Section Head for Programme: Maj Antero Puotiniemi
Sec for Programme: Maj Tella Puotiniemi
Asst Leader for Social Work: Gun-Viv Glad-Junger

Asst for Programme Section and Youth: Capt Natalia Penttinen
Asst for Home and Family: Maj Camilla Rahkonen
Section Head for Training and Education: Maj Petter Kornilow
School for Officer Training: Maj Petter Kornilow
Education: Maj Eija Kornilow
Section Head for Business Administration: Liisa Kaakinen
Asst Business Administrator: Capt Rodrigo Miranda
Finance: Liisa Kaakinen
Property: Timo Matomaa
Recycling Industry: Harri Lehti
Information Technology: Riku Leino
Section Head for Personnel: Maj Marja Meras
Section Head for Communication: Maj Eija Kornilow
Literature and Editorial: Maj Antero Puotiniemi
Public Relations: Maj Sirkka Paukku
Missing Persons: Maj Kirsti Reponen
Mission Sponsorships and Volunteers: Maj Camilla Rahkonen

SOCIAL CENTRES
Clothing Industry (Recycling Centres)
90580 Oulu, Ratamotie 22; tel: 44 757 7945
33880 Lempäälä, Rajasilta 1; tel: 44 757 7943
20300 Turku, Virusmäentie 65; tel: 44 757 7944
01260 Vantaa, Itäinen Valkoisenlähteentie 15; tel: 9 877 0270

Homes for Alcoholics
68600 Pietarsaari, Permontie 34; tel: 44 757 7938 (acc 15)
33500 Tampere, Pohjolankatu 25; tel: 44 757 7980 (acc 36)
20500 Turku, Hämeenkatu 18; tel: 44 757 7897 (acc 37)

Shelters for Men
00530 Helsinki, Alppikatu 25; tel: 9 7743130 (acc 234)
00550 Helsinki, Inarintie 8; tel: 44 757 7937 (acc 34)
28120 Pori, Veturitallinkatu 3; tel: 45 139 3292 (acc 25)

Shelters for Women
00530 Helsinki, Papinkuja 1; tel: 9 77431330 (acc 18)
00530 Helsinki, Castréninkatu 24-26 F 46 tel: 9 774313329 (acc 12)

Finland and Estonia Territory

Poor Relief Distribution Centres
Alppikatu 25, 00530 Helsinki; tel: 9 77431321
Hämeenkatu 28 B, 15140 Lahti; tel: 44 757 7910
Ratamotie 22, 90580 Oulu; tel: 44 757 7947
Pyynikintori 3, 33230 Tampere; tel: 44 757 7941
Vanha Hämeentie 29, 20540 Turku;
   tel: 44 757 7940

Service Centres
Alppikatu 25, 00530 Helsinki; tel: 9 77431316
Permontie 34, 68600 Pietarsaari; tel: 44 757 7938
Vanha Hämeentie 29, 20540 Turku;
   tel: 44 757 7940

Children's Day Care Centres
48100 Kotka, Korkeavuorenkatu 24;
   tel: 45 635 8085 (acc 36)
15140 Lahti, Hämeenkatu 28 A 5; tel: 3 878680
   (acc 94)
90140 Oulu, Artturintie 27; tel: 45 635 8087
   (acc 30)
06100 Porvoo, Joonaksentie 1; tel: 45 635 8089
   (acc 54)
28100 Pori, Mikonkatu 19; tel: 45 635 8088
   (acc 83)
95420 Tornio, Putaankatu 2; tel: 45 635 8090
   (acc 47)

Eventide Homes
02710 Espoo, Viherlaaksonranta 19;
   tel: 9 84938410 (acc 60)

20740 Turku, Sigridinpolku; tel: 40 508 1291
   (acc 25)

Senior Citizens' Unit
00760 Helsinki, Puistolantie 6 (acc 75)

Summer Camp Centre
03100 Nummela, Helsinki (acc 60)

Family Support Centre
00530 Helsinki, Hedvig House, Castréninkatu
   24-26 F; tel: 50 400 1708

Youth Camp
33480 Ylöjärvi, Sovelontie 91 (summer use)

ESTONIA REGION
Regional Headquarters: Kopli 8-14,
   10412 Tallinn; tel: [372] 6413330;
   fax: [372] 6413331
Regional Commander: Capt Daniel Henderson

Corps 4

Hope House (Lootusemaja): Laevastiku 1a,
   10313 Tallinn; tel: 6561048
Camp: Ranna 24, Loksa; tel: 6031012

**Below: a friend of the Army is
warmly greeted by Salvationists
on the streets of Helsinki**

FRANCE AND BELGIUM TERRITORY

Territorial leaders:
Colonels Massimo and Jane Paone

Territorial Commander:
Colonel Massimo Paone (1 Feb 2011)

Chief Secretary:
Lieut-Colonel Sylvie Arnal (1 Feb 2011)

Territorial Headquarters: 60 rue des Frères Flavien
75976 Paris Cedex 20, France

Tel: [33] (1) 43 62 25 00; fax: [33] (1) 43 62 25 56; website: www.armeedusalut.fr

Since 'La Maréchale' (eldest daughter of William and Catherine Booth) conducted The Salvation Army's first meeting in Paris on Sunday 13 March 1881, Salvationist influence has grown and remarkable social and spiritual results have been achieved. French officers commenced work in Algeria in 1934 and this work was maintained until 1970.

In Belgium, Salvation Army operations were pioneered on 5 May 1889 by Adjutant and Mrs Charles Rankin and Captains Velleema and Hass. Most of our work in Belgium operates within the Francophone part of the country so, from 1 January 2009, the former Belgium Command became a region linked administratively to France under the newly created France and Belgium Territory.

Zone: Europe
Countries included in the territory: Belgium, France
'The Salvation Army' in French: Armée du Salut; in Flemish: Leger des Heils
Languages in which the gospel is preached: French, Flemish
Periodicals: *Avec Vous, Espoir, Le Bulletin de la Ligue du Foyer, Le Fil, Le Magazine, L'Officier, Quand Même*

'JUMP' – 'Jeunes (young people) United, Motivated and Passionate for Jesus' – brought together young people from North France, Belgium and the Paris area for a Pentecost event (30-31 May 2009). Workshops on mission, the internet, Islam, and Salvation Army commitment and service provoked considerable interest for the delegates. Two young people were enrolled as soldiers during this weekend.

The 'Protestants En Fête' celebra-tion held in Strasbourg (29-31 October) brought together more than 10,000 people from French Protestant churches united in Christian witness. The President of the Senate, himself a Protestant, gave a greeting at the opening ceremony. He encouraged Protestants to assume their place in society, contributing a quiet testi-mony of values.

The Territorial Band gave several concerts in different parts of the city centre. A Salvation Army stand

Soldiers are enrolled at the 'JUMP for Jesus' youth event held in Paris during Pentecost weekend

was among many others providing information. Major Danièle César (Lyon Corps) was the one woman of three principal preachers during Sunday morning's worship in the 10,000-capacity Zenith Concert Hall.

The year ended with the President of the French Republic honouring Colonel Alain Duchêne (then TC) with the title Knight of the Legion of Honour and Mrs Martine Dumont (Director of Finance) as a Knight of the National Order of Merit.

In February 2010 representatives from corps and social services institutions attended a day forum on spiritual ministry in social centres. The important gifts of listening, respect and communication between directors, employees, service users and headquarters were highlighted during group discussions.

The European Zonal Conference (28-31 March) was hosted in Paris,

using the newly refurbished Palais de la Femme for meetings. The three Paris corps united for a praise, prayer and testimony meeting on Palm Sunday. Commissioners Barry and Raemor Pobjie (then zonal leaders for Europe, IHQ) gave an overview of the Army's work worldwide and especially in Europe. Many people made prayerful rededications to Christ at the close of this meeting.

The territory's first 'Design for Life' weekend was held in Lyon (23-25 April). Under the guidance of Major Mark Herbert (Territorial Candidates Secretary, UK) 20 young people from various parts of the territory discovered through clear Bible teaching some of the gifts used to build up the Body of Christ.

One hundred children's Bibles were purchased with donations from the home league helping-hand scheme. These were distributed to children attending corps in France and Belgium. One child who wrote a letter of thanks said: 'It is the most precious gift I have received.'

The territory seeks to invest in lives of all ages, from all backgrounds, to make a difference for the sake of God's Kingdom.

STATISTICS

Officers 186 (active 79 retired 107)
Employees 2,097
Corps 39 **Outposts** 2 **Institutions** 61
Senior Soldiers 1,172 **Adherents** 263
Junior Soldiers 118
Personnel serving outside territory Officers 12

THE SALVATION ARMY CONGREGATION – FRANCE

BOARD OF DIRECTORS

Col Massimo Paone, Col Jane Paone,
Lt-Col Sylvie Arnal, Maj Bernard Fournel,
Capt David McNeilly

STAFF

Women's Ministries: Col Jane Paone (TLWM)
Maj Pascale Glories (TSWM)
Candidates: Col Jane Paone
Education and Prisons: Maj Jean-Paul Thoni
Field: tba
Finance: Mr Alain Raoul
Retired Officers: Majs Christian and Joëlle Exbrayat
Territorial Band: B/M Mrs Arielle Mangeard

Belgium: Maj Jacques Rouffet (RO)
Maj Yvonne Rouffet (RPWM)

THE SALVATION ARMY FOUNDATION – FRANCE

BOARD OF DIRECTORS

President: Col Alain Duchêne
Secretary: Col Massimo Paone
Treasurer: Mr Olivier Ponsoye
Members: Mr Patrick Audebert, Mrs Irène Debu-Carbonnier, Mr Bernard Westercamp, Maj Pascale Glories

STAFF

Director General: Mr Alain Raoul
Director of Social Exclusion Programme:
Mr Olivier Marguery

Director of Care, Handicap and Dependence Programme: Mr Eric Yapoudjian
Director of Youth Programme: Mr Samuel Coppens
Director of Projects and Property Programme: Mr Bernard Guilhou
Communications: Mr David Germain
Director of Finance: Mrs Martine Dumont
Business Manager: Mr Bruno Fontaine
Missing Persons: Maj Dominique Glories
Publications: Mr Pierre-Baptiste Cordier
Spiritual Care: Capt Jean-Claude Ngimbi
Volunteers: Maj Dominique Glories

RETIRED PERSONS' RESIDENCE

74560 Monnetier-Mornex: Résidence Leirens,
Chemin St Georges; tel: (04) 50 31 23 12
(acc disabled 62)

SUMMER COLONY FOR CHILDREN AND YOUTH CENTRE

30530 Chamborigaud: Chausse;
tel/fax: (04) 66 61 47 08 (acc 100)

SOCIAL SERVICES
Centres for Men

57100 Thionville: 8 place de la République;
tel: (03) 82 83 09 60 (acc 105)
59018 Lille Cedex: Les Moulins de l'Espoir,
48 rue de Valenciennes, BP 184;
tel: (03) 20 52 69 09 (acc 299)
75013 Paris: La Cité de Refuge/Centre Espoir,
12 rue Cantagrel; tel: (01) 53 61 82 00
(acc 215)
75013 Paris: Palais du Peuple,
29 rue des Cordelières; tel: (01) 43 37 93 61
(acc 100)

Centres for Women (with or without children)

30900 Nîmes: Les Glycines (Home for Battered Wives), 4 rue de l'Ancien Vélodrome;
tel: (04) 66 62 20 68/ 66 04 99 49 (acc 52)
75011 Paris: Le Palais de la Femme,
94 rue de Charonne; tel: (01) 46 59 30 00
(acc 300)
94320 Thiais: Résidence Sociale,
7 blvd de Stalingrad; tel: (01) 48 53 57 15
(acc 57)

Centres for Men or/and Women (with or without children)

13003 Marseille: 190 rue Félix Pyat;
tel: (04) 91 02 49 37 (acc 130)
27380 Radepont: Château de Radepont;
tel: (02) 32 49 03 82 (acc 90)

68100 Mulhouse: Le Bon Foyer,
24 rue de L'Ile Napoléon; tel: (03) 89 44 43 56
(acc 113)

69006 Lyon: La Cité de L'Armée du Salut,
131 ave Thiers; tel: (04) 78 52 60 80
(acc 147)

74560 Monnetier-Mornex: Les Hutins;
tel: (04) 50 36 59 52 (acc 16)

75011 Paris: Résidence Catherine Booth,
15 rue Crespin du Gast; tel: (01) 43 14 70 90
(acc 108)

75020 Paris: Résidence Albin Peyron,
60 rue des Frères Flavien; tel: (01) 48 97 54 50
(acc 290)

76600 Le Havre: Le Phare, 191 rue de la Vallée;
tel: (02) 35 24 22 11 (acc 265)

76005 Rouen: 26 rue de Crosne;
tel: (02) 35 70 38 00 (acc 97)

78100 St Germain en Laye: La Maison Verte,
14 rue de la Maison Verte; tel: (01) 39 73 29 39
(acc 64)

81200 Aussillon: 23 blvd Albert Gaches;
tel (05) 63 98 23 95 (acc 16)

90000 Belfort: 3 rue de l'As de Carreau;
tel: (03) 84 21 17 33 (acc 48)

Work Rehabilitation and Recycling Centre

43400 Le Chambon sur Lignon: Pause Café,
Rte du Stade – Levée Ferrier;
tel: 09 61 01 11 70

Emergency Accommodation

75013 Paris: Centre d'accueil d'urgence,
12 rue Cantagrel; tel: (01) 53 61 82 00
(acc 58)

92200 Neuilly sur Seine: L'Amirale Georgette
Gogibus, 14 quai du Général Koenig;
tel: (01) 55 62 02 95

Municipal Shelters (managed by The Salvation Army)

51100 Reims: Le Nouvel Horizon,
10 rue Goïot; tel: (03) 26 85 23 09 (acc 184)

90000 Belfort: Plate-forme d'urgence sociale,
7 rue Colbert; tel: (03) 84 21 05 53
(acc 134)

Mother and Baby Home

75019 Paris: Résidence Maternelle les Lilas,
9 ave de la Porte des Lilas;
tel: (01) 48 03 81 90 (acc 77)

Children's Homes

35400 Saint-Malo:
La Maison des Garçons, 35 ave Eugene Herpin;
tel: (02) 99 40 21 97 (acc boys 12)

Le Nid, 23 ave Paul Turpin,
tel: (02) 99 40 21 94 (acc 24)

Training Centres for Children and Young People

30000 Nîmes: La Villa Blanche Peyron,
122 Impasse Calmette; tel: (04) 66 04 99 40
(acc 10)

34093 Montpellier Cedex 5: Institut Nazareth,
13 rue de Nazareth; tel: (0) 4 99 58 21 21;
fax: (0) 4 99 58 21 21 (acc 48)

67100 Strasbourg-Neudorf: Le Foyer du
Jeune Homme, 42 ave Jean Jaurès;
tel: (03) 88 84 16 50 (acc 50)

68100 Mulhouse: Marie-Pascale Péan,
42 rue de Bâle; tel: (03) 89 42 14 77
(acc 38)

77270 Villeparisis: Domaine de Morfondé;
tel: (01) 60 26 61 61 (acc 67)

Centres for Children and Young People (Day Care)

30000 Nîmes: Aire du Lycéen,
4/6 bd Victor Hugo; tel: (04) 66 21 02 88

69007 Lyon: L'Arche de Noé, 5 rue Félissent;
tel: (04) 78 58 29 66

Rehabilitation Centres for the Impaired

45410 Artenay: Château d'Auvilliers;
tel: (02) 38 80 00 14 (acc 68)

74560 Monnetier-Mornex: Résidence Leirens,
Chemin St Georges; tel: (04) 50 31 23 12
(acc 60)

93370 Montfermeil: MAS Le Grand Saule,
2 ave des Tilleuls; tel: (01) 41 70 30 40
(acc 50)

Eventide Homes

35400 Saint-Malo: Res Boris Antonoff,
12 rue du Tertre Belot; tel: (02) 99 21 08 70

42028 Saint-Etienne Cedex 01: La Sarrazinière,
Allée Amilcare Cipriani; tel: 04 77 62 17 92
(acc 137)

47400 Tonneins: Le Soleil d'Automne,
ave Blanche Peyron, Escoutet;
tel: (05) 53 88 32 00 (acc 50)

60500 Chantilly: L'Arc-en-Ciel, 5 blvd de la
Libération; tel: (03) 44 57 00 33 (acc 53)

83230 Bormes les Mimosas, Res Olive et Germain
Braquehais, 66 chemin de la Queirade;
tel: (04) 94 02 37 00

Senior Housing

75014 Paris: 9 bis, Villa Coeur-de-Vey;
tel: (01) 45 43 38 75

93230 Romainville: 2 rue Vassou

Girls at a summer camp in France spend time reading their Bibles. One hundred children's Bibles donated through the home league helping-hand scheme were distributed to corps in France and Belgium.

Short-term Care Home and Services
07800 St Georges-les-Bains: Le Château;
  tel: (04) 75 60 81 72 (acc 50)

Guest House
74560 Monnetier-Mornex: Les Hutins (Holiday
  Home); tel: (04) 50 36 59 52 (acc 8)

Conference and Holiday Centre
30530 Chamborigaud: Chausse;
  tel/fax: (04) 66 61 47 08 (acc 100)

BELGIUM REGION
Regional Headquarters: Place du Nouveau
  Marché aux Grains, 34, 1000 Brussels;
  tel: [32] (02) 513 39 04;
  fax: [32] (02) 513 81 49;
  websites:
  www.armeedusalut.be; www.legerdesheils.be

Regional leaders: Maj Jacques Rouffet (RO)
  Maj Yvonne Rouffet (RSWM) (1 Jan 2009)
Regional Sec: Maj Noélie Lecocq

SOCIAL SERVICES
Hostels for Men
Foyer Georges Motte, blvd d'Ypres 24,
  1000 Brussels; tel: (02) 217 61 36 (acc 75)
'Le Foyer', Centre d'accueil, rue Bodeghem
  27-29, 1000 Brussels; tel: (02) 512 17 92
  (acc 70)

Family Aid (EU Food Distribution)
Service d'Aide aux familles: blvd d'Ypres 26,
  1000 Brussels; tel: (02) 223 10 44

Guidance Centre (Housing Help and Debt Counselling)
102 rue de l'Église Ste Anne, 1180 Brussels;
  tel: (02) 414 19 16

Refugee Centre
'Foyer Selah', blvd d'Ypres 28, 1000 Brussels;
  tel: (02) 219 01 77 (acc 90)

Mother and Children's Home
Maison de la Mère et de l'Enfant,
  Chaussée de Drogenbos 225, 1180 Brussels;
  tel: (02) 376 17 01 (acc mothers 14,
  children 25)

Children's Home
'Clair Matin', rue des Trois Rois 88,
  1180 Uccle-Brussels; tel: (02) 376 17 40
  (acc 41)

SHOPS
Brussels: Foyer George Motte,
  blvd d'Ypres 24, 1000 Brussels
Quaregnon: 82A rue Monsville 7390,
  Quaregnon
Antwerp: Ballaerstraat 94, 2018 Antwerpen

CONFERENCE AND YOUTH CENTRE
Villa Meyerbeer, route de Barisart 256,
  4900 Spa; tel: (087) 77 49 00

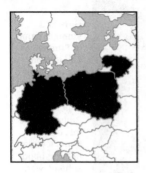

GERMANY AND LITHUANIA TERRITORY

Territorial leaders:
Commissioners Horst and Helga Charlet

Territorial Commander:
Commissioner Horst Charlet (12 Jun 2005)

Chief Secretary:
Lieut-Colonel Patrick Naud (1 May 2009)

Territorial Headquarters: 50677 Köln, Salierring 23-27, Germany

Tel: [49] (221) 20 8190; fax: [49] (221) 208 1957; email: NHQ@GER.salvationarmy.org;
website: www.heilsarmee.de

Salvation Army work in Germany began in Stuttgart on 14 November 1886 through the persistent sale of the Swiss *Kriegsruf* by Staff-Captain Fritz Schaaff who, after being converted in New York, was stationed in Switzerland and could not resist the call to bring the message over the border into his fatherland.

The Salvation Army was first registered as a limited company in Berlin in 1897 and was recognised throughout Germany as a church and public corporation on 10 October 1967 by law in Nordrhein-Westfalen. It is recognised as a religious association with public rights in the states of Berlin, Hessen, Schleswig-Holstein and Baden-Württemberg.

Salvation Army work in Lithuania having begun in 1998, the Germany Territory was redesignated the Germany and Lithuania Territory in September 2005. That same month, 'Project Warsaw' was launched to begin the Army's work in Poland (under IHQ) and on 1 July 2008 the Germany and Lithuania Territory took responsibilty for this work when a regional office for Poland was established in Dresden.

Zone: Europe
Countries included in the territory: Germany, Lithuania, Poland
'The Salvation Army' in German: Die Heilsarmee; in Lithuanian: Isganymo Armija; in Polish: Armia Zbawienia
Language in which the gospel is preached: German, Lithuanian, Polish
Periodicals: *Danke*, *Heilsarmee-Forum*, *Heilsarmee-Magazin*

WHEN General Shaw Clifton and Commissioner Helen Clifton (WPWM) led an Easter congress in Baunatal, Germany, some 650 people registered for all three days of meetings and workshops. 'Extraordinary', the congress slogan, fittingly portrayed all that occurred – from the large numbers of people moving to the place of prayer during meetings, to the strong Bible messages by the General and Commissioner Clifton,

to the variety of ways Jesus Christ was glorified.

Guest vocalist Kerry Sampson (UK) thrilled her listeners, as did the German Staff Band and a territorial youth choir formed for the congress. Praise groups from Lithuania and Poland also enhanced the meetings.

The 20th anniversary of the German Staff Band, celebrated in Solingen in June 2009, was marked by the visit of the Chicago Staff

Band (USA Central). More than 130 delegates participated in the Territorial Music Camp, which closed with a concert attended by 300 people. Sports events and a children's camp were very successful during the summer.

The ordination and commissioning of two women officers took place in July – the first commissioning to be held in Berlin for more than 70 years. Many people made public their commitment to Christ.

The then Chief of the Staff Commissioner Robin Dunster was guest leader at the Spiritual Day during territorial officers councils. This important visit brought much encouragement.

On 5 November the President of Churches Social Work in Germany awarded the Golden Crown Cross of the Diakonie to territorial leaders Commissioners Horst and Helga Charlet. The TC has been Chairman of the Diaconia Committee of Protestant Churches since 2004.

During the closing months of 2009 a special commission planned a three-year strategy to emphasise a year of silence, a year of vision and a year of mission. A strategy for the next 20 years is in preparation in relation to the development of spiritual life.

Several major projects are being developed in Poland and Lithuania, where the Army's work is growing and a significant number of people have become actively involved in the movement.

STATISTICS
Officers 155 (active 84 retired 71) **Cadets** 1 **Field Sergeants** 17 **Employees** 730
Corps 42 **Outposts** 6 **Institutions** 40
Senior Soldiers 1,029 **Adherents** 445 **Junior Soldiers** 65

STAFF
Women's Ministries: Comr Helga Charlet (TPWM) Lt-Col Anne-Dore Naud (TSWM)
Evangelisation and Field Programme: Maj Marsha Bowles
Editor: Maj Alfred Preuß
Finance and Fund-raising: Mr Hans Joachim Bode
IT Manager: Maj Hartmut Leisinger
Property: Mr Wilfried Otterbach
Public Relations and Internet: Maj Annette Preuß
Social: Maj Frank Honsberg
Staff Band: B/M Heinrich Schmidt
Trade: Maj Heidrun Edwards
Training and Candidates: Maj Marsha Bowles
Youth: Maj David Bowles

DIVISIONS
North-East: 12159 Berlin, Fregestr 13/14;
tel: (0) 30-859 8890; fax: (0) 30-859 889 99; email:
DHQ_NordOst@GER.salvationarmy.org;
Majs Reinhold and Ruth Walz
South-West: 45888 Gelsenkirchen, Hohenzollernstr 83; tel: (0) 0209-14908 546; fax (0) 0209-14908 545; email:
DHQ_SuedWest@GER.salvationarmy.org;
Majs Stephan and Andrea Weber

INVESTIGATION
Heckerstr 85, 34121 Kassel;
tel: (0) 561 2889945; fax: (0) 561 2889946;
email: Suchdienst@GER.salvationarmy.org;
Lt-Col Erika Siebel

SENIOR CITIZENS' RESIDENCES
12159 Berlin, Dickhardtstr 52-53 (acc apts 42)
45127 Essen, Hoffnungsstr 23 (acc apts 25)
44623 Herne, Koppenbergshof 2 (acc apts 5 flats 9)
50858 Köln, Rosenweg 1-5;
tel: (0)221-280 8979 (acc apts 42)
68159 Mannheim, G3, 1 + 20;
tel: (0)621-2 5361 (acc apts 31)
68165 Mannheim, Augartenstr 43, Haus Marie Engelhardt; tel: (0)621-44 27 28 (acc apts 19)
75175 Pforzheim, Pflügerstr 37-43;
tel: (0)7231-6 56 14 (acc apts 30)

SOCIAL SERVICES

Counselling

79106 Freiburg, Lehenerstr 115;
tel: (0)761-89 44 92; fax (0)761-500 99 98
20359 Hamburg, Counselling Centre, Talstr 11;
tel: (0)40-31 65 43
22117 Hamburg, Counselling for Alcoholics and
Rehabilitation Work, Oststeinbeckerweg 2-4;
tel: (0)40-713 65 64; fax: (0)40-713 44 37

Children's Day Nursery

12159 Berlin, Fregestr 13-14; tel: (0)30-850 72920;
fax: (0)30-850 729231 (acc 30)

Drop-in Cafés

79098 Freiburg, Löwenstr 1;
tel: (0)761-38 54616; fax: (0)761-38 546 22
22453 Hamburg, Borsteler Chaussee 23;
tel: (0)40-514 314 0; fax: (0)40-514 314 14
23552 Lübeck, An der Untertrave 48-49;
tel: (0)451-73394
90443 Nürnberg, Leonhardtstr 28;
tel: (0)911-28 73 156

Hostels

60314 Frankfurt, Windeckstr 58-60;
tel: (0)69-43 22 52 (acc 38)
73033 Göppingen, Markstr 58; tel: (0)7161-7 42 17;
fax: (0)7161-7 28 10 (acc 30)
37073 Göttingen, Untere Maschstr 13b;
tel: (0)551-4 24 84; fax: (0)551-5 31 14 22
(acc 24)
23552 Lübeck, Engelsgrube 62-64;
tel: (0)451-7 33 94; fax: (0)451-7 23 86 (acc 37)
80469 München, Pestalozzistr 36;
tel: (0)89-26 71 49; fax: (0)89-26 35 26 (acc 50)
70176 Stuttgart, Silberburgstr 139;
tel: (0)711-61 09 67/68; fax: (0)711-61 33 00
(acc 52)
65189 Wiesbaden, Schwarzenbergstr 7;
tel: (0)611-70 12 68; fax: (0)0611-71 40 21
(acc 191)

Nursing Homes

14163 Berlin, Goethestr 17-21; tel: (0)30-3289000;
fax: (0)30-32890022 (acc 51)
47805 Krefeld, Voltastr 50; tel: (0)2151-93 72 60;
fax: (0)2151-93 72626 (acc 65)

Therapeutic Rehabilitation Institutions

14197 Berlin, Hanauerstr 63; tel: (0)30-8 20 08 40;
fax: (0)30-8 20 08 430 (acc 60)
22453 Hamburg, Borsteler Chaussee 23;
tel: (0)40-514 314 0; fax: (0)40-514 314 0;
email: HamburgJJH@GER.salvationarmy.org
(acc 71)

34123 Kassel, Eisenacherstr 18;
tel: (0)561-570 35 90; fax: (0)561-570 359 22
(acc 85)
50825 Köln, Marienstr 116/118;
tel: (0)221-955 6090; fax: (0)221-5595 482
(acc 80)
90443 Nürnberg, Gostenhofer Hauptstr 47-49;
tel: (0)911-28 730; fax: (0)911-28 73 1103;
email:
NuernbergSozWerk@GER.salvationarmy.org
(acc 239, inc therapeutic workshops and
facilities for alcoholics and elderly men)

Therapeutic Workshops

22453 Hamburg, Borsteler Chaussee 23;
tel: (0)40-514 314 35;
fax: (0) 40-514 314 14
90443 Nürnberg, Leonhardstr 17-21;
tel: (0)911 28730

Women's Hostels

34134 Kassel-Niederzwehren, Am
Donarbrunnen 32; tel: (0)561-43113 (acc 7)
90443 Nürnberg, Gostenhofer Hauptstr 65;
tel: (0)911-272 3600 (acc 12)
65197 Wiesbaden, Königsteinerstr 24;
tel: (0)611-80 67 58; fax: (0)611-981 23 03
(acc 45)

CONFERENCE AND HOLIDAY CENTRE

24306 Plön, Seehof, Steinberg 3-4;
tel: (0)4522-5088200; fax: (0) 4522-5088202;
email: seehof@GER.salvationarmy.org
Conference and Holiday Home (acc 72 + 25)
Youth Camp (acc 50) Camping Ground and
3 holiday chalets and flats

LITHUANIA

Officer-in-Charge: Capt Susanne Kettler-
Riutkenen
Isganymo Armija, Lietuvoje, Tiltu 18, LT 91246
Klaipeda; tel/fax: [370] 46-310634;
email: klaipeda@isganymo-armija.org

POLAND

Regional Officer: Maj Patrick Granat
Warsaw Office: ul. Bialostocka 11 m. 21, 03-748
Warszawa, Poland; tel: (0) 048 691 283 891;
email: Warszawa@GER.salvationarmy.org
Starachowice Office: ul. Nowa 10, 27-200
Starachowice, Poland; tel: (0)048 60716 5903;
email starachowice@GER.salvationarmy.org;
Maj Denise McGarvey

GHANA TERRITORY

Territorial leaders:
Colonels Dennis L. and Sharon Strissel

Territorial Commander:
Colonel Dennis L. Strissel (1 Feb 2007)

Chief Secretary:
Lieut-Colonel Samuel Oklah (1 Jan 2011)

Territorial Headquarters: PO Box CT452 Cantonments, Accra, Ghana

Tel: [233] (21) 776 971; fax: [233] (021) 772 695; email: saghana@gha.salvationarmy.org

Salvation Army operations began in Ghana in 1922 when Lieutenant King Hudson was commissioned to 'open fire' in his home town of Duakwa. Ensign and Mrs Charles Roberts were also appointed to pioneer work in Accra.

Zone: Africa
Country included in the territory: Ghana
'The Salvation Army' in Ga: Yiwalaheremo Asrafoi Le; in Fanti and Twi: Nkwagye Dom Asraafo; in Ewe: Agbexoxo Srafa Ha La
Languages in which the gospel is preached: Bassa, Builsa, Dangme, English, Ewe, Fante, Frafra, Ga, Gola, Grushia, Twi
Periodical: *Salvationist Newsletter*

THE territory gives thanks to God as over the year 1,824 converts have been won for the Lord, 1,282 senior and 2,970 junior soldiers enrolled and five new openings established. Several new areas of work have been investigated by the Medical Social Department with possibilities being explored for future partnerships with district health offices and local communities.

'Serving Suffering Humanity' continued to be the main thrust in all activities undertaken; many marginalised adults and children were helped to realise their own self-worth and value in God's Kingdom.

There was a strong emphasis on partners in mission during the year, with projects at Asokore and Woe being funded and completed by mission teams from USA Central Territory. Four young Ghanaians travelled to the USA for summer camps, receiving valuable insight into the internationalism of The Salvation Army.

A three-day teachers conference, held in August 2009, involved 75 educational units and 125 teachers; it also marked the launching of the Association of Salvationist Teachers.

A new school block at Begoro, built by the district assembly, is nearing completion, the result of the commitment of the District

Chief Executive, who was a pupil at The Salvation Army's school. Much rejoicing was seen at Abobabo Secondary School, where a three-bedroom officers' quarters was commissioned, also two ablution blocks for the students.

Many special activities took place when a celebratory week for the Army's 87th anniversary at Duakwa was held in August 2009. The closing thanksgiving weekend meetings were conducted by territorial leaders Colonels Dennis and Sharon Strissel.

In line with the territory's Strategic Plan for Human Resource Development two seminars were held under the theme 'Leadership In Perspective'. Officers from across the territory were taken through various topics to enable them to build their leadership capacity and raise their self-awareness in ministry.

The submission of 20-year faith goals from all areas of the Army's ministry in the territory is bringing challenge to its officers, soldiers and various department heads. Strategies are now being strengthened to help the achievement of these goals.

Lieut-Colonel William Gyimah (then Chief Secretary) was awarded an Honorary Doctorate by the Pan African Clergy and Bible Seminary.

STATISTICS

Officers 259 (active 209 retired 50) **Cadets** 20 **Employees** 1,578
Corps 110 **Societies** 151 **Schools** 197 **Clinics** 9 **Social Centres** 8 **Day Care Centres** 66
Senior Soldiers 18,711 **Junior Soldiers** 6,787
Personnel serving outside territory Officers 10

STAFF

Women's Ministries: Col Sharon K. Strissel (TPWM) Lt-Col Philomina Oklah (TSWM) Lt-Col Theresa Adu-Manu (TLOMS) Maj Eva Kudezi (Women's Development and Training)
Business Administration: Maj Isaac Danso
Personnel: Lt-Col Mike Adu-Manu
  Asst to Sec for Personnel: Maj Eva Danso
Programme: Lt-Col Seth Agyei Appeateng
Communications and External Relations: Mr Kofi Sakyiamah
Editor: Maj Stephen Borbor
Extension Training: Capt Michael Eku
Finance: Maj Francis Amakye
Medical, Social and Community Services: Maj Heather Craig
Planned Giving: Maj Graeme Craig
Projects and Child Sponsorship: Capt Margaret Amponsah
Property: Maj Modesto Kudezi
Schools: Mrs Doris Mensah
Territorial Band: B/M Emmanuel Hackman
Training: Maj James Oduro
Youth and Candidates: Lt-Col Janet Agyei Appeateng

DIVISIONS

Accra: PO Box 166 Tema; tel: (022) 215 530; Majs Godfried and Felicia Oduro
Akim Central: PO Box AS 283, Asamankese; tel: (081) 23 585; Majs Peter and Grace Oduro-Amoah
Ashanti Central: PO Box 15, Kumasi; tel/fax: (051) 240 16; Majs Samuel and Juliana Kyeremeh
Ashanti North: c/o PO Box 477, Mampong, Ashanti; Majs Stephen and Cecilia Boadu
Central: PO Box 62, Agona Swedru; tel: (041) 20 285; Majs Edmund and Grace Abia
Nkawkaw: PO Box 3, Nkawkaw; tel: (0842) 22 208; Majs Edward and Mercy Addison
West Akim: PO Box 188, Akim Oda; tel: (0882) 2 305; Maj Jonas and Capt Constance Ampofo
Volta: PO Box 604, Ho, Volta Region; Majs Rockson and Emelia Oduro

DISTRICTS

Brong Ahafo: PO Box 1454, Sunyani; tel: (061) 23 513; Maj Stephen Amoaning
East Akim: PO Box KF 1218, Koforidua E/R; tel: (081) 22 580; Maj Edward Kyei
Northern: PO Box 233, Bolgatanga; tel: (072) 22 030; Capt Prosper Adua

Western: PO Box 178, Sekondi, C/R;
tel: (031) 23 763; Capt Alexander Siaw

TRAINING COLLEGE
PO Box CE 11991, Tema; tel: (022) 306 252/253

EXTENSION TRAINING CENTRE
PO Box CT 452, Cantonments, Accra;
tel: (021) 776 971; fax: (021) 772 695

CLINICS
Accra Urban Aid: PO Box CT 452, Cantonments,
Accra; tel: (021) 230 918 (acc 11, in maternity)
Accra Urban Aid Outreach: PO Box CT 452,
Cantonments, Accra; tel: (021) 246 764
(mobile outreach for street children)
Adaklu-Sofa: PO Box 604, Ho, V/R (acc 4,
inc maternity)
Anum: PO Box 17, Senchi, E/R (acc 11,
inc maternity)
Ba: PO Box 8, Ba, C/R (acc 4, inc maternity)
Begoro: PO Box 10, Begoro, E/R (acc 10,
inc maternity)
Duakwa: PO Box 2, Agona Duakwa, C/R (acc 30,
inc maternity)
Wenchi: PO Box 5, Wenchi, Akim Oda (acc 8,
including maternity)

HEALTH CENTRE
Wiamoase: PO Box 14, Wiamoase, Ashanti;
tel: (051) 32 613

EDUCATION
Sub-primary Schools 66, Primary Schools 79,
Junior Secondary Schools 40, Senior Secondary
Schools 2

SOCIAL WORK
Adaklu-Sofa Vocational Training Centre:
PO Box 604, Ho, V/R
Anidasofie Street Girls' Training Centre:
PO Box CT 452, Cantonments, Accra;
tel: (021) 246 764
Begoro Rehabilitation Centre: PO Box 10,
Begoro, E/R
Child Care Training Centre: PO Box 8, Ba, C/R
Community Rehabilitation Project:
PO Box 2, Agona Duakwa
Malnutrition Centre: PO Box 2, Agona
Duakwa, C/R
Rehabilitation Centre: PO Box 14, Wiamoase,
Ashanti
Voluntary Counselling and Testing Centre:
PO Box CT 452, Cantonments, Accra;
tel: (021) 776 971

Australians serving in Ghana – Majors Graeme and Heather Craig (THQ) and Miss Katharine Dale (Begoro Rehabilitation Centre) – fly the flag as they celebrate Australia Day

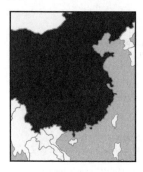

HONG KONG AND MACAU COMMAND

Command leaders:
Lieut-Colonels Samuel and Donni Pho

Officer Commanding:
Lieut-Colonel Samuel Pho (1 Jun 2009)

General Secretary:
Major Priscilla Nanlabi (1 Dec 2007)

**Command Headquarters: 11 Wing Sing Lane, Yaumatei,
Kowloon, Hong Kong**

Postal address: PO Box 70129, Kowloon Central Post Office, Kowloon, Hong Kong

Tel: [852] 2332 4531; fax: [852] 2771 6439; email: Hongkong@hkt.salvationarmy.org;
website: www.salvation.org.hk

In March 1930, at a meeting held at Government House, Hong Kong, The Salvation Army was requested to undertake women's work in the crown colony, a work pioneered by Majors Dorothy Brazier and Doris Lemon. This work was directed from Peking until, in 1935, the South China Command was established in Canton to promote wide evangelistic and welfare operations. In 1939 Hong Kong became the Army's administrative centre. Later, the inclusion of the New Territories determined that the Command Headquarters move to Kowloon. Since 1951 the General of The Salvation Army has been recognised as a Corporation Sole. From 1993, disaster relief and community development projects have been carried out in mainland China. In 1999, a pioneer officer was appointed to the Special Administrative Region of Macau and Salvation Army work began there officially on 25 March 2000. In 2001, an officer was appointed to the North/North Eastern Project Office in Beijing.

Zone: South Pacific and East Asia
Regions included in the command: Hong Kong and Macau (Special Administrative Regions of the People's Republic of China) and Mainland China
'The Salvation Army' in Cantonese: Kau Sai Kwan; in Filipino: Hukbo ng Kaligtasan; in Putonghua: Jiu Shi Jun
Languages in which the gospel is preached: Cantonese, English, Filipino, Putonghua
Periodicals: *Army Scene, The War Cry*

WITH 2010 being the 80th year of Salvation Army service in Hong Kong, on 1 January some 800 Salvationists from various Army units joined the launching march by the Shing Mun riverside, Shatin. All participants then gathered at Tin Ka Ping School playground to enjoy *punchai*, a traditional rural feast.

Celebration activities were planned throughout the year, leading up to an anniversary congress themed 'Thanksgiving, Commitment and Service'.

Commissioner Robert Street (then IS, SPEA) visited the command in May 2009 as guest speaker at a holiness seminar. He presented a series of lectures based on his book *Holiness Unwrapped*. The command has translated the book into Chinese for worldwide Chinese ministries.

The Salvation Army was very involved in emergency relief and rehabilitation service in several provinces in mainland China. The Global Chinese Ministry Training Centre conducted many seminars and courses for soldiers and local officers.

Four cadets entered the training college in the Ambassadors Of Holiness Session, which commenced on 1 September 2009. The command was delighted to welcome a cadet from Taiwan Region.

A change in the command's leadership came with the appointment of Lieut-Colonels Samuel and Donni Pho. Their installation took place on 1 June 2009 at William Booth Secondary School.

STATISTICS

Officers 53 (active 43 retired 8) **Cadets** 4 **Employees** 2,483
Corps 18 **Outpost** 1 **Institutions** 20 **Schools** 6 **Kindergartens** 7 **Nursery Schools** 17 **Social Centres and Hotels** 81
Senior Soldiers 2,365 **Adherents** 32 **Junior Soldiers** 378
Personnel serving outside command Officers 3

STAFF

Women's Ministries: Lt-Col Donni Pho (CPWM) Maj Ming-chun Connie Ip Kan (CSWM)
Asst to GS: Maj Simon Tso Kam-shing
China Development: Maj On Dieu Quang
Candidates: Capt Sara Tam Mei-shun
Community Relations: Envoy Simon Wong
Editor/Literary: Maj David Ip Kam-yuen
Educational Services: Maj Simon Tso Kam-shing
Emergency Services Coordinator: Ms Karen Ng Wai-sze
Finance: Ms Deidre Ashe

Human Resources: Ms Eva Lau
Property: Envoy Daniel Hui Wah-lun
Social: tba
Trade: Ms Karen Ng Wai-sze
Training: Maj Tony Ma Yeung-mo

DIVISION

1 Lung Chu St, Tai Hang Tung, Kowloon, HK; tel: 2195 0222; fax: 2319 0670; Maj Tommy Chan Hi-wai and Maj Helina Chan Lee Siu-king

OFFICER TRAINING COLLEGE AND GLOBAL CHINESE MINISTRY TRAINING CENTRE

1 Lung Chu St, Tai Hang Tung, Kln, PO Box 70129, Kowloon Central PO, Kln, HK; tel: 2195 0203; fax: 2319 1386

CHINA DEVELOPMENT

Hong Kong Head Office: tel: (852) 2783 2288; fax: (852) 2385 7823;
China Development Sec: Maj On Dieu Quang; tel: (852) 2783 2288;
email: cdd@hkt.salvationarmy.org
North/Northeast Regional Project Office – China: D-102 Jin Mao Apartment, 2 Guang Hua Lane, Chao Yang District, Beijing 100020, China;
tel: [86] (10) 6586 9331/2;
fax: [86] (10) 6586 8382;
email: nnerpo@hkt.salvationarmy.org
Xinghe Project Office – China: Room 520, Xinghe Municipal Government Bldg, Xinghe, 013650 Inner Mongolia, China; tel/fax: (86) 474 7212 010;
email: xho@hkt.salvationarmy.org
Yunnan Project Office – China: 6D, Unit 1, Block 8, Yin Hai Hot Spring Garden, Northern District, 173 Guan Xing Rd, Guan Shang, Kunming 650200, Yunnan, China;
tel: [86] (871) 7166 111/222;
fax: [86] (871) 7155 222;
email: ynpo@hkt.salvationarmy.org
The Salvation Army Campsite and Training Centre – China: Xinhge, Inner Mongolia, China; tel: (86) 474 7212980

EDUCATIONAL SERVICES
Kindergartens

Centaline Charity Fund: G/F, under Mei Mun House, Mei Tin Estate, Tai Wai, Shatin, NT; tel: 2886 2340; fax 2886 2343 (acc 224, 2 sessions) (acc 69 full-day)
Chan Kwan Tung: G/F & 1/F, The Salvation Army Headquarters, 11 Wing Sing Lane,

Yaumatei, Kln; tel: 2384 7831;
fax: 2388 5310 (acc 277, 2 sessions)

Fu Keung: Units 121-140, G/F, Fu Keung
House, Tai Wo Hau Estate, NT;
tel: 2614 4481; fax: 2439 0666 (acc 300,
2 sessions)

Hing Yan: G/F, Commercial Centre, Hau Tak
Estate, Tseung Kwan O, Kln; tel: 2706 6222;
fax: 2704 9262 (acc 270, 2 sessions)
plus Nursery (acc 108, 2 sessions)

Ng Kwok Wai Memorial: G/F, 22-30 Hoi
Shing Rd, Clague Garden Estate,
Tsuen Wan, NT; tel: 2499 7639;
fax: 2414 9214 (acc 360, 2 sessions)

Ping Tin: G/F, Ping Shing House, Ping Tin
Estate, Lam Tin, Kln; tel: 2775 5332;
fax: 2775 5412 (acc 270; 2 sessions)
plus Nursery (acc 42, 2 sessions)

Tin Ka Ping: G/F, No 15 Jat Min Chuen St,
Shatin, NT; tel: 2647 4227; fax: 2645 1869
(acc 524, 2 sessions)

Crèches (1 month - 2 years)

North Point: Podium Level 2, Healthy Village,
6 Healthy St, Central North Point, HK;
tel: 2856 0892; fax: 2856 1398 (acc 28
full-day)

Pak Tin: G/F, Wing C, Fu Tin House, Pak Tin
Estate, Pak Wan St, Shamshuipo, Kln;
tel: 2778 3588; fax: 2778 9622 (acc 16
full-day)

Nursery Schools (2 - 6 years)

Catherine Booth: 2/F, Salvation Army HQ,
11 Wing Sing Lane, Yaumatei, Kln:
tel: 2332 7963; fax: 2385 4167 (acc 110
full-day)

Hoi Fu: G/F, Wing B & C, Hoi Ning House,
Hoi Fu Court, Mongkok, Kln; tel: 2148 2477;
fax: 2148 1711 (acc 118 full-day)

Jat Min: 1/F, 15 Jat Min Chuen St, Jat Min
Chuen, Shatin, NT; tel: 2647 4897;
fax: 2646 6825 (acc 168 full-day)

Kam Tin: G/F, 103 Kam Tin Rd, Yuen Long, NT;
tel: 2442 3606; fax: 2442 0523 (acc 104 full-day)

Lai Chi Kok: 1/F, Prosperity Court, 168 Lai Chi
Kok Rd, Kln; tel: 2787 5788; fax: 2787 1581
(acc 100 full-day)

Lei Muk Shue: G/F, Wing B & C, Yeung Shue
House, Lei Muk Shue Estate, Kwai Chung,
NT; tel: 2420 2491; fax: 2619 9289 (acc 112
full-day)

Lok Man: 1/F, Block H, Lok Man Sun Chuen,
Tokwawan, Kln; tel: 2365 1994;
fax: 2764 8036 (acc 145 full-day)

Ming Tak: G/F, Wing B & C, Hin Ming Court,

Hang Hau, Tseung Kwan O, Kln;
tel: 2623 7555; fax: 2623 7551 (acc 126
full-day)

North Point: Podium Level 2, Healthy Village,
6 Healthy St, Central North Point, HK;
tel: 2856 0892; fax: 2856 1398 (acc 28
full-day)

Pak Tin: G/F, Wing C, Fu Tin House,
Pak Tin Estate, Pak Wan St, Shamshuipo, Kln;
tel: 2778 3588; fax: 2778 9622 (acc 104
full-day)

Sam Shing: G/F, adj to Moon Yu House,
Sam Shing Estate, Tuen Mun, NT;
tel: 2452 0032; fax: 2541 1347 (acc 104
full-day)

Tai Wo Hau: Units 215, 217, 219 & 221-232,
2/F, Fu Keung House, Tai Wo Hau Estate,
Tsuen Wan, NT; tel: 2614 7662;
fax: 2612 2571 (acc 126 full-day)

Tai Yuen: G/F, Tai Ling House,
Tai Yuen Estate, Tai Po, NT; tel: 2664 9725;
fax: 2666 9698 (acc 100 full-day)

Tin Ping: G/F, Units 106-110, Wing B,
Tin Hor House, Tin Ping Estate, Sheung
Shui, NT; tel: 2671 9972; fax: 2671 8436
(acc 116 full-day)

Tsuen Wan: 1/F, Clague Garden Estate,
22 Hoi Shing Rd, Tsuen Wan, NT;
tel: 2417 1400; fax: 2411 1926 (acc 182
full-day)

Wah Fu: 1/F-2/F, Wah Sang House,
Wah Fu Estate, HK; tel: 2551 6341;
fax: 2538 1229 (acc 126 full-day)

Wo Che: Bays 101-114, G/F, Tak Wo House,
Wo Che Estate, Shatin, NT; tel: 2604 0428;
fax:2608 0614 (acc 168 full-day)

Primary Schools

Ann Wyllie Memorial School: 100 Shing Tai Rd,
Heng Fa Chuen, HK; tel: 2558 2111;
fax: 2898 4377 (acc 732)

Centaline Charity Fund School: 9 Wah Ha St,
Chaiwan, HK; tel: 2556 2292; fax: 2556 2722
(acc 464)

Lam Butt Chung Memorial School: 8 Yat Tung St,
Yat Tung Estate, Tung Chung, Lantau, NT;
tel: 2109 0328; fax: 2109 0223 (acc 915)

Tin Ka Ping School: Pok Hong Estate,
Shatin, NT; tel: 2648 9283; fax: 2649 4305
(acc 732)

Secondary School

William Booth Secondary School,
100 Yuk Wah St, Tsz Wan Shan, Kln;
tel: 2326 9068;fax: 2328 0052 (acc 1,205)

HAITI: Responding to the devastating earthquake that hit the island in January 2010, The Salvation Army distributed more than five million meals

Urgent relief supplies are speedily unloaded at Petit Goave (*left*). In Haiti's capital, Port-au-Prince, an emergency camp in a sports ground behind The Salvation Army's compound (*below*) became home to some 20,000 people.

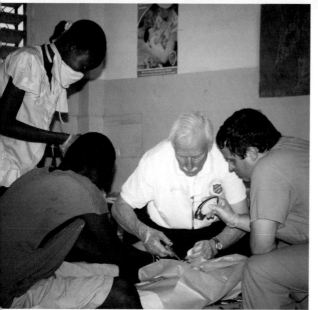

Amid extensive damage caused by the 7.0 magnitude earthquake, Salvationists in Port-au-Prince join in the search for survivors (*above*). Nearby, a Salvation Army doctor from the USA tirelessly seeks to save a life (*left*) during an operation in the Army's clinic.

A Salvation Army captain translates for a patient (*above*) being treated at the Army's health care centre in Port-au-Prince

A comforting embrace (*right*) and a prayer for strength are readily received by one of the disaster's many victims

PAKISTAN: As the worst floods for 80 years spread across the country in August 2010, Salvation Army emergency services personnel distributed relief packages to more than 13,000 families

The floods affected an estimated 14 million people, making more than a million homeless. A tent city near Hyderabad housed hundreds of families. Salvation Army emergency services distributed supplies of tents, mattresses, quilts, pillows and kitchen utensils.

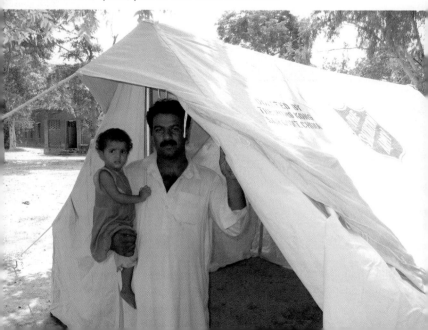

Transporting relief to flood-hit towns and villages (*left*), The Salvation Army distributed much-needed supplies among Christian and Muslim families. Grateful for assistance, two boys (*below*) happily wheel their goods back home.

CHILE: Salvation Army teams provided practical and spiritual support to communities affected by an 8.8 magnitude earthquake and tsunami in February and March 2010. During a three-week period of aftershocks, more than 15,000 people were helped as 14,000 rations of food were distributed to individuals and families (*left*). Southern areas of the country, particularly coastal regions, were most affected by the disaster so this was where The Salvation Army focused its main efforts. Volunteers helped with the clean-up (*above*). The Salvationists' prayers (*left*) were valued by the disaster victims and workers alike.

Special School

Shek Wu School, Area 8 Jockey Club Rd,
Sheung Shui, NT; tel: 2670 0800;
fax: 2668 5353 (acc 200)

GUEST ACCOMMODATION

Booth Lodge, 7/F, 11 Wing Sing Lane,
Yaumatei, Kln; tel: (852) 2771 9266;
fax: (852) 2385 1140;
email: boothlodge@salvationarmy.org.hk

RECYCLING PROGRAMME

Logistic Centre: 7/F Tat Ming Industrial
Building, 44-52 Ta Chuen Ping St,
Kwai Chung, NT; tel: 2332 4433;
fax: 2332 4411;
email: Recycling@hkt.salvationarmy.org

Family Stores

Aberdeen Store: No 8, Tung Sing Rd,
Aberdeen, HK; tel: 2873 4666
Kowloon City Store: 1/F, HICB Building,
78-82 Tam Kung Rd, To Kwa Wan, Kln;
tel: 2624 7878
Kwun Tong Store: No 237, G/F, Hay Cheuk Lau,
Garden Estate, Kwun Tong, Kln;
tel: 2331 2577
Macau Store: Ave Artur Tamag Barbosa,
BL 9, Fl R/C, Flat CF, Ed Jardim
Cidade – Man Seng Kok, Macau;
tel: (853) 2843 2888
Mongkok Store: Shop 1, G/F Xing Hua Ctr,
433 Shanghai St, Mongkok, Kln;
tel: 3422 3205
Nam Cheong Store: Shop 3-4, Nam Cheong
West Rail Station, Kln; tel: 2387 4933
North Point Store: G/F, Fok Ying Building,
379A King's Rd, North Point, HK;
tel: 2570 0138
Shau Kei Wan Store: G/F, Tung Hong Building,
139 Shau Kei Wan, Main Street East, HK;
tel: 2535 8113
Stanley Store: G/F, 98 Stanley Main St, HK;
tel: 3197 0070
Tai Hang Tung Store: G/F, 1 Lung Chu St,
Tai Hang Tung, Kln; tel: 2784 0689
Tin Hau Store: G/F, 29 Wing Hing St,
Tin Hau, HK; tel: 2887 5577
Wanchai Store: G/F, 31 Wood Rd,
Wanchai, HK; tel: 2572 2879
Western District Store: Shop A2, G/F,
Man Kwong Court, 12F-12G Smithfield Rd,
Kennedy Town, Western District, HK;
tel: 2974 0882
Yaumatei Store: G/F, 1A Cliff Rd,
Yaumatei, Kln; tel: 2332 4448

Yue Wan Store: Shop 29-30, Yue On House,
Yue Wan Estate, Chaiwan, HK;
tel: 2558 8655

SOCIAL SERVICES
Camp Service

Bradbury Camp: 6 Ming Fai Rd,
Cheung Chau, HK; tel: 2981 0358 (acc 108)
Ma Wan Youth Camp: Ma Wan Island, HK;
tel: 2986 5244 (acc 40)

Youth Service
Children and Youth Centres

Chuk Yuen: 2-4/F, Chuk Yuen Estate
Community Centre, Chuk Yuen South
Estate, Kln; tel: 2351 5321
Lung Hang: G/F, Sin Sum House, Lung Hang
Estate, Shatin, NT; tel: 2605 5569
Tai Wo Hau: 2-4/F, Tai Wo Hau Rd,
Tai Wo Hau Community Centre,
Kwai Chung, NT; tel: 2428 4581

Education and Employment Service

Education and Development Centre: 6 Salvation
Army St, Wanchai, HK; tel: 2572 6718

Integrated Services for Young People

Chaiwan: Podium Level Market Bldg,
Wan Tsui Estate, Chaiwan, HK;
tel: 2898 9750
Tai Po: 2/F, Tai Man House, Tai Yuen Estate,
Tai Po, NT; tel: 2667 2913
Tuen Mun: G/F, 13-24 Hing Ping House,
Tai Hing Estate, Tuen Mun, NT;
tel: 2461 4741
Tuen Mun East: 5/F Ancillary Facilities Block,
Fu Tai Estate, 9 Tuen Kwai Rd,
Tuen Mun, NT; tel: 2467 7200
Yaumatei: 1/F, Block 4, Prosperous Garden,
3 Public Square St, Kln; tel: 2770 8933

School Social Work Services

Tuen Mun: G/F, 13-24 Hing Ping House, Tai
Hing Estate, Tuen Mun, NT; tel: 2461 4741

Services for Young Night Drifters

Tuen Mun: 5/F Ancillary Facilities Block,
Fu Tai Estate, 9 Tuen Kwai Rd,
Tuen Mun, NT; tel: 2467 7200

Youth Special Projects

'Flying High' Child Development Project:
6 Salvation Army St, Wanchai, HK;
tel: 2892 1302
'Walk With You' Project: 6 Salvation Army St,
Wanchai, HK; tel: 2834 3483

Community Projects

'Home Optimisation Movement for the Elderly'
Community Service Team: Room 416,
Tsui Wing House, Tsui Ping Estate,
Kwun Tong, Kln

Integrated Service for Street Sleepers:
1/F, GIC Bldg, 345A Shanghai St, Kln;
tel: 2710 8911

Ngau Tam Mei Community Development
Projects: Lot 323 & 324 in DD104,
Ngau Tam Mei, Yuen Long, NT;
tel: 2482 7175

Sam Mun Tsai Community Development
Projects: 31 Chim Uk Village, Shuen Wan,
Tai Po, NT; tel: 2660 9890

Shamshuipo Family Support Networking
Team: Rm 69, 2/F Fuk Sing House,
63-69 Fuk Wing St, Shamshuipo, Kln;
tel: 2390 9361

So Uk Estate Community Service Team:
G/F, 145-146 Azalea Hse, So Uk Estate,
Shamshuipo, Kln; tel: 2728 3350

Sunrise House: 323 Shun Ning Rd,
Cheung Sha Wan, Kln; tel: 2307 8001
(acc 310)

Urban Renewal Social Service Team:
G/F, 140 Yee Kuk St, Shamshuipo, Kln;
tel: 3586 3094

Yee On Hostels: Unit 111-116, 1/F,
Hoi Yu House, Hoi Fu Court, Mongkok, Kln;
tel: 2708 9553 (acc 40)

Day Care Centres for Senior Citizens

Chuk Yuen: 141-150 Podium Level, Chui
Yuen House, Chuk Yuen (South) Estate, Kln;
tel: 2326 6683 (acc 44)

Hoi Yu: G/F, Hoi Lam House, Hoi Fu Court,
2 Hoi Ting Rd, Mongkok, Kln;
tel: 2148 1480 (acc 44)

Centres for Senior Citizens

Chuk Yuen: 1/F, Chuk Yuen (South) Estate
Community Centre, Kln; tel: 2320 8032

Hoi Lam: 1/F, Hoi Yu House, Hoi Fu Court,
2 Hoi Ting Rd, Mongkok, Kln;
tel: 2148 1481

Nam Tai: G/F, Nam Tai House, Nam Shan
Estate, Kln; tel: 2779 5983

Tai Po Multi-service: 2/F-3/F, Tai Po Community
Centre, 2 Heung Sze Wui St, Tai Po
Market, NT; tel: 2653 6811

Tai Wo Hau: 1/F, Tai Wo Hau Rd, Tai Wo
Hau Community Centre, Kwai Chung, NT;
tel: 2428 8563

Wah Fu: Unit 125-129, G/F, Wah Kin House,

Wah Fu Estate, Aberdeen, HK; tel: 2550 9971

Yaumatei Multi-service: 3/F, 11 Wing Sing Lane,
Yaumatei, Kln; tel: 2332 0005

Rehabilitation Hostels

Cheung Hong: 2/F & 3/F Hong Cheung Hse,
Cheung Hong Est, Tsing Yi, NT;
tel: 2432 1588 (acc 40)

Heng On Hostel: G/F, Heng Shan House,
Heng On Estate, Ma On Shan, NT;
tel: 2640 0581 (acc 62)

Lai King Home: 200-210 Lai King Hill Rd,
Kwai Chung, NT; tel: 2744 1511 (acc 100)

Community Day Rehabilitation Service

Shaukeiwan: 456 Shaukeiwan Rd,
Shaukeiwan, HK; tel: 2560 8123 (acc 40)

Tak Tin: G/F, Tak Yan House, Tak Tin Estate,
Lam Tin; tel: 2177 7122

Integrated Home Care Service Teams

Kwun Tong: Unit 1-2, Wing B, G/F,
Tak Lung House, Tak Tin Estate,
Lam Tin, Kln; tel: 2340 0100

Sai Kung: 4/F, Po Kan House, Po Lam Estate,
Tseung Kwan O, Kln; tel: 2701 5828

Tai Po (Tai Po Office):
2/F-3/F, Tai Po Community Centre,
2 Heung Sze Wui St, Tai Po Market, NT;
tel: 2653 6619

Tai Po (Tai Wo Office): Unit 126-128,
G/F Hang Wo House, Tai Wo Estate,
Tai Po, NT; tel: 2653 3941

Yau Tsim (Kowloon Central Office):
G/F & 1/F, Chee Sun Building,
161-165 Reclamation St, Yaumatei;
tel: 2300 1399

Yau Tsim (Yaumatei Office): 3/F, 11 Wing
Sing Lane, Yaumatei, Kln; tel: 2770 5266

Elderly Special Projects
CADENZA Community Projects

CDSMP: Rm 316, 3/F, Tai Po Community
Centre, 2 Heung Sze Wui St, Tai Po Market;
tel: 2651 1698

HSPTCM: Shop D, G/F, Phase 2, Prosperous
Gdn, 3 Public Square St, Kln; tel: 2782 1334

Senior Citizens Talent Advancement Projects

Tung Tau Centre: Unit 1-3, G/F, Yat Tung
House, Tung Tau Estate, Kln; tel: 2340 0266

Kwun Tong Centre: 1/F, Flat A, Yee On
Centre, 31 Yee On St, Kwun Tong, Kln;
tel: 2389 5568

Carer Project

3/F, 11 Wing Sing Lane, Yaumatei, Kln;
tel: 2782 2229

Residential Childcare Service

Tai Wo Hau Small Group Homes: Fu Yin House,
Wing K, Tai Wo Hau Estate, Kwai Chung, NT;
Home of Joy: Flat 214; tel: 2615 1709
(acc 8)
Home of Love: Flat 314; tel: 2615 1784
(acc 8)
Home of Peace: Flat 112; tel: 2615 1710
(acc 8)
Ping Tin Small Group Homes: Ping Wong House,
Ping Tin Estates, Lam Tin, Kln;
Home of Faithfulness: Flat 103;
tel: 2952 3691 (acc 8)
Home of Goodness: Flat 203;
tel: 2952 3692 (acc 8)
Home of Kindness: Flat 303;
tel: 2775 3542 (acc 8)
Wan Tsui Home for Boys: 115-128 G/F,
Chak Tsui House, Wan Tsui Estate,
Chai Wan, HK; tel: 2557 3290 (acc 48)
Yue Wan Boys' Hostel: 3-8 Yue Tai House,
Yue Wan Estate, Chaiwan, HK;
tel: 2558 4048 (acc 15)

Family Support Centre

Tung Chung: No. 4, G/F. Ying Yat House,
Yat Tung Estate, Tung Chung, NT;
tel: 3166 0030

Residences for Senior Citizens

Bradbury Home of Loving Kindness:
16 Tung Lo Wan Hill Rd, Tai Wai,
Shatin, NT; tel: 2601 5000 (acc 136)
Hoi Tai: 2/F, Hoi Tai House, Hoi Fu Court,
2 Hoi Ting Rd, Mongkok, Kln;
tel: 2148 2000 (acc 98)
Lung Hang: 3&4/F, Wing Sam House,
Lung Hang Estate, Shatin, NT;
tel: 2602 3696 (acc 155)
Nam Ming Haven for Women: G/F,
Nam Ming House, Nam Shan Estate,
Shek Kip Mei, Kln; tel: 2777 5484 (acc 38)
Nam Shan: 1&2/F, Nam Ming House,
Nam Shan Estate, Shek Kip Mei, Kln;
tel: 2777 5102 (acc 150)
Po Lam: 4/F, Po Kan House, Po Lam Estate,
Tseung Kwan O, Kln; tel: 2701 5828 (acc 141)
Tak Tin: 2/F, Tak King House, Tak Tin Estate,
Lam Tin, Kln; tel: 2347 8183 (acc 81)
Kam Tin: 103 Kam Tin Rd, Yuen Long, NT;
tel: 2944 1369 (acc 150)

Sheltered Housing

Grace Apartments: Flat 3-95, Lotus Tower 4,
297 Ngau Tau Kok Rd, Kln; tel: 2763 6367
Kei Lok Apartments: Rm 225, Block 5,
Prosperous Garden, Public Square St,
Yaumatei, Kln; tel: 2782 6655

Integrated Vocational and Rehabilitation Service

Heng On Integrated Vocational Rehabilitation
Service: G/F, Heng Kong House,
Heng On Estate, Ma On Shan, NT;
tel: 2640 0656 (acc 285)
On the Job Training Programme for People
with Disabilities: G/F, Heng Kong Hse,
Heng On Est, Ma On Shan, NT;
tel: 2640 0656 (acc 18)
Sunnyway – On the Job Training Programme
for Young People with Disabilities:
G/F, Heng Kong Hse, Heng On Est,
Ma On Shan, NT; tel: 2640 0656 (acc 30)
Talent Shop: G/F, Heng Sing House,
Heng On Estate, Ma On Shan, Shatin, NT;
tel: 2633 7116

Rehabilitation Special Projects

Share-Care New Scope Project: 200-210 Lai King
Hill Rd, Kwai Chung, NT; tel: 2744 1511
Family Support Service for Persons with
Autism: Room 201, 6 Salvation Army St,
Wanchai, HK; tel: 2893 2537

Social Enterprise

Digital Plus: Unit D, 5/F Kwun Tong Industrial
Centre, Phase 1, 472-484 Kwun Tong Rd,
Kln; tel: 3595 2320
Shatin Family Store: Shop No 70-72,
G/F Ming Yiu Lau, Jat Min Chuen, Shatin, NT;
tel: 2636 6113
Shatin Park Food Kiosk: Kiosk no 4, Shatin Park,
2 Yuen Wo Rd, Shatink, NT
The WARM Project (Wheelchair and Assistive
Device Re-engagement Movement): 1/F,
Flat A, Yee On Centre, 31 Yee On St,
Kwun Tong, Kln; tel: 2389 5568
Tuen Mun Family Store: Shop no 41-42, Chik
Lok Garden, Tuen Mun, NT; tel: 2618 2241

INDIA NATIONAL SECRETARIAT

Postal address: 37 Lenin Sarani (1st Floor), Dharamtala St, PO Box 8994, Kolkatta – 700 013, West Bengal, India

Tel: [91] (0) 33 2227 5780 ®/2249 7210 (O); email:IND_Secretariat@ind.salvationarmy.org; website: www.salvationarmy.org/ind

India is The Salvation Army's oldest mission field. Frederick St George de Latour Tucker, of the Indian Civil Service, read a copy of *The War Cry*, became a Salvationist and, as Major Tucker (later Commissioner Booth-Tucker), took the Indian name of Fakir Singh and commenced The Salvation Army's work in Bombay on 19 September 1882. The adoption of Indian food, dress, names and customs gave the pioneers ready access to the people, especially in the villages.

In addition to evangelistic work, various social programmes were inaugurated for the relief of distress from famine, flood and epidemic. Educational facilities such as elementary, secondary, higher secondary and industrial schools, cottage industries and settlements were provided for the depressed classes. Medical work originated in Nagercoil in 1895 when Captain (Dr) Harry Andrews set up a dispensary at the headquarters there. The medical work has grown from this. Work among the then Criminal Tribes began in 1908 at government invitation.

The Salvation Army is registered as a Guarantee Company under the Indian Companies Act 1913.

Publication: *The War Cry* (English)

THE National Secretariat for India serves the six Salvation Army territories within the country.

The Conference of Indian Leaders (COIL), established in 1989, meets annually to coordinate national Salvation Army affairs and give direction to the National Secretariat.

Several national offices had been established in earlier years, including the Editorial and Literary Office and the Audit Office. Since the establishment of The Salvation Army Health Services Advisory Council (SAHSAC) in 1986, a regionally based National Secretariat evolved to provide support to many aspects of Salvation Army work in India.

An administrative reorganisation took place in 2008. This led to all the Secretariat departments being brought together in one building under the leadership of a National Secretary with the result that, for the first time, the National Secretariat functions as a whole and not as separate departments.

THE SALVATION ARMY ASSOCIATION

Chairman: Comr M. C. James
National Sec: Lt-Col Davidson Varghese

Business Administration: Capt Emmanuel Masih
Communications: Maj Ashok K. Dushing
Editorial and Publications: Maj Sanjivani Dushing (Editor)
Human Resources Development and Education: Capt Hnamte Lalramliana
Social, Health and Emergencies: Capt Raj Paul Thamalapakula
Women's Advisory Council: Capt C. Lalhriatpuii

THE SALVATION ARMY CHRISTIAN RETREAT CONFERENCE CENTRE

'Surrenden', 15-18 Orange Grove Rd, Coonoor – 643 101, Nilgiris Dt, Tamil Nadu, S India; tel: (0423) 2230242

Right: a seminar for parents in **INDIA SOUTH EASTERN** deals with human trafficking

Above: the Territorial Songsters in **INDIA EASTERN** break the world record in bamboo dancing

Left: relief aid is distributed to tropical storm victims in **INDIA NORTHERN**

INDIA CENTRAL TERRITORY

Territorial leaders:
Commissioners M. Y. Emmanuel and T. Regina Chandra Bai

Territorial Commander:
Commissioner M. Y. Emmanuel (1 Dec 2006)

Chief Secretary:
Lieut-Colonel P. T. Abraham (1 Mar 2007)

Territorial Headquarters: 31 (15) Ritherdon Road, Vepery, Chennai 600 007

Postal address: PO Box 453, Vepery, Chennai 600 007, India

Tel: [91] (044) 2532 3148; fax: [91] (044) 2532 5987; email: ICT_mail@ICT.salvationarmy.org; website: www.salvationarmy.org/ind

The India Central Territory comprises three regions – North Tamil Nadu (Madras-Chennai), Karnataka and Andhra Pradesh. Salvation Army work commenced at Vijayawada in Andhra Pradesh in 1895 by Staff Captain Abdul Aziz, a person of Muslim background, with his friend Mahanada. Captain Abdul attended a revival meeting led by Captain Henry Bullard in 1884 at Bangalore and subsequently dedicated himself to be a Salvation Army officer. The territory was named the India Central Territory in 1992, with its headquarters at Madras (Chennai).

Zone: South Asia
States included in the territory: Andhra Pradesh, Karnataka, Tamil Nadu
'The Salvation Army' in Tamil: Ratchania Senai; in Telugu: Rakshana Sinyamu
Languages in which the gospel is preached: English, Tamil, Telugu
Periodicals: *Home League Magazine, Udyogasthudu, Yovana Veerudu, Yudha Dwani*

THE year 2009 began with the territorial theme – 'Sanctify Yourselves' – being announced and introduced at all corps throughout the territory. Events during the year were given this emphasis.

Conducting reviews of extension areas that had been opened, the Territorial Commander met extension officers at Bapatla and heard enthusiastic reports of progress. House visitation had attracted people to Sunday and weekday meetings (held in rented school buildings if there were no prayer halls or established church buildings); social and humanitarian services were established as a result of financial support from well-wishers. In some areas, friends donated musical instruments and other items to enhance the worship.

A Salvation Army flag was presented to the newly opened outpost at Sholinganalloor (Chennai Division). More than 60 adults and children were present; regular meetings are attracting increasing attendances.

Bible study classes have been started in all the children's homes. This is additional to the young people's usual attendance at Sunday school and other children's activities in nearby corps. With the support of the All-India Sunday School Association, training was conducted in five centres and 265 young people were equipped to teach Sunday school classes in their respective corps.

The visit of Commissioners Lalkiamlova and Lalhlimpuii (IS and ZSWM, South Asia) brought a spirit of revival to the territory. They conducted youth councils, when more than 3,000 delegates attended, and at the close of the event a number of young people dedicated themselves to fuller service in their corps.

During officers councils at Bapatla the next day, the IS presented 90-year-old Commissioner Mannam Samuel with the insignia of the Order of the Founder – in acknowledgement of 'his compassionate ministry to the marginalised and unreached people of India'. The TC conducted the ordination and commissioning of 31 officers of the Prayer Warriors Session.

Commemorating 127 years of The Salvation Army in India, a special function at Periamet Social Services Centre, Chennai, on 19 September 2009 was attended by the Mayor of Chennai and Sub-Collector, who both spoke warmly of the Army's ministry to the needy. Food parcels were supplied to underprivileged

people present for the occasion. Also, new clothing and dresses collected from Army friends and well-wishers have been distributed to 500 poor men and women.

With money raised through the helping-hand scheme, the Women's Ministries Department has provided disabled women with tricycles to assist them in their income-generating street sales.

STATISTICS

Officers 728 (active 554 retired 174) **Cadets** 31 **Employees** 518
Corps 272 **Outposts** 162 **Societies** 145 **Institutions** 14 **Schools and Colleges** 71 **Day Care Centres** 3 **Clinic** 1 **Homes and Hostels** 20
Senior Soldiers 71,529 **Adherents** 8,729 **Junior Soldiers** 9,928

STAFF

Women's Ministries: Comr T. Regina Chandra Bai (TPWM) Lt-Col C. Mariamma Abraham (TSWM) Maj S. Vimalakumari (THLS) Maj Yesuamma (TLOMS) Maj Rajeswari (S&GSS) Maj D. Mani Kumari (TWDO)
Editor: Maj B. Annamani
Education: Maj A. Nathaniel
Emergencies: Maj O. Philip Raju
Field: Maj S. P. Abbulu
Finance: Maj John Kumar Dasari
Human Resources Development: Maj K. Yesudas
Music and Creative Arts: Capt Prabathkumar
Evangelism and Outreach: Maj M. Prakasha Rao
Property and Projects: Maj B. G. Prakash Rao
Social: Maj K. Yesu Dhana Kumar
Sponsorship: Capt I. D. Ebenezer
Trade: Maj Yesamma (O-i-C)
Training: Maj John Williams
Youth: Maj B. Joseph

DIVISIONS

Bapatla: Bapatla, Guntur District, 522 101; tel: (086432) 23931; Majs D. Joshi and Leela Mani
Chennai: 109 Gangadeeswara Koil St, Chennai 600 084; tel: (044) 2641 5021; Majs K. Suvarna Raju and K. Jhansi Bai

Eluru: Adivarapupet, Eluru, West Godavari District, 534 005; tel: (08812) 237484; Majs S. Jayananda Rao and Christiansen

Gudivada: Krishna District, 521 301; tel: (08764) 243524; Majs M. Daniel and M. Rachel Raju

Hyderabad: 6d Walker Town, Padmarao Nagar, Secunderabad, 500 025; tel: (040) 27502610; Majs G. V. Ratnam and Rajakumari

Nellore: Dargamitta, Nellore, 524 003; tel: (0861) 2322 589; Majs P. Samuel Rathan and P. Ananda Kumari

Rajahmundry: Mallayapet, East Godavari District, 533 105; tel: (0883) 5579200; Majs K. Y. Raj Kumar Babu and K. Y. Krupa Bai

Tanuku: West Godavari District, 534 211; tel: (08819) 225366; Majs Kaki Sundar Rao and K. Dasaratna Kumari

Tenali: Ithanagar, Tenali, Guntur District, 522 201; tel: (08644) 225949; Majs M. P. Prasad and Krupamma

Vijayawada: nr Gymkhana Club, Eastside H. No 26-191/2, Ghandi Nagar, Vijayawada, 521 003; tel: (0866) 2575168; Majs K. Samuel Raju and K. Raja Kumari

DISTRICTS

Bangalore: Karnataka Main Rd, J. P. Nagar, Bangalore, 560 078, Karnataka State; Maj P. Rajan

Divi: PO Nagayalanka, Krishna District, 521 120; tel: (08671) 274991; Maj N. Jeeva Ratnam

Machilipatnam: The Salvation Army, Edepalli, Door No 15/344, Machilipatnam; Maj Chella Wycliff

Mandavalli: Station Rd, Mandavalli, Krishna District, 521 345; tel: (08677) 280503; Maj Chella Solomon Raju

Prakasam: Stuartpuram, Guntur District, 522 317; tel: (086432) 271131; Maj Valley Prabhadus

EXTENSION AREAS
(under THQ)

Chittor: The Salvation Army, c/o Kamalamma Samuel, D No 4 – 84, Balaji Nagar, Greamspet, Chittor

Kadapa: The Salvation Army, c/o Mr M. Ajay Kumar, D No 2/147 – 3, Balaji Nagar, Kadapa, 515 003; tel: (098660) 77318

Khammam: The Salvation Army, c/o Ch. Prabhakara Rao, D No 4-2-119, Sreenagar Colony, nr Mamatha Medical College, Khammam

Kurnool: The Salvation Army, c/o Y. A. Evangeline, D No 40 – 448, A1A,

Gipson Colony, Kurnool; tel: (09391) 107852

Mahabub Nagar: The Salvation Army, Venkateswara Colony, behind Jagadhamba Temple, Laxmi Nager Colony, Mahabub Nagar District

Nalgonda: The Salvation Army, H No 7-1-155/D/19/4, Aruna Nilayam, Srinagar Colony, Panagal Rd, Nalgonda PO and District

Rangareddy: The Salvation Army, H No 20 – 45, Madhuranagar, Shamshebad, Rangareddy District

Warangal: The Salvation Army, H No 7 – 91, Gorry Kunta Crossroad, Labour Colony, Warangal

TRAINING COLLEGE
Dargamitta, Nellore, 524 003; tel: (0861) 2322687

CONFERENCE AND TRAINING CENTRE
Vadarevu: nr Chirala, Prakasam District

HUMAN RESOURCES DEVELOPMENT
PB9, Nidubrolu, Guntur District 522 123; tel: (08643) 243447

EDUCATION
College (with hostel for boys and girls)
William Booth Junior College, Bapatla, Guntur District, 522 101; tel: (086432) 24259

Community College
Virugambakkam, Chennai

High Schools (with hostels for boys and girls)
Bapatla: Guntur District, 522 101; tel: (086432) 24282 (acc 300)
Stuartpuram: Prakasham District, 522 317; tel: (086432) 271131 (acc 150)

Upper Primary School
Dargamitta, Nellore, Nellore District

Elementary Schools (Telugu Medium)
Bapatla Division: Bethapudi, Chintayapalem, Gudipudi, Kattivaripalem, Mallolapalem, MR Nagar, Murukondapadu, Valluvaripalem, Perlipadu, Pasumarthivaripalem, Pedapalli, Parli Vadapalem, Yaramvaripalem, Yazali

Eluru Division: Bhogapuram, Dendulur, Gopavaram, Gandivarigudem, Kovvali, Musunur, Pathamupparru, Surappagudem, Velpucharla

Gudivada Division: Chinaparupudi, Edulamadalli, Guraza, Gajulapadu, Gudivada, Kodur, Kancharlapalem, Kornipadu, Mandavalli, Narasannapalem, Pedaparupudi, Ramapuram

Nellore Division: Alluru, Buchireddipalem, Chowkacherla, Iskapalli, Kakupalli, Kanapartipadu, Mudivarthi, Modegunta, North Mopur, Pallaprolu, Rebala

Tenali Division: Annavaram, Burripalem, Chukkapallivaripalem, Duggirala, Danthuluru, Emani, Ithanagar, Kollipara, Kattivaram, Nambur, Nelapadu

Prakasam District: Cherukuru, Stuartpuram

Primary Schools (English Medium)

The Haven, 21 Thiru Narayanaguru Rd, Choolai, Chennai 600 112; tel: (044) 26612784

Teachers' Colony, Vijayawada 500 008, Krishna District; tel: (0866) 2479854

Hyderabad, 6D Walker Town, Padmarao Nagar PO, Secunderabad 500 025 (with day care centre)

Nidubrolu; Villivakkam and Chennai; Hosur-Karnataka

English Medium High School

Teachers' Colony, Vijayawada 500 008; tel: (0866) 2479854

English Medium Matriculation School

The Haven, 21 Tiru Narayanaguru Rd, Choolai, Chennai 600 112; tel: (044) 2661 2784

English Medium Upper Primary School

B. H. Puram, Mangalagir Post, Vijayawada

Residential School

Tissot Sunrise School, PB9 Bapatla, 522 101; tel: (086432) 23336 (acc 125)

Vocational Training Centre

Adivarpet, Eluru, West Godivari District, 534 005 (with boys' hostel); tel: (08812) 550070

MEDICAL WORK

Evangeline Booth Hospital: Nidubrolu, Guntur District, 522 123; tel: (08643) 2522124 (acc 100)

Evangeline Booth Hospital (with home for the aged), Bapatla, Guntur District, 522 101; tel: (086432) 24134 (acc 75)

Clinic: Dindi, Nagayalanka PO, Nagayalanka Mandal, Krishna District, 521 120

HIV/Aids Programme

The Salvation Army, H. No 7-1-155/D/19/4, Aruna Nilayam, Srinagr Colony, Panagal Rd, Nalagonda PO

SOCIAL WORK
Children's Homes and Hostels
Boys' Hostels

Mallayyapet, Rajahmundry; tel: (0883) 2427926 (acc 40)

Virugambakkam, Chennai; tel: (044) 23772723 (acc 80)

Girls' Hostels

Adivarpet, Eluru; tel: (08812) 226048 (acc 60)

Catherine Booth Girls' Hostel, Tenali (acc 30)

Gudivada, Krishna District; tel: (08674) 240739 (acc 25)

'Home of Peace', Tanuku; tel: (08819) 229163 (acc 30)

Miriam Girls' Hostel, Kaikaluru, Mandavalli (acc 30)

Nagayalanka; tel: (08671) 274512 (acc 24)

Virugambakkam, Chennai; tel: (044) 23770400 (acc 70)

Boys' and Girls' Hostels

Nellore; tel: (0861) 2340202 (acc 120)

Stuartpuram, Bapatla Mandal; tel: (08643) 71307 (acc 80, 8 girls)

c/o William Booth Junior College, Bapatla, Guntur District, 522 101; tel: (086432) 24259

Old Age Home

Virugambakkam, Chennai; tel: (044) 23770400 (acc 70)

Working Women's Hostel

The Haven, 21 Thiru Narayanaguru Rd, Choolai, Chennai 600 112; tel: (044) 2532 1789

Day Care Centre

21 Thiru Narayanaguru Rd, Choolai, Chennai 600 112; tel: (044) 2532 1789

Red Shield Guest House

15/31 Ritherdon Rd, Vepery, Chennai 600 007; tel: (044) 2532 1821 (acc 60)

Waste Paper and Free Feeding Programmes

6D Walker Town, Secunderabad 500 025, AP

8 Perianna Maistry St, Periamet, Chennai-3

INDIA EASTERN TERRITORY

Territorial Commander:
Colonel Lalngaihawmi (1 Jan 2011)

Chief Secretary:
Lieut-Colonel Lalramhluna (1 Jan 2011)

Territorial Headquarters: PO Box 5, Aizawl 796001, Mizoram, India

Tel: [91] 389 2322290 (EPABX)/321864; fax: [91] 389 2326123;
email: IET_mail@IET.salvationarmy.org; website: www.salvationarmy.org/ind

Work in the region commenced on 26 April 1917 when Lieutenant Kawlkhuma, the first Mizo officer commissioned in India, returned to start the Army work. He was then joined by a group of earnest believers who shared his vision of an 'Army like a church, very much in line with The Salvation Army'. India Eastern became a separate command on 1 June 1991 and became a territory in 1993. Work was officially opened in Nepal on 26 April 2009

Zone: South Asia

States included in the territory: Arunachal Pradesh, Assam, Manipur, Meghalaya, Mizoram, Nagaland, Sikkim, Tripura, West Bengal; also the Federal Democratic Republic of Nepal (part)

'The Salvation Army' in Mizo: Chhandamna Sipai Pawl

Languages in which the gospel is preached: Adhibasi, Bengali, Bru, English, Hindi, Hmar, Manipuri (Meitei), Mizo, Nagamese, Nepali, Paite, Pali, Simte, Thadou, Vaiphai

Periodicals: *Sipai Tlangau* (Mizo *War Cry*), *The Officer* (Mizo), *Young Salvationist* (Mizo), *Chunnunpar* (Mizo Women's Ministries magazine) *Naupang Sipai* (Mizo *Young Soldier*)

SALVATION Army Youth (SAY) groups are enthusiastically engaged in evangelism and humanitarian ministry. At Aizawl Temple Corps, for example, the SAY group runs its 'Feed the Needs' programme, seeking out young people who have been ostracised because of their immoral or anti-social behaviour.

Unwanted, they resort to living in dire need on the streets. Christ's love compels the SAY members to regularly provide dinner to more than 350 of these street-dwellers. They share their faith and pray with them, and consequently some have started attending meetings at the corps.

Keen to be involved in the Army's expansion, SAY groups and young people's corps helped to construct three meeting halls, two missionary quarters and an outreach mission school. They raised the resources, visited the outreach centres and got involved 'hands on' in the building work. During the evenings they shared the gospel as they took part in meetings.

Marking the 93rd anniversary of The Salvation Army in Mizoram, SAY group members donated 763 units of blood to government hospitals in Aizawl. Other groups organised Christmas charity concerts in various locations. These raised funds to sponsor children in several homes and to purchase gifts for prisoners as well as Christmas presents for other needy recipients.

During the Christmas season a total of 92,247 rupees was received from the public through the Christmas Red Kettle Appeal on roadsides and in market places. Christmas gifts were purchased for patients at two tuberculosis hospitals, a hospice and an HIV/Aids hospital. A donation was also given to the Poor Fund at Aizawl Civil Hospital.

Mr P. C. Zoramsangliana – a government minister in Mizoram and assistant corps sergeant-major at Dawrpuivergthar – launched an anti-trafficking programme. He assured the territory of the government's support for this campaign.

The 22 members of the Territorial Songsters formed one of the teams among 11,200 youthful participants from Mizoram State who made a successful attempt to break the world record in bamboo dancing.

STATISTICS

Officers 288 (active 221 retired 67) **Cadets** 17 **Employees** 371
Corps 233 **Societies/Outposts** 100 **Social Institutions** 12 **Schools** 17
Senior Soldiers 35,258 **Adherents** 2,103 **Junior Soldiers** 9,673

STAFF

Women's Ministries: Col Lalngaihawmi (TPWM) Lt-Col Kawlramthangi (TSWM) Maj Thantluangi (THLS) Maj Vanlalnungi (Dir, Special Services) Maj Thanzuali (LOM) Maj K. C. Ropari (SAMF) Maj J Lalpianpuii (WDO) Maj K. Lalchhuanmawii (OSS)

Maj Biaksailovi (Prayer Fellowship)
Maj Lalchhuanmawii (Fundraising)
Maj Hoihniang (Retired and Pensioned Officers Fellowship) Maj Lalfakzuali (Literature) Maj Ramthanmawii (Officers' Children) Maj Lalbiaktluangi (FLC)
Lt Lalnunmawii (Asst to TPWM)
Community Health Action Network (CHAN): under THQ
Editor and Communications:
Maj Chawnghluna
Education: Maj Lalhriatpuia
Finance: Maj Shamu Meitei
Human Resources and Development:
Maj Khaizadinga
Music and Creative Arts: Maj Laithanmawia
Outreach: Maj Hrangngura
Personnel: Maj Thanhlira
Projects and Sponsorship: Maj Vanlalfela
Property and Legal: Maj Jonathan Thanruma
Public Relations: Maj Laithanmawia
Social: Maj Lianhlira
Territorial Songsters: S/L K. Zohmingthanga
Trade: Maj K. Lalrinawma
Training: Maj Zothanmawia
Youth and Candidates: Maj Lalmuansanga

DIVISIONS

Central North: PO Aizawl, 796 001, Mizoram; tel: (0389) 2317097; Majs Sangchhunga and Vanlalauvi
Central South: PO Kulikawn, 796005, Aizawl – Mizoram; tel: (0389) 2300246; Majs Lalhmingliana and Lalhlimpuii
Himalayan: 8 Bylane Zoo Narengi Rd, nr SBI Geeta Nagar Branch, PO Box 65, Guwahati – 781021, Assam; tel/fax: (0361) 2413405; Majs S. T. Dula and Malsawmi
Manipur: Salvation Rd, PO Churachanpur, 795 128, Manipur; tel: (3874) 233188; Majs Lianthanga and Ringliani
Southern: PO Lunglei, 796 701, Mizoram; tel: (95372) 2324027; Majs C. Dawngliana and H. Manthangi
Western: PO Kolasib, 796 081, Mizoram; tel: (3837) 220037; Majs S. Biakliana and Biakmawii

UNDER THQ

Nepal: PO Box 8975, EPC-1677, Kathmandu, Nepal; tel: 00977-1-5537552; mobile: 00977-9851093256; email: sangliana@sify.com; Majs Lalsangliana and Lalunsangi (Extension Officers)

TRAINING COLLEGE

Kolasib Vengthar, PO Kolasib, 796 081,
Mizoram; tel: (3837) 220466

EDUCATION
Special Residential Schools for the Physically Challenged

Mary Scott Home for the Blind: Kalimpong,
West Bengal; tel: (3552) 255252;
email: sa_msh_kpg@yahoo.co.in (acc 80)
School for Deaf and Dumb Children:
Darjeeling, West Bengal;
tel: (354) 2252332/2257645
email: sadeaf@sify.com (acc 50)

Higher Secondary Schools

Children's Training Higher Secondary School:
Churachandpur, Manipur; tel: (3874) 235097
Modern English Higher Secondary School:
Aizawl, Mizoram; tel: (389) 2323248

High Schools

Blue Mount: Behliangchhip, Zampui, Tripura
Booth Tucker Memorial School: Gahrodpunjee,
Cachar
Hermon Junior: Moreh, Manipur
School for the Blind (Junior High School):
Kalimpong

Middle Schools

Children's Education School: Zezaw, Manipur
Children's Training School: Singngat, Manipur
Booth Tucker: Thingkangphai, Manipur
Hermon Junior: Moreh, Manipur
SA Middle School: Saikawt, Manipur
School for the Deaf: Darjeeling
Willow Mount: Durtlang, Mizoram

Primary School

Integrated Primary School: Kolasib

Outreach Schools: 27

SOCIAL WORK
Home for Boys and Girls

Mary Scott Home for the Blind: Kalimpong,
West Bengal
Hostel for the Deaf and Dumb: Darjeeling,
West Bengal

Homes for Boys

Hostel for the Blind: Kolasib, Mizoram;
tel: (3837) 220236 (acc 25)
Enna In: Kolasib; tel: (3837) 221419 (acc 30)

Kawlkhuma Home: Lunglei; tel: (372) 224420
(acc 25)
Muanna In: Mualpui, Aizawl; tel: (389) 2320426
(acc 30)
Manipur Boys' Home: Mualvaiphei,
Churachandpur; tel: (3874) 235469 (acc 25)
Saiha Orphanage; tel: (3835) 226140 (acc 15)
Silchar Home (acc 20)

Home for Girls

Hlimna In: Keifang, Mizoram;
tel: (389) 2862278 (acc 65)

Motherless Babies' Homes

Aizawl: Tuikal 'A', Aizawl, Mizoram;
tel: (389) 2329868 (acc 35)
Manipur: Mualvaiphei, Churachandpur,
Manipur; tel: (3874) 235469 (acc 10)

Community Caring Programme

Churachandpur, Manipur; tel: (3874) 235469

Deafness Reduction Programme

Darjeeling, West Bengal

HIV/AIDS PROGRAMME
Community Health Action Network (CHAN)

Kawlkhuma Bldg, Tuikal 'A', PO Box 5,
Aizawl 796001; tel: (389) 2320202/2327609;
fax: (389) 2326106;
email: chanaizawl@sancharnet.in

CENTENARY PRESS

PO Box 5, Tuikal 'A', Aizawl, Mizoram;
tel: (389) 2329626

INDIA NORTHERN TERRITORY

Territorial leaders:
Commissioners Kashinath and Kusum Lahase

Territorial Commander:
Commissioner Kashinath Lahase
(1 Jan 2006)

Chief Secretary:
Lieut-Colonel Paul Christian (1 Dec 2006)

Territorial Headquarters: Flat No 103, Aashirwad Complex, D-1, Green Park, New Delhi 110 016, India

Tel: [91] (11) 2651 2394; fax: [91] (11) 2651 6912; email: INT_mail@INT.salvationarmy.org;

website: www.salvationarmy.org/ind

Shortly after arriving in India in 1882, Booth-Tucker visited major cities in northern India, including Allahabad, Delhi, Lucknow, Benares and Kolkata (Calcutta). Rural work was established later and operations were extended to Bihar and Orissa. The boundaries of the India Northern Territory have changed over the years; there have been headquarters in Gurdaspur, Bareilly, Lucknow, Benares and Kolkata and more recently Delhi. In 1947, part of the territory became Pakistan. The present territory was established on 1 June 1991.

Zone: South Asia
The territory is comprised of: the States of Bihar, Chattisgarh, Haryana, Himachal Pradesh, Jammu and Kashmir, Jharkhand, Orissa, Punjab, Uttar Anchal, Uttar Pradesh, Uttara Khand, West Bengal; the Union Territories of Delhi, Chandigarh, and the Andaman and Nicobar Islands
'The Salvation Army' in Hindi, Punjabi and Urdu: Mukti Fauj
Languages in which the gospel is preached: Bengali, English, Hindi, Kui, Nepali, Oriya, Punjabi, Santhali, Tamil, Urdu
Periodicals: *Home League Yearly* (Hindi and English), *Mukti Samachar* (Hindi and Punjabi), *The Officer* (Hindi), *Yuva Sipai* (Hindi)

MORE than 10,000 people attended meetings when the then Chief of the Staff, Commissioner Robin Dunster, supported by Lieut-Colonel Edna Williams (IHQ), campaigned in the territory (6-13 October 2009). Salvationists were greatly encouraged by the Chief's ministry and many made decisions for Christ at the mercy seat.

Commissioners Maxwell and Lenora Feener (territorial leaders of USA Southern) and Lieut-Colonels Henry and Doris Gonzalez (DC and DDWM, Texas Division) were special guests at the ordination and commissioning of 47 officers of the Prayer Warriors Session at Booth Tucker Hall, Batala (18 April 2010). The USA Southern Territory gave financial help to purchase 24 bicycles for new lieutenants (23 couples and a single officer) while Texas Division purchased bicycles for new cadets of the Friends Of Christ Session.

The day after the commissioning 3,000 young people gathered at Batala for a youth congress.

Four new corps were opened – in Mukerian District and the Patiala and Bajpur Extension Areas – while Ghoga Corps (Batala Division) and Gumtala Corps (Amritsar Division) were reopened.

People receiving daily meals at the Army's free feeding programme in Kolkata and New Delhi are attending Sunday meetings on a regular basis. Most of them are from non-Christian backgrounds but seeds of faith are being sown in their lives. Many street children who find a livelihood from garbage and waste tips are having their lives transformed while in The Salvation Army' care.

Women's Ministries officers are making regular visits into their local communities to give counselling regarding child labour and human trafficking, also providing health and sanitation education. Women officers at THQ are making *kurtas* and undertaking embroidery work as part of an income-generation programme.

Some 460 self-help groups and 12 federations are functioning effectively in the territory, particularly in rural areas. The programmes involve more than 5,500 women who live below the poverty line.

Salvation Army emergency relief teams distributed aid to victims of Cyclone Aila in West Bengal State. Food, tarpaulin for temporary shelters and ground mats were distributed to 300 families. When a tropical storm hit Bihar and West Bengal, 400 families received tarpaulin and bamboo.

STATISTICS

Officers 483 (active 393 retired 90)
Employees 271
Corps 153 **Outposts** 384 **Societies** 737
Institutions 33 **Schools** 9 **College** 1
Senior Soldiers 62,218 **Adherents** 2,432 **Junior Soldiers** 7,866

STAFF

Women's Ministries: Comr Kusum K. Lahase (TPWM) Lt-Col Anandi Christian (TSWM) Maj Mariam Parkash (THLS)
Church Growth: Maj Robin Kumar Sahu
Editor: Maj Yaqoob Masih
Education and Disasters: Maj Tarsem Masih
Field: Maj Parkash Masih
Finance: Maj Thomas Gera
   Territorial Auditor: Maj Sulakhan Masih
Human Resources: Maj Dilip Singh
Legal and Community Development:
   Maj Samir Patra
Music Ministry: Maj Swinder Masih
Property and Projects: Maj Kashmir Masih
Public Relations and Fundraising: Capt Robin
Social: Maj Joginder Masih
Spiritual Development: Maj Vijayapal Singh
Training: Maj Baldev Nayak
Youth and Candidates: Maj Philip Nayak

DIVISIONS

Amritsar: 25 Krishna Nagar, Lawrence Rd, Amritsar 143 001, Punjab; Majs Makhan and Sunila Masih
Angul: Sikhayak Pada, Angul Post, Angul District 759 122, Orissa; tel: 06764-211271; Majs Dilip and Nivedita Singh
Bareilly: 220 Civil Lines, Bareilly 243 001, UP; tel: 05812-427081; Majs Lazar and Sharbati Masih
Batala: Dera Baba Nanak Rd, Batala 143 505, Dist Gurdaspur, Punjab; tel: 01871-243038; Majs Gurnam and Razia Masih
Beas: Ajeet Nagar, Beas, Amritsar 143 201, Punjab; tel: 01853-273834; Majs Manuel and Anita Masih

Chandigarh: Surajpur Rd, Firojpur,
  PO Dhamala Via Pinjore, Dist Panchkula,
  Haryana 134 102; tel: 01733-654946;
  Majs Gian and Salima Masih
Dera Baba Nanak: Dist Gurdaspur,
  PO Dera Baba Nanak 143 604, Punjab;
  tel: 01871-247262; Majs Daniel and
  Parveen Gill
Gurdaspur: Jail Rd, Dist Gurdaspur 143 521,
  Punjab; tel: 01874-220622; Majs Piara and
  Grace Masih
Kolkata: 37 Lenin Saranee, Kolkata 700 013;
  tel: 033-55101591; fax: 033-22493910;
  Capts George and Veera Patric
Moradabad: Kanth Rd, nr Gandhi Ashram PAC,
  Moradabad 244 001; tel: 09897-358114;
  Majs Manga and Roseleen Masih

DISTRICTS

Jasidih: Deoghar Rd, Ramchanderpur, Jasidih,
  Jharkand – 814 142; Maj Chotka Hembrom
Mukerian: Rikhipura Mohalla,
  Dist Hoshiyarpur, Mukerian – 144 211,
  Punjab; tel: 01883-248733; Maj Peter Masih

EXTENSION WORK

Pathankot: Daulatpur Rd, Prem Nagar,
  nr FCI Godown, Pathankot – 145001, Punjab;
  tel: 09463-970566; Maj Salamat Masih
Patiala: c/o Mr Roshan Lal, H. No. 5193,
  Urban Estate, Patiala – 147002 Punjab;
  tel: 09872-39915; Maj Gurcharan Masih
Port Blair: Prothrapur, nr Atta Chakki,
  PO Garacharma, Port Blair – 744105,
  Andaman Nicobar Islands;
  Capt Arun Biswas
Shahjahanpur and Lucknow: 43A Church Rd,
  Vishnupuri, Aliganj, Lucknow – 226001, UP;
  Capt Sanjay Robinson
Taran Taran: Sandhu Ave, nr Shota Kazi
  Kot Rd, Ward 11, Taran Taran – 143401,
  Dist Amritsar, Punjab; Maj Piara Lal
Uttara Khand – Bajpur: c/o Mr Matloob Masih,
  Indira Colony, Baria Rd, Bajpur Udham
  Singh Nagar – 261 401, Uttara Khand;
  mobile: 91-9758635462; Maj Masih Dayal

TRAINING COLLEGE

Bareilly: 220 Civil Lines, Bareilly 243 001, UP;
  tel: 0581-2423304

MEDICAL WORK
Hospital

MacRobert Hospital: Dhariwal,
  Dist Gurdaspur 143 519, Punjab;
  tel: 01874-275152/275274 (acc 50)

Clinics

Social Service Centre: 172 Acharya Jagdish
  Chandra Bose Rd, Kolkata 700 014;
  tel: 033-22840441
Community Health Centre: 192-A, Arjun Nager,
  New Delhi 110 029; tel: 011-26168895
Eye Hospital: Surajpur Rd, Firojpur,
  PO Dhamala via Pinjore, Dist Panchkula,
  Haryana 134 102; tel: 01733-654946
HIV/Aids Clinic: 220 Civil Lines,
  Bareilly 243 001, UP; tel: 0581-2427081

EDUCATION
Senior Secondary School

Aliwal Rd, Batala 143 505, Dist Gurdaspur,
  Punjab; tel: 01871-242593 (acc 900)

Extension Branch

Gurdaspur School: The Salvation Army DHQ
  Compound, Jail Rd, Dist Gurdaspur,
  Punjab; tel: 01874-20622

English Medium Schools

Behala: 671 D. H. Rd, Hindustan Park, Behala,
  Kolkata 700034; tel: 033-23972692
Moradabad: Kanth Rd, opp Gandhi Ashram PAC,
  Moradabad 244 001, UP;
  tel: 0591-2417351/2429184 (acc 400)
William Booth Memorial School:
  220 Civil Lines, Bareilly 243001, UP;
  tel: 0581-2420007 (acc 200)

College

Catherine Booth College for Girls: Aliwal Rd,
  Batala 143 505, Dist Gurdaspur, Punjab;
  tel: 01871-242593 (acc 300)

Non-residential Tailoring Units

Dera Baba Nanak: Dist Gurdaspur, Punjab
Kancharapada: West Bengal
New Delhi: H-15, Green Park Extn,
  New Delhi – 110 016

SOCIAL WORK
Free Feeding Programmes

Kolkata: 172 Acharya Jagadish Chandra Rd,
  Kolkata 700 014 (beneficiaries 250)
New Delhi: 6 Malik Bldg, Chunamundi,
  Paharganj, New Delhi 110 055;
  tel: 011-23588433 (beneficiaries 150)

Homes for the Aged

Bareilly: 220 Civil Lines, Bareilly 243 001, UP;
  tel: 0581-2421432 (acc 20)
Dhariwal: MacRobert Hospital, Dhariwal,
  Dist Gurdaspur 143 519, Punjab;

tel: 01874-275152/275274 (acc 20)
Kolkata: 172 Acharya Jagadish Chandra Rd,
  Kolkata 700 014 (acc 15)

Homes for Boys

Angul: Angul 759 122, Orissa;
  tel: 06764-232829 (acc 10)
Batala: Aliwal Rd, Batala 143 505,
  Dist Gurdaspur (acc 60)
Bhubaneswar: AT – Damana, Plot No 275,
  PO, Housing Board, Chandra Sekhar Pur,
  Bhubaneswar – 751016, Orissa (acc 26)
Kolkata: 37 Lenin Saranee, Kolkata 700 013;
  tel: 033-55124567 (acc 30)
Moradabad: Kanth Rd, Moradabad 244 001, UP;
  tel: 0591-2417351 (acc 40)
Simultala: Simultala 811 316, Dist Jamui, Bihar
  (acc 43)

Homes for Girls

Angul: Angul 759 122, Orissa; tel: 06764-232829
  (acc 40)
Bareilly: 220 Civil Lines, Bareilly 243 001, UP;
  tel: 0581-2421432 (acc 40)
Batala: Aliwal Rd, Batala 143505,
  Dist Gurdaspur (acc 60)
Behala: 671 D. H. Rd, Hindustan Park, Behala,
  Kolkata 700034; tel: 033-23972692
  (acc 120)
Gurdaspur: Jail Rd, Dist Gurdaspur 143 521,
  Punjab (acc 100)

Hostels
Blind (Men)

172 Acharya Jagadish Chandra Rd, Kolkata
  700 014 (acc 30)

Working Men and Students

172 Acharya Jagadish Chandra Rd,
  Kolkata 700 014; tel: 033-22840441 (acc 200)

Young Women

Bareilly: 220 Civil Lines, Bareilly 243 001, UP;
  tel: 0581-2421432
Kolkata: 38 Lenin Saranee, Kolkata 700 013;
  tel: 033-22274281 (acc 50)
Ludhiana: 2230, ISA Nagari, Ludhiana – 141 008,
  Punjab

RED SHIELD GUEST HOUSE

Kolkata: 2 Saddar St, Kolkata 700 016;
  tel: 033-22861659 (acc 80)

TRANSIT HOUSE

New Delhi: P-2 S Extension, Part II,
  New Delhi 110 049; tel: 011-2625 7310

VEER PROJECT

Kolkata: 172 Acharya Jagadish Chandra Rd,
  Kolkata 700 014
New Delhi: 6 Malik Bldg, Chunamundi, Paharganj,
  New Delhi 110 055; tel: 011-2358 8433.

WASTE PAPER DEPARTMENT

6 Malik Bldg, Chunamundi, Paharganj,
  New Delhi 110 055; tel: 011-2358 8433

**Below: A Salvationist supervises
members of a self-help group
in making carrier bags from waste
cement bags. These are sold to
help support their families.**

INDIA SOUTH EASTERN TERRITORY

Territorial leaders:
Commissioners M. C. and Susamma James

Territorial Commander:
Commissioner M. C. James (1 Dec 2006)

Chief Secretary:
Lieut-Colonel Thumati Vijayakumar (1 May 2008)

**Territorial Headquarters: High Ground Road, Maharajanagar PO,
Tirunelveli – 627 011, Tamil Nadu, India**

Tel: [91] (462) 2574331/2574313; fax: [91] (462) 2577152;
email: ISE_mail@ISE.salvationarmy.org; website: www.salvationarmy.org/ind

The Salvation Army commenced operations in south-east India on 27 May 1892 as a result of the vision received by Major Deva Sundaram at Medicine Hill, while praying and fasting with three officers when the persecution in Southern Tamil Nadu was at its height. On 1 October 1970 the Tamil-speaking part of the Southern India Territory became a separate entity as the Army experienced rapid growth.

Zone: South Asia
States included in the territory: Pondicherry, Tamil Nadu
'The Salvation Army' in Tamil: Ratchaniya Senai; in Malayalam: Raksha Sainyam
Languages in which the gospel is preached: English, Malayalam, Tamil
Periodicals: *Chiruveeran* (Tamil), *Home League Quarterly*, *Poresatham* (Tamil), *The Officer* (Tamil)

INNOVATIVE fundraising by the territory's home league members and through sponsorship from USA Western made it possible to improve facilities at the training college. In April 2010 territorial leaders Commissioners M. C. and Susamma James presided at the opening, when a new prayer room and library were dedicated to the glory of God.

Commissioner Susamma James unveiled a plaque in recognition of Women's Ministries groups that had raised funds to provide the library. It is hoped this addition will provide relevant resources in the training of

cadets and aid the spiritual development of the territory's Salvationists for many years.

A memorial tower was erected to mark the inauguration of Kanyakumari Division. There was great rejoicing when the territorial leaders visited Attaikulam Corps, the first to be established in the territory when the Army 'opened fire' in 1892.

The vocational training centre in Aramboly continued to train physically disabled men and boys in practical skills that will enable them to produce income-generating goods. Government officials were among invited guests to the centre's 41st anniversary celebratory meal at which 100 women's saris were distributed.

The Community Empowerment Programme established a further 21 self-help groups, taking the territorial total to more than 200, administered in clusters. Ongoing training in leadership, finance and project management was delivered. Staff and community volunteers worked together to enable families to improve their circumstances.

At East Kalungadi, Nagercoil, income-generation schemes provided families with opportunities to educate their children. Members of the Shamma women's group earned much-needed income through raising milch animals and poultry.

In Kuruvilaikadu, a self-help group with 15 members enabled new housing and toilet facilities to be constructed for five members. Health and environmental issues are addressed; large numbers of the community are advised on issues such as HIV/Aids and waste disposal.

STATISTICS

Officers 636 (active 472 retired 164)
Employees 724
Corps 307 **Outposts** 181 **Societies** 75
Schools 19 **Institutions** 45
Senior Soldiers 48,027 **Adherents** 17,228
Junior Soldiers 4,922
Personnel serving outside territory Officers 16

STAFF

Women's Ministries: Comr L. Susamma James (TPWM) Lt-Col Keraham Manikyam (TSWM) Maj Retnam (THLS)
Sec for Business Administration: Maj Appavoo Sam Devaraj
  Finance and Audit: Maj Jebamony Jayaseelan

Legal: Maj Swamidhas Nalladhas
Projects: Maj Ponniah Ashok Sundar
Sponsorship: Capt Kezial
Supplies: Maj Masilamony Yesudhason
Sec for Personnel Administration:
  Maj Arulappan Paramadhas
HRD: Maj Chellaiyan Anbayan
Training: Maj Jeyaraj Daniel Jebasingh Raj
Sec for Programme Administration:
  Maj Chelliah Mony
Health: Maj S P Simon
Literature and Editorial: Maj Yesudian Ponnappan
Projects and Development: Mr Benjamin Dhaya
Public Relations: Maj Abraham Jeyasekhar
Youth: Maj Yacob Selvam

DIVISIONS

Azhagiapandipuram: KK Dist PO, 629 852; tel: (04652) 281952; Lt-Cols Perinbanayagam Suthananthadhas and Esther Evangelin
Kanyakumari: Kadaigramam, Suchindram PO, KK Dist 629 704; tel: (04652) 243955); Majs Sundaram Motchakan and Selvabai
Kulasekharam: Kulasekharam PO, 629 161 KK Dist; tel: (04651) 279446; Majs Chelliah Swamidhas and Joicebai
Marthandam: Pammam, Marthandam PO, 629 165; tel: (04651) 272492; Majs Nallathanbi Edwin Sathyadhas and Gnana Jessy Bell
Nagercoil: Vetturnimadam PO, Nagercoil 629 003; tel: (04652) 272787; Majs Tharmar Alfred and Rajabai
Palayamcottai: 28 Bell Amorses Colony, Palayamcottai 627 002; tel: (0462) 2580093; Majs Job William and Daisybai
Radhapuram: Radhapuram PO, 627 111; tel: (04637) 254318; Majs Asirvatham Devadhas and Jothi Vasanthakumari
Tenkasi: Tenkasi PO, 627 811; tel: (04633) 280774; Majs Abel Bailis and Abaranam
Thuckalay: Mettukadai, Thuckalay PO, 629 175; tel: (04651) 252443; Majs Devasundaram Samuel Raj and Kanagamony
Valliyoor: Valliyoor PO, 627 117; tel: (04637) 221454; Majs Jeyaraj Samraj and Jessie

DISTRICTS

Coimbatore: Daniel Ngr, K. Vadamaduai PO, 641 017; tel: (0422) 2461277; Maj Daniel Dhason
Erode: 155 Amman Nager, Erode 638 002; tel: (0424) 2283909; Maj S. Yesuretinam

Madurai: TPK Rd, Palanganatham PO,
625 003; tel: (0452) 2370169;
Maj Geevanantham Kumaradhas

Trichy: New Town, Malakovil,
Thiruvarumbur 620 013; tel: (0431) 2510464;
Maj Yovan Dhason

Tuticorin: 5/254 G, Caldwell Colony,
Tuticorin 628 008; tel: (0461) 2376841;
Maj Sebagnanam James

Pondicherry Extension Area: opp Mahatma
Dental College, Kamaraj Ngr,
Goremedu Check Post, Pondicherry 605 006;
tel: (0413) 2271933; Maj Gnanamony Moses

TRAINING COLLEGE
WCC Rd, Nagercoil 629 001; tel: (04652) 231471

RED SHIELD HOUSE AND RETREAT CENTRE
Muttom, via Nagercoil 629 202;
tel: (04651) 238321

MEDICAL WORK
Catherine Booth Hospital: Nagercoil 629 001;
tel: (04652) 275516/7; fax: (04652) 275489;
Administrator: Maj S. P. Simon

COMMUNITY HEALTH AND DEVELOPMENT PROGRAMMES
Catherine Booth Hospital, Nagercoil 629 001;
tel: (04652) 272068

Women's Micro-credit and Health Programme;
Community-based HIV/Aids Care and
Support Programmes; Reproductive and
Child Health Programme, Community Health
Centre; Voluntary Counselling and Testing
Centre cum STD Clinic Programme;
Community Eye Health Programme

EDUCATION
Higher Secondary School (mixed)
Nagercoil 629003; tel: (04652) 272647;
Headmaster: Mr M. Kingsly

Matriculation Higher Secondary School (mixed)
Nagercoil; tel: (04652) 272534;
Principal: Mr Monickadhas

Middle School (mixed)
Nambithoppu Middle School;
Headmaster: Mr Vethamuthu

Noble Memorial High School
Valliyoor; tel: (04637) 220380;
Headmaster: Mr A. Benjamin

Village Primary Schools: 9

Nursery and English Medium Primary Schools: 6

SOCIAL SERVICES
Hostels
Boys' Hostel: Nagercoil; tel: (04652) 272953
(acc 72)

Noble Memorial Boys' Hostel: Valliyoor;
tel: (04637) 221289 (acc 70)

Tucker Girls' Hostel: Nagercoil;
tel: (04652) 231293 (acc 135)

Girls' Hostel: Thuckalay; tel: (04651) 252764
(acc 100)

Motherless Babies' Home
Palayamcottai 627 002; tel (0462) 2584441

Child Development Centres
Chemparuthivilai, Chemponvilai, Kadaigramam,
Madurai, Nagercoil, Pondicherry, Thuckalay,
Valliyoor

Vocational Training Centre for the Physically Disabled (Men and Boys)
Aramboly 629 003; tel: (04652) 263133

Vocational Training Centre for Women and Home League Retreat Centre
Nagercoil 629 003; tel: (04652) 232348

Rural Development and Vocational Training Centre
Chemparuthivilai 629 166; tel: (04651) 253292

Vocational Training Institute
Kilkothagiri Junction, 643 216 Nilgris

Industrial Training School
Aramboly; tel: (04652) 262198

RETIRED OFFICERS' HOME
Catherine Booth Hospital, Nagercoil 629 001

INDIA SOUTH WESTERN TERRITORY

Territorial leaders:
Colonels Samuel and Bimla Charan

Territorial Commander:
Colonel Samuel Charan (1 Jan 2011)

Chief Secretary:
Lieut-Colonel Masilamony Ponniah (1 Jul 2008)

Territorial Headquarters: The Salvation Army, Kowdiar, Thiruvananthapuram, Kerala

Postal address: PO Box 802, Kowdiar, Thiruvananthapuram 695 003, Kerala State, India

Tel: [91] (471) 2314626/2723238; fax: [91] (471) 2318790;

email: ISW_mail@ISW.salvationarmy.org; website: www.salvationarmy.org/ind

Salvation Army work commenced in the old Travancore State on 18 March 1894 by Captain Yesudasen Sanjivi, who was a high-caste Brahmin before his conversion. His son, Colonel Donald A. Sanjivi, became the first territorial commander from Kerala. The work spread to other parts of the state through the dedication of pioneer officers, including Commissioner P. E. George. The India South Western Territory came into being on 1 October 1970 when the Southern India Territory divided into two. The territory has its headquarters at Thiruvananthapuram and comprises the entire Malayalam-speaking area known as Kerala State.

Zone: South Asia
State included in the territory: Kerala
'The Salvation Army' in Malayalam: Raksha Sainyam; in Tamil: Ratchania Senai
Languages in which the gospel is preached: English, Malayalam, Tamil
Periodicals: *Home League Quarterly* (Malayalam/English), *The Officer* (Malayalam), *Youdha Shabdam* (Malayalam), *Yuva Veeran* (Malayalam)

FOCUSING on the development of teenagers and young girls, the first-ever Junior Home League rallies were held in all divisions and districts. The lives and minds of hundreds of Junior Miss Home Leaguers were empowered and enriched through seminars, classes and discussions, and consequently the territorial leadership anticipates that the young generation will be moulded into an effective force in leading the Army's ministry throughout the territory.

Junior Miss Home Leaguers have shown their concern for other people's needs by raising substantial funds for the helping-hand scheme. Also, young Salvationists became positively involved in contemporary issues through a counselling centre for victims of sex-trafficking.

Divisional youth camps were inspiring events where many young people committed themselves to God's service within The Salvation Army. A divisional youth secretaries' training course emphasised the development of Sunday schools. Vacation Bible schools, themed 'A Life So Blessed', were held in many corps and attracted 11,000 students, many non-Salvationists being among that number.

'A Day With Christ' – a special prayer campaign throughout the territory – led to many people claiming blessings from God, including healing of the sick. The establishing of prayer cells at territorial and divisional level is resulting in the development of people's lives, spiritually and physically.

The territory's HIV/Aids team was involved in a programme for more than 2,000 HIV/Aids patients. In Kollam District the divisional HIV/Aids team coordinator is involved in the Government's HIV/Aids policy-making body.

Heavy monsoon rains devastated many houses in backwater regions, and chickungunya fever became a major health issue all over Kerala State. The Salvation Army responded to the needs of people affected in numerous areas.

CSM (Dr) John Syamkutty was admitted to the Order of the Founder. As Chief Medical Officer at Evangeline Booth Hospital, Puthencruz, he has 'addressed the needs of leprosy patients with extraordinary dedication, deep love and compassion' for more than 30 years. Founders' Day was marked across the territory by the planting of trees to help combat global warming.

STATISTICS

Officers 696 (active 460 retired 236) **Cadets** 16 **Employees** 174
Corps 333 **Societies and Outposts** 460 **Schools** 16 **Institutions** 20
Senior Soldiers 42,311 **Adherents** 15,179 **Junior Soldiers** 3,960
Personnel serving outside territory Officers 10

STAFF

Women's Ministries: Col Bimla Charan (TPWM) Lt-Col Sathiabama Ponniah (TSWM) Maj Elizabeth Solomon (THLS) Maj Lillybai Samuelkutty (TLOMS) Lt-Col Mariamma Davidson (TSSFS, pro-tem)
Business Administration: Maj K. M. Gabriel
Personnel: Maj John Suseelkumar
Programme: Maj K.M Solomon
Editor: Maj Charles V. John
Education: Maj Simson Samuelkutty
Field: tba
Finance: tba
HRD: Lt-Col Davidson Varghese (pro-tem)
Projects: Maj C. J. Bennymon
Property: Major P. S. Johnson
Social: Capt Roy Joseph
Territorial Evangelist and Church Growth Sec: Maj Jacob George
Training: Maj John Samuel
Youth and Candidates: Maj O. P. John

DIVISIONS

Adoor: Adoor 691 523; tel: 0473-4229648; Majs Rajan K. John and Susamma Rajan
Cochin: Erumathala PO, Alwaye 683 105; tel: 0484-2638429; Majs D. Gnanadasan and D. I. Sosamma Gnanadasan
Kangazha: Edayirikapuzha PO, Kangazha 686 541; tel: 0481-2494773; Majs C. S. Yohannan and L. Rachel Yohannan
Kattakada: Kattakada 695 572; tel: 0471-2290484; Majs Sam Immanuel and Rachel Immanuel
Kottarakara: Kottarakara 691 506; tel: 452650; Majs N. J. George and M. C. Ruth George
Malabar: Veliyamthode, Chandakunnu PO, Nilambur 679 342; tel: 2222824; Majs D. Sathiyaseelan and Aleyamma Sathiaseelan
Mavelikara: Thazhakara, Mavelikara 690 102;

tel: 2303284; Majs P. J. Yohannan and Annamma Yohannan

Nedumangadu: Nedumangadu 695 541; tel: 2800352; Majs T. J. Simon and Ammini Simon

Neyyattinkara: Neyyattinkara 695 121; tel: 2222916; Majs M. Samuel and K. Thankamma Samuel

Peermade: Kuttikanam PO, Peermade 685 501; tel: 232816; Majs Rajamani Christuraj and Mary Christuraj

Tiruvella: Tiruvella 689 101; tel: 2602657; Majs Davidson Daniel and M. V. Estherbai Davidson

Thiruvananthapuram: Parambuconam, Kowdiar PO, Thiruvananthapuram 695 003; tel: 2433215; Majs P. K. Philip and Rachel Philip

DISTRICTS

Kottayam: Manganam PO, Kottayam 686 018; tel: 0481-2577481; Maj D. Gnanadasan

Punalur: The Salvation Army, PPM PO, Punalur; tel: 0475-2229218; Maj V. D. Samuel

TRAINING COLLEGE

Kowdiar, Thiruvananthapuram 695 003; tel: 2315313

TERRITORIAL PRAYER CENTRE FOR SPIRITUAL EMPOWERMENT

Kowdiar PO, Thiruvanathapuram 695 003; tel: 0471-2723237

MEDICAL WORK
Hospitals

Evangeline Booth Community Hospital: Puthencruz 682 308; tel: Ernakulam 2731056

Evangeline Booth Leprosarium: Puthencruz 682 308; tel: Ernakulam 2730054 (acc 200) Administrator for EB Hospitals: Maj P.V Stanley Babu

General Hospital: Kulathummel, Kattakada 695 572, Thiruvananthapuram Dist; tel: Kattakada 2290485 (acc 60)

Medical Centre

Kanghaza 686 541, Edayappara; tel: Kangazha 2494273 (acc 12)

EDUCATION
Higher Secondary School (mixed)

Thiruvananthapuram 695 003; tel: 2315488 (acc 1,371)

Primary Schools: 15 (acc 2,640)

SOCIAL WORK
Boys' Homes

Kangazha 686 541 (acc 30)
Kottarakara 691 506 (acc 30)
Kowdiar, Thiruvananthapuram 695 003 (acc 20)
Mavelikara 690 102 (acc 25)

Community Development Centres

North: Trikkakara, Cochin 682 021
South: Konchira, Thiruvananthapuram 695 607; tel: 0472-2831540

Girls' Homes

Adoor 691 523 (acc 25)
Kowdiar, Thiruvananthapuram 695 003 (acc 24)
Nedumangad 695 541 (acc 30)
Peermade, Kuttikanam 685 501 (acc 30)
Thiruvalla 689 101; tel: 0469-2831540 (acc 25)

Vocational Training Centre for Women

Nedumangad 695 541 (acc 25)

Young Men's Training Centres

Thazhakara, Mavelikara 690 102
Thiruvananthapuram 695 003

Printing Press

Kowdiar, Thiruvananthapuram 695 003; tel: 0471 2725358

ITI and Computer Training Centre

Kowdiar, Thiruvananthapuram; tel: 2318524

Tailoring Centres

Adoor, Cochin, Kangazha, Kattakada, Kottarakara, Malabar, Neyyattinkara, Peermade

Young Women's Hostel (Goodwill Hostel)

Thiruvananthapuram 695 003; tel: 2319917 (acc 20)

Working Women's Hostel

Thrikkakara, B. M. C. PO, Ernakulam

Youth Centre

Kowdiar, Thiruvananthapuram 695 003

RED SHIELD GUEST HOUSES

Kowdiar, Thiruvananthapuram 695 003; tel: 0471-2319926
Kovalam, Thiruvananthapuram; tel: 0471 2485895

RETIREMENT COTTAGES FOR OFFICERS

Thiruvananthapuram (cottages 4)

INDIA WESTERN TERRITORY

Territorial Commander:
Commissioner P. Mary Rajakumari
(1 Aug 2007)

Chief Secretary:
Lieut-Colonel K. C. David (1 Jan 2011)

Territorial Headquarters: Sheikh Hafizuddin Marg, Byculla, Mumbai 400 008

Postal address: PO Box 4510, Mumbai 400 008, India

Tel: [91] (022) 2308 4705/2307 1140; fax: [91] (022) 2309 9245;
email: IWT_mail@iwt.salvationarmy.org; website: www.salvationarmy.org/ind

The Salvation Army began its work in Bombay (later Mumbai) in 1882 as a pioneer party led by Major Frederick Tucker and including Veerasoriya, a Sri Lankan convert, invaded India with the love and compassion of Jesus. Bombay (Mumbai) was the capital of Bombay Province, which included Gujarat and Maharashtra, and the first headquarters in India was in a rented building at Khetwadi. From these beginnings the work of God grew in Bombay Province. Various models of administration were tried for the work in Gujarat and Maharashtra until the India Western Territory was established in 1921.

Zone: South Asia
States included in the territory: Gujarat, Maharashtra, Madhya Pradesh, Rajasthan
'The Salvation Army' in Gujarati and Marathi: Muktifauj
Languages in which the gospel is preached: English, Gujarati, Hindi, Marathi, Tamil
Periodicals: *Home League Quarterly* (Gujarati and Marathi), *The Officer* (Gujarati and Marathi), *The War Cry* (Gujarati and Marathi), *The Young Soldier* (Gujarati and Marathi)

THE year 2009 was proclaimed a year of 'Living With Jesus', with personal witness being encouraged throughout the territory. Soldiers Renewal Day was also a notable territorial occasion that resulted in revival in the lives of Salvationists.

The year was one of non-stop campaigns in the territory's five extension areas, outstanding progress being reported in Sangli Extension (Maharasthra State). The extension officer enlisted six local church pastors along with their church members to join The Salvation Army.

In this strongly Hindu area, God is abundantly blessing the Army; numbers at meetings are increasing and there are plans to elevate the work in Sangli to district status.

Officers participated in international as well as territorial conferences; such opportunities will prove to be of great benefit to the Army's work in the territory.

Salvation Army delegates joined members of the Baptist, Presbyterian and Mennonite Churches at two theological conferences at Kolkatta's

Senate Centre for Extension and Pastoral Theological Research. Commissioner P. Mary Rajakumari (TC) was one of the main speakers among the church leaders.

The CARE Programme Centre organised a workshop for all officers in Mumbai, THQ employees and specially invited guests who are workers among the city's slum-dwellers. A swine flu awareness workshop held at the THQ Conference Hall focused on the current situation in India and especially Maharasthra State.

Responding to the General's international calls to prayer, many corps observed these with great respect and fasting. 'Prayer for Peace' and 'Prayer for Sex Trafficking' vigils were attended by a total of more than 29,000 people.

At the start of 2010 the territory was encouraged by the visit of Commissioners Lalkiamlova and Lalhlimpuii (IS and ZSWM for South Asia). As well as conducting a territorial review, they visited Pune, Anand and Ahmedabad and led councils for officers in Mumbai. Commissioner Lalhlimpuii addressed a women's rally.

The new year brought news that NORAD (Norwegian Agency for Development Cooperation) is giving its support to the community development programme in Anand, through the HIV/Aids programme at Emery Hospital. NORAD will provide technical and medical help to many people who are in need.

STATISTICS
Officers 614 (active 394 retired 220) **Cadets** 24 **Employees** 301

Corps 250 **Outposts** 342 **Institutions** 20 **Day Schools** 12

Senior Soldiers 36,604 **Adherents** 3,712 **Junior Soldiers** 9,277

STAFF
Women's Ministries: Comr P. Mary Rajakumari (TPWM) Lt-Col G. Marykutty David (TSWM) Maj Indumati G. Christian (THLS - Gujarati) Maj Sudina Gaikwad (THLS - Marathi); Maj Persis P. Christian (LOMS - G) Maj Shanta Kamble (LOMS - M) Maj Jassi (SAMF - G) Maj Ratnamala Randive (SAMF - M) Maj Indira Chauhan (SSM - G) Maj Ruth Mahida (ROS - G) Maj Shobha Jadhav (ROS - M)

Editor: Maj Surendra Chopde (Marathi) Maj Ruth Macwan (Gujarati)

Education: Maj Jashwant Chauhan (Gujarati)

Field: Maj Gabriel I. Christian (Gujarat) Maj Benjamin Gaikwad (Maharashtra)

Finance: Maj Jashwant D. Mahida

Human Resources: Maj Paul V. Macwan (Gujarat) Maj Shashikala Vanjare (Maharashtra)

Projects: Maj Benjamin Randive

Property: Maj Prabhudas J. Christian (Gujarat)

Property and Development: Maj J. P. Salve (Maharashtra)

Public Relations: Maj Benjamin Randive

Social: Maj Jashwant Chauhan (Gujarat) Maj B. P. Jadhav (Maharashtra)

Training: Maj Nicolas Damor (Gujarat); Maj Ratnakar D. Kale (Maharashtra)

Youth: Maj Yusuf Daud (Gujarat) Maj Sanjay Wanjare (Maharashtra)

DIVISIONS
Gujarat
Ahmedabad: Behrampura, Ahmedabad 380 022; tel: (079) 2539 4258; Majs Yakub and Sophia Macwan

Anand: Amul Dairy Rd, Anand 388 001; tel: (02692) 240638; Majs Jashwant and Sunita Macwan

Matar: Behind Civil Court, Matar District, Kheda 387 530; tel: (02694) 285482; Majs Rasik and Ramila Christian

Nadiad: Nadiad, District Kheda 387 002; tel: (0268) 2558856; Majs David K. and Vimlaben Sevak

Panchmahal: Dohad, Panchmahal 389 151; tel: (02673) 221771; Majs Paul and Febiben Maganlal

Petlad: Sunav Rd, Post Petlad,
District Anand 388 450; tel: (02679) 221527;
Majs Punjalal and Margaret Macwan

South Gujarat: Khambla Zampa, PO Vansda,
396 580 District Navsari; Majs Kantilal and
Eunice K. Parmar

Maharashtra

Ahmednagar: Fariabagh, Sholapur Rd,
414 001; tel: (95241) 2358194; Majs Devdan
and Maria Kasbe

Mumbai: Sankli St, Byculla,
Mumbai 400 008; tel: (022) 2300 3990;
Majs Suresh and Martha Pawar

Pathardi: Pathardi, District Ahmednagar
414 102; tel: (952428) 223116; Majs Vijay
and Rajani Dalvi

Pune: 19 Napier Rd, 411 040;
tel: (9520) 2636 3198; Majs Gulab and
Meena Pathare

Satara: Satara, District Satara 415 001;
tel: (952162) 234006; Majs Ashok and
Sheela Mandgule

Shevgaon: Shevgaon, District Ahmednagar
414 502; tel: (952429) 223191;
Majs Jagannath and Kusum Tribhuwan

Shrirampur: District Ahmednagar 413 709,
Tal Shrirampur; Majs Bhausaheb and
Pushpa Magar

DISTRICT

Songadh: Maj Joseph Mahida

EXTENSION AREAS

Madhya Pradesh: Capt Savsing Bhabhor
Rajasthan: Maj James Solomon
Sangli: Maj Sunil Waghmare

TRAINING COLLEGES

Gujarat: Anand 388 001, District Anand,
Amul Dairy Rd; tel: (02692) 254801

Maharashtra: Fariabagh, Ahmednagar 414 001;
tel: (95241) 2355950

EDUCATION
Boarding Schools (Boys and Girls)

William Booth Memorial Children's Home
and Hostel: Anand 388 001, District Anand,
Gujarat; tel: (2692) 255580 (acc 226)

William Booth Memorial Primary and High
Schools: Farlabagh, District Ahmednagar
414 001, Maharashtra;
tel: (022) 95241 2324267 (acc 513)

Day Schools

Anand:
William Booth Memorial High School,
Amul Dairy Rd; tel: (2692) 254901 (acc 276)
English Medium Primary School (acc 260)
William Booth Primary School (acc 476)

Ashakiran: Primary School, Satara; under DHQ
(acc 130)

Dahod: English Medium School (acc 210)

Dynanjot: English Medium School,
Vishrantwadi 411 015; tel: (9520) 2669 2761
(acc 25)

Muktipur: PO Bareja 382 425,
District Ahmednabad; tel: 02718 233318
(acc 93)

Mumbai: Tucker English Medium School,
Sankli St, Byculla, Mumbai 400 008;
tel: (022) 307 7062 (acc 652)

Vadodara: English Medium School:
Chhani Rd, Vadodra; tel: (0265) 277 5361
(acc 150)

MEDICAL WORK

Emery Hospital: Amul Dairy Rd, Anand 388 001,
District Anand, Gujarat; tel: (2692) 253737
(acc 160)

Evangeline Booth Hospital: Ahmednagar 414 001,
Maharashtra; tel: (022) 95241 2325976
(acc 172)

Community-Based Aids Programme and
Confidential Aids Counselling Clinic: Byculla,
Mumbai; tel: (022) 2309 3566

HUMAN RESOURCES DEVELOPMENT CENTRES

Anand (Gujarat):
Faujabad Comp, Ananda 388 001
Ahmednagar (Maharashtra):
tel: (022) 95241 2358489

SOCIAL WORK
CARE Programme Centre

Byculla, Mumbai:
Community-based Aids Programme;
Confidential Aids Counselling Clinic;
Aruna Children's Programme;
Asha Deep Tailoring Programme;
tel: (022) 309 3566;

Farm Colony

Muktipur 382 425, Post Bareja,
District Ahmedabad; tel: (02718) 33318

Feeding Programme

Mumbai (under King Edward Home);
tel: (022) 23071346

147

Homes
Children
Mumbai: Sion Rd, IOB Bldg, Sion (E) 400 022;
tel: (022) 2409 4405 (acc 170)
Pune: Hope House, Gidney Park, Salisbury Park,
Plot 41 No 554/2, Pune 411 037;
tel: 9529 24271728 (acc 50)

Elderly Men
Mumbai 400 008: 122 Maulana Azad Rd,
Byculla; tel: (022) 23071346; (acc 50)

Industrial
King Edward Home: 122 Maulana Azad Rd,
Byculla, Mumbai 400 008; tel: (022) 2307 1346

Physically Handicapped Children
Joyland, Anand 388 001, District Anand,
Gujarat; tel: (02692) 251891 (acc 60)

'Ray of Hope' Home
Vansda: under DHQ (acc 63)

Hostels
Blind Working Men
Ahmedabad: Locoshed, Rajpur-Hirpur,
Ahmedabad, Gujarat; tel: (079) 2294 1217;
(acc 40)
Mumbai 400 008: Sankli St, Byculla;
tel: (022) 2305 1573 (acc 70)

Young Men
Satara: under DHQ; tel: (952162) 234006
(acc 30)

Young Women
Anand: District Kheda, Gujarat;
tel: (02692) 254499 (acc 50)
Baroda: Nava Yard, Chhani Rd,
Vadodara; tel: (0265) 2775361
Mumbai 400 008: Concord House,
Morland Rd, Byculla; tel: (022) 2301 4219
(acc 63)
Pune: c/o DHQ, 19 Napier Rd, Pune 411 040
(acc 16)

RED SHIELD HOTEL
30 Mereweather Rd, Fort, Mumbai 400 039;
tel: (022) 2284 1824; fax: (022) 2282 4613
(acc 450)

New Chief of the Staff welcomed to IHQ

Arriving at International Headquarters on their first day in office as Chief of the Staff and World Secretary for Women's Ministries, Commissioners Barry C. and Sue Swanson (*centre*) are greeted by the General and Commissioner Helen Clifton (WPWM)

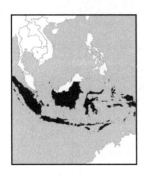

INDONESIA TERRITORY

Territorial leaders:
**Commissioners Basuki and
Marie Kartodarsono**

Territorial Commander:
Commissioner Basuki Kartodarsono
(1 Oct 2006)

Acting Chief Secretary:
Lieut-Colonel Mickey McLaren (1 Dec 2010)

Territorial Headquarters: Jalan Jawa 20, Bandung 40117

Postal address: Post Box 1640, Bandung 40016, Indonesia

Tel: [62] (22) 4207029/4205056; fax: [62] (22) 423 6754;

website: www.salvationarmy.or.id

The Salvation Army commenced in Indonesia (Java) in 1894. Operations were extended to Ambon, Bali, East Kalimantan, Sulawesi (Central, North and South), Sumatra (North and South) and East Nusa Tenggara, Aceh and Papua. A network of educational, medical and social services began.

Zone: South Pacific and East Asia
Country included in the territory: Indonesia
'The Salvation Army' in all Indonesian languages: Bala Keselamatan
Languages in which the gospel is preached: Indonesian with various dialects such as Batak, Daa, Dayak, Javanese, Ledo, Makassarese, Moma, Niasnese, Tado and Uma
Periodicals: *Berita Keselamatan* (*The War Cry*), *Cakrawala* (*Waves of Hope*), *Home League Programme*, *Sunday School Programme*, *Medical Fellowship Bulletin*, *Oasis Fajar* (Daily Devotions)

THE highlight of 2009 was the 115th Anniversary Congress in Palu, Central Sulawesi, attended by a number of overseas guests as well as Indonesian Salvationists and adherents. Retired General Paul Rader and Commissioner Kay Rader were the keynote speakers for this significant event.

On 30 September 2009 another earthquake struck Indonesia, this time hitting West Sumatera. The 7.9 magnitude quake caused much damage to a large part of Padang City. Casualty figures were 1,117 people killed and 1,214 wounded. Large numbers of houses and schools were destroyed.

Supported by the International Emergency Services, IHQ, the territory's relief team arrived on the scene the day after the disaster. For three weeks they provided medical care, tents, blankets, mats and milk, and later began building a simple housing complex of 126 houses.

On 24 February 2010 The Salvation Army dedicated to God's glory 65 houses then handed them over to beneficiaries from three villages. Five months later the other 61 houses were handed over.

On 4 February 2010 the territorial commander officially opened and dedicated to God a new residential care centre at Jogyakarta Boys' Home, Central Java. This was funded by generous donors after the former building was destroyed by an earthquake in 2006. All the boys are excited to be in their new home.

The Army has been establishing an agriculture-related self-help programme in Central Sulawesi. During a pastoral visit in March 2010 the territorial leaders participated in the first rice harvesting and other ongoing agricultural activities in Kalawara.

In April 2010 Lieut-Colonel Helen Starrett and Miss Lindsey Bailey from The Salvation Army World Service Office worked with the Women's Ministries Department to facilitate seminars on human trafficking. Under a theme 'Hands that Heal', these events attracted 70 participants in both Medan and Bandung, where trafficking is more prevalent because of people's poverty and vulnerability.

STATISTICS

Officers 700 (active 561 retired 139) **Cadets** (1st Yr) 19 (2nd Yr) 18 **Employees** 1,671 **Corps** 274 **Outposts** 119 **Kindergartens** 14 **Primary Schools** 64 **Secondary Schools** 18 **High Schools** 5 **Technical High School** 1 **Theological University** 1 **Hospitals** 6 **Clinics** 13 **Academies for Nurses** 2 **Social Institutions** 20 **Senior Soldiers** 27,056 **Adherents** 16,524 **Junior Soldiers** 7,880 **Officers serving outside Territory** 5

STAFF

Women's Ministries: Comr Marie Kartodarsono (TPWM), Lt-Col June McLaren (TSWM) Maj Anastasia Poa (HL)

Sec for Business Administration: Lt-Col Yohanes Sayuti **Finance:** Maj Sri Widajati Goni **Chief Auditor:** Mr Anton Priyono **Property:** Maj John Umasanthiram **Information Technology:** Kadek White **Sec for Programme:** Lt-Col Selly Poa **Social Services:** Maj Ernie Lasut **Corps Growth and Education:** Maj Benjamin Goni **Legal and Parliament:** Maj Sasmoko Hertjahjo **Youth and Children's Ministries:** Capt Alberth Sarimin **Sec for Personnel:** Lt-Col Jones Kasaedja **Spiritual Life Development Sec:** Maj Mulyati Mitra Sumarta **Candidates:** Maj Risma Manurung **Literature and Editorial:** Maj Sasmoko Hertjahjo **Projects:** Mr Martyn Smith **Public Relations:** Maj Spener Tetenaung Jl. Kramat Raya 55, Jakarta Pusat; tel: (021) 391 4518; fax: (021) 392 8636 **Training:** Maj Immanuel Supardi

DIVISIONS

Jawa and Bali: Jalan Dr Cipto 64b, Kelurahan Bugangan, Semarang 50126, Jateng; tel: (024) 355 1361; Majs Gidion and Lidia Rangi

Kulawi: Bala Keselamatan Post Office, Kulawi 94363, Sulteng; tel/fax: (0451) 811 017; Majs Indra and Helly Mangiwa

Manggala (West Palu, Central Sulawesi): c/o Jalan Miangas 1-3, Palu 94112; Majs Imanuel and Henny Duhu

Palu Timur (East Palu): Jalan Miangas 1, Kantor Pos Palu 94112; tel: (0451) 426 821; fax: (0451) 425 846; Majs Yusak and Widiawati Tampai

Palu Barat (West Palu): Jalan Miangas 1-3, Palu 94112, Sulteng; mobile: 0816 4304498; Majs Wayan and Herlina Widyanoadi

Regional East Indonesia: Jl Dr Sutomo No 10, Makasar; tel/fax: (0411) 312 919; Majs Made Sadia and Syastiel Lempid

Sulawesi Utara (North Sulawesi): Jalan A. Yani 15, Manado 95114; tel/fax: (0431) 864 052; Majs I. Made and Margaretha Petrus

Sumatera Utara: Jl. Sei Kera 186 Medan 20232, Sumatera Utara; tel: (061) 4510284; Majs Marthen and Yulin Pandorante

DISTRICTS

Under Jawa and Bali Division
East Kalimantan: Maj Ezra Mangela
Under East Palu Division
Kamarora: Capt Yonas Parese
Maranatha: Maj Jantje Kasumba
Palolo: Capt Yahya Benyamin
Palu: Maj Hesron Mpapa
Under West Palu Division
Dombu: Maj Robert Sumbasubu
Pakawa: Capt Bambang Tadewatu
Porame: Maj Elias Sale
Rowiga : Capt Sopani Laia
Wawugaga: Capt Yusdimer Momi
Under Manggala Division
Lalundu: Capt Gunawan Mantaely
Malino: Capt Resman Manurung
North Mamuju: Capt Aser Yupa
Under Kulawi Division
Gimpu: Maj I. Ketut Putrayasa
Kantewu: Maj Jusuf Tarusu
Karangana: Maj Janji Rusanto
Kulawi: Maj Nogerto Mariono
Lindu: Maj Lewi Bagalatu
Tobaku: Capt Hendry Simanjuntak
Under North Sumatera Division
Nias: Maj Alex Kedoh

OFFICER TRAINING COLLEGE

Jalan Kramat Raya 55, Jakarta 10450, PO Box
3203, Jakarta 10002; tel: (021) 310 8148;
fax: (021) 391 0410

EDUCATION

Central Sulawesi: 79 schools (acc 7,118),
1 theological university (acc 223)
East Kalimantan: 1 school (acc 52)
Jawa: 14 schools (acc 1,110)
Kalawara: 4 schools (acc 400)
North Sumatra: 2 schools (acc 62)
South Sulawesi: 4 schools (acc 106)

MEDICAL WORK
General Hospitals (Jawa)

Bandung: Bungsu Hospital, Jalan Veteran 6;
tel: (022) 423 1550/1695; fax: (022) 423 1582
(acc 49) (poli-clinic attached)
Semarang: William Booth Hospital, Jalan Let
Jen S. Parman 5 Semarang, 50232;
tel: (024) 841 1800/844 8773;
fax: (024) 844 8773 (acc 100) (eye and
general clinic attached)
Surabaya: William Booth Hospital,
Jalan Diponegoro 34;
tel: (031) 561 4615/4616/5349;
fax: (031) 567 1380 (acc 200) (maternity

hospital and 3 poli-clinics attached)
Turen: Bokor Hospital, Jalan Jen A. Yani 89,
Turen near Malang; tel: (0341) 824 453/002;
fax: (0341) 823 878 (acc 150) (poli-clinic
and outpost clinic attached)

General Hospital and Clinics (Sulawesi)

Palu: Woodward Hospital, Jalan L. H.
Woodward 1, Kantor Pos Palu, Sulawesi
Tengah; tel: (0451) 421 769/482 914/426 361;
fax: (0451) 423 744 (acc 110)

Branch Hospitals

Ampera: under Woodward Hospital
Kulawi: Bethesda Hou Popakauria

Clinics

Central Sulawesi: Gimpu, Kantewu, Kulawi,
Mamu, Manusi Ampera, Panii
East Kalimantan: Long Merah, Muara Batuq,
Muara Mujan
North Sulawesi: Amurang, Kumelembuai,
Makasili
Regional East Indonesia: Ambon

Maternity Hospital

Makassar, Sulawesi Selatan: Catherine Booth
Mother and Child Hospital, Jalan Arif,
Rate 15 or Post Box 33;
tel: (0411) 873 803/852 344;
fax: (0411) 873 803 (acc 53) (poli-clinic
attached)

Academies for Nurses' Training

Palu: under Woodward Hospital (acc 345)
Surabaya: under William Booth Hospital
(acc 155)

SOCIAL WORK
Babies' and Toddlers' Home

Surabaya: Matahari Terbit, Jalan Kombes
Pol Durjat 10-12, Surabaya 60262;
tel: (031) 534 1132; fax: (031) 532 2118
(acc 60)

Boys' Homes

Bandung: Maranatha, Jalan Dr Cipto 7;
tel: (022) 423 0480 (acc 80)
Denpasar, Bali: William Booth Home, Jalan
Kebo Iwa No 29, Banjar Liligundi,
Ubung Kaja, Denpasar, Bali (acc 200)
Kalawara: Bahagia, Kantor Pos Palu,
Sul Teng (acc 60)
Medan: William Booth Home, Jalan K. L. Yos
Sudarso 10, Lorong 1A; tel: (061) 661 3840
(acc 90)

The territorial leaders begin the first rice harvesting of a self-help programme run by The Salvation Army in Central Sulawesi

Semarang: Betlehem, Jalan Musi Raya 2, Kel Rejosari, Semarang 50125; tel: (024) 355 3287 (acc 80)

Surabaya: Imanuel, Jalan Gatotan 36; tel: (031) 352 2932 (acc 60)

Tompaso: Wisma Anugerah, Post Box 1100, Manado/Desa Liba, Kecamatan Tompaso 95693, Kab Minahasa; tel: (0431) 371 524 (acc 80)

Yogyakarta: Tunas Harapan, Jalan Kenari 7, Miliran Post Box 1095; tel: (0274) 563598 (acc 32)

Children's Homes

Bandung: William Booth Home, Jalan Jawa 18; tel: (022) 420 5549 (acc 90)

Denpasar: Anugerah, Jalan Hos Cokroaminoto 34; tel/fax: (0361) 426 484 (acc 60)

Jakarta: Catherine Booth Home, Pondok Cabe (acc 100)

Malang: Elim, Jalan Panglima Sudirman 97; tel: (0341) 362 905 (acc 80)

Manado: Bukit Harapan, Jalan Arnold Manonutu 501, Post Box 118; tel: (0431) 863 394 (acc 60)

Medan: Evangeline Booth Home, Jalan Samanhudi 27; tel: (061) 414 2148 (acc 80)

Palu: Sejahtera, Jalan Maluku 18, Palu 94112; tel: (0451) 424 586 (acc 80)

Centre for Homeless People

Semarang: Eben Haezer, Jalan Dr Cipto 64a, Kelurahan Bugangan, Semarang 50126, Jateng; tel: (024) 771 0501/354 2536 (acc 100) (dairy farm attached)

Eventide Homes

Bandung: Senjarawi, Jalan Jeruk 7; tel: (022) 727 1369 (acc 100)

Semarang: Bethany, Jalan Musi Raya 4-6; tel: (024) 354 4855 (acc 60)

Turen: Tresno Mukti, Jalan Achmad Yani 180; tel: (0341) 825 290 (acc 50)

Students' Hostels

Bandung: Jalan Dr Cipto 7; tel: (022) 423 0480 (acc 32)

Bandung: Jalan Jawa 18; tel: (022) 420 5549 (acc 32)

Medan: Jalan Samanhudi 27; tel: (061) 414 2148 (acc 30)

Surabaya: Jalan Gatotan 36; tel: (031) 352 2932 (acc 24)

Yogyakarta: Jalan Kenari 7, Miliran; tel: (0274) 563 598 (acc 8)

THQ GUEST HOUSE

Jalan Jawa 20; tel: (022) 420 7029 (acc 10)

ITALY COMMAND

Command leaders:
Lieut-Colonels Daniel and Eliane Naud

Officer Commanding:
Lieut-Colonel Daniel Naud (1 Sep 2009)

General Secretary:
Major Massimo Tursi (1 Aug 2007)

Command Headquarters: Via degli Apuli 39, 00185 Rome, Italy

Tel: [39] 06 447406300/06 4941089; fax: [39] 06 490078;
email: Italy_Command@ity.salvationarmy.org; website: www.esercitodellasalvezza.org

The Salvation Army flag was unfurled in Italy on 20 February 1887 by Major and Mrs James Vint and Lieutenant Fanny Hack, though subsequent difficulties necessitated withdrawal. In 1890 Fritz Malan (later lieut-colonel) began meetings in his native village in the Waldensian Valleys. In 1893 Army work was re-established. In a decree of the President on 1 April 1965, The Salvation Army was recognised as a philanthropic organisation competent to acquire and hold properties and to receive donations and legacies. It received legal status as a religious body/church on 20 March 2009.

On 8 October 2007 The Salvation Army began operations in Greece, the work being linked to the Italy Command with the command leadership giving guidance and support to future development. Thessaloniki was identified as the centre of the new undertaking and Captains Polis Pantelidis and Maria Konti-Galinou, UK officers of Greek nationality, were entrusted with the task of launching the Army's mission in their home country.

Zone: Europe
Countries included in the command: Greece, Italy
'The Salvation Army' in Italian: Esercito della Salvezza; in Greek: O Stratos Tis Sotirias
Languages in which the gospel is preached: Greek, Italian
Periodicals: *Il Bollettino del Dipartimento Società e Famiglia, Il Grido di Guerra*

THROUGH the year Salvationists at Castelvetrano Corps, on the island of Sicily, maintained a monthly ministry to 640 people. Newcomers were attracted to the corps as a result of personal contacts made by the officer during a campaign in October 2009. A second campaign is planned.

On the island of Ischia the Concordia Centre hosted 42 Salvationists and people from other churches for a traditional family camp during the first 10 days of September.

In northern Italy, the annual youth camp in Bobbio Pellice during August was a very positive experience. The event ended with a public concert in which the camp youth band played an important part.

A special event at the social services centre in Rome was the inauguration of a new fully equipped dental unit. This project aims to provide free assistance to the centre's clients while offering treatment to the public at very reasonable rates. The unit was

Another group of young Italians choose to serve Jesus Christ as soldiers in The Salvation Army

opened during the visit of Commissioners Barry and Raemor Pobjie (then zonal leaders for Europe).

In the cosmopolitan city of Thessaloniki, birthplace of Christianity in Europe, the Army's activities – such as a soup run and contacting on the streets of the red light district – have been intensified. Other opportunities are being seized to raise awareness of The Salvation Army in Greece.

Three cadets from Italy and Greece are being trained in London. This strong indication that people are responding to God's calling to ministry brings joy and hope for the future.

STATISTICS
Officers 47 (active 23 retired 24) **Auxiliary-Captains** 3 **Auxiliary-Lieutenants** 3 **Employees** 9
Corps 17 **Outposts** 15 **Institutions** 7
Senior Soldiers 231 **Adherents** 100 **Junior Soldiers** 59

STAFF
General's Personal Representative to the Vatican: Lt-Col Daniel Naud
Women's Ministries (and Resources): Lt-Col Eliane Naud (CPWM) Maj Anne-Florence Tursi (CSWM)
Finance: Capt Patricia Pavoni
Property: Maj. Massimo Tursi

Public Relations and Social: Capt. Emanuele Pavoni
Training: Maj. Anne-Florence Tursi
Family Tracing: Maj Angela Dentico
Candidates: Maj Lidia Bruno

SOCIAL WORK
Centre for the Homeless
Centro Virgilio Paglieri, Via degli Apuli 41, 00185 Roma; tel: 06 4451351; fax: 06 4456306 (acc 200)

Workers' Lodge
Villa Speranza, Contrada Serra 57a, 85100 Potenza; tel/fax: 0971 51245 (acc 6)

Holiday Centres
Le Casermette, Via Pellice 4, 10060 Bobbio Pellice (To); tel/fax: 0121 957728; email: direzione@centrovacanzebobbio.com; www.centrovacanzebobbio.com (acc 206)
Concordia, Via Casa di Majo 36, 80075 Forio d'Ischia (Na); tel/fax: 081 997324; email: concordia@esercitodellasalvezza.org (acc 55)
L'Uliveto, Via Stretta della Croce 20, 84030 Atena Lucana (Sa); tel/fax: 0975 76321 (acc 80)

Guest Houses
Florence: Villa delle Rose, Via Aretina 91, 50136 Firenze; tel/fax: 055 660445 email: davidcavanagh@esercitodellasalvezza.org (acc 13)
Rome: Foresteria, Via degli Apuli 41, 00185 Roma; tel/fax: 06 44 51 351; email: foresteriaroma@esercitodellasalvezza.org (acc 70)

GREECE
Notara 1 Pylaia, GR 555 35, Thessaloniki, Greece; tel: 00 30 2310 315027; www.salvationarmy.gr; Capts Polycarpos Pantelidis and Maria Konti-Galinou

JAPAN TERRITORY

Territorial leaders:
Commissioners Makoto and Kaoru Yoshida

Territorial Commander:
Commissioner Makoto Yoshida (1 Jun 2006)

Chief Secretary:
Lieut-Colonel Naoshi Hiramoto (1 Mar 2004)

**Territorial Headquarters: 17, 2-chome, Kanda Jimbocho,
Chiyoda-ku, Tokyo 101-0051, Japan**

Tel: [81] (03) 3237 0881; fax: [81] (03) 3237 7676; website: www.salvationarmy.or.jp

In 1895 a small group of pioneer officers from Britain arrived in Japan at Yokohama to start operations. In spite of great difficulties, work was soon established. Of several outstanding Japanese who were attracted to The Salvation Army, the most distinguished was Commissioner Gunpei Yamamuro OF, prominent evangelist and author, whose book *The Common People's Gospel* has been reprinted more than 500 times.

Zone: South Pacific and East Asia
Country included in the territory: Japan
Language in which the gospel is preached: Japanese
Periodicals: *Home League Quarterly*, *The Officer*, *The Sunday School Guide*, *Toki-no-Koe*, *Toki-no-Koe Junior*

THE territory continued to place emphasis on integrated mission in terms of holistic ministry. This was particularly encouraged within Salvation Army-run hospitals. As of April 2010, business sections of hospitals were united into one department to handle all the business matters of each hospital.

As in previous years, a special seminar was held for new employees of social institutions and hospitals to make them aware of the spirit of The Salvation Army, since most of them are neither Salvationists nor Christians. A DVD of the 2008 Salvation Army Mission Seminar, which emphasised integrated mission, was produced and distributed to every Salvation Army centre.

A primary concern continuing to be the shortage of officers, a 24-hour prayer chain was organised in connection with Candidates Sunday in October 2009. More than 600 prayer warriors joined the chain. God honoured their faith and provided another three cadets and two lieutenants for the territory.

The territory especially rejoiced in the commissioning of three officers of the Prayer Warriors Session in March 2010, since no officers had been commissioned the previous year.

The rural community development project in Papua New Guinea, carried out in partnership with Japan International Cooperation Agency (JICA), successfully concluded. So impressed and inspired by what had been achieved, JICA staff strongly recommend starting another project in PNG. The Sepik Rural Water and Primary Health Care Programme was commenced in November 2009 and runs until the middle of 2012.

A building project in Ichigaya was launched in October 2009 with support from Territorial Advisory Board members. This is a property investment that will be a significant financial source for the territory. The building was scheduled for completion in October 2010.

At the invitation of New Zealand, Fiji and Tonga Territory, and sponsored by Wellington Citadel Band, a young bandswoman participated in the National Youth Band Camp.

STATISTICS

Officers 172 (active 81 retired 91) **Cadets** (1st Yr) 1 (2nd Yr) 3 **Employees** 1,068
Corps 47 **Outposts** 12 **Institutions** 20 **Hospitals** 2
Senior Soldiers 2,851 **Adherents** 37 **Junior Soldiers** 101

STAFF

Women's Ministries: Comr Kaoru Yoshida (TPWM) Lt-Col Seiko Hiramoto (TSWM)
Business Administration: Maj Jiro Katsuchi
Candidates: Maj Kyoko Yoshida
Editor: Sis Keiko Saito
Literary: Maj Kazumitsu Higuchi
Medical: Maj Naoko Harita
Music: B/M Hajime Suzuki
Personnel: Maj Chieko Tanaka
Programme: Maj Kazumitsu Higuchi
Social: Maj Naoko Harita

Staff Band: B/M Hajime Suzuki
Staff Songsters: S/L Mikako Ebara
Training: Maj Tsukasa Yoshida
Youth: Capt Kazuyuki Ishikawa

DIVISIONS

Hokkaido: Nishi 1-13-1, Minami-4-jo, Chuo-ku, Sapporo-shi 064-0804; tel: (011) 231 2805; fax: (011) 231 2825; Majs Kojiro and Yumi Tokunaga

Kanto-Tohoku: 5 Yoriai-cho, Takasaki-shi, Gunma Ken 370-0822; tel: (027) 323 1337; fax: (027) 323 1334; Majs Haruhisa and Hiromi Ota

Nishi Nihon: 3-6-20 Tenjinbashi, Kita-ku, Osaka-shi 530-0041; tel: (06) 6351 0084; fax: (06) 6351 0093; Majs Nobuhiro and Yasuko Hiramoto

Tokyo-Tokaido: 4-11-3 Taihei, Sumida-ku, Tokyo 130-0012; tel: (03) 5819 1460; fax: (03) 5819 1461; Majs Kenji and Chiaki Fujii

TRAINING COLLEGE

1-39-5 Wada Suginami-ku, Tokyo 166-0012; tel: (03) 3381 9837

MEDICAL WORK

Booth Memorial Hospital: 1-40-5 Wada, Suginami-ku, Tokyo 166-0012; tel: (03) 3381 7236; fax: (03) 5385 0734 (acc hospital 179, hospice 20)

Kiyose Hospital: 1-17-9 Takeoka, Kiyose-shi, Tokyo, 204-0023; tel: (042) 491 1411/3; fax: (042) 491 3900 (acc hospital 117, hospice 25)

SOCIAL WORK

Alcoholic Rehabilitation Centre

Jiseikan, 1-17-60 Takeoka, Kiyose-shi, Tokyo 204-0023; tel: (042) 493 5374 (acc 50)

Rehabilitation Centre (Men)

2-21-2 Wada Suginami-ku, Tokyo 166-0012 tel: (03) 5860 2990 (acc 15)

Social Service Centre (Men) (Bazaar)

2-21-2 Wada Suginami-ku, Tokyo 166-0012; tel: (03) 5860 2992

Working Men's Homes

Jijokan, 2-17-10 Tsukishima, Chuo-ku, Tokyo 104-0052; tel: (03) 5860 2994 (acc 35)

Shinkokan, 87 Akagishita-machi, Shinjuku-ku,
Tokyo 162-0803; tel: (03) 3269 4901 (acc 40)

Women's Homes

Fujinryo: 1-43-11 Wada Suginami-ku,
Tokyo 166-0012; tel: (03) 3381 0992 (acc 40)
Shinseiryo: 4-11-14 Shibazaki-cho,
Tachikawa-shi, Tokyo 190-0023;
tel: (042) 522 2306 (acc 70)

Children's Homes

Aikoen: 1-3 Aoyama-cho, Kure-shi,
Hiroshima 737-0023; tel: (0823) 21 6374
(acc 30)
Kibokan: 2-16-11, Nakahodzumi, Ibaraki-shi,
Osaka 567-0034; tel: (0726) 23 3758 (acc 65)
Kiekoryo: 4-12-10 Kami Ikedai, Ota-ku,
Tokyo 145-0064; tel: (03) 3729 0357 (acc 35)
Sekoryo: 2-21-1 Wada, Suginami-ku,
Tokyo 166-0012; tel: (03) 3381 0545 (acc 50)
Toyohama-Gakuryo: 3082-5 Toyoshima,
Toyohama-cho, Kure-shi, Hiroshima 734-0101;
tel: (08466) 8 2029 (acc 60)

Day Nurseries

Kikusui Kamimachi Hoikuen: 2-52 Kikusui
Kamimachi 3-jo, Shiroishi-ku, Sapporo-shi
003-0813; tel: (011) 821 2879 (acc 90)
Kure Hoikusho: 1-4 Aoyama-cho,
Kure-shi 737-0023; tel: (0823) 21 4711 (acc 60)
Sano Hoikuen: 182 Asanuma-cho, Sano-shi
327-0831; tel: (0283) 22 4081 (acc 126)
Shiseikan Hoikuen: Nishi 7, Minami 3-jo,

Chuo-ku, Sapporo-shi 060-0063;
tel: (011) 204 9560 (acc 120)
Soen Hoikusho: Nishi 14-1, Kita 5-jo, Chuo-ku,
Sapporo-shi 060-0005; tel: (011) 221 6630
(acc 60)

Home for the Aged

Keisen Home: 1-17-61 Takeoka, Kiyose-shi,
Tokyo 204-0023; tel: (042) 493 5161/2 (acc 50)

Hostel

Kyoto Hostel: 37 Tokushoji-machi,
Tominokoji-dori 4-jo Sagaru, Shimogyo-ku,
Kyoto-shi 600-8051; tel: (075) 363 3926
(acc 16)

Senior Citizens' Housing and Care Centre

Grace: 1-40-15 Wada, Suginami-ku,
Tokyo 166-0012; tel: (03) 3380 1248;
fax: (03) 3380 1206 (acc 100)

Care House

Izumi: 1-17-24 Takeoka, Kiyose-shi,
Tokyo 204-0023; tel: (042) 496 7575 (acc 32)

RETIRED OFFICERS' APARTMENTS

Olive House: 1-39-12 Wada, Suginami-ku,
Tokyo 166-0012
Osaka Central Hall 5F: 3-6-20 Tenjinbashi,
Kita-ku, Osaka 530-0041
Tokiwa House: 1-17-12 Takeoka, Kiyose-shi,
Tokyo 204-0023

HONG KONG AND MACAU COMMAND: Many elderly representatives were among 800 Salvationists who joined a march launching the 80th year of Salvation Army service in Hong Kong. Participants then gathered to enjoy *punchai*, a traditional rural feast.

KENYA EAST TERRITORY

Territorial Commander:
Commissioner Hezekiel Anzeze
(1 Mar 2008)

Chief Secretary:
Colonel Steven Howard (1 Jun 2009)

Territorial Headquarters: Marist Lane, Karen, Nairobi, Kenya

Postal address: Box 24927, Karen 00502, Nairobi, Kenya

Tel: [254] (020) 240-3260; fax: [254] (020) 240-3263

In 1896 three Salvationists went to Kenya to work on the building of a new railway and made their witness while based at the Taru Camp. The first official meetings were held in Nairobi in April 1921, led by Lieut-Colonel and Mrs James Allister Smith. The first cadets were trained in 1923. On 1 March 2008, the Kenya Territory was divided into two and Kenya East Territory and Kenya West Territory were created.

Zone: Africa
Country included in the territory: Kenya
'The Salvation Army' in Kiswahili: Jeshi La Wokovu
Languages in which the gospel is preached: English, Kiswahili and a number of tribal languages
Periodicals: *Sauti ya Vita* (English and Kiswahili)

FORTY-EIGHT new corps opened during 2009, four districts were elevated to division status and three new districts were created. Open-air meetings continued to be an effective means of proclaiming the gospel. Uniformed Salvationists on the march invited many people to attend meetings, where they received Jesus Christ as their saviour.

'Raised Up to Holiness' is the current territorial theme and Salvationists are being encouraged to read through the Bible following a schedule published in *The War Cry*. A series of articles challenged people on the subject of spiritual disciplines. The territory established a Spiritual Life Development Office and commenced a one-year training programme to educate and encourage officers.

Spiritual growth has also been evident in small groups, Bible study and women's ministries seminars focusing on spiritual disciplines. A women officers' retreat, 'Growing in Grace and Knowledge', has been planned.

In April 2010 the Territorial Youth Convention took place, based on the 'Raised Up to Holiness' theme. During the week several hundred young people were taught and challenged on various aspects of holy living. Their passion and their hunger for a deeper experience of the Lord were evident.

The Water, Sanitation and Hygiene (WASH) project benefited 40 schools by providing toilet and washing facilities. Jointly sponsored by Sweden and Latvia Territory and Switzerland, Austria and Hungary Territory, this three-year project has attracted requests from many other schools wishing to improve the health and welfare of their students.

The Karibu Centre is a partnership between The Salvation Army and Orphans Overseas (an American charitable group) which began in 2009 and opened its own building in Thika in May 2010. The centre started with feeding programmes for street children and developed a day programme for slum children up to the age of four.

A residential programme assisted pregnant teenagers and expanded to accommodate babies who had been abandoned at the district hospital or elsewhere. It is hoped that the babies can be integrated back into their families or adopted within Kenya.

STATISTICS

Officers 510 (active 438 retired 72) **Cadets** 51 **Employees** 128
Corps 341 **Outposts** 382 **Pre-primary Schools** 4 **Primary Schools** 146 **Secondary Schools** 40 **Institutions** 13
Senior Soldiers 70,665 **Junior Soldiers** 61,025

STAFF

Women's Ministries: Col Janice Howard (TLWM)
Business Administration: Lt-Col Lalbulliana
Personnel: Lt-Col Gabriel Kathuri
Programme: Maj Luka Khayumbi
Audit: Maj Bilha Rewa
Finance:
Projects: Marshall Currie

Property: Mr John Kamau
Social: Maj Joyce Mbungu
Education: Capt John Mutune
Territorial Band: B/M Samuel Odiara
Territorial Songsters: S/L Javan Malika
Trade: Mr Joshua Mugera
Training (National): Maj Enock Lufumbu
Youth: Capt Martin Kimeu
   Candidates: Capt Jane Kasyoka

DIVISIONS

Coast: PO Box 98277, Mombasa; tel: 041-490629; Majs Samson and Mary Mwangi
Embu: PO Box 74, Embu; tel: 068-20107; Lt-Cols Julius and Phyllis Mukonga
Kangundo: PO Box 324, Kangundo; tel: 044-21049; Lt-Cols Nahashon and Zippora Njiru
Kibwezi: PO Box 428, Sultan Hamud; tel: 044-52200; Majs Peter and Annah Mutuku
Machakos: PO Box 160, Machakos; tel: 044-21660; Majs Simon and Zippora Mbuthu
Nairobi: PO Box 31205, Nairobi; tel: 020-767208; Majs John and Mary Olewa
Thika: PO Box 809, Thika; tel: 067-22056; Majs Lucas and Agnes Kithome
Westlands: PO Box 25240, Nairobi; Capts Jonathan and Alice Barasa
Yatta: PO Box 29 Kithimani; Majs Boniface and Esther Munyekhe

DISTRICTS

Kathiani: PO Box 2, Kathiani; Maj Nathan Musieni
Kilome: PO Box 85, Nunguni; Capt Samwel Opuka
Kirinyaga: PO Box 21, Kerugoya; Capt Thomas Musyoki
Makueni: PO Box 40, Wote; tel: 044-77 Makueni; Capt Samuel Kang'ara
Matungulu: PO Box 422, Tala; Maj Gideon Nako
Meru: PO Box 465, Nkubu, Meru; tel: 064-51207; Maj Ibrahim Lorot
Mwala: PO Box 19, Mwala; Maj Matthew Wangubo
Nakuru: PO Box 672, Nakuru; tel: 051-212455; Maj Joseph Mwanga

NATIONAL TRAINING COLLEGE
PO Box 4467, Thika; tel: 0733-629411

EDUCATIONAL WORK
SA Sponsored Primary Schools: 15

SA Sponsored and Managed Secondary Schools: 26

Special Schools
Visually Handicapped
High School
Thika: PO Box 704, Thika; tel: 067-22092
(acc 163)
Primary Schools
Likoni: PO Box 96089, Mombasa;
tel: 041-451101 (acc 120)
Thika: PO Box 80, Thika; tel: 067-21691
(acc 297)

Physically Disabled
Primary Schools
Joytown: PO Box 326, Thika; tel: 067-21291
(acc 215)
Secondary School
Joytown: PO Box 1370, Thika; tel: 067-30588
(acc 110)

Multi-Handicapped Special Units
Joytown: PO Box 326, Thika; tel: 067-21291
(acc 22)
Njoro Special School: PO Box 359, Njoro
Thika Primary School: PO Box 80, Thika;
tel: 067-21691

SOCIAL SERVICES
Children's Homes
Kabete: PO Box 210-00606 Sarit Centre,
Nairobi; tel: 020-442766 (acc 114)
Mombasa: PO Box 90531, Mombasa;
tel: 041-224387 (acc 40)
Thika: Karibu Children's Centre, PO Box 1625,
Thika 01000

Community Centre
Kibera: PO Box 21608, Nairobi; tel: 020-567064

Girls' Hostel
Nairobi: PO Box 31354, Nairobi;
tel: 020-765750

Vocational Training Centres
Variety Village: PO Box 1472, Thika;
tel: 020-2106603
Nairobi Girls' Centre: PO Box 31304, Nairobi;
tel: 020-766375 (acc 60)

NIGERIA: The first Salvation Army building in Mali – the corps hall at Sogonyiko (*right*) – was opened during a visit from THQ leaders, pictured below with Mali's new Salvationists

KENYA WEST TERRITORY

Territorial leaders:
Commissioners Joash and Florence Malabi

Territorial Commander:
Commissioner Joash Malabi (1 Nov 2010)

Chief Secretary:
Colonel Benjamin Mnyampi (1 Jul 2010)

Territorial Headquarters: Mumia Highway Rd, Kakamega, Kenya

Postal address: PO Box 660, Kakamega 50100, Kenya

In 1896 three Salvationists went to Kenya to work on the building of a new railway and made their witness while based at the Taru Camp. The first official meetings were held in Nairobi in April 1921, led by Lieut-Colonel and Mrs James Allister Smith. The first cadets were trained in 1923. On 1 March 2008, the Kenya Territory was divided into two and Kenya East Territory and Kenya West Territory were created.

Zone: Africa
Country included in the territory: Kenya
'The Salvation Army' in Kiswahili: Jeshi La Wokovu
Languages in which the gospel is preached: English, Kiswahili and a number of tribal languages
Periodicals: *Sauti ya Vita* (English and Kiswahili)

HIGHLIGHTS in the year included the inauguration of three new districts – Lugari, Madzuu and Sabatia – and the elevation of Kitale District to divisional status. This not only reflects the growth of The Salvation Army in those areas, but also gives further evidence of the territory's intention to bring leadership closer to the people.

An emphasis on evangelism is also evident in the registering of 2,446 first-time commitments to Christ, contributing to the enrolment of 2,485 senior soldiers and 4,294 junior soldiers.

The territory's second annual school of music took place in August, when 120 musicians and leaders deepened their spiritual lives and developed their musical proficiency. Supported by Salvationists from Del Oro and Golden State Divisions (USA Western), instrumentalists, vocalists and dancers committed themselves to the highest standards of Salvation Army musicianship.

Commissioners Amos and Rosemary Makina (IS and ZSWM, Africa) opened and dedicated to God the new Territorial Headquarters building, completed nearly two years to the day that construction began. Staff now occupy a modern and spacious headquarters and are grateful to USA Western, Southern and Central Territories for their generous support.

While in Kakamega, Commissioners Makina conducted the territory's first review, led officers councils and then presided over a large rally of Salvationists at Bukhungu Stadium.

The entire staff and cadets from the National Officers Training College visited the territory to conduct 10-day spiritual campaigns in eight of the divisions and districts. The outreach and results of this effort were phenomenal: meeting attendances of over 30,000; some 3,000 homes and 14,300 people visited; 2,100 seekers for salvation and 2,800 commitments to holy living.

History was also made in November 2009 when a commissioning of officers in Kenya occurred outside of Nairobi for the first time. More than 16,000 people gathered, again in Kakamega's Bukhungu Stadium, to witness the ordination and commissioning of 41 members of the Prayer Warriors Session. For many in attendance, it was their introduction to such an event.

The Psycho-Social Support (PSS) programme, a community-based effort to address the needs of children and youth relative to HIV/Aids, is especially targeting orphans and vulnerable children who, as a result of their situation, encounter rejection, humiliation, poor education and lack of parental care and support. Hope, healing and empowerment were brought to almost 3,000 young people, meeting in 66 PSS clubs in 50 different communities.

The territory's 2010 Self-Denial Appeal ingathering reported a 67 per cent increase over that raised in 2009, demonstrating that Kenya West Salvationists are not only committed to sharing the gospel of Christ close to home but in distant places of the world as well.

Kenya West enters its third year of existence with the intention of 'Growing Stronger through Bible Study and Prayer' – and by God's grace that will happen.

STATISTICS

Officers 700 (active 468 retired 232) **Cadets** 50 **Envoys/Employees** 170
Corps 328 **Outposts** 970 **Pre-primary Schools** 131 **Primary Schools** 280 **Secondary Schools** 33 **Institutions** 3
Senior Soldiers 113,707 **Junior Soldiers** 118,382

STAFF

Women's Ministries: Comr Florence Malabi (TLWM) Col Grace Mnyampi (TSWM) Maj Linet Wolayo (TDCM) Capt Gaudencia Omukonyi (TJHLS)
Business Administration: Lt-Col Timothy Mabaso
Personnel: Maj Johnstone Wolayo
Programme: Lt-Col Herman Mbakaya
Audit: Maj Jacob Olubwayo
Editor: Capt Julius Omukonyi
Education: Capt Fridah Kimaswoch
Finance: Capt Patrick Kimaswoch
Information Technology: Capt Brown Musasia
Projects: Capt Isaac Siundu
Property: Mr Moses Maruti
Public Relations: Capt Julius Omukonyi
Social: Maj Jacoba de Ligt
Sponsorships: Capt Jane Wanyama
Statistics: Capt Leah Kitaa
Youth: Capt Pelegi Wanyama
    Candidates: Capt Felisters Madegwa

DIVISIONS

Bungoma: PO Box 1106, Bungoma; tel: 055-30589; Lt-Col Tiras and Mebo Mbaja

Eldoret: PO Box 125, Eldoret; tel: 053-22266;
Lt-Col Sarah Wanyama

Kakamega: PO Box 660, Kakamega;
tel: 331-20344; Majs Harun and Beatrice
Chepsiri

Kitale: PO Box 548, Kitale; tel:054-30259;
Majs Fredrick and Jesica Khamalishi

Mbale: PO Box 80, Maragoli; tel: 056-51076;
Majs Isaac and Naomi Kivindyo

Musudzuu: PO Box 278, Seremi;
tel: 056-45055; Lt-Cols Peter and
Jescah Dali

Shigomere: PO Box 125, Khwisero;
tel: 056-20260; Majs William and
Florence Mutungi

Tongaren: PO Box 127, Tongaren; Majs Moses
and Gladys Shavanga

DISTRICTS

Bunyore: PO Box 81, Bunyore; Capt Reuben
Malaba

Elgon: PO Box 274, Malakisi; tel: 055-20443;
Capt Henry Changalwa

Kapsabet: PO Box 409, Kapsabet; Maj Sarah
M'tetu

Lugari: PO Box 15, Matete; Capt Amos
Malabi

Kimilili: PO Box 220, Kimilili; Maj Frederick
Omuzee

Kisumu: PO Box 288, Kisumu; tel: 057-2025632;
Maj Isaac Liviala

Madzuu: PO Box 381, Vihiga; Maj Wellington
Ongaya

Migori: PO Box 59, Suna, Migori; Maj James
Mukubwa

Sabatia: PO Box102, Wodanga; Maj Rosemary
Matunde

Turkana: PO Box 118-30500, Lodwar;
tel: 054-21010; Maj Joshua Kitonyi

Webuye: PO Box 484, Webuye; Maj Meshack
Wanjia

EDUCATIONAL WORK

SA Sponsored Kindergartens: 131
SA Sponsored Primary Schools: 280
**SA Sponsored and Managed Secondary
Schools:** 33

Special Schools
Schools for Visually Impaired
Kibos Primary School: PO Box 477, Kisumu;
(acc 230)
Kibos Secondary School: PO Box 77, Kisumu;
tel: 057-43135

Schools for Physically Impaired
Joyland Primary School: PO Box 1790, Kisumu;
tel:057-41864/50574 (acc 230)
Joyland Secondary School: PO Box 19494,
Kisumu (acc 174)

School for Hearing Impaired
Chekombero Primary School: PO Box 93,
Wodanga via Maragoli (60 pupils)

School for Mentally Challenged
Madegwa Primary School: PO Box 52,
Maragoli (55 pupils)

Inclusive School
Joy Valley Primary School – Kimatuni:
PO Box 1293, Bungoma (236 pupils)

SOCIAL SERVICES
Feeding Programmes for Destitutes
Kisumu: PO Box 288, Kisumu; tel: 057-4151
Shinoyi Community Centre

Health Centre
Kolanya: PO Box 88, Malakisi via Bungoma

Workshop
Kibos: PO Box 477, Kisumu (acc 12)

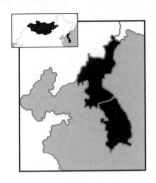

KOREA TERRITORY

Territorial leaders:
**Commissioner Park, Man-hee and
Commissioner Kim, Keum-nyeo**

Territorial Commander:
Commissioner Park, Man-hee
(1 Oct 2010)

Chief Secretary:
Colonel Park, Chong-duk (1 Oct 2010)

**Territorial Headquarters: The Salvation Army Building,
5th and 6th floors, 476 Choong Chung Ro 3-ga, Sudaemun Ku,
Seoul 120-837, Republic of Korea**

Postal address: The Salvation Army, Central PO Box 1192, Seoul 100-709, Republic of Korea

Tel: [82] (2) 720 9494 (Korean); [82] (2) 720 9403 (English);

email: korea@kor.salvationarmy.org; website: www.salvationarmy.or.kr

Responding to a request while visiting Japan in 1907, the Founder despatched Commissioner George Scott Railton to survey prospects on the Korean peninsula. As a result, in October 1908 Colonel and Mrs Robert Hoggard (née Annie Johns) arrived with a group of officers to 'open fire' in Seoul. During the Korean conflict, which took place from 1950 to 1953, five Korean officers and a corps sergeant-major were martyred.

Outreach work in Mongolia was officially commenced in October 2008.

Zone: South Pacific and East Asia
Countries included in the territory: Republic of Korea (South Korea), Democratic People's Republic of Korea (North Korea), Mongolia
'The Salvation Army' in Korean: (pronounced) 'Koo Sei Goon'
Language in which the gospel is preached: Korean, Mongolian
Periodicals: *Home League Programme Helps*, *Loving Hands* (sponsorship magazine), *The Officer*, *The War Cry*

UNDER the 2009 territorial theme, 'Let's Create A New History', several significant events took place. A Mongolian corps in the Seoul Division, located on the training college campus, is the first non-Korean corps in the territory. Commissioner Chun, Kwang-pyo (then TC) led the opening meeting on 15 April 2009, attended by 330 officers and soldiers along with 16 people from Mongolia.

Following on from The Salvation Army opening fire in Ulaanbaatar, Mongolia, in October 2008, the Kwachun Mongolian Corps will act as a bridge between its members' home country and Seoul for future expansion of ministries in both locations.

The groundbreaking ceremony for The Salvation Army Office, Mongolia, was carried out on 16 December.

Launched on 2 July 1909, *The War Cry* has continued publication throughout the years and so its centenary was marked by a thanksgiving. After the celebration gathering, current and past editors met in a forum to reflect on the significance of this monthly publication and to discuss its development and effectiveness.

The annual Territorial Youth Power Camp was organised by the Youth Department for three days in August. Under the theme 'Jesus Generation', 600 young delegates attended special events relevant to their generation's concerns.

The itinerary also included a concert with nationally famous gospel singers and a musical performed by Salvationist youth. During the dedication meeting led by the TC 20 young people publicly registered a commitment to officership.

Six corps held centenary celebrations during 2009-10. The centenary of the officer training college was also celebrated (2-5 February) with events that included seminars in which Salvationists, other Christians and leading theologians participated. The main theme centred on 'The Future of the Korean Church' and 'Challenges of Theological Education'.

At the ordination and commissioning of the Prayer Warriors Session (20 February) the territory's new lieutenants received their appointments. Shortly after came the public welcome to cadets of the Friends Of Christ Session (11 March).

Also in March, the annual Temperance Campaign was held throughout the territory. During these days, in all divisions, united open-air witness is held and visits are made to schools, prisons and other centres within local communities. This year 75,500 copies of a specially themed edition of *The War Cry* were distributed at campaign events.

STATISTICS

Officers 752 (active 604 retired 148) **Cadets** (1st Yr) 27 (2nd Yr) 30 **Employees** 947

Corps 251 **Outposts and Societies** 20 **Institutions** 37 **School** 1 **Child Day Care Centres** 6 **Conference Centres** 4 **Corps Child Day Care Centres** 23 **Students Study Centres (and after-school programmes)** 35 **Counselling Centres** 6 **Food Banks** 18 **Sarangbang Centres** 3 **Special Service Vehicle Units** 4 **HIV/Aids Care and Prevention Team Units** 2 **Bridge Centre for the Homeless** 1 **Self-Support Training Centres** 5 **Community Centres** 17 **Day Care Centres for the Elderly** 9

Senior Soldiers 42,418 **Adherents** 10,221 **Junior Soldiers** 6,636

Personnel serving outside territory Officers 15

STAFF

Women's Ministries: Comr Kim, Keum-nyeo (TPWM) Col Yoon, Eun-sook (TSWM) Lt-Col Yeo, Keum-soo (THLS) Lt-Col Chun, Soon-ja (TLMS) Lt-Col Lee, Ok-kyung (TSAMFS) Maj Pyo, Choon-yun (TSSS)

Sec for Personnel: Lt-Col Lim, Hun-taek
 Editor and Education: Capt Kim, Jong-sun
 Literary: Capt Lee, Bo-tak
 Development Ministry: Capt Park, Sung-ha
 Overseas Service Bureau: Capt Lee, Bo-tak

Sec for Programme: Lt-Col Lim, Young-sik
 Church Growth: Capt Chung, In-ok
 Social: Maj Lee, Soo-keun
 Youth: Maj Kim, Byoung-moo
 Music: Capt Kim, Hai-du

Sec for Business: Lt-Col Kim, Un-ho
  Finance and Audit: Maj Kim, Young-tae
  Information Technology: Capt Lee, Hyun-hee
  Property: Maj Lee, Ki-yong
  Public Relations: Capt Hong, Bong-shik
  Child Sponsorship: Capt Hong, Bong-shik
  Trade: Capt Kim, Sook-yung
Territorial Archivist: Lt-Col Kim, Joon-chul
Training: Maj Hwang, Sun-yup

DIVISIONS

Choong Buk: 704 Doosan Hansol 1 cha
  Apartments 101 dong, 447-15 Kaeshin
  Dong, Heungduk Ku, Chung Ju, Choong
  Book 361-746; tel: (043) 276 1634;
  fax: (043) 263 6387; Maj Kim, Nam-sun
Choong Chung: 603 Oosung Apartments
  126 dong, 640 Chunglim dong, Suh ku,
  Taejon, Choong Nam Do 302-795;
  tel: (042) 584 2891; fax: (042) 584 2892;
  Maj Park, Nai-hoon and Maj Kil, Soon-boon
Choong Saw: 401 Hyundai Apartments 3-cha
  302 dong, 388-2 Ssangyong dong, Suh Buk
  Ku, Chonan, Choong Nam Do 330-091;
  tel: (041) 572 0855; fax: (041) 578 0855;
  Maj Kwon, Sung-dal and Maj Kim, Moon-ok
Chulla: 375-21 Song San Dong, Chung Eup,
  Chun Buk 580-200; tel: (063) 536 1190;
  fax: (063) 536 1191; Maj Ahn, Guhn-shik and
  Maj Yang, Shin-kyong
Kyung Buk: #901 Doosan We've Apartments
  102 dong, Sung Dang 2 dong 728-1,
  Dahl suh ku, Taegu 704-980;
  tel: (053) 322 3695; fax: (053) 322 3694;
  Maj Choo, Seung-chan and Maj Lee, Ok-hee
Kyung Nam: 1306 Green Core Apartments
  301 dong, 216 7 Manduk 3 dong, Buk ku,
  Pusan, Kyung Sang Nam Do 616-782;
  tel: (051) 337 0789; fax: (051) 337 2292;
  Maj Kang, Jik-koo and Maj Kim, Chung-sook
Seoul: The Salvation Army Office Building,
  #705, 58-1 Shinmoonro 1-ga, Chongno gu,
  Seoul 110-061; tel: (02) 720 9543;
  fax: (02) 720 9546; Lt-Col Yang, Tae-soo and
  Lt-Col Chun, Ok-kyung
Seoul South: 602, Soojung Hanyang Apartments
  235-dong, 1086 Sunboo 3-dong, Danwon Ku,
  Ansan, Kyunggi-do 425-765;
  tel: (031) 413 7811; fax: (031) 413 7812;
  Lt-Col Chun, Joon-hong and Lt-Col Shin,
  Myung-ja
Suh Hae: 301 Dongshin Apartments 204 dong,
  Eupnae Dong 624-1, Sosan, Choong Nam
  356-758; tel: (041) 667 2580;
  fax: (041) 667 2576; Maj Kim Jong-koo
  and Maj Kim, Kye-suk

MONGOLIA OFFICE

Apartment 9 Narlii Zam 145th, District 13th
  Mini District 6, Ulaanbaatar Bayanzurkh,
  Mongolia; tel: (976) 7016 5355;
  mobile: (976) 9191 7261; Capt Lee, Min-ho
  and Capt Chang, Mi-hyun

CONFERENCE CENTRES

Territorial Retreat and Conference Centre:
  Paekhwasan (Mount Paekhwa) (acc 1,000)
Choong Chung Div: Taejon Central Corps,
  Taejon (acc 400)
Seoul Div: Ah Hyun Corps, Kangwondo
  (acc 300)
Seoul Div: Youngwol Corps (acc 50)

OFFICER TRAINING COLLEGE

83-2 Chungang-dong, Kwachun, Kyunggi-do
  427-010; tel: (02) 502 9505/2927;
  fax: (02) 502 7160

RETIRED OFFICERS' RESIDENCE

'Victory Lodge' Silver Nursing Home (acc 50)

SCHOOL

Inpyung Technical High School (acc 1,340)

TERRITORIAL HERITAGE CENTRE

1st floor, The Salvation Army Central Hall,
  1-23 Chung dong, Choong Ku,
  Seoul 100-120

THE SALVATION ARMY BUILDING

476 Choong Chung Ro 3-ga, Sudaemun Gu,
  Seoul 120-837

THE SALVATION ARMY
CENTRAL HALL

1-23 Chung dong, Choong Ku, Seoul 100-120

THE SALVATION ARMY OFFICE
BUILDING (THE SAOB)

58-1 Shinmoon ro 1-ga, Chongno Ku,
  Seoul 110-061

SOCIAL MINISTRIES
Adult Rehabilitation Centre (ARC)

Iljook

Bridge Centres (drop-in centres)

Seoul (acc 530)

Centres for the Handicapped

Kunsan:
    Catherine Centre for the Handicapped (acc 54)
    Day Care Centre for the Handicapped (acc 25)

There was joyous celebration at the official opening of Kwachun Mongolian Corps, in Seoul Division. Located on the training college campus, it is the first non-Korean corps in the territory.

Suwon:
Support Centre for the Handicapped
(acc 5)
Rehabilitation Centre for the Handicapped
(acc 15)
Day Care Centre for the Handicapped
(acc 15)

Children's Homes
Kunsan (acc 75), Seoul Broadview (acc 160),
Taegu (acc 61), Taejon No 1 (acc 50),
Taejon No 2 (acc 75) Sarangsaem (acc 7)

Community Centres
Community Centres: Hapchong, Hongeun,
Kang Buk, Myung Chun, Samyang Dong,
Suh San Suklim, Youngwol
Corps Welfare Centres: An Sung Gongdo,
Booyuh, Cheju, Mosan, Najoo, Seogwipo,
Taegu, Suh An Sung Home Helper Centre
for the Elderly, Taegu Chil Kok Centre for
the Elderly, Yoju
Self-Support Training Centres: Asan, Bohryung,
Nonsan, Sosan, Tai An,

Corps Day Care Centres
Bahnyawol, Boo Nam, Chin Chang, Chun Kok,
Hap Duk, Kang Buk, Keumbit Namoo
(Hongeun), Kim Chon, Kwachun, Masan
(Moonwha), Mindalae, Mosan, Myung Chun,
Osan Saetbyeol (Star), San Kok, Sharon,
Sok Cho, Suhdaemun, Suh Taegu, Suh San
Suk Lim, Taegu, Wonju, Yul Mok

Counselling and Friendship Centres
Chonan Counselling Centre for Women,
Tong Taegu, Taegu, Suh Taejon, Tong Taejon,
Taejon

Family Welfare Centres
Bohryung Multicultural Family Support Centre

**Food Banks, Food Markets and
Distribution Centres**
Asan, Bohryung, Cheju, Chun An, Kwachun,
Mapo #1, Mapo #2 Nonsan, Seogwipo,
Song Dong, Sosan, Sudaemun #1,
Sudaemun #2, Suh Chung Ju, Taejon, Taian,
Yea San, Yeoju

HIV/Aids Care and Prevention Programme Units

Pusan Shelter; Red Ribbon Centre, Seoul

Oori Jip (transitional housing for those leaving children's homes)

Ah Hyun (acc 6), Choongdong (Seoul Broadview Children's Home) (acc 2), Chun Yun (acc 3), Yung Chun (acc 4)

Sarangbang Centres (hostels for the homeless)

Buk Ah Hyun Dong (acc 30), Iljook (acc 59), Mangu Dong (acc 75), Sudaemun (acc 50)

Self-Support Training Centres

Boryung, Nonsan, Taian

Senior Citizens' Services

Residential

Ansung Nursing Home (acc 60), Ansung Peace Village Nursing Home (acc 71), Kwachun Home for the Elderly (acc 30), Kwachun Nursing Home (acc 50), Mulwoori, Namdong Peace Village (acc 71), Pusan Home for the Elderly (acc 71), Sooyong, Sun Chang Welfare Centre for the Elderly (acc 30), 'Victory Lodge' Silver Nursing Home, Kwachun (acc 60), Yongho

Day Centres

Hapjung Day Centre for the Elderly (acc 14), Hongjae Dong Day Care Centre for the Elderly (acc 20), Mooan 'Silver Centre' for the Elderly (acc 5), Najoo Day Centre for the Elderly (acc 10), Namdong Day Centre for the Elderly (acc 71), Suhsansung Day Centre for the Elderly (acc 20), Suwon Day Care Centre for the Elderly (acc 15), Wolsung Day Care Centre for the Elderly (acc 18)

Welfare Centre

Ansung Welfare Centre for Seniors

Special Service and Relief Services

9 programmes, 4 vehicles

Students' Study Centres (and after-school programmes)

1318 Happy Zone (Cheju), 1318 Happy Zone (Onyang), Asan, Baesan, Boo Nam, Buk Choon Chun, Buk Gumi, Cheju, Chew Kok, Chin Hae, Chisan, Chun An, Chun Kok, Daniel (Eonyak), Doriwon, Eden, Haram (Nonsan), Hongjae, Keumsan, Mil Yang, Oh Ka, Sae Chung Ju, Sae Sungnam, Seogwipo, Seoul Broadview, Shim Chon, Shinchang, Suh Taegu Pisan 4-dong, Taegu, Taegu Chil Kok, Wadong, Yea San, Yong Dong, Yoju, Youngwol

Student Accommodation

Taejon (university students, acc 23)

Thrift Stores

Seoul: Sudaemun; Yun Hie

Thrift Stores and Sally's Coffee

Seoul: Ah Hyun; Daehangno

Food Markets, Thrift Stores and Sally's Coffee

Seoul: Seon Dong; Buk Ah Hyung Dong; Mapo #1 (no Sally's Coffee); Mapo #2

Vocational Training and Support Centres

Chung Daoon House, Taejon (acc 30); Sally Home, Pusan (acc 22)

Women's Homes

Chonan House of Hope (acc 10); Doori Home, Seoul (acc 35); Taejon Women's Refuge Shelter (acc 55)

LATIN AMERICA NORTH TERRITORY

Territorial leaders:
Colonels Tito and Martha Paredes

Territorial Commander:
Colonel Tito Paredes (1 Aug 2010)

Chief Secretary:
Lieut-Colonel Josue Cerezo (1 Mar 2011)

Territorial Headquarters: Avenida 11, Calle 20, San José, Costa Rica

Postal address: Apartado Postal 125-1005, Barrio México, San José, Costa Rica

Tel: [506] 2257-7535; fax: [506] 2257-5291; email: lan_leadership@lan.salvationarmy.org

The Salvation Army's work commenced in the Isthmus of Panama (1904), Costa Rica (1907), Cuba (1918), Venezuela (1972), Guatemala (1976), Colombia (1985), El Salvador (1989), Dominican Republic (1995) Honduras (2000) and Nicaragua (2010).

Legal recognition was given to El Ejército de Salvación by the Republic of Panama (1946), Costa Rica (1975), Guatemala (1978), Colombia (1988), The Dominican Republic (1995), El Salvador (1996) and Honduras (2001). The territory was formed on 1 October 1976, then reformed on 1 September 1998, when Mexico became a command.

Zone: Americas and Caribbean
Countries included in the territory: Colombia, Costa Rica, Cuba, Dominican Republic, El Salvador, Guatemala, Honduras, Nicaragua, Panama, Venezuela
'The Salvation Army' in Spanish: Ejército de Salvación
Languages in which the gospel is preached: English, Kacchikel, Spanish
Publications: *Voz de Salvación (Salvation Voice), Arco Iris de Ideas (Rainbow of Ideas)*

SIXTEEN new officers – from Cuba, Colombia, Costa Rica, El Salvador and Dominican Republic – were ordained and commissioned in December 2009. The celebration weekend for the Prayer Warriors Session took place in the Blas Roca Theatre, Havana, Cuba, with Commissioners Maxwell and Leonora Feener (territorial leaders, USA Southern) and Texas Divisional Band as special guests.

Cuba's music and drama groups participated in meetings where a strong spirit of Salvationism was evident.

Costa Rica hosted the welcome meeting for the Ambassadors Of Holiness Session. The then territorial leaders, Colonels Oscar and Ana Rosa Sánchez, and Chief Secretary Lieut-Colonel Zoilo Pardo received cadets from Honduras, El Salvador, Costa Rica and Venezuela for officer training.

Earlier in the year members of the Future Officers' Fellowship met in Cuba. Many knelt at the mercy seat to affirm their commitment to service as Salvation Army officers.

'La Esperanza' Refuge in Costa Rica was reopened in May. The centre serves 130 people with breakfast every day. Ten people with alcohol dependency who attended the refuge were admitted to the rehabilitation centre in San Jose.

In June an initiative by league of mercy members in Colombia included leading meetings in residential homes for the elderly. Members also preached the gospel in the open-air and visited people in the community. A prayer ministry took place among drug addicts, homeless people and residents in care homes.

When a men's camp was held in Panama in July, delegates from every corps and outpost participated. Major Federico Larrinaga (USA Eastern) was the guest speaker.

In Cuba seven corps held a successful holiday Bible school. The programme included songs, games and lessons. Staff also visited children and their families. The young people participated with enthusiasm and some received Christ as their saviour.

Conquistadores del Reino ('Conquerors of the Kingdom') was the theme of the annual youth camp in September. Captain Mark Hall (Canada and Bermuda) led the young people in sessions based on the Book of Joshua.

The Dominican Republic Region celebrated Youth Week in October. Salvationists took every opportunity to speak with young people in the community and invited them to planned events.

After floods hit El Salvador in November more than 13,000 people received food, clothing, cleaning products and spiritual support from Salvationists. Members of corps, including young people, visited more than 2,500 people in several affected areas.

STATISTICS

Officers 148 (active 131 retired 17)
   Employees 230
Corps 56 **Outposts** 17 **Institutions** 8 **Schools** 11
   Day Care Centres 9 **Children's Development
   Centres** 8 **Vocational Training Centres** 4
   Feeding Centres 14 **Camps** 2
Senior Soldiers 2,811 **Adherents** 1,063 **Junior
   Soldiers** 1,224

STAFF

Women's Ministries: Col Martha Paredes
   (TPWM) Lt-Col Ruth Cerezo (TSWM)
Business Administration: Maj Esteban Calvo
Personnel: under CS's Office
Programme: Maj Max Mayorga
Candidates: Maj Ileana Calvo
Editorial: Maj Ileana Calvo
Education: Maj Javier Obando
Finance: Maj Esteban Calvo
Projects and Sponsorship: Maj Esteban Calvo
Social: Maj Max Mayorga
Training: Maj Javier Obando

DIVISIONS

Colombia: Apartado Aéreo 17756 Santa Fe de
   Bogotá, Colombia; tel: (571) 263 2633;
   fax: (571) 295 2921; email:
   coldiv_leadership@lan.salvatonarmy.org;
   Majs José and Hilda Santiago
Costa Rica: Apartado Postal 6227-1000,
   San José, Costa Rica; tel: (506) 2221 8266;
   fax: (506) 2223 0250; email:
   crdiv_leadership@lan.salvationarmy.org;
   Majs Jorge and Idali Méndez
Cuba: Calle 96 Nª 5513 entre 55 Y 57,
   Marianao CP 11400, Ciudad de la Habana, Cuba;
   tel: (53) 7260-2171; fax: (53) 7267-2537;
   email: ejdivcuba@enet.cu; Capts Orestes and
   Sandra Linares
Guatemala: Apartado Postal 1881, Guatemala CA;

Members of a mission team in Costa Rica conduct a children's meeting

2a Avenida 3-10, Sector A4 San Cristóbal 1,
Zona 8 de Mixco, Guatemala;
tel (502) 2472-4804/4803; fax: (502) 2472-4668;
email: divgua.lan@gmail.com
Panama: Apartado Postal 0843-01134 Balboa,
Ancón Panamá, República de Panamá,
Balboa Calle La Boca, Calle Julio Linares
Edificio 0792, República de Panamá;
tel: (507) 228-0148; Maj Deisy Costas

REGIONS
Dominican Republic: Ejército de Salvación,
Apartado Postal M215, Oficina Postal Los
Mameyes, Calle 4ta, Esquina 26 De Enero,
Santo Domingo Este, Dominican Republic;
tel: 1(809) 335 2678; fax: 1(809) 335 2678;
email: armyregion@gmail.com; Maj Gerardo
Góchez
El Salvador: Apartado Postal No 7,
Centro de Gobierno, Calle 15 de Septiembre,
Nº 119 y Nº 121 Barrio Candelaria,
San Salvador; tel: (503) 2237-0267;
fax: (503) 2270-9155; email:
ejercito-salvacion@salnet.net; Majs Donald
and Jean Wilson
Honduras work (under THQ): Colonia El
Hogar, Bloque B, Casa Nº11 Tegucigalpa,
Apartado Postal 6590, Honduras;

tel/fax: (504) 232-4927/235-9855;
email: obrahondurastegu@gmail.com;
Capt Quelvin Cañas
Venezuela: Calle San Juan de Dios Melián,
Entre calle san Rafael y la Segunda de
Cabudare Riviera Departamento 1,
Cabudare-Barquisimento, Venezuela;
tel: (058) 251 261-6318;
email: ejercitodes.venz@yahoo.es;
Maj Pedro López

PIONEER WORK
Nicaragua: Reparto Miraflores de donde fue
el Restaurante Munich, 1 cuadra al Sur,
2 cuadras arriba y media cuadra al Sur;
Maj Enrique Molina

TRAINING COLLEGE
Calle Puente de Piedra, 1 km norte del Puente
de Piedra, Barrio Los Angeles, San Rafael de
Heredia, Costa Rica; Postal address: Apartado
173-3015 San Rafael de Heredia, Costa Rica;
tel: (506) 2262 0061; fax: (506) 2262 0733

SOCIAL SERVICES
Institutions
Centre for Homeless
Costa Rica: Refugio de Esperanza: Avenida 9

Zona Roja, San José; tel: (506) 2233-2059 (acc 30)

Disabled Centre
Costa Rica: Hogar Sustituto 'Tierra Prometida', Carretera Interamericana 100 metros sur de Autos Mundiales, Pérez Zeledón; tel: (506) 2771-2517 (acc 13)

Residential Homes for the Elderly
Cuba: William Booth Home, Calle 84 No 5525 e/55 y Lindero, Mariano, CP 11400, Ciudad de la Habana; tel: (537) 260-1118
Panama: Hogar Jackson Home, Avenida Amador Guerrero y Calle 3 No 2014, Colón; tel: (507) 441-3371 (acc 30)

Residential Homes for Children
Panama: Hogar Dr Eno (Girls), Transísmica, Sabanitas, Colón; tel: (507) 442-0371 (acc 20)
Venezuela: Hogar Nido Alegre, Calle 71 # 14 A63, Juana de Avila, Apdo Postal 1464 Maracaibo 4001; Estado de Zulia, Venezuela; tel: (58-261) 798-3761 (acc 50)

Adult Rehabilitation Centres
Costa Rica:
Centro Modelo: Calle Naranjo, Concepción de Tres Ríos, Cartago; tel: (506) 2273-6307
Refugio de Esperanza Liberia: Frente a la Estación de Bomberos, Guanacaste; tel: (506) 2666-5567/2664-4691
Cuba: Centro de Rehabilitación de Alcoholicos: Carretera de Vertienes Km 3 #335, Reparto Río Verde Camagüey CP 71200; tel: (53) 3225-8230

EDUCATIONAL WORK
Kindergartens
Dominican Republic: Moca, Prolongación Sánchez #12, Moca; tel: (1809) 578-9712 (acc 20)
El Salvador: Merliot Corps: Jardines del Volcán, Calle El Jabali # 36, Ciudad Merliot, La Libertad; tel: (503) 2278-4982 (acc 60)
Panama: Panamá Templo: Calle 25 y Avenida Cuba-Este; tel: (507) 262-2545 (acc 30)

Kindergartens and Schools
Dominican Republic:
Cotui: 16 de Agosto N° 98, Cotui, Sánchez Ramírez; tel: (809) 585-3393 (acc 40)
Tres Brazos: Calle Matadero N° 70 (acc 20)
Guatemala:
Chimaltenango: 7a Avenida y 1a Calle, Zona 1,

Villas del Pilar; tel: (502) 7839-6585 (acc 150)
Maya: Manzana #2, Lote 262, Zona 18, Conia Maya; tel: (502) 2260 1519
Mezquital: 4a Calle 3-99, Zona 12, Colonia Mezquital; tel: (502) 2479-8443 (acc 150)
Satelite: Lote 5, Manzana 27, Proyecto 2, Ciudad Satelite, Mixto; tel: (502) 484-3052 (acc 30)
Tierra Nueva: Sector B-1, Manzana D, Lote 3, Colonia Tierra Nueva 11, Chinautla; tel: (502) 2484-1255 (acc 150)
Honduras: San Pedro Sula: Colonia Trejos – IV Etapa, Calle 22E, 21-23 Avenida, Town House No 1, San Pedro Sula, Honduras; Apartado Postal No 2270, San Pedro Sula, Honduras; tel/fax: (504) 556 7238
Panama: Calle 11 y 1/2, La Pulida, Río Abajo; tel: (507) 224-7480 (acc 40)

Kindergarten, Primary and Secondary School
Guatemala: Limón: Colegio William Booth, Centro Communal 'El Limón' Costado Derecho, Zona 18; tel: (502) 2260-0723 (acc 395)

Health-Education in Hospitals
Honduras:
Avanzada de Tegucigalpa: Hospital Materno Infantil (4 classrooms); tel: (504) 232-4927
Avanzada San Pedro Sula: Hospital Mario Catarino Rivas (2 classrooms); tel: (504) 556-7238

Day Care Centres
Colombia: San Cristóbal Sur, Bogotá: Calle 12 Sur # 11-71 Este, Barrio San Cristóbal Sur, Santa Fe de Bogotá; tel: (571) 333-0606/289-2672
Costa Rica:
Central Corps: Avenida 16, Entre Calle 5 y 7 San José; tel: (506) 2233-6850 (acc 35)
León XIII: Ciudadela León XIII, Detrás de la Escuela de León XIII, San José; tel: (506) 2231-1786 (acc 80)
Limón Central: Av 4 entre Calles 7 y 9; tel: (506) 2758-0657 (acc 75)
Pavas: Villa Esperanza de Pravas, Contiguo Al Instituto Nacional de Aprendizaje, San José; tel: (506) 2231-1786 (acc 80)
El Salvador:
Merliot Corps: Jardines del Volcán, Calle El Jabali # 36, Ciudad Merliot, La Libertad; tel: (503) 2278-8249 (acc 60)

Latin America North Territory

Guatemala: Escuela – Satélite: Lote 5, Manzana 27, Proyecto 2, Ciudad Satélite, Mixco; tel: (502) 484-3052 (acc 15)

Panama:
Templo Central: Calle 25 y Av Cuba-Este; tel: (507) 262-2545 (acc 20)
Río Abajo: Calle 11 y 1/2 y la Pulida; tel: (507) 224-7480 (acc 25)

Children's Development Centres

Colombia:
Armenia Outpost: Carrera 11 # 14-19 Barrio Guayaquil; tel: (576) 746-8591
Nuevo Kennedy: Avda Calle 43 Sur #79 B47, Barrio Nuevo Kennedy, Santa Fe de Bogotá, Colombia; tel: (57) 1 264 9161
Ibague, Tolima: Carrera 4ta Sur # 20A-34, Barrio Yuldaima, Apartado Aéreo 792; tel: (578) 260-8032
Robledo, Medellín: Carrera 84B # 63-73, Barrio Robledo, Medellín, Antioquía; tel: (094) 234-8250
San Cristóbal Sur, Bogotá: Calle 12 Sur # 11-71 Este, Barrio San Cristóbal Sur, Santa Fe de Bogotá; tel: (571) 333-0606/289-2672

El Salvador:
Cuerpo Central: Calle 15 de Septiembre # 199 y # 121, Barrio Candelaria, San Salvador; tel: (503) 270-5273 (acc 246)

Venezuela: Maracaibo: Calle 10 (99E) #62-09, Barrio Simón Bolivar, Apartado postal 322, Maracaibo 4001, Estado Zulia

Vocational Training Centres

Cuba:
Cuerpo Central: Computer Centre, Calle 96 Nª 5513 entre 55 y 57, Marianao 11400, La Habana; tel: (53) 260-2171
Diezmero: Dressmaking, Calle 3ra Nª 25304 entre 2da y Martí Diezmero San Miguel del Padrón, CP 130000 Guevara, La Habana

Guatemala: Mecanografía: Satelite Lote 5, Manzana 27, Proyecto 2, Ciudad Satelite, Mixto; tel: (502) 484-3052 (acc 30)

Venezuela: Centro Vocacional – Carpenteria y Costura, Calle 71 # 14 A-63, Cuartel Juana de Acila, Apartado Postal 1464

Feeding Centres

Costa Rica:
Liberia: 500 mts Norte Estación de Bomberos 100 Este y 50 Norte, Barrio San Roque; tel: (506) 2666-3603 (acc 100)

Limón 2000: Barrio Limón 2000 frente al Predio El Aragón, Alameda # 4; tel: (506) 2797-1602 (acc 30)
Nicoya: Escuela de San Martín 900 al Oeste, Barrio San Martín; tel: (506) 2685-5531 (acc 100)
Sagrada: Costado Este de la Escuela Carolina Dent, Barrio Sangrada Familia
Salitrillos: Salitrillos de Aserri, de las Prestaciones, 300 metros al sur; tel: (506) 2230-4668 (acc 80)
San Isidro del General: Barrio Los Angeles, Apartado Postal 7-8000; tel: (506) 2770-6756 (acc 150)
Santa Cruz: Barrio Tulita Sandino, 300 este del IDA Guanacaste; tel: (506) 2680-0724 (acc 100)

Colombia: Comedor de Ancianos, Carrera 5ta Sur # 20A-34, Barrio Yulduima, Ibague, Tolima

Cuba:
Comedor William Booth: Calle 96 No 5513 entre 55 y 57

Panama:
Colon: Avenida Amador Guerrero 14201, Apartado 1163; tel: (507) 441-4570 (acc 75)
Chilibre: Transistmica, Lote No 175, Chilibre; tel: (507) 216-2501 (acc 100)

Venezuela: Simón Bolívar, Calle 10 (99E) #62-09, Barrio Simón Bolivar, Apartado postal 322, Maracaibo 4001, Estado Zulia

Camps

El Salvador: Km 50, Carretera a la Herradura, Caserio los Novios, Hacienda del Cauca; tel: (503) 2354-4530 (acc 150)

Guatemala: Tecpán: Calle Tte Coronel Jack Waters, Barrio Poromá, Colonia Iximché; tel: (502) 7840-3998 (acc 100)

LIBERIA COMMAND

Officer Commanding:
Lieut-Colonel Festus Oloruntoba
(1 Jul 2010)

General Secretary:
Major Charles Swansbury (1 Feb 2009)

Command Headquarters: 17th Street, Sinkor, Monrovia

Postal address: PO Box 20/5792, Monrovia, Liberia

The Salvation Army opened fire in Liberia in May 1988 as part of the Ghana and Liberia Territory, with Major and Mrs Leonard Millar as pioneer officers. This happened after more than 10 years of letters being written to International Headquarters by church pastors asking that they become part of the movement. Liberia was given separate command status on 1 January 1997. Neighbouring Sierra Leone became part of the command on 1 January 2010, with Captains John and Rosaline Bundu as pioneer officers.

Zone: Africa
Countries included in the command: Liberia, Sierra Leone
Languages in which the gospel is preached: Bassa, English, Gola, Krahn, Pele

HISTORY was made on 4 December 2009 when Captains John and Rosaline Bundu left Liberia en route to Freetown to pioneer the opening of The Salvation Army in neighbouring Sierra Leone. Having originated from Sierra Leone, but meeting the Army and becoming officers in Liberia, the captains had for many years felt called to be among those who would work towards the expansion of the Army further along the West African coast.

As from 1 January 2010 Sierra Leone became the 119th country in which the Army is established. Just four months later the first 25 soldiers were enrolled in a ceremony broadcast live on national radio.

Following the establishment of the Education Secretariat in October 2008, the Salvation Army Schools System remained financially self-sufficient throughout the 2008-09 academic year, this after some years of fiscal uncertainty. Teacher training workshops were held in Monrovia and at regional centres, to upgrade the educational standard of teaching staff.

A graduation ceremony in August 2009 for 360 students marked the completion of the first academic year of the vocational and technical training centre. Appreciation was expressed in recognition of the valuable support from Norway, Iceland and The Faeroes Territory in making provision to facilitate the vocational programmes.

Additional support from that same territory will enable the mobile clinic to be maintained for a five-year period.

The clinic travels to remote areas where there is no other medical service.

The hostel for boys was closed as the remaining five residents exceeded the threshold of 18 years of age and were assisted into independent living.

Nine cadets of the Prayer Warriors Session were ordained and commissioned as lieutenants in an exuberant celebratory weekend at the William Booth Compound in Paynesville.

A visit by Commissioners Amos and Rosemary Makina (IS and ZSWM, Africa) coincided with the production of a new Liberia Command lappa. Women wearing these outfits provided a colourful backdrop to traditional ceremonies of greeting during a women's rally.

STATISTICS

Officers 59 Auxiliary-Captains 10 Envoys 4
Corps Leaders 4 Cadets 9 Employees 198
Corps 21 Outposts 18 Schools 12 (pupils 2,992)
Child Day Care Centres 8 Clinic 1 Mobile
Clinic 1
Senior Soldiers 2,028 Adherents 54 Junior
Soldiers 424

STAFF

Women's Ministries: Maj Denise Swansbury
(CSWM) Maj Etta Gaymo (LOMS)
Capt Lydia McKay (JMHLS)
Education Secretariat: Mr David Massaquoi
(Dir Education) Mr Elijah Sowen (Dep Dir
Education) Mr Julius Fayiah, Mr Christian
Smith (Education Officers)
Field: Maj Ben Gaymo
Finance: tba
High School Coordinator: Maj Denise
Swansbury
Projects: Maj Denise Swansbury
Protocol and Communications: Envoy Momo
Douwee
Trade: Miss Maria Gee
Vocational and Technical Training Centre
Programme Coordinator: Mr Tweh Wesseh
Youth and Candidates: Capt Morris McKay

DISTRICT

Grand Bassa: c/o CHQ, PO Box 20/5792,
Monrovia; Capt Anthony Sio

SECTIONS

(c/o CHQ, PO Box 20/5792, Monrovia)
Bomi: Capt Edwin Kpadebah
Bong: Capt Amos Barnard
Buchanan City: Capt Jerry Duwah
Bushrod Island: Maj William Zogar
Compound Three: Capt Jonah Roberts
Grand Gedeh: Capt Shad Joloe
Margibi: Capt Amos Diah
Monrovia City: Capt Phillip Boweh
Mount Coffee: Maj Hilton Youngar
Paynesville: Capt Samson Kanmoe
Sinoe: Capt Broton Weah

SCHOOLS AND COLLEGES

(c/o CHQ, PO Box 20/5792, Monrovia)
Salvation Army Vocational Technical and
Training College; Programme Coordinator:
Mr Tweh Wesseh BSc, LLB; Programme
Consultant: Mr Taweh Johnson MSc
William Booth High School; Principal: Mr Brima
Dennis MA
John Gowans Junior and Senior High School;
Principal: Mr Morris Sargba BSc
Bill Norris Primary, Elementary and Junior High
School; Principal: Mr Richard Zekor
Albert Orsborn Primary and Elementary School;
Principal: Capt Amos Diah
Bramwell Booth Primary and Elementary
School; Principal: Mr Davison Paye
Len Millar Primary and Elementary School;
Mr Egbinda Brima BSc
Paul A. Rader Primary and Elementary School;
Principal: Mr Andrew Sagely
William Booth Primary and Elementary School;
Principal: Mr Lansana Kamara

CLINIC

William Booth Clinic: c/o CHQ, PO Box 20/5792,
Monrovia; Administrator: Mrs Korlu Smoke
Geh; Physcian Asst: Mr Johannson David

SIERRA LEONE (under CHQ)

Officer-in-charge: Capt John Bundu
The Salvation Army, 39 Upper Brook St,
Freetown, Sierra Leone

MALAWI COMMAND

Command leaders:
Colonels Henry and Catherine Nyagah

Officer Commanding:
Colonel Henry Nyagah (1 Jul 2010)

General Secretary:
Major Francis Nyambalo (1 Feb 2007)

Command Headquarters: PO Box 51140, Limbe, Malawi

tel: [265] 1 917073 / 981142 email: MAL_Leadership@mal.salvationarmy.org

The Salvation Army began operations in Malawi on 13 November 1967 and was granted official government recognition on 2 October 1973. The Malawi Division was part of the Zimbabwe Territory until 1988, when it was integrated into the Zambia Command, which was given territorial status and became known as the Zambia and Malawi Territory. The Army's work in Malawi has grown and developed and on 1 October 2002 it became a separate region. Further growth and expansion of the work in Malawi resulted in the region being elevated to command status on 1 February 2004.

Zone: Africa
Country included in the command: Malawi
'The Salvation Army' in Chichewa: Nkhondo ya Chipulumutso
Languages in which the gospel is preached: Chichewa, English, Lomwe, Sena, Tumbuka

AN inspiring congress in September 2009 was conducted by Africa zonal leaders Commissioners Amos and Rosemary Makina, IHQ, near the place where The Salvation Army began its ministry in Malawi.

More than 2,000 Salvationists travelled for miles on foot, by bicycle and in the back of trucks while some marched to the congress site along dusty roads. As they met for worship in small and large groups God blessed them abundantly.

Commissioner Amos Makina opened the extension to Command Headquarters. The building was funded through the generosity of USA Central Territory.

Commissioner Margaret Sutherland visited the command to conduct officers councils at the beginning of the year. During the visit of Commissioners Barry and Sue Swanson (the then territorial leaders, USA Central) 14 officers were ordained and commissioned. These were the first cadets to be trained in Malawi since the Army commenced work in 1967.

Two districts were elevated to division status and two new districts were formed during the year.

An earthquake at the end of 2009 caused considerable damage to communities near Karonga on the northern shore of Lake Malawi.

With funding from International Emergency Services, IHQ, the command provided hundreds of people with temporary shelters, food and clothing. As a result three new outposts have opened and the fledgling Army in the area is well recognised.

A group of divisional leaders from the United Kingdom visited Mchinji and observed the Army's work among victims of human trafficking. Boys who have been taken from their homes to work on tobacco farms are rescued, rehabilitated and returned to their families.

Projects providing facilities such as clean water, health education, food supplies and 'bush' ambulances are flourishing within the growing Army in Malawi.

STATISTICS

Officers 78 (active 72 retired 6) **Cadets** (1st year 20) **Employees** 94
Corps 37 **Outposts** 14 **Outreach Units and New Openings** 61
Senior Soldiers 5,758 **Junior Soldiers** 1,696
Personnel serving outside command Officers 2

STAFF

Women's Ministries: Col Catherine Nyagah (CPWM) Maj Jamiya Nyambalo (CSWM)
Business: Mr Lameck Adam
Development Services: Narelle Gurney
Extension Training and Candidates: Capt Robert Mtengowalira
Property: Capt Godfrey Chagwa
Training: Maj Samuel Oklah
Youth: Capt Luke Msikita

DIVISIONS

Blantyre: PO Box 51749, Limbe; tel: 01 655 901; Maj Effort and Capt Annet Paswera
Central: PO Box 40058, Kanengo, Lilongwe; tel: 01 716 869; Capts Alfred and Pamela Banda

Phalombe: PO Box 99, Migowi; tel: 01 481 216; Majs Gerald and Ellen Chimimba
Shire Valley: PO Box 48, Chiromo; Capts Paul and Doreen Kholowa

DISTRICTS

Northern: PO Box 1129, Mzuzu: Capt Dickson Mpakula
Upper Shire: P/Bag 8, Ntcheu CDSS, Ntcheu; Capt Dyson Chifudzeni

OFFICER TRAINING COLLEGE AND EXTENSION TRAINING CENTRE

Ndirande Ring Rd, Chinseu, Blantyre; PO Box 51140, Limbe

COMMUNITY DEVELOPMENT PROGRAMMES

Adult Literacy
Blantyre, Central, Phalombe and Shire Valley Divisions, Northern District

Agriculture, Irrigation, Food Security Programme
Shire Valley Division

Child Advocacy
Central Division

Feeding/Food for Work
Chikwawa, Migowi, Nguludi, Nsanje

HIV/Aids Home-based Care
Bangwe, Migowi, Nguludi, Nsanje

Micro-credit Schemes
All divisions and districts

Orphans and Vulnerable Children
All divisions and districts

Rural Women Empowerment (inc boreholes)
Blantyre, Central and Shire Valley Divisions

Solar power (Small Business) Enterprise
Blantyre Division

SOCIAL SERVICES

Hans Andersen Memorial Youth Centre for Child Anti-Trafficking: PO Box 167, Mchinji

MEXICO TERRITORY

Territorial leaders:
Commissioners David and Grace Bringans

Territorial Commander:
Commissioner David Bringans (1 Jul 2009)

Chief Secretary:
Lieut-Colonel Douglas Danielson
(1 Mar 2011)

Territorial Headquarters: San Borja #1456, Colonia Vértiz Narvarte, Delegación Benito Juárez, México 03600, DF

Postal address: Apartado Postal 12-668, México 03020, DF

Tel: [525] 55575-1042; 55559-5244/9625; fax: [525] 55575-3266; email: mexico@salvationarmy.org;
website: www.ejercitodesalvacionmx.org

In 1934, a group known as the Salvation Patrol was commenced in Mexico by Alejandro Guzmán. In October 1937, he was presented with a flag by General Evangeline Booth at the USA Southern Territory Congress in Atlanta, Georgia. The Salvation Patrol then became absorbed into the international Salvation Army, operating under the supervision of DHQ in Dallas, Texas, later becoming part of Latin America North Territory. On 1 September 1998 it was made a command and, on 1 October 2001, it became a territory.

Zone: Americas and Caribbean
Country included in the territory: Mexico
'The Salvation Army' in Spanish: Ejército de Salvación
Language in which the gospel is preached: Spanish
Publications: *El Grito de Guerra (The War Cry), El Eslabon (The Link)*

DRUGS, guns and violence are part of life in Mexico but so too is The Salvation Army – the compassionate 'Army without guns' whose dedicated personnel reach out with the gospel of hope and give practical assistance to people in need.

In August 2009 the training college welcomed 11 cadets of the Ambassadors Of Holiness Session. The following month eight officers, with guest lecturer Lieut-Colonel Ruth Cerezo (then TSWM), attended the Brengle Institute held in Chile for Latin American territories.

'Building God's Kingdom' – through personal holiness, strong and united corps, and mission in the community – was the territorial theme for 2010. Resources were provided to equip every corps to teach and promote this theme.

In January, 49 personnel from the Army's 19 children's homes attended a conference in Metepec. The territory has since published two manuals of guidelines for the care and protection of children.

In March, 43 members of the Future Officers' Fellowship travelled to Mexico City for meetings led by the Territorial Youth and Candidates Secretary. For the first time candidates for officership were assessed by selected officers, a local officer and a psychologist.

Youth and children's camps were held to teach and encourage young people. Teams of young people held successful missions in corps. Their enthusiasm and innovative methods brought beneficial results in growing God's Kingdom.

On 4 April, Mexicali in Baja California experienced a 7.2 earthquake, causing loss of life and damage to buildings including the Army hall. Emergency vehicles from USA Southern Territory delivered food and water to 500 people.

Women's ministries are flourishing in the territory, with women actively involved in their communities. Four home league camps, held during March and April, were attended by 264 delegates.

Territorial leaders Commissioners David and Grace Bringans travelled more than 10,000 kilometres in Noroeste and Rio Bravo Divisions, visiting officers at every corps and centre. They enrolled 36 senior soldiers, 33 junior soldiers and 11 home league members.

The territory gratefully acknowledges the generosity of donors and mission partner territories. This support has made it possible to renovate corps and centre buildings and give practical help to many children and adults.

STATISTICS
Officers 154 (active 126 retired 28) **Auxiliary-Captains** 4 **Sergeants** 6 **Cadets** (1st Yr) 9 (2nd Yr) 6 **Employees** 42
Corps 48 **Outposts** 10 **Institutions** 51
Senior Soldiers 1,919 **Adherents** 332 **Junior Soldiers** 1,095

STAFF
Women's Ministries: Comr Grace Bringans (TPWM)
Personnel: Maj Humberto García
Programme: Capt Luis Camarillo
Education: Maj Leticia García
Finance: Maj Jannette Sáenz
Legal: Maj Humberto García
Property: Maj James Hood
Public Relations: Capt Rene Rodriguez
Social: Maj Sallyann Hood
Training: Maj Victor Váldes
Youth and Candidates: Capt Nohemí Camarillo

DIVISIONS
Capital: Alicante No 88, Colonia Álamos Delegación Benito Juárez, 03400 México, DF; Apartado Postal 13-013, México, DF 03501; tel: 5590-9220; fax: 5590-9603; Maj Guadalupe Galván
Noroeste: Tamborel No. 601, Colonia Santa Rosa, Chihuahua, Chihuahua CP31050; tel: (614) 435-5968; tel/fax: (614) 420-4002; Majs Facundo and Bersábe Vera
Río Bravo: Lombardo Toledano No 2709, Colonia Alta Vista Sur, 64740 Monterrey, Nuevo León; Apartado Postal # 1097, 64000 Monterrey, Nuevo León, México; tel: (81) 8359-5711; fax: (81) 8359-9115; Majs Manuel and Ana Campos

REGION
Sureste: Calle 19 No 116 x 22 y 24, Colonia México, Mérida, Yucatán 97128; tel: (999) 944-6415; Maj Jorge Martínez

TRAINING COLLEGE
Calle Monte Albán No 510, Colonia Independencia, México 03630, DF; tel: (55) 5672-7986; fax: (55) 5672-0608

SOCIAL SERVICES
Children's Care Centres
Ciudad Juárez, Chihuahua: Ulises Irigoyen #1674 Colonia Chaveña, CP 32060; tel: (656) 1614-2828 (acc 150)
Chihuahua, Chihuahua: Tamborel 601, Colonia Santa Rosa, CP 31050; tel: (614) 1420-4002 (acc 70)

Culiacán, Sinaloa: Cuauhtémoc #40 Sur, Colonia Las Vegas, Esquina Alba de Acosta, Cerca de KZ4, CP 80090; tel: (667) 715-1043 (acc 27)

La Gloria, Tijuana, Baja California: Avenida Benito Juárea No 26, Poblado 'La Gloria', Colonia La Joya, Tijuana, BC 22674 (acc 45)

Matamoros, Tamaulipas: Calle Sonora #15 Esquina San Pedro, Colonia Esperanza, CP 87310; tel: (868) 810-1369 (acc 15)

Mexicali, Baja California: Avenida Aguascalientes #2300, Colonia Santa Clara; tel: (686) 553-1194 (acc 20)

México, DF: Imprenta #225, Colonia Morelos, CP 15270; tel: (55) 5789-0554; fax: (55) 5702-3666 (acc 30)

Nuevo Laredo, Tamaulipas: Avenida Santos Degollado #1217, Sector Centro, CP 8800; tel: (867) 712-1455 (acc 30)

Puerto Vallarta, Jalisco: Sonora No 232, Colonia Mjoneras, Apartado Postal 75-C Terminal Marítima, CP 48321; tel: (322) 290-1587 (acc 30)

Reynosa, Tamaulipas: Allende #465 Poniente, Colonia Centro, CP 88500; tel: (899) 922-5463 (acc 25)

San Luis Potosí, San Luís Potosí: Bolívar #1426 Barrio San Miguelito, CP 78339; tel: (444) 815-4530 (acc 30)

Tampico, Tamaulipas: Avenida Central #501, Colonia Moctezuma, CP 89250; tel: (833) 212-0365 (acc 35)

Tapachula, Chiapas: Avenida 11 Sur #44, Colonia 16 de Septiembre, entre la 18y20, Oriente; tel: (962) 625-6733 (acc 50)

Tijuana, Baja California: Calle Aquiles Serdán #11585, Colonia Libertad, Parte Baja, CP 22300; tel: (664) 683-2694 (acc 15)

Torreón, Coahuila: Calle 21, #373 Nte, CP 27000; tel: (871) 7136-023 (acc 65)

Villahermosa, Tabasco: Calle Fco Sarabia #304, Colonia Segunda del Águila, CP 86080; tel: (993) 315-2694 (acc 30)

Children's Homes

Acapulco, Guerrero: Avenida de los Cantiles #16, Fraccionamiento Mozimba, CP 39460; tel: (744) 446-0359 (acc 90)

Chihuahua, Chihuahua: Tamborel #601, Colonia Santa Rosa, CP 31050; tel: (614) 420-4002 (acc 70)

Coatzacoalcos, Veracruz: Gutiérrez Zamora #1120 Colonia Centro, CP 96400; tel: (921) 214-5923 (acc 50)

Cuernavaca, Morelos: Avenida Atlacomúlco #124, Colonia Acapantzingo, CP 62440; tel: (777) 312-8207/ 8238 (acc 45)

Culiacán, Sinaloa: Chuahutémoc #40 Sur, Colonia Las Vegas, Esquina Alba de Acosta, Cerca de KZ4, CP 80090; tel: (667) 715-1043 (acc 27)

Guadalajara, Jalisco: Calzada Revolución #2011, Sector Reforma, CP 44800; tel: (33) 3635-4192 (acc 100)

Matamoros, Tamaulipas: Calle Sonora #15, Esquina San Pedro, Colonia Esperanza, CP 87310; tel: (868) 810-1369 (acc 30)

Mazatlán, Sinaloa: Calle Ángel Flores s/n, Colonia El Venadillo CP 82129; tel: (669) 980-7609 (acc 30)

Mérida, Yucatán: Calle 103, #506 Ax 62, Colonia Delio Moreno Cantón, CP 97268; tel: (999) 928-5153 (acc 30)

México, DF: Avenida Encino Grande #550, Tetelpán, VAO, CP 17000; tel: (55) 5585-0144 (acc 120)

Nuevo Laredo, Tamaulipas: Avenida Santos Degollado 1217, CP 88000; tel: (867) 712-1455 (acc 30)

Puebla, Puebla: Calle 16 Sur #704, Colonia Analco Centro, CP 72000; tel: (222) 242-6047 (acc 35)

Reynosa, Tamaulipas: Allende #465 Poniente, Colonia Centro, CP 88500; tel: (899) 922-5463; fax: (899) 930-9028 (acc 25)

Saltillo, Coahuila: Durazno #354, Colonia del Valle, CP 25000; tel: (844) 436-2005 (acc 40)

San Luis Potosí, San Luis Potosí: Bolívar #1426, Barrio San Miguelito, CP 78339; tel: (444) 815-4530 (acc 30)

Tampico, Tamaulipas: Avenida Central #501, Colonia Moctezuma, CP 89250; tel: (833) 212-0365 (acc 55)

Torreón, Coahuila: Calle 21, #373 Nte, CP 27000; tel: (871) 7136-023 (acc 50)

Veracruz, Veracruz: Revillagigedo #1507, Colonia México, CP 91756; tel: (229) 934-1927 (acc 50)

Villahermosa, Tabasco: Calle Fco Sarabia #304, Colonia Segunda del Águila, CP 86080; tel: (993) 315-2694 (acc 30)

Clinic and Dispensary

México DF: Clínica de Salud Mental, Calle Imprenta No 221 Colonia Morelos, CP 15270; tel: (55) 5794-1994

Feeding Centres
(Senior Citizens and Children)

Alvarado, Veracruz: Ignacio Ramírez #87, CP 95250, Apartado Postal 1; tel: (297) 973-2191 (acc 160)

Can Cún, Quintana Roo: Avenida Talleres entre 109 y 111 región 94, Manzana 80

Lote 28, Can Cún, Quintana Roo;
tel/fax: (998) 840-1074 (acc 30)

Ciudad Juárez: Ulises Irigoyen No 1674,
Colonia Chaveta, CP 32060, Apartado
Postal 807; tel/fax: (656) 614-2828/632-0068
(acc 60)

Ciudad Madero, Tamaulipas: Calle Elena Alanís
No 510 Norte, Esquinta Río Verde,
Colonia Ampliación, Candaleario Garza,
Diudad Madero, Tamaulipas, Apartado
Postal 103, Cd Madero, Tamaulipas;
tel: (833) 211-7661 (acc 25)

Cocotitlán, Estado de México: Acercamiento
Nacional No 31, Esq con Abasolo,
Colonia Centro, Cocotitlán, Estado de México
56680 (acc 25)

Culiacán, Sinaloa: Chuahutémoc #40 Sur,
Colonia Las Vegas, Esquina Epitacio Alba de
Acosta, Cerca de KZ4, CP 80090;
tel: (667) 715-1043 (acc 33)

El Paso Texas, Mérida, Yucatán: Calle 159 #251,
Colonia Emiliano Zapata III, Mérida,
Yucatán 9720 (acc 50)

Genaro Vázquez, Nuevo León: Manzana Heroica
Lote 13, Colonia Genaro Vázquez, Monterrey,
Nuevo Léon (acc 70)

Hermosillo, Sonora: Calle Ignacio M. Altamirano
No 574, Colonia Benito Juárez, Hermosillo,
Sonora 83110; tel: (622) 118-6709 (acc 50)

La Gloria, Tijuana, Baja California: Avenida
Benito Juárea No 26, Poblado 'La Gloria',
Colonia La Joya, Tijuana, BC 22674 (acc 30)

Mexicali, Baja California: Avenida Aguascalientes
#2300, Colonia Santa Clara, CP 21110;
tel: (686) 553-1194 (acc 30)

México, DF (Corps #3): Norte 68 #3742,
Colonia M. de Río Blanco, CP 07880;
tel: (55) 5751-3598 (acc 20)

México, DF (Corps #6): Calle 12 #68 Esquina
Avenida Pantitlán, Colonia Provenir, CP 57430,
Netzahualcoyotl, Estado de México;
tel/fax: (55) 5200-1839 (acc 30)

Monclova, Coahuila: Benjamín Garza #1221,
Colonia Primero de Mayo, CP 25760;
tel: (866) 631-3502 (acc 50)

Nogales, Sonora: Calle San Juan #191,
Colonia Benit Juárez, CP 84015;
tel/fax: (631) 312-4647 (acc 45)

Piedras Negras: Victoria No 805 Nte,
Colonia Centro, CP 26030;
tel/fax: (878) 782-2707 (acc 50)

Puerto Vallarta, Jalisco: Sonora 232 Colonia
Mojoneras, Puerto Vallarta, Jalisco 48300;
tel: (322) 290-1587 (acc 60)

Querétaro, Querétaro: Heriberto Jara No 211,
Colonia Lázaro Cárdenas, Querétaro,

Querétaro 76087; tel: (442) 222-9623
(acc 25)

Sabinitas, Nuevo León: Calle Plutarco Elías
Calles #401, Colonia 6 de Marzo, Guadalupe,
NL 67160; tel: (81) 8299-5981 (acc 75)

Saltillo, Coahuila: Sosténes Rocha 170,
Colonia Chamizal, CP 25180;
tel: (844) 135-3458 (acc 35)

San Juan Ixhuatepec, Estado de México:
Tenochtitlan #10, Administración San Juan
Ixhuatepec, Tlanepantla, Edo de México,
CP 54180; tel: (55) 5715-0649 (acc 80)

Tijuana, Baja California: Calle Aquiles Serdán
#11585, Colonia Libertad, CP 22300, Apartado
Postal 5-G; tel: (664) 683-2694 (acc 45)

Toluca, Estado de México: Calle Pangue
Iztaccihuati #3, Colonia Parques Nacionales,
Toluca, Estado de México 50100;
tel: (722) 278-7335 (acc 25)

Xochitepec, Morelos: Calle Hidalgo
S/N esquina Jalisco, Colonia Lázaro Cárdenas,
Xochitepec, Morelos 62790;
tel/fax: (777) 361-3628 (acc 40)

(Men)

Mexicali, Baja California: Avenida
Aguascalientes #2300, Colonia Santa Clara,
CP 21110; tel: (686) 553-1194 (acc 50)

Nogales, Sonora: San Juan No. 141, Esquina
Sierra Mariposas, Colonia Benito Juárez, CP
84015; tel: (631) 312-4647 (acc 50)

Nuevo Laredo, Tamaulipas: Avenida Santos
Degollado No. 1217 Sector Centro, CP 88000;
tel: (867) 712-1455 (acc 50)

Night Shelters (Men)

Mexicali, Baja California: Avenida
Aguascalientes #2300, Colonia Santa Clara,
CP 21110; tel: (686) 553-1194 (acc 50)

México, DF: La Esperanza, Labradores #85,
Esquina con Imprenta, Colonia Morelos,
México 15270 DF; tel: (55) 5789-1511 (acc 125)

Monterrey, Nuevo León: Carvajal y de la
Cueva #1716 Nte, Colonia Primero de Mayo,
CP 64580; tel: (81) 8375-0379 (acc 80)

Piedras Negras, Coahuila: Victoria #805 Nte,
Colonia Centro CP 26030; tel: (878) 782-2707
(acc 50)

Tijuana, Baja California: Calle Aquiles Serdán
#11585, Colonia Libertad, Porte Baja, CP
22300; tel: (664) 683-2694 (acc 180)

Vocational Training Centre

México DF: Labradores #85 Esquina con
Imprenta, Colonia Morelos, CP 15270;
tel: (55) 5789-1511

MOZAMBIQUE COMMAND

Command leaders:
Lieut-Colonels Torben and Deise Eliasen

Officer Commanding:
Lieut-Colonel Torben Eliasen
(1 Mar 2008)

General Secretary:
Major Celestino Pepe Pululu (1 Mar 2008)

Command Headquarters: Avenue Filipe Samuel Magaia, 860, Maputo, Mozambique

Postal address: PO Box 4099, Maputo, Mozambique

Tel: [258] 2132 8145; fax: [258] 2132 8146

The Salvation Army's evangelistic endeavours in Mozambique were pioneered in 1916 by Mozambican converts returning from South Africa. The work was recognised by the Mozambique government in 1986 and officially registered in June 2005. Previously part of the Southern Africa Territory, Mozambique became a separate command on 1 March 2008.

Zone: Africa
Country included in the command: Mozambique
'The Salvation Army' in Portuguese (the official language): Exército de Salvação
Languages in which the gospel is preached: Portuguese, Chona, Chopi, Gitonga, Makhuwa, Ndau, Sena, Tchewa, Tsonga, Tswa
Periodicals: *Devocionias para Encontros da Liga do Lar* (Home League resource manual)

THE command has corps and outposts in eight of Mozambique's 10 provinces and is now working in the remaining two – Niassa and Cabo Delgado. Divisions have been formed so that the rapidly expanding work can be developed and supervised more efficiently .

In 2010 three new administrative regions opened: Central-North Division in Beira, South Division in Maxixe, and Maputo District based at Command Headquarters in Maputo.

The first administrative conference was held under the inspiring leadership of Commissioner Robin Forsyth (IHQ) and new divisional leaders were appointed.

While some Army buildings are rented or unfinished, two DHQs – for Central-North and South Divisions – are undergoing construction. Due to open in early 2011, these buildings will provide facilities for officers to meet for spiritual renewal, direction and celebration.

Most corps buildings in Mozambique are made from local

straw or clay, so the command strategy is to build at least one brick structure in each province. Funding from mission partner territories, CHQ and local corps make this possible. A mission team from Australia Southern Territory visited Mocuba Corps and got involved in building work; this is nearing completion.

Many people have been saved and sanctified to serve God through The Salvation Army's ministry in Mozambique.

STATISTICS

Officers 51 **Employees** 20
Corps 41 **Outposts** 59 **Day Care Centres** 5
  HIV Home-based Care and OVC Projects 4
  Adult Literacy Projects 50
Senior Soldiers 3,598 **Junior Soldiers** 1,387

STAFF

Women's Ministries: Lt-Col Deise Eliasen
  (CPWM) Maj Veronica Pululu (CSWM)
Education: Maj Maria Gutierrez
Finance: Capt Dini Varte
Projects: Capt Mario Nhacumba
Property: Capt Feliz Nhaduate
Sponsorship: Lt-Col Deise Eliasen
Training: Maj Hugo Gutierrez
Youth and Candidates: Capt Celeste
  Nhacumba

DIVISIONS

Central-North: Beira; tel: (258) 843897200;
  Majs Manoel and Irene Nhelenhele
South: Maxixe; tel: (258) 843897199;
  Capts João and Graça Guiamba

DISTRICT

Maputo: c/o CHQ, Maputo; tel: (258) 843036570

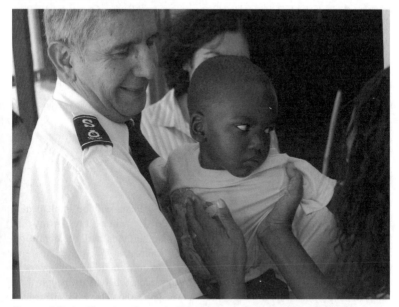

On a visit to Maputo, Commissioner Jorge Ferreira (TC, South America West) gets to see the Salvation Army-run nursery and day-care centre

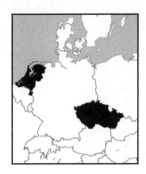

THE NETHERLANDS AND CZECH REPUBLIC TERRITORY

Territorial leaders:
Commissioners Hans and Marja van Vliet

Territorial Commander:
Commissioner Hans van Vliet (1 Jun 2010)

Chief Secretary:
Colonel Pieter Dijkstra (25 Mar 2008)

Territorial Headquarters: Spoordreef 10, 1315 GN Almere, The Netherlands

Tel: [31] (36) 5398111; fax: [31] (36) 5331458; email: ldhnl@legerdesheils.nl;
websites: www.legerdesheils.nl; www.armadaspasy.cz

Captain and Mrs Joseph K. Tyler, English officers, and Lieutenant Gerrit J. Govaars, a gifted Dutch teacher, commenced Salvation Army work in the Gerard Doustraat, Amsterdam, on 8 May 1887. Operations soon spread throughout the country and reached Indonesia (then The Netherlands East Indies) in 1894. Further advances were made in 1926 in Surinam and in 1927 in Curaçao.

Salvation Army operations in Czechoslovakia commenced in 1919, the pioneer being Colonel Karl Larsson. Evangelistic and social activities were maintained until suppressed in June 1950. After the opening of the central European borders, The Salvation Army's work was re-established and The Netherlands Territory was asked to take charge of the redevelopment. By the end of 1990 centres were reopened in Havirov, Prague, Brno and Ostrava and the work has grown steadily since then.

On 1 February 2002 the territory was renamed The Netherlands and Czech Republic Territory.

Zone: Europe
Countries included in the territory: Czech Republic, The Netherlands
'The Salvation Army' in Dutch: Leger des Heils; in Czech: Armáda Spásy
Languages in which the gospel is preached: Czech, Dutch
Periodicals: *Dag In Dag Uit*, *Heils-en Strijdzangen*, *InterCom*, *Strijdkreet*, (all Dutch), *Prapor Spásy* (Czech)

THE Salvation Army in The Netherlands launched its 'Revive the Church' plan. Meetings with officers, soldiers and lay staff in which they could give opinions and ideas helped the territory's leaders to make important proposals and decisions. These will assist spiritual development and numerical growth in corps. Plans will be implemented by 2012, when the Army in The Netherlands will celebrate its 125th anniversary.

A new corps building was opened in Leeuwarden, where many people from the neighbourhood have become regular visitors at the Army. Some have been enrolled as soldiers or adherents.

In several cities, community centres under the name *Bij Bosshardt* were opened in memory of Lieut-Colonel Alida Bosshardt OF. Her idea was to have 'a living room for the neighbourhood' where people come for coffee, a meal, a chat and help. The territory hopes to establish more of these centres in the next few years.

A television programme broadcast at Christmas drew attention to the Army's second-hand clothes collection and shops. The Army was also involved in creating the TV series *Filthy Rich and Homeless*, which starred four young business people who wanted to know what it feels like to live and survive on the streets.

An increasing number of projects for job training have been set up. There is now a pasta production facility, a laundry, a packaging line and a catering centre.

During the territory's Day of Reflection 2010 more than 300 people came together to discuss in workshops and meetings the essence of the Army's holiness theology.

In the Czech Republic, the year 2010 marked the 20th anniversary of The Salvation Army recommencing service after being banned by the communist regime in 1950. Various celebrations were planned, with every town where the Army works organising open days, garden parties, street activities and exhibitions.

These have provided excellent opportunities for Armáda Spásy to emphasise its religious credentials as well as its ministry to people in need.

STATISTICS

Officers 370 (active 138 retired 231)
  Cadets (1st Yr) 3 (2nd Yr) 6 **Employees** 5,274
Corps 70 (99 local service centres) **Business Units** 17 (187 local service centres)
Senior Soldiers 4,488 **Adherents** 1,244
  Junior Soldiers 473

STAFF
The Salvation Army Church
Women's Ministries: Comr Marja van Vliet (TPWM) Col Alida Dijkstra (TSWM)
Adult Ministries: see Field Programme Support
Field: Col Alida Dijkstra (pro-tem)
Field Programme Support (inc Youth and Adult Ministries): Mr Bert Onstwedder/Mr Alex van Zoeren
Candidates: Maj Tineke van de Wetering
Editor-in-Chief: tba
Education and Training: Maj Hendrika Scholtens
Finance and International Projects: Cadet Harm Slomp
Finance, Accommodation and Dataprocessing: Mr Bert Barink
Literary: Maj Simon M. van der Vlugt
Music: Mr Roel van Kesteren
Sponsorships: Maj Marijke van Dalen

DIVISIONS
Central: Piccolostraat 13, 1312 RC Almere; tel: (36) 536 51 06; Maj Elsje Klarenbeek
North/East: Gein 27, 8032 BB Zwolle; tel: (38) 452 67 13; fax: (38) 452 67 19; Majs Teunis and Hendrika Scholtens
South: Wittebrem 22, 3068 TM Rotterdam; tel: (10) 4557921; Majs Johannes and Annetje den Hollander

THE SALVATION ARMY MAIN FOUNDATION
Board of Administration
Chairman: Comr Hans van Vliet (TC)

Staff
Secretary: Col Pieter Dijkstra (CS)
Financial Sec and Managing Director: Cadet Harm Slomp

THE SALVATION ARMY SERVICES FOUNDATION
Board of Administration
Chairman: Comr Hans van Vliet (TC)
Vice-Chairman: Col Pieter Dijkstra (CS)

The Netherlands and Czech Republic Territory

Official (non-voting) Sec: Cadet Harm Slomp
Members: Mr G. L. Telling, Mrs L. M. Welschen-van der Hoek, Mr P. Visser

Staff

Managing Director: Envoy Ed Bosma
Central Purchasing: Mr Egbert Oostra
Communications: Mrs Hella van der Schoot
Family Tracing: Maj Jaap de Ruiter
Finance and Information Technology: Mr Joop Rozema
Fundraising and Marketing: Mr Will van Heugten
Human Resources: tba
Information Technology: Mr. Friso van den Berg

ReSHARE BV (Recycling Services)

Koopvaardijweg 15, 4906 CV Oosterhout;
tel: (0900) 9900099
Depot: Hattem
Director Operations: Capt Robert Paul Fennema

THE SALVATION ARMY FUNDRAISING FOUNDATION
Board of Administration

Chairman: Comr Hans van Vliet (TC)
Vice-Chairman: Col Pieter Dijkstra (CS)
Official Sec: Cadet Harm Slomp RA
Members: Mrs F. H. van Ham-Laning,
Mr C. Hendriks, Mr J. de Widt,
Mr F. B. A. M. van Oss, Mrs J.W. Immink

Staff

Managing Director: Envoy Ed Bosma
Director Operations: Mr Will van Heugten

All activities of the Foundation are to be executed by The Salvation Army Services Foundation.

THE SALVATION ARMY FOUNDATION FOR WELFARE AND HEALTH CARE

Care for the Homeless (total acc 3,313): night shelter (acc 417); day care (acc 668); 24-hour shelter (acc 1,478); care for vulnerable people (acc §646); young people (acc 218); supervised
living (acc 532); preventative homelessness projects, ambulatory programs (57 FTE)
Substance Misuse Services (total acc 63): residential (acc 20); supervised living (acc 43); ambulatory programs (3 FTE)
Probation Services: ambulatory programmes (134 FTE); day training centres (acc 40)
Health Care and Care for the Elderly (total

capacity 1,395): permanent stay (acc 355); hospice care (acc 19); temporary stay (inc medical care of homeless) (acc 175); day care (acc 20); ambulatory programmes (inc home care) (94 FTE); supervised living (acc 237); psychiatric clinic (acc 57)
Custody Care (total pupils 2,351): ambulatory programmes (156 FTE)
Care for Children and Young People: residential care (acc 379); day care (acc 4)
Prevention and Social Rehabilitation Services (total acc 152): community centres (6); ambulatory programmes (acc 122 FTE); work coaching (acc 152)

Board of Administration

Chairman: Comr Hans van Vliet (TC)
Vice-Chairman: Col Pieter Dijkstra (CS)
Sec/Treasurer: Cadet Harm Slomp
Members: Mrs G. W. van Montfrans-Hartman,
Mr D. J. Rutgers, Mrs M. Trompetter,
Mr J. Wienen

Staff

Managing Director: Lt-Col Christina A. Voorham
Deputy Director: Mr Hermanus M. van Teijlingen
Executive Sec: Mr Jeroen Hoogteijling
Finance, Property, HRM and ICT: Mr Ruud de Vries
Managers: Mr Marinus A. J. Timmer,
Mr Josephus J. Sesink, Rev Johannes J. Blom
Risk Management and Internal Control: Mr Piet van Keulen
Main Office: Spoordreef 10, 1315 GN Almere;
tel: (36) 539 82 50; fax: (36) 534 07 10

CENTRES FOR LIVING, CARE AND WELFARE
Central Region

Managing director: Mr Harrie de Heer
Information: Aïdadreef 8, 3561 GE Utrecht;
tel: (30) 274 91 21
Northern Region
Managing director: Mr Cornel Vader
Information: Kwinkenplein 10-A, 9712 GZ,
Groningen; tel: (50) 317 26 70
South-Western Region
Managing director: Mrs Joanne Blaak-van de Lagemaat
Information: Kromhout 110, 3311 RH
Dordrecht; tel: (78) 632 07 00
Gelderland
Managing director: Mr Jan Jans
Information: Hoenderloseweg 108, 7339 GK

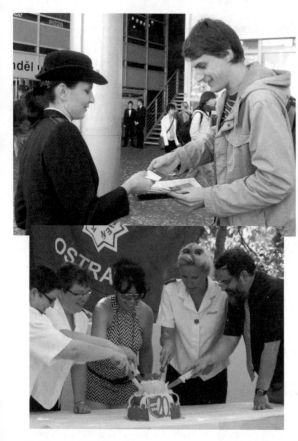

A Salvationist distributes leaflets about The Salvation Army as an open-air meeting is held in Prague, to mark the 20th anniversary of the Army recommencing its work in the Czech Republic. A number of celebrations around the country provided opportunities for *Armáda Spásy* to emphasise its religious credentials.
In Ostrava, the Czech Republic's third largest city located close to the Polish border, Salvationists and friends of the Army gathered to cut a 20th anniversary cake.

Ugchelen; tel: (55) 538 03 33

Flevoland

Managing director: Mr Evert Dijkstra
Information: Spoordreef 12, 1315 GN Almere;
tel: (36) 549 68 00

Northern Holland

Managing director: Mr Dik van den Hoek
Information: Mariettahof 25, 2033 WS
Haarlem; tel: (23) 553 39 33

Overijssel

Managing director: Mr Elzo Edens
Information: Eiffelstraat 1 – 117, 8013 RT
Zwolle; tel: (38) 467 19 40

Limburg/Brabant

Managing director: Mr Hans Martin Don
Information: Mariastraat 13, 6211

EP,Maastricht; tel: (43) 350 33 84

Amsterdam Goodwill Centres

Managing director: Envoy Henk Dijkstra
Information: Rode Kruisstraat 24b, 1025 KN
Amsterdam; tel: (20) 630 11 11

The Hague Goodwill Work

Managing director: Maj Germen Stoffers
Information: St Barbaraweg 4, 2516 BT
Den Haag; tel: (70) 311 55 40

Rotterdam Centres for Social Services

Managing director: Mr Johan Koeman
Information: Kooikerweg 28, 3069 WP
Rotterdam; tel: (10) 222 98 88

Probation Services Leger des Heils Jeugdzorg

Managing director: Mr Bert Sprokkereef
Central Office: Zeehaenkade 30, 3526 LC

The Netherlands and Czech Republic Territory

Utrecht; tel: (88) 090 10 00
HOTEL AND CONFERENCE CENTRE
'Belmont', Goorsteeg 66, 6718 TB Ede;
tel: (31) 848 23 65 (50 twin-bedded rooms;
14 conference rooms acc varying 12-375;
during summer 96 extra beds available,
in tents acc 160)

CZECH REPUBLIC
Officer-in-charge: Maj Mike Stannett
(1 May 2008)

National Headquarters: Armáda spásy
Nat Petrzilkova 2565/23, 158 00 Praha 5;
tel: (00420) 251 106 424;
fax: (00420) 251 106 442
email: info@armadaspasy.cz;
website: www.armadaspasy.cz

STATISTICS
Officers 19 **Employees** 342
Corps 8 **Community Centres** 15 **Institutions** 20
Senior Soldiers 67 **Adherents** 53 **Junior
Soldiers** 8

STAFF
Asst Officer-in-charge: Maj Ruth Stannett
Personal Assistant: Pavla Vopeláková
Nat Director Residential Social Services:
Maj Rein van Wagtendonk
Training: Capt Aleš Malach
Editorial: Maj Attie van Wagtendonk
Finance: Mrs Hana Kosová

CENTRES
Hostels for Men and Women and Night Shelters
Brno: Dům Josef Korbel Mlýnská 25,
602 00 Brno; tel: 543 212 530 (acc 136)
Krnov: Csl armády 837 bcd, Opavské předměstí,
794 01 Krnov; tel: 554 612 296 (acc 85,
includes mothers and children)
Opava: Nákladní 24, 746 01 Opava;
tel: 553 712 984 (acc 48)
Prague: Dům Bohuslava Bureš, Tusarova 60,
170 00 Praha 7;tel: 220 184 000 (acc 220)

Hostels for Men and Night Shelters
Havířov: Hostel, Na spojce 2, 736 01 Havířov;
tel: 596 810 197 (acc 53)
Karlovy Vary: Nákladní 7, 360 05 Karlovy Vary;
tel: 353 569 267 (acc 45)
Opava: Nákladní 24, 746 01 Opava;
tel: 553 712 984 (acc 48)
Ostrava: U Nových Válcoven 9,
709 00 Ostrava-Mariánské Hory;

tel: 596 620 650 (acc 114)
Šumperk: Vikyrovicka 1495, Šumperk-Luže;
tel: 583 224 634 (acc 35)

Homes for Mothers and Children
Havířov: Dvorákova 21/235, 736 01 Havířov;
tel: 596 810 221 (acc 18 mothers plus children)
Krnov: Csl armády 837 bcd, Opavské předměstí,
794 01 Krnov; tel: 554 612 296 (acc 85,
includes hostel for men and women)
Ostrava: Gen Píky 25, Ostrava-Fifejdy 702 00;
tel: 596 611 962 (acc women 30, mothers 10,
children 15-20)
Opava: Rybárská 86, 746 01 Opava;
tel: 553 714 509 (acc mothers 11, children 33)
Přerov: 9 kvetna 2481/107, 750 02 Přerov;
tel: 581 210 769 (acc 45)

Alternative Punishment Programme
Opava: Nákladní 24, 746 01 Opava;
tel: 553 712 984

Azylovy Dům for Families
Stankova 4, 602 00, Brno; tel: 543 212 530
(acc 12 flats)

Elderly Persons Project
Domov Přistav: Holvekova 38, 718 00, Ostrava-
Kunčičky; tel: 596 238 163 (acc 40)

Farm Rehabilitation Project
Strahovice č.16, 747 24 pošta, Chuchelná;
mobile: 737 215 396 (acc 4)

Follow-up Care (for alcoholics)
Dům pod svahem, Pod Svahem 1, 736 01,
Havířov-Šumbark; tel: 596 881 007

Prevention Project (against homelessness)
Palackeho 25, 702 00 Ostrava – Přívoz;
tel: 596 133 417/112 009 (25 flats)

Prison Work
Šumperk: Štefánikova 1, 787 01, Šumperk;
tel: 737 215 396

Youth Centre
Brno-Bystrc: Kubickova 23, 635 00 Brno-Bystrc;
tel: 546 221 756

NEW ZEALAND, FIJI AND TONGA TERRITORY

Territorial leaders:
Commissioners Donald C. and Debora K. Bell

Territorial Commander:
Commissioner Donald C. Bell (1 Mar 2009)

Chief Secretary:
Colonel Graeme Reddish (1 Mar 2009)

Territorial Headquarters: 204 Cuba Street, Wellington, New Zealand

Postal address: PO Box 6015, Wellington 6141, New Zealand

Tel: [64] (04) 384 5649; fax: [64] (04) 802 6258; website: www.salvationarmy.org.nz

On 1 April 1883 Salvation Army activities were commenced at Dunedin by Captain George Pollard and Lieutenant Edward Wright. Social work began in 1884 with a home for ex-prisoners. Work was begun officially in Fiji on 14 November 1973 by Captain Brian and Mrs Beverley McStay, and in Tonga on 9 January 1986 by Captain Tifare and Mrs Rebecca Inia.

Zone: South Pacific and East Asia
Countries included in the territory: Fiji, New Zealand, Tonga
'The Salvation Army' in Maori: Te Ope Whakaora
Languages in which the gospel is preached: English, Fijian, Hindi, Korean, Maori, Rotuman, Samoan, Tongan and Vietnamese
Periodical: *War Cry*

A FOCUS on discipleship and soldiership resulted in the highest number of cadets since 1986 – a total of 40 by 2010, including six in Fiji. A redeveloped curriculum for Pacific cultures was introduced into the school for officer training in Fiji.

'Delve' weekends encouraged people to explore God's call to officership. This has resulted in more candidates and Salvationists committed to serve in corps and centres.

'Caring for people, transforming lives and reforming society by God's power' remains the territory's mission statement and its vision.

The Haurora programme to meet the needs of people on the margins of society commenced in October 2009. It was developed after a New Zealand gang asked The Salvation Army to help them turn their backs on addiction, especially to methamphetamine. Whole families receive an intensive seven-week treatment period followed by reintegration aftercare. This has been successful in reducing harm to gang members, their families and the wider community.

Many New Zealanders are calling for changes to the nation's out-of-control drinking culture. The Salvation Army has made submissions to the Government and released substantial reports on alcohol taxation and people seriously affected by alcohol abuse.

The Army expressed the view that framing the debate in terms of consumer choice and personal responsibility trivialised the damage to society caused by the misuse of alcohol.

The territory continued to invest in its young people. A website (www.firezone.co.nz) was launched in early 2010 to connect its vibrant youth community.

In January 2010 the Creative Arts Camp brought together musicians, vocalists, songwriters, film-makers, photographers, actors and writers aged between 16 and 30. Throughout the eight-day camp spirituality was developed alongside artistic talents, and a strong call to holiness was affirmed.

Prayer, particularly 24/7 prayer initiatives, continued to underpin the life and mission of the Army and proved a fruitful strategy for the growth of God's Kingdom.

The territory continued to emphasise four specific goals: discipleship, making new soldiers, fighting poverty and working together. This strategic mission plan proved so valuable in shaping an innovative 'one Army' approach that the decision was taken to include its sequel, 'The Next Chapter', at the territorial congress in October 2010.

STATISTICS

Officers 538 (active 316 retired 222) **Cadets** (1st Yr) 20 (2nd Yr) 8 **Employees** 2,788
Corps 94 **Plants** 5 **Outposts** 5 **Recovery Churches** 10 **Institutions** 82
Senior Soldiers 5,565 **Adherents** 1,456 **Junior Soldiers** 718
Personnel serving outside territory Officers 19

STAFF

Women's Ministries: Comr Debora K. Bell (TPWM) Col Wynne Reddish (TSWM)
Business Administration: Maj Bruce Vyle
  Audit: Mr Graeme Tongs
  Finance: Maj David Bateman
  Information Technology: Mr Mark Bennett
  Property: Mr Ian McLaren
  Public Relations: Maj Robbie Ross
  Trade: Mr George Borthwick
  Communications: Maj Christina Tyson
Personnel: Lt-Col Wilfred Arnold
  Asst (Officer Resources and Overseas Service): Maj Tanya Dunn
  Asst (Pastoral Care): Lt-Col Margaret Arnold
  Human Resources: Mr Paul Geoghegan
  Booth College of Mission:
    Principal: Maj David Noakes
    School for Bible and Mission: Maj Garth Stevenson
    Centre for Leadership Development: Caroline Jewkes
    Education Consultant and Registrar: Alison Mawson
  Candidates: Maj Yvonne Westrupp
Programme: Lt-Col Lyndon Buckingham
  Asst: Lt-Col Bronwyn Buckingham
  Social Programme: Maj Campbell Roberts
  Creative Ministries: Matthew Pethybridge
  National Youth Bandmaster: Grant Pitcher
  Youth: Capt Rebecca Gane
  Planned Giving: Maj Sandra Mellsop
  SpiritSong: Vocal Leader Denise Hewitt
  Children's Ministries: Capt Brenda Luscombe
Book Production: Maj Christina Tyson
Moral and Social Issues Council: Maj Ian Hutson
Overseas Development Consultant: Maj Vyvyenne Noakes
Social Policy and Parliamentary Unit: Maj Ian Kilgour
Territorial Events Co-Ordinator: Joanne Poole

DIVISIONS

Central: 204 Cuba St, Wellington 6011, PO Box 6421, Wellington 6141;

tel: (04) 384 4713; fax: (04) 802 6267;
email: cdhq@nzf.salvationarmy.org;
Majs Rod and Jenny Carey

Midland: 12 Vialou St, PO Box 500,
Hamilton 3240; tel: (07) 839 2242;
fax: (07) 839 2282;
email: Midland_dhq@nzf.salvationarmy.org;
Majs Andrew and Yvonne Westrupp

Northern: 369 Queen St, PO Box 5035,
Auckland 1001; tel: (09) 337 1318;
fax: (09) 379 4152;
email: ndhq@nzf.salvationarmy.org;
Maj Heather Rodwell

Southern: 71 Peterborough St, Christchurch 8013,
PO Box 25-207, Christchurch 8144;
tel: (03) 377 0799; fax: (03) 377 3575;
email: southern@nzf.salvationarmy.org;
Majs Clive and Lesley Nicolson

FIJI DIVISION

Headquarters: PO Box 14412, Suva, Fiji;
tel: [679] 331 5177; fax: [679] 330 3112
Divisional leader: Majs Iliesa and Litiana Cola;
email: dhq_fiji@nzf.salvationarmy.org
Corps 11 Corps Plant 1 Outposts 4

School for Officer Training and Leadership Training

tel: (679) 330 7749; fax: (679) 330 7010;
email: SFOT_FIJI@nzf.salvationarmy.org

Community Ministries Offices

Eastern: Grantham Rd, Raiwai, Suva;
tel: (679) 337 2122
Western: 38 Sukanaivalu Rd, Waiyavi Lautoka;
tel: (679) 664 5471

Family Care Centres

Labasa: Sarwan Singh St, Nasea, Labasa;
tel: (679) 881 1898 (acc 12)
Lautoka: 160 VM Pillai Rd, Drasa-Vitogo,
Lautoko; tel: (679) 665 0952 (acc 16)
Suva: 21 Spring St, Toorak, Suva;
tel: (679) 330 5518 (acc 18)

Court and Prison Officers

Lautoka; tel: (679) 665 0952/664 5471
Suva; tel: (679) 331 5440

Farm Project: Farm 80, Lomaivuna;
tel: (679) 368 0771 (acc 10)

Girls' Home: Mahaffy Dr, Suva;
tel: (679) 331 3318 (acc 20)

Raiwai Hostel
Hostel for young male tertiary students,
Grantham Rd, Suva; tel: (679) 338 7438
(acc 20)

Red Shield House
Hostel for young females, 37 Moala St, Samabula,
Suva; tel: (679) 338 1347 (acc 9)

Sewing Skills Programmes
Labasa: Lot 2 Batinikama, Siberia Rd;
tel: (679) 881 4822
Lautoka: 38 Sukanaivalu Rd, Waiyavi;
tel: (679) 666 3712
Sigatoka: Kulukulu Subdiv'n;
tel: (679) 650 0782
Suva: 50 MacGregor Rd; tel: (679) 3307 746

Tiny Tots Kindergartens
Ba: 6 Old Kings Rd, Yalalevu;
tel: (679) 667 0155 (acc 15)
Labasa: Lot 2 Batinikama, Siberia Rd, Labasa;
tel: (679) 881 4822 (acc 15)
Lautoka: 38 Sukanaivalu Rd, Waiyavi Lautoka;
tel: (679) 666 3712 (acc 50)
Lomaivuna: Farm 80, Lomaivuna;
tel: (679) 360 1238 (acc 15)
Nadi: Lot 30-32, Goundar St, Namaka, Nadi;
tel: (679) 670 0405 (acc 15)
Nasinu: Yaka Place, Valelevu, Nasinu;
tel: (679) 339 3744 (acc 30)
Suva Central: 50 MacGregor Rd, Suva;
tel: (679) 3307 746 (acc 30)

TONGA REGION

Regional Headquarters: Mosimani Building,
cnr Hala Fatafehi and Mateialona, Nuku'alofa,
PO Box 1035, Nuku'alofa, Tonga;
tel: (676) 23-760; fax (676) 28-731;
email: rhq_tga@nzf.salvationarmy.org
Regional leaders: Majs Rex and Geraldine
Johnson
Corps 4 Corps Plant 1

Community Ministries

Mosimani Building, cnr Hala Fatafehi and
Mateialonga, Nuku'alofa, Tonga

Court and Prison Work: Nuku'alofa

Addiction Programme

Mosimani Building, cnr Hala Fatafehi and
Mateialonga, Nuku'alofa, Tonga;
tel: (676) 23760;
email: rhq_tga@nzf.salvationarmy.org

Kindergartens:
Sopu, Nuku'alofa; tel: (676) 26370 (acc 30)
Kolovai; tel: (676) 11737 (acc 25)

Mobile Health Clinic: Popua and Patangata
Community

BOOTH COLLEGE OF MISSION (BCM)
**School for Officer Training (SFOT); Centre
for Leadership Development; School of
Bible and Mission**
20 William Booth Grove, Upper Hutt 5018;
PO Box 40-542, Upper Hutt, 5140;
tel: (04) 528 8628; fax: (04) 527 6900
Principal, BCM and SFOT: Maj David Noakes

FAMILY TRACING SERVICE
PO Box 6015, Wellington 6015;
tel: (04) 382 0710; fax: (04) 802 6257;
email: familytracing@nzf.salvationarmy.org

ARCHIVES AND MUSEUM
202-204 Cuba St, PO Box 6015, Wellington 6141;
tel: (04) 382 0732; fax(04) 802 6259;
email: archives@nzf.salvationarmy.org;
Maj Garry Mellsop

FARM
Jeff Memorial Farm, Kaiwera RD 2, Gore;
tel: (03) 205 3572

INDEPENDENT LIVING UNITS
Ashburton: Wilson Court, 251-255 Tancred St
(units 3)
Auckland: 353 Blockhouse Bay Rd (units 20)
New Plymouth: Bingham Court, 46 Murray St,
Bell Block (units 10)
Blenheim: 35 George St (units 7)
Carterton: 204 High St South (units 8)
Christchurch: 794 Main North Rd, Belfast
(units 10)
Gisborne: Edward Murphy Village,
481 Aberdeen Rd (units 30)
Hamilton: Nawton Village, 57 Enfield St
(units 40)
Kapiti: 41 Bluegum Rd, Paraparaumu Beach
(units 18)
Mosgiel: Elmwood Retirement Village,
22 Elmwood Dr (units 30); 17 Cedar Cres
(units 30)
Oamaru: Glenside, 9 Arthur St (units 12)
Papakura: 91 Clevedon Rd (units 6)
Wellington:
Summerset Units, Newtown: 182a Owen St
(units 11); 210, 212, 214 Owen St (units 3);
226 Owen St (units 9)

RETIRED OFFICERS'
ACCOMMODATION (under THQ)
Auckland: Lang Court, 9 Willcott St (units 6);
6D Liston St, Northcote (unit 1);
19 Splendour Cl, Henderson (unit 1)
Wellington: 176, 176a, 178, 178a Queens Dr,
Lyall Bay (units 4)

YOUTH CAMPS AND CONFERENCE
CENTRES
Blue Mountain Adventure Centre: RD 1,
Owhango 3989; tel: (07) 892 2630;
website: www.bluemountainadventure.co.nz

SOCIAL SERVICES (under THQ)
Addiction and Supportive
Accommodation Services
National Office: Level 2, 369 Queen St,
PO Box 7342, Wellesley St, Auckland 1141;
tel: (09) 337 1351; fax: (09) 377 1249
National Manager: Maj Lynette Hutson; email:
lynette_hutson@nzf.salvationarmy.org

**Bridge Programme: Community and
Residential Programmes (Treatment of
Alcohol and Drug Dependency)**
Auckland: Bridge Centre, PO Box 56-442,
7-15 Ewington Ave, Mt Eden, Auckland 1024;
tel: (09) 630 1491; fax: (09) 630 8395;
email: akbridge@xtra.co.nz (acc assessment 21,
treatment 16, day clients 7)
Christchurch: The Bridge Programme, PO Box
9070, Tower Junction, Christchurch 8149;
Addington, 35 Collins St, Christchurch 8324;
tel: (03) 338 4436; fax: (03) 338 4312; email:
christchurch_bridge@nzf.salvationarmy.org
(acc 26)
Dunedin: PO Box 934, Dunedin 9054,
160 Crawford St, Dunedin 9016;
tel: (03) 477 9852; fax: (03) 477 1493; email:
Dunedin_bridge@nzf.salvationarmy.org (acc 7)
Hamilton: Midland Regional Residential and Detox
Centre, 227 Baverstock Rd, Hamilton 3200;
PO Box 15 673, Hamilton 3204;
tel: (07) 839 6871; fax: (07) 839 6872
Invercargill: 110 Leven St, PO Box 74,
Invercargill 9840; tel: (03) 218 3094;
fax: (03) 218 7934; email:
Invercargill_bridge@nzf.salvationarmy.org
Manukau: Bridge Centre, 16b Bakerfield Place,
PO Box 76075, Manukau City 2241;
tel: (09) 261 0887; fax: (09) 263 9325;
email: mkbridge@xtra.co.nz
Waikato: The Bridge Programme, 25 Thackeray St,
Hamilton 3204; tel: (07) 839 6871;
fax: (07) 839 6872

Waitakere: Bridge Centre, 17 James Laurie St, PO Box 69 005, Glendene, Waitakere City 0645; tel: (09) 835 4069; fax: (09) 835 4690; email: wkbridge@xtra.co.nz

Wellington: 22-26 Riddiford St, PO Box 6033, Wellington 6141; tel: (04) 389 6566; fax: (04) 389 7110; email: wbridge@nzf.salvationarmy.org (acc 24)

Whangarei: Northland Bridge, PO Box 1746, Whangarei 0140, 6 Alexander St, Whangarei 0110; tel: (09) 430 7500; fax: (09) 430 7501

Oasis Centres: Treatment Centres for Gambling

Auckland: PO Box 41-309, St Lukes, Auckland 1346; 726 New North Rd, Auckland 1025; tel: (09) 846 0660; fax: (09) 846 0440

Christchurch: PO Box 9070, Addington, Tower Jctn, Christchurch 8149; 126 Bealey Ave; tel: (03) 365 9659; fax: (03) 365 7585; email: oasisch@xtra.co.nz

Dunedin: PO Box 934, Dunedin 9054, 160 Crawford St, Dunedin 9016 ; tel: (03) 477 9852; fax: (03) 477 1493; email: Dunedin_oasis@nzf.salvationarmy.org

Hamilton: 2nd Floor, Cecil House, Garden Pl; Postal address: 25 Thackeray St, Hamilton 3204; tel: (07) 839 7053; fax: (07) 839 4428

Queenstown: 29 Camp St, PO Box 887, Queenstown 9348; tel: (03) 442 5103; fax: (03) 442 9644

Wellington: 22 Riddiford St, PO Box 6033, Wellington 6141; tel: (04) 389 6566; fax: (04) 389 7110

Community Addictions Programme

Invercargill: Social Service Centre, PO Box 74, Invercargill 9840, cnr Gala and Leven Sts; tel: (03) 218 3094; fax: (03) 218 7934

Kaitaia: PO Box 495, Kaitaia 0441, 40 Commerce St; tel: (09) 408 6180; fax: (09) 408 3365

Kaikohe: PO Box 748, Kaikohe 0440, 2 Station Rd, Kaikohe 0405; tel: (09) 401 2865

Tauranga: PO Box 164, Tauranga 3140, 375 Cameron Rd; tel: (07) 578 4264; fax: (07) 578 4536

Supportive Accommodation Services

Auckland: Epsom Lodge: PO Box 26-098, Auckland 1344; 18 Margot St, Epsom, Auckland 1344; tel: (09) 524 0252; fax: (09) 524 9604 (acc men 90)

Christchurch: Addington Supportive Accommodation Services Social Services Centre, PO Box 9057, Tower Junction, Christchurch 8149; 62 Poulson St, Addington, Christchurch 8024; tel: (03) 338 5154; fax: (03) 338 4390 (acc 70)

Invercargill: PO Box 74, Invercargill 9840; cnr Gala and Leven Sts; tel: (03) 218 3094; fax: (03) 218 7934 (acc 35)

Temuka: Bramwell Booth House (Intellectual Disability): PO Box 57, Temuka 7948, Milford Rd; tel: (03) 615 9570; fax: (03) 615 9571 (acc 18)

Wellington: (Intellectual Disability) PO Box 6033, 26 Riddiford St; tel: (04) 389 0594; fax: (04) 389 1130 (acc 12)

Reintegration Services

Christchurch: 62 Poulson St, PO Box 9057, Temuka 7948, Christchurch 8024; tel: (03) 338 2643; fax: (03) 338 4390

Wellington: PO Box 40328, Upper Hutt 5140; tel: (04) 527 7462; fax: (04) 528 9445

Mothercraft Centre

Bethany, 35 Dryden St, Grey Lynn, Auckland 1021; tel: (09) 376 1324; fax: (09) 376 1307; website: www.bethanycentre.org.nz (acc antenatal 14, mothers and babies 7)

Employment Plus

National Office: 204 Cuba St, PO Box 6015, Wellington 6141; tel: (04) 382 0714; fax: (04) 382 0711; toll free: 0800 437 587

National Manager: Mr Mark Pickering; email: m.pickering@eplus-salvationarmy.org.nz

National Mission Directors: Majs Wayne and Joanne Jellyman; email: wayne_jellyman@nzf.salvationarmy.org joanne_jellyman@nzf.salvationarmy.org

Finance Service Bureau: 12 Vialou St, PO Box 5347, Frankton, Hamilton; tel: (07) 834 3195; fax: (07) 834 3198

Regions

Auckland: 16b Bakerfield Pl, PO Box 76 075, Manukau City 2241; tel: (09) 261 1063; fax: (09) 262 4103; email: t.huri@eplus-salvationarmy.org.nz

Bay of Plenty: 21 Mill Rd, PO Box 2046, Kopeopeo, Whakatane 3159; tel: (07) 308 7448; fax: (07) 307 0297; email: p.rodgers@eplus-salvationarmy.org.nz

Central: 148 Manchester St, PO Box 569, Feilding 4740; tel: (06) 323 9017;

fax: (06) 323 9620; email:
a.adams@eplus-salvationarmy.org.nz
Lower South: 160 Crawford St, Dunedin;
PO Box 784, Dunedin 9054; tel: (03) 476 7111;
fax: (03) 476 7188; email:
b.lee@eplus-salvationarmy.org.nz
Northern: 12 Kaka St, PO Box 1524,
Whangarei 0140; tel: (09) 438 4470;
fax: (09) 438 6500;
email: g.eilering@eplus-salvationarmy.org.nz
Upper South: Level 2, Science Alive Building,
Moorhouse Ave, PO Box 7198, Christchurch
8240; tel: (03) 379 4736; fax: (03) 377 2989;
email: d.dixon@eplus-salvationarmy.org.nz
Waikato: 182 Grandview Rd, Grandview,
PO Box 5347, Hamilton 3200;
tel: (07) 846 5216; fax: (07) 846 5217; email:
a.murphy@eplus-salvationarmy.org.nz

Home Care Services

National Office: 71 Seddon Rd, Hamilton 3204;
PO Box 9417, Hamilton 3240;
tel: (07) 848 2157; fax: (07) 846 1026;
email: homecare.hamilton@xtra.co.nz
Service Centres: Auckland, Hamilton, Paeroa,
Rotorua, Tauranga

SOCIAL SERVICES (under DHQ)
Community Ministries

Aranui: 34 Portsmouth St, Christchurch 8061;
tel/fax: (03) 388 1072
Auckland City: PO Box 27-153, 691 Mt Albert Rd,
Royal Oak; tel: (09) 625 7940;
fax: (09) 625 6045
Blenheim: Cnrs George and Henry Sts,
PO Box 417 Blenheim 7240; tel: (03) 578 0862;
fax: (03) 578 0990
Carterton: PO Box 145, Carterton 5743;
204-210 High St South, Carterton 5713;
tel: (06) 379 7176; fax: (06) 379 6109;
email: carterton_corps@nzf.salvationarmy.org
Christchurch: PO Box 1015, Christchurch 8140;
32 Lichfield St, Christchurch 8011;
tel: (03) 366 8128; fax: (03) 366 8295
Dunedin: 160 Crawford St, PO Box 934,
Dunedin 9016 tel: (03) 477 9852;
fax: (03) 477 1493
Feilding: 124 Manchester St, Feilding;
tel: (06) 323 4718; email:
feilding_corps@nzf.salvationarmy.org
Foxton: Avenue Rd, Foxton 4814; PO Box 51,
Foxton 4848; tel: (06) 363 8669; email:
foxton_corps@nzf.salvationarmy.org
Gisborne: PO Box 1086, 389 Gladstone Rd;
tel: (06) 868 9468; fax: (06) 868 1395;
email: Gisborne_corps@nzf.salvationarmy.org

Gore: 21 Irwell St; tel: (03) 208 4443
Hamilton: The Nest, PO Box 8020, Kahikatea Dr;
tel: (07) 843 4509; fax: (07) 843 3865;
incl Mary Bryant Family Home,
24 Ohaupo Rd; tel: (07) 843 4509; email:
the_nest@nzf.salvationarmy.org (acc 8)
Hastings: PO Box 999, cnr Warren St and
Ave Rd; tel: (06) 876 5771; fax (06)870 9331;
email: hastings_corps@nzf.salvationarmy.org
Hornby: 23 Manurere St, Christchurch 8042;
PO Box 16 967, Christchurch 8441;
tel: (03) 349 6268; fax: (03) 344 5376
Hutt City: cnr Kings Cres and Cornwall St,
Lower Hutt 5010; PO Box 30745, Lower Hutt;
tel: (04) 570 0273; fax: (04) 570 0274;
email: huttcity_corps@nzf.salvationarmy.org
Invercargill: PO Box 252, Invercargill 9840;
105 Tay St, Invercargill 9810;
tel/fax: (03) 214 0223
Linwood: 177 Linwood Ave, Christchurch 8067;
tel: (03) 389 3723
Manukau City: PO Box 76-075, 16b Bakerfield Pl,
Manukau City; tel: (09) 262 2332;
fax: (09) 262 4103
Motueka: PO Box 85, Motueka 7143;
tel: (03) 528 9338; fax: (03) 528 5109
Napier: PO Box 3086, 36 Faraday St;
tel: (06) 834 0759; fax: (06) 834 0759;
email: napier_cfs@nzf.salvationarmy.org
Nelson: 57 Rutherford St, Nelson 7010;
PO Box 22, Nelson 7040; tel: (03) 548 4807;
fax: (03) 548 4810
North Shore City: 407 Glenfield Rd, Glenfield,
Auckland, PO Box 40555, Glenfield;
tel: (09) 441 2554; fax: (09) 441 7599
North Taranaki: PO Box 384, cnr Powderham
and Dawson Sts, New Plymouth;
tel: (06) 758 9338; fax (06) 758 2325; email:
northtaranaki_corps@nzf.salvationarmy.org
Palmerston North: 431 Church St,
Palmerston North 4410; PO Box 869,
Palmerston North 4440; tel: (06) 358 7455;
fax: (06) 358 2314; email:
palmerstonnorth_cfs@nzf.salvationarmy.org
Porirua: PO Box 53-025, Cannons Creek 5243;
cnr Warspite Ave and Fantame St,
Porirua East 5024; tel: (04) 235 6266;
fax: (04) 235 6482; email:
porirua_cm@nzf.salvationarmy.org
Queenstown: PO Box 887, Queenstown 9348;
Camp St, Queenstown 9300; tel: (03) 442 5103;
fax: (03) 442 9644
Rotorua: 1115 Haupapa St; tel: (07) 346 8113;
fax: (07) 346 8075; email:
rotorua_cfs@nzf.salvationarmy.org

Sydenham: 17 Southampton St;
  Christchurch 8023; tel: (03) 331 7483;
  fax: (03) 332 8395
Tauranga: PO Box 164, 375 Cameron Rd;
  tel: (07) 578 5505; fax: (07) 578 4536; email:
  tauranga_corps@nzf.salvationarmy.org
Timaru: 206 Wai-iti Rd, Timaru 7910;
  tel/fax: (03) 684 7139
Tokoroa: PO Box 567; tel: (07) 886 9812;
  fax 886 9051; email:
  tokoroa_cfs@nzf.salvationarmy.org
Upper Hutt: 695 Fergusson Dr,
  Upper Hutt 5018; tel: (04) 528 6745;
  fax: (04) 528 6748; email:
  upper_hutt_corps@nzf.salvationarmy.org
Waitakere City: PO Box 21-708, Henderson,
  7-9 View Rd; tel: (09) 837 4471;
  fax: (09) 837 1246
Wellington: 26 Riddiford St, Newtown,
  Wellington 6021; tel: (04) 389 0594;
  fax: (04) 389 1130;
  Counselling Service: 26 Riddiford St,
  Newtown, Wellington 6021;
  tel: (04) 389 0594; fax: (04) 389 1130;
  email:
  wellingtoncfs@nzf.salvationarmy.org
  614 Youth Services: 1 Ghuznee St,
  Wellington 6011; PO Box 27459,
  Wellington 6141; tel: (04) 384 6119;
  fax: (04) 384 6115

Early Childhood Education Centres

Gisborne: 'Noah's Young Ones',
  PO Box 1086, 389 Gladstone Rd, Gisborne;
  tel: (06) 868 9468; fax: (06) 868 1395
  (roll 24)
Hamilton: The Nest Educare, PO Box 8020,
  Kahikatea Dr; tel: (07) 843 4066;
  fax: (07) 843 3865 (roll 50)
Masterton: Cecilia Whatman Early Childhood
  Education Centre, 132-140 Ngaumutawa Rd,
  Masterton 5810; tel: (06) 378 7316 (roll 38)
Upper Hutt: William Booth Educare,
  PO Box 40-542 Upper Hutt;
  tel: (04) 528 8628/527 6929 (roll 25)
Waitakere: Kidz Matter 2US, PO Box 21-708,
  Henderson; tel: (09) 837 4471;
  fax: (09) 837 1246 (roll 25)
Wellington:
  Britomart ECEC, 126 Britomart St,
  Berhampore, Wellington 6002;
  tel: (04) 389 9781 (roll 28)
  Wellington Bridge – Te Matua Tamariki
  Home-based ECE Service, PO Box 6033,
  Wellington 6002

COURT AND PRISON SERVICE

National Consultant: PO Box 7342, Auckland;
  tel: (09) 337 1351; fax: (09) 337 1249;
  mobile: 027 478 9758
Auckland: PO Box 7342, Wellesley St, Auckland;
  tel: (09) 916 9267; fax: (09) 309 9751;
  cellphone: 027 478 4457
Alexandra: 21 Aronui Rd; tel: (03) 448 9436;
  cellphone: 021 264 4765
Ashburton: PO Box 248; tel: 03 308 7610,
  cellphone 027 227 7029
Blenheim: PO Box 417; tel: (03) 578 0862;
  fax: (03) 578 0990
Christchurch: PO Box 25 207; tel: (03) 377 0799;
  fax: (03) 377 3575; mobile: 027 435 7915
Dunedin: 44a Filleul St; tel: (03) 477 9852;
  fax: (03) 477 1493; mobile: 027 496 7194
Gore: 21 Irwell St; tel/fax: (03) 208 4443
Hamilton: tel: (07) 843 4509; fax: (07) 843 3865;
  mobile: 027 280 9673
Invercargill: 14 Trent St; tel/fax: (03) 217 1131;
  mobile: 027 436 9796
North Shore: PO Box 40 034, Glenfield;
  tel: (09) 337 1351
Manukau: PO Box 76 075; tel/fax: (09) 525 2473;
  mobile: 027 478 4429
Kaitaia: PO Box 391; tel: (09) 408 3362;
  fax (09) 408 3362
Lower Hutt/Upper Hutt: PO Box 31 363,
  Lower Hutt; tel: (04) 389 0594;
  fax: (04) 389 1130
Palmerston North: PO Box 869;
  tel/fax: (06) 353 3459
Porirua: PO Box 53 025, Porirua East;
  tel: (04) 914 3260; mobile: 027 482 7437;
  fax: (04) 914 3262
Tauranga: PO Box 164, Tauranga;
  tel: (07) 578 5505; mobile: 027 6764 155
Thames: PO Box 142, Thames; tel: (07) 868 5495
Timaru: 206 Wai-iti Rd; tel/fax: (03) 684 7139
Waitakere: mobile: 027 243 0586
Wellington: PO Box 5094; tel: (04) 918 8063;
  fax: (04) 918 8098
Westport: tel: (03) 789 8085; fax: (03) 789 8058
Whangarei: tel: (09) 983 5460

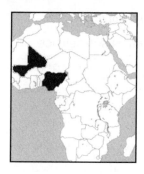

NIGERIA TERRITORY

Territorial leaders:
Commissioners Mfon and Ime Akpan

Territorial Commander:
Commissioner Mfon Akpan (1 Dec 2010)

Chief Secretary:
Lieut-Colonel Godfrey Payne (1 Jul 2010)

Territorial Headquarters: 6 Shipeolu St, Igbobi, Shomolu, Lagos

Postal address: Box 3025, Shomolu, Lagos, Nigeria

Tel/fax: [234] (1) 774 9125; email: nig_leadership@nig.salvationarmy.org

Salvation Army operations began in Nigeria in 1920 when Lieut-Colonel and Mrs George H. Souter landed in Lagos, to be followed later by Staff-Captain and Mrs Charles Smith with 10 West Indian officers. Following an invitation for the Army to establish a presence in Mali, with registration being given on 29 November 2007, a response was undertaken under local leadership until work in the country became official in February 2008 with the appointment of officers.

Zone: Africa
Countries included in the territory: Mali, Nigeria
'The Salvation Army' in Yoruba: Ogun Igbala Na; in Ibo: Igwe Agha Nzoputa; in Efik: Nka Erinyana; in Edo: Iyo Kuo Imienfan; in Urhobo: Ofovwi re Arhc Na; in Hausa: Soldiogi Cheta
Languages in which the gospel is preached: Calabari, Edo, Efik/Ibibio, English, French, Hausa, Ibo, Ijaw, Tiv, Urhobo, Yoruba
Periodicals: *Salvationist, The Shepherd, The War Cry*

THE first Salvation Army building in Mali – the corps hall at Sogonyiko – was opened during a campaign weekend in September 2009. The event was given extensive media coverage. Government representatives, church music groups, Malian Salvationists and friends were among those who attended.

A police-escorted march and open-air meetings with a small brass band made an impact in the community, where people refer to the Army as 'The Hallelujah Church'. Fifteen people accepted Christ as Saviour.

Converts recorded in Mali during the year totalled 353 and 377 soldiers were enrolled. On 1 April 2010 Mali became a region, with Majors Eugene and Odile Dikalembolovanga appointed as the regional leaders.

Salvationists in Nigeria responded to a number of emergency crises. In Jos, they provided food for 150 families, including 40 physically disabled people; elsewhere, clothing was distributed to people caught up in a fire in a Lagos suburb.

Through its prison ministry the Army continued to meet the needs of inmates. Women's Ministries staff of Lagos Division visited the Ikoyi

Prison women's wing to hand out children's and adults' clothing.

Physically disabled children and eye patients successfully received corrective surgery in Oji River Rehabilitation Centre. Projects relating to micro-credit loans and people living with HIV/Aids continued to be effective.

The Territorial Junior Soldiers Rally took place at Akure in September. More than 2,500 young people attended and nine junior soldiers were enrolled during the rally. This has led to renewed enthusiasm in many corps.

Port Harcourt was the venue for the Territorial Men's Fellowship Congress. Themed 'Rooted and Built Up in Christ for Mission', the congress aimed at urging men to demonstrate Christian faith and principles in their families, corps and communities. The four-day congress was attended by some 300 delegates representing every divsion, district and section in the territory.

STATISTICS

Officers 383 (active 305 retired 78) **Cadets** 23
Employees 114
Corps 181 **Societies and Outposts** 173
Institutions 12 **Schools** 32 **Clinics** 9
Senior Soldiers 29,700 **Adherents** 3,990
Junior Soldiers 6,824
Personnel serving outside territory Officers 3

STAFF

Women's Ministries: Comr Ime Akpan (TPWM) Lt-Col Diane Payne (TSWM) Lt-Col Patience Akpan (THLS) Lt-Col Theresa Baah (Junior Miss and Young Women's Sec) Lt-Col Norma Kwenda (Development and Grace Families Sec) Maj Edith Uzoho (Medical Fellowship and Retd Officers Sec)

Business Administration: Lt-Col Peter Kwenda
Editor/Literary: Capt Ifesinachi Ijioma
Extension Training: Maj Michael Olatunde
Field Programme: Lt-Col Samuel Baah
Finance: Joseph Vaikhuma
Personnel: Lt-Col Joseph U. Akpan
Prison Chaplain: Maj Benson Erhuwumnsee
Projects: Helen Vaikhuma
Property: Lazarus Akpadiaha
Public Relations: Maj Obed Mgbebuihe
Social: Maj Ebenezer O. Abayomi
HIV/Aids: Abraham Leka
Sponsorship: Maj Comfort Abayomi
Statistics: Maj Benson Erhuwumnsee
Training: Maj Gabriel O. Adepoju
Youth and Candidates: Maj Gabriel Ogungbenle

DIVISIONS

Akwa Ibom Central: c/o Afia Nisit PA, via Uyo; Majs Udoh and Esther Uwak
Akwa Ibom East: PO Box 20, Ikot Ubo, via Eket; Majs Paul and Edina Onyekwere
Akwa Ibom South West: c/o Abak PO Box 23, Abak; Majs Michael and Roseline Oyesanya
Akwa Ibom West: PO Box 47, Etinan; Majs Michael and Comfort Sijuade
Anambra East: Umuchu; Majs Edwin and Agnes Okorougo
Anambra West: 5 Urenebo St, Housing Estate, PO Box 1168, Onitsha, Anambra State; Majs Friday and Glory Ayanam
Ibadan: PO Box 261, Ibadan, Oyo State; Majs Patrick and Blessing Orasibe
Imo Central: based at Orogwe, Owerri; Majs Chika B. and Virginia Ezekwere
Lagos City: PO Box 2640, Surulere, Lagos State; Majs Benson and Celine Mgbebuihe
Ondo/Ekiti: PO Box 51, Akure, Ondo State; Majs Raphael and Esther Ogundahunsi

DISTRICTS

Abia: 2-8 Market Rd, PO Box 812, Aba, Abia State; Maj Simon Ekpendu
Cross River: PO Box 11, Calabar, Cross River State; tel: (087) 220284; Maj Samuel Edung
Edo/Delta: PO Box 108, Benin City, Edo State; Maj Vincent Adejoro
Lagos West: PO Badagry, Lagos State; Maj Silas Olebunne
Imo North: PO Box 512, Akokwa; Maj Godspower Sampson
Northern: PO Box 512, Jos, Plateau State; Maj Edet Essien

Ogun: PO Box 46, Ado Odo, Ogun State;
Maj Bramwell Chukwunwem
Rivers: PO Box 1161, Port Harcourt, Rivers State;
Capt Joseph Mbagwu

SECTIONS
Akwa Ibom South East: PO Box 25,
Ikot Abasi; Maj Maurice Akpabio
Enugu/Ebonyi: PO Box 1454, Enugu;
4 Moorehouse St, Ogui, Enugu State;
Maj Martins Ujari

TRAINING COLLEGE
4 Shipeolu St, PO Box 17, Shomolu, Igbobi,
Lagos; tel: (01) 774 9125

SOCIAL SERVICES
THQ-based Prison Ministry
Badagry Prison, Ikoyi Prison, Kirikiri Maximum
Security, Kirikiri Minimum Security, Kirikiri
Women's Prison

Corps-based Prison Ministry
Afaha Eket, Agbor, Badagry, Benin Central,
Ibadan Central, Port Harcourt Corps Team

Medical Centres
Ado Odo Medical Centre: Ado Odo Corps,
PO Box 46, Ado Odo, Ogun State (acc 2)
Gbethromy Training and Medical Centre:
c/o Badagry PO, Badagry, Lagos State (acc 8)
Iyara Health Centre: c/o Ado Irele, Ondo State
(acc 3)
Lagos Central Corps Clinic: 11 Odunlami St,
PO Box 125, Lagos State (acc 2)
Nda Nsit Clinic/Maternity: Nda Nsit Corps,
via Uyo, Akwa Idom State (acc 2)
Nkoro Corps Mobile Clinic: Nkoro Corps,
via Boni PO Box, Rivers State (acc 4)
Oji River Eye Clinic: Oji River PO Box
Ubrama Health Centre/Clinic: Ubrama PO Box,
Ahoada Alaga, Rivers State
Umucheke Corps Clinic: via Uruala PO,
Ideato L/G. A., Imo State (acc 4)

HIV/Aids Action Centre and Voluntary Counselling and Testing Centre
11 Odunlami St, PO Box 125, Lagos

Social Centres/Institutions/Programmes
Akai Children's Home: PO Box 1009, Eket,
Akwa Ibom State (acc 35)
Benin Rehabilitation Centre: 20A First East
Circular Rd, PO Box 108, Benin City,
Edo State (acc 17)

Oji River Rehabilitation Centre: Oji River PO,
via Enugu, Enugu State (acc 64)
Orphans/Vulnerable Children Centre/Orphans
Psycho-Social Centre – Akai: PO Box 1009,
Eket Akwa Ibom State

SCHOOLS
Nursery
Aba Corps, Agbor Corps, Akai Corps,
Akokwa Corps, Amauzari Corps,
Benin Corps, Ibughubu Corps, Ikot Inyang Eti,
Ile Ife Corps, Ivue Corps, Jos Corps,
Mpape Corps, Onitsha Corps, Osumenyi Corps,
Somorika Corps, Suleja, Umucheke Corps,
Umuchu Corps, Umudike Corps

Primary
Aba Corps, Akai, Amauzari Corps,
Benin Corps, Ile Ife, Ikot Inyang Eti,
Ivue Corps, Jos Corps, Mpape Corps,
Onitsha Corps, Somorika Corps, Suleja

Secondary
Ilesha Corps, Ile-Ife, Orogwe

VOCATIONAL TRAINING CENTRES
Afia Nsit-Nsit: PO Box 8, Afia Nsit Urua Nko,
Akwa Ibom State (acc 8)
Abak: PO Box 23, Abak, Akwa Ibom State
(acc 4)
Amauzari: via Owerri PO, Imo State (acc 4)
Enugu: 4 Moorhouse St, PO Box 1454,
Ogui, Enugu State (acc 6)
Ibesit: Ibesit Corps, Anang PA, Ukanafun LGA,
Akwa Ibom State (acc 3)
Ikot Okobo Training Centre: PO Box 493,
Eket, Akwa Ibom State (acc 156)
Ilesha VTC: Ilesha Corps, PO Box 91, Ilesha,
Oyo State (acc 30)
Ile-Ife VTC: Ile-Ife Corps, PO Box 113, Ile-Ife,
Oyo State
Orogwe VTC: Orogwe Corps, via Owerri PO,
Imo State (acc 235)
Supare VTC: Supare Corps, PMB 257,
via Ikare Akoko, Ondo State (acc 30)
Umuogo VTC: Umuogo Corps, c/o Amuzu PA,
via Owerri, Imo State (acc 8)

MALI REGION
Regional Headquarters: Armée du Salut/The
Salvation Army, Rue N° 477, Porte N° 39,
Immeuble Drissa, Dissa, Hamdallaye-ACI 2000,
Bamako; tel: (223) 7465 30 76/2023 83 15
Regional leaders: Majs Eugene and Odile
Dikalembolovanga

NORWAY, ICELAND AND THE FÆROES TERRITORY

Territorial leaders:
Commissioners Clive and Marianne Adams

Territorial Commander:
Commissioner Clive Adams (1 Dec 2010)

Chief Secretary:
Colonel Jan Peder Fosen (1 Dec 2010)

Territorial Headquarters: Kommandør T I Øgrims plass 4, 0165 Oslo, Norway

Postal address: Box 6866, St Olavs Plass, 0130 Oslo, Norway

Tel: [47] 22 99 85 00; fax: [47] 22 20 84 49; email: nor.leadership@frelsesarmeen.no;

website: www.frelsesarmeen.no

Commissioners Hanna Ouchterlony and George Scott Railton with Staff-Captain and Mrs Albert Orsborn 'opened fire' in Oslo (Kristiania) on 22 January 1888. Work began in Iceland on 12 May 1895, pioneered by Adjutant Christian Eriksen, Captain Thorstein Davidsson and Lieutenant Lange, and spread to The Færoes in 1924.

Zone: Europe
Countries included in the territory: Iceland, Norway, The Færoes
'The Salvation Army' in Norwegian: Frelsesarmeen; in Icelandic: Hjálpraedisherinn; in Færoese: Frelsunarherurin
Languages in which the gospel is preached: English, Færoese, Icelandic, Norwegian
Periodicals: *Krigsropet, Uni-Form* (both Norwegian), *Herópid* (Icelandic)

TWO exciting innovations in The Salvation Army's annual programme in Norway were a concerted political engagement in the build-up to the 2009 parliamentary election and the hosting of the National Street Football Championships as part of the territorial congress weekend. Both were successful and should open doors to new possibilities.

The Army's political engagement included the production of a newspaper in which five Salvationists, all well-known figures in public life, wrote challenging articles on ethical topics and Salvationist teaching.

The Christmas Kettle Appeal was yet again a great success, setting a record figure of almost 23.5 million kroner. In addition to kettles on the streets and internet donations, for the second year running donation coupons could be purchased in Co-op shops instead of putting cash in a collecting tin. Customers bought coupons valued at 20, 50 or 100 kroner with their groceries, raising some 1.8 million kroner.

In the Western Division 70 young people and leaders came together for a New Year Conference arranged for teenagers at Stavanger Corps. Four youths gave their lives to Christ.

The corps at Brevik has experienced considerable growth in young people's work, especially among teenagers. Some 200 of them meet bi-weekly for Bible teaching and recreational activities such as paintball and archery. Many of the young people have accepted Christ as their saviour.

A corps plant is being registered at Alta, where six solders, an adherent and a small group of friends meet in a monthly house fellowship. Also, a Fretex second-hand clothing centre has been established.

There was much public interest in the 85th anniversary celebrations of Salvation Army ministry in The Færoes. Prominent guests were among an audience reminded by the then TC, Commissioner Carl Lydholm, that the Army came to the islands as an initiative from Denmark, his father being one of the pioneer officers. Service in The Færoes has been expanded with the opening of new facilities for community work among homeless and alcoholic-dependant people.

In Iceland the necessary renewal of mission focus was accomplished in Keflavik. The Salvation Army moved in as the American Air Force vacated their base. A corps has been successfully established; the number of adherents is growing and some are preparing for soldiership.

STATISTICS

Officers 405 (active 186 retired 219) **Cadets** 7 **Employees** 1,329
Corps 109 **Outposts** 328 **Institutions** 38 (incl slum posts) **Industrial Centres/Second-hand Shops** 47
Senior Soldiers 5,440 **Adherents** 1,371 **Junior Soldiers** 78
Personnel serving outside territory Officers 20

STAFF

Women's Ministries: Comr Marianne Adams (TPWM) Col Birgit T. Fosen (TSWM) Lt-Col Brit Knedal (Home and Family)
Asst CS: Maj Arne Undersrud
Sec for Business Administration: Lt-Col Thorgeir Nybo
Financial Sec: Maj Eli Nodland Hagen
  Chief Accountant: Egil Hognerud
  Missionary Projects: Maj Magna Våje Nielsen
Property: Dag Tellefsen
Sec for Communication: Maj Inger Marit Nygård
  Section for Information and Marketing: Andrew Hannevik
  Editor: Hilde Dagfinrud Valen
Sec for Personnel: Maj Lise O. Luther
Sec for Field and Programme: Lt-Col Jan Øystein Knedal
  Asst Sec for Field and Programme: Maj Anne-Lise Undersrud
  Community Services: Col Birgit T. Fosen
  Music: Maj Jan Harald Hagen
    Territorial Band: B/M John Philip Hannevik
  Over 60s: Maj Leif-Erling Fagermo
  Youth and Children: Maj Henrik Bååth
    Mission Team: Janne Nielsen
Sec for Social Services: Lindis Evja (pro tem)
  Alcohol and Drug Rehabilitation: Capt Knut Haugsvær
  Children and Family Services: Anne Hernæs Hjelle (pro tem)
  Day Care Centres for Children: Anne-Dorthe Nodland Aasen
  Family Tracing: Maj Erling Levang
  Welfare and Development: Elin Herikstad
  Work Rehabilitation and Recycling (Fretex): Thor Fjellvang
  'Sally Ann': Bent Undnesseter

JELØY RESOURCE CENTRE:

1516 Moss, Nokiavn 30; Maj Jostein Nielsen (Director)
Training College: 1385 Asker, Brendsrudtoppen, 40; tel: 66 76 49 70; fax: 66 76 49 71;

Maj Frank Gjeruldsen (Training Principal)
Jeløy Folk High School: 1516 Moss,
Nokiavn, 30b; tel: 69 91 10 70;
fax: 69 91 10 80; Maj Wenche Walderhaug
Midjord (Principal)
CO-Worker School: 1516 Moss, Nokiavn, 30;
Maj Jostein Nielsen (Principal)

DIVISIONS

Central: Heimdalsgt 14, PO Box 2869, Tøyen,
0608 Oslo; tel: 23 24 49 20; fax: 23 24 49 21;
Lt-Col Elisabeth Henne
Eastern: Kneika 11, PO Box 40, 3056
Solbergelva; tel: 32 87 12 90;
fax: 32 87 12 01; Majs Per Arne and
Lillian Pettersen
Iceland and The Færoes: Kirkjurstræti 2,
IS 121 Reykjavik; tel: (00354) 552 0788;
fax: (00354) 562 0780; Majs Paul William
and Margaret Marti
Midland: Knausv 12, Smeby, PO Box 3002,
2318 Hamar; tel: 62 52 21 83; fax: 62 54 91 08;
Maj Brith-Mari Heggelund
Northern: Bjørkvn 12, PO Box 8255 Jakobsli,
7458 Trondheim; tel: 73 57 14 20;
fax: 73 57 16 93; Majs Bernt Olaf and
Hildegard Ørsnes
North Norway: Skolegt 6, PO Box 177,
9252 Tromsø; tel: 77 68 83 70;
fax: 77 68 81 51; Maj Gro-Merete Berg
Western: Kongsgt 50, PO Box 553,
4003 Stavanger; tel: 51 56 41 60;
fax: 51 56 41 61; Lt-Cols Odd and Grethe Berg

SOCIAL SERVICES

Head Office: 0165 Oslo, Kommandør T. I.
Øgrims plass 4 ; tel: 22 99 85 00

Children's and Youths' Homes

3018 Drammen, Hotvedtveien 57; tel: 23 69 19 90
3028 Drammen, Bolstadhagen 61;
tel: 32 20 45 80
1441 Drøbak, Nils Carlsensgt 31; tel: 64 90 51 30;
fax: 64 91 51 31
1112 Oslo, Nordstrandsvn 7; tel: 23 16 89 10;
fax: 23 16 89 19
2021 Skedsmokorset, Flesvigs vei 4;
tel: 63 83 67 10
4011 Stavanger, Vidarsgt 4; tel: 51 52 11 49;
fax: 51 52 66 31
7037 Trondheim, Øystein Møylas veg 20 B;
tel: 73 95 44 33, fax: 73 95 44 39
1540 Vestby, Soldammen, Gjølstadveien 73;
tel: 64 98 04 70; fax: 64 98 04 71

Day Care Centres for Children

1385 Asker, Brendsrudtoppen 60; tel: 66 78 74 86;
fax: 66 79 02 64
5011 Bergen, Skottegt 16; tel: 55 23 08 83;
fax: 55 23 47 45
1441 Drøbak, Nils Carlsensgt 31; tel: 64 93 15 09;
fax: 64 93 15 73
0664 Oslo, Regnbuevn 2C; tel: 23 03 93 30,
fax: 23 03 93 39
4017 Stavanger, Auglendsdalen 62; tel: 51 88 68 80

Family Centre

0487 Oslo, Kapellvn 61; tel: 22 09 86 20,
fax: 22 09 86 21

Home-Start Family Contact

Avd Drammen: 3007 Drammen, Rådhusgt 19,
tel: 478 93 800
Avd Nedre Eiker: 3007 Drammen, Rådhusgt 19,
tel: 478 93 800
Avd Lillehammer: 2609 Lillehammer,
Fossvegen 15 B; tel: 40 24 66 38
Avd Gamle Oslo: 0561 Oslo, Heimdalsgt 14 B;
tel: 90 61 76 74
Avd Østensjø: 0686 Oslo, Vetlandsveien 99/100;
tel: 23 43 89 10

Old People's Welfare Centre

0661 Oslo, Malerhaugvn 10b; tel: 22 57 66 30;
fax: 22 67 09 34

Slum and Goodwill Centres

6005 Ålesund, Giskegt 27; tel: 70 12 18 05;
fax: 70 12 18 05
5808 Bergen, Ladegårdsgt 21; tel: 55 56 34 70;
fax: 55 56 34 71
0656 Oslo, Borggt 2; tel: 23 03 74 494004

Hostels

5812 Bergen, Bakkegt 7; tel: 55 30 22 85,
fax: 55 30 22 90
8001 Bodø, Kongensgt 16; tel: 75 52 23 38;
fax: 75 52 23 39
5501 Haugesund, Sørhauggt 215; tel: 52 72 77 01;
fax: 52 72 35 30
0561 Oslo, Heimen, Heimdalsgt 27 A;
tel: 23 21 09 60; fax: 22 68 00 98
0656 Oslo, Schweigaardsgt 70; tel: 23 24 39 00;
fax: 23 24 39 09
0354 Oslo, Sporveisgt 33; tel: 22 95 73 50;
fax: 22 95 73 51
3111 Tønsberg, Farmannsvn 26; tel: 33 31 54 09;
fax: 33 31 07 74
7041 Trondheim, Furulund, Lade Allè 84;
fax: 73 90 70 40

FO-100 Torshavn, N Winthersgt 3;
tel: (00298) 31 73 93; tel: 73 90 70 30

Self-catering Accommodation for Female Drug Addicts

8000 Bodø, Prinsensgate 151B; tel: 75 52 39 90;
fax 75 52 23 39

Work-rehabilitation Programme among Alcohol and Drug Addicts (The Job)

0650 Oslo, Schweigaardsgt 68;
tel: 61 60 06 84
2609 Lillehammer, Morterudveien 15;
tel: 61 60 06 84
6400 Molde, Spolertbakken 3

Rehabilitation Homes for Alcohol and Drug Addicts

4017 Stavanger, Auglendsdalen 64;
tel: 51 82 87 00; fax: 51 82 87 82
4463 Ualand, Heskestad; tel: 51 40 50 13;
fax 41 40 50 11

Day Care Centres (Alcohol and Drug Addicts)

0187 Oslo, Urtegaten 16 A/C; tel: 23 03 66 80;
fax: 23 03 66 81
4379 Egersund, Bedehusgaten 3; tel: 51 46 70 00
1301 Sandvika, Kinoveien 4; mobile: 40 48 63 70
7012 Trondheim, Hvedingsveita 3;
tel: 73 52 09 00; fax: 73 51 03 97
8001 Bodø, Kongensgt 16

Supervisons of Residence (Alcohol and Drug Addicts)

0561 Oslo, Heimdalsgt 27A; tel: 23 121 09 73

Health Clinics for Drug Addicts

0650 Oslo, Borggt 2, tel: 22 08 36 70
0187 Oslo, Urtegt 16 A/C; tel: 22 67 43 45

Prison Work

5032 Bergen, Bakkegt 7
0666 Oslo, Ole Deviksv 20; tel: 23 06 92 35,
fax: 22 65 57 74
0650 Oslo, Borggt 2
4002 Stavanger, Kongensgt 50

Home for Prisoners

0666 Oslo, Ole Deviksv 20; tel: 23 06 92 35;
fax: 22 65 57 74

Work Rehabilitation and Recycling Centres (FRETEX)

(including 44 second-hand shops)
6002 Ålesund, Korsegt 6; tel: 70 12 71 75;
fax: 70 12 71 75

5852 Bergen, Sandalsringen 3; tel: 55 92 59 00;
fax: 55 92 59 10
8013 Bodø, Notveien 17; tel: 75 21 03 50
3036 Drammen, Kobbevikdalen 71;
tel: 32 20 83 50; fax: 32 20 83 51
4110 Forsand, Myra Industriområde;
tel: 51 70 39 07
3550 Gol, Sentrumsvn. 63; tel: 32 07 98 80;
fax: 32 07 98 81
9406 Harstad, Storgt 34; tel: 77 00 24 77;
fax: 77 00 24 71
7080 Heimdal, Heggstadmyra 2; tel: 72 59 59 15;
fax: 72 59 59 19
7550 Hommelvik, Havneveien; tel: 73 98 72 00;
fax: 73 98 72 01
2050 Jessheim, Storgata 11; tel: 67 49 04 30;
fax: 67 49 04 31
9900 Kirkenes, Pasvikvn 2; tel: 78 97 02 40;
fax: 78 97 02 41
2615 Lillehammer, Storgt 91; tel: 61 24 65 50;
fax: 61 24 65 51
1515 Moss, Bråtengt; tel: 64, 69 27 50 69;
fax: 69 27 11 14
0668 Oslo, Ole Deviksvei 20; tel: 23 06 92 00;
fax: 23 06 92 01
3208 Sandefjord, Basen, Bugårdsgata 7;
tel: 33 52 27 38
4315 Sandnes, Tornerosevn 7; tel: 51 95 13 00
3735 Skien, Bedriftsvn 58; tel: 35 59 89 44;
fax: 35 59 57 44
9018 Tromsø, Skattøravn 39; tel: 77 67 22 88;
fax: 77 67 22 87

Second-hand Shops

Ålesund (2), Bergen (5), Bodø, Bryne, Drammen,
Fredrikstad, Gol, Harstad, Haugesund,
Jessheim, Jørpeland, Kirkenes, Kristiansand,
Lillehammer, Lillestrøm, Lyngdal, Mandal,
Molde, Moss, Oslo (5), Sandnes (2), Sandvika,
Skien, Stavanger (3), Stjørdal, Tromsø,
Trondheim (5), Tønsberg, Voss

Art Galleri

Bergen

Cafe

3016 Drammen, Torget Vest Rådhusgata 2

ICELAND

Convalescent Home: Skólabraut 10, PO Box 115,
IS-172 Seltjarnarnes; tel: [354] 561 2090;
fax: [354] 561 2089
Guest Home: PO Box 866, IS-121 Reykjavik;
tel: [354] 561 3203; fax: [354] 561 3315

PAKISTAN TERRITORY

Territorial leaders:
Colonels Robert and Marguerite Ward

Territorial Commander:
Colonel Robert Ward (1 Feb 2008)

Chief Secretary:
Lieut-Colonel Yousaf Ghulam (1 Oct 2007)

Territorial Headquarters: 35 Shahrah-e-Fatima Jinnah, Lahore

Postal address: PO Box 242, Lahore 54000, Pakistan

Tel: [92] (042) 3758 1644/3756 9940; fax: [92] (042) 3757 2699;

website:www.salvationarmy.org/pakistan

The Salvation Army began work in Lahore in 1883 and was eventually incorporated under the Companies Act of 1913 on 9 October 1968.

Zone: South Asia
Country included in the territory: Pakistan
Languages in which the gospel is preached: English, Punjabi, Pashto, Urdu
Periodicals: *Home League Annual, The War Cry* (in Urdu)

THE territory experienced a year of both great blessing and challenge. The theme 'Forward With Prayer' was a reminder of the need to advance with guidance and power from the Lord.

Thirty-nine cadets were welcomed into the Ambassadors Of Holiness Session. For the first time both women and men needed the same level of education to be accepted for officer training.

When Lieut-Colonels Wayne and Myra Pritchett (IHQ) led the territory's third Brengle seminar in two years the officer-delegates were challenged to teach, preach and model holiness. The zonal leaders for South Asia, Commissioners Lalkiamlova and Lalhlimpuii, conducted an IHQ

review of the territory that proved a great encouragement.

Funding from mission partners, the United Kingdom Territory, facilitated the opening of a hall and officers' quarters in Nishat Colony (Lahore), a quarters in Bhattiabad (Karachi) and the purchase of a building in 66 Quarters (Islamabad) with a sizeable roof, to accommodate the congregation in worship. Mala Singh became the second hall in two years to be built with funds from the helping-hand scheme.

A number of events took place for the first time in the territory: a 15 years' service review for newly promoted majors, a prayer conference led by Commissioner Lyn Pearce (then World Secretary for Women's Ministries) and training for leaders of young women's fellowships. The Women's Ministries team visited every division to conduct leaders workshops and to review women's groups.

The 'Sally Ann' programme provides income as other territories and 'Sally Ann' shops place orders for goods. The sustainable livelihood development project continues to expand and a skills development programme has commenced in Islamabad.

A team of officers responded to two man-made disasters, the first due to military action taken against militant forces. Thousands of families on the western border of the country were displaced. Tents, eating and cooking utensils, bedding and latrines were provided and led to an invitation to commence a permanent community service in Mardan.

Then when homes were destroyed and people killed as a result of violence against Christians in Koriyan and Gojra, officers responded with pastoral care, beds, food and utensils.

STATISTICS

Officers 390 (active 305 retired 85) **Cadets** (2nd Yr) 39 **Employees** 171
Corps 134 **Societies** 544 **Institutions** 7 **Schools** 3 **Training and Resource Centres** 2
Senior Soldiers 52,112 **Adherents** 8,988 **Junior Soldiers** 14,586

STAFF

Women's Ministries: Col Marguerite Ward (TPWM) Lt-Col Rebecca Yousaf (TSWM)
Projects: Col Marguerite Ward
'Sally Ann': Faisal Yacoob

Secretary for Business Administration: Maj Dennis Gensler
Chief Accountant: Andrew Lee
Editor: Capt Raja Azeem Zia
Finance: tba
Property: Capt MacDonald Chandi
Secretary for Personnel: Lt-Col Morris John
Candidates: Capt Rebecca Samuel
Mission Training and Education Coordinator: Maj Rosemary Cowdery
Training: Maj Colin Cowdery
Secretary for Programme: Maj Samuel Tari
Asst Sec for Programme: Maj Lynn Gensler
Prayer Coordinator: Maj Victoria Samuel
Social Services and Sponsorship: Capt Diana MacDonald
Youth: Capt Samuel John

DIVISIONS

Faisalabad: Jamilabad Jamia Salfia Rd, Faisalabad; tel: (041) 8783472; Majs Shafqat Masih and Perveen Shafqat
Islamabad: William Booth Village, Khana Kak (Majaraj Plaza) Iqbal Town, Islamabad; mobile: 0300 4805838; Capts Washington Daniel (DO) and Azra Washington
Jaranwala: Water Works Rd, nr Telephone Exchange, Jaranwala; tel: (041) 4312423; Majs Salamat Masih and Grace Salamat
Jhang: Yousaf Shah Rd, Jhang Saddar; tel: (047) 7611589; Majs Michael Gabriel and Shamim Gabriel
Karachi: 78 NI Lines, Frere St, Saddar, Karachi 74400; tel: (021) 2254260; Lt-Col Zarina Veru
Khanewal: Chak Shahana Rd, Khanewal 58150; tel: (065) 2553860; Majs Walter Emmanuel and Mussaraf Walter
Lahore: The Salvation Army, Bahar Colony, Kot Lakhpat, Lahore; tel: (042) 35834568; Majs Samuel Barkat and Margaret Samuel
Sahiwal: Karbala Rd, Sahiwal; tel: (040) 4466383; Capts Haroon Ghulam (DO) and Jennifer Haroon
Sheikhupura: 16 Civil Lines Rd, Qila, Sheikhupura; tel: (056) 3786521; Majs Javed Yousaf (DO) and Surriya Javed

DISTRICT

Hyderabad: Bungalow No 9, 'E' Block, Unit No 11, Latifabad 11, Hyderabad; tel: (022) 3813445; Maj Khuram Shahzada

TRAINING COLLEGE

Ali Bridge, Canal Bank Rd North, Tulspura, Lahore; tel: (042) 36582450; email: sacollege@cyber.net.pk

CONFERENCE CENTRE

Lahore: 35 Shahrah-e-Fatima Jinnah,
PO Box 242, Lahore 54000;
tel: (042) 37581644 ext 338

MISSION TRAINING AND EDUCATION CENTRE

35 Shahrah-e-Fatima Jinnah, PO Box 242,
Lahore 54000; tel: (042) 37581644

SOCIAL SERVICES

Boarding Hostels

Boys

Jhang: Yousaf Shah Rd, Jhang Saddar;
tel: (047) 7624763 (acc 50)

Girls

Lahore: 35 Shahrah-e-Fatima Jinnah, PO Box 242,
Lahore 54000; tel: (042) 37569940 (acc 50)

Children's Homes

Karachi Boys' Home: Site Metroville,
PO Box 10682, Karachi 75700;
tel: (021) 6650513 (acc 50)
Joyland Girls' Home: 90-B Block, Model Town,
Lahore; tel: (042) 35850190 (acc 50)

Sheikhupura Children's Home: 16 Civil Lines,
Qilla, Sheikhupura; tel: (056) 3614378 (acc 50)

EDUCATION

Schools

Azam Town Secondary School, Street 6,
100 Foot Rd, Azam Town, Karachi 75460;
tel: (021) 5384223
Shantinagar Educational Institute:
Chak No 72/10-R, Shantinagar, Khanewal;
tel: (065) 2019633
Tibba Coaching Centre: Chak No 72/10-R, Tibba,
Shantinagar, Khanewal; tel: (065) 2023151

REHABILITATION CENTRES FOR DISABLED

Karachi: Manzil-e-Umead, PO Box 10735,
Site Metroville, Karachi 75700;
tel: (021) 6650434
Lahore: Manzil-e-Shifa, 35 Shahrah-e-Fatima
Jinnah, PO Box 242, Lahore 54000;
tel: (042) 37582391

In Pakistan a donkey and branches cut from nearby palm trees are not an unusual sight as this Salvation Army procession takes place on Palm Sunday

PAPUA NEW GUINEA TERRITORY

Territorial Commander:
Commissioner Andrew Kalai (1 Jun 2005)

Chief Secretary:
Lieut-Colonel Neil Webb (1 Jun 2010)

Territorial Headquarters: Angau Dr, Boroko, National Capital District

Postal address: PO Box 1323, Boroko, NCD, Papua New Guinea

Tel: [675] 325-5522/5507; fax: [675] 323 3282; website: www.png.salvationarmy.org

The Salvation Army officially commenced in Papua New Guinea on 31 August 1956 and the first meeting was conducted on Sunday 21 October at the Royal Police Constabulary Barracks in Port Moresby. The first officers appointed to the work there were Major Keith Baker, Mrs Major Edna Baker and Lieutenant Ian Cutmore. On 4 July 1994, after 38 years as part of the Australia Eastern Territory, Papua New Guinea became an independent command and on 9 December 2000 was elevated to territory status.

Zone: South Pacific and East Asia
Country included in the territory: Papua New Guinea
Languages in which the gospel is preached: English, Hiri Motu, Pidgin and many local languages
Periodicals: *Tokaut*

MOVING forward intentionally and steadfastly, The Salvation Army in Papua New Guinea continues to grow.

A highlight of the year came when two village tribes who had been fighting each other for more than 20 years, came together in a peace agreement brokered by The Salvation Army in conjunction with other churches. Warriors from each village handed in their guns and received Bibles in return.

Six new officers were ordained and commissioned. As there are more cadets than there is accommodation capacity at the officer training college, four cadets are training outside the territory.

An officer has been appointed to the Solomon Islands with a view to the Army opening fire there.

The territory hosted a visit from Sydney Youth Band (Australia Eastern). Playing to at least 2,500 people during its short stay, the band brought exciting music and positive Christian witness in each of the three major cities it visited.

The first Territorial Men's Convention, held in Lae, attracted more than 500 delegates for the weekend, at the end of which 50 men rededicated themselves to the Lord. A number of 'Women Only Weekends' were also held around the territory, with large numbers attending on each occasion.

The first training for divisional leaders took place. Delegates from across the territory joined with THQ staff for a much-appreciated week of refreshment and renewal.

Supported by greatly appreciated funding from mission partners territories and others, various territorial projects were successfully completed. Japan Territory, with JICA (Japan International Cooperation Agency) and the European Union, funded rural water supply and sanitation projects that will benefit eight communities.

AusAid funding was secured for further HIV/Aids work, and for the first time the government offered funding to conduct health and social projects that will contribute to achieving the United Nations Millennium Development Goals.

An almost entirely new cabinet has been appointed at THQ, and its members continue to give the supportive and co-ordinated leadership to the territory established by their predecessors.

STATISTICS

Officers 254 (active 221 retired 33) **Cadets** (1st Yr) 15 (2nd Yr) 12 **Employees** 385 **Corps** 54 **Outposts** 78 **Institution** 1 **Motels** 2 **Schools** 8 **Health Centre and Sub Centres** 6 **Community Health Posts** 19 **Counselling Centres** 3 **Staff Clinic** 1 **Senior Soldiers** 6,654 **Adherents** 4,710 **Junior Soldiers** 1,722

STAFF

Women's Ministries: Lt-Col Christine Webb (TSWM)
Business Administration: Maj Philip Maxwell
Personnel: Maj Iveme Yanderave

Programme: Maj Rex Johnson
Leadership Development: Maj Joe Nato
Editorial/Literature: tba
Property: tba
Projects: tba
Public Relations and Planned Giving: Capt John Kerari
SALT: Capt Gandi Igoto
Training: Capt Patricia Kerari
Youth Resources Co-ordinator: Capt Kila Apa

DIVISIONS

North Coastal: PO Box 667, Lae, Morobe Province; tel: 472 0905; fax: 472 0897; Capts David and Rita Vele
North Eastern: PO Box 343, Kainantu, Eastern Highlands Province; tel: 537 1220; tel/fax: 537 1482; Majs Steven and Eva'aso Nehaya
North Western: PO Box 365, Goroka, Eastern Highlands Province; tel: 532 1382; fax: 532 1218; Majs Christian and Tilitah Goa
South Central: PO Box 4227, Boroko, National Capital District; mobile: 7285 0568; fax: 321 6008; Majs Dinunu and Ridia Nenewa
South Eastern: PO Box 49, Kwikila, Central Province; 2-way Radio Cell call no: 8564; tel: 329 5008; Majs Rabona and Gabi Rotona
Gulf Regional Office: PO Box 132, Kerema, Gulf Province; tel/fax: 648 1384; Maj Vari and Capt Nellie Burava
Sepik District Office: PO Box 184, Wewak, East Sepik Province; tel/fax: 456 1642; Majs Bugave and Tomuna Kada

OFFICER TRAINING COLLEGE

PO Box 5355, Boroko, National Capital District; tel: 323 0553; fax: 325 6668

SALT COLLEGE

PO Box 343, Kainantu, Eastern Highlands Province; tel/fax: 737 1125

EDUCATION SERVICES

Mary and Martha Child Care Centre, Koki (acc 35)
Boroko Primary School (acc 781)
Lae Primary School (acc 704)
Goroka Elementary School (acc 150)
Kainantu Elementary School (acc 172)
Kerowagi Elementary School (acc 150)
Tamba Elementary School (acc 120)
Koki Secondary School (acc 289, Grades 9 to 12)

After more than 20 years of fighting each other in a remote area of Papua New Guinea, warriors from two feuding tribes hand over their guns to The Salvation Army and receive Bibles in return. The men and their families are now reading the gospel of love and peace.

Boroko FODE Centre (acc 610) (inc Boroko Driving School

Kimbe Computer School (acc 30)

Community Health Workers Training School

Private Mail Bag 3, Kainantu, Eastern Highlands Province; tel/fax: 537 1404 (acc 40)

SOCIAL PROGRAMME
Community Services and HIV/Aids

Courts and Prison Ministry, Missing Persons, Welfare Feeding Projects

House of Hope: Ela Beach Care and Counselling Centre; tel: 320 0389

Jim Jacobsen Centre: PO Box 901, Lae, Morobe Province; tel/fax: 472 1117

DEVELOPMENT SERVICES

Onamuga Development Project: Private Mail Bag 3, Kainantu, Eastern Highlands Province

Literacy Programmes: each division

HEALTH SERVICES PROGRAMMES

North Coastal: PO Box 667 Lae, Morobe Province; tel: 472 0905, fax 472 0897
Community Health Posts: Pongani, Waru

North Eastern: Private Mail Bag 3, Kainantu,
Eastern Highlands Province; tel/fax: 537 1279
Onamuga Health Centre (acc 35)
Community Health Posts: Barokira, Kokopi, Norikori, Pitanka, Yauna

North Western: PO Box 365, Goroka, Eastern Highlands Province; tel: 532 1382; fax: 532 1218
Health Sub Centre: Misapi
Community Health Posts: Kamila, Kwongi

South Central PO Box 4227, Boroko, National Capital District; tel: 321 6000; fax: 321 6008
Community Health Posts: Ilavapari, Lapari, Papa, Sogeri

South Eastern: PO Box 49, Kwikila, Central Province
Health Sub Centre: Boregaina (acc 10)
Community Health Posts: Dirinomu, Kokorogoro, Kwaipo, Matairuka, Meirobu

MOTELS

Goroka: PO Box 365, Goroka, Eastern Highlands Province; tel: 532 1382; fax: 732 1218 (family units 2, double units 4, house 1)

The Elphick: PO Box 637, Lae, Morobe Province; tel: 472 2487; fax: 472 7487 (double rooms 8)

THE PHILIPPINES TERRITORY

Territorial leaders:
Commissioners Malcolm and Irene Induruwage

Territorial Commander:
Commissioner Malcolm Induruwage
(2 Apr 2006)

Chief Secretary:
Lieut-Colonel Ronald Clinch (1 May 2009)

Territorial Headquarters: 1843 Leon Guinto Sr St, 1004 Malate, Manila

Postal address: PO Box 3830, Manila 1099, The Philippines

Tel: [63] (2) 524 0086/88; fax: [63] (2) 521 6912 local 120

email: saphl1@phl.salvationarmy.org

The first Protestant preaching of the gospel in The Philippines was done by Major John Milsaps, a chaplain appointed to accompany US troops from San Francisco to Manila in July 1898. Major Milsaps conducted open-air and regular meetings and led many into a saving knowledge of Jesus Christ.

The advance of The Salvation Army in The Philippines came at the initiative of Filipinos who had been converted through contact with The Salvation Army in Hawaii, returned to their homeland and commenced meetings in Panay, Luzon, Cebu and Mindanao Islands during the period 1933-37. On 6 June 1937 Colonel and Mrs Alfred Lindvall officially inaugurated this widespread work.

The Salvation Army Philippines was incorporated in 1963 as a religious and charitable corporation under Company Registration No 24211. The Salvation Army Social Services was incorporated in 1977 as a social welfare and development corporation under Company Registration No 73979 and The Salvation Army Educational Services was incorporated in 2001 as an educational corporation under Company Registration No A200009937.

Zone: South Pacific and East Asia
Country included in the territory: The Philippines
'The Salvation Army' in Filipino: Hukbo ng Kaligtasan; in Ilocano: Buyot ti Salakan
Languages in which the gospel is preached: Antiqueño (Kinaray-a), Bagobo, Bicolano, Cebuano, English,
  Filipino (Tagalog), Hiligaynon (Ilonggo), Ilocano, Korean, Pangasinan, T'boli, Waray
Periodical: *The War Cry*

THE disastrous Typhoon Ondoy dominated the last part of 2009 in The Philippines. With the support of International Emergency Services, IHQ, the territory responded to bring significant relief and support to many thousands of people displaced by the devastation in the main island of Luzon.

The Salvation Army was one of the first agencies to provide food and supplies, and led the way in bringing relief to isolated areas often overlooked by a resource stretched nation. In many areas Salvationists delivered food by boat to families living on their rooftops.

Supporting territories and commands made this an international response to a huge disaster, which was recognised by government at an appreciation ceremony the following February.

The annual Red Shield Appeal during December 2009 also saw a good response from the public at all Christmas kettle sites in recognition of the Army's relief work during the typhoon. Much-needed funds were raised for the territory's social work.

'Press Onward, Looking Unto Jesus' was the theme launched at the 2010 new year rallies conducted throughout the territory. It was fitting that the Territorial Executive Council concentrated on The General's call to look forward and set goals for the next 20 years. The challenge was accepted to work towards doubling the size and strength of The Salvation Army in The Philippines in that period.

The establishment of five corps plants in Palawan, a main island in The Philippines and one where The Salvation Army has only recently commenced work, has reflected this desire to significantly grow God's Army. Five new soldiers were trained by their corps officers to take the gospel back to their respective mountain villages and start the Army's work. Indigenous people are being helped with livelihood projects; community centres have been established in conjunction with the commencement of corps activities.

As the territory continued its advance, it eagerly anticipated the opening and dedication of a new territorial headquarters, to be conducted by former Chief of the Staff Commissioner Robin Dunster, who initiated the building plans when TC in The Philippines.

STATISTICS

Officers 222 (active 173 retired 49) **Cadets** 11 **Envoys/Field Sgts** 6 **Employees** 50

Corps 78 **Societies, Outposts and Outreaches** 75 **Institutions** 2 **Social Programmes** 23

Senior Soldiers 6,513 **Adherents** 3,493 **Junior Soldiers** 1,231

Personnel serving outside territory Officers 11 Layworker 1

STAFF

Women's Ministries: Comr Irene Induruwage (TPWM) Lt-Col Robyn Clinch (TSWM)

Sec for Business Administration: Lt-Col Knud David Welander

  Finance: Maj Estelita Bautista

  Christian Bookstore: Lt-Col Ma Luisa Menia

  Information Technology: Mr Victor Benganan Jr

  Property: Mr Alfredo Agpaoa Jr

Sec for Personnel Administration: Lt-Col Elnora Urbien

  Candidates: Maj Quintin Casidsid

  Training and Development: Capt Ruby Casimero

Sec for Programme Administration: Lt-Col Virgilio Menia

  Social Programme: Maj Susan Tandayag

  Corps Programme: Capt David Casimero

  Training Principal: Maj Linda Manhardt

  Training and Development/Education Services: Capt Ruby Casimero

  Editor: Lt-Col Robyn Clinch

  Gospel Arts Coordinator: Mr Nicanor Bagasol

  Legal Consultant: Mr Paul Stephen Salegumba

  Public Relations Coordinator: Mr Efren Bargan

The Philippines Territory

DIVISIONS

Central Philippines: 20 Senatorial Dr,
Congressional Village, Project 8,
Quezon City; tel: (02) 929 6312;
fax: (02) 453 8208;
email: Central@phl.salvationarmy.org;
Majs David and Elsa Oalang

Mindanao Island: 344 NLSA Rd, Purok
Bayanihan, San Isidro, Lagao 9500 General
Santos City; tel: (083) 302 3798;
email: Mid@phl.salvationarmy.org;
Majs Joel and Susan Ceneciro

Northern Luzon: Doña Loleng Subd.,
Nancayasan 2428 Urdaneta Pangasinan City;
tel: (075) 656 2383;
email: Northern@phl.salvationarmy.org;
Majs Alexander and Jocelyn Genabe

Visayas Islands: 731 M. J. Cuenco Ave,
Cebu City; tel/fax: (032) 505 6972/6054;
email: Vid@phl.salvationarmy.org;
Maj Myline Joy Flores

TRAINING COLLEGE

Pantay Rd, Sitio Bukal Brgy, Tandang Kutyo,
Tanay, Rizal; tel: (02) 654 2909;
fax: (02) 654 2895

UNDER THQ

Sponsorship/Scholarship Programme;
Missing Persons/Family Tracing Service;
Emergency Disaster Relief

SOCIAL SERVICES
Residential Social Centres
(Abused girls/children)

Bethany Home: 20 Senatorial Dr,
Congressional Village, Project 8,
Quezon City (acc 40)

(Street children)

Joyville Home: Pantay Rd, Sitio Bukal,
Tanay, Rizal (acc 25)

Learning Centres

Asingan Educational Services Inc: Bautista St,
Poblacion, 2439 Asingan, Pangasinan
Caloocan: Cnr Langaray and Dagat-dagatan Ave,
Caloocan City
Cebu: 731 M. J. Cuenco Ave, 6000 Cebu City
Iloilo: Arroyo St, 5000 La Paz, Iloilo City
Tondo: 1815 Velasquez St, 1012 Tondo,
Manila

Child Care Centres

Bagong Silang: Phase 7 B-Blk 6, Lot 3A,
Package 3, Bagong Silang Tala,
Caloocan City

Bulalacao: Bulalacao, 5214 Oriental Mindoro
Dagupan: Puelay District, 2400 Dagupan City
Davao: Blk 14, Lot 10, Kingfisher St,
RPJ Village II, Seaside Subd, Matina Aplaya,
Matina, 8000 Davao City
General Santos: 344 NLSA Rd, Purok
Bayanihan, San Isidro, Lagao,
9500 General Santos City
Laoag: 50 Buttong, 2900 Laoag City,
Ilocos Norte
Legazpi: 332 San Roque, Governor St,
San Roque, Legazpi City
Mariveles: Porto del Sur, National Rd,
2105 Mariveles, Bataan
Olongapo: Camia St, Sta Rita,
2200 Olongapo City
Quezon City 2: 20 Senatorial Dr,
Congressional Village, Project 8,
Quezon City
Signal Village: Daisy St, Zone 6, Signal Village,
Taguig, Metro Manila
Sta Barbara: 20 Poblacion Norte,
2419 Sta Barbara, Pangasinan

Nutrition, Feeding and Day Care Centres

Dasmarinas: Blk 11, Lot 6, San Antonio de
Padua II Area E, DBB, Dasmarinas, Cavite
Makati: 3493 Honda St, Pinagkaisahan,
1200 Makati City
Signal Village: Daisy St, Zone 6,
Signal Village, Taguig, Metro Manila

(under the Newman Feeding Scheme)

Bella Luz: Barangay Bella Luz 3318,
San Mateo, Isabela
Camiling: Cacamilingan Sur 2306, Camiling,
Tarlac
Manila Central Corps: 1414 Leon Guinto Sr St,
Ermita, Manila
Quezon City 1: 115 Batanes St, Galas,
Quezon

Dormitories for Students and Working Women

Baguio: 35-37 P. Guevarra St, Aurora Hill,
2600 Baguio City (acc 50)
Makati: 3493 Honda St, Pinagkaishan,
1200 Makati City (acc 12)
Quezon City 1: 67 Batanes St, Galas,
Quezon City (acc 12)
San Jose Mindoro: 3090 Roxas St,
Doña Consuelo Subd, 5100 San Jose,
Occidental Mindoro (acc 12)

Programmes for Minorities

Bulalacao: Bulalacao, 5214 Oriental Mindoro

The Philippines Territory

Lake Sebu: T'boli Village, Lake Sebu
Wali: Bo Wali, Maitum, Saranggani
   Province

Skills Training
Lapu-lapu: Vincent Drive, Gun-ob 6015,
   Lapu-lapu City

Livelihood Support
Ansiray Fishcages: Ansiray, 5100 San Jose,
   Occidental Mindoro
Badipa: Bayaos, Urdaneta, Pangasinan

Bautista: Nibaliw Norte, 2424 Bautista,
   Pangasinan
Bella Luz Cooperative Store: Brgy Bella Luz,
   3318 San Mateo, Isabela
Caguray: Magsaysay Occidental Mindoro
Camangaan Agricultural Cooperative:
   Bo Camangaan, Rosales, 2442 Pangasinon
Malingao: Bo Malingao, Tubod, 9202
   Lanao del Norte
Nasukob: Nasukob, 5214 Bulalacao,
   Oriental Mindoro
Orani: 163 Calero St, Orani, 2112 Bataan

INDIA CENTRAL: The gospel is preached in a village as Salvationists conduct an open-air meeting, while at a Salvation Army school (below) the pupils have their daily Bible classes

Ozamis: Carmen Annex, 7200 Ozamis City

Pahanocoy Tricycad: Florence Ville Subd, Pahanocoy, 6100 Bacolod City

Palili: 163 Calero St , Orani 2112 Bataan

Patnongon: Real St, 5702 Patnongon, Antique

Signal Village: Daisy St, Zone 6, Signal Village, Taguig, Metro Manila

Agricultural Assistance

Bella Luz: Barangay Bella Luz, 3318 San Mateo, Isabela

Cabayaoasan Agricultural Cooperative: Cabayaoasan, 2413 Mangatarem, Pangasinon

Nasukob Agricultural Loan: Nasukob, 5214 Bulalacao

Santa Agricultural Loan: Mabibila Sur, Santa, Ilocos Sur

Wali: Bo Wali, Maitum, Saranggani Province

Micro-Credit Enterprise Projects

Almacen: Barangay Almacen, 2111 Hermoza, Bataan

Ansiray: 5100 San Jose, Occidental Mindoro

Badipa: Bayaoas, Urdaneta, Pangasinan

Bautista: Nibaliw Norte 2424 Bautista, Pangasinan

Bulalacao: Bulalacao 5214, Oriental Mindoro

Cacutud: 34-B Misael St, Diamond Subd, Balibago, Angeles City

Liloan: Catherine Booth Development Centre, Tayud, Liloan, 6002 Cebu City

Magsaysay: Burgos St, Magsaysay, Occidental Mindoro

Malingao: Bo Malingao, Tubod, 9202 Lanao del Norte

Mariveles: Porto del Sur, National Rd, 2105 Mariveles, Bataan

Merville: 128 Sitio Malaya, Brgy Merville, Paranaque City

Nasukob: Nasukob 5214 Bulalacao, Oriental Mindoro

Orani: 163 Calero St, Orani, 2112 Bataan

Ozamis: Carmen Annex, 7200 Ozamis City

Pasay: 511 Inocencio St, Pasay City

Sampaloc: Sitio, Hinadiongan, Sampaloc, Tanay, Rizal 1080

San Jose Mindoro: 3090 Roxas St, Doña Consuelo Subd, 511 San Jose, Occidental Mindoro

Signal Village: Daisy St, Zone 6, Signal Village, Taguig, Metro Manila

Sta Ana: 2439 Asingan, Pangasinan

Wali: Wali, Maiturn, 9515 Saranggani Province

Water Systems

Bulalacao: Bulalacao, 5214 Oriental Mindoro

Camangaan: Bo Carmangaan, Rosales 2442, Pangasinon

Lopez: San Vicente St, Barangay Magsaysay, Lopez, Quezon

Lourdes: Barangay Lourdes, Lopez, Quezon

Mariveles: Porto del Sur, National Rd, 2105 Mariveles, Bataan

Nasukob: Nasukob, 5214 Bulalacao, Oriental Mindoro

Palili: c/o The Salvation Army, 163 Calero St, Orani 2112, Bataan

Sampalac: Sitio, Hinadiongan Sampalac Tanay, Rizal 1080

Upper Katalicanan: c/o Midsayap Corps, Poblacion 8, Midsayap 9410, North Cotabato

Housing Project

Lopez, Quezon: Abines St, Talolong, Lopez, Quezo

Anti-Human Trafficking Projects

Bacolod; Cebu; Darapuay; Dasmarinas; Davao; Diamond/Cacutud; General Santos; Iligan; Laoag; Lapu-Lapu; Mariveles Corps; Olongapo; Orani; Pasay; Quezon City 2; Sinamar; San Jose Mindoro

HEALTH
Barangay Health Workers in Rural Corps
Botica sa Barangay

Cabayaosan Corps: Cabayaosan, Mangatarem Pangasinan

San Jose Occidental Mindoro: 3090 Roxas St, Doña Consuelo Subd, San Jose Occidental Mindoro

HIV/Aids Programmes

Ansiray; Bacolod; Bella Luz; Bulalacao; Cantamuak; Cebu; Dagupan; Darapuay; Dasmarinas; Davao; Diamond/Cacutud; Diffun; General Santos; Iligan; Lake Sebu; Laoag; La Paz; Lapu-Lapu; Lebe; Legaspi; Mariveles Nasukob; Olongapo; Orani; Pandanan; San Jose Antique; San Jose Mindoro; Santiago; Sinamar; Tacloban; Tondo; Urdaneta; Villa Ros; Wali

PORTUGAL COMMAND

Command leaders:
Lieut-Colonel Gordon and Susan Daly

Officer Commanding:
Lieut-Colonel Gordon Daly
(1 Oct 2010)

Command Headquarters: Rua Dr Silva Teles, 16, 1050-080 Lisboa

Postal address: Apartado 14109, 1064-002 Lisboa, Portugal

Tel: [351] (21) 780 2930; fax: [351] (21) 780 2940;
email:Portugal_Command@POR.salvationarmy.org; website: www.exercitodesalvacao.pt

On 25 July 1971, official recognition was given to the first corps established in Portugal. The work was started in the northern city of Porto by a group of evangelical Christians. On 28 January 1972, Major and Mrs Carl S. Eliasen arrived in Lisbon to start work there and to supervise the existing activities.

On 4 July 1974 The Salvation Army was recognised by the Ministry of Justice as a religious and philanthropic organisation. All social activities are incorporated in Centro Social do Exército de Salvação which was constituted in Portugal on 26 March 1981 (Public Utility Register 16/82 dated 10 March 1982). On 8 March 2007 The Salvation Army was registered as a Collective Religious Person (the legal term for a church) and on 10 September 2009 became an Established (*Radicada*) Collective Religious Person, by decree from the Minister of Justice.

Zone: Europe
Country included in the command: Portugal
'The Salvation Army' in Portuguese: Exército de Salvação
Language in which the gospel is preached: Portuguese
Periodicals: *O Salvacionista, Ideias & Recursos* (for Women's Ministries)

ON 10 September 2010 The Salvation Army was recognised as *Pessoa Colectiva Religiosa Radicada* (an established church) in the country. This enhanced status will benefit the command, such as in allowing Salvation Army officers to officiate at marriages.

The command has issued its first book, The Salvation Army in The Body of Christ. Two thousand copies were printed in a Portuguese-English edition with financial support from the International Literature Programme, IHQ.

'Integral Mission' was the theme for the year and was taken up by Xabregas Shelter for the Homeless (Lisbon) when it held an open day on the International Day for the Eradication of Poverty (17 October 2009) and transformed its premises into an art gallery. Paintings from known artists, sculptures and drawings were exhibited and poetry was read. The day ended with a praise and thanksgiving meeting. Hundreds of people attended this event.

In Évora meetings commenced at a

214

new plant on 10 May 2009, less than one year after officers were appointed to the city. In Castelo Branco the new hall was opened on 26 July, offering excellent facilities to the community.

The National Congress, led by Commissioners Peder and Janet Refstie (Brazil), saw waves of seekers kneeling at the mercy seat. Enthusiastic young people attended the second EuroMusic school, a number coming from other countries in Europe.

In January 2010 two candidates entered the training college in São Paulo, Brazil. Porto Community Centre rented another shop in order to expand its services to the local community.

As a response to the Haiti earthquake The Salvation Army, Micah Challenge and the Evangelical Alliance organised a fundraising concert with Christian bands and singers. More than 800 people gathered in Lisbon to support this event.

STATISTICS

Officers 16 **Cadets** (1st Yr) 2 **Employees** 126
Mission Areas with Corps 6 **Institutions** 7
Senior Soldiers 81 **Adherents** 59 **Junior Soldiers** 33
Personnel serving outside command Officers 2

STAFF

Women's Ministries: Lt-Col Susan Daly (CPWM)
Finance: Maj Arlette Reichenbach
Projects: Maj Mendes Reichenbach
Social: Dra Sandra Martins Lopes

SOCIAL SERVICES
Children's Home
Centro de Acolhimento Novo Mundo,

Ave Desidério Cambournac, 14, 2710-553 Sintra; tel: 219 244 239; fax: 219 249 688 (acc 14)

Clothing and Food Distribution Centre
Rua Escola do Exército, 11-B, 1150-143 Lisboa; tel: 213 528 137; fax: 213 160 732

Thrift Shop
Chelas: Rua Rui de Sousa, Lote 65-A Loja C, 1900-802 Lisboa
Rua D Jerónimo de Azevedo, 640-Loja, 4550-241 Porto; tel: 22 6172769

Day Centres for the Elderly and Home Help Services
Colares: Av dos Bombeiros Voluntários, Várzea de Colares, 2705-180 Sintra; tel: 219 288 450; fax: 219 288 458
Lisboa: Rua Capitão Roby, 19 (Picheleira), 1900-111 Lisboa; tel: 218 409 108; fax: 218 409 112
Porto: Av Vasco da Gama, 645, Lojas 1 e 2, Ramalde, 4100-491 Porto; tel: 226 172 769; fax: 226 171 120

Eventide Homes
Nosso Lar: Av dos Bombeiros Voluntários, Várzea de Colares, 2705-180 Colares; tel: 219 288 450; fax: 219 288 458 (acc 30)
Marinel: Rua das Marinhas, 13, Tomadia, Praia das Maçãs, 2705-313 Colares; tel: 219 288 480; fax: 219 288 481 (acc 50)

Night Shelter for the Homeless
Rua da Manutenção, 7 (Xabregas) – 1900-318 Lisboa; tel: 218 680 908; fax: 218 680 913 (acc 75)

HOLIDAY AND CONFERENCE CENTRES
Casa Marinel, Av José Félix da Costa, 9, Praia das Maçãs – 2705-312 Colares (information from CHQ)
Vivenda Boa Nova, Rua do Vinagre, 9, 2705-354 Colares; tel: 219 291 718 (holiday bookings to CHQ)

RWANDA AND BURUNDI COMMAND

Command leaders:
Majors Stephen and Grace Chepkurui

Officer Commanding:
Major Stephen Chepkurui (1 Apr 2010)

General Secretary:
Captain Jean Clénat (1 Apr 2010)

Command Headquarters: Plot 11737, Kibagabaga Road, Kimironko, Kimironko Sector, Kigali

Postal address: PO Box 812, Kigali, Rwanda

Tel: [250] 587639; fax: [250] 511812; email: Rwanda@rwa.salvationarmy.org

As a result of civil war and genocide in Rwanda, The Salvation Army became actively involved in relief work in September 1994. Operations were concentrated in Kayenzi Commune, part of the Gitarama Prefecture. Following mission work by officers from Zaïre, Uganda and Tanzania in 1995, officers were appointed from Congo (Brazzaville) to develop corps and mission work in Kayenzi Commune. Kayenzi Corps officially began its ministry on 5 November 1995. The Salvation Army was officially registered as a church in Rwanda on 15 September 2008.

In 1983, Justin Lusombo-Musese (a Congolese born in Burundi) was introduced by a friend to some of William Booth's writings and learned about The Salvation Army's early history. Justin and the friend were so enthused they decided to become members of the Army. Over the ensuing years they persistently requested International Headquarters to start Army operations in Burundi, and on 5 August 2007 the work was officially recognised with the warranting of Justin Lusombo-Musese and his wife Justine Fatouma as auxiliary-captains. The Rwanda Region was redesignated Rwanda and Burundi Region in October 2008 and upgraded to command status on 1 April 2010.

Zone: Africa
Countries included in the command: Burundi, Rwanda
The Salvation Army in Kinyarwanda: Ingabo Z'Agakiza
Languages in which the gospel is preached: English, French, Kinyarwanda, Kirundi, Kiswahili
Periodical: *Salvationist News*

THE region became Rwanda and Burundi Command on 1 April 2010. When the inauguration ceremony was led by then Chief of the Staff Commissioner Robin Dunster, an enthusiastic 5,000-strong congregation welcomed the announcement by dancing and singing praises.

This special meeting celebrated 15 years since the Army was established in Rwanda. Guests included visitors from IHQ, Uganda Command and Kenya East Territory, with Nairobi Central Band and Timbrel Brigade providing music.

On 22 December 2009, The Salvation Army in Rwanda was officially accepted as a member of the Protestant Council of Churches. This will give the Army many more opportunities for future ministry.

The Women's Ministries Congress, the first in the region, took place in November at Kayenzi Secondary School and the guest speaker was Commissioner Rosemary Makina (ZSWM for Africa, IHQ).

Training in community project management support systems was held in June, led by Major Ted Horwood and Mrs Hanna Ferguson (International Projects and Development Services, IHQ). This creative and challenging training placed the community at the centre of each project and gave clear guidelines to help each delegate evaluate the work of corps and individuals.

STATISTICS

Officers 18 **Auxiliary-Captains** 2 **Corps Leaders** 18 **Employees** 30
Corps 11 **Outreach Unit** 3 **Outposts** 12 **Societies** 4 **Pre-School Facility** 2 (acc 170)
Senior Soldiers 1,536 **Adherents** 343 **Junior Soldiers** 790

STAFF

Women's Ministries: Maj Grace Chepkurui (CPWM) Capt Elianise Clénat (CSWM)
Accountant: Albine Batamuliza
Education: Capt Dancille Ndagijimana
Emergency Response: Capt Brian Martin
Extension Training: Capt Dancille Ndagijimana
Finance: tba
HIV/Aids Coordinator: Capt Beatrice Ayabagabo
Information Technology: Mr Pascal Igiraneza
Projects: Capt Brian Martin
Public Relations: Capt Emmanuel Ndagijimana
Social: tba
Sponsorship: Capt Amanda Martin
Youth and Candidates: Capt Emmanuel Ndagijimana

DISTRICT

Kayenzi: PO Box 812, Kigali; Maj Joseph Wandulu

SECTIONS

Kigali: c/o PO Box 812, Kigali
Muhanga: c/o PO Box 812, Kigali
Nyagatare: c/o PO Box 812, Kigali

BURUNDI

Ruhero II, Boulevard de l'Independence, Parcelle No 1416, Bujumbura, Burundi; Aux-Capts Justin and Justine Lusombo-Musese; mobile: 257 79996148; email: lusombo@yahoo.com

Commissioner Robin Dunster (then Chief of the Staff) leads a 5,000-strong congregation in the joyous inauguration of the Rwanda and Burundi Command

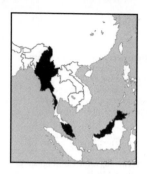

SINGAPORE, MALAYSIA AND MYANMAR TERRITORY

Territorial Commander:
Colonel Gillian Downer (1 Jul 2010)

Chief Secretary:
Lieut-Colonel Bob Lee (1 May 2009)

Territorial Headquarters: 20 Bishan St 22, Singapore 579768

Postal address: Ang Mo Kio Central, PO Box 640, Singapore 915605

Tel: [65] 6555 0188; fax: [65] 6552 8542; website: www.salvationarmy.org.sg

In May 1935 Salvation Army work began in Singapore. It spread to Penang (1938), Melaka and Ipoh (1940), Kuching (Sarawak) (1950), Kuala Lumpur (1966) and Kota Kinabalu (Sabah) (1996).

'The General of The Salvation Army' is a 'corporation sole' by The Salvation Army Ordinance 1939 in the Straits Settlements; by The Salvation Army (Incorporation) Ordinance 1956 in the Federation of Malaya; and by the Missionary Societies Order 1957 in the Colony of Sarawak.

Adjutant Taran Das (Reuben Moss), who was attached to the Lahore headquarters in India, was appointed to open the work in Burma (now Myanmar) by Commissioner Booth Tucker in January 1915. Myanmar Salvationists have, since 1966, developed their witness and service despite the restriction on reinforcements from overseas. In 1994 Myanmar was joined to the Singapore and Malaysia Command. The command was elevated to territory status on 1 March 2005.

Zone: South Pacific and East Asia
Countries included in the territory: Malaysia, Myanmar, Singapore
'The Salvation Army' in Chinese: (Mandarin) Chiu Shi Chen, (Cantonese) Kau Shai Kwan, (Amoy, Hokkien) Kiu Se Kun; Bahasa: Bala Keselamatan; Myanmar: Kae Tin Chin Tat; Tamil: Retchania Senai
Languages in which the gospel is preached: Burmese, Chin (Mizo, Zahau, Dai), Chinese (Amoy, Cantonese, Hokkien, Mandarin), English, Bahasa, Malay, Tamil, Telegu
Periodical: *The War Cry*

ON 1 May 2009 newly installed Territorial Commander Colonel Keith Burridge urged the territory: 'Go and make disciples – now! There is no greater priority at this time.' The territory reports an encouraging response to that challenge.

More than 200 delegates from 20 corps in Upper Myanmar gathered in the Tahan district for their first-ever youth rally. Later, 412 young people from 28 corps in the Kalay and Tamu districts gathered for a children's camp. Many received Christ into their lives for the first time. Myanmar Region reported continued growth throughout the year.

A growing number of children within Salvation Army homes in Malaysia and Myanmar continue to benefit from child sponsorship programmes, with more than 500 children currently receiving support. Without sponsorship many of them would not finish their education and subsequently be unable to earn a proper living.

The ordination and commissioning of the Prayer Warriors Session in Singapore was a God-glorifying occasion as the TC told the new lieutenants to be 'extravagant in prayer, hard work and loving people'.

The eagerly anticipated visit of the then zonal leaders for SPEA, Commissioners Robert and Janet Street, included leadership of the 2010 Zonal Conference in Singapore. Visits were made to Peacehaven Nursing Home and The Haven and Gracehaven Children's Homes before the commissioners moved to Myanmar for the Prayer Warriors Session's ordination and commissioning in Yangon.

The new lieutenants were the first of many people to kneel at the mercy seat, including several young people affirming their calling to full-time service. The presentation of flags to officers acknowledged that their corps plants had been elevated to corps status.

Hopehaven Centre for Special Needs Children in Melaka, West Malaysia, returned to its newly refurbished premises after a two-year absence. It is hoped that the expanded programme will be further upgraded to provide a professional centre of excellence for special needs education. In East Malaysia, the corps at Kota Kinabalu celebrated the opening of its new hall.

In March, the Dementia Care Programme at Bedok Multiservice Centre was officially launched during the 10th anniversary celebrations of Peacehaven Nursing Home.

News of the sudden death of Colonel Keith Burridge (TC), who was promoted to Glory from his quarters in Singapore on 19 April 2010, shocked the territory. He and his wife had been the territorial leaders for just 11 months.

STATISTICS
Officers 131 (active 118 retired 13) **Cadets** 16 **Employees** 699
Corps 48 **Outposts** 22 **Institutions** 16 **Kindergarten** 2 **Day Care Centres** 17
Senior Soldiers 2,398 **Adherents** 456 **Junior Soldiers** 525

STAFF
Women's Ministries: Col Gillian Downer (TPWM) Lt-Col Wendy Lee (TSWM)
Editor: Maj Katrina Thomas
Finance: Mdm Koh Guek Eng
Human Resources: Mrs Toh-Chia Lai Ying
Programme: Maj Darrell Thomas
Property: Mr John Ng
Public Relations: Mr Gregory Lee
Projects: Lt-Col Bob Lee
Training: Lt-Col Bob Lee
Youth and Candidates: Capt Hary Haran

SCHOOL FOR OFFICER TRAINING (Singapore and Malaysia)
500 Upper Bukit Timah Rd, Singapore 678106; tel: 6349 5333

SINGAPORE
Children's Homes
Gracehaven: 3 Lorong Napiri (off Yio Chu Kang Rd), Singapore 547528; tel: 6488 1510 (acc 160)
The Haven: 350 Pasir Panjang Rd, Singapore 118692; tel: 6774 9588/9 (acc 50)

Day Care Centres for Children
Ang Mo Kio Child Care Centre: Blk 610 Ang Mo Kio Ave 4, #01-1227 Singapore 560610; tel: 6452 4862 (acc 89)
Bukit Batok East Child Care Centre: Blk 247

Bukit Batok East Ave 5, #01-86 Singapore
650247; tel: 6562 4976 (acc 73)

Bukit Panjang Child Care Centre: Blk 402
Fajar Rd, #01-217 Singapore 670402;
tel: 6760 2624 (acc 82)

Tampines Child Care Centre: Blk 159
Tampines St 12, #01-95 Singapore 521159;
tel: 6785 2976 (acc 90)

Day Care Centres for the Elderly

Bedok Multiservice Centre for the Elderly:
Blk 121, #01-161/163 Bedok North Rd,
Singapore 460121; tel: 6445 1630
(acc 60)

Bedok Rehabilitation Centre: Blk 121,
#01-163 Bedok North Rd,
Singapore 460121; tel: 6445 1630
(acc 35)

Family Support Services

Blk 42, Beo Cresc, #01-95 Singapore 160042;
tel: 6273 7207

Hostels

Peacehaven Nurses' Hostel: 9 Upper Changi Rd
North, Singapore 507706; tel: 6546 5678
(acc 100)

Young Women's Hostel: The Haven,
350 Pasir Panjang Rd, Singapore 118692;
tel: 6774 9588/9 (acc 10)

Retreat Centre

Praisehaven, 500 Upper Bukit Timah Rd,
Singapore 678106; tel: 6349 5302
(acc 210)

Nursing Home

Peacehaven, 9 Upper Changi Rd North,
Singapore 507706; tel: 6546 5678 (acc 401)

Prison Support Services – Kids In Play

9 Upper Changi Rd North,
Singapore 507706;
tel 6546 5868 (130 families)

Red Shield Industries

309 Upper Serangoon Rd, Singapore 347693;
tel: 6288 5438

Youth Development Centres

Bukit Panjang Youth Hub Centre: Fajar Rd,
#01-267 Singapore 670404; tel: 6763 0837
(acc 70)

Youth Development Centre: Blk 65 Kallang
Bahru, #01-305 Singapore 330065;
tel: 6291 6303; under Balestier Corps

EAST MALAYSIA
Boys' Home

Kuching Boys' Home: Jalan Ban Hock,
93100 Kuching; PO Box 547, 93700 Kuching,
Sarawak, Malaysia; tel: (082) 24 2623 (acc 30)

Children's Home

Kuching Children's Home: 138 Jalan Upland,
93200 Kuching; PO Box 106, 93700 Kuching,
Sarawak, Malaysia; tel: (082) 24 8234 (acc 60)

Kindergarten

Kuching Kindergarten: Sekama Rd,
93300 Kuching, Sarawak, Malaysia;
PO Box 44, 93700 Kuching, Sarawak,
Malaysia; tel: (082) 333981 (acc 100)

Corps Community Services

Bintulu Corps and Community Services:
S/Lot 1362, 1st Floor Tanjung Batu
Commercial Centre, Jalan Tun Razak,
97000 Bintulu; Sarawak; tel: (086) 315 843

Kota Kinabalu Corps and Community Services:
Lot 1, Taman Seri Kiansom Lorong Seri
Kiansom, Inanam, Kota Kinabalu, Malaysia;
tel: (088) 433766

Kuching Corps and Community Services:
Sekama Rd 93300, Kuching, Sarawak,
Malaysia; PO Box 44, 93700 Kuching,
Sarawak, Malaysia; tel: (082) 333981

Red Shield Industries

Ground–1st Flr, 1 Jalan Ang Cheng Ho,
93100 Kuching; tel: 082 410564

WEST MALAYSIA

Liaison and Public Relations Office:
26-1 Jalan Puteri, 4/2 Bandar Puteri,
47100 Puchong, Selangor Darul Ehsan,
Malaysia; tel: (06) 8061 4929

Boys' Homes

Ipoh Boys' Home: 4367 Jalan Tambun,
31400 Ipoh; PO Box 221, 30720 Ipoh,
Perak, Malaysia; tel: [60] (05) 545 7819
(acc 60)

Centre for Special Children

Hopehaven Centre for Special Children:
321 Jalan Parameswara, 75000 Melaka,
Malaysia; tel: [60] (06) 283 2101 (acc 100)

Children's Homes

Ipoh Children's Home: 255 Kampar Rd,
30250 Ipoh, Perak, Malaysia;
tel: (05) 254 9767; fax: (05) 242 9630
(acc 50)

Melaka Lighthouse Children's Home:
404 Taman Sinn, Jalan Semabok 75050,
Melaka, Malaysia;tel: (06) 283 2101 (acc 25)
Penang Children's Home: 8A Logan Rd,
10400 Penang, Malaysia; tel: (04) 227 0162
(acc 60)

Day Care Centre for Children
Banting Day Care Centre: 30 Jalan Cendana 15,
Taman Mihhibah, Banting 42700 (acc 50)

Kindergarten
Banting Day Care Centre: 30 Jalan Cendana 15,
Taman Mihhibah, Banting 42700 (acc 50)
Batang Melaka Kindergarten: J7702 Main Rd,
Batang Melaka 77500, Selandar, Malaysia;
tel: (06) 446 1601 (acc 50)
Kuala Lumpur Kindergarten: 1 Lingkungan
Hujan, Overseas Union Garden, 58200 KL,
Malaysia; tel: (03) 7782 4766 (acc 60)

Homes for the Aged
Joyhaven Home for the Elderly: 1 Jalan 12/17,
Seksyen 12, 46200 Petaling Jaya, Selangor,
Malaysia; tel: (03) 7958 6257 (acc 25)
Perak Home for the Aged: Jalan Bersatu,
Jelapang, 30020 Ipoh, Perak, Malaysia;
tel: (05) 526 2108 (acc 50)

Corps Community Services
Banting Corps Community Services: 30 Jalan
Cendana 15, Taman Mihhbah, Banting 42700
(acc 50)
Kuala Lumpur Community Services: 26-1 Jalan
Puteri 4/2, Bandar Puteri 47100, Puchong,
Selangor, Malaysia; tel: (03) 8061 4929
(acc 50)
Penang Corps Community Services: 53 Perak Rd,
10150 Penang, West Malaysia;
tel: (04) 2290921

Social/Community Services
Melaka State Community Services: 321 Jalan
Parameswara, 75000 Melaka, Malaysia;
tel: (06) 283 1203

MYANMAR REGION
Headquarters: 176-178 Anawrahta St,
Botahtaung, East Yangon 11161, Myanmar;
Postal address: GPO Box 394, Yangon,
Myanmar; tel: [95] (1) 294267/293307;
fax: [95] (1) 298067
Regional Officer: Maj Ian Marshall
(1 Oct 2010)

DISTRICTS
Central: District Office, Mandalay
Kalaymyo: District Office, D-group, Tahan,
Kalemyo; tel: [95] (73) 21396
Tamu: District Office, Kanan Corps, Kanan
Township

SCHOOL FOR OFFICER TRAINING (Myanmar)
50 Byaing Ye O Zin St, Tarmway, Yangon,
Myanmar; tel: [95] (1) 543694

Boys' Home
406 Banyadala Rd, Tarmway, Yangon,
Myanmar; tel: [95] (1) 541462 (acc 50)

Children's Home
50 Bago Rd, Pyu, Myanmar (acc 50)

Girls' Home
50 Byaing Ye O Zin St, Tarmway, Yangon,
Myanmar; tel: [95] (1) 543961
(acc 50)

Day Care Centre for Children
Tarmway Corps

SOUTH AMERICA EAST TERRITORY

Territorial Commander:
Colonel Susan McMillan (1 May 2010)

Chief Secretary:
Lieut-Colonel Ricardo Bouzigues
(1 Jul 2008)

Territorial Headquarters: Avda Rivadavia 3257 (C1203AAE), Buenos Aires, Argentina

Postal address: Casilla de Correos 2240 (C1000WAW) Buenos Aires, Argentina

Tel/fax: [54] (11) 4864-9321/9348/9491/1075; email: ejersaljefatura@SAE.salvationarmy.org;

website: www.ejercitodesalvacion.org.ar

Four officers, who knew no Spanish, established The Salvation Army in Buenos Aires in 1890. Operations spread to other South American nations, of which Paraguay (1910), Uruguay (1890) and Argentina now comprise the South America East Territory.

The Salvation Army was recognised as a juridical person in Argentina by the Government Decree of 26 February 1914 (No A 54/909); in Uruguay by the Ministry of the Interior on 17 January 1917 (No 366537); and in Paraguay by Presidential Decree of 28 May 1928 (No 30217).

Zone: Americas and Caribbean
Countries included in the territory: Argentina, Paraguay, Uruguay
'The Salvation Army' in Spanish: Ejército de Salvación
Language in which the gospel is preached: Spanish, Korean, Guaraní
Periodicals: *El Oficial*, *El Salvacionista*

THE Salvation Army's centenary in Paraguay was celebrated during 2010 with a regional congress in Asuncion. Salvationists were strengthened in their faith and encouraged to pray for the continued growth of God's Kingdom in their country.

Youth officers from the territory's three divisions and four districts, meeting in June 2009 to determine the way forward for youth and children's work, have prepared action plans for the next five years.

In October a territorial men's camp attracted 220 delegates from the three countries within the territory.

Discussion topics included human trafficking and pornography. Through sponsorship from Switzerland, Austria and Hungary Territory, the Women's Ministries Department arranged divisional camps attended by 400 women. Workshops dealt with trafficking and domestic violence.

In December Commissioners Kurt and Alicia Burger (territorial leaders, Switzerland, Austria and Hungary) were special guests at the ordination and commissioning of nine officers of the Prayer Warriors Session. In March 2010 the Friends Of Christ Session was welcomed and the

Ambassadors Of Holiness Session returned for their second-year training.

Dr Roger Green (USA Eastern) addressed territorial officers councils on 'The Foundations of the William and Catherine Booth Theology' and held a seminar for soldiers on this subject. Major Ian Swan (Booth College, Canada and Bermuda) spoke at the annual seminar for officers in their first five years of service.

Nueva Chicago, Chacabuco and Saladillo Outposts in Buenos Aires were elevated to corps status. Three students' residences were opened.

The territory is now seeking to strengthen local officer leadership, to establish and train pastoral care councils at every corps, and to develop the thrift store operations so as to increase the sustainability of the Army's programmes.

STATISTICS

Officers 149 (active 118 retired 31) **Cadets** 18 **Employees** 166
Corps 42 **Outposts** 13 **Institutions** 40
Senior Soldiers 1,736 **Adherents** 571 **Junior Soldiers** 451

STAFF

Women's Ministries: Col Susan McMillan (TPWM) Lt-Col Sonia Bouzigues (TSWM)
Personnel: Maj Wendy Johnstone
Programme: Maj Hugh Pizzirusso
Business Administration: Maj Pablo Nicolasa
Education: Maj Wendy Johnstone
Finance: Mr Sergio Cerezo (Accountant in charge)
Legal: Mr Rene Menares
Literature and Editor: Lt-Col Sonia Bouzigues
Music and Gospel Arts: S/L Omar Pérez
Pastoral Care: Maj Bartolo Aguirre
Projects/Sponsorship/Missing Persons: Mrs Claudia Franchetti
Property: Mr Rolando Ramírez
Red Shield/Thrift Store Operations: Maj Miguel Del Bello

Social: Maj Bartolo Aguirre
Training: Maj Estela Nicolasa
Youth: Maj Hugh Pizzirusso
   Candidates: Maj Wendy Johnstone

DIVISIONS

Buenos Aires: Avda Rivadavia 3257 – Piso 2 (C1203AAE), Buenos Aires, Argentina; tel: (011) 4861 1930/9499; Majs Dantón and Juana Moya
Central Argentina: Urquiza 2142, (S2000AOD) Rosario Pcia de Santa Fe, Argentina; tel/fax: (0341) 425 6739; Majs Rafael and Karina Giusti
Uruguay: Hocquart 1886, (11800) Montevideo, Uruguay; tel: (598) (2) 409 7581; Majs Raúl and Lidia Bernao

DISTRICTS

Central West Argentina: Felix Frías 434/6, (X5004AHJ) Córdoba, Argentina; tel: (351) 423-3228; Maj Roberto Juarez
North East Argentina: Brignole 126, (H3500BOF) Resistencia, Prov De Chaco, Argentina; tel: (3722) 466-529; Maj Cristina Escudero
Paraguay: Héroes de la Independencia y Vietnam, Casilla 2008, (CP 2160) San Lorenzo, Paraguay; tel/fax: 595 (21) 577 082; Maj Thore Paulsen
Southern Argentina: Moreno 759 (B8000FWO), Bahía Blanca, Pcia de Buenos Aires; tel/fax: (291) 4533 642; Capt Diego Barth

TRAINING COLLEGE

Avda Tte Gral Donato Álvarez 465/67, (C1406BOC) Buenos Aires; tel/fax: (011) 4631 4815

COMMUNITY AND DAY CARE CENTRES

Argentina: Pellegrini 376, (E3200AMF) Concordia (Entre Ríos); tel: (345) 421 1751 (acc 20)
Uruguay: Sarandí 1573, (60,000) Paysandú; tel: (72) 22709 (acc 84)

CONFERENCE CENTRES AND YOUTH CAMP

Argentina
   Parque General Jorge L. Carpenter, Avda Benavídez 115, (Paraguay y Uruguay) (B1621) Benavídez, Pcia de Buenos Aires; tel: (03488) 458644
   Parque El Oasis, Ruta 14 Km 7 Camino Público a Rosario – Zona Rural (Santa Fe); tel: (341) 495 0003

SOCIAL SERVICES
Counselling and Labour Exchange
Argentina: Loria 190, (C1173ACD) Buenos
Aires; tel: (11) 4865 0074

Boys' Home
Uruguay: El Lucero, J. M. Blanes 62,
(50,000) Salto; tel: (732) 32740 (acc 30)

Children's Homes (mixed)
Argentina: Evangelina, Monroe 1166,
(B1878IPP) Quilmes, Pcia de Buenos Aires;
tel: (11) 4253 0623 (acc 32)
Paraguay: El Redil, Dr Hassler 4402 y
MacArthur, Asunción; tel: [595] (21) 600 291
(acc 40)

Eventide Homes
Argentina
Catalina Higgins Home, Calle Mitre,
54 No 2749, (1650) Villa Maipú, San
Martín, Pcia de Buenos Aires;
tel: (11) 4753 4117 (acc 54)
Eliasen Home, Primera Junta 750,
(B1878IPP) Quilmes, Pcia de Buenos Aires;
tel: (011) 4254 5897 (acc 37)
Uruguay: El Atardecer, Avda Agraciada 3567,
(11800) Montevideo;
tel: (2) 308 5227/309 5385 (acc 75)

Industrial Homes
Argentina
Avda Hipólito Irigoyen 4750, (B1814ABQ)
Lanús Oeste, Buenos Aires;
tel: (11) 4241-4756
Avda Sáenz 580, (C1437DNS) Buenos Aires;
tel: (11) 4911 7561/0781/7585
Calle 4 Nº 711, (B1900) La Plata, Buenos Aires;
tel: (0221) 483-6152
Cañada de Gómez 2322, (1440EGV)
Buenos Aires
Gral Juan O'Brien 1260, (1137ABD)
Buenos Aires; tel: (011) 4305-5021
Einstein 705, (B1688DBO) Villa Santos Tesei,
Buenos Aires; tel: (011) 4450-3606
Barrio ULM, Cnel Bogado Nº 5, (H3730QA)
Charata, Chaco; tel: (03731) 421-292
Salta 3197, Barrio San Javier, (H3500BOF)
Resistencia, Chaco; tel: (03722) 466 529
Godoy Cruz 348, (M5500GOQ) Mendoza,
tel: (0261) 429-6113
Amenábar 581, (S2000OQK) Rosario;
tel: (0341) 482 0155
Génova 2592, (S2000AOD) Rosario;
tel: (0341) 438-1898

Uruguay Félix Laborde 2577, (12000)
Montevideo; tel: (00598-2) 508-7766

Night Shelters
(Men)
Argentina
Copahué 2032, (C1288ABB) Buenos Aires;
tel: (11) 438 6750 (acc 75)
Maza 2258 (C1240ADV) Buenos Aires;
tel: (11) 4912 0843 (acc 86)

(Women and Children)
Argentina
José I. Rucci 1231, (B1822CJY) Valentín
Alsina, Pcia de Buenos Aires;
tel: (11) 4228 4328 (acc 34)
O'Brien 1272, (C1137ABD) Buenos Aires;
tel: (11) 4304 8753 (acc 38)

Students' Homes
Argentina
Bat de Junín 2921, (S3000ASQ) Santa Fe;
tel: (342) 452 0563 (acc 28)
Calle 4, No 711, (1900) La Plata, Pcia de
Buenos Aires; tel: (0221) 483 6152 (acc 16)
Félix Frías 434/6, (X5004AHJ) Córdoba;
tel: (351) 423 3228 (acc 15)
Godoy Cruz 352, (M5500GOQ) Mendoza,
Pcia de Mendoza; tel: (261) 429 6113 (acc 6)
San Martín 964 (U9100BET) Trelew, (Chubut);
tel: (2965) 433 125 (acc 20)

Women's Residence
Argentina: Esparza 93, (C1171ACA)
Buenos Aires; tel: (11) 4861 3119 (acc 56)

Primary School
Argentina: EEGB No 1027 Federico Held,
Barrio ULM, (H3730BQA) Charata,
Pcia del Chaco; tel: (3731) 421 292 (acc 450)

Technical School
Argentina: 'Major Juan C. Costen and Friends
of Germany', Coronel Bogado s/n, Bo OLM,
(H3730BQA) Charata, Pcia del Chaco;
tel: (3731) 421 292

Health Centre
Argentina: Pcia del Chaco, Coronel Bogado 4,
Barrio ULM, (H3730BQA) Charata;
tel: (3731) 421 292

Medical Clinic
Paraguay: Héroes de la Independencia y
Vietnam, Villa Laurelty, San Lorenzo;
tel: [595] 21 577 082

SOUTH AMERICA WEST TERRITORY

Territorial leaders:
Commissioners Jorge A. and Adelina Ferreira

Territorial Commander:
Commissioner Jorge A. Ferreira (1 Feb 2007)

Chief Secretary:
Lieut-Colonel William A. Bamford III (1 May 2010)

Territorial Headquarters: Avenida España No 44, Santiago, Chile

Postal address: Casilla 3225, Santiago, Chile (parcels/courier service: Avenida España No 44, Santiago Centro, Santiago, Chile)

Tel: [56] (2) 671 8237/695 7005; fax: [56] (2) 698 5560; email: saw_leadership@saw.salvationarmy.org

Salvation Army operations were commenced in Chile soon after the arrival of Brigadier and Mrs William T. Bonnet to Valparaíso on 1 October 1909. The first corps was opened in Santiago on 28 November, with Captain David Arn and Lieutenant Alfred Danielson as officers. Adjutant and Mrs David Thomas, with Lieutenant Zacarías Ribeiro, pioneered the work in Peru in March 1910. The work in Bolivia, started in December 1920, was planned by Brigadier Chas Hauswirth and established by Adjutant and Mrs Oscar E. Ahlm. Quito saw the Army's arrival in Ecuador on 30 October 1985 under the command of Captain and Mrs Eliseo Flores Morales.

Zone: Americas and Caribbean
Countries included in the territory: Bolivia, Chile, Ecuador, Peru
'The Salvation Army' in Aymara: Ejercitunaca Salvaciananaca; in Quechua: Ejercituman Salvacionman; in Spanish: Ejército de Salvación
Languages in which the gospel is preached: Aymara, Quechua, Spanish
Publications: *El Grito de Guerra* (*The War Cry*), *El Trébol* (Women's Ministries annual magazine and programme aids)

THE Salvation Army's centenary in Chile was highlighted by the Centennial Congress in Santiago, led by General Shaw Clifton and Commissioner Helen Clifton (WPWM) in November 2009. With the motto 'To Celebrate the Past, Sanctify the Present, and Prophesy the Future' more than 1,000 people – dignitaries and Government representatives among them – filled the hall with songs, music and testimonies.

A 13-metre-long mercy seat, in the form of a huge map of Chile, became the sacred focal point for the congress, as more than 200 seekers knelt there throughout the weekend.

The congress also included the presentation of a Latin version of the musical *Spirit* and the launch of Enrique Lalut's book, *The Path of Glory*, recording the Army's first 100 years in Chile.

But the territory is not only Chile. 'From the Equator to the Antarctic' is the phrase often used to describe the territory's geographic extension, and Salvationists in the four countries within the territory are working hard for the glory of God.

Along the coast and in the mountains and valleys, officers and soldiers served diligently in ministering to their needy communities. They offer material aid, encouragement and most of all the gospel of Jesus.

This was clearly shown when a devastating 8.8 magnitude earthquake struck in Chile during the early hours of 27 February 2010. Salvation Army emergency services were immediately mobilised to provide support and comfort in affected communities. Strong aftershocks more than two weeks after the earthquake and a subsequent tsunami heightened the feeling of fear.

Salvationists and other volunteers distributed aid throughout the country. More than 14,000 rations of food were supplied to individuals and families. In Concepción, around the epicentre of the earthquake, family baskets were distributed at a camp in the centre of the city. Chile Central Division sent 20 tons of food, clothing and water to the cities of Concepción and Hualpén, including goods purchased with funds received from overseas.

The territory's goal is to change people's lives and living conditions. The Army's schools, nurseries, day care centres, shelters, homes, clinics and community centres all seek to achieve this purpose as Salvationists continue to preach God's love by action, word and example.

STATISTICS

Officers 293 (active 268 retired 34) **Cadets** (1st Yr) 3 (2nd Yr) 3 **Employees** 974
Corps 84 **Outposts** 19 **Schools and Vocational Institutes** 16 **Day Nurseries** 29 **Community Centres** 40 **Hospital** 1 **Health Centres** 3 **Mobile Clinic** 1 **Community Health** 1 **Pre-Primary Schools** 2 **Institutions** 35
Senior Soldiers 4,416 **Adherents** 510
Junior Soldiers 1,977

STAFF

Women's Ministries: Comr Adelina de Ferreira (TPWM) Lt-Col G. Lorraine Bamford (TSWM)
Business Administration (Legal): Lt-Col María de Alarcón
Personnel: Lt-Col David Alarcón
Programme: Maj Cecilia Bahamonde
Editor and Literary: Maj Cecilia Bahamonde
Education: Maj Víctor García
 Schools: Maj Eduardo Salinas
Enterprise Development: Maj Jaime Herrera
Finance: Capt Manuel Márquez
League of Mercy/Golden Age: Maj Cecilia Bahamonde
Property and Public Relations: Maj Juan Elena Espinoza
Social and Sponsorship: Capt Paulina de Márquez
Trade: Capt Manuel Márquez
Training: Maj Angela de García
 Candidates: Maj Sonia de Salinas

DIVISIONS

Bolivia Altiplano: Calle Cañada Strongest 1888, Zona San Pedro, Casilla 926, La Paz, Bolivia; tel: 591 (2) 249 1560; fax: 591 (2) 248 5948; Majs Eliseo and Remedios Flores
Bolivia Central: Calle Rico Toro 773 Zona Queru Queru, Casilla 3594, Cochabamba, Bolivia; tel: 591 (4) 445 4281/468 1147
 fax: 591 (4) 411 5887; Majs Sixto and Aída Alí
Chile Central: Agustinas 3020, Casilla 3225, Santiago, Chile; tel/fax: 56 (2) 681 4992/5277; Majs Hernán and Glenda Espinoza
Chile South: Av Caupolicán 990, Casilla 1064, Temuco, Chile; tel: 56 (45) 215 850; fax: 56 (45) 271 425; Majs Antonio and Lilian Arguedas
Ecuador: Tomás Chariove 149-144 y Manuel Valdivieso, El Pinar Bajo, Casilla 17,10.7179, Quito, Ecuador; tel/fax: 593 (2) 243 5422/ 244 7829; Maj Maria Flores
Peru: Calle Zaragoza 215, Urbanización Parque San Martín, Pueblo Libre, Lima 21, Apartado 690, Lima 100;

In Quinta Normal, Santiago Province, the corps officer visits the home of a Salvationist caught up in the devastation of the earthquake that hit Chile

tel: 51 (1) 653 4965/6; fax: 51 (1) 653 4968;
Majs Alex and Luz Nesterenko

DISTRICT
Chile North: Sucre 872, Casilla 310, Antofagasta, Chile; tel: 56 (55) 280 668/224 094;
Maj Luis Cisternas

TRAINING COLLEGE
Coronel Souper 4564, Estación Central, Casilla 3225, Santiago, Chile;
tel: 56 (2) 776 2425/5153; fax: 56 (2) 779 9187

SALVATION ARMY CAMP GROUNDS
Bolivia
'Chapare', Población Chimoré, Chapare;
tel: 591 7642 8777
'Eben-Ezer', Puente Villa, Comunidad Tarila, Provincia Nor Yungas

Chile
Complejo Angostura, Panamericana Sur km 55, Paine, Región Metropolitana, Casila 3225, Santiago; tel: 591 (2) 825 0398
Villa Frontera, Parcela 16, Calle San Martín, Villa la Frontera, Arica

EDUCATIONAL WORK
Vocational Institutes
Bolivia
'Lindgren' Murillo 4364, Barrio Central Viacha, La Paz; tel/fax: 591 (2) 280 0969 (acc 200)
'William Booth' – Oruro, Sucre 909, Oruro;
tel: 591 (2) 525 1369; fax: 591 (2) 511 3512

Aymara Bible Institute
Bolivia
La Paz, Prolongación Illampu 1888, Zona San Pedro

Schools
Bolivia
'William Booth' – Villa Cosmos: Uraciri Patica 2064, Barrio Cosmos 79, Unidad Vecinal C, La Paz; tel: 591 (2) 288 0118
'William Booth' – Oruro: Sucre 909, Oruro;
tel: 591 (2) 525 –1369; fax: 591 (2) 511 3512 (acc 800)
'William Booth' – Viacha: Murillo 4364, Barrio Central, Viacha; tel: 591 (2) 280 0969 (acc 200)

Chile
Arica: Av Cancha Rayada 3839, Segunda Etapa Población Cardenal Silva Henríquez, Casilla 203; tel/fax: 56 (58) 211 100 (acc 678)
Calama:
Aníbal Pinto 2121, Casilla 62, Calama;
tel/fax: 56 (55) 311 216/345 802
Catalina Booth – Calama, Irene Frei 2875, Villa Esmeralda, Casilla 347, Calama;
tel/fax: 56 (55) 360 458 (acc 800)
Osorno: William Booth, Zenteno 1015, Casilla 317, Osorno; tel: 56 (64) 247 449;
tel/fax: 56 (64) 233 141 (acc 879)
Puerto Montt:
Naciones Unidas – Antuhue, Presidente Ibáñez 272, Casilla 277; tel: 56 (65) 286 236 (acc 1,207 journey)
Ejército de Salvación, Séptimo de Línea 148,

227

Población Libertad, Casilla 277;
tel/fax: 56 (65) 254 047/251 918 (acc 363)
Santiago: Ejército de Salvación, Herrera 185,
Santiago; tel: 56 (2) 681 7097 (acc 400)

Peru

Eduardo Palací, Av Progreso 1032, Urb San
Gregorio, Vitarte, Lima; tel/fax: 51 (1) 356 0461
(acc 500)
Miguel Grau, Av 29 de Diciembre 127, Trujillo;
tel/fax: 51 (44) 255 571 (acc 300)

Ecuador

Ejército de Salvación – Cayambe, Calle H 1
393 Morales, Urbanización Las Orquídeas,
Cayambe, Casilla 17.10.7179, Quito;
tel: 593 (2) 211 0196 (acc 150)
Ejército de Salvación – Manta, Avenida 201,
entre Calles 116 y 117, Barrio, La Paz;
tel: 593 (5) 292 0147 (acc 40)

Pre-Primary Schools
Chile

Santiago:
El Bosque, Las Vizcachas 858, Población
Las Acacias, Comuna de El Bosque;
tel: 56 (2) 529 4242 (acc 45)
Ejército de Salvación N°1619, Pudahuel (and
Initial Grades of Primary) Mapocho 9047,
Comuna de Pudahuel, Santiago;
tel: 56 (2) 643 1875 (acc 160)

MEDICAL WORK
Bolivia

Harry Williams Hospital: Av Suecia 1038-1058,
Zona Huayra K'assa, Casilla 4099,
Cochabamba; tel: 591 (4) 422 7778/474 5329/
447 45612 (30 beds)
Community Extension Programme: Av Suecia
1038-1058, Zona Huayra K'assa, Casilla 4099,
Cochabamba; tel/ fax: 591 (4) 422 7778/
474 5329/447 45612

Ecuador

Dental Clinic and Medical Centre: Quito Sur,
Calle Apuela S 25-182 y Malimpia, Santa Rita,
Casilla 17 107179, Quito; tel: 593 (2) 284 5529
Health Clinic: Calles Uruguay y Ecuador,
Barrio Las Américas, Casilla 08 01 73,
Esmeraldas; tel: 593 (6) 271 0439

SOCIAL WORK
Emergency and Social Welfare Office:
Chile Central, Mapocho 4130, Comuna de
Quinta Normal, Casilla 3225 Santiago;
tel: 56 (2) 775 1566

Men's Shelters
Bolivia

Calle Prolongación Illampu 1888,
Zona San Pedro, Casilla 926, La Paz;
tel: 591 (2) 231 1189 (acc 100)

Chile

Villagrán 9, Casilla 1887, Valparasío;
tel: 56 (32) 221 4946 (acc 170)

Peru

Calle Colón 138/142, Apartado 139, Callao;
tel: 51 (1) 429 3128 (acc 24)

Transit House (Women)
Chile

Calle Zenteno 1499, Casilla 3225, Santiago;
tel: 56 (2) 554 1767 (acc 15)

Pregnant Teens Refuge
Ecuador

Av 201, entre calles 116 y 117, Barrio La Paz,
Casilla 13-05-149, Manta; tel: 593 (5) 292 0147
(acc 20)

Student Residence Halls
Bolivia

Cochabamba: 'Tte - Coronel Rosa de Nery' (Girls),
Calle Lanza S-0555, Casilla 3198,
Cochabamba; tel: 591 (4) 422 6553 (acc 30)
La Paz: 'Remedios Asín' (Girls), Cañada
Strongest 1888, Casilla 926, La Paz;
tel: 591 (2) 248 0502 (acc 20)
Oruro: 'Tte - Coronel Jorge Nery Torrico' (Boys),
Calle Junin 459, entre 6 de Octubre y Potosí;
Casilla 86, Oruro; tel: 591 (2) 528 6885
(acc 24)

Chile

Santiago: 'El Faro' (Boys), Santiago Concha 1333,
Casilla 3225, Santiago; tel: 56 (2) 555 3406
(acc 24)

Peru

Lima: 'Catalina Booth' (Girls), Jirón
Huancayo 245, Apartado 690, Lima 100;
tel: 51 (1) 433 8747 (acc 20)
San Martín: 'Las Palmeras' – Tarapoto, Jirón
Amoraca 212, Distrito Morales, Apartado 88,
Tarapoto, San Martín; tel: 51 (42) 527 540
(acc 20)

Children's Homes
Bolivia

Cochabamba:
'Evangelina Booth' (Girls), Francisco

Viedma 1054, Villa Montenegro, Casilla 542;
tel: 591 (4) 424 1560 (acc 60)
'Oscar Ahlms' (Boys), Km 19.5 Carretera a
Oruro cruce San Jorge, Calle Boliviar s/n,
Comunidad de San Jorge, Vinto, Casilla 542;
tel: 591 (4) 435 6264 (acc 48)
La Paz: 'María Remedios Asín' (Boys),
Murillo 434, Barrio Central Viacha,
Casilla 15084; tel/fax: 591 (2) 280 0404
(acc 50)

Chile
Llo Lleo: 'El Redil' (Boys), Arzobispo
Valdivieso 410, Casilla 61, Llo Lleo;
tel: 56 (35) 282 054 (acc 52)
Temuco: 'Los Copihues' (Girls), Calle Los
Sauces 0202, Población Las Quilas,
Casilla 1064, Temuco;
tel: 56 (45) 234 028/275 008 (acc 60)

Eventide Home
Chile
'Otoño Dorado', Av La Florida 9995, La Florida,
Casilla 3225, Santiago; tel: 56 (2) 287 5280;
tel/fax: 56 (2) 287 1869 (acc 48)

Day Care Centres for the Aged
Chile
'Los Lagos', Berlín 818, Población Los Lagos,
Angol; tel: 56 (45) 712 583 (acc 20)

Ecuador
Cayambe, Calle Montalvo 220, Las Orquideas,
Cayambe; tel: 593 (2) 236 1273 (acc 60)

Day Nurseries
Bolivia
Cochabamba:
'Catalina Booth', Lanza S-0555, Zona Central,
Casilla 542; tel: 591 (4) 422 7123 (acc 150)
La Chimba, Av Cañada Cochabamba 2572,
Zona La Chimba, Casilla 542;
tel: 591 (4) 428 3079 (acc 75)
'Mi Casita' – El Temporal, Calle J. Mostajo s/n,
Zona El Temporal,Casilla 542;
tel: 591 (4) 445 0809 (acc 70)
'Wawasninchej' – Huayra K'assa,
Av Suecia 1083, Zona Huayra K'assa,
Casilla 542; tel: 591 (4) 422 4808 (acc 50)
La Paz: 'Refugio de Amor', Villa 8 de Diciembre,
Calle Rosendo Gutiérrez 120, Barrio Alto
Sopocachi, Casilla 926; tel 591 (2) 241 0470
(acc 25)
Santa Cruz:
'Gotitas de Amor', Calle Corumba 2360
(esq Calle Cañada Larga), Barrio Lazareto,

Casilla 2576; tel: 591 (3) 346 3531 (acc 40)
'La Roca', Calicanto, Comunidad La Serena
Calicanto, Kilómetro 8, Carretera antigua a
Santa Cruz, Casilla 542; tel: 591 (4) 433 8338
(acc 35)

Chile
Antofagasta: Lautarito, Castro 5193, Población
Lautaro, Casilla 581; tel/fax: 56 (55) 380 719
(acc 70)
Concepción: Catalina Booth, Hipólito Salas 760;
tel: 56 (41) 223 0447 (acc 24)
Copiapó: Gotitas, Av Carlos Condell 1535,
Los Salares, Casilla 436; tel: 56 (52) 216 099
(acc 32)
Iquique: Las Estrellitas, Esmeralda 862,
Casilla 134; tel/fax: 56 (57) 421 325 (acc 38)
Rancagua: Hijitos de Dios, Iquique 24
(esquina Bolivia), Población San Francisco;
tel: 56 (72) 239 028 (acc 20)
Santiago:
Arca de Noé, El Fundador 13678, Población
Santiago de la Nueva Extremadura,
La Pintana, Casilla 3225; tel: 56 (2) 542 4523
(acc 58)
La Estrellita, Maipú 284, Maipú, Casilla 3225;
tel: 56 (2) 531 2638 (acc 40)
Las Acacias, Las Vizcachas 858, Población
Las Acacias, El Bosque, Casilla 3225;
tel: 56 (2) 529 4242 (acc 52)
Marta Brunet, Montaña Adentro 01650,
Puente Alto, Casilla 3225,
tel: 56 (2) 572 9340 (acc 50)
Neptuno, Los Aromos 833, Lo Prado,
Casilla 3225; tel: 56 (2) 773 5154 (acc 40)
Puente Alto, Soldaditos de Jesús, Santo
Domingo 90, Puente Alto, Casilla 3225;
tel: 56 (2) 419 0110/850 3331 (acc 86)
Rayitos de Sol, Av Brasil 73, Casilla 3225;
tel: 56 (2) 699 3595; fax: 56 (2) 688 4755
(acc 90)
Temuco: Padre Las Casas, Los Misioneros 1354,
Comuna de Padre Las Casas, (acc 20)
Valdivia: Rayito de Luz, Picarte 1894;
tel/fax: 56 (63) 214 404 (acc 120)
Valparaíso: Faro de Ángeles, Calle Santa
Martha 443, Cerro Playa Ancha, Casilla 1887;
tel: 56 (32) 228 1160 (acc 76)

Ecuador
Guayaquil: Nueva Esperanza, Av Martha de
Roldós km 5½, Vía Daule, Casilla 09.01.10478;
tel: 593 (4) 383 0351 (acc 60)
Manta: Arca de Noé, Av 201, entre calles
116 y 117, Barrio La Paz, Casilla 13-05-149;
tel: 593 (5) 292 0147 (acc 30)

Quito:
  El Ranchito: Manzana 44, Lote 801-802,
    Rancho Alto, Casilla 7110.7179;
    tel 593 (2) 338 2408/9 (acc 50)
  Gotitas de Miel: Montalvo 220, Cayambe,
    Casilla 17.10.7179; tel: 593 (2) 236 1273
    (acc 100)
La Colmena:
  Calle Pomasqui 955 y Pedro Andrade,
    La Colmena, Casilla17.01.1120;
    tel: 593 (2) 258 1081/228 4776 (acc 60)
  Mi Casita: Apuela S 25-182 y Malimpia,
    Santa Rita, Casilla 17.107179;
    tel: 593 (2) 284 5529 (acc 40)
Mi Hermoso Redil: Urbanización Sierra Hermosa,
  Calle 5, lotes 237-239, Parroquia de Carapungo;
  tel: 593 (2) 282 6835 (acc 100)

Food Aid Programmes
Chile:

Calle Ejército casa 721, Pobl Oscar Bonilla 2,
  Ancud; tel: 56 (65) 622 045 (acc 80)
Avanzada Bonilla, Río Lauca 1162, Pobl Bonilla,
  Antofagasta; tel: 56 (55) 761 312

Peru

Chiclayo: PP.JJ. Sto Toribibio de Mogrovejo MZ
  A Lote 17, Chiclayo; tel: 51 (74) 208 216
  (neighbour) (acc 100)
El Porvenir: Calle Synneva Vestheim 583,
  Cacerío El Porvenir, Provincia Rioja,
  Dpto San Martín (acc 50)

Development Integral Centres and Nutritional Centres
Bolivia

Achachicala, La Paz (acc 150)
Corqueamaya, La Paz (acc 70)
El Tejar, La Paz (acc 245 journey)
Lacaya, La Paz (acc 75)
Nueva Vida, Santa Cruz (acc 250)
Potosí (acc 30)
Tiahuanacu, La Paz (acc 200)
Yaurichambi, La Paz (acc 75)
Villa Cantería, Potosí (acc 50)
Villa Cosmos, La Paz (acc 250)
Villa Fátima, La Paz (acc 50 journey)
Villa 8 de Diciembre, La Paz (acc 90)
Viacha, La Paz (acc 250 journey)
Zona Este de Oruro, Oruro (acc 150 journey)

Ecuador

Bastión Popular, Guayaquil (acc 100)
El Rancho, Quito (acc 100)
Mi Casita, Quito Sur (acc 120)
Nido Alegre, La Colmena, Quito (acc 150)

Nueva Esperanza, Guayaquil (acc 160)
Pedacito de Cielo, Esmeraldas (acc 200)
William Booth, Cayambe (acc 150)

Peru
Moquegua (acc 60)

Day Care Centre (without corps/outposts)
Chile:
Nido Alegre, Santiago (acc 40)

Community Day Centres/School-age Day Care Centres (attached to corps/outposts)
Bolivia

Batallón Colorados, Sucre (acc 60)
El Temporal, Cochabamba (acc 75)
'El Vergel', Chapare (acc 60)
Fortín del Niño, Uspha Ushpha, Santa Cruz
  (acc 100)
Huayra K'assa, Cochabamba (acc 50)
La Chimba, Cochabamba (acc 80)
La Roca, Calicanto, Santa Cruz (acc 25)
Pacata, Cochabamba (acc 200)
Parotani, Cochabamba (acc 60)
Pockonas, Sucre (acc 50)
Primero de Mayo, Santa Cruz (acc 300)
Tarija (acc 50)

Peru

Buenos Aires, Trujillo (acc 50)
La Esperanza, Trujillo (acc 40)
San Martín de Porras, Lima (acc 40)
Tacna (acc 60)
Vitarte, Lima (acc 80)

Workshop
Ecuador

Tailoring Workshop and Sewing Centre:
  Calle Apuela S25-182 y Malimpia,
  Santa Rita, Casilla 17.10.7179, Quito;
  tel: 593 (2) 284 5529

Enterprise Development

Warehouse: Coronel Souper 4564,
  Estación Central, Casilla 3225, Santiago,
  Chile; tel: 56 (2) 764 1917

SOUTHERN AFRICA TERRITORY

Territorial leaders:
Commissioners André and Silvia Cox

Territorial Commander:
Commissioner André Cox (1 Oct 2008)

Chief Secretary:
Lieut-Colonel William Langa (1 Nov 2010)

Territorial Headquarters: 119-121 Rissik Street, Braamfontein, Johannesburg 2001

Postal address: PO Box 1018, Johannesburg 2000, South Africa

Tel: [27] (011) 718 6700; fax: [27] (011) 718 6790;

email: CS_SouthernAfrica@SAF.salvationarmy.org; website: www.salvationarmy.co.za

On 4 March 1883 Major and Mrs Francis Simmonds with Lieutenant Alice Teager 'opened fire' in Cape Town. Other officers were sent to the island of St Helena in 1886 to consolidate work commenced (in 1884) by Salvationist 'Bluejackets'. Social services began in 1886. The Salvation Army's first organised ministry among the African people was established in 1888 in Natal and, in 1891, in Zululand. Work in Swaziland was commenced in 1960. Having previously been in Namibia from 1932 to 1939, the Army re-established a presence in the country in January 2008 under the leadership of Major Lenah Jwili, a South African national, and was given official recognition on 11 March 2008.

Zone: Africa
Countries included in the territory: Lesotho, Namibia, Island of St Helena, South Africa, Swaziland
'The Salvation Army' in Afrikaans: Die Heilsleër; in IsiXhosa: Umkhosi wo Sindiso; in IsiZulu: Impi yo Sindiso; in SeSotho: Mokhosi oa Poloko; in SiPedi: Mogosi wa Pholoso; in Tshivenda: Mbi ya u Tshidza; in Tsonga: Nyi Moi Yoponisa
Languages in which the gospel is preached: Afrikaans, English, IsiXhosa, IsiZulu, SeSotho, Shangaan, SiPedi, Tshivenda, Tsonga, Tswana
Periodicals: *Echoes of Mercy, Home League Highlights, Home League Resource Manual, Outer Circle Newsletter, SAMF Newsletter, The Reporter, The War Cry*

A DEFINING statement emerged from the strategic planning workshop held in May 2009: 'The Salvation Army is a vibrant movement, with people of integrity, coming alongside communities, together enabling growth and transformation of the whole person through the full expression of the gospel of Jesus Christ.'

Convened with representatives from territorial and divisional headquarters, corps and social institutions, the workshop brought together issues raised in previous mission confer-ences and at the 2008 Territorial Leaders Conference.

An online forum enabled people to participate in shaping the strategic plan. Five priorities were identified:

youth and children, leadership development, community engagement, Salvation Army community life and business. The territory plans to focus on these for five years.

In June 2009 Envoy Mrs Coral Yon (St Helena) was awarded the MBE. The presentation took place at the official residence of the Governor (His Excellency Mr Andrew Gurr) and was witnessed by territorial leaders Commissioners André and Silvia Cox.

Envoy Yon is the corps's first St Helenian leader. The citation also recognised her career in the public sector including the police, health and social services. She established a much-needed crèche in a densely populated area of the island and continues to work with youth and vulnerable members of the community.

The Army's work in Namibia is progressing. At Windhoek the first local officers were commissioned. At Okahandja Society, the second opening in Namibia, senior soldiers, junior soldiers and home league members have been enrolled. Uniforms for the soldiers at Okahandja were lovingly sewn by home league women of Windhoek.

When the 2010 FIFA World Cup was hosted by South Africa, mission teams worked in every division throughout the tournament. The country suffers a high level of violent crime, including kidnapping, assault and human trafficking. An anti-trafficking task team was established to raise awareness, provide education,

victim support and prevent trafficking of vulnerable and migrant children.

An extensive campaign by the public relations department, assisted by an advertising company, ensured that The Salvation Army's anti-trafficking message was heard, seen and read. Billboards were displayed on major routes in Gauteng Province. A free helpline was launched by the Army for community members who were concerned about or had something to report on trafficking in their neighbourhood.

STATISTICS

Officers 276 (active 174 retired 102) **Auxiliary-Captains** 19 **Cadets** 13 **Employees** 535
Corps 183 **Societies and Outposts** 53 **Mission Team** 1 **Schools** 3 **Hospitals** 2 **Institutions** 24 **Day Care Centres** 18 **Goodwill Centres** 23 **Nursery Schools** 3
Senior Soldiers 22,296 **Adherents** 1,021 **Junior Soldiers** 2,849

STAFF

Women's Ministries: Comr Silvia Cox (TPWM) Lt-Col Thalitha Langa (TSWM) Lt-Col Fikile Khoza (THLS), Maj Marieke Venter (Anti-Trafficking)
Business Administration: Capt Garth Niemand
  Finance: Maj Daniel Moukoko
  Financial Consultant: Mr John Pugsley
  Information Technology: Mr Andrew Geer
  Property: Mr Stan Eland
  Public Relations: Capt Piet Semeno
  Trade: Mr Gavin Blackwood
Personnel: Lt-Col Jabulani Khoza
  Human Resources: Mr Leon Schmahl
  Retired Officers: Comr William Mabena
Programme: Lt-Col Robert Donaldson
  Field Programme: tba
    Anti Human Trafficking: Maj Marieke Ventner
    Child Sponsorship: Capt Prudence Mahlobo
    Family Tracing: Lt-Col Veronica Trollip
    Projects and Emergencies: tba
    Statistician: Maj Arschette Moukoko

...**Youth:** Capt Themba Mahlobo
Social Programme: Capt Robert Hendricks
  Community Care Ministries: Lt-Col Fikile
  Khoza
  Medical Ministries: Capt (Dr) Felicia
  Christians
Training Principal: Maj Lenah Jwili
Candidates: Capt Themba Mahlobo
Education: Maj Frankie Burgoyne
Editorial and Literary: Capt Noluntu Semeno

DIVISIONS

Central: PO Box 756, Rosettenville,
  Johannesburg 2130; tel: (011) 435-0267;
  fax: (011) 435-2835; Majs Alistair and
  Marieke Venter
Eastern Cape: PO Box 12514, Centralhill,
  Port Elizabeth 6006; tel: (041) 585-5363;
  fax: (041) 586-3521; Majs Daniel and
  Tracey Kasuso
Eastern Kwa Zulu/Natal: PO Box 1267,
  Eshowe 3815; tel: (035) 474-1132;
  fax: (035) 474-1132; Majs Johannes and
  Veliswa Raselalome
Mid Kwa Zulu/Natal: PO Box 100061,
  Scottsville, Pietermaritzburg 3209;
  tel: (033) 386-3881; fax: (033) 386-8019;
  Majs Shadrack and Rosannah Ntshangase
Mpumalanga/Swaziland: PO Box 1571,
  Nelspruit 1200; tel: (013) 741-2869;
  fax: (013) 741-1205; Majs Solomon and
  Mercy Mahlangu
Northern: PO Box 3549, Makhado 0920;
  tel/fax: (015) 516-6658; Majs Keith and
  Yvonne Conrad
Northern Kwa Zulu/Natal: PO Box 923,
  Vryheid 3100; tel: (034) 982-3113;
  fax: (034) 983-2882; Majs Albert and
  Peggy Shekwa
Western Cape: PO Box 18179, Wynberg,
  Cape Town 7824; tel: (021) 761-8530/6;
  fax: (021) 761-8539; Majs Patrick and
  Margaret Booth

St Helena: The Salvation Army, Jamestown,
  Island of St Helena, South Atlantic Ocean;
  tel: 09 (290) 2703; fax: 09 (290) 2052;
  email: salvationarmy@cwimail.sh;
  Envoy Coral Yon

THQ OUTREACH – NAMIBIA

The Salvation Army, PO Box 26820,
  Windhoek, Namibia; tel: [00] (264) 61223881;
  mobile: 264 813087518;
  email: salvationarmy@iway.na;
  Capt Robert and Lt Juanita Wright

COLLEGE FOR OFFICER TRAINING

PO Box 32902, Braamfontein 2017,
  Johannesburg; tel: (011) 718 6762

DAY CARE CENTRES FOR PRE-SCHOOL CHILDREN

Central: Benoni, Eldorado Park, Galashewe,
  Katlehong, Lethlabile, Mangaung
Mpumalanga/Swaziland: Barberton, Emangweni,
  Pienaar
Mid Kwa Zulu/Natal: Hammarsdale, Imbali,
  Kwa Mashu, Umlazi
Northern: Messina
Northern Kwa Zulu/Natal: Ezakheni, Madadeni,
  Mondlo, Ulundi, Vryheid
Western Cape: Bonteheuwel, Mitchells Plein,
  Manenburg

DAY CARE CENTRES FOR SENIOR CITIZENS

Central: Benoni, Krugersdorp, Pretoria,
  Vereeniging
Eastern Cape: East London, Port Elizabeth
Mid Kwa Zulu/Natal: Pietermaritzburg
Western Cape: Goodwood

GOODWILL CENTRES

Benoni: PO Box 17299, Benoni West 1503
Family Mission Centre: PO Box 351,
  Krugersdorp 1740
Hind House: PO Box 13012, Vincent 5217
Hope Goodwill House: PO Box 100-213,
  Scottsville 3209
Sally Ann Cottage: PO Box 2090, Vereeniging
  1930

HEALTH SERVICES

Booth Hospital: 32 Prince St, Oranjezicht, Cape
  Town 8001; tel: (021) 465-4896/46 (acc 84)
Carl Sithole Wellness, VCT and Art Support
  Centre: PO Box 180, Orlando, Soweto 1840
Mountain View Hospital: PO Salvation 3110,
  via Vryheid, Natal; tel: (034) 967-1544
  (acc 88) (with Mountain View Mobile Clinic)
Msunduza Community and Primary Health Care
  Centre and Mbuluzi Clinic: Box 2543, Mbabane,
  Swaziland; tel: (268) 404-5243

RETIRED OFFICERS RESIDENCES

Citadel Court: Vrede St Gardens, Cape Town 8001
Emmarentia Flats: PO Box 85214, Emmarentia
  2029, Johannesburg; tel: (011) 646-2126
Ephraim Zulu Flats: PO Box 49, Orlando 1804,
  Soweto; tel: (011) 982-1084
Sunset Lodge: 10 World's View Cl, World's View,
  Doonside 4135, Natal

SOCIAL SERVICES

Crèches
Bridgman Crèche: PO Box 62, Kwa Xuma 1868;
88, 3b White City, Jabavu 1856;
tel: (011) 982-5574 (acc 140)
Carl Sithole Crèche: Carl Sithole Centre,
PO Box 180, Orlando 1804; tel: (011) 986-7417
(acc 40)

Children's Homes
Bethany: Carl Sithole Centre, Klipspruit,
PO Box 180, Orlando 1804;
tel: (011) 986-7417 (acc 110 children 6-18 yrs)
Bethesda: Zodwa's House, Carl Sithole Centre,
PO Box 180, Orlando 1804, Soweto (acc 32
children 2-6 yrs)
Ethembeni (Place of Hope): 63 Sherwell St,
Doornfontein, Johannesburg 2094;
tel: (011) 402-8101 (acc 60 children 0-3 yrs)
Firlands: Fourth Ave, PO Box 44291,
Linden 2104; tel: (011) 782-5556/7 (acc 60
children 3-18 yrs)
Joseph Baynes House: 89 Trelawney Rd,
Pentrich, PO Box 212275, Oribi 3205, Natal;
tel: (033) 386-2266 (acc 72 children 0-18 yrs)
Strathyre: Eleventh Ave, Dewetshof,
PO Box 28240, Kensington 2101,
Johannesburg; tel: (011) 615-7327/7344
(acc 50 children 3-18 yrs)

Community Programme
Thusanong/Osizweni: Home-based Community
Care and Counselling Programme, Carl Sithole
Centre, Klipspruit, Soweto, PO Box 180,
Orlando 1804; tel: (011) 986-7417

Street Children's Home
Musawenkosi: PO Box 14794, Madadeni
Township 2951 (acc 16 boys 7-18 yrs)

Eventide Home (men)
Beth Rogelim: Cape Town 8005, 22 Alfred St;
tel: (021) 425-2138 (acc 52)

Eventide Homes (men and women)
Emmarentia: Johannesburg, PO Box 85214,
Emmarentia 2029, 113 Komatie Rd;
tel: (011) 646-2126 (acc 40)
Ephraim Zulu Senior Citizen Centre: Orlando
1804, PO Box 49; tel: (011) 982-1084 (acc 100)
The Salvation Army Albert Baumann Frail Care
Home: Doonside, 4135, 10 World's View Cl,
PO Box 53, World's View, 4125, South Coast,
Natal; tel: (031) 903-3139 (acc 76)
Thembela: Durban 4001, 68 Montpelier Place;
tel: (031) 321-6360 (acc 53)

Homes for Abused Women
Beth Shan, PO Box 19713, Pretoria West 0117,
Pretoria (acc 15 women)
Care Haven: PO Box 38186, Gates Ville 7766,
Cape Town; tel: (021) 638-5511;
fax: (031) 637-0226;
email: careaid@iafrica.co.za
(acc 18 women, 60 children)
Durban Family Care, PO Box 47122,
Greyville 4023, Durban; tel: (031) 309-1395
(acc 45)
Haven of Hope Home, PO Box 2304,
North End 6056, Port Elizabeth;
tel: (041) 373-4317 (acc 32)

Men's Homes
Beth Rogelim: 22 Alfred St, Cape Town 8005;
tel: (021) 425-2138 (acc 100)
Bloemfontein Men's Home: 23 Fountain St,
Bloemfontein 9301; tel: (051) 447-2626
(acc 28)

Rehabilitation Centres
Hesketh King Treatment Centre: PO Box 5,
Elsenburg 7607, Cape; tel: (021) 884-4600
(acc 60)
Mountain Lodge: PO Box 168,
Magaliesburg 2805; tel: (014) 577 2155
(acc 60)

Social Centres
Durban Family Care Centre: PO Box 47122,
Greyville, Durban 4023; tel: (031) 309-1395
(acc 70)
Haven of Hope Home: PO Box 2304, North End,
Port Elizabeth 6056; tel: (041) 373-4317
(acc 60)
Johannesburg Social Services: Simmonds St Ext,
Johannesburg 2001; tel: (011) 832-1227;
fax: (011) 833-6259 (acc 56)
Pretoria Family Care Centre: PO Box 19713,
Pretoria West 0117; tel: (012) 327-3005
(acc 80)

SCHOOLS
Bethany Combined School: Carl Sithole
Centre, PO Box 180, Orlando 1804;
tel: (011) 986-7417
Mathunjwa High School: PO Box 923,
Vryheid 3100
William Booth Primary School: Mountain View,
PO Salvation 3110; tel: (034) 967-1533

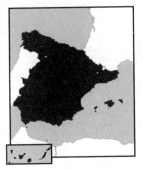

SPAIN COMMAND

Command leaders:
Lieut-Colonels Luis E. and Aída A. Castillo

Officer Commanding:
Lieut-Colonel Luis E. Castillo
(1 Jul 2008)

Command Headquarters: Hermosilla 126 Lc 1, 28028 Madrid

Postal address: Ejército de Salvación, c/ Hermosilla, 126 Local 1, 28028 Madrid, Spain

Tel: [34] 91 356 6644; fax: [34] 91 361 4782; email: Spain_Command@SPA.salvationarmy.org;
website: www.ejercitodesalvacion.es

Following the appointment of Captain and Mrs Enrique Rey to La Coruña on Ascension Day 1971, it was announced on 24 December 1971 that The Salvation Army had been granted the status of a Legal Person, enjoying full legal rights in the country and permitted to carry on its work without let or hindrance.

Zone: Europe
Country and autonomous communities included in the territory: Canary Islands, Mallorca, Spain
'The Salvation Army' in Spanish: Ejército de Salvación
Languages in which the gospel is preached: English (Mallorca, Denia), Filipino, Spanish

IN June 2009 the Comunidad de Madrid (Regional Government) invited an officer from the command to participate in a conference supported by Real Madrid Football Club. The positive influence of sport on young people in communities was the focus of this gathering, which complemented the 'Christ and Sports' programme that aims to win young people for Christ.

In October some 400 Salvationists from across Spain welcomed General Shaw Clifton and Commissioner Helen Clifton (WPWM) to the command. During the weekend of celebration, delegates at men's and women's rallies appreciated the international leaders' ministry.

At a youth rally the young people were challenged on the subject of life in the Spirit.

In the 'Salvationist Festival', and later in Sunday's holiness and salvation meetings, people responded to Christ by seeking salvation or in consecrating their lives more fully to him. Some expressed their desire to become Salvation Army officers.

The Greater New York Divisional Youth Band and Chorus (USA Eastern) supported this significant event and visited Madrid, Denia, Alicante and Barcelona. Their music and witness made a great impact on people in these places.

Despite a difficult financial climate in Spain, Salvationists have worked hard to secure the resources necessary for the Army's mission. The command gratefully acknowledges all who have contributed to enable the spreading of God's Word, trusting the Lord for future growth of his Kingdom.

STATISTICS

Officers 28 (active 26 retired 2) **Employees** 34
Corps 11 **Outposts** 5 **Institution** 1 **Thrift Shops** 14
Senior Soldiers 545 **Adherents** 48 **Junior Soldiers** 92
Personnel serving outside command Officers 2

STAFF

Women's Ministries: Lt-Col Aída Castillo (CPWM)
Business Administration: Maj Ambrosio Aycón
Programme and Evangelism: Maj Miguel Aguilera
Finance: Maj Fortunato Echeverría
Accountant: Fausta Gonzales
Training: Maj Angélica Aguilera

SOCIAL SERVICES
Food and/or Clothing Distribution Centres

Alicante 03006: c/ Deportista César Porcel, 11 Bajo
Barcelona 08024: c/ del Rubí 18
Denia, Alicante 03700: c/ San José 14 B
La Coruña 15010: c/ Francisco Añón 9
Las Palmas 35014: Plaza de los Ruiseñores, Local 8 alto, Miller Bajo
Madrid 28028: c/ Hermosilla, 126, Local 4
Madrid 28038: Avda Rafael Alberti, 18 Bis
Mallorca 07015: Cala Mayor, Avda Joan Miró 285
Mallorca 07015: Palma Nova, c/ Jardiel Poncela 2
Tenerife 38006: c/ Marisol Marín 10
Valdemoro-Madrid 28340: c/Bretón de los Herreros 10

Emergency Feeding Kitchens

Barcelona 08024: c/ del Rubí 18
La Coruña 15010: c/ Francisco Añón 9

Eventide Home (men and women)

Finca El Apostolado, Vereda del Alquitón 9, Arganda del Rey, Madrid 28500 (acc 35)

Homeless Day Care Centre

La Coruña 15010: 'Sen Teito' c/ Francisco Añón 9 (acc 25)

Social Emergency Apartments

La Coruña 15010: c/ Francisco Añón 9 (acc 25)

CONFERENCE, RETREAT AND HOLIDAY CENTRE

Camp Sarón, Partida Torre Carrals 64, 03700 Denia, Alicante; tel: 96 578 2152; fax: 96 643 1206; website: www.campsaron.com (acc 60)

Spain's National Timbrel Brigade featured in the General's visit to the command

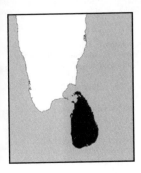

SRI LANKA TERRITORY

Territorial leaders:
Colonels Lalzamlova and Nemkhanching

Territorial Commander:
Colonel Lalzamlova (1 Jun 2006)

Chief Secretary:
Lieut-Colonel William Mockabee
(1 Oct 2010)

Territorial Headquarters: 53 Sir James Peiris Mawatha, Colombo 2

Postal address: PO Box 193, Colombo, Sri Lanka

Tel: [94] 011 232 4660/232 2159; fax: [94] 011 243 6065; website: www.sri.salvationarmy.org

Salvation Army work began in Ceylon (now Sri Lanka) on 26 January 1883 under the leadership of Captain William Gladwin. 'The General of The Salvation Army' is a corporation Sole by Ordinance No 11 of 1924.

Zone: South Asia
Country included in the territory: Sri Lanka
'The Salvation Army' in Sinhala: Galavime Hamudava; in Tamil: Ratchaniya Senai
Languages in which the gospel is preached: English, Sinhala, Tamil
Periodical: *Yudha Handa* (*The War Cry*)

FOUR officers of the Prayer Warriors Session were ordained and commissioned in meetings conducted by Commissioners Lalkiamlova and Lalhlimpuii (zonal leaders, South Asia). During their visit, in December 2009, the commissioners carried out a territorial review and were updated on the training college's major programme of renovation.

Commissioner Lalkiamlova returned to the territory the next month to preside over the 2010 Zonal Conference (18-23 January 2010). Commissioner Christine MacMillan (Director, International Social Justice Commission) was guest lecturer at the South Asia College for Officers

(27 January-25 February). Both events were held in Colombo.

In March, training meetings were held to equip corps officers in implementing the territorial theme, 'A Year Of Restoration'. Selected Bible readings in English, Sinhala and Tamil were made available for every centre.

Two women officers have been appointed as divisional and district leaders and significant growth has taken place under their leadership.

A three-year foster care and child development project, giving assistance to 200 tsunami orphans, concluded in five centres. Closing ceremonies took place with guardians and children expressing thanks for the support to help rebuild their lives.

The Combatting Human Trafficking Project entered its final year. The focus has been on prevention and raising awareness in areas of high vulnerability.

Small projects facilitated by the Women's Ministries Department benefited various communities. Funding from IHQ and partner territories enabled various mission and development projects and emergency response. The territory gratefully acknowledges this support.

A reunion for former residents of children's homes paved the way for a local sponsorship scheme. An encouraging number who attended pledged to support the Army's social work.

Sports ministry was developed as a means of outreach to children and youth. Three officers and two young people were trained in India in partnership with International Sports Coalition (India) and Sports Men In Action (Sri Lanka). It is hoped that sports ministry with a biblical emphasis will shape the future of the territory's youth work.

The territory released a video of its work and property; also, the book *Soldiers of the Cross*, the story of faithful Sri Lankan pioneer officers, was published in Sinhalese.

STATISTICS

Officers 145 (active 98 retired 47) Cadets 4 Employees 151
Corps 44 Corps Plants 5 Social Homes and Hostels 11 Community Centres 5 Day Care Centre 1 Corps-based Child Care Centres 6 Health Centre 1 Conference Centre 1
Senior Soldiers 3,768 Adherents 848 Junior Soldiers 559
Personnel serving outside territory Officers 2

STAFF

Women's Ministries: Col Nemkhanching (TPWM) Lt-Col Debra Mockabee (TSWM) Maj Nilanthi Philip (THLS & WDO) Maj Usha Rani Zachariah (LOMS)
Candidates: Maj Ajantha Fernando
Community Services Development: tba
Editorial: Maj Shanthi Seneviratne
Field and Human Resources Development: Maj Packianathan Jayaratnasingham
Finance: Maj Jupalli Zachariah
Combating Human Trafficking Programme: Mrs Swarna De Silva
Information Technology: Miss Coojanie Heendeniya
Projects: tba
Property: tba
Public Relations, Legal and Fund-raising: Maj Alister Philip
Social Services: Maj Nihal Hettiarachchi
Training: Maj Newton Fernando
Youth: Capt Wijenama Wijesinghe

DIVISIONS

Rambukkana: Mawanella Rd, Rambukkana; tel: 035 226 5179; email: salrambu@sltnet.lk; Majs Ranjit and Vijayashri Senaratne
Western: 11 Sir James Peiris Mawatha, Colombo 2; tel: 011 232 4660 ext 214; Maj Chandra Jayaratnasingham

DISTRICTS

Kandy: 26 Srimath Bennet Soysa Veediya, Kandy; tel: 08 223 4804; Maj Kokila Muthusamy
Northern: Kandy Rd, Kaithady; tel: 0213 217450; Maj Newton Jacob

SECTIONS

Eastern: 135 Trincomalee St, Batticaloa; tel: 065 222 4558; fax: 065 222 4768 (AST Link Communication & Agency Post Office – Batticaloa); Maj M. Puvanendran
Southern: Weerasooriya Watte, Patuwatha-Dodanduwa; tel: 091 227 7146; Maj Shelton Fernando

TRAINING COLLEGE

77 Ananda Rajakaruna Mawatha, Colombo 10;

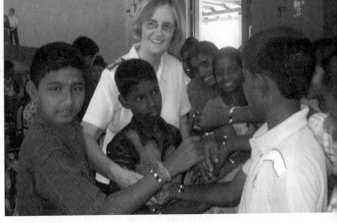

At a Sunday school rally in the Northern District, young people get to meet an officer from New Zealand, Major Colleen Marshall

tel: 011 268 6116; email:
sritraining.college@sri.salvationarmy.org

SOCIAL SERVICES
Children's Homes
Batticoloa Girls' Home: 135 Trincomalee St,
Batticaloa; tel: 065 222 4558 (acc 16)
Dehiwela Girls' Home: 12 School Ave,
Dehiwela; tel: 271 7049 (acc 50)
Rajagiriya Boys' Home: Obeysekera Rd,
Rajagiriya; tel: 286 2301 (acc 30)
Shalom Children's Home and Centre: Kandy Rd,
Kaithady; tel: 0213 210779 (acc boys 16,
girls 22, remandees 10)
Sunshine Home: 127 E. W. Perera Mawatha,
Colombo 10 (acc remandees 34)
Swedlanka Boys' Home: South Pallansena Jaya
Mawatha, Kochchikade; tel: 031 227 7964
(acc 25)
The Haven: 127, E. W. Perera Mawatha,
Colombo 10; tel: 011 269 5275
(acc babies 10, children 10)

Hostels
Dehiwela Eventide Home for Women: 8 School
Ave, Dehiwela; tel: 272 8542 (acc 34)
Hope House Home for Employed Disabled
Men: 11 Sir James Peiris Mawatha,
Colombo 2; tel: 011 232 4660 ext 200 (acc 12)
Ladies' Hostel (1): 18 Sri Saugathodaya
Mawatha, Colombo 2; tel: 011 311 7783
(acc 82)
Ladies' Hostel (2): 30 Union Pl, Colombo 2;
tel: 011 311 7735 (acc 78)
Rajagiriya Elders' Home and Iris Perera Home:
1700 Cotta Rd, Rajagiriya; tel: 288 5947
(acc men 20, women 22)
Rajagiriya Young Men's Hostel: Obeysekera Rd,
Rajagiriya; tel: 286 2301 (acc 10)

Rawathawatte Hostel for Women: 14 Charles Pl,
Rawathawatte, Moratuwa; tel: 421 3018
(acc working girls 28)
The Haven: 127 E. W. Perera Mawatha,
Colombo 10; tel: 269 5275 (acc unwed
mothers 14, elderly women 10,
rehabilitation 10)

Community Centres
Dias Place: 16, Dias Place, Colombo 11;
tel: 242 3912
Hope House: 11 Sir James Peiris Mawatha,
Colombo 2; tel: 011 232 4660 ext 200
Rambukkana: Mawanella Rd, Rambukkana;
tel: 035 226 5179

Child Day Care Centres
Amparai: Main Rd, Amparai; tel: 063 222 3779
Kudagama: Kudagama, Dombemada;
tel: 035 3950361
Hewadiwela: Hewadiwela; tel: 035 226 6785
Talampitiya: Mahagama, Kohilegedera,
Talampitiya; tel: 037 223 8278
Wattegama: 34 Nuwaratenne Rd, Wattegama;
tel: 081 3803319
Rathmeewela, Menikdiwela

HEALTH SERVICES
Physiotherapy Unit: Colombo; tel 011 232 4660
ext 204

CONFERENCE CENTRE
Rambukkana Conference Centre for Camp:
Mawanella Rd, Rambukkana;
tel: 035 2265179

KALUTARA ESTATE AND CAMP CENTRE
Galapatha, Kalutara

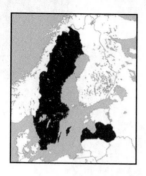

SWEDEN AND LATVIA TERRITORY

Territorial Commander:
Commissioner Marie Willermark
(1 Feb 2011)

Chief Secretary:
Colonel Johnny Kleman (1 Jun 2010)

Territorial Headquarters: Nybrogatan 79B, 114 41, Stockholm, Sweden

Postal address: Box 5090, SE 102 42 Stockholm, Sweden

Tel: [46] (08) 562 282 00; fax: [46] (08) 562 283 91; email: fralsningsarmen@fralsningsarmen.se;
website: www.fralsningsarmen.se

Commissioner Hanna Ouchterlony, inspired by the first Army meeting held on Swedish soil in Värnamo in 1878 led by the young Chief of the Staff, Bramwell Booth, began Salvation Army work in a Stockholm theatre on 28 December 1882. The first women's home and a men's shelter were opened in 1890. Work among deaf and blind people was inaugurated in 1895. The Salvation Army was re-established in Latvia on 18 November 1990 and two months later, on 23 January 1991, The Salvation Army in Latvia became a juridical person. On 15 November 1994 the Sweden Territory was renamed the Sweden and Latvia Territory.

Zone: Europe
Countries included in the territory: Latvia, Sweden
'The Salvation Army' in Swedish: Frälsningsarmén; in Latvian: Pestíšanas Armija; in Russian: Armiya Spaseniya
Languages in which the gospel is preached: Latvian, Russian, Swedish
Periodical: *Stridsropet*

REORGANISATION of the territory was implemented during the year to maximise mission resources in the areas of personnel and finance. Part of the THQ building was sold and the remaining premises renovated and modernised to accommodate a smaller staff complement.

The closure of the four divisional headquarters has meant greater responsibility at corps level. The Programme Office continued to develop social and corps community work in order to serve people in need. Projects for unemployed people have been established.

The territory held 24/7 prayer initiatives in October and November 2009.

Whilst a number of corps closed, there was a new opening in partnership with the Finland and Estonia Territory. Outposts developed from cell groups and corps in both Sweden and Latvia enrolled soldiers and welcomed adherents.

A series of six 'Hearing Days' was held, giving Salvationists opportunity to present and discuss various subjects including 'Increased Freedom – Increased Responsibility' and 'Visionary and Servant Leadership'. The new strategy document for the territory was introduced.

For the fourth year running The Salvation Army and the Christian newspaper *Dagen* participated in the annual week-long event held by political parties on the island of Gotland. Using the theme 'G' (as in God), the Army in collaboration with *Dagen* held seminars on issues such as euthanasia, loneliness and freedom.

'A Glorious Mixture' was the theme of a successful summer camp held at the Army's scouting centre, Högaberg. Children and adults from many corps and social centres participated in Bible teaching, scouting activities, music, drama and sports.

After attending Bible classes at Ågestagården Conference Centre, 50 teenagers publicly declared their Christian faith in the annual Confirmation Ceremony at Stockholm Temple.

In Latvia new regional leaders were appointed and two cadets were welcomed for training. Three Latvian cadets were among the 10 members of the Prayer Warriors Session ordained and commissioned as officers during the commissioning in Stockholm.

Latvian television featured the opening of a crisis centre for women and children in Skangale. Soldiers and recruits who were formerly homeless have been accommodated at a halfway house in Riga.

STATISTICS
Officers 351 (active 142 retired 209)
Cadets (1st Yr) 2 (2nd Yr) 7
Employees 1,077
Corps (incl Community and Family Services) 136 **Outposts** 20 **Hotels/Guest Homes** 2
Senior Soldiers 4,909 **Adherents** 727 **Junior Soldiers** 148
Personnel serving outside territory Officers 13

STAFF
Women's Ministries: Comr Marie Willermark (TPWM) Col Eva Kleman (TSWM)
Sec for Business Administration: Capt Elisabeth Beckman
Editor-in-Chief: Maj Bert Åberg
Fundraising: Mr Mats Wiberg
Legacies: Maj Margaretha Andersson
Sec for Personnel: Lt-Col Kenneth Nordenberg
Human Resources Responsibility: Mrs Eva Malmberg
Training College: Maj Mona Stockman
People's High School: Mr Magnus Wetterberg
Sec for Programme: Lt-Col Britt-Marie Alm
Asst Sec for Programme: Maj Sonja Blomberg,
Development Officers: Col Kristina Frisk, Col Kehs David Löfgren, Maj Gunilla Olausson, Maj Leif Öberg
Area Experts:
Corps Development: Capt Mia-Lisa Alhbin
Social Work: Maj Sonja Blomberg
Youth: Mrs Gunnel Lerne
International Development: Mr Christian Lerne
Child Sponsorship: Mrs Anna-Carin Wiberg Löw
'Sally Ann' – Trading Programme:
Sally Ann Sverige AB:
email: sallyann@fralsningsarmen.se
website: www.sallyann.se
Manager: Mr Lars Beijer
Chair of Board:
Shop: Hornsgatan 98, 118 21 Stockholm

TRAINING
Training College
Frälsningsarméns Officersskola, Ågestagården, Bonäsvägen, 5, 123 52 Farsta;
tel: (08) 562 281 50; fax: (08) 562 281 70

People's High Schools

Ägesta Folkhögskola: Bonäsvägen 5,
123 52 Farsta; tel: (08) 562 281 00;
fax (08) 562 281 20
Älvsjö Bransch: Älvsjö Gårdsväg 9,
125 30 Älvsjö; tel: (08) 647 52 77;
fax: (08) 556 233 15

CONFERENCE CENTRE/GUEST HOMES

Smålandsgården, Örserum, 563 91 Gränna;
tel: (0390) 300 14; fax: (0390) 304 17
(acc 67)
'Lännerstahemmet', Djurgårdsvägen 7,
132 46 Saltsjö-Boo; tel: (08) 715 11 58;
fax: (08) 747 11 76

SOCIAL SERVICES
Work Among Alcoholics
Treatment Centre for Substance Abusers

'Kurön', 178 92 Adelsö; tel: (08) 560 518 80;
fax: (08) 560 514 05 (acc 63)

Rehabilitation Centres

Göteborg: 'Lilla Bommen', S:t Eriksgatan 4,
411 05 Göteborg; tel: (031) 60 45 56;
fax: (031) 711 83 67 (acc 63)
Göteborg: 'Nylösegården', Skaragatan 3,
415 01 Göteborg; tel: (031) 25 59 59;
fax: (031) 21 99 86 (acc 20)
Örebro: 'Gnistan', Bruksgatan 13,
702 20 Örebro; tel: (019) 32 38 40;
fax: (019) 32 37 72 (acc 11)
Stockholm: 'Värtahemmet', Kolargatan 2;
115 42 Stockholm; tel: (08) 545 835 00;
fax: (08) 545 835 07 (acc 42)
Stockholm Tyresö: 'Källan',
Wättingegårdsväg 1, 135 40 Tyresö;
tel: (08) 448 73 50; fax: (08) 448 73 59
(acc 20)
Sundsvall: 'Klippangården', Fredsgatan 38,
852 38 Sundsvall; tel: (060) 17 31 74;
fax: (060) 17 52 10 (acc 16)
Uppsala: 'Sagahemmet', Storgatan 2 A,
753 31 Uppsala; tel: (018) 10 08 01;
fax: (018) 12 12 39 (acc 26)

Night Shelters

Örebro: 'Gnistan', Bruksgatan 13, 702 20 Örebro;
tel: (019) 32 38 40; fax: (019) 32 37 72
(acc 10)
Stockholm: 'Midsommarkransen',
Midsommarslingan 1-3, 126 32 Hägersten;
tel: (08) 19 13 30; fax: (08) 744 20 78
(acc 27)

Sundsvall: 'Klippangården', Fredsgatan 38,
852 38 Sundsvall; tel: (060) 17 31 74;
fax: (018) 12 12 39
Uppsala: 'Sagahemmet', Storgatan 2 A,
753 31 Uppsala; tel: (018) 10 08 01;
fax: (018) 12 12 39 (acc 10)

Drop-in Centre

Stockholm: Bergsundsstrand 51, 117 38
Stockholm; tel: (08) 34 85 98;
fax: (08) 31 97 85

Harbour Light Corps

'Fyrbåkskåren', S:t Pauligatan 1, 416 60
Göteborg; tel: (031) 19 58 08

Advisory Services

Stockholm: 'Eken' Counselling Centre,
Hornsgatan 98, 118 21 Stockholm;
tel: (08) 55 60 80 76
Uppsala: 'Brobygget', S:t Persgatan 20,
753 20 Uppsala; tel: (018) 71 05 44;
fax: (018) 14 84 59

Work Among Children and Families
Pre-Schools

Jönköping: 'Vårsol', Von Platensgatan 10,
553 13 Jönköping; tel: (036) 71 15 02;
fax: (036) 71 21 90 (acc 17)
Umeå: 'Krubban', N Slevgränd 123,
906 27 Umeå; tel: (090) 18 05 90;
fax: (090) 18 27 88 (acc 18)
Västra Frölunda: 'Morgonsol', Poppelgatan 11,
426 74 Västra Frölunda; tel/fax: (013) 29 10 29
(acc 34)

Work Among Mother and Children

Stockholm: Frälsningsarméns Mamma –
barnarbete, Gotlandsgatan 73 C,
116 38 Stockholm; tel: (08) 21 47 92

School and Treatment Centre for Adolescents

'Sundsgården', 179 96 Svartsjö;
tel: (08) 560 428 21; fax: (08) 560 425 00
(acc 27)

Treatment Centre for Families

'FAM-Huset', Hagvägen 1, 513 32 Fristad;
tel: (033) 21 01 62; fax: (033) 21 01 63
(acc adults 8, babies 8)

Emergency Diagnostic and Short-term Treatment Centre

'Vårsol', Von Platensgatan 10, 553 13 Jönköping;

tel: (036) 16 74 58; fax: (036) 71 21 90
(acc 6)

Group Homes for Adolescents

Jönköping: 'Vårsols Ungdomsboende',
V:a Storgatan 21, 553 15 Jönköping;
tel: (036) 17 32 75; fax: (036) 17 32 74
(acc 6)
Stockholm: 'Locus', Grev Turegatan 66,
114 38 Stockholm; tel: (08) 667 21 82;
fax: (08) 667 21 87 (acc 14)

Family Centres with Advisory Service

'Vårsols Familjecenter', V:a Storgatan 21,
553 15 Jönköping; tel: (036) 17 32 72;
fax: (036) 17 32 74
393:s Familjecenter, Södermannagatan 46,
116 40 Stockholm; tel: (08) 664 60 32

Salvation Army Refugee Aid

Jönköping SARA: V:a Storgatan 21,
553 15 Jönköping; tel: (036) 17 32 75;
fax: (036) 17 32 74

Vacation Centres for Children

Gävle: 'Rörberg', Hedesundavägen 89,
818 91 Valbo; tel: (026) 330 19 (acc 15)
Luleå: 'Sunderbyn', Sunderbynvägen 323,
954 42 Södra Sunderbyn;
tel: (0920) 26 57 25 (acc 15)
Malmö: 'Kotten', Klockarevägen 20,
236 36 Höllviken; tel: (040) 45 05 24
(acc 15)

Centre for Elderly People

'Dalen', Kapellgatan 14, 571 31 Nässjö;
tel: (0380) 188 11 (acc 20)

Recreation Centre for Elderly People

Malmö: 'Furubo', Klockarevägen 22, 236 36
Höllviken; tel: (040) 45 39 13

Multicultural Ministries

'Akalla', Sibeliusgången 6, 164 73 Kista;
tel: (08) 750 62 16; fax: (08) 751 71 61

Women Emergency Residence

Stockholm: 'Skogsbo', Box 112,
132 23 Saltsjö Boo; tel: (08) 21 47 92

Second-hand Shops

Head office: Stensätravägen 3B,
127 39 Skärholmen; tel: (08) 563 169 50;
fax: (08) 563 169 60
Shops: Borås, Eskilstuna, Falun, Gävle,
Göteborg, Halmstad, Jönköping, Karlstad,
Linköping, Luleå, Malmö (2), Norrköping,
Skellefteå, Stockholm (7), Sundbyberg,
Sundsvall, Trollhättan, Umeå, Uppsala (2),
Västerås, Örebro

LATVIA REGION (under THQ)

Regional Headquarters: Bruninieku iela 10A,
LV 1001 Riga; tel: [371] 673 10037;
fax: [371] 673 15266;
email: info@pestisanasarmija.lv;
website: www.pestisanasarmija.lv
Regional leaders: Lts Peter and Rut
Baronowsky

STATISTICS

Officers 14 (active 13 retired 1) **Cadets** (2nd
Yr) 3 **Envoys** 3 **Employees** 122
Corps 7 **Outposts** 5 **Institutions** 2
Senior Soldiers 231 **Adherents** 216 **Junior
Soldiers** 18

SOCIAL SERVICES

Leontine Gorkša Children's Home:
Agenskalna iela 3, LV 1048 Riga;
tel: [371] 760 17 00
Maternity and Child Health Centre:
Bruninieku iela 10A, LV 1001 Riga;
tel/fax: [371] 672 71384
'Patverums' Day Centre for Children at Risk:
Bruninieku iela 10 A, LV 1001 Riga;
tel: [371] 731 14 63
Skangale School Home: Liepa pag,
Césu rajons, LV 4128 Liepa;
tel: [371] 641 02220; fax: [371] 641 02221

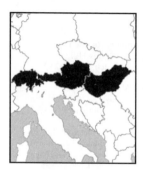

SWITZERLAND, AUSTRIA AND HUNGARY TERRITORY

Territorial leaders:
Commissioners Kurt Burger and Alicia Burger-Pedersen

Territorial Commander:
Commissioner Kurt Burger (1 Sep 2007)

Chief Secretary:
Colonel Franz Boschung (1 Oct 2007)

Territorial Headquarters: Laupenstrasse 5, Bern, Switzerland

Postal address: Die Heilsarmee, Postfach 6575, 3001 Bern, Switzerland

Tel: [41] (31) 388 05 91; fax: [41] (31) 388 05 95; email: info@swi.salvationarmy.org

websites: www.heilsarmee.ch; www.armeedusalut.ch; www.salvationarmy.ch

On 10 December 1882 Salvation Army operations were commenced in the Salle de la Réformation, Geneva, by the Maréchale, Catherine Booth, and Colonel Arthur S. Clibborn. Bitter opposition was encountered but now the Army is recognised as an evangelical and social force throughout the Confederation. The Salvation Army's constitution consists of Foundation Salvation Army Switzerland; Cooperative Salvation Army Social Organisation; Salvation Army Immo Ltd.

Work first commenced in Austria on 27 May 1927 in Vienna. Unofficial meetings had been held earlier, but the official opening was conducted by Lieut-Commissioner Bruno Friedrich and Captain Lydia Saak was the officer-in-charge. 'Verein der Heilsarmee' was legally recognised by the Austrian Federal Ministry on 8 May 1952.

The Salvation Army's operations in Hungary were commenced on 24 April 1924 by Colonel Rothstein with two German women-officers. The evangelistic and social activities were maintained until suppressed in 1950. After the opening of the central European borders, The Salvation Army was officially re-established on 3 November 1990 by General Eva Burrows.

Zone: Europe

Countries included in the territory: Austria, Hungary, Switzerland

'The Salvation Army' in German: Die Heilsarmee; in French: Armée du Salut; in Hungarian: Az Üdvhadsereg; in Spanish: Ejército de Salvación

Languages in which the gospel is preached: French, German, Hungarian, Spanish

Periodicals: *Espoir* (French), *Dialog* (German), *Dialogue* (French), *IN* (French and German), *Just 4 U* (French), *Klecks* (German), *Trampoline* (French), *Trialog* (German)

RECRUITING new Salvationists and officers has proved difficult in a society where personal commitment is unpopular. Nevertheless, 2009 was an encouraging year. Within the territory, 57 senior and 85 junior soldiers were enrolled, and 179 adherents welcomed into The Salvation Army.

In July a new corps was opened in a region where an officer-couple had pioneered for several years. The school for officer training developed an officially acknowledged degree course in Christian Leadership Education.

By involving officers, soldiers and employees in plans for the future, the territory substantiated its corporate strategy and began its implementation in 2009. The key elements – 'to worship, to win, to grow, to serve' – are linking the Army's strong evangelistic focus to its publicly acknowledged social work. The overall goal is to bring people into contact with the love of Jesus Christ.

In Austria, while the men's hostel celebrated its 10th anniversary, building work began on another social services centre, which will provide 60 living quarters. Corps ministry within local communities concentrated on supporting people living on the margins of society.

In Hungary, economic hardship means a helping hand from The Salvation Army is needed more than ever. Homeless people, families, mothers and children escaping domestic violence, prisoners and people suffering physical and mental illness have all benefited from the Army's services.

A new facility for the refuge for abused women and children is being constructed and the infrastructure of the men's shelter is to be upgraded. Additionally, a project development is planned in Budapest's 6th and 17th districts, where the Army already operates.

Salvationists in Switzerland celebrated God with a huge 'Be On Fire!' event. It ranged from classical music to sensitive worship interludes to latest dance and rap performances. Some 1,500 visitors enjoyed two days of celebration and fellowship.

Donations through direct mailing campaigns throughout the year reached a record increase of six per cent, affirming the public's strong trust in The Salvation Army's work. By the end of the year investments that had been lost because of the worldwide recession had been recovered.

STATISTICS
(Switzerland and Austria)

Officers 424 (active 188 retired 236) **Cadets** (2nd Yr) 2 **Employees** 1,613

Corps 65 **Outposts** 8 **Institutions** 45 **Thrift Stores** 25

Senior Soldiers 2,876 **Adherents** 968 **Junior Soldiers** 397

Personnel serving outside territory Officers 14 Layworkers 1

STAFF

Dept of Evangelisation: Maj Fritz Schmid
  Society and Family: Comr Alicia Burger-Pedersen (TPWM) Col Hanny Boschung (TSWM) Maj Christianne Winkler (Women's Ministries & Seniors Sec) Capt Barbara Bösch (Family Work)
  Music and Gospel Arts: Mr Micael Dikantsa
  Youth: Capt Thomas Bösch
Dept of Social Work: Sgt Erhard Meyner-Dätwyler
  Social French Part: Mr Michel Bonjour
  Social German Part: Mr Christian Rohrbach
  Prison Work: Maj Samuel Winkler
  Family Tracing: Maj Martha Mosimann
  Refugees: Mr Jakob Amstutz
  Thrift Stores: Mr David Küenzi
Dept of Personnel: Maj Marianne Meyner-Stettler
  Candidates: Maj Daniela Zurbrügg-Jäggi
  Training: Maj Hervé Cachelin
  Personnel Administration: Sgt Christian Hefti

Dept of Finance and Business Administration:
Sgt Andreas Stettler
Finance Controlling Evangelisation:
Maj Peter Zurbrügg
Finance Controlling Social: Mr Michael
Lippuner
Finance Controlling THQ: Sgt Kenneth Hofer
Property: Mr Marc Hendry
Mission and Development: Aux-Capt Markus
Muntwiler
Dept of Communication: Sgt Martin Künzi
Editor-in-Chief: Mrs Gabrielle Keller
Fundraising: Sgt Christoph Bitter
Information Technology: Mr Martin Schweizer
Museum and Archives: Maj Corinne Gossauer
Trade Shop: Mrs Hanni Butler

DIVISIONS

Bern: Gartenstrasse 8, 3007 Bern;
tel: (031) 380 75 45; fax: (031) 380 75 42;
Majs Bernhard and Regina Wittwer
Division Romande: Rue de l'Ecluse 16,
2000 Neuchâtel; tel: (032) 729 20 81;
Majs Jacques and Claude-Evelyne Donzé
Nordwestschweiz: Breisacherstrasse 45,
4057 Basel; tel: (061) 691 11 50;
fax: (061) 691 12 59; Majs August and
Ruth Martin
Ost-Division: Eidmattstrasse 16, 8032 Zürich;
tel: (044) 383 69 70; fax: (044) 383 52 48;
Comrs Werner and Paula Frei

SCHOOL FOR OFFICER TRAINING

4012 Basel, Habsburgerstrasse 15, Postfach 54,
CH-4012 Basel; tel: (061) 387 91 11;
fax: (061) 381 77 63

SOCIAL WORK
Social Services Advice Bureaux
4053 Basel: Frobenstrasse 18; tel: (061) 272 00 07;
fax: (061) 273 29 00
3007 Bern: Gartenstrasse 8; tel: (031) 380 75 40;
fax: (031) 380 75 42
2503 Biel-Bienne: Oberer Quai 12;
tel: (032) 322 53 66; fax: (032) 322 60 64
1018 Lausanne: Rue de la Borde 22;
tel: (021) 646 46 10
8400 Winterthur: CASA, Wartstrasse 9;
tel: 052 202 77 80
8032 Zürich: Eidmattstrasse 16; tel: 044 383 16 96
8005 Zürich: Luisenstrasse 23; tel: 044 272 85 20

Adult Rehabilitation Centres
1201 Genève: Centre-Espoir, Rue Jean-Dassier 10;
tel: (022) 338 22 00; fax: (022) 338 22 01
(acc 109)

3098 Köniz: Buchseegut, Buchseeweg 15;
tel: (031) 970 63 63; fax: (031) 970 63 64
(acc 40) (with gardening and workshop)
1003 Lausanne: Foyer Féminin,
Ave Ruchonnet 49; tel: (021) 310 40 40;
fax: (021) 310 40 42 (acc 23)
1005 Lausanne: La Résidence, Place du Vallon 1a;
tel: (021) 320 48 55; fax: (021) 310 39 34
(acc 38)
5022 Rombach (Aarau): Obstgarten,
Bibersteinstrasse 54; tel: (062) 839 80 80;
fax: (062) 839 80 89 (acc 34)
2024 St-Aubin: Le Devens, Socio-medical Home;
tel: (032) 836 27 29; fax: (032) 836 27 28
(acc 34)
9205 Waldkirch: Hasenberg; tel: (071) 434 61 61;
fax: (071) 434 61 71 (acc 48) (agriculture
and workshop)

Community Centres
Hochfeld, Bern; Eidmattegge, Zürich; Gelber
Stern, Zürich; Open Heart, Zürich; Genève.

Emergency Shelters
1201 Genève: Accueil de Nuit, Chemin
Galiffe 4; tel: (022) 388 22 00;
fax: (022) 338 22 01 (acc 40)
1005 Lausanne: La Marmotte, Rue du Vallon 17;
tel: (021) 311 79 12 (acc 30)

Holiday Flats
3715 Adelboden: Chalet Bethel;
tel: (033) 673 21 62 (acc 20)

Homes for the Aged
3013 Bern: Lorrainehof, Lorrainestrasse 34-38;
tel: (031) 330 16 16; fax: (031) 330 16 00
(acc 50 + 10 flats) (health care)
1814 La Tour-de-Peilz: Le Phare-Elim,
Ave de la Paix 11, case postale 444;
tel: (021) 977 33 33; fax: (021) 977 33 90
(acc 44) (health care)
1201 Genève: Résidence Amitié (health care),
Rue Baudit 1; tel: (022) 919 95 95;
fax: (022) 740 30 11 (acc 52) (health care)
2000 Neuchâtel: Le Foyer, Rue de l'Ecluse 18;
tel: (032) 729 20 20 (acc 30) (health care)

Homes for Children
8344 Bäretswil: Sunnemätteli Home for
Handicapped Children, Wirzwil,
Rüggenthalstrasse 71; tel: (044) 939 11 88;
fax (044) 979 10 45 (acc 16)
4054 Basel: Kinderhaus Holee,
Nenzlingerstrasse 2; tel: (061) 301 24 50;
fax: (061) 301 24 44 (acc 24)

Young Salvationists rehearse in the delightful woodland setting of the territory's music and gospel arts camp

8932 Mettmenstetten: Kinderheim Paradies;
tel: (044) 768 58 00; fax: (044) 768 58 19
(acc 24)
3110 Münsingen: Kinderheim Sonnhalde,
Standweg 7; tel: (031) 721 08 06;
fax: (031) 721 42 72 (acc 24)

Hostels for Men
4058 Basel: Rheinblick, Rheingasse 80;
tel: (061) 666 66 77; fax: (061) 666 66 78
(acc 53)
8004 Zürich: Dienerstrasse 76; tel: (044) 298 90 80;
fax: (044) 242 41 71 (acc 26)
8005 Zürich: Geroldstrasse 27;
tel: (043) 204 10 20; fax: (043) 204 10 21
(acc 25)

Hostels for Men and Women
3006 Bern: Passantenheim, Muristrasse 6;
tel: (031) 351 80 27; fax: (031) 351 46 97
(acc 43)
2503 Biel: Haus am Quai, Oberer Quai 12;
tel: (032) 322 68 38; fax: (032) 322 60 64
(acc 24)
3600 Thun: Passantenheim, Waisenhausstrasse 26;
tel: (033) 222 69 20; fax: (033) 222 69 25
(acc 15)

8400 Winterthur: Wartstrasse 40;
tel: (052) 208 90 50; fax: (052) 208 90 59
(acc 34)
8026 Zürich: Molkenstrasse 6;
tel: (044) 298 90 00; fax: (044) 242 38 97
(acc 85)

Hostel for Women
4058 Basel: Frauenwohnheim,
Alemannengasse 7; tel: (061) 681 34 70;
fax: (061) 681 34 72 (acc 37)

Young Women's Residence
4059 Basel: Schlössli, Eichhornstrasse 21;
tel: (061) 335 31 10; fax: (061) 335 31 29
(acc 14)

Refugee Work
Main Office: 3008 Bern: Effingerstrasse 67;
tel: (031) 380 18 80; fax: (031) 398 04 28
(12 centres, 6 coordination offices)

Social Flats
3012 Bern: Begleitetes Wohnen,
Waldheimstrasse 16; tel: (031) 302 02 35
(acc 25 flats)

Switzerland, Austria and Hungary Territory

HOTELS

4055 Basel: Alegria B&B, Habsburgerstrasse 15;
tel: (061) 387 91 10; fax: (061) 381 77 63
1204 Genève: Bel' Espérance, Rue de la
Vallée 1; tel: (022) 818 37 37;
fax: (022) 818 37 73 (acc 65 beds, 40 rooms)
3852 Ringgenberg: Guesthouse, Vordorf 264;
tel: (033) 822 70 25; fax: (033) 822 70 74
(acc 24 beds, 12 rooms)

YOUTH CENTRES
Under THQ
3715 Adelboden (acc 75)

Under DHQ
Nordwestschweiz: 4462 Rickenbach, Waldegg
(acc 100)
Division Romande: 1451 Les Rasses (acc 150)
Ost-Division: 8712 Stäfa (acc 55)

AUSTRIA
City Command: AT-1020 Vienna
Salztor-Zentrum, Grosse Schiffgasse 3;
tel: [43] (1) 214 48 30;
fax: [43] (1) 214 48 30 55;
City Commander: Maj Hans-Marcel Leber

Hostel for Men
AT-1020 Vienna: SalztorZentrum,
Grosse Schiffgasse 3; tel: [43] (1) 214 48 30 27;
fax: [43] (1) 214 48 30 55 (acc men 60,
sheltered housing 42, external flats 21)

HUNGARY REGION
Regional Headquarters: Bajnok utca 25,
HU-1063 Budapest VI, Hungary;
tel: [36] (1) 332 3324; fax: [36] (1) 373 0010;
email: kozponti@swi.salvationarmy.org;
website: www.udvhadsereg.org
Regional Officer: Capt Andrew Morgan

STATISTICS
Officers 13 (active 10 retired 3) Employees 57
Corps 4 Outposts 1 Institutions 3
Senior Soldiers 35 Adherents 18 Junior
Soldiers 5

STAFF
Asst Regional Officer: Capt Darlene Morgan
Administrative Assistant: Laura Halmaghi
Finance: Katalin Kabai

SOCIAL WORK
Hostel for Men
'Új Remenység Háza', HU-1086 Budapest VIII,
Dobozi utca 29; tel: [36] (1) 314 2775
(acc 98)

Rehabilitation Home for Women
'Válaszút Háza', HU-1171 Budapest XVII,
Lemberg utca 38-42; tel: [36] (1) 259 1095
(acc 24)

Refuge for Maltreated Women and Children
'Fény Hazá', IV utca 16, HU-1172 Budapest XVII;
tel/fax: [36] (1) 257 9461 (acc 20, inc mothers
with children)

Day Drop-In Centre
HU-1171 Budapest XVII, Lemberg utca 38-42;
tel: [36] (1) 259 1095 (acc 50)

SOUTHERN AFRICA: The fledgling Salvation Army in Namibia is growing, as more soldiers are enrolled during a visit by the territorial leaders, Commissioners André and Silvia Cox

TAIWAN REGION

Regional leaders:
Majors Michael and Annette Coleman

Regional Commander:
Major Michael Coleman (1 May 2008)

Regional Headquarters: 3/F, 273 Tun Hwa South Road, Section 2, Da-an District, Taipei 106

Postal address: PO Box 44-100, Taipei, Taiwan

Tel: [886] (02) 2738 1079/1171; fax: [886] (02) 2738 5422;

email: RHQAdmin@taw.salvationarmy.org; website: www.salvationarmy.org.tw

Pioneered in 1928 by Colonel Yasowo Segawa, Salvation Army work in Taiwan was curtailed by the Second World War. Following initiatives by two American servicemen, operations were officially re-established in October 1965 by Colonel and Mrs George Lancashire. Taiwan has been a separate region since 1997.

Zone: South Pacific and East Asia
Country included in the region: Taiwan
'The Salvation Army' in Taiwanese (Hokkien): Kiu Se Kuen; in Mandarin: Chiu Shih Chun
Languages in which the gospel is preached: English, Mandarin, Taiwanese (Hokkien)
Periodical: *Taiwan Regional News*

THE second half of 2009 was dominated by the relief work carried out in response to Typhoon Morakot. Taiwan's worst storm in recorded history struck on 8 August, killing more than 650 people, making 25,000 homeless, and causing US$6.6 billion worth of infrastructure damage.

Salvationists were quick to volunteer their help in the relief operations and are continuing to support victims. The relief work conducted by The Salvation Army included cleaning homes and villages, distributing cleaning material, clothes and educational material, and providing water filters and power generators

to schools in remote locations.

A new five-year strategy, launched at the 'Discover Vision' Congress in June 2009, formally began at the beginning of 2010, but even prior to that the consultation and planning phases inspired mission focus and growth that resulted in a 30 per cent increase in indoor attendances for 2009.

There has been a growing interest in developing mission capacity. Several corps stepped up evangelism training programmes for soldiers and began a number of outreach initiatives.

The region continues to strengthen

its support structures through training (in such fields as leadership and finance), also reviewing and upgrading its strategic focus and the use of specialist expertise.

STATISTICS
Officers 18 (active 16 retired 2)
Corps with Community Centres 5 **Social Services Centres** 3
Senior Soldiers 185 **Adherents** 83 **Junior Soldiers** 34

STAFF
Women's Ministries: Maj Annette Coleman (RPWM) Maj Mary Tsou (WMO)
Administration Officer: Maj Stephen Tsou

Regional Mission and Resource Officers:
(Programme Development) Maj Robert Duncan
(Social Programmes) Maj Leanne Duncan
Youth: Capt Grace Weng

SOCIAL SERVICES
Homeless
Taipei Homeless Caring Centre: c/o 1/F, No 42, Lane 65, Jin Si St., Taipei 103

Youth
Puli Youth Services Centre: No 192 Pei Hwang Rd, Puli Town, Nantou County 545 (acc 60)

COMMUNITY SERVICES
Puli Community Development Centre:
c/o No 62-1, Shueitou Rd, Puli Town, Nantou County 545

UNITED KINGDOM: As members of Chalk Farm Band played on the Garden Terrace at the House of Commons, a number of residents who had been helped by The Salvation Army's Homelessness Services told their stories to MPs and peers during a parliamentary reception. Later in the year the Speaker of the House of Commons, John Bercow MP (*left*), supported the Army's Soup Kitchen Challenge Day, when soup was provided by the Covent Garden Food Company.

The Salvation Army's World Youth Convention took place in Stockholm, Sweden, during July 2010. More than 1,000 delegates represented 94 of the 121 countries where the Army is operating.

Although from many different countries, and displaying varied cultures, the youth convention delegates found no difficulty in making friends. Each day they celebrated enthusiastically and witnessed to being one in Christ Jesus with their fellow Salvationists from around the world.

Musicians and creative arts groups in the 'Praise Party' provided a vibrant and God-glorifying occasion during the convention as musicians and dancers from (*left to right*) Zambia, Mizoram (India), Australia and Indonesia expressed their joy in varied ways

Principal guest speaker at the convention, General Shaw Clifton (*above left*) also led the closing meeting of dedication. The mercy seat was lined several times and the stage filled to overflowing with delegates kneeling at drums. Many sought a deeper relationship with Jesus; others responded to the General's call to full-time service for God as Salvation Army officers.

BRAZIL: A young Salvationist teaches music to children from the slums of the *favelas* in Rio de Janeiro, where The Salvation Army is seeking to provide young people with better opportunities in life

LIBERIA: Salvationists enthusiastically proclaim their faith in Jesus as they march through one of the poorer districts of Monrovia

ZAMBIA: Dressed in colourful *chitenge* wear, women participate in their territorial home league rally. The territory has a vibrant expression of ministry among women.

CONGO BRAZZAVILLE: Home league members at the Ouenze Corps express the joy they find in worshipping Jesus in The Salvation Army

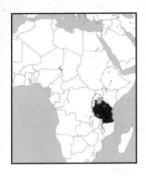

TANZANIA TERRITORY

Territorial leaders:
Colonels Hezekiel and Mirriam Mavundla

Territorial Commander:
Colonel Hezekiel Mavundla (1 Feb 2008)

Chief Secretary:
Lieut-Colonel Christopher Mabuto
(1 Jul 2010)

Territorial Headquarters: Kilwa Road, Dar es Salaam

Postal address: PO Box 1273, Dar es Salaam, Tanzania

Tel/fax: [255] (22) 2850468/2850542

Adjutant and Mrs Francis Dare began Salvation Army work in Tabora, Tanzania (formerly known as Tanganyika), in November 1933, as part of the East Africa Territory. In 1950, at the request for assistance from the Colonial Governor, The Salvation Army set up Mgulani Camp, where the Tanzania Headquarters is now located. Tanzania became a separate command on 1 October 1998 and was elevated to territory status on 1 February 2008.

Zone: Africa
Country included in the territory: Tanzania
'The Salvation Army' in Kiswahili: Jeshi la Wokovu
Languages in which the gospel is preached: Kiswahili and various tribal languages

BUILDING on the themes of the past two years – 'United in Christ' and 'Forward Together' – the territory continues to encourage its people to work together in harmony, advancing with one purpose.

Tanzania is a large country with many tribes and clans, but in some areas this has caused tension among communities. In most of these areas the Church, including The Salvation Army, has worked amid difficult situations. The message of unity has been preached wherever possible, with Jesus' words as the key verse: 'Remain united to me, and I will remain united to you' (John 15:4, *GNB*).

Projects continue to be a vehicle that takes the message of hope and salvation to communities. Kids clubs run in some of the corps provide opportunities to introduce children to the gospel.

Kwetu Counselling Centre, part of the territory's anti-human-trafficking programme, continues to rescue girls from the streets of Dar es Salaam and provide shelter and advice before they are reunited with their parents and relatives.

There are encouraging signs around the territory as Salvationists work together in building and renovating their corps halls and officers' quarters. They make bricks and collect stones for laying solid foundations for these buildings. With money from the home league helping-hand scheme, many officers' quarters have been renovated and others newly furnished.

Two women's Bible conferences were conducted under the leadership of Commissioners Hope Mungate and Vinece Chigariro (Zimbabwe). Using the theme 'Rise, Woman, Stand and Press On', the visiting speakers brought encouragement and spiritual renewal to the delegates.

In February 2010 the territory's first public relations seminar was held at THQ, conducted by Major Daniel Kasuso (Southern Africa). This will help in creating a Public Relations Department within the territory.

STATISTICS
Officers 133 (active 126 retired 7) **Cadets** (2nd Yr) 12 **Employees** 155
Corps 65 **Outposts** 64 **Schools** 2 **Day Care Centres** 17 **Hostel** 1
Senior Soldiers 5,845 **Junior Soldiers** 3,671

STAFF
Women's Ministries: Col Mirriam Mavundla (TPWM) Lt-Col Anne Mabuto (TSWM) Maj Tamali Mwalukani (LOMS/ SAMF)
Education: Maj Musa Magaigwa
Field: Maj Wilson Mwalukani
Finance: Maj Yesuvadian Manoharan
Projects: Mr Frederick Urembo
Property: Capt Peter Tingo
Social Services: Maj Joy Paxton
Sponsorship: Maj Vethamony Manoharan
Training: Maj Lynda Levis
Youth and Candidates: Maj Fanuel Ndabila

DIVISIONS
Mbeya: PO Box 1214, Mbeya; tel: (025) 2560009; Majs Samuel and Mary Mkami
Tarime: PO Box 37, Tarime; tel: (028) 2690095; Majs Yohana and Jesinala Msongwe

DISTRICTS
Coastal: PO Box 7622, Dar es Salaam; tel: (022) 2860365; Capt James Mwita
Mwanza: PO Box 11267, Mwanza; tel: (028) 40123; Capt James Gitangita
Serengeti: PO Box 28, Mugumu; tel: (028) 2621434; Capt Christopher Ighoty

TRAINING COLLEGE
PO Box 1273, Dar es Salaam

AGRICULTURE DEVELOPMENT PROGRAMME
PO Box 1273, Dar es Salaam

EDUCATIONAL WORK
College for Business Management and Administration
Shukrani International College for Business Management and Administration, PO Box 535, Mbeya; tel: (00255) (0)25 2504404; fax: (00255) (0)25 2500202

Primary School for the Physically Handicapped
Matumaini School, PO Box 1273, Dar es Salaam; tel: (022) 2851861 (acc 175)

Secondary School
Itundu School, PO Box 2994, Mbeya

SOCIAL SERVICES
Kwetu Counselling and Psycho-Social Support Services: PO Box 1273, Dar es Salaam
Mbagala Girls' Home: PO Box 1273, Dar es Salaam
Mgulani Hostel and Conference Centre: PO Box 1273, Dar es Salaam; tel: (022) 2851467 (acc 110)
Vocational Training Workshop: PO Box 1273, Dar es Salaam

Anti-Human Trafficking Programmes

Rehabilitation and Reunification Services for Orphans and Vulnerable Children

PROJECTS
Community counselling, Community psycho-social support programme for orphans and vulnerable children, Gardening and farming activities, Goat banks schemes, Home-based care services, Literacy classes, Micro-credit schemes, Nutrition programmes, Primary health care, Training and economic empowerment for rural women, Water and sanitation programmes

UGANDA COMMAND

Command leaders:
Lieut-Colonels Moses and Sarah Wandulu

Officer Commanding:
Lieut-Colonel Moses Wandulu (1 Jul 2007)

General Secretary:
Major Eugene Bamanabio (1 Jan 2010)

Command Headquarters: Plot 78-82 Lugogo Bypass, Kampala

Postal address: PO Box 11776, Kampala, Uganda

Tel: [256] 41 533901; Kampala mobile: [256] 752 375782

The Salvation Army opened fire in Uganda in 1931 when Captain and Mrs Edward Osborne unfurled the flag in Mbale, as part of the East Africa Territory. In September 1977 the Army's religious teaching was banned and in June 1978 its ministry, including social work, was proscribed. In 1980 Majors Leonard and Dorothy Millar began work with the persecuted Salvationists to re-establish The Salvation Army. Uganda became a separate command on 1 November 2005.

Zone: Africa
Country included in the command: Uganda
'The Salvation Army' in Kiswahili: Jeshi La Wokovu; in Luganda: Eje Liobulokozi
Languages in which the gospel is preached: English, Kiswahili, Luganda and a number of tribal languages

AS the command structures developed, demand for services increased and the need for a long-term strategy to effectively manage and deploy mission resources became urgent. In April 2010, officers and employees from every department of the Army's work participated in a three-day workshop in Mbale.

Facilitated by Dr Paul Bukuluki (Medical Anthropologist Consultant, Makerere University, Kampala) and Mr Peter Kayiira Byansi (Africa Social Development and Health Initiatives Consultancy), the delegates created a five-year strategy to define the way forward for the Army in Uganda.

This strategic plan – to provide mission priorities and objectives, and to formulate policies and guidelines to ensure best practice – will be reviewed annually.

Heavy rains in Bududa and Manafwa caused landslides in which lives were lost and property was destroyed. The Command Projects Office organised the distribution of food, mosquito nets and clothing to people affected by the disaster.

Thirty delegates benefited from training in community project management support systems, given by Major Lalsangpuii and Mrs Hanna Ferguson (International Projects and Development Services, IHQ) in April.

'Seek God's Face and Make A Difference' was the theme of the Women Leaders' Conference held in May at the training college in Jinja. Led by Lieut-Colonel Sarah Wandulu (CPWM) and Major Brigitte Bamanabio, (CSWM), the women had opportunity to learn new things. They also donated 53,300 shillings for necessary repairs to the college.

STATISTICS

Officers 61 (active 56 retired 4) **Envoys** 2
Corps leaders 94 **Cadets** 24 **Employees** 86
Corps 75 **Outposts and Outreach Centres** 18
Pre-primary Schools 2 **Day Care Centre** 1
Primary Schools 11 **Vocational Centres** 3
Institutions 3
Senior Soldiers 7,271 **Junior Soldiers** 6,540
Personnel serving outside the command
Officers 2

STAFF

Women's Ministries: Lt-Col Sarah Wandulu (CPWM) Maj Brigitte Bamanabio (CSWM) Maj Nolega Imbiakha (CCMS/Retired Officers Sec)
Field: Maj Daniel Imbiakha
Finance: Capt Patrick Sithole
Projects: Maj Emmanuel Sichibona
Property: tba
Social Services: Capt Christine Ambenge
Statistics: Capt Jesline Sithole
Training: Maj Trustmore Muzorori
Youth: Capt Christine Ambenge
Candidates: Capt Jesline Sithole

DIVISION

Central: PO Box 11776, Kampala; Majs Emmanuel and Irene Sichibona
Eastern: PO Box 168, Tororo; Majs Fred and Grace Walukano
Mbale: PO Box 2214, Mbale; Majs Peter and Elizabeth Soita

Southern: P.O. Box 2012, Busia, Majs Moses and Achola Itwalume
West: P.O.Box 73, Kigumba via Masindi; Majs Bramwell and Margaret Simiyu

DISTRICTS

Mulimani: c/o PO Box 168, Tororo; Majs George and Annette Musamali
Sebei: c/o PO Box 2214, Mbale; Maj Esau Wekala

TRAINING COLLEGE

Jinja

SOCIAL SERVICES

Children's Home
Tororo: PO Box 48, Tororo; tel: 045-45244 (acc 54)

Community Centre
Kampala: PO Box 11776, Kampala; tel: 041-532517

Home for Children with Physically Disabilities
Home of Joy, PO Box 1186, Kampala; tel: 041-542409 (acc 30)

Vocational Training Workshops
Kampala (carpentry, catering, tailoring): PO Box 11776, Kampala
Lira (carpentry, tailoring, building): PO Box 13, Lira
Mbalala (carpentry, tailoring): PO Box 11776, Mbalala

PROJECTS

'Peace for African Child' (Education Programme)
PO Box 11776, Kampala

SAU-OVC Programme
HIV/Aids Education for Orphans and Vulnerable Children: PO Box 11776, Kampala; tel: 041-533113

WORTH Programme
Income Generation for Women: PO Box 2214, Mbale; tel: 045-79295

UNITED KINGDOM TERRITORY WITH THE REPUBLIC OF IRELAND

Territorial leaders:
Commissioners John and Elizabeth Matear

Territorial Commander:
Commissioner John Matear (2 Apr 2006)

Chief Secretary:
Colonel Brian Peddle (1 Jun 2009)

Territorial Headquarters: 101 Newington Causeway, London SE1 6BN, UK

Tel: [44] 20 7367 4500; email: thq@salvationarmy.org.uk;

website: www.salvationarmy.org.uk

The foundation of the territory dates from the earliest formation of The Salvation Army – prior to the adoption of that title in 1878 – when in July 1865 the Founder, William Booth, took charge of a mission to the East End of London. Certain UK corps were first established as Christian Mission stations.

Throughout the Army's history its work in this geographical area has been organised in a variety of forms and territories, but before 1990 these were all part of International Headquarters administration. However, on 1 November 1990 a restructuring occurred so that now the United Kingdom Territory is separate from International Headquarters and under a single command similar to that of the Army's other territories.

Zone: Europe
Countries included in the territory: Channel Islands, Isle of Man, Republic of Ireland, United Kingdom of Great Britain and Northern Ireland
Languages in which the gospel is preached: English, Korean, Urdu, Welsh
'The Salvation Army' in Welsh: Byddin Yr Iachawdwriaeth
Periodicals: *Kids Alive!*, *Salvationist*, *The War Cry*

MARKET research in 2009 showed that as well as considering The Salvation Army to be caring, compassionate and trustworthy, the public also associated the movement most strongly with homelessness and then with bands, uniforms and religion. Salvationists themselves know it is their Christian faith that is the first motivation of their lives and work, and the territory has continued to promote its strategic mission priority of making disciples.

The rebranding of hostels as 'Lifehouses' in February 2010 – a name chosen by service users – showed a continued commitment to rebuilding the lives of the homeless. As part of this, the Employment Plus scheme created 'animateur' roles for hundreds of unemployed young people.

Meanwhile the *Seeds of Exclusion 2009* report released in July carried further detailed research and analysis into the causes of social exclusion – probably the most important research by The Salvation Army in the UK since William Booth's social manifesto *In Darkest England and the Way Out*.

Concern with social justice was also emphasised when a 'think-tank' met in February 2010, and when soon-to-be Deputy Prime Minister Nick Clegg gave the first of a series of lectures at THQ in March 2010. The previous May he had visited Logos House, Bristol, and commended the contribution of faith communities.

In November 2009 the then Prime Minister Gordon Brown provided a video message for the territory's annual carol concert in London's Royal Albert Hall.

When a General Election was called for spring 2010, the Army issued a manifesto challenging all political parties to maintain funding and support faith-based initiatives. In a time of national financial stringencies, public fundraising held up surprisingly well, with the Army ranked as the seventh largest charity based on voluntarily donated income, and one of the most cost-effective. A poll of MPs and peers in November 2009 voted the Army the Best Social, Religious or Family Charity.

As usual there was a host of imaginative programme and mission initiatives over the year, many on a local basis. In 135 corps an experiment in engaging with Back To Church Sunday in September 2009 brought positive results.

Many centres revitalised their programmes for children, some by creating 'messy church' activities and others by fostering new links with schools. A children's sports camp, 'In Touch', was run in east London in July 2009, and it was planned to roll out the pattern in other locations in 2010.

The ALOVE youth programme in 2009 focused on discipleship, in line with the territory's strategic mission priority, emphasising training, while at the same time developing strategies to reach excluded young people through alternative education such as RockSchool and Starfish.

Two major new social centres were opened on the south coast in December 2009: Booth Centre replaced the Mountbatten Centre in Southampton, and Catherine Booth House relocated to new premises in Southsea. In Scotland the Eva Burrows First-Stop Project in Cambuslang was inaugurated in February 2010. In the same month the planned development of the William Booth College began.

The year 2009 saw the 50th anniversary of over-60 clubs, celebrated at the New Horizons holiday week, Bognor Regis, in September; and of The Salvation Army Housing Association, marked at the Hopetown Centre in July. Other anniversaries included 30 years of the International Staff Songsters and 125 years of the Family Tracing Service.

In her role as Moderator of the Free Churches, Commissioner Betty Matear signed a personal covenant with the other three presidents of Churches Together in England at a CTE conference in September 2009, a sign of friendship and joint commitment to unity and mission.

The Best of Both Worlds, the autobiography of Colonel Brindley Boon, was published in time for the Gospel Arts Concert in June 2009 just three months after his promotion to Glory. The year also saw the release of *A Moment in Time* (a CD version of the book *The Time ... the Place*) and numerous music CDs and DVDs.

THE SALVATION ARMY TRUSTEE COMPANY

Registered Office: 101 Newington Causeway, London SE1 6BN

THE SALVATION ARMY (REPUBLIC OF IRELAND)

Registered Office: 114 Marlborough St, Dublin 1, Republic of Ireland

STATISTICS

Officers 2,701 (active 1,223 retired 1,478)
 Cadets (1st Yr) 23 (2nd Yr) 23 (+ 14 distance learning cadets) **Employees** 5,262
Corps/Outreach Centres/New Plants 696
 Social Services Centres 115 **Red Shield Defence Services Clubs** 24 **Mobile Units for Service Personnel** 11
Senior Soldiers 30,902 **Adherents** 9,469
 Junior Soldiers 4,464
Personnel serving outside territory Officers 76 Layworkers 5

STAFF

Women's Ministries: Comr Elizabeth Matear (TPWM) Col Rosalie Peddle (TSWM)
Asst Chief Sec: Lt-Col Sylvia Hinton

Executive Sec to Territorial Leadership: Lt-Col Sylvia Hinton
International Staff Band: B/M Dr Stephen Cobb
International Staff Songsters: S/L Mrs Dorothy Nancekievill
Sec for Business Administration: Lt-Col David Hinton
 Asst Sec for Business Administration (Risk and Research): Mr David Rice
 Company Sec: Maj Alan Read
 Finance: Maj Alan Read
 Internal Audit: Mr Phil Goss
 Property: Mr Keith Manners
 Strategic Information: Mr Martyn Croft
 SAGIC: Mr John Mott
 Trade: Mr Trevor Caffull
Sec for Communications: Lt-Col Marion Drew
 Editor-in-Chief and Publishing Sec: Maj Leanne Ruthven
 Editors: *Salvationist*: Maj Stephen Poxon
  The War Cry: Maj Nigel Bovey
  Kids Alive!: Mr Justin Reeves
 Head of Media: Cathy Le Feuvre
 Public Affairs Officer: Dr Helen Cameron
 Territorial Ecumenical Officer: Maj John Read
 International Heritage Centre: Maj Stephen Grinsted (Director)
 Schools and Colleges Unit: Maj Stephen Grinsted (Director)
 Marketing and Fundraising: Mr Julius Wolff-Ingham
Sec for Personnel: Lt-Col George Pilkington
 Asst Sec for Personnel: Maj Angela Irving
 Human Resources (Employees): Mr Ian Hammond
 Overseas Services Sec: Maj Pam Cameron
 Pastoral Care Unit: Maj Stephen Gowler
 Retired Officers Sec: Maj James Williams
 Safeguarding: Mr Dean Juster
Sec for Programme: Lt-Col Ian Barr
 Asst Sec for Programme: Maj Ivor Telfer
 Asst Sec for Programme: Maj Hannelise Tvedt
 Anti-Trafficking Response: Maj Anne Read
 Employment Plus: Maj Ivor Telfer
 Evangelism: Maj Paul Main
  Adult and Family Ministries: Majs John and Lorna Smith
  Children's and Youth Ministries: Majs Mark and Andrea Sawyer (ALOVE) Maj Denise Cooper
  Mission Development Unit: Maj Noel Wright
  Music Ministries: B/M Dr Stephen Cobb
 International Development: Maj Heather Poxon

Family Tracing: Maj Graham Kinsley
Research and Development: Mr Richard Bradbury
Social Services: Maj Ray Irving (SocS Sec); Maj Jane Cowell (Deputy – Head of Operations); Homelessness Services: Mr Mitch Menagh; Older People's Services: Mrs Elaine Cobb
Red Shield Defence and Emergency Services: Maj Muriel McClenahan
Special Events: Mr Melvin Hart

WILLIAM BOOTH COLLEGE

Denmark Hill, London SE5 8BQ;
tel: (020) 7326 2700; fax: (020) 7326 2750
Principal: Maj Norman Ord
Directors of School for Officer Training: Training Programme: Capt Sheila Dunkinson Spiritual Programme: Capt Gordon Cotterill
Director of School for In-Service Training and Development: Maj Judith Payne
Territorial Candidates Director: Maj Mark Herbert

INTERNATIONAL HERITAGE CENTRE (including The William Booth Birthplace Museum, Nottingham) AND SCHOOLS AND COLLEGES UNIT

Denmark Hill, London SE5 8BQ;
tel: (020) 7737 3327;
email: heritage@salvationarmy.org.uk;
Director: Maj Stephen Grinsted

SCOTLAND SECRETARIAT

12a Dryden Rd, Loanhead, Midlothian EH20 9LZ; tel: (0131) 440 9100; fax: (0131) 440 9111;
Scotland Sec: Lt-Col Alan Burns

DIVISIONS

Anglia: 2 Barton Way, Norwich NR1 1DL; tel: (01603) 724 400; fax: (01603) 724 411; Maj David Jackson (DC) Maj Joy Allchin (DDWM)
Central North: 80 Eccles New Rd, Salford, Gtr Manchester M5 4DU; tel: (0161) 743 3900; fax: (0161) 743 3911; Majs Melvyn and Kathleen Jones
Central South: 16c Cowley Rd, Uxbridge, UB8 2LT; tel: (01895) 208800; fax: (01895) 208811; Maj Christine Bailey
East Midlands: Paisley Grove, Chilwell, Nottingham NG9 6DJ; tel: (0115) 983 5000; fax: (0115) 983 5011; Lt-Cols Mike and Wendy Caffull

East Scotland: 12a Dryden Rd, Loanhead, Midlothian EH20 9LZ; tel: (0131) 440 9100; fax: (0131) 440 9111; Lt-Cols Alan and Alison Burns
Ireland: 12 Station Mews, Sydenham, Belfast BT4 1TL; tel: (028) 9067 5000; fax: (028) 9067 5011; Majs Alan and Linda Watters
London Central: 1 Tiverton St, London SE1 6NT; tel: (020) 7378 1021; fax: (020) 7378 1026; Lt-Cols Michael and Joan Parker
London North-East: Maldon Rd, Hatfield Peverel, Chelmsford CM3 2HL; tel: (01245) 383000; fax: (01245) 383 011; Maj Carol Bailey
London South-East: 1 East Court, Enterprise Rd, Maidstone ME15 6JF; tel: (01622) 775000; fax: (01622) 775011; Lt-Cols Anthony and Gillian Cotterill
North Scotland: Deer Rd, Woodside, Aberdeen AB24 2BL; tel: (01224) 496000; fax: (01224) 496011; Majs Denis and Olive Lomax
North-Western: 16 Faraday Rd, Wavertree Technology Park, Liverpool L13 1EH; tel: (0151) 252 6100; fax: (0151) 252 6111; Majs Michael and Lynn Highton
Northern: Balliol Business Park West, Newcastle upon Tyne NE12 8EW; tel: (0191) 238 1800; fax: (0191) 238 1811; Majs Melvin and Suzanne Fincham
South and Mid Wales: East Moors Rd, Ocean Park, Cardiff CF24 5SA; tel: (029) 2044 0600; fax: (029) 2044 0611; Majs Peter and Sandra Moran
South-Western: 6 Marlborough Court, Manaton Close, Matford Business Park, Exeter EX2 8PF; tel: (01392) 822100; fax: (01392) 822111; Maj Martin Hill (DC) Maj Hélène Carey (DDWM)
Southern: 6-8 Little Park Farm Rd, Segensworth, Fareham PO15 5TD; tel: (01489) 566800; fax: (01489) 566811; Lt-Cols Graham and Kirsten Owen
West Midlands: 102 Unett St North, Hockley, Birmingham B19 3BZ; tel: (0121) 507 8500; fax: (0121) 507 8511; Maj Samuel Edgar (DC) Maj Amanda White (DDWM)
West Scotland: 4 Buchanan Court, Cumbernauld Rd, Stepps, Glasgow G33 6HZ; tel: (0141) 779 5000; fax: (0141) 779 5011; Majs Victor and Miriam Kennedy
Yorkshire: 1 Cadman Court, Hanley Rd, Morley, Leeds LS27 0RX; tel: (0113) 281 0100; fax: (0113) 281 0111; Lt-Cols William and Gillian Heeley

CONFERENCE CENTRES

Carfax: Bath BA2 4BS; tel: (01225) 462089
St Christopher's: 15 Sea Rd, Westgate-on-Sea,
   Kent; tel: (01932) 782196
Sunbury Court (incl Recreation Centre and Log
   Cabin): Lwr Hampton Rd, Sunbury-on-Thames,
   Middlesex TW16 5PL; tel: (01932) 782196

CONFERENCE AND YOUTH CENTRE

Sunbury Court, Log Cabin and Recreational
   Centre: Lwr Hampton Rd, Sunbury-on-Thames,
   Middlesex TW16 5PL; tel: (01932) 782196

SELF-CATERING ACCOMMODATION

Caldew House: Sebergham, Cumbria;
   tel: (01225) 462089 (large house)
St Christopher's: Westgate-on-Sea, Kent;
   tel: (01932) 782196 (5 flats)
Sunbury Court, Log Cabin and Recreational
   Centre: Lower Hampton Rd, Sunbury-on-
   Thames, Middlesex TW16 5PL;
   tel: (01932) 782196

FAMILY TRACING SERVICE

101 Newington Causeway, London SE1 6BN;
   tel: (020) 7367 4747; fax: (020) 7367 4723

FARM

Hadleigh: Castle Lane, Hadleigh, Benfleet,
   Essex; tel: (01702) 558550

HOTELS

Bath: Carfax Hotel, Gt Pulteney St, Bath
   BA2 4BS; tel: (01225) 462089
Bournemouth: Cliff House, 13 Belle Vue Rd,
   Southbourne, Dorset BH6 3DA;
   tel: (01202) 424701 (office);
   (01202) 425852 (guests)
Westgate-on-Sea: St Christopher's, 15 Sea Rd,
   Westgate-on-Sea, Kent CT8 8SA;
   tel: (01932) 782196

INSURANCE CORPORATION

The Salvation Army General Insurance
   Corporation Ltd, Faith House,
   23-24 Lovat Lane, London EC3R 8EB;
   tel: 0845 634 0260; fax: 0845 634 0263

PASTORAL CARE UNIT

Administration (inc Trauma Care Programme):
   101 Newington Causeway, London SE1 6BN;
   tel: (020) 7367 6580;
   After-office hours mobile: 0779 699 1579
Counselling Services: 1 Water Lane, Stratford,
   London E15 4LU; tel: (020) 8536 5480;
   fax: (020) 8536 5489

Pastoral Support:
   London Central, London North-East, UKT
      personnel departing/arriving from overseas;
      tel: (020) 7367 6580; mobile: 07796 991579
   Central South, London South-East, Southern,
      South-Western; tel: (01895) 252794
   Central North, North-Western, South and Mid
      Wales, West Midlands; tel: (01282) 697378
   Northern, Yorkshire, East Midlands, Anglia:
      tel: (01924) 420407
   Scotland and Ireland: tel: (01506) 854474
Director: Maj Stephen Gowler

TRADE (SP&S)

Head Office (and shop): 66-78 Denington Rd,
   Denington Industrial Estate, Wellingborough,
   Northants NN8 2QH; tel: (01933) 445445
   (mail order); fax: (01933) 445415
Shop: 1 Tiverton St, London SE1 6NT

TRADING (SA TRADING CO LTD)

66-78 Denington Rd, Denington Industrial
   Estate, Wellingborough, Northants NN8 2QH
Textile Recycling Division:
   tel: (01933) 441086; fax: (01933) 445449;
   email: paul.ozanne@satradingco.org
Charity Shops Division:
   tel: (01933) 441807; fax: (01933) 442942;
   email: reception@satradingco.org

SOCIAL SERVICES DEPARTMENT
Centres for Older People

Bath: Smallcombe House, Bathwick Hill, BA2 6EJ;
   tel: (01225) 465694; fax: (01225) 465769
   (acc men and women 32, sheltered flat 1)
Buxton: The Hawthorns, Burlington Rd,
   SK17 9AR; tel: (01298) 23700;
   fax: (01298) 28761 (acc 34)
Coventry: Youell Court, Skipworth Rd,
   Binley CV3 2XA; tel (024) 76561300;
   fax: (024) 76561306 (acc 40)
Edinburgh:
   Davidson House, 266 Colinton Rd, EH14 1DT;
      tel: (0131) 441 2117 fax: (0131) 441 2109
      (acc 40)
   Eagle Lodge, 48 Ferry Rd, EH5 2DL;
      tel: (0131) 551 1611; fax: (0131) 551 1644
      (acc 33)
Glasgow: Eva Burrows Day Centre, Clyde Place,
   Halfway, Cambuslang G72 7QT;
   tel: (0141) 646 1461 (places 112)
Hassocks: Villa Adastra, 79 Keymer Rd,
   BN6 8QH; tel: (01273) 842184;
   fax (01273) 841420 (acc 40, day centre 20)
Holywood: The Sir Samuel Kelly Memorial
   Home, 39 Bangor Rd, Co Down BT18 0NE;

tel: (028) 9042 2293; fax: (028) 9042 7361 (acc 39)

London:

Alver Bank, 17 West Rd, Clapham SW4 7DL; tel: (0207) 7627 8061; fax: (0207) 720 2150 (acc 30)

Glebe Court, 2 Blackheath Rise, Lewisham SE13 7PN; tel: (020) 8297 0637; fax: (020) 8852 7298 (acc 42)

Rookstone, Lawrie Park Cres, Sydenham SE26 6HH; tel: (020) 8778 0317; fax: (020) 8778 0314 (acc 30)

North Walsham: Furze Hill House, 73 Happisburgh Rd, NR28 9HD; tel: 01692 502703 (acc 40, day centre 22)

Nottingham: Notintone House, Sneinton Rd, NG2 4QL; tel: (0115) 950 3788; fax: (0115) 959 8604 (acc 40)

Prestwich: Holt House, Headlands Dr, Hilton Lane, Gtr Manchester M25 9YF; tel: (0161) 773 0220; fax: (0161) 798 6428 (acc 31)

Sandridge: Lyndon, 2 High St, Sandridge, St Albans AL4 9DH; tel: (01727) 851050 fax: (01727) 831744 (acc 32)

Southend-on-Sea: Bradbury Home, 2 Roots Hall Drive, SS2 6DA; tel: (01702) 435838; fax: (01702) 435877 (acc 34)

Tunbridge Wells: Sunset Lodge, Pembury Rd, TN2 3QT; tel: (01892) 530861 (acc 20)

Weston-super-Mare: Dewdown House, 64 Beach Rd, BS23 4BE; tel: (01934) 417125; fax: (01934) 631064 (acc 40)

Centres for Families (Residential)

Belfast:

Glen Alva, 19 Cliftonville Rd, BT14 6JN; tel: (028) 9035 1185 (acc family units 20, max 77 residents)

Thorndale Parenting Assessment/Family Centre, 8 Duncairn Ave, Antrim Rd, BT14 6BP; tel: (028) 9035 1900 (acc family units 34, single bedsits 4, max 125 residents)

Leeds: Mount Cross, 139 Broad Lane, Bramley LS13 2JP; tel: (0113) 257 0810 (acc flats 28, max 78 residents)

Portsmouth: Catherine Booth House, 23 St Paul's Rd, Southsea PO5 4AE; tel: (023) 9273 7226 (acc family units 21, max 40 residents)

Refuge from Domestic Abuse (women with children)

Birmingham: Shepherd's Green House; address and telephone confidential; contact via West Midlands DHQ (acc 16 families, 4 single women, max 44 residents)

Centres for People with Learning Difficulties

Kilbirnie: George Steven Centre, Craigton Rd, KA25 6LJ; tel: (01505) 683 233

Plymouth: Pilgrim House, Courtfield Rd, PL3 5BB; tel: (01752) 223435

Stoke: Lovatt Court, Lovatt St, Stoke-on-Trent ST4 7RL; tel: (01782) 415621

Centres for the Single Homeless

Accrington: Accrington Crossroads, Empress St, BB5 1SG; tel: (01254) 389157 (acc 11)

Belfast:

Centenary House, 2 Victoria St, BT1 3GE; tel: (02890) 320320 (acc direct access 80)

Calder Fountain (attached to Centenary House) (registered care 28, resettlement 12)

Birmingham: William Booth Centre, 72 Shadwell St, B4 6HA; tel: (0121) 236 6554; (acc 64)

Blackburn: Bramwell House, Heaton St, BB2 2EF; tel: (01254) 677338 (acc 55)

Bradford: Lawley House, 371 Leeds Rd, BD3 9NG; tel: (01274) 731221 (acc direct access 51, resettlement 12)

Braintree: New Direction Centre, David Blackwell House, 25-27 Bocking End, CM7 9AE; tel: (01376) 553373 (acc 14)

Bristol: Logos House, Wade St, BS2 9EL; tel: (0117) 955 2821 (acc 69)

Cardiff: Crichton House Outreach Services, Dowlais Court, Vale Rd, Splott CF24 2LS; tel: (02920) 440391 (acc 55)

Cardiff: Northlands, 202 North Rd, CF14 3XP; tel: (029) 2061 9077 (acc 26)

Coventry: 1 Lincoln St, CV1 4JN; tel: (024) 7625 1437 (acc 99)

Darlington: Tom Raine Court, Coburg St, DL1 1SB; tel: (01325) 489242 (acc 37)

Dublin: Granby Centre, 9-10 Granby Row, Dublin 1, Eire; tel: [353] (1) 872 5500 (acc units 101)

Dundee:

Strathmore Lodge, 31 Ward Rd, DD1 1NG; tel: (01382) 225448 (acc 25)

Burnside Mill, Milnes East Wynd, DD1 5BA; tel: (01382) 203278 (acc 20)

Edinburgh:

Ashbrook, 492 Ferry Rd, EH5 2DL; tel: (0131) 552 5705 (acc 30)

The Pleasance, 1 The Pleasance, EH8 9UE; tel: (0131) 556 9674 (acc 37)

Glasgow:

Eva Burrows 1st Stop Project, Eva Burrows Centre, Clyde Place, Halfway, Cambuslang

G72 7QT; tel: (0141) 643 9680 (acc 32)

Hope House, 14 Clyde St, G1 5JH;
tel: (0141) 552 0537 (acc 96)

Wallace of Campsie House, 30 East Campbell St,
G1 5DT; tel: (0141) 552 4301; (acc 52)

William Hunter House, 70 Oxford St, G5 9EP;
tel: (0141) 429 5201 (acc 37)

Grimsby: Brighowgate House, 34 Brighowgate,
DN32 0QW; tel: (01472) 242648 (acc 46)

Hull: William Booth House, 2 Hessle Rd,
HU1 2QQ; tel: (01482) 225521 (acc 113)

Huntingdon: Kings Ripton Court,
Kings Ripton Rd, Sapley PE17 2NZ;
tel: (01480) 423800 (acc 36)

Ipswich: Lyndon House, 107 Fore St, IP4 1LS;
tel: (01473) 251070 (acc 39)

Isle of Man: David Gray House,
6 Drury Terrace, Douglas IM2 3HY;
tel: (01624) 662814 (acc 13)

Leamington Spa: Eden Villa, 13 Charlotte St,
CV31 3EB; tel: (01926) 450708 (acc 11)

Liverpool:
Ann Fowler House, Fraser St, L3 8JX;
tel: (0151) 207 3815 (acc 38)

Darbyshire House, 380 Prescot Rd, L13 3DA;
tel: (0151) 228 0925 (acc 45)

London:
David Barker House, 115a Blackfriars Rd,
SE1 8HW (acc 45)

Booth House, 153-157 Whitechapel Rd,
E1 1DF; tel: (020) 392 9497 (acc 150)

Cambria House, 37 Hunter St, King's Cross
WC1N 1BG; tel: (020) 7841 0230 (acc 48)

Edith Road, 10-12 Edith Rd, Hammersmith,
W14 9BA; tel: (020) 7603 1692 (acc 25)

Edward Alsop Court, 18 Great Peter St,
Westminster, SW1 2BT;
tel: (020) 7233 0296 (acc 108)

Hopetown, 60 Old Montague St, Whitechapel,
E1 5NF; tel: (020) 539 9240 (acc 99)

Riverside House, 20 Garford St, West India
Dock Rd, E14 8JG; tel: (020) 068 0950
(acc 40)

Manchester: 1 Wilmott St, Chorlton-on-Medlock,
M15 6BD; tel: (0161) 236 7537 (acc 113)

Newcastle upon Tyne:
39 City Rd, NE1 2BR; tel: (0191) 233 9150
(acc 69)

Cedar House, Denmark St, Byker, NE6 2UH;
tel: (0191) 224 1509 (acc direct access 18,
resettlement flats 6)

Nottingham:
Acorn Lodge, 4 Campbell St, St Ann's,
NG3 1GZ (acc 12); tel: (0115) 915 9010

Sneinton House, 2 Boston St, NG1 1ED;
tel: (0115) 950 4364 (acc 70)

Perth: 16 Skinnergate, PH1 5JH;
tel: (01738) 624360 (acc 41)

Plymouth: Devonport House and Zion House,
24 Park Ave, PL1 4BA; tel: (01752) 562170
(acc 72)

Reading: Willow House, Willow St, RG1 6AB;
tel: (0118) 959 0681 (acc 38)

Rochdale: Providence House, 2 High St,
OL12 0NT; tel: (01706) 645151 (acc 73)

St Helens: Salisbury House, 1 Phoenix Brow,
WA9 1SA; tel: (01744) 744800 (acc 68)

Salford: 1 James St (off Oldfield Rd), M3 5HP;
tel: (0161) 831 7020/7040 (acc 38)

Sheffield: Charter Row, 126 Charter Row, S1 4HR;
tel: (0114) 272 5158 (acc 56)

Skegness: Witham Lodge, Alexandra Rd,
PE25 3TL; tel: (01754) 899151 (acc 30)

Southampton: The Booth Centre, 57 Oxford St,
SO14 3DL (acc 46)

Stoke-on-Trent: Vale St, ST4 7RN;
tel: (01782) 744374 (acc 60 + 4 training flats)

Sunderland: Swan Lodge, High St East,
SR1 2AU; tel: (0191) 565 5411 (acc 65)

Swindon: Booth House, 1 Spring Close,
SN1 2BF; tel: (01793) 401830 (acc 50)

Warrington: James Lee House, Brick St,
Howley, WA1 2PD; tel: (01925) 636496
(acc 54)

Children's Homes/Centres (Residential)

Dublin:
Lefroy Night Light, 12-14 Eden Quay,
Dublin 1, Eire; tel: [353] (1) 874 3762
(acc 7 overnight emergency beds)

Lefroy Support Flats, 12-14 Eden Quay,
Dublin 1, Eire; tel: [353] (1) 874 3762
(acc 7)

Leeds: Spring Grove, 139 Broad Lane, Bramley
LS13 2JJ; tel: (0113) 257 7552
(acc 6 female care leavers)

London: The Haven, Springfield Rd, SE26 6HG;
tel: (020) 8659 4033 (acc 12)

Day Care, Early Years Education and Contact Centres for Children

Bath: The Mews Nursery, The Mews Out of
School Club and Green Park Out of School
Club, Carfax Hotel, Henrietta Mews,
BA2 6LR; tel: (01225) 332 593
(registered for 40 total)

Birmingham: Sally Ann's Pre-School and
Out of School Club @ Elmwood Church,
45 Hamstead Hill, B20 1BU;
tel: (0121) 523 734 (registered for 64 total)

Leeds: Copper Beech Day Nursery and
Rainbow After-School Club, 137 Broad Lane,

Bramley, LS13 2JP; tel: (0113) 256 5820
(registered for 62 total)

There are a further 5 Day Nurseries, 23 Pre-schools/ Playgroups, 2 Crèches, 10 Out-of-School Clubs and 8 Child Contact Centres attached to social centres and corps

Domiciliary Care (elderly)

Community Care Service (Angus): Chapel St,
Forfar, DD8 2AB; tel: (01307) 469393

Drop In Centres

Edinburgh: Regener8+, 25 Niddry St, Edinburgh
EH1 1LG; tel: (0131) 523 1060

Norwich: Pottergate Arc, 28 Pottergate, NR2 1DX;
tel: (01603) 663496

Southampton: H2O Project, Princess St,
Northam SO14 5RP; tel: (023) 8022 4632

Employment Training Centres

Hadleigh: Castle Ave, Castle Lane, Hadleigh,
Benfleet, Essex SS7 2AS;
tel: (01702) 426260

Norwich: Employment 2000, Calvert St;
tel: (01603) 761175

Night Shelter

Dublin: Cedar House, Marlborough Pl, Dublin 1,
Eire; tel: [353] (1) 873 1241
(acc 48)

Outreach Teams

Bristol: Logos House, Bridge Project, Little
George St, BS2 9EL; tel: (0117) 955 0074
(acc 24)

Cardiff: Bus Project, Ty Gobaith, 240 Bute St,
CF1 5TY; tel: (029) 2048 0187

London: Faith House, 11 Argyle St, King's Cross
WC1H 8EJ; tel: (020) 7837 5149

York: Homeless Prevention/Resettlement,
Gillygate, YO31 7EA; tel: (01904) 630470

Prison Ministries

Prison Ministries Officer, THQ,
101 Newington Causeway,
London SE1 6BN; tel: (020) 7367 4866

Probation Hostel

Isle of Man: David Gray House, 6 Drury Tce,
Douglas, IM2 3HY; tel: (01624) 662814 (acc 9)

Red Shield Services

UK THQ: 101 Newington Causeway,
London SE1 6BN; tel: (020) 7367 4851

HQ Germany: SAHQ/CVWW, Block 1,
NAAFI Complex, BFPO 15;
tel: [49] (5221) 24627

Sheltered Housing

London: Alver Bank, 17 West Rd, Clapham,
SW4 7DL; tel: (020) 7627 8061
(acc single 6, double 2)

Tunbridge Wells: Charles Court, Pembury Rd,
TN2 3QY; tel: (01892) 547439
(acc single 9, double 8)

Addiction Service

Bristol: Bridge Project, Little George St,
BS2 9EL; tel: (0117) 935 1255
(acc 24)

Cardiff: Bridge Project, Ty Gobiath,
240 Bute St, CF1 5TY; tel: (029) 2048 0187
(acc 23)

Dublin: York House, Alcohol Recovery Unit
(inc short-term intervention), Longford St
Little, Dublin 2, Eire; tel: (00 353-1) 476 3337
(acc 80)

Highworth: Gloucester House (Residential
Rehabilitation Centre), 6 High St, Swindon
SN6 7AG; tel: (01793) 762365 (acc 12,
halfway house 3, day programme 5)

London:
Greig House, 20 Garford St, West India
Dock Rd, E14 8JG; tel: (020) 7987 5658
(acc 36)

Riverside House 'Specialist' Homeless Centre
for People with Addiction Issues,
20 Garford St, West India Dock Rd,
E14 8JG; tel: (020) 7068 0950 (acc 31)

Riverside House Harbour Recovery Project
(inc detoxification), 20 Garford St, West
India Dock Rd, E14 8JG;
tel:(020) 7068 0950 (acc 40)

Stirling: Harm Reduction Service, SA Hall,
Drip Rd, FK8 1RA; tel: (01786) 448923

Offering Hope to Trafficked Women

The Jarrett Community

Biomedical Services

Biomedical Support Services are provided across
social work disciplines in partnership with the
University of Kent, Canterbury

THE UNITED STATES OF AMERICA

National leaders:
Commissioners William A. and Nancy L. Roberts

National Commander:
Commissioner William A. Roberts (1 Nov 2010)

National Chief Secretary:
Colonel David Jeffrey (1 Jul 2007)

National Headquarters: 615 Slaters Lane, PO Box 269, Alexandria, VA 22313-0269, USA

Tel: [1] (703) 684 5500; fax: [1] (703) 684 3478; website: www.salvationarmyusa.org

The Salvation Army began its ministry in the United States in October 1879. Lieutenant Eliza Shirley left England to join her parents who had migrated to America in search of work. She held meetings that were so successful that General William Booth sent Commissioner George Scott Railton and seven women officers to the United States in March 1880 to formalise the effort. Their initial street meeting was held on the dockside at Battery Park in New York City the day they arrived.

In only three years, operations had expanded into California, Connecticut, Indiana, Kentucky, Maryland, Massachusetts, Michigan, Missouri, New Jersey, New York, Ohio and Pennsylvania. Family services, youth services, elderly services and disaster services are among the many programmes offered in local communities throughout the United States, in Puerto Rico, the Virgin Islands, the Marshall Islands and Guam.

The National Headquarters was incorporated as a religious and charitable corporation in the State of New Jersey in 1982 as 'The Salvation Army National Corporation' and is qualified to conduct its affairs in the Commonwealth of Virginia.

Zone: Americas and Caribbean
Periodicals: *The War Cry, Women's Ministries Resources, Word & Deed – A Journal of Theology and Ministry, Young Salvationist*

DURING the year National Headquarters published its first online annual report, providing a readily accessible account of Salvation Army service and ministry throughout the nation. A recent poll showed Americans viewed The Salvation Army as one of the top ten most trusted non-profit organisations.

August 2009 saw 163 Salvationists meeting together in Colorado Springs for the 40th National Seminar on Evangelism. For many years this event has equipped thousands of people in ministry.

Dallas Cowboys owner Jerry Jones hosted the 13th annual National Red Kettle Campaign kick-off at Texas Stadium on Thanksgiving Day. Grammy-nominated rock band Daughtry performed live during the half-time show.

Despite the economic recession people contributed a record-breaking $139 million to the campaign, including an increasing number of online donations. A seven per cent increase over last year's record total

As a Board of Trustees member at Asbury University, Commissioner Israel Gaither (then USA National Commander) addresses an event marking the change in designation from college to university

was appreciated since demand for social services greatly increased during the holiday season.

Since January 2010 the Army has been actively serving earthquake survivors in Haiti. The UN designated The Salvation Army the lead organisation to coordinate relief for 20,000 displaced Haitians.

As long-term recovery continues, the Army's partnerships with hunger relief organisation Numana Inc, as well as UPS, FedEX, DHL and more than 86,000 volunteers, have been integral in preparing and delivering food to survivors.

NATIONAL STATISTICS
(incorporating all USA territories)

Officers 5,335 (active 3,422 retired 1,913)
Cadets (1st Yr) 146 (2nd Yr) 137 **Employees** 59,841
Corps 1,241 **Outposts** 25 **Institutions** 805
Senior Soldiers 82,792 **Adherents** 15,956
Junior Soldiers 24,601

STATISTICS
(National Headquarters)
Officers (active) 26 **Employees** 80

STAFF

Women's Ministries: Comr Nancy L. Roberts (NPWM); tel: (703) 684 5503; Col Barbara Jeffrey (NSWM, NRVAVS); tel: (703) 684 5504

Asst Nat Chief Sec: Maj Joan Canning; tel: (703) 684 5508

Nat Treasurer and Nat Sec for Business Administration: Lt-Col Gary W. Haupt; tel: (703) 684 5507

Nat Sec for Personnel: Lt-Col Suzanne H. Haupt; tel: (703) 684 5512

Nat Sec for Programme: Lt-Col Mark Israel; tel: (703) 684 5527; fax: (703) 519 5880

Nat Social Services Sec: Maj Betty A. Israel; tel: (703) 684 5533; fax: (703) 519 5889

Nat Community Relations and Development Sec: Maj George Hood; tel: (703) 684 5526; fax: (703) 684 5538

Nat Editor-in-Chief and Literary Sec: Maj Edward Forster; tel: (703) 684 5523; fax: (703) 684 5539

Salvation Army World Service Office (SAWSO): Lt-Col Daniel L. Starrett, jr; tel: (703) 684-5524; fax: (703) 684 5536

ARCHIVES AND RESEARCH CENTRE
Email: Archives@usn.salvationarmy.org

USA CENTRAL TERRITORY

Territorial leaders:
Commissioners Paul R. and Carol Seiler

Territorial Commander:
Commissioner Paul R. Seiler (1 May 2010)

Chief Secretary:
Colonel Néstor R. Nüesch (1 May 2010)

Territorial Headquarters: 10 W Algonquin Rd, Des Plaines, IL 60016-6006, USA

Tel: [1] (847) 294-2000; fax: [1] (847) 294-2295; website: www.usc.salvationarmy.org

The Salvation Army was incorporated as a religious and charitable corporation in the State of Illinois in 1913 as 'The Salvation Army' and is qualified to conduct its affairs in all of the states of the territory.

Zone: Americas and Caribbean
USA states included in the territory: Illinois, Indiana, Iowa, Kansas, Michigan, Minnesota, Missouri, Nebraska, North Dakota, South Dakota, Wisconsin
'The Salvation Army' in Spanish: Ejército de Salvación; in Swedish: Frälsningsarmén
Languages in which the gospel is preached: English, Korean, Laotian, Russian, Spanish, Swedish
Periodical: *Central Connection*

THE entire territory was affected by the world economic crisis and some regional unemployment rates were triple the national average. Territorial faith stimulus grants exceeding $2 million encouraged community partnerships in serving the newly poor. In spite of the economic climate the territory raised a record $7.3 million for World Services/Self-Denial Appeals.

The final phase of the national three-year 'Come Join Our Army' soldier-enrolment initiative in the territory saw significant broad-based growth that reversed a decade-long decline in membership.

The then territorial leaders Commissioners Barry C. and E. Sue Swanson focused on prayer as the foundation for ministry. Appointed the territory's first prayer ambassador, Commissioner Sue Swanson established a 24/7 website.

Online meetings were introduced at the Power Point Prayer Summit, held in June 2009 during the commissioning weekend for 17 cadets of the Witnesses For Christ Session. The college for officer training later welcomed 23 members of the Ambassadors Of Holiness Session.

The TC gathered 200 officers, soldiers and employees at a conference to generate creative ideas on six strategic priorities: prayer, multi-cultural and youth ministries, soldier vitality, candidate recruitment and urban mission. A new office for urban mission was established.

Colonel Paul Seiler (then CS) launched a pilot programme linking individual corps with partners in mission to broaden knowledge, develop relationships and increase World Services/Self-Denial Appeal fundraising.

In the summer, six other countries and America's Midwest welcomed six mission teams of young adults and four interns, while 24 adults travelled overseas on three territorial mission teams. More than 100 Salvationists served on divisional and corps teams.

During the 2010 Vancouver Winter Olympics, 11 members of the territory raised awareness of human trafficking.

The Ray and Joan Kroc Corps Community Centre in Omaha, Nebraska had more than 2,400 members within six months of opening. Groundbreaking ceremonies took place at the Quincy, Illinois and Green Bay, Wisconsin Kroc Centres. The centre at Grand Rapids, Michigan began the final stage of fundraising.

Chicago Kroc Centre was officially declared a corps before the building was completed. The centre rents school premises and had seen exceptionally high levels of soldiership and attendance at its programmes. Activities began at South Bend, Indiana Kroc Corps.

A programme by Notre Dame University students to mentor young band players has been very successful and this was demonstrated when children were featured during a joint concert featuring the university symphonic winds and the Chicago Staff Band (CSB).

The summer of 2009 held two other music highlights, including a CSB tour of northern Europe and the 75th anniversary of the acclaimed Central Music Institute, which has been intrinsic to the territory's strong tradition of musical excellence.

Emergency disaster services responded effectively and compassionately to seasonal tornadoes, flooding and winter storms. Salvationists from the territory already serving in Haiti when the January 2010 earthquake struck were on hand to provide immediate assistance and were supported by a succession of 10 USA Central teams deployed for two weeks each.

New fundraising technologies introduced at Christmas included wireless credit card machines at Christmas kettle stands, Facebook, email kettles and text donations, and online 'Angel Tree' shopping.

STATISTICS

Officers 1,177 (active 757 retired 420) **Cadets** (1st Yr) 23 (2nd Yr) 23 **Employees** 8,076
Corps 265 **Institutions** 172
Senior Soldiers 16,934 **Adherents** 2,554 **Junior Soldiers** 3,724
Personnel serving outside territory Officers 27

STAFF

Women's Ministries: Comr Carol Seiler (TPWM) Col Rebecca Nüesch (TSWM)

Maj Dorene Jennings (TCCMS)
Personnel: Lt-Col Jeffrey Smith
Programme: Lt-Col Richard E. Vander Weele
Business: Lt-Col Merle Heatwole
Adult Rehabilitation Centres: Maj Graham Allan
Audit: Maj David Clark
Candidates: Lt-Col Dawn Heatwole
Community Relations and Development: Maj John Wilkins
Corps Mission and Adult Ministries: Maj Phillip Aho
Evangelism and Corps Growth: Capt Carol J. Lewis
Finance: Maj Randall Polsley
Information Technology: Mr Ronald E. Shoults
Multicultural Ministries: Maj Mary Hammerly
Music and Gospel Arts: B/M William F. Himes, jr, OF
Pastoral Care Officers: Majs Larry and Margo Thorson
Property: Maj Cheryl Lawry
Resource Officer and Development: Lt-Col Dorothy R. Smith
Resource Connection Dept: Mr Robert Jones
Risk Management: Maj James C.Hoskin
Social Services: Maj Geoffrey Allan
Training: Maj Paul Fleeman
Youth: Maj Gail Aho

DIVISIONS

Eastern Michigan: 16130 Northland Dr, Southfield, MI 48075-5218;
tel: (248) 443-5500; Lt-Cols Norman S. and Diane Marshall
Heartland: 401 NE Adams St, Peoria, IL 61603-4201; tel: (309) 655-7220; Maj Evelyn Diaz
Indiana: 3100 N Meridian St, Indianapolis, IN 46208-4718; tel: (317) 937-7000; Majs Richard and Vicki Amick
Kansas and Western Missouri: 3637 Broadway, Kansas City, MO 64111-2503; tel: (816) 756-1455; Majs Charles and Sharon Smith
Metropolitan: 5040 N Pulaski Rd, Chicago, IL 60630-2788; tel: (773) 725-1100; Lt-Cols Ralph and Susan Bukiewicz
Midland: 1130 Hampton Ave, St Louis, MO 63139-3147; tel: (314) 646-3000; Majs Lonneal and Patty Richardson
Northern: 2445 Prior Ave, Roseville, MN 55113-2714; tel: (651) 746-3400; Lt-Cols Daniel and Rebecca Sjögren
Western: 3612 Cuming St, Omaha,

NE 68131-1900; tel: (402) 898-5900; Majs Paul and Renea Smith
Western Michigan and Northern Indiana: 1215 E Fulton, Grand Rapids, MI 49503-3849; tel: (616) 459-3433; Majs Thomas and Jacalyn Bowers
Wisconsin and Upper Michigan: 11315 W Watertown Plank Rd, Wauwatosa, WI 53226-0019; tel: (414) 302-4300; Majs Robert E. and Nancy Thomson, jr

COLLEGE FOR OFFICER TRAINING

700 W Brompton Ave, Chicago, IL 60657-1831; tel: (773) 524-2000

UNDER THQ
Conference Centre
10 W Algonquin, Des Plaines, IL 60016-6006

SOCIAL SERVICES
Adult Rehabilitation Centres
Chicago (Central), IL 506: N Des Plaines St; tel: (312) 738-4367 (acc 200)
Chicago (North Side), IL 60614: 2258 N Clybourn Ave; tel: (773) 477-1771 (acc 140)
Davenport (River Valley), IA 52806: 4001 N Brady St; tel: (563) 323-2748 (acc 86)
Des Moines, IA 50309-4897: 133 E 2nd St; tel: (515) 243-4277 (acc 58)
Flint, MI 48506: 2200 N Dort Highway; tel: (810) 234-2678 (acc 121)
Fort Wayne, IN 46802: 427 W Washington Blvd; tel: (260) 424-1655 (acc 75)
Gary, IN 46402: 1351 W 11th Ave; tel: (219) 882-9377 (acc 110)
Grand Rapids, MI 49507-1601: 1491 S Division Ave; tel: (616) 452-3133 (acc 126)
Indianapolis, IN 46202-3915: 711 E Washington St; tel: (317) 638-6585 (acc 103)
Kansas City, MO 64106: 1351 E 10th St; tel: (816) 421-5434 (acc 132)
Milwaukee, WI 53202-5999: 324 N Jackson St; tel: (414) 276-4316 (acc 100)
Minneapolis, MN 55401-1039: 900 N 4th St; tel: (612) 332-5855 (acc 125)
Omaha, NE 68131-2642: 2551 Dodge St; tel: (402) 342-4135 (acc 95)
Rockford, IL 61104-7385: 1706 18th Ave; tel: (815) 397-0440 (acc 72)
Romulus, MI 48174-4205: 5931 Middlebelt; tel: (734) 729-3939 (acc 111)
St Louis, MO 63108-3211: 3949 Forest Park Ave; tel: (314) 535-0057 (acc 102)
South Bend, IN 46601-2226: 510-18 S Main St; tel: (574) 288-2539 (acc 67)

Southeast, MI 1627: W Fort St, Detroit,
MI 48216; tel: (313) 965-7760;
toll-free: 1-(800) SA Truck (acc 360)
Springfield, IL 62703-1003: 221 N 11th St;
tel: (217) 528-7573 (acc 89)
Waukegan, IL 60085-6511: 431 S Genesee St;
tel: (847) 662-7730 (acc 100)

UNDER DIVISIONS
Emergency Lodges
Alton, IL 62002: 525 Alby
Alton, IL 62002: 14-16 E 5th St
Ann Arbor, MI 48108: 3660 Packard Rd
Belleville, IL 62226: 4102 W Main St
Benton Harbor, MI 49022: 645 Pipestone St
Bloomington, IL 61701: 601 W Washington St
Champaign, IL 61820: 2212 N Market St
Chicago, IL 60640: 800 W Lawrence
Columbia, MO 65203: 602 N Ann St
Davenport, IA 52803-5101: 301-307 W 6th St
Decatur, IL 62523: 137 Church St
Detroit, MI 48208-2517: 3737 Humboldt
Detroit, MI 48208-2517: 3737 Lawton
Grand Island, NE 68801-5828; 818 W 3rd St
Hutchinson, KS 67504-0310: 200 S Main
Independence, MO 64050-2664:
14704 E Truman Rd
Indianapolis, IN 46204: 540 N Alabama St
Jefferson City, MO 65101: 907 Jefferson St
Kankakee, IL 60901: 148 N Harrison
Kankakee, IL 60901: 541 E Court Ave
Kansas City, KS 66102: 6721 State Ave
Kansas City, MO 64127: 6935 Bell Rd
LaCrosse, WI 54601: 223 N 8th St
Lafayette, IN 47904-1934: 1110 Union St
Lawrence, KS 66044: 946 New Hampshire St
Madison, WI 53703: E 630 Washington Ave E
Mankato, MN 56001-2338: 700 S Riverfront Dr
Milwaukee, WI 53205: 1730 N 7th St
Monroe, MI 48161: 815 E 1st St
O'Fallon, MO 63366-2938: 1 William Booth Dr
Olathe, KS 66061: 400-402 E Santa Fe
Omaha, NE 68131: 3612 Cuming St
Peoria, IL 61603: 417 NE Adams St
Peoria, IL 61603: 414 NE Jefferson St
Quincy, IL 62301: 400 Broadway
Rockford, IL 61104: 1706 18th Ave E
St Cloud, MN 56304: 400 Highway 10
St Joseph, MO 64501: 618 S 6th St
St Louis, MO 63132: 10740 W Page Ave
Sheboygan, WI 53081: 710 Pennsylvania Ave
Sioux Falls, SD 57103-0128: 800 N Cliff Ave
Somerset, WI 54025: 203 Church Hill Rd
Springfield, IL 62701: 100 N 9th St
Springfield, MO 65802: 636 N Boonville

Warren, MI 48091: 24140 Mound Rd
Waterloo, IA 50703: 218 Logan Ave
Waterloo, IA 50703: 229 Logan Ave
Waterloo, IA 50703: 603 S Hanchett Rd
Waukesha, WI 53188: 445 Madison St
Wichita, KS 67202-2010: 350 N Market

Senior Citizens' Residences
Chicago, IL 60607: 1500 W Madison
Columbus, IN 47201: 300 Gladstone Ave
Grandview, MO 64030: 6111 E 129th St
Indianapolis, IN 46254-2738: 4390 N High
School Rd
Kansas City, KS 66112: 1331 N 75th St
Minneapolis, MN 55403-2116: 1421 Yale Pl
Oak Creek, WI 53154: 150 W Centennial Dr
Oak Creek, WI 53154: 180 W Centennial Dr
Omaha, NE 68131: 923 38th St
St Louis, MO 63118: 3133 Iowa St

Harbour-Light Centres
Chicago, IL 60607: 1515 W Monroe St;
tel: (312) 421-5753
Clinton Township, MI 48043: 42590 Stepnitz
Detroit, MI 48201: 3737 Lawton;
tel. (313) 361-6136
Indianapolis, IN 46222: 2400 N Tibbs Ave;
tel: (317) 972-1450
Kansas City, KS 66102: 6721 State Ave;
tel: (913) 232-5400
Minneapolis, MN 55403: 1010 Currie;
tel: (612) 338-0113
Monroe, MI 48161: 3580 S Custer
St Louis, MO 63188: 3010 Washington Ave

Substance Abuse Centres
Detroit, MI 48216: 3737 Humboldt
Grand Rapids, MI 49503: 72 Sheldon Blvd SE;
tel: (616) 742-0351
Kansas City, MO 64127: 5100 E 24th;
tel: (816) 483-3679
Minneapolis, MN 55403: 1010 Currie Ave;
tel: (612) 338-0113

Transitional Housing
Appleton, WI 54914: 105 S Badger Ave
Champaign, IL 61820: 502 N Prospect
Cheboygan, MI 49712: 444 S Main St
Duluth, MN 55806: 215 S 27th Ave W
Grand Rapids, MI 49503: 1215 E Fulton St
Green Bay, WI 54301: 626 Union Ct
Jefferson City, MO 65101: 907 Jefferson St
Joplin, MO 64801: 320 E 8th St
Kansas City, KS 66102: 6723 State Ave
Kansas City, MO 64111: 101 W Linwood Blvd

Lawrence, KS 66044: 946 New Hampshire
Minneapolis, MN 55403: 1010 Currie
New Albany, IN 47151: 2300 Green Valley Rd
Olathe, KS 66061: 400 E Santa Fe
Omaha, NE 68131: 3612 Cuming St
Pekin, IL 61554: 243 Derby St
Pine Lawn, MO 63120: 4210 Peyton Ln
Rochester, MN 55906: 20 First Ave NE
Rockford, IL 61104: 416 S Madison
Steven's Point, WI 54481: 824 Fremont
St Louis, MO 63118: 2740 Arsenal
St Paul, MN 55108: 1471 Como Ave W
Sioux Falls, SD 57103-0128; 800 N Cliff Ave
Springfield, MO 65802: 10740 W Chestnut
  Expway
Waterloo, IA 50703: 149 Argyle St
Wausau, WI 54401-4630: 113 S Second St
Wichita, KS 67202-2010: 350 Market

Child Day Care

Benton Harbor, MI 49023: 1840 Union St
Bloomington, IN 47404-3966: 111 N Rogers St
Chicago, IL 60621: 845 W 69th St
DeKalb, IL 60115-0442: 830 Grove St
Emporia, KS 66801: 327 Constitution St
Kansas City, KS 66117: 500 N 7th St

Kansas City, MO 64111: 500 W 39th St
Lansing, MI 48901-4176:
  525 N Pennsylvania Ave
Menasha, WI 54911: 1525 Appleton Rd
Mishawaka, IN 46544: 1026 Dodge Ave
Oak Creek, WI 53154: 8853 S Howell Ave
Olathe, KS 66051: 420 E Santa Fe
Omaha, NE 68131: 3612 Cuming St
Pekin, IL 61554: 243 Derby St
Peoria, IL 61603: 210 Spalding Ave
Plymouth, MI 48170: 9451 S Main St
Rockford, IL 61101: 210 N Kilburn
Rockford, IL 61104: 220 S Madison
Royal Oak, MI 48073: 3015 N Main St
Sheboygan, WI 53081: 1125 N 13th
Topeka, KS 66601: 1320 E 6th St
Traverse City, MI 49685-0063: 1239 Barlow St

Emergency Diagnostic and Short-term Treatment Centre

Edwin Denby Memorial Children's Home:
  20775 Pembroke Ave, Detroit, MI 48219;
  tel: (313) 537-2130 (acc 40)
Wilcox Residential Programmes: North Platte,
  NE 69101-2268, 1121 W 18th St;
  tel: (308) 534-4164

Teenage boys study Scripture weekly with their corps officer, Major Bill Cox, at Escanaba, Michigan. Youth ministry is one of six strategic priorities in the USA Central Territory.

Youth Group Homes
North Platte, NE 69101-2258: 1121 W 18th St
Omaha, NE 68131-1998: 3612 Cuming St

Emergency Shelter Care of Children
Kansas City, MO 64111: 101 W Linwood Blvd
North Platte, NE 69101: 704 S Welch Ave
Oak Park, IL 60302-1713: 924 N Austin
Omaha, NE 68131: 3612 Cuming St
St Paul, MN 55108-2542: 1471 Como Ave W
Wichita, KS 67202-2010: 350 N Market

Head Start Programmes
Chicago, IL 60651: 4255 W Division
Chicago, IL 60644: 500 S Central
Chicago, IL 60651: 1345 N Karlov
Chicago, IL 60607: 1 N Ogden
Chicago, IL 60621: 945 W 69th St
Chicago, IL 60649: 1631 E 71st St
Saginaw, MI 48602: 2030 N Carolina St

Homes (each of the following have facilities for unmarried mothers)
Detroit, MI 48219-1398: 20775 Pembroke Ave
Grand Rapids, MI 49503: 1215 E Fulton St;
    tel: (616) 459-9468 (Teen-parent centre)
Omaha, NE 68131-1998: 3612 Cuming St

Latchkey Programmes
DeKalb, IL 60115-0442: Camp 'I Can Do It'
DeKalb, IL 60115-0442: 830 Grove St
Evanston, IL 60201-4414: 1403 Sherman Ave
Gary-Merrillville, IN 46408-4420:
    4800 Harrison St
Huntington, IN 46750: 1424 E Market St
Huron, SD 57350: 237 Illinois St SW
Indianapolis, IN 46203-1944: 1337 Shelby St
Kokomo, IN 46902: 1101 S Waugh
Jacksonville, IL 62650: 331 W Douglas St
Newton, IA 50208: 301 N 2nd Ave E

North Platte, NE 69101: 421 E 6th St
Omaha, NE 68131: 3612 Cuming St
Pekin, IL 61554: 243 Derby St
Royal Oak, MI 48073: 3015 N Main Sts
Springfield, MO 65802: 1707 W Chestnut
    Expway
St Louis, MO 63113: 2618 N Euclid Ave
St Louis, MO 63143: 7701-15 Rannells Ave
Wyandotte, MI 49192-3498: 1258 Biddle Ave

Residential Services for Mentally Ill
Omaha, NE 68131: 3612 Cuming St

Permanent and/or Supportive Housing
Coon Rapids, MN 55433: 10347 Ibis Ave
Indianapolis, IN 46204: Barton Center,
    222 E Michigan St
Jefferson City, MO 65101: 907 Jefferson St
Joplin, MO 64801: 320 E 8th St
Kansas City, KS 66102: 6723 State Ave
Kansas City, MO 64111: 101 W Linwood
Minneapolis, MN 55403: 53 Glenwood Ave
Rochester, MN 55906: 120 S Broadway
St Louis, MO 63103: 205 N 18th St
St Louis, MO 63132: 10740 W Page Ave
St Paul, MN 55108: 1471 Como Ave W

Foster Care
Wichita, KS 67202: Kock Center, 350 N Marat

Medical/Dental Clinics (SA owned and occupied)
Grand Rapids, MI 49503: 1215 E Fulton St
Rochester, MN 55906: 120 S Broadway
Sheboygan, WI 53081: 710 Pennsylvania Ave

In addition, a number of fresh-air camps, youth centres, community centres, red shield clubs, day nurseries, family service and emergency relief bureaux are attached to corps and divisions

USA EASTERN TERRITORY

Territorial leaders:
Commissioners R. Steven and Judith A. Hedgren

Territorial Commander:
Commissioner R. Steven Hedgren
(1 Aug 2010)

Chief Secretary:
Colonel William R. Carlson (1 Aug 2010)

Territorial Headquarters: 440 West Nyack Road, PO Box C-635, West Nyack, New York 10994-1739, USA

Tel: [1] (845) 620-7200; fax: [1] (845) 620-7756; website: www.salvationarmy-usaeast.org

The Salvation Army was incorporated as a religious and charitable corporation in the State of New York in 1899 as 'The Salvation Army' and is qualified to conduct its affairs in all of the states of the territory.

Zone: Americas and Caribbean
USA states included in the territory: Connecticut, Delaware, Kentucky, Maine, Massachusetts, New Hampshire, New Jersey, New York, Ohio, Pennsylvania, Rhode Island, Vermont
Other countries included in the territory: Puerto Rico, Virgin Islands
'The Salvation Army' in Korean: Koo Sei Kun; in Norwegian: Frelsesarmeen; in Spanish: Ejército de Salvación; in Swedish: Frälsningsarmén
Languages in which the gospel is preached: Creole, English, Korean, Laotian, Portuguese, Russian, Spanish, Swedish
Periodicals: *¡Buenas Noticias!* (Spanish), *Cristianos en Marcha* (Spanish), *Good News!* (English and Korean), *Priority!*, *Ven a Cristo Hoy* (Spanish)

GENERAL Shaw Clifton and Commissioner Helen Clifton (TPWM) joined Salvationists in Boston, Massachusetts, for the 'Holiness Ablaze – Living Examples' weekend to celebrate the 125th anniversary of the sanctification experience of Samuel Logan Brengle on Boston Common, on 9 January 1885.

As Salvationists gathered on a snowy January afternoon at the large, elevated bandstand, a dramatic re-enactment of Brengle's testimony was followed by the singing of 'O God of Burning, Cleansing Flame', led by Commissioner Lawrence R. Moretz (then TC). 'Send the fire!' was the sung prayer of the crowd kneeling in the snow around the gazebo.

The Brengle Holiness Institute was attended by 250 delegates – soldiers, officers and the cadets from the school for officer training – and included worship meetings and lecture sessions in which noted Salvation Army leaders and academics spoke about the Army's holiness theology.

Following news of the devastating earthquake in Haiti, the territory sent two officers, Lieut-Colonel (Dr) Herbert Rader and Captain (Dr) Cindy-Lou Drummond, to lead the Army's medical team.

Lieut-Colonel Rader reported seeing miracles amid the difficult conditions: 'Patients were coming in wheelbarrows; people were being carried on doors and just deposited there with their injuries and illnesses, pre-existing conditions of all sorts. Somehow, no one died.'

'For Such A Time As This' (a Scripture reference from the Book of Esther) was the theme of the Social Services Conference held in March at the Territorial Conference Centre, West Nyack. Delegates considered the past, present and future of Salvation Army social ministry.

Three hundred delegates attended the annual Candidates and Students Seminar.

A new building for Montclair Citadel Corps, New Jersey, was dedicated to the glory of God in March and a Ray and Joan Kroc Corps Community Centre opened in Dayton, Ohio, in May.

A dental clinic, set up in Western Pennsylvania Division in April, is reaching people who would otherwise go without dental care. Leading the opening and dedication ceremony, the TC said: 'This is a great day for our holistic mission.'

The General and Commissioner Clifton returned to the territory for the ordination and commissioning of 42 lieutenants and three captains of the Prayer Warriors Session. During the weekend, the territory also bade farewell to its leaders of eight years as Commissioners Lawrence R. and Nancy A. Moretz entered retirement. They received their retirement certificates from the General.

Commissioner Lawrence Moretz presented to the General the territory's World Services offering of $12 million.

STATISTICS

Officers 1,660 (active 1,039 retired 621) **Cadets** 85 **Employees** 10,100
Corps 375 **Outposts** 2 **Institutions** 83
Senior Soldiers 21,373 **Adherents** 7,815 **Junior Soldiers** 8,544
Personnel serving outside territory Officers 48 Layworker 1

STAFF

Women's Ministries: Comr Judith A. Hedgren (TPWM) Col Marcella Carlson (TSWM) Lt-Col Sharon Tillsley (TMFS) Lt-Col Judy LaMarr (TCCM, TWAS) Lt-Col Susan Gregg (OCS)
Personnel: Lt-Col Mark W. Tillsley
Programme: Lt-Col Kenneth W. Maynor
Business: Lt-Col James W. Reynolds
Territorial Ambassadors for Evangelism: Lt-Cols Howard and Patricia Burr
Territorial Ambassadors for Holiness: Majs David and Jean Antill
Territorial Ambassador for Prayer/Spiritual Formation: Lt-Col Cheryl A. Maynor
ARC Commander: Lt-Col Timothy Raines
Audit: Maj John Cramer
Community Relations/Development: Maj John Hodgson
Education: Maj Edward Russell
Finance: Maj Glenn C. Bloomfield
Information Technology: Mr Paul Kelly
Legal: Maj Thomas A. Schenk
Literary: Linda D. Johnson
Mission and Culture: Maj William R. Groff
Music: B/M Ronald Waiksnoris
  New York Staff Band: B/M Ronald Waiksnoris
  Territorial Songsters: S/L William Rollins

Officers' Services/Records: Maj Deborah K. Goforth

Pastoral Care and Spiritual Special: Lt-Col Gary Asperschlager.

Property/Mission Expansion: Maj Hubert S. Steele III

Risk Management: Mr Samuel C. Bennett

Social Services: Maj Florence Townsend

Supplies/Purchasing: Maj Ronald Lugiano

Training: Maj Stephen Banfield

Youth and Candidates: Maj Kevin Stoops

DIVISIONS

Eastern Pennsylvania and Delaware: 701 N Broad St, Philadelphia, PA 19123; tel: (215) 787-2800; Lt-Cols Donald W. and Renee P. Lance

Empire State: 200 Twin Oaks Dr, PO Box 148, Syracuse, NY 13206-0148; tel: (315) 434-1300; Maj Donald D. and Arvilla Hostetler

Greater New York: 120 West 14th St, New York, NY 10011-7393; tel: (212) 337-7200; Lt-Cols Guy D. and Henrietta Klemanski

Massachusetts: 25 Shawmut Rd, Canton, MA 02021-1414; tel: (339) 502-5934; Majs William H. and Joan I. Bode

New Jersey: 4 Gary Rd, Union, NJ 07083-5598, PO Box 3170, Union, NJ 07083; tel: (908) 851-9300; Majs Donald and Vicki Berry

Northeast Ohio: 2507 E 22nd St, 44115-3202, PO Box 5847, Cleveland, OH 44101-0847; tel: (216) 861-8185; Majs Ricardo J. and Mirtha N. Fernandez

Northern New England: 297 Cumberland Ave, PO Box 3647, Portland, ME 04104; tel: (207) 774-6304; Majs David E. and Naomi R. Kelly

Puerto Rico and Virgin Islands: 306 Ave De La Constitución 00901-2235, PO Box 71523, San Juan PR, 00936-8623; tel: (787) 999-7000; Maj Jorge L. and Capt Limaris Marzan

Southern New England: 855 Asylum Ave, PO Box 628, Hartford, CT 06142-0628; tel: (860) 543-8400; Lt-Col Barbara A. Hunter

Southwest Ohio and Northeast Kentucky: 114 E Central Parkway, PO Box 596, Cincinnati, OH 45201; tel: (513) 762-5600; Majs Ronald R. and Dorine M. Foreman

Western Pennsylvania: 700 N Bell Ave, Carnegie, PA 15106; tel: (412) 446-1500; Majs Robert J. and Lynette Reel

SCHOOL FOR OFFICER TRAINING

201 Lafayette Ave, Suffern, NY 10901-4798; tel: (845) 357-3501

THE SALVATION ARMY RETIREMENT COMMUNITY

1400 Webb St, Asbury Park, NJ 07712; tel: (732) 775-2200; Maj Jean Booth (Administrator) (acc 32)

SOCIAL SERVICES

Adult Rehabilitation Centres

*(*Includes facilities for women)*

Akron, OH 44311: 1006 Grant St, PO Box 1743; tel: (330) 773-3331 (acc 83)

Albany, NY 12206: 452 Clinton Ave, PO Box 66389; tel: (518) 465-2416 (acc 90)

Altoona, PA 16602: 200 7th Ave, PO Box 1405, 16603 (mail); tel: (814) 946-3645 (acc 39)

Binghamton, NY 13904: 3-5 Griswold St; tel: (607) 723-5381 (acc 62)

*Boston (Saugus), MA 01906: 209 Broadway Rte 1; tel: (781) 231-0803 (acc 125)

Bridgeport CT 06607: 1313 Connecticut Ave; tel: (203) 367-8621 (acc 50)

Brockton, MA 02301: 281 N Main St; tel: (508) 586-1187 (acc 56)

Brooklyn, NY 11217: 62 Hanson Pl; tel: (718) 622-7166 (acc 136)

Buffalo, NY 14217-2587: 1080 Military Rd, PO Box 36, 14217-0036; tel: (716) 875-2533 (acc 90)

Cincinnati, OH 45212: 2250 Park Ave, PO Box 12546, Norwood, OH 45212-0546; tel: (513) 351-3457 (acc 175)

Cleveland, OH 44103: 5005 Euclid Ave; tel: (216) 881-2625 (acc 159)

Columbus, OH 43207: 1675 S High St; tel: (614) 221-4269 (acc 122)

*Dayton, OH 45402: 913 S Patterson Blvd; tel: (937) 461-2769 (acc 72)

Erie, PA 16501: 1209 Sassafras St, PO Box 6176, 16512; tel: (814) 456-4237 (acc 50)

*Harrisburg, PA 17110: 3650 Vartan Way, PO Box 60095, 17106-0095; tel: (717) 541-0203 (acc 100)

*Hartford, CT 06132: 333 Homestead Ave, PO Box 320440; tel: (860) 527-8106 (acc 110)

Hempstead, NY 11550: 194 Front St; tel: (516) 481-7600 (acc 100)

Jersey City, NJ 07302: 248 Erie St; tel: (201) 653-3071 (acc 75)

Mount Vernon, NY 10550: 745 S Third Ave; tel: (914) 664-0800 (acc 80)

Newark, NJ 07101: 65 Pennington St, PO Box 815; tel: (973) 589-0370 (acc 125)

New Haven, CT 06511: 301 George St; tel: (203) 865-0511 (acc 45)

*New York, NY 10036: 535 W 48th St;
tel: (212) 757-7745 (acc 140)
Paterson, NJ 07505: 31 Van Houten St,
PO Box 1976, 07509; tel: (973) 742-1126
(acc 89)
*Philadelphia, PA 19128: 4555 Pechin St;
tel: (215) 483-3340 (acc 138)
Pittsburgh, PA 15203: 44 S 9th St;
tel: (412) 481-7900 (acc 127)
Portland, ME 04101: 30 Warren Ave,
PO Box 1298, 04104; tel: (207) 878-8555
(acc 60)
Poughkeepsie, NY 12601: 570 Main St;
tel: (845) 471-1730 (acc 50)
*Providence, RI 02906: 201 Pitman St;
tel: (401) 421-5270 (acc 129)
*Rochester, NY 14611: 745 West Ave;
tel: (585) 235-0020 (acc 135)
San Juan, PR 00903: ARC, Fernández Juncos Ave,
cnr of Valdés #104, Puerta de Tierra,
PO Box 13814, 00908; tel: (787) 722-3301
(acc 36)
Scranton, PA 18505: 610 S Washington Ave,
PO Box 3064; tel: (570) 346-0007 (acc 62)
Springfield, MA 01104: 285 Liberty St,
PO Box 1569, 01101-1569 (mail);
tel: (413) 785-1921 (acc 70)
*Syracuse, NY 13224: 2433 Erie Blvd East;
tel: (315) 445-0520 (acc 100)
Toledo, OH 43602: 27 Moorish Ave,
PO Box 355 43697; tel: (419) 241-8231
(acc 60)
Trenton, NJ 08638: 436 Mulberry St,
PO Box 5011; tel: (609) 599-9801 (acc 86)
Wilkes-Barre, PA 18702: 163 Hazle St,
PO Box 728, 18703-0728; tel: (570) 822-4248
(acc 52)
*Wilmington, DE 19801: 107 S Market St;
tel: (302) 654-8808 (acc 81)
*Worcester, MA 01603: 72 Cambridge St;
tel: (508) 799-0520 (acc 115)

ATTACHED TO DIVISIONS
Adult Day Care
Buffalo, NY 14202: Golden Age Center,
950 Main St; tel: (716) 883-9800 (acc 300)
Carlisle, PA 17013: 20 East Pomfret St,
PO Box 309; tel: (717) 249-1411
Lancaster, OH 43130: 228 W. Hubert Ave,
tel: (740) 687-1921, ext 111 (acc 50)
Syracuse, NY 13202: 749 S Warren St;
tel: (315) 479-1313

Extended In-home Service for the Elderly
Syracuse, NY 13202: 749 S Warren St;
tel: (315) 479-1309

Adult Rehabilitation
Kenmore, NY 14217: 1080 Military Rd;
tel: (716) 875-2533 (acc 90)

Day Care Centres
Akron, OH 44303: Child Development Center,
135 Hall St; tel: (330) 762-8177 (acc 69)
Boston, MA 02124: 26 Wales St;
tel: (617) 436-2480 (acc 70)
Bronx, NY 10451: 425 E 159th St;
tel: (718) 742-2346 (acc 45)
Bronx, NY 10457: 2121 Washington Ave;
tel: (718) 563-1530 (acc 69)
Brooklyn, NY 11212: Day Care Center, 280
Riverdale Ave; tel: (718) 345-2488 (acc 100)
Brooklyn, NY 11212: Sutter Day Care and
Family Day Care, 20 Sutter Ave;
tel: (718) 773-3041/(718) 735-6519 (acc 75
and 248)
Brooklyn, NY 11216: 110 Kosciusko St;
tel: (718) 857-7264 (acc 39)
Brooklyn, NY 11221: 1151 Bushwick Ave;
tel: (718) 455-0100 (acc 60)
Brooklyn, NY 11231: Family Day Care
Redhook and Fiesta Day Care Center,
80 Lorraine St; tel: (718) 834-8755
(acc 62 and 65)
Cambridge, MA 02139: 402 Massachusetts Ave,
PO Box 390647; tel: (617) 547-3400
(acc 28)
Cincinnati, OH 45202: 3501 Warsaw Ave;
tel: (513) 251-1451 (acc 112)
Cleveland, OH 44103: 6010 Hough Ave;
tel: (216) 432-0505 (acc 40)
Danbury, CT 06813-0826: 15 Foster St,
PO Box 826; tel: (203) 792-7505 (acc 30)
Hartford, CT 06105: 121 Sigourney St;
tel: (860) 543-8488 (acc 69)
Jersey City, NJ 07034: 562 Bergen Ave,
PO Box 4237, Bergen Stn;
tel: (201) 435-7355 (acc 70)
Lexington, KY 40508: 736 W Main St;
tel: (859) 252-7709 (acc 80)
Meriden, CT 06450-0234: 23 St Casimir Dr,
PO Box 234; tel: (203) 235-6532 (acc 27)
Morristown, NJ 07960: 95 Spring St,
PO Box 9150; tel: (973) 538-0543 (acc 95)
New York, NY 10034: 3732 10th Ave;
tel: (212) 569-4300 (acc 63)
Philadelphia (Germantown), PA 19133: 2601
North 11th St; tel: (215) 225-2700 (acc 131)
Providence, RI 02905: 20 Miner St;
tel: (401) 781-7238 (acc 110)
Syracuse, NY 13202:
Cab Horse Commons, 677 S Salina St;
tel: (315) 479-1305

Salvationists in Boston, Massachusetts, kneel in prayer on the snowy ground during the 'Holiness Ablaze – Living Examples' weekend held to celebrate the 125th anniversary of the sanctification experience of Samuel Logan Brengle on Boston Common in 1885

749 S Warren St; tel: (315) 479-1334
South Salina Street Infant Care Center,
  667 S Salina St; tel: (315) 479-1329
School Age Day Care, 749 S Warren St;
  tel: (315) 479-1334
Wilmington, DE 19899: 107 W 4th St;
  tel: (302) 472-0712 (acc 110)

Family Centres

Newark, NJ 07102: Newark Area Services
  Kinship Care, 45 Central Ave;
  tel: (973) 623-5959
  Grand Family Success Center,
  699 Springfield Ave; tel: (973) 373-5062
Oil City, PA 16301: The Salvation Army
  Dental Center, 217 Sycamore St;
  tel: (814) 677-4056

Development Disabilities Services

Bronx, NY 10457: Topping Ave Residence,
  1638-1640 Topping Ave; tel: (718) 466-1567
  (acc 8)
Brooklyn, NY 11220: Centennial House,
  426 56th St; tel: (718) 492-4415 (acc 9)
Brooklyn, NY 11237: Decade House,

315 Covert St; tel: (718) 417-1583 (acc 10)
Brooklyn, NY 11206: Millennium House,
  13 Pulaski St; tel: (718) 222-0736
  (acc 13)
Glendale, NY 11385: Glendale House,
  71-29 70th St; tel: (718) 381-7329 (acc 13)
Jamaica, NY 11423: Family Care,
  90-23 161st St; tel: (718) 206-9171 (acc 15)
Philadelphia, PA 19123: Developmental
  Disabilities Program, 701 N Broad St,
  Administrative Offices; tel: (215) 787-2804
  (community homes 46, acc 100)
South Ozone Park, NY 11420: Hope House,
  115-37 133rd St; tel: (718) 322-1616
  (acc 9)
Springfield, OH 45501: Hand N'Hand Activity
  Center for Adults with Disabilities,
  15 S Plum St; tel: (937) 322-3434
St Albans, NY 11412: Pioneer House, 104-14
  186th St; tel: (718) 264-8350 (acc 12)

Evangeline Residence

New York, NY 10011: 123 W 13th St (Markle
  Memorial Residence); tel: (212) 242-2400;
  fax: (212) 229-2801 (acc 286)

Family Counselling

Boston, MA 02118: Family Service Bureau, 1500 Washington St; tel: (617) 236-7233; fax: (617) 236-0123

Buffalo, NY 14202: Emergency Family Assistance, Family Court Visitation Program, Spouse Abuse Education Workshop, 960 Main St; tel: (716) 883-9800

Cincinnati, OH 45210: Cincinnati Family Service Bureau, 131 E 12th; tel: (513) 762-5660

Covington, KY 41014: N Kentucky Family Service Bureau, 1806 Scott Blvd; tel: (859) 261-0835

Newport, KY 41072: N Kentucky Family Service Bureau, 340 W 10th St; tel: (859) 431-1063

Rochester, NY 14604-4310: Rochester Emergency Family Assistance, 70 Liberty Pole Way, PO Box 41210; tel: (716) 987-9540

San Juan, PR 00921-2118: Family Services for Victims of Crime, 1327 Americo Miranda Ave, PO Box 10601, 00922-0601; tel: (787) 749-0027, 0029

Syracuse, NY 13202:
    Family Services, 749 S Warren St; tel: (315) 479-3651
    Family Place Visitation Center, 350 Rich St; tel: (315) 474-2931

Foster Home Services

Allentown, PA 18109: Foster Care In-Home Placement Services, Adoption Services and Administrative Services, 425 Allentown Dr, Suite 1; tel: (610) 821-7706

Group Homes for Adolescents

Fall River, MA 02720: Gentle Arms of Jesus Teen Living Center, 429 Winter St; tel: (508) 324-4558 (acc 15)

New York, NY 10027: Lenox House, 131 W 132nd St; tel: (212) 926-1236 (acc men 12)

Harbour Light Centres

Boston, MA 02118: Adult Women's Emergency Shelter, 407-409 Shawmut Ave, PO Box 180130; tel: (617) 536-7469 (acc 74)

Cleveland, OH 44115-2376: Harbor Light Complex, 1710 Prospect Ave; tel: (216) 781-3773 (acc 221)

Pittsburgh, PA 15233: 865 W North Ave; tel: (412) 231-0500 (acc 50)

Hotels, Lodges, Emergency Homes

Akron, OH 44302: Booth Manor Emergency Lodge, 216 S Maple St; tel: (330) 762-8481 ext 194 (acc 67)

Allentown, PA 18102: Hospitality House, 344 N 7th St; tel: (610) 432-0128 (acc 65)

Bellaire, OH 43906: 315 37th St; tel: (740) 676-6225 (acc 40)

Brooklyn, NY 11207: Bushwick Family Residence, 1675 Broadway; tel: (718) 574-2701 (acc families 87)

Brooklyn, NY 11203: Kingsboro Men's Shelter, 681 Clarkson Ave; tel: (718) 363-7738 (acc 80)

Bronx, NY 10456: Franklin Women's Shelter and Referral, 1122 Franklin Ave; tel: (347) 417- 8200 (acc 200)

Buffalo, NY 14202: 960 Main St, Emergency Family Shelter; tel: (716) 884-4798 (acc 96)

Cambridge, MA 02139-0008: Day Drop-in Shelter for Men and Women/Night Shelter for Men, 402 Mass Ave, PO Box 390647; tel: (617) 547-3400 (acc 200/50)

Carlisle, PA 17013: Genesis House (Men's Emergency Housing), 24 E Pomfret St; tel: (717) 249-1411

Chester, PA 19013: Stepping Stone Program, 151 W 15th; tel: (610) 874-0423 (acc 35)

Cincinnati, OH 45210: Emergency Shelter, 131 E 12th; tel: (513) 762-5655 (acc 24)

Cleveland, OH 44115: Zelma George Family Shelter, 1710 Prospect Ave; tel: (216) 641-3712 (acc 110)

Concord, NH 03301: McKenna House (Adult Shelter), 100 S Fruit St; tel: (603) 228-3505 (acc 29)

Dayton, OH 45402:
    Women and Children's Homeless Shelter, 138 S Wilkinson St; tel: (937) 228-8241 (acc 27)
    Men's Homeless Shelter, 624 S Main St; tel: (937) 228-8210 (acc 55)

East Stroudsburg, PA 18301: 226 Washington St; tel: (570) 421-3050

Elizabeth, NJ 07201: 1018 E Grand St; tel: (908) 352-2886 (acc 45)

Elmira, NY 14902: 414 Lake St, PO Box 293; tel: (607) 732-0314 (24-hour Domestic Violence Hotline); Victims of Domestic Violence Safe House (acc 15)

Elmira, NY 14901: Our House, 401-403 Division St; tel: (607) 734-0032 (acc 20)

Hartford, CT 06105: Family Shelter, 225 S Marshall St; tel: (860) 543-8423 (acc 27)

Jamaica, NY 11434: Springfield Family Residence, 146-80 Guy R. Brewer Blvd; tel: (718) 521-5090 (acc families 90)

Jamestown, NY 14702: ANEW Center Shelter for Domestic Violence, Residential/Non-

Residential Program, PO Box 368;
tel: (716) 483-0830; 24-hour Hotline
tel: (800) 252-8748
Johnstown, PA 15901: Emergency Shelter;
tel: (814) 539-3110 (acc 24)
Laconia, NH 03246: The Carey House,
6 Spring St; tel: (603) 528-8086 (acc 30)
Lexington, KY 40508: Early Learning Center
Families, 736 W Main St; tel: (859) 252-7706
(acc 129)
Montclair, NJ 07042-2776: 68 N Fullerton Ave;
tel: (973) 744-8666 (acc 18)
Newark, OH 43055: 250 E Main St;
tel: (740) 345-3289 (acc 18)
New Britain, CT 06050: 78 Franklin Sq;
tel: (860) 225-8491 (acc 25 men)
Norristown, PA 19404: 533 Swede St;
tel: (610) 275-9225 (acc 41)
Northport, NY 11768-0039: Northport Veterans'
Residence, 79 Middleville Rd, Bldg 11,
PO Box 300 (mail); tel: (631) 262-0601
(acc 87)
Perth Amboy, NJ 08862-0613: Care House,
Seasonal Emergency Shelter, 433 State St;
tel: (732) 826-7040 (acc men 20)
Philadelphia, PA 19107: Eliza Shirley House,
1320 Arch St; tel: (215) 568-5111 (acc 125)
Philadelphia, PA 19123: Red Shield Family
Residence, 715 N Broad St;
tel: (215) 787-2887 (acc 100)
Pittsburgh, PA 15206: Family Caring Center,
6017 Broad St; tel: (412) 362-0891
(acc 40)
Pottstown, PA 19464: Lessig-Booth Family
Residence, 137 King St; tel: (610) 327-0836
(acc 32)
Queens (Jamaica), NY 11435: Briarwood Family
Residence, 80-20 134th St; tel: (718) 268-3395
(acc 91)
Rochester, NY 14604-4310: Men's Emergency
Shelter, Booth Haven, 70 Liberty Pole Way,
PO Box 41210; tel: (585) 987-9500
(acc 39)
Rochester, NY 14604-4310: Women's Shelter,
Hope House, 100 West Ave, PO Box 41210;
tel: (585) 697-3430 (acc 19)
Rochester, NY 14604-4310: Safe Haven
Emergency Shelter, 70 Liberty Pole Way,
PO Box 21210; tel: (585) 987-9540
(acc 16)
San Juan, PR 00903: Homeless Shelter, Proyecto
Esperanza, Fernández Juncos, cnr Valdés;
tel: (787) 722-2370
Schenectady, NY 12305: Evangeline Booth
Home and Women's Shelter, 168 Lafayette St;
tel: (518) 370-0276

Syracuse, NY 13202:
Parenting Center, 667 S Salina St;
tel: (315) 479-1330
Emergency Lodge, 749 S Warren St;
tel: (315) 479-1332
Trenton, NJ 08601: Homeless Drop In Center,
575 E State St; tel: (609) 599-9373
Waterbury, CT 06720: 74 Central Ave;
tel: (203) 756-1718 (acc 29)
West Chester, PA 19380: Railton House,
101 E Market St; tel: (610) 696-7434
(acc 17)
Wilmington, DE 19899: Booth Social Service
Center, 104 W 5th St; tel: (302) 472-0764
(acc 52)
Wooster, OH 44691: 24-Hour Open Door
Emergency Shelter, 437 S Market St;
tel: (330) 264-4704 (acc 44)
Zanesville, OH 43701: 515 Putnam Ave;
tel: (740) 454-8953 (acc 35)

HIV Services

Bronx, NY 10458: 601 Crescent Ave;
tel: (718) 329-5410; fax: (718) 329-5409
Newark, NJ 07102: 45 Central Ave;
tel: (973) 623-5959; fax: (973) 848-1556
New York, NY 10010: 340 East 24th St;
tel: (212) 585-6085; fax: (646) 335-6311

Homeless Youth and Runaways

Rochester, NY 14604-1210: Genesis House,
35 Ardmore St, PO Box 41210;
tel: (585) 235-2600 (acc 14)
Syracuse, NY 13205: Barnabas House,
1912 S Salina St; tel: (315) 475-9720 (acc 8)
Syracuse, NY 13205: Booth House and Host
Home, 264 Furman St; tel: (315) 471-7628
(acc 8)

Transitional Housing Programme

Allentown, PA 18101; Fleming Hospital House,
344 N 7th St; tel: (610) 432-0128
Arlington, MA 02474-6597: Wellington House,
8 Wellington St (Single Resident Occupancy);
tel: (781) 648-2636 (acc 20)
Buffalo, NY 14202: 984 Main St;
tel: (716) 884-4798
Carlisle, PA 17013; Stuart House, 20 E Pomfret St;
tel: (717) 249-1411 (acc 41)
Cincinnati, OH 45210: (families with children)
19 & 21 E 15th St; tel: (513) 762-5660
Cleveland, OH 44103: Railton House, 6000
Woodland; tel: (216) 361-6778 (acc 56)
Cleveland, OH 44115:
Pass Programme, 1710 Prospect Ave;
tel: (216) 619-4722 (acc 75)

Cleveland, OH 44115: Project Share,
2501 E 22nd St; tel: (216) 623-7492 (acc 29)

Lancaster, PA 17603: 131 South Queen St;
tel: (717) 397-7565 (acc 21)

Norristown, PA 19404; Faith and Bridge
Programmes, 533 Swede St; tel: (610) 275-4183

Perth Amboy, NJ 08862-0613: Care House
Transitional Shelter, 433 State St;
tel: (732) 826-7040 (acc veterans 11,
homeless men 7)

Philadelphia, PA 19103: Mid-City Apartments
Permanent Housing, 2025 Chestnut St;
tel: (215) 569-9160 (acc 60)

Philadelphia, PA 19147: Reed House Permanent
Housing, 1320 S 32nd St; tel: (215) 755-6789
(acc 66)

Pottstown, PA 19464: Transitional Housing,
137 King St; tel: (610) 326-1621

Syracuse, NY 13205:
Transitional Family Apartments, 1482 S State St;
tel: (315) 475-7663
Transitional Living Project Apartments (youth),
1941 S Salina St; tel: (315) 475-9720

Women's Shelter, 1704 S Salina St;
tel: (315) 472-0947

West Chester, PA 19380: William Booth Initiative,
101 E Market St; tel: (610) 696-8746
(acc7)

Wilkes Barre, PA 18703: Kirby House;
17 S Pennsylvania Ave; tel: (570) 824-8741

Youth Service and Emergency Shelter

Syracuse, NY 13205: Barnabas, 1941 S Salina St;
tel: (315) 475-9744

Senior Citizens' Residences

Cincinnati, OH 45224: Booth Residence for the
Elderly and Handicapped, 6000 Townvista Dr;
tel: (513) 242-4482 (acc 150)

New York, NY 10025: Williams Residence,
720 West End Ave; tel: (212) 316-6000;
fax: (212) 280-0410 (acc 367)

Philadelphia, PA 19139: Booth Manor,
5522 Arch St; tel: (215) 471-0500 (acc 50)

Philadelphia, PA 19131: Ivy Residence,
4051 Ford Rd; tel: (215) 871-3303 (acc 75)

USA SOUTHERN: Salvationists of Florida Division load a small plane at Fort Lauderdale to take personnel and emergency supplies to Haiti, after the island had been struck by a 7.0 magnitude earthquake. The plane made several trips, piloted by a Salvationist from Fort Lauderdale Corps.

USA SOUTHERN TERRITORY

Territorial leaders:
Commissioners Maxwell and Lenora Feener

Territorial Commander:
Commissioner Maxwell Feener
(1 Jul 2006)

Chief Secretary:
Colonel Terry W. Griffin (2 Jul 2007)

Territorial Headquarters: 1424 Northeast Expressway, Atlanta, GA 30329-2088, USA

Tel: [1] (404) 728 1300; fax: [1] (404) 728 1392; website: www.salvationarmysouth.org

The Salvation Army was incorporated as a religious and charitable corporation in the State of Georgia in 1927 as 'The Salvation Army' and is qualified to conduct all its affairs in all of the states of the territory.

Zone: Americas and Caribbean
USA states included in the territory: Alabama, Arkansas, Florida, Georgia, Kentucky, Louisiana, Maryland, Mississippi, North Carolina, Oklahoma, South Carolina, Tennessee, Texas, Virginia, West Virginia, District of Columbia
Languages in which the gospel is preached: English, Haitian-Creole, Korean, Laotian, Spanish, Vietnamese
Periodical: *Southern Spirit*

THE territory continued its Christ-centred mission, as Salvationists were actively engaged in four priority areas: Fervent Prayer; Effective Visitation; Sunday School/Discipleship; Dynamic Worship. The call to fervent prayer was augmented with a 24/7 territorial prayer website (www.armybattlecry.org).

An emphasis on Bible study at Sunday school and in midweek meetings led to increased attendances and several small group studies being established. Attempts at dynamic worship resulted in worship that is relevant, interactive and Christ-centred.

The national emphasis on recruitment – 'Come Join Our Army' – steadily increased. A highlight of this was the recognition of more than 75 new senior and junior soldiers in an event prior to the commissioning in June 2009.

A representative of this group, Dorothy Helm of Jackson Corps (Mississippi), testified through a video recording. Dorothy led a life of drugs, sex and alcohol abuse until her mother took her to the

Army's Centre of Hope. Invited to attend Sunday meetings and the weekly Bible study class at the corps, she later surrendered her life to Christ. Dorothy was enrolled a soldier and became fully involved in the corps, making it her ministry to visit areas where once she was an addict.

The ordination and commissioning of the Witnesses For Christ Session saw 52 new lieutenants sent to all corners of the territory and two returning to Korea to commence their service as officers.

The Territorial Bible Conference (16-23 August), themed 'Lift Jesus Higher … Experience His Power', was held at Lake Junaluska, North Carolina. Commissioners William and Marilyn Francis (Canada and Bermuda) were the guest leaders.

General Shaw Clifton and Commissioner Helen Clifton (WPWM) met Salvationists of the territory in October. They led the morning devotions at THQ, where the General accepted a $3 million cheque for the grant-aided territories' Centralised Pension Fund – the first instalment towards a pledge of $20 million.

In a public meeting at Atlanta Temple Corps later that day General Clifton gave the Bible message and many people responded to his invitation to kneel at the mercy seat.

The territory published a series of podcasts (video and audio streams on the internet) demonstrating the role of the Army's Emergency Disaster Services. These can be viewed at www.disaster.salvationarmyusa.org

In contrast to the previous five years, the period under review was absent of major hurricanes. However, EDS teams were called into action for tornadoes, ice storms, floods, major fires and a host of other catastrophes where victims needed food, water, emotional and spiritual care, and hope for the future.

When the January 2010 earthquake struck Haiti, the Florida Division immediately sent personnel and emergency supplies in a small plane from Fort Lauderdale to the stricken island. The plane made several trips, piloted by a Salvationist from Fort Lauderdale Corps.

STATISTICS

Officers 1,438 (active 942 retired 496) **Cadets** (1st Yr) 36 (2nd Yr) 42 **Employees** 14,974
Corps 344 **Societies/Outposts** 11 **Institutions** 274
Senior Soldiers 27,821 **Adherents** 2,421 **Junior Soldiers** 6,989
Personnel serving outside territory Officers 29

STAFF

Women's Ministries: Comr Lenora Feener (TPWM) Col Linda Griffin (TSWM) Maj Susan Ellis (CCMS/Outreach)
Personnel: Lt-Col Charles White
Programme: Lt-Col Edward Hobgood
Business: Lt-Col John R. Jones
Adult Rehabilitation Centres Command: Lt-Col Mark Bell
Audit: Maj Eugene Broome
Community Relations and Development: Maj Mark Brown
Evangelism and Adult Ministries: Maj Otis Childs
Employee Relations: Murray Flagg PhD
Finance: Maj Stephen Ellis
Legal: Maj Charles Powell
Multicultural Ministries: Maj Vivian Childs
Music: Mr Nicholas Simmons-Smith
Officers' Health Services: Maj Jeanne Johnson
Property: Mr Robert L. Taylor
Retired Officers: Maj Hilda Howell

USA Southern Territory

Social Services: Mr Kevin Tompson-Hooper
Supplies and Purchasing: Maj Robert Bagley
Training: Maj Alan Hofer
Youth: Maj Art Penhale
Candidates: Maj Susan Brown

DIVISIONS

Alabama-Louisiana-Mississippi: 1450
Riverside Dr, PO Box 4857, 39296-4857,
Jackson, MS 39202; tel: (601) 969 7560;
fax: (601) 968-0273; Majs Samuel A. and
Nancy Henry

Arkansas and Oklahoma: 5101
N Pennsylvania Ave, PO Box 12600,
73157, Oklahoma City, OK 73112;
tel: (405) 840 0735; fax: (405) 840 0460;
Majs Kenneth and Dawn Luyk

Florida: 5631 Van Dyke Rd, Lutz, FL 33558,
PO Box 270848, 33688-0848, Tampa, FL;
tel: (813) 962 6611; fax: (813) 962 4098;
Lt-Cols Vernon and Martha Jewett

Georgia: 1000 Center Pl, NW, 30093,
PO Box 930188, 30003 Norcross, GA 30003;
tel: (770) 441-6200; fax: (770) 441-6214;
Majs James E. and Linda Arrowood

Kentucky and Tennessee: 214-216
W Chestnut St, Box 2229, 40201-2229,
Louisville, KY 40202; tel: (502) 583 5391;
fax: (502) 625 1199; Majs John and
Marthalyn Needham

Maryland and West Virginia: 814 Light St,
Baltimore, MD 21230; tel: (410) 347 9944;
fax: (410) 539 7744; Maj Sandra Defibaugh

National Capital and Virginia: 2626
Pennsylvania Ave NW, PO Box 18658,
Washington, DC 20037; tel: (202) 756 2600;
fax: (202) 464-7200; Majs Kelly and
Donna Igleheart

North and South Carolina: 501 Archdale Dr,
Box 241808, 28224-1808, Charlotte, NC
28217-4237; tel: (704) 522 4970;
fax: (704) 522 4980; Majs Willis and
Barbara Howell

Texas: 6500 Harry Hines Blvd, PO Box 36607,
75235, Dallas, TX 75235; tel: (214) 956 6000;
fax: (214) 956 9436; Lt-Cols Henry and
M. Dorris Gonzalez

SCHOOL FOR OFFICER TRAINING
1032 Metropolitan Pkwy, SW Atlanta, GA 30310;
tel: (404) 753 4166; fax: (404) 753 3709

ATTACHED TO DIVISIONS
Alcoholic Rehabilitation
Fort Worth, TX 76103: 1855 E Lancaster
(women only, acc 13)

Greenville, SC 29609: 419 Rutherford St (acc 40)
Mobile, AL 36604: 1009 Dauphin St (acc 30)

Child Care Centres
Annapolis, MD 21403: 351 Hilltop Ln (acc 80)
Austin, TX 78767: 4523 Tannehill Hill (acc 26)
Clearwater, FL 34625: 1625 N Belcher Rd
(acc 66)
Charlottesville, VA 22204: 207 Ridge St (acc 50)
Decatur, AL 36604: 100 Austinville Rd SW
Freeport, TX 77541-2620: 1618 Ave J (acc 85)
Irving, TX 75061: 250 E Grauwyler (acc 62)
Jacksonville, FL 32202: 318 N Ocean St
(acc 125)
Lakeland, FL 33801: 835 N Kentucky (acc 45)
Lynchburg, VA 24501: 2215 Park Ave (acc 40)
Naples, FL 34104: 3180 Estey Ave (acc 124)
Nashville, TN 37207: 631 Dickerson Rd
(acc 37)
Salisbury, MD 21804: 415 Oak St (acc 52)
West Pasco, FL 34673: PO Box 1050, Port
Richey (acc 161)

Children's Residential Care
Birmingham, AL 35212: Youth Emergency
Services, 6001 Crestwood Blvd (acc 33)
Dallas, TX, 75220: Casa Youth Runaway
Shelter, 2640 Webb Chapel Ext (acc 16)
St Petersburg, FL 33733: Children's Village,
PO Drawer 10909 (acc 24)
St Petersburg, FL 33733: Sallie House
Emergency Shelter, PO Drawer 10909 (acc 18)

Family Resident Programme
Alexandria, VA 22301: 2525 Mt Vernon Ave
(acc 40)
Albany, GA 31721: 304 W 2nd Ave (acc 12)
Amarillo, TX 79101: 400 S Harrison (acc 40)
Arlington, TX 76013: 711 W Border (acc 30)
Athens, GA 30606: 484 Hawthorne Ave (acc 52)
Atlanta, GA 30310: 400 Luckie St NW (acc 328:
men 156 women 150 Harbour Light 22)
Augusta, GA 30904: 2020 Gardner St (acc 109)
Austin, TX 78701: 501 E 8th St (acc 60)
Austin, TX 78767: 4523 Tannehill Ln (Women
and Children Shelter) (acc 26)
Baltimore, MD 21030: 1114 N Calvert St (acc 75)
Beaumont, TX 77701: 1078 McFadden (acc 10)
Bradenton, FL 34205: 1204 14th St W (acc 102)
Brunswick, GA 31520: 1620 Reynolds St
(acc 16)
Cambridge, MD 21613: 200 Washington St
(acc 10)
Charleston, WV 25302: 308, 308A, 310,
312 Ohio St (16)
Charlottesville, VA: 207 Ridge St NW (acc 36)

281

Chattanooga, TN 37403: 800 N McCallie Ave (acc 72)

Clearwater, FL 33756: 1527 E Druid Rd (acc 64)

Columbus, GA 31909: 1718 2nd Ave (acc 39)

Corpus Christi, TX 78401: 513 Josephine (acc 28)

Dalton, GA 30720: 1101A North Thorton Ave (acc 24)

Daytona Beach, FL 32114: 560 Ballough Rd (acc 49)

Enid, OK 73701: 222 W Pine (acc 8)

Ft Lauderdale, FL 33312: 1445 W Broward Blvd (acc 251)

Ft Myers, FL 33901: 2163 Stella St (acc 134)

Fort Worth, TX 76103: 1855 E Lancaster Ave (acc 62)

Gainesville, FL 32601: 639 E University Ave (acc 24)

Gainesville, GA: 711 Dorsey St (acc 52)

Griffin, GA 30224: 329 N 13th St (acc 32)

Hagerstown, MD 21740: 534 W Franklin St (acc 30)

Harrisonburg, VA 22801: 895 Jefferson St (acc 72)

Hollywood, FL 33020: 1960 Sherman St (acc 140)

Houston, TX 77004: 1603 McGowen (acc 42)

Jacksonville, FL 32201: PO Box 52508 (acc 123)

Lakeland, FL 33801: 835 N Kentucky Ave (acc 166)

Louisville, KY 40203: 209 E Breckinridge (acc 35)

Louisville, KY 40203: 817 S Brook St (acc 18)

Lynchburg, VA 24501: 2215 Park Ave (acc 22)

Macon, GA 31206: 2312 Houston Ave (acc 131)

Melbourne, FL 32901: 1080 S Hickory St (acc 48)

Memphis, TN 38105: 696 Jackson Ave (acc 120)

Miami, FL 33142: 1907 NW 38th St (acc 238)

Nashville, TN 37207-5608: 631 Dickerson Rd (acc 53)

Newport News, VA 23602: 11931 Jefferson Ave (acc 30)

N Central Brevard, Cocoa, FL 32922: 919 Peachtree St (acc 17)

Norfolk, VA 23502: Hope Village, 5525 Raby Rd (acc 65)

Ocala, FL 34475: 320 NW 1st Ave (acc 118)

Orlando, FL 32804: 400 W Colonial Dr (acc 198)

Panama City, FL 32401: 1824 W 15th St (acc 48)

Parkersburg, WV 24740: 534-570 Fifth St (acc 56)

Pensacola, FL 32505: 1310 North S St (acc 28)

Richmond, VA 23220: 2 W Grace St (acc 52)

Rome, GA 30161: 317 E First Ave (acc 26)

San Antonio, TX 78212: 515 W Elmira 78212 (acc 300)

Sarasota, FL 34236: 1400 10th St (acc 226)

Savannah, GA 31405: 3100 Montgomery St (acc 120)

St Petersburg, FL 33733: PO Drawer 10909 (acc 112)

Tampa, FL 33602: 1603 N Florida (acc 192)

Texarkana, TX 71854: 316 Hazel (acc 46)

Thomasville, GA 31792: 208 South St (acc 9)

Titusville, FL 32796: 1212 W Main (acc 16)

Tulsa, OK 74103: 102 N Denver (acc 100)

Tyler, TX 75701: 633 N Broadway 75702

Valdosta, GA 31601: 317 Virginia Ave (acc 9)

Washington, DC 20009: 1434 Harvard St NW (acc 60)

Waycross, GA 31501: 977 Tebeau St (acc 11)

West Palm Beach, FL 33402: PO Box 789 (acc 95)

Wheeling, WV 26003: 140 16th St (acc 32)

Winchester, VA 22603: 300 Ft Collier Rd (acc 48)

Winter Haven, FL 33882: PO Box 1069 (acc 40)

Williamsburg, VA 7131: Merrimac Trail (acc 17)

Harbour Light Centres

Atlanta, GA 30313: 400 Luckie St (acc 327)

Dallas, TX 75235: 5302 Harry Hines Blvd (acc 309)

Houston, TX 77009: 2407 N Main St (acc 308)

Washington, DC 20002: 2100 New York Ave, NE (acc 207)

Senior Citizens' Centres

Arlington, TX 76013: 712 W Abrams

Beaumont, MS 1502: Bolton Ave

Birmingham, '614 Birmingham', AL 35203: 2410 8th Ave N

Brooklyn, MS: Carnes Rd

Dallas Cedar Crest, TX 75203: 1007 Hutchins Rd

Dallas Oak Cliff, TX 75208: 1617 W Jefferson Blvd

Dallas Pleasant Grove, TX 75217-0728: 8341 Elam Rd

Ft Worth, TX 76106: 3023 NW 24th St

Ft Worth, TX 76119-5813: 1909 E Seminary Dr (acc 121)

Houston Aldine/Westfield, TX 77093: 2600 Aldine Westfield

Houston Pasadena, TX 77506: 45/6 Irvington Blvd

Houston Temple, TX 77009: 2627
    Cherrybrook Ln 77502
Jacksonville, FL 32202: 17 E Church St
Lufkin, TX 75904: 305 Shands
Montgomery, AL 36107: 900 Bell St
Oklahoma City, OK 73109: 311 SW 5th St
    (includes 5 drop-in centres)
San Antonio Citadel, TX 78201:
    2810 W Ashby Pl
San Antonio Dave Coy Center, TX 78202:
    226 Nolan St
San Antonio Hope Center, TX 78212:
    521 W Elmira
Sarasota, FL 34236: 1400 10th St
Shreveport, LA 71163: 200 E Stoner
St Petersburg, FL 33713: 3800 9th Ave N

Senior Citizens' Residences

Atlanta, GA 30306: William Booth Towers,
    1125 Ponce de Leon Ave NE (acc 99)
Charlotte, NC 28202-1727: William Booth
    Gardens Apts, 421 North Poplar St (acc 130)
Cumberland, MD 21502-0282: William Booth
    Towers, 220 Somerville Ave (acc 113)
Fort Worth, TX 76119-5813: Catherine Booth
    Friendship House, 1901 E Seminary Dr
    (acc 157)
Gastonia, NC 28054: Catherine Booth Gardens
    Apts, 1336 Union Rd (acc 82)
High Point, NC 27263: William Booth Gardens
    Apts, 123 SW Cloverleaf Place (acc 76)
Houston, TX 77009: William Booth Gardens
    Apts, 808 Frawley (acc 62)
Ocala, FL 34470: Evangeline Booth Gardens
    Apts, 2921 NE 14th St (acc 64)
Orlando, FL 32801: William Booth Towers,
    633 Lake Dot Circle (acc 168)
Orlando, FL 32801: Catherine Booth Towers,
    625 Lake Dot Circle (acc 125)
Pasadena, TX 77502: Evangeline Booth,
    2627 Cherrybrook Ln (acc 62)
San Antonio, TX 78201-5397: William Booth
    Gardens Apts, 2710 W Ashby Pl (acc 95)
San Antonio, TX 78201: Catherine Booth Apts,
    2810 W Ashby Pl (acc 62)
Tyler, TX 75701: William Booth Gardens Apts,
    601 Golden Rd (acc 132)
Waco, TX 76708-1141: William Booth Gardens
    Apts, 4200 N 19th (acc 120)
Waco, TX 76708-1141: Catherine Booth Appts,
    N 19th

Service Centres

Alexander City, AL 35010: 823 Cherokee Rd
Americus, GA 31709: 204 Prince St
Bainbridge, GA 39818: 600 Scott St

Bay City, TX 77414: 1911 7th St
Borger, TX 79008-1046: 1090 Coronado
    Center Cir 79008-1046
Bogalusa, LA 70427: 400 Georgia Ave
Boone, NC 28607: High Country 7979,
    Hwy 105 South
Brownwood, TX 76801: 403 Lakeway
Bushnell, FL 33513: PO Box 25 (Sumter County)
Carrollton, GA 30112: 115 Lake Carroll Blvd
Carthage, MS 39051: 610 Hwy 16 West, Suite A
Cleburne, TX 76031: 111 S Anglin
Columbia, MD 21045: PO Box 2877 (Howard
    County)
Corinth, MS 38835: 2200 Lackey Dr
Covington, GA 30014: 5193 Washington St
Culpeper, VA 22701: 102 Main St, #304
Douglas, GA 31533: 110 S Gaskin Ave
Dublin, GA 31921: 1617 Telfair St
East Pasco, Dade City, FL 33523: 14445 7th St
Eden, NC 27288: 314 Morgan Rd
Elberton, GA 30635: 262 N McIntosh St
Elizabethtown, KY 42701: 1006 N Mulberry
Enterprise, AL 366331: 1919-B E Park Ave
    (Coffee County)
Fernandina Beach, FL 32034: 421 S 9th St
Fort Payne, AL 35967: 450 Gault Ave N
    (Dekalb County)
Frankline, VA, 23851: Western Tidewater
    Svc Ctr, 50l N Main St
Fulton, MS 38843: 414 E Main St
Glen Burnie, MD 21061: 511 S Crain Hwy
Gonzales, LA 70737: 218 Bayou Narcisse
Guntersville, AL 35976: 1336 Gunter Ave
    (Marshall County)
Hopewell, VA 23860: 222 N Main St, Suite 218
Houma, LA 70363: 1414 E Tunnel Blvd.
Houston, MS 38851: 114 Washington St
Immokalee, FL 34142: 2050 Commerce Ave,
    Unit 3A
Jackson, GA 30233: 178 N Benton St (Jackson/
    Butts County)
Jacksonville, FL 32256: 10940 Beach Blvd
Jacksonville, FL 32204: Towers, 900 W Adams St
Jasper, AL 35502: 207 20th St E (Walker County)
Kaufman, TX 75142: 5 Oak Creek Dr
    (mail PO Box 217)
LaBelle, FL 33935: 180 N Main St
Lebanon, TN, 37087: 215 University Ave
Lenoir, NC 28645: 108 Morganton Blvd
Lewisburg, WV 24901: 148 Maplewood Ave
    (Greenbriar Valley)
Lewisville, TX 75067: 207 Elm St 75057
McDonough, GA 30253: 401 Race Track Rd
McGehee, AR 71654: 102 E Oak St (Desha
    County)
Milledgeville, GA 31061: 420 S Wilkinson St

Mocksville, NC 27028: 279 N Main St (Davie County)

Morganton, NC 28655: 420-B W Fleming Dr

Nacogdoches, TX 75963: 118 E Hospital Suite 101

Natchez, MS 39120: 509 N Canal St

New Braunfels, TX 78130: 373-B Landa St

Newnan, GA 30264: 670 Jefferson St

Okmulgee, OK 74447-0123: 105-111 E 8th St

Oneonta, AL 35121: 333 Valley Rd (Blount County)

Opelika, AL 36801: 720 Columbus Pkwy (Lee County)

Oxford, MS 38655: 2617 W Oxford Loop, Ste 4

Ozark, AL 36360: 154 E Broad St (Dale County)

Pleasanton, TX 78064: 2132 2nd St (mail PO Box 951)

Pontotoc, MS 38863: 187 Hwy 15 N

Putnam County, WV 25177: 720 N Winfield Rd, St Albans, WV

Sallisaw, OK: PO Box 292, Fort Smith, AR 72902

San Marcos, TX 78667: 1658 I-35 S

Scottsboro, AL 35768: 1501 E Willow St (Jackson County)

Spencer, WV 25276: 145 Main St (Roane County)

Starksville, MS 39759: 501 Hwy 12 W

St Mary's, GA 31558: 1909 Osborne Rd

Sylacauga, AL 35150: 100 E 3rd St (Talledega South)

Talladega, AL 35160: 215 E Battle St (Talledega North)

Tarpon Springs, FL 34689: 209 S Pinellas Ave

Thomasville, AL 36784: 122 W Wilson Ave

Troy, AL 36081: 509 S Brundidge St

Union, SC 29379: 215 S Mountain St

Vidalia, GA 30475: 204 Jackson St

Warrenton, VA 20186: 26 S Third St

Wellsburg, WV 26070: 491 Commerce St

Westminster, MD 21157: 300 Hahn Rd

Yadkinville, NC 27055: 111 E Main St (Yadkin County)

Spouse House Shelters

Cocoa, FL: 919 Peachtree St 32922 (PO Box 1540, 32923) (acc 20)

Panama City, FL 32401: 1824 W 15th St (PO Box 540, 32412) (acc 46)

Port Richey, FL 34673: PO Box 5517 Hudson, FL 34674-5517 (acc 32)

Roanoke, VA 24016 (acc 60)

Warner Robins, GA 31093: 96 Thomas Blvd (acc 18)

SOCIAL SERVICES
Adult Rehabilitation Centres (including industrial stores)

Alexandria, VA 22312: Northern Virginia Center, 6528 Little River Turnpike (acc 120)

Atlanta, GA 30318-5726: 740 Marietta St, NW (acc 132)

Austin, TX 78745: 4216 S Congress (acc 118)

Baltimore, MD 21230: 2700 W Patapsco Ave (acc 115)

Birmingham, AL 35234:
1401 F. L. Shuttlesworth Dr (acc 107)

Charlotte, NC 28204: 1023 Central Ave (acc 116)

Dallas, TX 75235-7213: 5554 Harry Hines Blvd (acc 137)

Fort Lauderdale, FL 33312-1597:
1901 W Broward Blvd (acc 99)

Fort Worth, TX 76111-2996: 2901 NE 28th St (acc 109)

Houston, TX 77007-6113: 1015 Hemphill St (acc 167)

Hyattsville, MD 20781: (Washington, DC, and Suburban Maryland Center) 3304 Kenilworth Ave (acc 151)

Jacksonville, FL 32246: 10900 Beach Blvd (acc 121)

Memphis, TN 2649 Kirby Whitten Rd, 38133-4734 (acc 86)

Miami, FL 33127-4981: 2236 NW Miami Court (acc 134)

Nashville, TN 37213-1102: 140 N First St (acc 86)

New Orleans, LA 70121-2596: 200 Jefferson Highway (acc 50)

Oklahoma City, OK 73106-2409: 2041 NW 7th St (acc 81)

Orlando, FL 32808-7927: 3955 W Colonial Dr (acc 105)

Richmond, VA 23220-1199: 2601 Hermitage Rd (acc 81)

San Antonio, TX 78204: 1324 S Flores St (acc 110)

St Petersburg, FL 33709-1597: Suncoast Area Center, 5885 66th St N (acc 119)

Tampa, FL 33682-2949: 13815 N Salvation Army Lane (acc 131)

Tulsa, OK 74106-5163: 601-611 N Main St (acc 86)

Virginia Beach, VA 23462: Hampton Roads Center, 5560 Virginia Beach Blvd (acc 123)

In addition, 10 fresh-air camps and 344 community centres, boys'/girls' clubs are attached to the division

USA WESTERN TERRITORY

Territorial leaders:
**Commissioners James M. and
Carolyn R. Knaggs**

Territorial Commander:
Commissioner James M. Knaggs
(1 Jul 2010)

Chief Secretary:
Colonel William Harfoot (1 Jul 2008)

**Territorial Headquarters: 180 E Ocean Boulevard,
PO Box 22646 (90801-5646), Long Beach, California 90802-4709, USA**

Tel: [1] (562) 436-7000; website: www.usw.salvationarmy.org

The Salvation Army was incorporated as a religious and charitable corporation in the State of California in 1914 as 'The Salvation Army' and is qualified, along with its several affiliated separate corporations, to conduct its affairs in all of the states of the territory.

Zone: Americas and Caribbean
USA states included in the territory: Alaska, Arizona, California, Colorado, Hawaii, Idaho, Montana, Nevada, New Mexico, Oregon, Utah, Washington, Wyoming, Guam (US Territory)
Other countries included in territory: Republic of the Marshall Islands, Federated States of Micronesia
'The Salvation Army' in Cantonese: Kau Shai Kwan; in Japanese: Kyu-sei-gun; in Mandarin (Kuoyo): Chiu Shi Chuen; in Spanish: Ejército de Salvación
Languages in which the gospel is preached: Cantonese, Chamarro, Chuukese, English, Hmong, Korean, Laotian, Mandarin, Marshallese, Filipino, Pohnpeian, Portuguese, Spanish, and Tlingit
Periodicals: *Caring, New Frontier, Nuevas Fronteras* (Spanish)

THE 'Come Join Our Army' emphasis is bearing fruit in the West. Senior and junior soldiers have been enrolled on the island of Chuuk and in Kolonia Corps at Pohnpei, both islands located in the Federated States of Micronesia.

The then territorial leaders Commissioners Philip and Patricia Swyers enrolled more than 200 soldiers at Commissioning 2009 (13-14 June). Sixteen cadets of the Witnesses For Christ Session and four auxiliary-captains were commissioned as officers. Commissioner Israel Gaither (then National Commander) and Commissioner Eva Gaither took part in the weekend activities, themed 'Army of the Lord'.

Meetings conducted by Commissioners Gaither in Oakland, California and Seattle, Washington saw 250 senior and junior soldiers enrolled. Additionally, enrolments took place in numerous other locations.

On 12 September 2009, 43 cadets

of the Ambassadors Of Holiness Session were welcomed.

The territory opened two new Ray and Joan Kroc Corps Community Centres in 2009 – Coeur d'Alene, Idaho and Salem, Oregon. Commissioners Swyers carried out the groundbreaking for the Hawaii Kroc Centre due to open in 2011, while the new Phoenix South Mountain Kroc Centre's groundbreaking took place in March 2010, with the visiting International Staff Band providing music for the occasion.

The ISB's visit to the territory (26 March-4 April) took in programmes and meetings at Tustin Ranch, Pasadena, Oakland and Sacramento, California, as well as Las Vegas, Nevada, Coeur d'Alene, Idaho and Seattle, Washington. The band blessed, inspired, challenged and won the hearts of its audiences.

Also in the area of music, the Territorial Band toured the United Kingdom in October 2009, inspiring audiences and sharing the gospel in eight locations, from Worthing in the south, to Cardiff in Wales and Sunderland in the north. In January 2010 the band ministered in Las Vegas, Nevada.

The Territorial Youth Band conducted workshops and presented a concert in Billings, Montana; the Territorial Youth Chorus visited Mesa, Arizona.

The Western Music Institute hosted leaders of both the ISB (Bandmaster Dr Stephen Cobb) and the International Staff Songsters (Songster Leader Dorothy Nancekievill), who challenged and inspired the delegates to excellence.

Rural communities in Alaska received visits from Father Christmas thanks to 'Operation Santa Claus' run by Alaska National Guard and The Salvation Army. Helpers flew into remote villages, often in a C130 Hercules cargo plane, to distribute gifts and Christmas cheer.

Following the devastating earthquake in Haiti, a number of USA Western officers and soldiers were deployed to assist with relief and recovery efforts.

The territory partnered with Numana (a non-profit corporation whose goal is to save starving people in the world) on the 'Million Meals for Haiti' project. Teams of Salvationists and many other volunteers worked throughout the day to package more than a million meals at two sites. Volunteers prepared meal packages containing six meals per bag.

The Salvation Army in El Centro, California, near the Mexican border, took emergency disaster vehicles into Mexico to serve 500 of those people hardest hit by Easter Sunday's 7.2-magnitude earthquake.

STATISTICS

Officers 1,000 (active 626 retired 374) **Cadets** 71 **Employees** 8,821

Corps 254 **Outposts** 12 **Institutions** 273

Senior Soldiers 16,787 **Adherents** 3,188 **Junior Soldiers** 5,422

Personnel serving outside territory Officers 37 Lay Personnel 5

USA Western Territory

STAFF

Women's Ministries: Comr Carolyn R. Knaggs (TPWM) Col Susan Harfoot (TSWM)
Personnel: Lt-Col David E. Hudson
 Asst Sec for Personnel (Officer Development): Maj Charlene Bradley
 Asst Sec for Personnel (Officer Services): Maj Eloisa Martin
Business: Lt-Col Ron Strickland
 Asst Sec for Business: Maj John Reed
Programme: Lt-Col Judith E. Smith
 Assoc Sec for Programme: Lt-Col Pamela Strickland
 Asst Sec for Programme: Mr Martin Hunt
ARC Command: Maj Man-Hee Chang
Audit: Maj Joe Frank Chavez
Candidates and Recruitment: Maj John P. Brackenbury
Community Care Ministries: Lt-Col Sharron Hudson
Community Relations/Development: Maj Robert L. Rudd
Education: Maj Jeffrey A. Martin
Finance: Lt-Col Don McDougald (pro tem)
Gift Services: Ms Kathleen Durazo
Human Resources: Ms Margaret (Miki) Webb
Information Technology: Mr Clarence White
Legal: Mr Michael Woodruff
Multicultural Ministries: Maj Elicio Marquez
Music: Mr Neil Smith
Officer Care and Development: Maj William Nottle
Older Adult Ministries: Maj Evelyn Chavez
Property: Maj William Raihl
Risk Management: Mr John McCarthy
Senior Housing Management: Mrs Susan Lawrence
Social Services: Maj Allie Laura Niles
Spiritual Life Development: Maj Glen A. Madsen
 Assoc Sec for Spiritual Life Development: Maj Linda L. Madsen
Supplies and Purchasing: Mr Robert Jones
Training: Maj Stephen C. Smith
Western Bible Conference Sec: Maj Cathyrn Russell
Youth: Major Ivan P. Wild

DIVISIONS

Alaska: 143 E 9th Ave, Anchorage, AK 99501-3618 (Box 101459, 99510-1459); tel: (907) 276-2515; Majs Douglas and Sheryl Tollerud
Cascade: 8495 SE Monterey Ave, Happy Valley, OR 97086; tel: (503) 794-3200; Lt-Col Eda Hokom

Del Oro: 3755 N Freeway Blvd, Sacramento, CA 95834-1926 (Box 348000, 95834-8000); tel: (916) 563-3700; Majs Douglas F. and Colleen Riley
Golden State: 832 Folsom St, San Francisco, CA 94107-1123 (Box 193465, 94119-3465); tel: (415) 553-3500; Lt-Cols Joe E. and Shawn Posillico
Hawaiian and Pacific Islands: 2950 Manoa Rd, Honolulu, HI 96822-1798 (Box 620, 96809-0620); tel: (808) 988-2136; Majs Edward A. and Shelley Hill
Intermountain: 1370 Pennsylvania St, Denver, CO 80203-2475 (Box 2369, 80201-2369); tel: (303) 861-4833; Majs Victor R. and Joan Doughty
Northwest: 111 Queen Anne Ave N, Suite 500 Seattle, WA 98109-4955 (Box 9219, 98109-0200); tel: (206) 281-4600; Lt-Cols Douglas and Diane O'Brien
Sierra Del Mar: 2320 5th Ave, San Diego, CA 92101-1679; tel: (619) 231-6000; Maj Linda Markiewicz
Southern California: 180 E Ocean Blvd, Long Beach, CA 90802-4709; Lt-Cols Victor A. and Rose-Marie Leslie
Southwest: 2707 E Van Buren St, Phoenix, AZ 85008-6039 (Box 52177, 85072-2177); tel: (602) 267-4100

COLLEGE FOR OFFICER TRAINING

30840 Hawthorne Blvd, Rancho Palos Verdes, CA 90275-5301; tel: (310) 377-0481; fax: (310) 541-1697

SOCIAL SERVICES
Adult Rehabilitation Centres (Men)

Anaheim, CA 92805: 1300 S Lewis St; tel: (714) 758-0414 (acc 145)
Bakersfield, CA 93301: 200 19th St; tel: (661) 325-8626 (acc 57)
Canoga Park, CA 91304: 21375 Roscoe Blvd; tel: (818) 883-6321 (acc 52)
Denver, CO 80216: 4751 Broadway; tel: (303) 294-0827 (acc 98)
Fresno, CA 93721: 804 S Parallel Ave; tel: (559) 490-7020 (acc 110)
Honolulu, HI 96817: 322 Sumner St; tel: (808) 522-8400 (acc 77)
Long Beach, CA 90813: 1370 Alamitos Ave; tel: (562) 218-2351 (acc 94)
Lytton, CA 95448: 200 Lytton Springs Rd, Healdsburg, PO Box 668, Healdsburg, 95448; tel: (707) 433-3334 (acc 75)
Oakland, CA 94607: 601 Webster St, PO Box 24054, 94623; tel: (510) 451-4514 (acc 132)

Pasadena, CA 91105: 56 W Del Mar Blvd;
tel: (626) 795-8075 (acc 107)
Phoenix, AZ 85004: 1625 S Central Ave;
tel: (602) 256-4500 (acc 142)
Portland, OR 97214: 6655 NE 82nd Ave
(acc 76)
Riverside County, CA 92570: 24201 Orange Ave,
Perris, PO Box 278, Perris 92570;
tel: (951) 940-5790 (acc 125)
Sacramento, CA 95814: 1615 D St, PO Box 2948,
95812; tel: (916) 441-5267 (acc 91)
San Bernardino, CA 92408: 363 S Doolittle Rd;
tel: (909) 889-9605 (acc 122)
San Diego, CA 92101: 1335 Broadway;
tel: (619) 239-4037 (acc 132)
San Francisco, CA 94110: 1500 Valencia St;
tel: (415) 643-8000 (acc 112)
San Jose, CA 95126: 702 W Taylor St;
tel: (408) 298-7600 (acc 96)
Santa Monica, CA 90404: 1665 10th St;
tel: (310) 450-7235 (acc 56)
Seattle, WA 98134: 1000 4th Ave S;
tel: (206) 587-0503 (acc 117)
Stockton, CA 95205: 1247 S Wilson Way;
tel: (209) 466-3871 (acc 80)
Tucson, AZ 85713: 2717 S 6th Ave;
tel: (520) 624-1741 (acc 85)

Adult Rehabilitation Centres (Women)

Anaheim, CA 92805: 1300 S Lewis St;
tel: (714) 758-0414 (acc 30)
Arvada, CO 80002: Cottonwood,
13455 W 58th Ave; tel: (303) 456-0520
(acc 30)
Fresno, CA 93704: Rosecrest, 745 E Andrews St;
tel: (559) 490-7020 (acc 14)
Pasadena, CA 91107: Oakcrest Women's
Program, 180 W Huntington Dr;
tel: (626) 795-8075 (acc 14)
Phoenix, AZ 85003: Lyncrest Manor,
344 W Lynwood St (acc 14)
San Francisco, CA 94116: Pinehurst Lodge,
2685 30th Ave; tel: (415) 681-1262 (acc 27)
Seattle, WA 98102: The Marion-Farrell House,
422 11th Ave E; tel: (206) 587-0503 (acc 14)

UNDER DIVISIONS

Clinics

Kalispell, MT 59901: 110 Bountiful Dr;
tel: (406) 257-4357
Lodi, CA 95240: 525 W Lockeford St;
tel: (209) 367-9560
Oxnard/Port Hueneme, CA: 622 W Wooley Rd;
tel: (805) 483-9235
San Diego, CA 92123: Door of Hope,
2799 Health Center Dr; tel: (858) 279-1100

Family Services

Anchorage, AK 99501: 1712 'A' St;
tel: (907) 277-2593
Anchorage, AK 99508: Booth Memorial Youth
and Family Services, 3600 E 20th Ave;
tel: (907) 279-0522 (acc 20)
Apache Junction, AZ 85219: Apache Junction
Service Center, 605 E Broadway Ave;
tel: (480) 982-4110
Denver, CO 80205: 2201 Stout St;
tel: (303) 295-3366
El Cajon, CA 92021: 1011 E Main St;
tel: (619) 440-4686
Havre, MT 59501: Service Ext, Social Service
Center, 605 2nd St, PO Box 418;
tel: (406) 265-6411
Honokaa, HI 96727: Prevention Program,
45-511 Rickard Pl; tel: (808) 959-5855
Honolulu, HI 96819: 1931 N King St;
tel: (808) 841-5565
Honolulu, HI 96816: Family Treatment
Services, 845 22nd Ave; tel: (808) 739-4952
(acc 41)
Kent, WA 98032: S King County Service Center,
1209 Central Ave #145; tel (253) 852-4983
Mesquite, NV 89048: Mesquite Service Center,
780 Hafen Ln #D; tel: (775) 751-8199
Moses Lake, WA 98837: Service Ext, Social
Service Center, 310 S Cedar, PO Box 1000;
tel: (509) 766-5875
Oakland, CA 94607: 379 12th St;
tel: (510) 645 9710
Olympia, WA 98501: Social Services,
824 5th Ave E; tel: (360) 352-8596
Pasco, WA 99301: Social Services,
310 N 4th Ave; tel: (509) 547-2138
Phoenix, AZ 85034-2177: 2702 E Washington;
tel: (602) 267-4122
Renton, WA 98055: Food Bank and Multi-
Service Center, 206 S Tobin St;
tel: (425) 255-5969
Riverside, CA 92501: 3695 1st;
tel: (951) 784-3571
Sacramento, CA 95814: 1225 North 'B' St;
tel: (916) 469-4632
San Diego, CA 92101: Social Services;
tel: (619) 231-6000
San Diego, CA 92115: Kroc Family Service
Center, 6845 University Ave;
tel: (619) 269-1430
San Francisco, CA 94103: 520 Jesse St;
tel: (415) 575-4848
Seattle, WA 98101-1923: Emergency Family
Assistance, 1101 Pike St; tel: (206) 447-9944
Spokane, WA 99209: 2020 N Division;
tel: (509) 325-6821

Tiyan, Guam: 613-615 E Sunset Blvd;
tel: (671) 477-3528
Tucson, AZ 85716: 3525 E 2nd St #1;
tel: (520) 546-5969
Vancouver, WA 98684: 7509 NE 47th Ave;
tel: (360) 694-9503
Walla Walla, WA 99362: Service Ext, Social
Service Center, 827 W Alder St;
tel: (509) 529-9470
Wenatchee, WA 98801: 1205 Columbia St S;
tel: (509) 662-8864
Yakima, WA 98907: Social Services,
9 S 6th Ave; tel: (509) 453-3139
Yuba City, CA 95991: 401 Del Norte Ave;
tel: (530) 216-4530
Yucca Valley, CA 92284: Service Ext,
56659 Twenty-nine Palms Hwy;
tel: (760) 228-0114

Adult Care Centres

Anchorage, AK 99508: Serendipity Adult
Day Services, 3550 E 20th Ave;
tel: (907) 279-0501 (acc 35)
Henderson, NV 89015: 830 E Lake Mead Dr;
tel: (702) 565-8836 (acc 49)
Honolulu, HI 96817: 296 N Vineyard Blvd;
tel: (808) 521-6551 (acc 57)
San Pedro, CA 90731-2351: 138 S Bandini;
tel: (310) 832-7228 (acc 30)
Torrance, CA 90503: 4223 Emerald St;
tel: (310) 370-4515 (acc 40)

Alcoholic and Drug Rehabilitation Services

Anchorage, AK 99503-7317: Box 190567,
99519-0567 Clitheroe Center;
tel: (907) 276-2898 (acc 58)
Bell, CA 90201-6418: Bell Shelter, 5600
Rickenbaker Rd 2a/b; tel: (323) 263-1206
Honolulu, HI 96816-4500: Women's Way/Family
Treatment Services, 845 22nd Ave;
tel: (808) 739-4952 (acc 41)
Honolulu, HI 96817: Addiction Treatment
Services, 3624 Waokanaka St;
tel: (808) 595-6371 (acc 80)
Admin Office: 2228 Liliha Street, #304;
tel: (808) 529-1480
Honolulu, HI 96822-1757: Therapeutic Living,
845 22nd Ave; tel: (808) 739-4931
Los Angeles, CA 90007: Hope Harbor,
3107 S Grand Ave; tel: (213) 744-8186
Los Angeles, CA 90073: The Haven-Victory
Place, 11301 Wilshire Blvd, Bldg 212;
tel: (310) 478-3711 ext 48761 (acc 200)
Marysville, CA 95901: The Depot Family Crisis
Center, 408 J St; tel: (530) 216-4530

Tiyan, GU 96921: Lighthouse Recovery Center,
155003 Corsair Ave, PO Box 23038, GMF
GU 96921, E Agana; tel: (671) 477-7671

Child Day Care Centres

Anchorage, AK 99508: Booth Memorial Youth
and Family Services Infant Nursery,
3600 E 20th Ave; tel: (907) 279-0522
Aurora, CO 80011: Aurora After School
Program, 802 Quari Ct, Box 31739,
80041-0739; tel: (303) 366-7585 (acc 123)
Boise, ID Booth, 83702: 1617 N 24th, Box 1216
83701; tel: (208) 343-3571 (acc 15)
Bozeman, MT 59715: 32 S Rouse, Box 1307,
59771-1307; tel: (406) 586-5813 (acc 14)
Broomfield, CO 80020: Broomfield After-School
Program, PO Box 1058, 1080 Birch St;
tel: (303) 635-3018
Colorado Springs, CO 80903-4023: Children's
Development Center, 709 S Sierra Madre;
tel: (719) 578-9190 (acc 30)
Denver, CO 80205-4547: Denver Red Shield
Tutor Program, 2915 High St;
tel: (303) 295-2108 (acc 250)
Denver, CO 80219-1859: Denver Citadel Tutor
Program, PO Box 280750, 80228-0750,
4505 W Alameda Ave; tel: (303) 922-4540
(acc 15)
Globe, AZ 85501: Box 1743, 85502,
161 E Cedar St; tel: (928) 425-4011 (acc 20)
Honolulu 96816: (FTS-Kula Kokua),
(FTS-Therapeutic Nursery), 845 22nd Ave;
tel: (808) 739-4922 (acc 24, 12)
Kailua-Kona, HI 96740: (Ohana Keiki)
75-223 Kalani St, Box 1358 96745;
tel: (808) 329-7780 (acc 326)
Los Angeles, CA 90026: Alegria Day/After-School
Care, 2737 Sunset Blvd; tel: (323) 454-4200
(acc 90)
Los Angeles, CA 90021: LA Day Care,
836 Stanford Ave; tel: (213) 623-9022
(acc 250)
Los Angeles, CA 90025: Bessie Pregerson
Childcare, Westwood Transitional Village,
1401 S Sepulveda Blvd; tel: (310) 477-9539
(acc 64)
Los Angeles, CA 90001: Siemen Family
Center, 7655 Central Ave;
tel: (323) 277-0732 (acc 62)
Modesto, CA 95354: 625 'I' St, PO Box 1663,
95353 (mail); tel: (209) 342-5220 (acc 60)
Monterey, CA 93942: 1491 Contra Costa,
Seaside, PO Box 1884, 93955 (mail);
tel: (831) 899-4915 (acc 105)
Oakland, CA 94611: Box 510, Booth Memorial
CDC, 2794 Garden St; tel: (510) 535-5088

Pomona, CA 91767: Box 2562, 91769,
490 E Laverne Ave; tel: (909) 623-1579
(acc 66)

Portland, OR 97296: 2640 NW Alexandra Ave;
tel: (503) 239-1248 (acc 18)

Riverside, CA 92501: 3695 1st St;
tel: (909) 784-4495 (acc 108)

Sacramento, CA 95817: 2550 Alhambra Blvd;
tel: (916) 451-4230

San Francisco, CA 94103: Harbor House,
407 9th St; tel: (415) 503-3000 (acc 66)

Santa Fe Springs, CA 90606: Infant/Pre-School
and After-School Care, 12000 E Washington
Blvd; tel: (310) 696-7175 (acc 57)

Seattle, WA 98103: Little People Preschool and
Child Care, 9501 Greenwood Ave N,
Box 30638, 98103-0638; tel: (206) 782-3142
(acc 65)

Tacoma, WA 98405: Joyful Noise Child Care,
1100 S Puget Sound Ave; tel: (253) 752-1661
(acc 47)

Tustin, CA 92680: Creator's Corner Pre-School,
10200 Pioneer Rd; tel: (714) 918-0659
(acc 90)

Emergency Shelters, Hospitality Houses

Anchorage, AK 99501:
Eagle Crest Transitional Housing, 438 E 9th
Ave; tel: (907) 276-5913 (acc 76)
McKinnell House, 1712 'A' Street;
tel: (907) 276-1609 (acc 110)

Bell, CA 90201: 5600 Rickenbacker;
tel: (323) 263-1206 (acc 484)

Boise, ID 83702: 1617 N 24th St;
tel: (208) 343-3571 (acc 24)

Cheyenne, WY 82001: Sally's House,
1920 Seymour St, PO Box 385, 82003 (mail);
tel: (307) 634-2769 (acc 6)

Colorado Springs, CO 80909: Bridge House,
2641 E Yampa St; tel: (719) 227-8773 (acc 7)

Colorado Springs, CO 80909-4037:
2649 E Yampa St, Freshstart Transitional
Family Housing; tel: (719) 227-8773 (acc 61)

Colorado Springs, CO 80903-4023: R. J.
Montgomery New Hope Center, 709 S Sierra
Madre; tel: (719) 578-9190 (acc 200)

Denver, CO 80221-4115: Denver New Hope
(Lambuth) Family Center, 2741 N Federal
Blvd; tel: (303) 477-3758 (acc 84)

El Centro, CA 92244: 375 N 5th St;
tel: (760) 352-8462

El Paso, TX 79905: Box 10756-79997, 4300 E
Paisano Dr; tel: (915) 544-9811 (acc 136)

Fresno, CA 93711-3705: Gabelcrest Women's
Transitional Home, 1107 W Shaw;
tel: (559) 226-6110 (acc 48)

Glendale, CA 91204-2053: Nancy Painter
Home, 320 W Windsor Rd;
tel: (213) 245-2424 (acc 19)

Grand Junction, CO 81502: Women's and Family
Shelter, 915 Grand Ave, PO Box 578, 0578
81501 (mail); tel: (907) 242-3343 (acc 10)

Grass Valley, CA 95945: Booth Family Center,
12390 Rough and Ready Hwy;
tel: (530) 272-2669 (acc 46)

Helena, MT 59601: Transitional Housing,
1905 Henderson; tel: (406) 442-8244 (acc 8)

Hilo, HI 96720: Interim Home for Youth,
1786 Kinoole St, Box 5085;
tel: (808) 959-5855 (acc 18)

Honokaa, HI 96727: Residential Group Home,
45-350 Ohelo St, PO Box 5085, Hilo,
HI 96720; tel: (808) 775-0241

Honolulu, HI 96816: FTS-Supportive Living,
845 22nd Ave; tel: (808) 732-2802 (acc 24)

Kahului, HI 96732-2256: Safe Haven Drop-in
Center, 45 Kamehameha St;
tel: (808) 877-3042

Kailua-Kona, HI 96740: Youth Shelter,
75-235 Kalani St, PO Box 5015, Hilo, HI 96720;
tel: (808) 935-4411 (acc 8)

Kodiak, AK 99615-6511: Kodiak, Beachcombers
Transitional Housing, 1855 Mission Rd;
tel: (907) 486-8740 (acc 10)

Las Vegas, NV 89030:
Safehaven Shelter, 31 W Owens Ave;
tel: (702) 639-0277 (acc 22)
Pathways, 37 W Owens Ave;
tel: (702) 639-0277 (acc 42)
Lied Transitional Housing, 45 W Owens Ave;
tel: (702) 642-7252 (acc 70)
Emergency Lodge, 47 W Owens Ave;
tel: (702) 639-0277 (acc 167)
PATH – Petaluma Area Transitional Housing,
33 W Owens Ave; tel: (702) 651-0123
(acc 34)
Horizon Crest Apts, 13 W Owens Ave;
tel (702) 399-3255

Lodi, CA 95240-2128: Hope Harbor Family
Service Center, 622 N Sacramento St;
tel: (209) 367-9560 (acc 54)

Lodi, CA 95240: Hope Avenue,
331 N Stockton Ave (acc 26)

Long Beach, CA 90810: The Village at Callebrio,
2260 Williams St; tel: (562) 388-7600 (acc 82)

Los Angeles, CA 90073: Naomi House (for
women veterans), Exodus Lodge (for mentally
ill), The Haven, 11301 Wilshire Blvd, Bldg 212,
Los Angeles; tel: (310) 478-3711 ext 48761
(acc 100)

Los Angeles, CA 90015: Alegria (HIV/Aids
housing) Aids Project, Transitional Housing,

2737 Sunset Blvd; tel: (323) 454-4200 (acc 195); Emergency Shelter, 832 W James M. Woods Blvd; tel (213) 438-0933

Los Angeles, CA 90028: The Way In (teen counselling) Drop In Center/Emergency Housing, 5941 Hollywood Blvd, Box 38668, 90038-0668; tel: (213) 468-8666 (acc 4)

Los Angeles, CA 90025-3477: Westwood Transitional Housing, 1401 S Sepulveda Blvd; tel: (310) 477-9539 (acc 60)

Marysville, CA 95901-5629: The Depot Family Crisis Center, 408 'J' St; tel: (530) 216-4530 (acc 67)

Marysville, CA 95901: Transitional Living Program, 5906 B Riverside Dr; tel: (530) 216-4530 (acc 45)

Medford, OR 97501-4630: 1065 Crews Rd; tel: (541) 773-7005 (acc 43)

Modesto, CA 95354: Berberian Shelter, 320 9th St; tel: (209) 525-8954 (acc 110)

Nampa, ID 83651: 1412 4th St South; tel: (208) 461-3733 (acc 54)

Oakland, CA 94601: Family Emergency Shelter, 2794 Garden St, Box 510, 94604 (mail); tel: (510) 437-9437 (acc 65)

Olympia, WA 98501: Hans K. Lemcke Lodge, 808 5th Ave SE; tel: (360) 352-8596 (acc 86)

Petaluma, CA 94975: PATH – Petaluma Area Transitional Housing, PO Box 750684; tel: (707) 769-0716 (acc 15)

Phoenix, AZ 85008: Kaiser Family Center, 2707 E Van Buren, Elim House, PO Box 52177, 85072; tel: (602) 267-4122 (acc 114)

Portland, OR 97296: Women's Shelter, 2640 NW Alexandra Ave; tel: (503) 239-1248 (acc 10)

Portland, OR 97208: Women and Children's Family Violence Center, PO Box 2398; tel: (503) 239-1254 (acc 53)

Sacramento, CA 95814-0603: Emergency Shelter, 1200 N 'B' St; tel: (916) 442-0331 (acc 134)

Salem, OR 97303:
1901 Front St NE; tel: (503) 585-6688 (acc 83)
105 River St NE; tel: (503) 391-1523 (acc 6)
1960 Water St NE; tel: (503) 566-7267 (acc 10)

San Bernardino, CA 92411: Hospitality House, 925 W 10th St; tel: (909) 888-4880 (acc 78)

Sand City, CA 93955: Good Samaritan Center, 800 Scott St; tel: (831) 899-4988 (acc 60)

San Diego, CA 92101: STEPS, 825 7th Ave; tel: (619) 669-2200 (acc 30)

San Francisco, CA 94103: SF Harbor House, 407 9th St; tel: (415) 503-3000 (acc 52)

San Francisco, CA 94102: Railton Place

(Permanent and Transitional Housing), 242 Turk St; tel: (415) 345-3142 (acc 110)

San Jose, CA 95112: Emmanuel House, 405 N 4th St, Box 2-D, 95109-0004 (mail); tel: (408) 282-1175 (acc 78)

Santa Ana, CA 92701 (Orange County): 818 E 3rd St; tel: (714) 542-9576 (acc 52)

Santa Barbara, CA 93101: 423 Chapala St; tel: (805) 962-6281 (acc 40)

Santa Fe Springs, CA 90606: Transitional Living Center, 12000 E Washington Blvd, Box 2009, 90610; tel: (562) 696-9562 (acc 116)

Santa Rosa, CA 95404: Transitionanl Living Program; tel (707) 535-4271 (acc 33)

Seaside, CA 93955:
Casa De Las Palmas Transitional Housing, 535 Palm Ave; tel: (831) 392-1762 (acc 54)
Two-Step-Two Transitional Housing, 1430 Imperial St; tel: (831) 899-4988 (acc 16)

Seattle, WA 90101: Julia Sampson Women's Shelter (Emergency Financial Assistance), 1101 Pike St, PO Box 20128; tel: (206) 447-9944 (acc 20)

Seattle, WA: Catherine Booth House (Shelter for Abused Women), Box 20128, 98102; tel: (206) 324-4943 (acc 37)

Seattle, WA 98134: William Booth Center – Emergency Shelter and Transitional Shelter/Living, 811 Maynard Ave S; tel: (206) 621-0145 (acc 183)

Seattle, WA 98136: Hickman House (Women), 5600 Fauntleroy Way SW, Box 20128, 98102; tel: (206) 932-5341 (acc 35)

Spokane, WA 99201:
Family Shelter, 204 E Indiana Ave, Box 9108, 99209-9108; tel: (509) 325-6814 (acc 48)
Sally's House (Foster Care Home), Box 9108, 99209-9108, 222 E Indiana; tel: (509) 392-2784 (acc 14)

Spokane, WA 99207-2335: Transitional Housing, 127 E Nora Ave; tel: (509) 326-7288 (acc 96)

Tacoma, WA 98405: Jarvie Family/Women's Emergency Shelter, 1521 6th Ave, Box 1254, 98401-1254; tel: (253) 627-3962 (acc 72)

Tucson, AZ 85705: 1021 N 11th Ave; tel: (520) 622-5411 (acc 91)

Tucson, AZ 85716: SAFE Housing, 3525 E 2nd St #1; tel: (520) 323-6080

Ventura, CA 93001-2703: 155 S Oak St; tel: (805) 648-5032 (acc 51)

Watsonville, CA 95076-5048: Supportive Housing Program for Women, 232 Union St; tel: (831) 763-0131 (acc 60)

Whittier, CA 90602: 7926 Pickering Ave, PO Box 954, 90608; tel: (562) 698-8348 (acc 17)

Harbour Light Centres

Denver, CO 80205: Denver Harbor Light, 2136 Champa St; tel: (303) 296-2456 (acc 80)

Portland, OR 97204: 30 SW 2nd St, Box 5635, 97228-5635; tel: (503) 239-1259 (acc 143)

San Francisco, CA 94103-4405: 1275 Harrison St; tel: (415) 503-3000 (acc 109)

Residential Youth Care and Family Service Centres

Anchorage, AK 99508: Booth Memorial Youth and Family Services, 8600 E 20th Ave; tel: (907) 279-0522 (acc 20)

Boise, ID 83702: Family Day Care Center, 1617 N 24th St, Box 1216, 83701; tel: (208) 343-3571 (acc 15)

Los Angeles, CA 90028: The Way In (teen counselling) Transitional Housing, 5941 Hollywood Blvd, Box 38668, 90038-0668; tel: (213) 468-8666 (acc 20)

Portland, OR 97210: 2640 NW Alexandra Ave, Box 10027; tel: (503) 239-1248 (acc 33)

San Diego, CA 92123: Door of Hope Haven, Transitional Living Center, 2799 Health Center Dr; tel: (858) 279-1100

San Francisco, CA 94102: Railton Place Foster Youth Housing, 242 Turk St; tel (415) 345-3400 (acc 27)

Adult Rehabilitation Programmes (Men)

Albuquerque, NM 87102: 400 John St SE, Box 27690, 87125-7690; tel: (505) 242-3112 (acc 36)

Anchorage, AK 99503: 660 E 48th Ave; tel: (907) 562-5408 (acc 61)

Chico, CA 95973: 13404 Browns Valley Dr; tel: (530) 342-2199 (acc 30)

El Centro, CA 92244: 375 N 5th St; tel (760) 352-8462

Grand Junction, CO 81502: 903 Grand Ave, Box 578, 81502; tel: (970) 242-8632 (acc 32)

North Las Vegas, NV 89030: 211 Judson St, Box 30096; tel: (702) 649-2374 2035 Yale St; tel (702) 649-2374

Reno, NV 89512-1605: 2300 Valley Rd; tel: (775) 688-4570 (acc 85)

Salt Lake City, UT 84102-2030: 252 South 500 East; tel: (801) 323-5817 (acc 51)

San Bernardino, CA 92410: Path to Prosperity, 730 W Spruce; tel: (909) 884-2364

San Diego, CA 92101-6304: STEPS, 825 7th Ave; tel: (619) 669-2200

Adult Rehabilitation Programmes (Women)

Chico, CA 95973: 13404 Browns Valley Dr; tel: (530) 342-2199 (acc 20)

Grand Junction, CO 81502: Adult Rehabilitation Program – Women's Residence, 915 Grand Ave, PO Box 578, 0578-81501 (mail); tel: (907) 242-8632 (acc 10)

Las Vegas, NV 89030: 39 W Owens; tel: (702) 649-1469 (acc 42)

North Las Vegas, NV 89030: 39 W Owens; tel: (702) 649-1469

Ogden, UT 84401-3610: Women's Rehabilitation Program, 2615 Grant Ave; tel: (801) 621-3580 (acc 29)

Senior Citizens' Housing

Albuquerque, NM: Silvercrest, 4400 Pan Am Fwy NE, 87107; tel: (505) 883-1068 (acc 55)

Broomfield, CO 80020-1876: Silvercrest, 1110 E 10th Ave; tel: (303) 464-1994 (acc 85)

Chula Vista, CA 91910: Silvercrest, 636 3rd Ave; tel: (619) 427-4991 (acc 73)

Colorado Springs, CO 80909-7507: Silvercrest I, 904 Yuma St; tel: (719) 475-2045 (acc 50)

Colorado Springs, CO 80909-5097: Silvercrest II, 824 Yuma St; tel: (719) 389-0329 (acc 50)

Denver, CO 80219-1859: Silvercrest, 4595 W Alameda Ave; tel: (303) 922-2924 (acc 66)

El Cajon, CA 92020: Silvercrest, 175 S Anza St; tel: (619) 593-1077 (acc 73)

El Sobrante, CA 94803-1859: Silvercrest, 4630 Appian Way #100; tel: (510) 758-1518 (acc 63)

Escondido, CA 92026: Silvercrest, 1303 Las Villas Way; tel: (760) 741-4106 (acc 75)

Eureka, CA 95501-1264: Silvercrest, 2141 Tydd St; tel: (707) 445-3141 (acc 152)

Fresno, CA 93721-1041: Silvercrest, 1824 Fulton St; tel: (559) 237-9111 (acc 158)

Glendale, CA 92104: Silvercrest, 323 W Garfield; tel: (818) 543-0211 (acc 150)

Hollywood, CA 90028: Silvercrest, 5940 Carlos Ave; tel: (323) 460-4335 (acc 140)

Lake View Terrace, CA 91354: Silvercrest, 11850 Foothill Blvd; tel: (818) 896-7580 (acc 150)

Los Angeles, CA 90006: Silvercrest, 947 S Hoover St; tel: (213) 387-7278 (acc 120)

Mesa, AZ 85201: Silvercrest, 255 E 6th St; tel: (480) 649-9117 (acc 81)

Missoula, MT 59801: Silvercrest, 1550 S 2nd St W #125; tel: (406) 541-0464 (acc 50)

N Las Vegas, NV 89030: Silvercrest, 2801 E Equador Ave; tel: (702) 643-0293 (acc 60)

Oceanside, CA 92056: Silvercrest, 3839 Lake Blvd; tel: (760) 940-0166 (acc 67)

Pasadena, CA 91106: Silvercrest, 975 E Union St;
tel: (626) 432-6678 (acc 150)

Phoenix, AZ 85003: Silvercrest, 613 N 4th Ave;
tel: (602) 251-2000 (acc 125)

Portland, OR 97232: Silvercrest, 1865 NE Davis;
tel: (503) 236-2320 (acc 78)

Puyallup, WA 98373: Silvercrest, 4103 9th St SW;
tel: (253) 841-0785 (acc 40)

Redondo Beach, CA 90277: Mindeman Senior
Residence, 125 W Beryl St;
tel: (310) 318-2827/0582 (acc 54)

Reno, NV 89512-2448: Silvercrest,
1690 Wedekind Rd; tel: (775) 322-2050 (acc 59)

Riverside, CA 92501: Silvercrest, 3003 N Orange;
tel: (951) 276-0173 (acc 72)

San Diego, CA 92101: Silvercrest, 727 E St;
tel: (619) 699-7272 (acc 122)

San Francisco, CA 94133-3844: SF Chinatown
Senior Citizens' Residence, 1450 Powell St;
tel: (415) 781-8545 (acc 9)

San Francisco, CA 94107-1132: Silvercrest,
133 Shipley St; tel: (415) 543-5381 (acc 514)

Santa Fe Springs, CA 90670: Silvercrest,
12015 Lakeland Rd; tel: (562) 946-7717
(acc 25)

Santa Monica, CA 90401: Silvercrest,
1530 5th St; tel: (310) 393-5336 (acc 122)

Santa Rosa, CA 95404-6601: Silvercrest,
1050 3rd St; tel: (707) 544-6766 (acc 186)

Seattle, WA 98103, Silvercrest,
9543 Greenwood Ave N #105;
tel: (206) 706-0855 (acc 75)

Stockton, CA 95202-2645: Silvercrest,
123 N Stanislaus St; tel: (209) 463-4960
(acc 84)

Tulare, CA 93274: 350 North 'L' St;
tel: (559) 688-0704 (acc 65)

Turlock, CA 95380: Silvercrest, 865 Lander Ave;
tel: (209) 669-8863 (acc 82)

Ventura, CA 93004: Silvercrest, 750 Petit Ave;
tel: (805) 647-0110 (acc 130)

Wahiawa, HI 96786-1961: Silvercrest Residence,
520 Pine St #101; tel: (808) 622-2785
(acc 159)

Senior Citizens' Nutrition Centres

Anchorage, AK 99501: Older Alaskans' Program
(OAP), 1712 'A' Street; tel: (907) 349-0613

Denver, CO 80205-4547: Denver Red Shield,
2915 High St; (tel): (303) 295-2107

Fresno, CA 93712-1041: 1824 Fulton St;
tel: (559) 233-0319

Phoenix, AZ: Laura Danieli Senior Activity
Center, 613 N 4th Ave; tel: (602) 251-2005

Portland, OR 97232-2822: Rose Centre – Senior
Citizens' Program, 211 NE 18th Ave;
tel: (503) 239-1221

Redondo Beach, CA 90277-2056:
Home-delivered meals, 125 W Beryl St;
tel: (310) 318-2827

Salinas, CA 93906-1519: 2460 N Main St;
tel: (831) 443-9655

San Diego, CA 92101-1679: Senior Citizens'
Program (9 Locations), 2320 5th Ave;
tel: (619) 446-0212

San Francisco, CA 94107-1125: Senior Meals
Program, 850 Harrison St; tel: (415) 777-5350
(5 locations)

San Jose, CA 95112: 359 N 4th St;
tel: (408) 282-1165

Tucson, AZ 85705; Nutrition and Home
Delivered Meals, 1021 N 11th Ave;
tel: (520) 792-1352

Tulare, CA 93274-4131: 314 E San Joaquin Ave;
tel: (559) 687-2520

Turlock, CA 95380-5815: 893 Lander Ave;
tel: (209) 667-6091

Watsonville, CA 95076-5203: 29-A Bishop St;
tel: (831) 724-0948

A volunteer in Bell, California, seals a meal bag at one of the territory's 'One Million Meals For Haiti' events

In addition there are 14 fresh-air camps and 35 youth community centres attached to divisions, as well as 557 service units in the territory

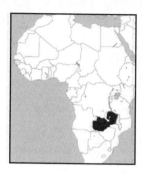

ZAMBIA TERRITORY

Territorial leaders:
Colonels John and Dorita Wainwright

Territorial Commander:
Colonel John Wainwright (1 Mar 2008)

Chief Secretary:
Lieut-Colonel Bislon Hanunka (1 Mar 2008)

Territorial Headquarters: 685A Cairo Road, Lusaka

Postal address: PO Box 34352, Lusaka 10101, Zambia

Tel: [260] 1 238291/228327; fax: [260] 1 226784

In 1922 emigrants from villages on the north bank of the Zambezi River working in a mica mine near Urungwe were converted. They carried home the message of salvation to their chief, and established meeting places in their villages. Two years later, Commandant Kunzwi Shava and Lieutenant Paul Shumba were appointed to command the new opening. The Zambia Division in the Rhodesia Territory became the Zambia Command in 1966. In 1988, the Malawi Division was transferred from the Zimbabwe Territory to form the new Zambia and Malawi Territory. The Zambia and Malawi Territory became the Zambia Territory on 1 October 2002 when Malawi became an independent region.

Zone: Africa
Country included in the territory: Zambia
Languages in which the gospel is preached: Chibemba, Chinyanja, Chitonga, English, Lozi

THE main highlight of the year under review was the Territorial Congress (17-21 September 2009), when General Shaw Clifton and Commissioner Helen Clifton (WPWM) were special guests together with the Soweto Songsters from Southern Africa Territory. This was the first such congress for nine years and attracted 10,000 people. The theme, 'Growing In Holiness', was aligned to the territorial emphasis on holiness teaching.

The world leaders' visit brought inspiration and encouragement, attracting wide media interest. At a thanksgiving service in the Anglican Cathedral, Lusaka, the Honourable Minister of Defence represented the State President. The High Commissioners of Britain and Zimbabwe were also present.

The congress provided opportunity for the launch of the territorial plan for 2010-2015 under the theme, 'Now Is The Time ...'. This has at its heart a call to evangelism, spiritual development, tackling social justice issues, and a strong determination to make significant progress in self-support.

The territory has developed close links with the government in seeking to respond to the increasing evil of human trafficking across Zambian borders.

A Brengle Institute held at Chikankata (8-12 June) was led by Commissioner Margaret Sutherland and attended by 22 delegates. Officers were encouraged to explore the doctrine of holiness in the context of local culture and officers prepared essays on the topic, 'Holiness Today – An African Perspective'.

The ordination and commissioning of 24 officers of the Prayer Warriors Session took place in Lusaka (14-15 November). The weekend events began with a Silver Star meeting, marking the first occasion when cadets' fathers were admitted to the Fellowship of the Silver Star.

The first married woman divisional commander was appointed, to Lusaka North West Division. A new district – Central North – was inaugurated and the district officers were welcomed at a meeting held in Kabwe.

The Ambassadors Of Holiness Session – with 34 cadets, the largest number in the territory's history – was welcomed in February 2010. Also during February, Commissioner Lyn Pearce (then WSWM) was the special guest at the Territorial Women's Ministries Seminar and then at a spiritual leadership seminar titled 'Go Deeper'.

With generous support from USA territories, 'Salvation Studio' started broadcasting from Chikankata Mission to a catchment area of some 50 kilometres. The territory took steps to develop its prison chaplaincy work and to seek new openings of service.

STATISTICS

Officers 222 (active 203 retired 19) **Cadets** 34 **Employees** 422

Corps 128 **Societies** 36 **Outposts** 149 **New Openings** 48 **Hospital** 1 **High School** 1 **Old People's Home** 1 **Farm** 1

Senior Soldiers 23,204 **Adherents** 2,604 **Junior Soldiers** 6,208

Personnel serving outside territory Officers 5

STAFF

Women's Ministries: Col Dorita Wainwright (TPWM) Lt-Col Melody Hanunka (Asst TPWM) Maj Jessie Magaya (TSWM) Maj Rodinah Chalwe (THLS) Capt Rachel Kandama (TJHLS) Lt-Col Marie Mata (TLOMS)

Sec for Personnel: Lt-Col Metson Chilyabanyama

Extension Training/Human Resources: Capt Aubey Hatukupa

Sec for Programme/Spiritual Life Sec: Lt-Col Jean-Baptiste Mata

Community Development and Micro-Credit: Maj Ireen Hachamba

Education: Maj Brighton Hachitapika

Faith-based Facilitation and HIV/Aids Services: Maj Angela Hachitapika

Men's Fellowships/Prisons: Maj Adeck Mwiinga

Projects: Chris and Erin Hann

Social Services: Maj Patricia Hangoma

Sponsorship: Elijah Hazemba

Territorial B/M: Brave Hanunka

Territorial S/L: Jericho Milambo

Youth and Candidates: Capt Ginger Kandama

Sec for Business Administration: tba

Finance and Audit: Capt Donald Hangoma

Property: Maj Bexter Magaya

Spiritual Life Centre Manager: Capt Jane Hatukupa

Trade: Capt Wilson Chiwoya

Training: Maj James Weymouth

DIVISIONS

Lusaka North West: PO Box 33934, Lusaka; Lt-Col Rosemary Chilyabanyama (DC) Capt Besnart Chiwoya (DDWM)

Lusaka South East: PO Box 34352, Lusaka; tel: (01) 221960; Majs Richard and Eunice Mweemba

Mapangazya: P Bag S2, Mazabuka; Maj Saraphina Milambo (DC) Maj Florence Shavanga (DDWM)

Mazabuka: PO Box 670017, Mazabuka; tel: (032) 30420; Majs Bernard and Dorothy Chisengele

Southern: PO Box 630537, Choma; Majs Cason and Mary Sichilomba

DISTRICTS

Central North: Maj Elisha Mankomba

Copperbelt: PO Box 70075, Ndola; tel: (02) 680302; Maj Isaac Kauseni

Siavonga: PO Box 59, Siavonga; tel: (01) 511362; Capt Clifford Chikondo

SECTION (reporting to THQ)

Eastern: PO Box 510199, Chipata; tel: (097) 881828; Capt Kennedy Mizinga

TRAINING COLLEGE

PO Box 34352, Lusaka, 10101; tel: (260) 211 261 755; email: zsaotc@gmail.com

CHIKANKATA MISSION

P Bag S2, Mazabuka

Mission Director: Maj Joster Chenda

CHIKANKATA HEALTH SERVICES

P Bag S2, Mazabuka; tel: (01) 222060; email: administration@chikankata.com

Development Director: Dr Trevor Kaile

Administration: Maj Edward Shavanga

Business Manager: Mr Anthony Watson

Manager/Aids Management Training Services: tba

Manager/Community Health and Development: Mr Charles Mang'ombe

Manager/Nursing Education: Mrs Z. Ngalande

Hospital Chaplain: Maj Rotinah Sitwala

Senior Medical Officer: Dr Zairemthiamma

Medical Clinics (under Chikankata)
Chaanga, Chikombola, Nadezwe, Nameembo, Syanyolo

Youth Project (under Chikankata)
Chikombola

CHIKANKATA HIGH SCHOOL

P Bag S1, Mazabuka; tel: (01) 220820; email: administration@chikankata.sch.zm

Headmaster: Mr Oscar Mwanza

Matron: Maj Christine Chenda

OLD PEOPLE'S HOME AND VOCATIONAL TRAINING CENTRE

Mitanda Home for the Aged: PO Box 250096, Kansenshi, Ndola; tel: (02) 680460; email: mitanda@zamtel.zm:

Centre Manager: Maj Park, Ok-Young

PRE-SCHOOL GROUPS

Chikankata, Chikanzaya, Chipapa, Chipata, Chitumbi, Choma, Dundu, George, Hapwaya, Ibbwe Munyama, John Laing, Kakole, Kalomo, Kanyama, Kawama, Kazungula, Lusaka Citadel, Maamba, Magoye, Mitchel, Mukwela, Mumbwa, Ngangula, Njomona, Nkonkola, Petauke, Peters, Siavonga, Sikoongo, Sinazongwe, Situmbeko

COMMUNITY SCHOOLS

Chelstone, Chipata (Lusaka), Choma, George, John Laing, Kanyama, Kasiwe, Kawama, Luanshya, Maamba, Mbala, Monze, Petauke

COMMUNITY WORK

Agriculture Projects: Chikankata, Chitumbi, Dundu, Hamabuya, Malala, Ngamgula

Feeding Programme: Lusitu

Health Centres: George, John Laing

HIV/Aids Training, Counselling: Chikankata, THQ

Micro-Credit Projects:
Eastern: Chipata
Lusaka North West: Mumbwa
Mapangazya: Chikankata
Mazabuka: Magoye, Monze, Nakambala, Njomona

FARM (income-generating)

PO Box 250096, Kansenshi, Ndola; tel: (02) 680460

ZIMBABWE TERRITORY

Territorial Commander:
Commissioner Vinece Chigariro
(1 Mar 2008)

Chief Secretary:
Colonel Wilfred Varughese
(1 Aug 2008)

Territorial Headquarters: 45 Josiah Chinamano Avenue, Harare

Postal address: PO Box 14, Harare, Zimbabwe

Tel: [263] (4) 736666/7/8, 250107/8; fax: [263] (4) 726658; email: ZIMTHQ@zim.salvationarmy.org;
website: www.salvationarmy.org/Zimbabwe

A pioneer party led by Major and Mrs Pascoe set out from Kimberley, South Africa, on 5 May 1891 in a wagon drawn by 18 oxen, arriving in Fort Salisbury on 18 November. The then Rhodesia became a separate territory on 1 May 1931. Work spread to Botswana where The Salvation Army was officially recognised in 1997.

Zone: Africa
Countries included in the territory: Botswana, Zimbabwe
'The Salvation Army' in Ndebele: Impi yo Sindiso; in Shona: Hondo yo Ruponiso
Languages in which the gospel is preached: Chitonga, English, Ndebele, Shona, Tswana
Periodicals: *Zimbabwe Salvationist, ZEST* (women's magazine)

'ROOTED In Holiness' was the theme of the 2009 Territorial Corps Cadet Congress aimed to deepen the spiritual life of corps cadets. They were taught to be prayerful and self-reliant, and vibrant stewards of God's resources.

The Eastern Women's Rally was held to empower women and raise awareness of sex-trade trafficking. Delegates were urged to help protect young women and girls in the fight against this modern-day slavery. Commissioner Silvia Cox (TPWM, Southern Africa) led the rally and donated a baby cupboard and blouses to every active woman officer in the territory.

The territory raised US$251,885

for its thanksgiving appeal, while the helping-hand scheme realised US$90,457 and US$10,881 was contributed to the Founder's Legacy Fund in support of officers' children and retired officers – all further proof of God's resources being inexhaustible during difficult economic times.

Wanting to see education standards improving in schools, and so producing better students, Hunyani Rotary Club donated nearly 800 educational books to Salvation Army schools.

The Korean Mission Team of 10 Salvationists visited the territory during August 2009 to monitor and evaluate the mission partnership project at Watyoka Corps. They explored new areas to support the territory and donated a borehole pump at Bumhudzo Hospital Home. They also participated at annual divisional congresses.

In a move to ease the water crisis, six boreholes were drilled in Matebeleland and Braeside in Harare. Switzerland, Austria and Hungary Territory sponsored the drilling of the boreholes. The communities are now drinking clean water.

Salvationists who gathered at the training college cheered as 40 cadets of the Witnesses For Christ Session marched into the hall at the start of their commissioning meetings. Later, 42 cadets of the Ambassadors Of Holiness Session were welcomed.

Commissioner Amos Makina (IS for Africa, IHQ) officially opened the territorial computer lab at the training college. This will be an asset to cadets' studies, as well as helping officers become more efficient and effective in their ministry.

A planned-giving and self-reliance seminar sought to move all centres in the territory further towards financial independence.

STATISTICS

Officers 591 (active 476 retired 115) **Cadets** 40
Employees 1,430
Corps 404 **Societies** 213 **Outposts** 181
Institutions/Social Centres 5 **Hospitals** 4
Schools: Pre-Schools 51 **Primary** 33
Secondary 13 **Boarding** 4 **Vocational Training** 7
Senior Soldiers 123,967 **Adherents** 5,898
Junior Soldiers 19,329
Personnel serving outside territory Officers 16

STAFF

Women's Ministries: Comr Vinece Chigariro (TPWM) Col Prema Wilfred (TSWM)
Lt-Col Ellen Nyereyemhuka (TLOMS)
Lt-Col Orlipha Ncube (THLS)
Sec for Business: Lt-Col Langton Zipingani
Sec for Personnel: Lt-Col Dubayi Ncube
Sec for Programme: Lt-Col Funny Nyereyemhuka
Audit: Maj Moyo Marasha
Development Services: Capt Criswell Chizengeya
Education: Maj Henry Chitanda
Finance: Maj Sheila Chitanda
Human Resources Development: Lt-Col Beauty Zipingani
Medical and Social: Capt Elizabeth Garland
Property: Capt Tendai Kadzvatsva
Public Relations: Maj Itai Mutizwa
Sponsorship: Capt Joice Chizengeya
Statistics: Capt Alice Marondo
Territorial Bandmaster: B/M M. Mtombeni
Territorial Songster Leader: S/L K. E. Mushababiri
Trade: Capt Tsaurai Mukwamuri
Training: Maj Abraham Lincoln Mudda
Youth and Candidates: Capt Absolom Makanga

DIVISIONS

Bindura: PO Box 197, Bindura; tel: (071) 6689;
Maj Anna Karengesha
Chiweshe: PO Box 98, Glendale;
tel: (077) 214524; Maj Margeret Siamoya
Greater Harare: PO Box 1496, Harare;
tel: (04) 747359; Majs Onai and Deliwe Jera
Guruve: c/o Box 150, Guruve; tel: (058) 505;
Maj Isiah Motsi
Harare Central: c/o Highfield Temple;
Stand # 3300, Old Highfield; tel: 663 159;
Majs Sammy and Ellen Nkoma
Harare Eastern: PO Box 26, Zengeza;
tel: (070) 22639; Majs Eliud and Aidah Nabiswa
Harare West: c/o Dzivarasekwa Corps,
PO Box 37, Dzivarasekwa; tel: (04) 216 293;
Maj Crisia Nyarubero
Hurungwe: PO Box 269, Karoi;
tel: (064) 629229; Majs Chatonda and Joyce Theu
Kadoma: PO Box 271, Kadoma;
tel: (068) 23338; Majs Casman and Martha Chinyembe
Makonde: PO Box 33, Chinhoyi; tel: (067) 2107;
Majs Frederick and Rosemary Masango
Masvingo: PO Box 314, Masvingo;
tel: (039) 63308; Majs Isaac and Charity Mhembere

Greater Harare junior soldiers on the march at their divisional rally

Matebeleland: PO Box 227 FM, Famona, Bulawayo; tel: (09) 46934; Majs Tineyi and Rumbidzai Mambo

Midlands: PO Box 624, Kwekwe; tel: (055) 3992; Majs Edwin and Tambudzai Jeremiah

Mupfure: PO Box 39, Mt Darwin; tel: (076) 529; Majs Clever and Daphine Kamambo

Semukwe: PO Box Maphisa Township, Maphisa; tel: (082) 396; Majs Final and Pfumisai Mubaiwa

DISTRICTS

Manicaland: PO Box DV8, Dangamvura, Mutare; tel: (020) 30014; Capt Sipho Mbangwa

Murehwa: PO Box 268, Murehwa; tel: (078) 2455; Maj Lovemore Chidhakwa

AREAS

Hwange: PO Box 130, Dete; tel: 018 237; Area Coordinator: Maj Peter Nikisi

TRAINING COLLEGE

PO Box CR95, Cranborne; tel: (04) 742298; fax: (04) 742575

MASIYE TRAINING CAMP

PO Box AC800 Bulawayo; tel: (09) 60727; Camp: tel: (0838) 222/261; tel/fax: (0838) 228; emails: info@masiye.com (camp), info@byo.masiye.com (town office)

EDUCATION

Boarding Schools

Bradley Secondary School: P Bag 909 Bindura; tel: (071) 3421 (acc 516)

Howard High School: PO Box 230, Howard; tel: (0758) 45921 (acc 908)

Mazowe High School: P Bag 211A, Harare; tel: (075) 25603 (acc 670)

Usher Secondary School: P Bag P5271, Bulawayo; tel: (083) 2904 (acc 560)

MEDICAL

Athol Evans Hospital Home: Chiremba Rd, Queensdale, PO Box CR70, Cranborne; tel: (04) 572121; email: aec.sec@zol.co.zw (acc 164)

Bumhudzo Hospital Home: St Mary's Township, PO Box ZG 48, Zengeza, Harare; tel: (070) 24911; 'C' scheme hospital home (acc 55); 'B' scheme residential (acc 55)

Howard Hospital: PO Box 190, Glendale; tel: (0758) 2433; emails: howard.hospital@africaonline.co.zw, pthistle@healthnet.zw (acc 144)

Tshelanyemba Hospital: PO Tshelanyemba, Maphisa; tel: (082) 254; email: tshelanyemba.hosp@healthnet.zw (acc 103)

SOCIAL SERVICES

Bulawayo

Enterprise House: Josiah Tongogara St/ 12th Ave, PO Box 3208; tel: (09) 60012 (acc men 65)

Ralstein Home: Masotsha Ndhlovu Ave; tel: (09) 61972 (acc mixed 30)

Harare

Braeside Social Complex: General Booth Rd, Braeside, PO Box CR66, Cranborne; tel: (04) 742001 (acc women 20, men 64)

Arcadia Girls' Hostel: Jampies St, Arcadia; tel: (04) 770082 (acc 28)

Howard

Weaving and Dressmaking School: PO Howard; tel: (0758) 45921

Biographical Information

Based on information received by 30 November 2010

1. The following list contains the names of all active officers with the rank of lieut-colonel and above, and other officers holding certain designated appointments.

2 (a) The place and date in parenthesis immediately following the name denote the place from which the officer entered Army service and the year of service commencement. Officers commissioned prior to 1 January 1973 have their active service dated from the conclusion of the first year of training. After 1 January 1973 active service begins at the date of commissioning following a two-year session of training.

(b) Details of married women officers' entry to active service are shown separately, including maiden name. If a wife was trained separately from her husband the word *and* joins the two entries, but if trained together the word *with* joins them.

(c) At the end of each entry of married officers a joint record of their service in other countries is given. Where applicable this includes countries each served in individually before marriage.

3. Where an officer is serving in a territory/command other than his/her own this is indicated by including the territory/command of origin after the corps from which he/she entered training. In all other instances the information given implies that the officer is serving in his/her home territory.

4. Details of appointments (where not given in this section) may be ascertained under the territorial or departmental headings.

5. A key to abbreviations is given on pages 348-349.

A

ABAYOMI, Ebenezer (Ife Ife, 1988); Maj, Nig. b 4 Apr 60; and
  ABAYOMI, Comfort (Ife Ife, 1990) m 1990; Maj, Nig. b 12 Dec 63.

ABEL, Bailis (Chenkody, 1980); Maj, Ind SE. b 20 Feb 53; and
  ABARANAM, Bailis (Chadayanvilai, 1972) m 1980; Maj, Ind SE. b 23 Aug 48.

ABBULU, Sankurati Pedda (Achanta, 1978); Maj, Ind C. b 2 Jan 50; with
  ABBULU, Vimala (née Kumari) m 1970; Maj, Ind C. b 10 Dec 53. Served in Tanz.

ABRAHAM, Puthenparambil T. (Karimala, Ind SW, 1972); Lt-Col, CS, Ind C. b 17 Feb 48; and
  ABRAHAM, Mariyamma (Central Adoor, Ind SW, 1975) m 1975; Lt-Col, TSWM, Ind C. b 30 Mar 52. Served in Ind SW

ABIA, Edmund (Somanya, 1993); Maj, Gha. b 14 Mar 62; with
  ABIA, Grace (née Awo) m 1991; Maj, Gha. b 15 Feb 69.

ADAMS, Clive (Claremont, S Afr, 1983); Comr, TC, Nor. b 5 Jan 57; and
  ADAMS, Marianne (née Jokobsen) (Oslo 3, 1985) m 1990; Comr, TPWM, Nor. b 10 Feb 60. Served in S Afr, UK, at IHQ and in Nor (CS/TSWM).

ADDISON, Edward (Swedru, 1981); Maj, Gha. b 24 Jan 54. Ww Lt Margaret, pG 1983; and

ADDISON, Mercy (née Simpson) (Swedru, 1985) m 1985; Maj, Gha. b 4 Nov 60.

ADEPOJU, Gabriel (Ibadan, 1986); Maj, Nig. b 17 Jul 60. MSc, BA (Relig Studies); and
  ADEPOJU, Comfort (Ibadan, 1994) m 1994; Maj, Nig. b 15 Aug 70.

ADU-MANU, Mike (Jamasi, 1987); Lt-Col, Gha. b 10 Apr 48; with
  ADU-MANU, Theresa (née Asante Pinamang) m 1970; Lt-Col, Gha. b 1 Apr 48.

AGUILERA, Miguel (Lo Valledor, S Am W, 1978); Maj, Brz. b 9 Jul 55; and
  AGUILERA, Angélica (née Cortes) (Lo Valledor, Chile, S Am W, 1978) m 1979; Maj, Brz. b 11 Sep 58. Served in S Am W, Sp and L Am N.

AHN, Guhn-shik (Oh Ka, 1985); Maj, Kor. b 23 Dec 57; and
  YANG, Shin-kyong (Sudaemun, 1984) m 1985; Maj, Kor. b 5 Jul 54.

AKPAN, Joseph (Calabar, 1980); Lt-Col, Nig. b 30 Sep 58; with
  AKPAN, Patience m 1978; Lt-Col, Nig. b 15 May 62.

AKPAN, Mfon Jaktor (Igbobi, 1969); Comr, TC, Nig. b 21 Jul 49; and
  AKPAN, Ime Johnnie (née Udo) (Ikot Udobia, 1974) m 1974; Comr, TPWM, Nig. b 9 Nov 53. Served in Con (Braz) (CS/TSWM, TC/TPWM).

ALARCÓN, David (Punta Arenas, 1980);

Lt-Col, S Am W. b 24 Jun 56; and
ALARCÓN, María (née Arredondo)
(Rancagua, 1980) m 1982; Lt-Col, S Am W.
b 3 Mar 55.

ALÍ, Sixto (El Tejar, 1990); Maj, S Am W.
b 28 Mar 63; with
ALÍ, Aída (née Cáceres) m 1988; Maj,
S Am W. b 8 Mar 68.

ALLAN, Geoffrey (Detroit Brightmoor, MI,
1977); Maj, USA C. b 27 Feb 46. BA (Ed),
MA (Sec Ed); with
ALLAN, Marian (née Botu) m 1965; Maj,
USA C. b 8 Jun 43. RN (Nursing).

ALLAN, Graham (Kokomo, IN, 1975); Maj,
USA C. b 24 Feb 49. BA (Counselling/Bus
Adm), AA (Bus); with
ALLAN, Vickie (née Hardebeck) m 1969;
Maj, USA C. b 26 Jan 50.

ALLCHIN, Joy (néeMuskett) (Aylsham, 1981);
Maj, UK. b 13 Feb 60; and
ALLCHIN, Clifford (Gravesend, 1981)
m 1982; Maj, UK. b 26 Feb 58.

ALLEMAND, Carolyn (née Olckers) (Cape
Town Citadel, S Afr, 1980); Lt-Col, UK.
b 4 Oct 55. Served in S Afr, at IHQ and in
S Am E. m 1989; Lt-Col Gustave, ret 2006.

ALLEY, Kelvin (Belconnen, Aus E, 1987); Maj,
Aus Nat and Aus E. b 3 Apr 54. BA (Admin),
BDiv, DMin; with
ALLEY, Julie (née Stewart) m 1975; Maj,
Aus E. b 19 Jun 56. Dip Min. Served in PNG.

ALM, Britt-Marie (née Johansson) (Hisingskåren,
1970); Lt-Col, Swdn. b 28 Dec 45.

AMAKYE, Francis (Achiase, 1995); Maj, Gha.
b 25 Jul 65; with
AMAKYE, Jemima (née Agyei Yeboah)
m 1992; Maj, Gha. b 3 May 65.

AMBITAN, Harold (Manado 1, 1973); Lt-Col,
Indon. b 9 May 49; and
AMBITAN, Deetje (née Malawau) (Bandung,
1972) m 1975; Lt-Col, Indon. b 8 Jun 49.

AMICK, Richard (Hutchinson, KS, 1978);
Maj, USA C. b 24 Nov 54. BA (Bus Adm);
and
AMICK, Vicki (née Anderson) (Grand
Haven, MI, 1978) m 1979; Maj, USA C.
b 29 Jun 55.

AMPOFO, Jonas (Asiakwa, 1981); Maj, Gha.
b 6 Oct 1950; with
AMPOFO, Constance (née Nyamekye)
m 2004; Capt, Gha. b 14 Apr 57.

ANDERSEN, Henrik (Copenhagen Gartnergade,
1986); Maj, Den. b 30 Aug 61; with
ANDERSEN, Lisbeth (née Bjarkam)
m 1984; Maj, Den. b 17 Apr 64. Served in
Swdn and UK.

ANZEZE, Hezekiel (Naliava, 1980); Comr,
TC, Ken E. b 15 Mar 49. Ww Comr Clerah,
pG 2005.

APPAVOO, Sam Devaraj (Muttacaud, 1976);
Maj, Ind SE. b 23 Jun 51; and
KANAGARETNAM, Sam Devaraj
(Anducode, 1975) m 1977; Maj, Ind SE.
b 19 Oct 54.

APPEATENG, Seth (Manso, 1989); Maj, Gha.
b 9 Jun 62; with
APPEATENG, Janet (née Nkansah) m 1987;
Maj, Gha. b 12 Dec 67.

ARGUEDAS, Antonio (Callao, 1974); Maj,
S Am W. b 9 Sep 53; and
ARGUEDAS, Lilian (née Sánchez) (Lima
Central, 1981) m 1981; Maj, S Am W.
b 24 Nov 58.

ARNAL, Sylvie (Alès, 1977); Lt-Col, CS, Frce.
b 13 Apr 53. Served in Zaï and Con (Braz).

ARNOLD, Wilfred D. (Hamilton, 1973);
Lt-Col, NZ. b 22 May 45. BSoc Sc,
MA (Soc Wk), CQSW; with
ARNOLD, Margaret D. (née Fitness)
m 1966; Lt-Col, NZ. b 6 Jul 45. BN, RGON,
Grad Dip Soc Sc. Served in Aus S and Sing.

ARROWOOD, James (Winston-Salem Central,
NC, 1983); Maj, USA S. b 23 Jan 56; with
ARROWOOD, Linda (née Portis) m 1975;
Maj, USA S. b 16 Feb 57.

ARULAPPAN, Paramadhas (Elanthiady, 1972);
Maj, Ind SE. b 11 May 54; and
ARULAPPAN, Retnam Paramadhas
(Changaneri, 1974) m 1976; Maj, Ind SE.
b 30 May 51.

ASIRVATHAM, Devadhas (Palliyady, 1971);
Maj, Ind SE. b 20 May 51; and
JOTHI, Vasanthabai Devadhas (Manakarai,
1973) m 1973; Maj, Ind SE. b 11 Apr 53

ASPERSCHLAGER, Gary C. (Orange, NJ,
1976); Lt-Col, USA E. b 20 Apr 46. BS (Biol),
MA (Div); and
ASPERSCHLAGER, Pearl A. (née Samson)
(White Plains, NY, 1973) m 1976; Lt-Col,
USA E. b 20 Aug 46. BA (Ed).

AYANAM, Friday S. (Akai, 1988); Maj, Nig.
b 2 Oct 64; with
AYANAM, Glory m 1986; Maj, Nig.
b 28 Apr 64. Served in Zimb.

B

BAAH, Samuel (Duakwa, Gha, 1987); Lt-Col,
Nig. b 13 Mar 63; with
BAAH, Theresa (née Kumi) m 1984; Lt-Col,
Nig. b 10 Sep 64. Served in Gha.

BAHAMONDE, Cecilia (Lo Vial, 1983); Maj,
S Am W. b 23 Mar 63.

BAILEY, Carol (Greenock, 1977); Maj, UK. b 13 May 57.

BAILEY, Christine (Barking, 1975); Maj, UK. b 15 Apr 49. BA (Hons) (Soc Sci – Pol), PGCE. Served in S Am E.

BAILEY, F. Bradford (Kansas City [Westport Temple], MO, USA C, 1982); Lt-Col, IHQ. b 4 May 58. BS (Soc Work); with **BAILEY, Heidi J.** (née Chandler) m 1978; Lt-Col, IHQ. b 17 Jul 54. Served in USA C, Sp (OC/CPWM) and S Am W (CS/TSWM).

BAKEMBA, Prosper (Mabenga, 1982); Lt-Col, Con (Braz). b 21 Oct 49; with **BAKEMBA, Monique** (née Mafoua) m 1980; Lt-Col, Con (Braz). b 28 Jun 52.

BAKER, Gary (Nundah, 1976); Maj, Aus E. b 23 Sep 48; with **BAKER, Judith** (née Wells) m 1969; Maj, Aus E. b 3 Jun 49.

BAMANABIO, Eugene (Mfilou, Con (Braz), 1990); Maj, GS, Uga. b 10 Jul 62; with **BAMANABIO, Brigitte** (née Locko-Oumba) m 1988; Maj, CSWM, Uga, b 13 Dec 1963. Served in Con (Braz) and Rwa.

BAMFORD, William A. III (Quincy, MA, USA E, 1989); Lt-Col, CS, S Am W. b 11 Jun 57. BS (Pharm), MS (Org Ldrshp); with **BAMFORD, G. Lorraine** (née Brown) m 1980; Lt-Col, TSWM, S Am W. b 25 Jul 53. BA (Mod Langs). Served in USA E.

BANFIELD, Stephen (Quincy, MA, 1978); Maj, USA E. b 17 Mar 53. BA (Psych); with **BANFIELD, Janet Mae** (née Anderson) m 1976; Maj, USA E. b 27 Apr 55.

BARASA, Jonathan (Bungoma, 1996); Capt, Ken E. b 23 Jun 70; with **BARASA, Alice** (née Nafula) m 1994; Capt, Ken E. b 12 Aug 73.

BARKAT, Samuel (Thal, 1973); Maj, Pak. b 7 Aug 51; with **SAMUEL, Margaret** m 1971; Maj, Pak. b 7 Aug 52.

BARNARD, Rodney (Norwood, 1982); Lt-Col, Aus S. b 7 Apr 49; with **BARNARD, Jennifer** (née Rowe) m 1970; Lt-Col, Aus S. b 5 Nov 50. Served in UK.

BARR, John M. (Ian) (Saltcoats, 1972); Lt-Col, UK. b 10 Aug 50. BD (Hons), MA Cert Ed. Served at ITC. m 1974; Lt-Col Christine, ret 2009.

BATEMAN, David (Lower Hutt, 1988); Maj, NZ. b 17 Dec 60. Dip Bus, Cert Mgmt (NZIM); with **BATEMAN, Margaret** (née Allott) m 1983; Maj, NZ. b 19 Nov 58. BN, RGON.

BAUTISTA, Estelita (née Baquirin) (Asingan, 1994); Maj, Phil. b 12 Nov 62. BS (Comm); and **BAUTISTA, David** (Asingan, 1996) m 1996; Capt, Phil. b 12 May 61. BSc (Industrial Ed).

BECKMAN, Elisabeth (née Sundström) (Stockholm Temple, 2006); Capt, Swdn, b 18 Jan 65.

BELL, Donald C. (Spokane, WA, USA W, 1978); Comr, TC, NZ. b 12 Oct 49. BA (Econ & Hist), JD (Law); and **BELL, Debora K.** (née Perry) (Hobbs, NM, 1977) m 1979; Comr, TPWM, NZ. b 6 Feb 56. Served at USA Nat, in USA W (CS/TSWM) and NZ (CS/TSWM).

BELL, Mark (Hagerstown, MD, 1977); Lt-Col, USA S. b 27 Mar 51; with **BELL, Alice** (née Armendariz) m 1975; Lt-Col, USA S. b 26 Sep 54.

BERG, Gro (née Egeland) (Stavanger, 1985); Maj, Nor. b 11 Oct 62; and **BERG, Pål Thomas** (Nord Odal II, 1985) m 1985; Maj, Nor. b 12 Aug 62.

BERG, Odd (Harstad, 1969); Lt-Col, Nor. b 4 Mar 47; and **BERG, Grethe** (née Knetten) (Ski, 1969) m 1971; Lt-Col, Nor. b 12 May 48. Served in Nor, UK, Den and Ger (CS/TSWM).

BERNAO, Raul (Trelew,1983); Maj, S Am E. b 11 Oct 61; and **BERNAO, Lidia** (née Lopez) (Santiago del Estero, 1981) m 1984; Maj, S Am E. b 20 Feb 59.

BERRY, Donald E. (Kearny, NJ, 1976); Maj, USA E. b 9 Jun 49; with **BERRY, Vicki** (née Van Nort) m 1970; Maj, USA E. b 15 Jan 50. BA (Engl), MA (Strategic Comms & Ldrshp)

BIAKLIANA, S. (Hnahthial, 1981); Maj, Ind E. b 15 Feb 56; and **BIAKMAWII** (Dolchera, 1982) m 1982; Maj, Ind E. b 10 Aug 62.

BLOMBERG, Sonja (née Waern) (Kristinehamn 1994); Maj, Swdn. b 1 May 56; and **BLOMBERG, Christer** (Kristinehamn 1994) Maj, Swdn. b 16 Jul 54.

BLOOMFIELD, Glenn C. (Philadelphia NE, PA, 1972); Maj, USA E. b 25 Feb 50; and **BLOOMFIELD, Carol** (née Thompson) (Cleveland Temple, OH, 1971) m 1972; Maj, USA E. b 1 Jun 48.

BOADU, Stephen (Topremang 1985); Maj, Gha. b 17 Jul 61; with **BOADU, Cecilia** (née Ofori) m 1983; Maj, Gha. b 4 Apr 63.

BODE, William H. (Alliance, OH, 1970); Maj, USA E. b 6 Sep 49, and **BODE, Joan I.** (née Burke) (Brooklyn 8th Ave, NY, 1969) m 1971; Maj, USA E. b 30 Aug 48.

BONAZEBI, Philippe (Makaka, 1992); Maj, Con (Braz). b 14 Sep 63; with **BONAZEBI, Julie Rose** (née Kouba) m 1988; Maj, Con (Braz). b 15 Jul 70.

BOND, Eric (St Catharines, ON, 1987); Maj, Can. b 24 Dec 46. BA (Teachers Cert); with **BOND, Donna** (née Williams) m 1968; Maj, Can. b 10 Mar 49.

BOND, Linda (St James, Winnipeg, Can, 1968); Comr, TC, Aus E. b 22 Jun 46. BRelig Ed, MTS. Served in UK, Can (CS), USA W (TC) and at IHQ.

BOOTH, Patrick (Paris-Central, Frce, 1989); Maj, S Afr. b 12 Jan 55; with **BOOTH, Margaret** (née Miaglia) m 1983; Maj, S Afr. b 31 Jul 61. Served in Frce and UK

BOSCHUNG, Franz (Basle 2, 1977); Col, CS, Switz. b 21 Sep 49; with **BOSCHUNG, Hanny** (née Abderhalden) m 1971; Col, TSWM, Switz. b 7 Apr 50. Served in Con (Braz).

BOSH, Larry (Mansfield, OH, USA E, 1966); Comr, IHQ (IS Am & Carib). b 9 Jun 46. BS (Acct), MBA; and **BOSH, Gillian** (née Reid) (Akron Citadel, OH, USA E, 1960) m 1967; Comr, IHQ (ZSWM Am & Carib). b 4 Dec 40. Served at IHQ, USA Nat (Nat CS/NSWM, NRVAVS) and in USA E (CS/TSWM)

BOUZIGUES, Ricardo (Colegiales, 1976); Lt-Col, CS, S Am E. b 12 Sep 52. BA (Pract Theol), MA (Theol); and **BOUZIGUES, Sonia** (née Alvez) (Cordoba, 1979) m 1979; Lt-Col, TSWM, S Am E. b 12 Nov 54.

BOWERS, Thomas M. (Moline, IL, 1978); Maj, USA C. b 19 Sep 55; with **BOWERS, Jacalyn G.** (née Thorson) m 1975; Maj, USA C. b 20 Mar 55. AA (Soc).

BOWLES, Marsha-Jean (née Wortley) (Woodstock, ON, Can, 1990); Maj, Ger. b 2 Mar 62; with **BOWLES, David** m 1981; Maj, Ger. b 20 Jul 60. Served in Can.

BREKKE, Birgitte (née Nielsen) (Copenhagen Temple, 1980); Col, TC, TPWM, Den. b 17 Sep 54. SRN. Served in Nor, Sri Lan, Ban (CPWO), UK, E Eur, Pak (TPWM) and at IHQ. Ww Col Bo, pG 2007

BROWN, Rosemarie (Kingston Central,

Jamaica, 1978); Maj, Carib. b 17 Oct 57. Served at ICO.

BRINGANS, David (Albion, Aus E, 1970); Comr, TC, Mex. b 25 May 47; with **BRINGANS, Grace** (née Palmer) m 1968; Comr, TPWM, Mex. b 21 Sep 46. Served in NZ, HK, Vietnam, Tai (RC/RPWM) and Sing (GS/CSWO, TC/TPWM), .

BUCKINGHAM, Lyndon (Whangarei, 1988); Lt-Col, NZ. b 13 Feb 62; with **BUCKINGHAM, Bronwyn** (née Robertson) m 1986; Lt-Col, NZ. b 21 Jun 65. Served in Can.

BUEYA, Nsoki Joseph (Kavwaya, 1981); Lt-Col, DR Con. b 12 Jul 48; with **BUEYA, Germaine** (née Nkenda Mbuku) m 1978; Lt-Col, DR Con. b 10 Jun 52.

BUKIEWICZ, Ralph (Milwaukee West, WI, 1980); Lt-Col, USA C. b 3 Mar 60; and **BUKIEWICZ, Susan** (née Cunard) (Dearborn Heights, MI, 1981) m 1981; Lt-Col, USA C. b 9 May 58.

BURGER, Kurt (Los Angeles Congress Hall, CA, USA W, 1972); Comr, TC, Switz. b 26 Aug 46. BS (Bus Adm), BA (Psych), MBA (Bus Adm), Cert CPA; and **BURGER, Alicia** (née Pedersen) (San Bernardino, CA, USA W, 1976) m 1988; Comr, TPWM, Switz. b 6 Jul 46. Served in USA W.

BURN, Margaret (née Cain) (Lincoln Citadel, 1966); Lt-Col, UK. b 12 Nov 46.

BURNS, Alan (Harlow, 1976); Lt-Col, UK. b 1 May 54. BSc (Hons), MA (Evan); and **BURNS, Alison** (née Hitchin) (Regent Hall, 1979) m 1981; Lt-Col, UK. b 8 Oct 52. Served at IHQ.

BURR, W. Howard (Lexington, KY, 1973); Lt-Col, USA E. b 8 Nov 47. BA (Psych), MS (Ed Adm); with **BURR, Patricia** (née Stigleman) m 1970; Lt-Col, USA E. b 29 Jun 51.

BURROWS, David (Skipton, UK, 1970); Lt-Col, IHQ. b 30 Apr 47. SRN. Served in Pak, Tanz (OC) and Mal (OC). m 1972; Lt-Col Jean, ret 2009.

C

CACHELIN, Hervé (Biel, 1979); Maj, Switz. b 16 Feb 57; and **CACHELIN, Deborah** (née Cullingworth) (Catford, UK, 1981) m 1983; Maj, Switz. b 2 Jul 57. Served in Aus E and UK.

CAFFULL, Michael (Worthing, 1978) Lt-Col, UK. b 20 Dec 55. MA (Miss Ldrshp); and **CAFFULL, Wendy** (née Hart) (Southend Citadel, 1977) m 1978; Lt-Col, UK.

303

b 24 Mar 57. BA (Pastoral Care with Psych). Served at IHQ.

CAIRNS, Philip (Campsie, 1982); Lt-Col, Aus E. b 5 Feb 51. Dip Mus Ed, Dip Min, MTh; with
CAIRNS, Janice (née Manson) m 1972; Lt-Col, Aus E. b 7 Oct 48. ATCL, LTCL, Grad Dip Chrstn Counselling.

CALDWELL, Bradley J. (Shreveport, LA, USA S, 1993); Maj, E Eur. b 31 Aug 64. MA (Div). BA (Phil); with
CALDWELL, Anita Maye (née Howard) m 1989; Maj, E Eur. b 1 Dec 56. BA (Rel). Served in USA S.

CALLANDER, Ian (Fairfield, Aus S, 1977); Maj, E Eur. b 7 Aug 55. BTh; and
CALLANDER, Vivien (née Wiseman) (Adelaide Congress Hall, Aus S, 1977) m 1978; Maj, E Eur. b 7 May 53. BPhys. Served in Aus S.

CALVO, Esteban (Concepcion de Rios, 1987); Maj, L Am N. b 23 Jan 63; and
CALVO, Ileana (née Jimenez) (Concepcion de Rios, 1986) m 1989; Maj, L Am N. b 5 Jun 66.

CAMARGO, Iolanda (Niterói, Brz, 1969), Maj, Asst TSWM, Brz. b 6 Aug 49.

CAMARILLO, Luís (Mexico # 1, 2001); Capt, Mex. b 25 Apr 73; with
CAMARILLO, Nohemí (née Martinez) m 1999; Capt, Mex. b 20 May 73. BA (Adm).

CAMPBELL, Mark T. (Wollongong, 1985); Maj, Aus E. b 4 May 60. MA Th, BAL; with
CAMPBELL, Julie A. (née Woodbury) m 1983; Maj, Aus E. b 17 Sep 59.

CAMPOS Manuel (Mexicali, 1980); Maj, Mex. b 14 Jun 58; with
CAMPOS Ana (née Flores) m 1978; Maj, Mex. b 26 Jul 57.

CANNING, Joan (Moncton, NB, Can, 1983); Maj, Asst CS, USA Nat. b 27 Sep 62. BA (Bible and Theol). Served in Can and at IHQ.

CAPSEY, Mary (Leeds Central, UK, 1984); Lt-Col, IHQ. b 10 Mar 59. SRN, SCM, MSc (Health Ed & Prom). Served in UK, Gha, Belg, Con (Braz) and Zimb.

CAREY, Hélène (née Paulus) (Liege, Belg, 1972); Maj, UK, b 24 Dec 50; and
CAREY, Graham (Southend Citadel, 1972) m 1975; Maj, UK b 28 Nov 50. Served in Belg and Free

CAREY, Roderick (Dunedin Fortress, 1982); Maj, NZ. b 19 Mar 58. Dip BRS, BTh; with
CAREY, Jennifer (née Cross) m 1980; Maj, NZ. b 5 Feb 61. Served Aust S.

CARLSON, William (Staten Island Port Richmond, NY, 1971); Col, USA E.

b 9 Jan 48. BA (Soc Studies); and
CARLSON, Marcella (née Brewer) (Staten Island Port Richmond, NY, 1971) m 1971; Col, USA E. b 18 Sep 49.

CASTILLO, Luis (Antofagasta, S Am W, 1977); Lt-Col, OC, Sp. b 7 Jan 48; and
CASTILLO, Aída (Quinta Normal, 1968) m 1972; Lt-Col, CPWM, Sp. b 5 Nov 49. Served in S Am W (CS/TSWM), Mex (CS/TSWM) and S Am E (CS/TSWM).

CASTOR, Onal (Aquin, Haiti, 1979); Col, TC, Carib. b 20 Jul 55; and
CASTOR, Edmane (née Montoban) (Duverger, Haiti, 1980) m 1980; Col, TPWM, Carib. b 1 Oct 57. Served in USA S, Con (Kin) and Carib (CS/TSWM).

CENECIRO, Joel (Manila, 1989); Maj, Phil. b 23 May 66. BA (Biblical Studies), MA (Chrstn Studies); and
CENECIRO, Susan (née Pudpud) (Tondo, 1989); Maj, Phil. b 31 Oct 66. B Min.

CEREZO, Josué (Monterrey, Mex, 1985); Lt-Col, CS, L Am N. b 16 May 57; with
CEREZO, Ruth (née Garcia) m 1983; Lt-Col, TSWM, L Am N. b 22 Oct 60. Served in Mex (CS/TSWM).

CHAGAS, Edgar (São Paulo Central, 1988); Maj, Brz. b 24 Feb 58. BA (Phys) MA (Sci); with
CHAGAS, Sara (née Parker) m 1982; Maj, Brz. b 26 Aug 60. BA (Psychol).

CHALWE, Frazer (Chikumbi, 1989); Maj, Zam. b 25 Jan 65; with
CHALWE, Rodinah (née Mukunkami) m 1986; Maj, Zam. b 8 May 68.

CHANG, Man-Hee (San Francisco Korean, CA, 1993); Maj, USA W. b 31 Mar 58. BA (Bus Adm), MBA (Bus Adm); with
CHANG, Stephanie (née Shim) m 1983; Maj, USA W. b 1 Jun 59. BA (Math).

CHARAN, Samuel (Rampur, Ind N, 1978); Col, TC, Ind SW. b 1 Apr 53; with
CHARAN, Bimla Wati m 1974; Col, TPWM, Ind SW. Served in Ind N, Ind SW (CS/TSWM) and Ind E (CS/TSWM, TC/TPWM).

CHARLET, Horst (Berlin-Neukölln, 1969); Comr, TC, Ger. b 1 May 46. Dip SW, Dip Soc Pedagogue; with
CHARLET, Helga (née Werner); Comr, TPWM, Ger. b 18 Oct 48. Served in Ger (CS/TSWM)

CHAUHAN, Jashwant Soma (Tarapur, 1979); Maj, Ind W. b 20 Feb 52; with
CHAUHAN, Indiraben m 1976; Maj, Ind W. b 8 Jun 56.

CHELLAIYAN, Anbayan (Perai, 1982); Maj, Ind SE. b 9 Apr 55. BA, BD; and

Biographical Information

DITCH, Saroja Bai Anbayan (Vannioor, 1984) m 1984; Maj, Ind SE. b 31 May 61.

CHELLIAH, Moni (Osaravillai, 1976); Maj, Ind SE. b 18 May 55. MA; and
MALLIKA, Moni (Alady, 1978) m 1978; Maj, Ind SE. b 6 Mar 57.

CHELLIAH, Swamidhas (Kannankulam, 1977); Maj, Ind SE. b 21 Apr 55; and
JOICEBAI, Swamidhas (Kaliancaud, 1973) m 1977; Maj, Ind SE. b 16 Feb 53.

CHENDA, Joster (Matero, 1981); Maj, Zam. b 10 Jun 57; and
CHENDA, Christine (née Chingala) (Libala, 1983) m 1983; Maj, Zam. b 3 Mar 62.

CHEPKURUI, Stephen (Cheptais, Ken, 1982); Maj, OC, Rwa. b 22 Feb 58; and
CHEPKURUI, Grace (née Madolio) (Vigeze, Ken, 1980) m 1985; Maj, CPWM, Rwa. b 15 May 55. Served in E Afr, Tanz (GS/CSWM) and Rwa (RC/RPWM).

CHEPSIRI, Harun (Toroso, 1995) Capt, Ken W. b 20 Sep 65; with
CHEPSIRI, Beatrice (née Cherop) m 1992; Capt, Ken W. b 6 Jul 68.

CHIGARIRO, Vinece (Gunguwe, 1975); Comr, TC, TPWM, Zimb. b 7 Mar 54. Served in Tanz (GS) and Zimb (TC, TPWM).

CHILYABANYAMA, Metson (Chitumbi, 1987); Lt-Col, Zam. b 30 Oct 55; with
CHILYABANYAMA, Rosemary (née Mboozi) m 1982; Lt-Col, Zam. b 8 Aug 61.

CHINYEMBA, Casman (Chimbumu, 1989); Maj, Zimb. b 7 Jan 62; with
CHINYEMBA, Martha (née Gomo) m 1988; Maj, Zimb. b 16 Oct 63. Served in Tanz.

CHISENGELE, Bernard (Monze, 1983); Maj, Zam. b 1 Jan 51; and
CHISENGELE, Dorothy (née Mweemba) (Kaumba, 1985) m 1985; Maj, Zam. b 14 Nov 59.

CHITANDA, Sheila (née Mvere) (Kwekwe, 1992); Maj, Zimb. b 15 Oct 68; and
CHITANDA, Henry (Chinhoyi, 1991) m 1992; Maj, Zimb. b 6 Apr 66.

CHIWOYA, Besnart (née Mvula) (Kawama 1997); Capt, Zam. b 28 Jul 64; with
CHIWOYA, Wilson m 1987; Capt, Zam. b 22 Jun 62.

CHOO, Seung-chan (Yung Deung Po, 1980); Maj, Kor. b 15 Jun 50; with
LEE, Ok-hee m 1978; Maj, Kor. b 2 Aug 54.

CHRISTIAN, Gabriel Ibrahim (Muktipur, 1983); Maj, Ind W. b 24 Dec 59; and
CHRISTIAN, Indumati (née Samual Macwan) (Petlad Central, 1985) m 1986; Maj, Ind W. b 30 Aug 62.

CHRISTIAN, Paul (Bhalej, Ind W, 1978);
Lt-Col, CS, Ind N. b 22 Sep 48; and
CHRISTIAN, Anandiben (née Kalidas) (Ghoghawada, Ind W, 1980) m 1980; Lt-Col, TSWM, Ind N. b 12 Jul 57. Served at Ind Cent Off and in Ind W (CS/THLS).

CHRISTURAJ, Rajamani (Elappara, 1983); Maj, Ind SW. b 27 Dec 61; and
CHRISTURAJ, Mary (née Mathew) (Elampally, 1983) m 1983; Maj, Ind SW. b 11 May 59.

CHRISTIAN, Rasik Paul (Chunel, 1988); Maj, Ind W. b 7 Sep 65; and
CHRISTIAN Ramilaben (née Samuel) (Piplag, 1990) m 1990; Maj, Ind W. b 17 Apr 68.

CHUN, Joon-hung (Yong Dong, 1978); Lt-Col, Kor. b 20 Jun 48; with
SHIN, Myung-ja m 1976; Lt-Col, Kor. b 28 Sep 49.

CHUNG, Edmund L. (Manhattan Citadel, USA E, 1976); Lt-Col, IHQ. b 8 Aug 48. BS (Chem), MS (Management); and
CHUNG, Carolynne J. (née Wiseman) (Lexington, KY, USA E, 1976) m 1977. BA, MA (Org Ldrshp); Lt-Col, IHQ. b 28 Jul 46. Served in USA E, USA Nat and UK.

CLÉNAT, Jean (Aquin, Haiti, Carib, 2001); Capt, GS, Rwa. b 8 Oct 73; and
CLÉNAT, Elianese (née Pierre) (Gros Morne, Haiti, Carib, 1998) m 2002; Capt, CSWM, Rwa. b 8 Oct 73. Served in Carib.

CLIFTON, Shaw (Edmonton, UK, 1973); General (see page 26); with
CLIFTON, Helen (née Ashman) m 1967; Comr, World President of Women's Ministries, IHQ. b 4 May 48. BA (Eng Lang/Lit) (Hons), PGCE. Served at IHQ, in Zimb, USA E, Pak (TC/TPWO), NZ (TC/TPWM) and UK (TC/TPWM).

CLINCH, Ronald (Launceston, Aus S, 1986); Lt-Col, CS, Phil. b 6 Sep 54. BEd; with
CLINCH, Robyn (née Mole) m 1982; Lt-Col, TSWM, Phil. b 8 Nov 60.

COCHRANE, William (Barrhead, 1975); Comr, IHQ (IS to CoS). b 7 Sep 54. Served in UK (CS).

COLA, Iliesa (Raiwai, 1995); Maj, NZ. b 7 Nov 55; with
COLA, Litiana (née Vuidreketi) m 1982; Maj, NZ. b 8 Mar 62.

COLEMAN, Michael T. (Kwinana, Aus S, 1986); Maj, RC, Tai. b 4 Nov 54; with
COLEMAN, Annette (née Willey) m 1976; Maj, RPWM, Tai. b 23 Oct 55. BSc. Served in Aus S.

CONDON, James (Shoalhaven, Aus E, 1971), Comr, IHQ (IS SPEA). b 29 Nov 49; and

CONDON, Jan (née Vickery) (Uralla, Aus E, 1971) m 1972; Comr, IHQ (ZSWM SPEA). b 25 Jan 47. Served in UK, PNG (CS/TSWM) and Aus E (CS/TWSM).

CONRAD, Keith (Matroosfontein, 1988); Maj, S Afr. b 31 Mar 62; with
CONRAD, Yvonne (née Jansen) m 1984; Maj, S Afr. b 13 Mar 63. Served in NZ.

COSTAS, Deisy (Achachicala, Bolivia, S Am W, 1981); Maj, L Am N. b 21 Jan 56.

COTTERILL, Anthony (Regent Hall, 1984); Lt-Col, UK. b 9 Dec 57. BA (Hons); with
COTTERILL, Gillian (née Rushforth) m 1979; Lt-Col, UK. b 15 Sep 57. SRN.

COWDERY, Colin (Eastleigh, UK, 1980); Maj, Pak. b 7 Dec 49. BA; with
COWDERY, Rosemary (née Thomas) m 1966; Maj, Pak. b 4 Oct 49.

COWLING, Alison (Macleans, Aus E, 1978); Maj, Asst CS, Can. b 10 Feb 50. Served in Aus E and at IHQ.

COX, André (Geneva 1, Switz, 1979); Comr, TC, S Afr. b 12 Jul 54; with
COX, Silvia (née Volet) m 1976; Comr, TPWM, S Afr. b 18 Nov 55. Served in Switz, Zimb and Fin (TC/TPWM).

CRAIG, Heather (née Mackay) (Parramatta, Aus E, 1986); Maj, Gha. b 31 Dec 57; and
CRAIG, Graeme (Rockhampton, Aus E, 1984) m 1986; Maj, Gha. b 10 Feb 56. Served in Aus E.

CRITCH, Shawn (La Scie, NL, 1990) Maj, Can. b 26 Jun 67. CGA; and
CRITCH, Brenda (née Cooper) (St John's Temple, NL, 1990) m 1991; Maj, Can. b 25 Jul 63. BSc N.

D

DALI, Peter (Ebushibungo, Ken, 1978); Lt-Col, Ken W. b 2 Mar 52; and
DALI, Jessica (née Kavere) (Masigolo, Ken, 1978) m 1979; Lt-Col, Ken W. b 25 Dec 55. Served in Ken, Tanz, at IHQ, in Gha (CS/TSWM), Zim (CS/TSWM) and Lib (OC/CPWM).

DALY, Gordon (Wellington South, NZ, 1977), Lt-Col, OC, Port. b 5 Mar 54; and
DALY, Susan (née Crump) (Te Aroha, NZ, 1976) m 1977; Lt-Col, CPWM, Port. b 22 Oct 54. DL Th. Served in NZ, Carib, S Am W and Sing.

DAMOR, Nicolas Maganlal (Jalpa, 1979); Maj, Ind W. b 1 Jun 55; and
DAMOR, Flora (née David) (Dilsar, 1980) m 1980; Maj, Ind W. b 26 Apr 58.

DANIELS, Frank (Katanning, 1967); Lt-Col,
Aus S. b 10 Apr 47; and
DANIELS, Yvonne (née Knapp) (Melbourne City Temple, 1972) m 1972; Lt-Col, Aus S. b 4 Oct 47.

DANIELSON, Douglas (El Paso, TX, USA W, 1987); Lt-Col, CS, Mex. b 19 Aug 58. BSc (Cmptr Sci), MA(Missiology). Ww Lt-Col Rhode, pG 2010. Served in USA W.

DANSO, Isaac (Asene, 1991); Maj, Gha. b 22 Feb 1960; with
DANSO, Eva (née Amoah) m 1988; Maj, Gha. b 1 Jul 61.

DASARI, John Kumar (Pathamupparru, 1991); Maj, Ind C. b 7 Jan 61; with
DASARI, Mani Kumari m 1986; Maj, Ind C. b 3 May 66. BTh, MA.

DAVID, K. C. (Puthuchira, Ind SW, 1978); Lt-Col, CS, Ind W. b 5 Jan 53. BA; and
DAVID, Gracy Marykutty (Thevalapuram, Ind SW, 1981) m 1981; Lt-Col, TSWM, Ind W. b 12 Nov 55. Served in Ind SW and at Ind Nat.

DAVIDSON, Daniel (Trivandrum Central, 1985); Maj, Ind SW. b 6 May 53. BA; with
DAVIDSON, M.V. Estherbai m 1984, Maj, Ind SW. b 1 Jun 61.

DAWNGLIANA, C. (Chhilngchip, 1981); Maj, Ind E. b 1 Oct 55; and
H. MANTHANGI (Champhai, 1982) m 1982; Maj, Ind E. b 20 Sep 61.

DEFIBAUGH, Sandra (Staunton, VA, 1978); Maj, USA S. b 19 Jan 51. Served at USA Nat.

DEN HOLLANDER, Johannes A. (Treebeek, 1990); Maj, Neth. b 21 Nov 56, with
DEN HOLLANDER, Annetje C. (née Poppema) m 1978; Maj, Neth. b 4 May 57.

DEVASUNDARAM, Samuel Raj (Vadasery, 1974); Maj, Ind SE. b 21 Sep 54; and
KANAGAMONY, Samuel Raj (Brahmapuram, 1978) m 1978; Maj, Ind SE. b 5 Feb 52.

DIAKANWA, Wante Emmanuel (Kintambo, 1985); Maj, DR Con. b 23 Dec 50; with
DIAKANWA, Madeleine (née Sitwakemba Luzizila) m 1974; Maj, DR Con. b 11 Nov 55.

DIANDAGA, Frédéric (Nzoko, 1988); Maj, Con (Braz). b 26 May 55; and
DIANDAGA, Claudia (née Bayekoula) (Ouenze, 1990) m 1990; Maj, Con (Braz). b 29 Oct 66.

DIAZ, Evelyn (Oakbrook Terrace, IL, 1981); Maj, USA C. b 1 Jun 60. AA (Pract Min). Served in Swdn.

DIJKSTRA, Pieter H. (Amsterdam West, 1979); Col, CS, Neth. b 27 Jan 48; with
DIJKSTRA, Alida (née Voorn); Col, TSWM,

Neth. b 21 Nov 50. Served in Cze R.

DONALDSON, Robert (Dunedin South, NZ, 1987); Lt-Col, S Afr. b 8 Jul 61. BSc, LTh; with
DONALDSON, Janine (née Hamilton) m 1983, Lt-Col, S Afr. b 23 Sep 62. Served in NZ and Zamb.

DONZÉ, Jacques (St Aubin, 1988); Maj, Switz. b 16 Feb 64; with
DONZÉ, Claude-Evelyne (née Roth) m 1983; Maj, Switz. b 5 Feb 63. Served in Belg.

DOUGHTY, Victor (Boscombe, 1979); Lt-Col; Maj, USA W. b 25 Mar 54. BA (Soc Anthrplgy), MSW (Soc Wk), CERT (Soc Wk); with
DOUGHTY, Joan (née Ritchie) m 1980; Maj, USA W. b 7 May 55.

DOWNER, Gillian (Great Yarmouth, UK, 1977); Col, Sing (TC, TPWM). b 18 Mar 54. Served in UK, Phil, Vietnam, HK, Tai, Sing (GS and CS) and at IHQ.

DREW, Marion (Boscombe, 1979); Lt-Col, UK. b 12 Jan 49. BA (French & Law), Dip Inst Linguists. Served at ICO.

DUHU, Imanuel (Surabaya 2, 1992); Maj, Indon. b 1 Aug 63; and
DUHU, Henny (Tumpaan, 1990) m 1995; Maj, Indon. b 2 Jul 67.

DUSHING, Ashok K. (Byculla Central, Ind W, 1991); Maj, Ind Nat. b 16 Jun 62; with
DUSHING, Sanjivani m 1989; Maj, Ind Nat. b 10 May 68. BA. Served in Ind W.

E

EDGAR, Samuel (Londonderry, 1969); Maj, UK. b 26 Feb 49. Served at ITC and in Ger.

EGGER, Paulette (Vallorbe, 1977); Maj, Switz. b 22 Nov 55.

ELIASEN, Anna Riitta (née Hamalainen) (Erie Central, PA, 1967); Lt-Col, USA E. b 11 Aug 45. BS (Org Mgmt), MA (MDIV Theol). Served in UK, Brz, S Am E, Sp and Fin (CS). Ww Lt-Col Samuel, pG 1997.

ELIASEN, Torben (Bosque, Brz, 1983); Lt-Col, OC, Moz. b 28 Nov 60; and
ELIASEN, Deise Calor (née de Souza) (Rio Comprido, Brz, 1985) m 1985; Lt-Col, CPWM, Moz. b 22 Feb 66. BA (Jrnlsm). Served in Brz (CS)

ELLIS, Stephen R. (Atlanta Temple, GA, 1989); Maj, USA S. b 25 Oct 62. BA (Eng), MA (Div), MBA; with
ELLIS, Susan (née Kennedy) m 1984; Maj, USA S. b 27 Apr 62. ABJ (PR). Served in Ger.

EMMANUEL, Muthu Yesudhason (Neduvaazhy, Ind SE, 1974); Comr, TC, Ind C. b 8 May 51; and

REGINA, Chandra Bai (Valliyoor, Ind SE, 1978) m 1978; Comr, TPWM, Ind C. b 3 Mar 55. Served in Ind SE, Ind N (CS/TSWM) and Ind E (TC/TPWM).

EMMANUEL, Walter (Green Town, 1983); Maj, Pak. b 7 Jul 57; with
WALTER, Mussaraf (née Ullah) m 1981; Maj, Pak. b 1 Dec 65.

ESPINOZA, Hernán (Santiago, 1971); Maj, S Am W. b 30 Jul 52; and
ESPINOZA, Glenda (née Aicón) (Puerto Montt, 1971); Maj, S Am W. b 16 Oct 49

EZEKWERE, Chika Boniface (Umuchu, 1978); Maj, Nig. b 1 Jan 49; with
EZEKWERE, Virginia Ete m 1976; Maj, Nig. b 1 Jan 54.

F

FEENER, Maxwell (Port Leamington, NL, Can, 1966); Comr, TC, USA S. b 5 Jul 45, with
FEENER, Lenora (née Tippett) m 1967; Comr, TPWM, USA S. b 26 Dec 45. Served in Can, S Afr (CS/TSWM) and USA S (CS/TSWM).

FERGUSON, Lester (Nassau, Bahamas, 1988); Maj, Carib. b 1 Sep 65. BA (Bible and Theol), MA (Chrstn Ed), MDiv; and
FERGUSON, Beverely (née Armstrong) (Bridgetown Central, Barbados, 1999) m 1999; Capt, Carib. b 12 Dec 64.

FERNANDEZ, Ricardo J. (Caparra Temple, PR, 1996); Maj, USA E. b 3 Jun 60; with
FERNANDEZ, Mirtha N. (née Benitez) m 1979; Maj, USA E. b 4 Jan 57.

FERNANDO, Newton (Handugala, 1981); Maj, Sri Lan. b 30 Aug 60; and
FERNANDO Ajantha (née Marasinghalage) (Talampitiya, 1984) m 1984; Maj, Sri Lan. b 8 Jun 61.

FERNIHOUGH, Robyn (Subiaco, 1993); Maj, Aus S. b 27 Dec 63.

FERREIRA, Jorge Alberto (Cordoba, S Am E, 1972); Comr, TC, S Am W. b 24 Jun 53; and
FERREIRA, Adelina (née Solorza) (Lauis, S Am E, 1974) m 1979; Comr, TPWM, S Am W. b 19 Sep 55. Served in S Am E (CS/TSWM) and L Am N (TC/TPWM).

FINCHAM, Melvin (Croydon Citadel, 1981); Maj, UK. b 20 May 56; and
FINCHAM, Suzanne (née Kenny) (Stockport Citadel, 1981) m 1981; Maj, UK. b 19 Jan 59.

FINGER, Raymond (Hawthorn, 1974); Comr TC, Aus S. b 11 Jul 51; and
FINGER, Aylene (née Rinaldi) (Maylands, 1976) m 1976; Comr, TPWM, Aus S.

307

b 17 Apr 53. Served in Aus S (CS/TSWM).

FLEEMAN, W. Paul (Royal Oak, MI, 1976); Maj, USA C. b 23 Dec 48. BA (Psychol), MA (Relig), MDiv (Counselling/Ed); with
FLEEMAN, Paula (née Cloyd) m 1973; Maj, USA C. b 14 Jun 54.

FLINTOFF, Ethne (Dunedin North, NZ, 1971); Lt-Col, OC, Ban. b 11 Nov 46. RN, RM. Served in NZ, Ind W, Ind N and Pak.

FLORES, Eliseo (Cochabamba, 1977); Maj, S Am W. b 28 Jul 56; and
FLORES, Remedios (née Gutiérrez) (Oruro, 1977) m 1978; Maj, S Am W. b 6 Apr 55.

FLORES, María (Calama, 1985); Maj, S Am W. b 16 Mar 63.

FLORES, Myline Joy (Lebe, 1988); Maj, Phil. b 2 May 63. BMin.

FOREMAN, Ronald R. (Concord, NH, 1978); Maj, USA E. b 17 Sep 1952. BA (Socio) MSW (Soc Wk), EJD (Gen Law); with
FOREMAN, Dorine (née Long); m 1972; Maj, USA E. b 6 Apr 1955. BSW (Soc Wk), MSW (Soc Wk). Served at USA Nat.

FORSTER, Malcolm (St Helier, UK, 1971); Lt-Col, S Afr. b 26 Mar 51; and
FORSTER, Valerie (née Jupp) (Croydon Citadel, UK, 1978) m 1979; Lt-Col, S Afr. b 5 Jun 55. Served in UK, at ITC, in Zam & Mal, Gha & Lib, Mal (OC/CPWM) and Tanz (OC/CPWM).

FORSYTH, Robin W. (Edinburgh Gorgie, UK, 1968); Comr, IHQ (IS Prog Res). b 30 Aug 1946; with
FORSYTH, Shona (née Leslie) m 1966; Comr, IHQ (Chaplain). b 25 Mar 1948. Served in Aus S, Mex, UK, L Am N (TC/TPWM) and NZ (CS/TSWM).

FOSEN, Jan Peder (Haugesund, 1976); Col, CS, Nor. b 18 Nov 55; and
FOSEN, Birgit (née Taarnesvik) (Trondheim, 1981) m 1979; Col, TSWM, Nor. b 27 Aug 49.

FRANCIS, William (Paterson, NJ, USA E, 1973); Comr, TC, Can. b 5 Mar 44. BA (Mus/Hist), MDiv, Hon DD; with
FRANCIS, Marilyn (née Burroughs) m 1965; Comr, TPWM, Can. b 3 Feb 43. BA (Mus), MA. Served in USA E (CS/TSWM) and at IHQ (IS/SWM Am and Carib).

FRANS, Roy (Surabaya 4, Indon, 1977); Comr, IHQ (Rep to UN, SPEA). b 30 Oct 50; and
FRANS, Arda (née Haurissa) (Jakarta 1, Indon, 1978) m 1978; Comr, IHQ (Rep to UN, SPEA) b 10 May 44. Served in Indon, Aus E, Sing, Ban, Sri Lan (TC/TPWM), at IHQ (IS/ZSWM SPEA) and in Neth (TC/TPWM).

FREIND, John (Floreat Park, 1981); Maj,

Aus S. b 11 Dec 55; with
FREIND, Wendy (née Morris) m 1977; Maj, Aus S. b 5 Aug 53.

FUGE, Walter J. (Anacortes, WA, USA W, 1972); Lt-Col, IHQ. b 18 Aug 52. MBA (Bus Adm), BS (Bus & Mngmnt), CERT (Data Analyst) (Internal Audit); and
FUGE, Ardis (née Muus) (Monterey, CA, USA W, 1974) m 1974; Lt-Col, IHQ. b 31 Jan 53. Served in USA W.

FUJII, Kenji (Kyobashi, 1982); Maj, Jpn. b 25 Feb 60; and
FUJII, Chiaki (née Inoue) (Kiyose, 1981) m 1987; Maj, Jpn. b 17 Nov 59.

G

GABRIEL, K. M. (Kaithaparambu, 1981); Maj, Ind SW. b 15 Nov 55; and
GABRIEL, Molamma (Vappala, 1986) m 1986; Maj, Ind SW. b 10 May 67.

GAIKWAD, Benjamin Yacob (Bodhegaon, 1974); Maj, Ind W. b 3 Oct 48; and
GAIKWAD, Sudina P. (née Makasare) (Bodhegaon, 1975) m 1975; Maj, Ind W. b 23 Oct 57.

GALVÁN, Guadalupe (Savo Loredo, 1975); Maj, Mex; b 28 Mar 51. Served in USA S and L Am N.

GARCÍA, Angela (née Sanguinetti) (Lima, 1982); Maj, S Am W. b 15 Oct 1953; and
GARCÍA, Víctor (Trujillo, 1982) m 1983; Maj, S Am W. b 21 Jan 1955. Served in USA C and L Am N.

GARCÍA, Humberto (Monterrey, 1990); Maj, Mex. b 19 Jan 57. LLM; with
GARCÍA, Leticia (née Castañeda) m 1981; Maj, Mex. b 9 Mar 59. BA (Primary Ed).

GARLAND, Elizabeth (Dulwich Hill, Aus E, 1998); Capt, Zimb. b 23 May 68. BA (Nursing), SRN, MA (PHC), MA (Health and Int Dev). Served in Aus E and Gha.

GARRAD, Rob (Skegness, UK, 1971); Lt-Col, IHQ. b 16 Jan 52. Served in UK and Rus.

GENABE, Alexander (Cebu, 1981); Maj, Phil. b 27 Mar 58; and
GENABE, Jocelyn (née Willy) (Baguio, 1993) m 1993; Maj, Phil. b 10 Feb 60. BSN, BSSW.

GENSLER, Dennis K. (Buffalo, NY, USA E, 1977); Maj, Pak. b 30 Nov 55; and
GENSLER, Lynn R. (née Luyk) (New Kensington, PA, USA E, 1979) m 1979; Maj, Pak. b 3 Aug 58. Served in USA E.

GEORGE, N. J. (Moncotta, 1978); Maj, Ind SW. b 24 Dec 51; and
RUTH, M. C. (Moncotta, 1977) m 1979,

Maj, Ind SW. b 23 Apr 48.

GERA, Thomas (EBLH, Bapatla, Ind C. 1988); Maj, Ind N. b 12 Jul 65; with
GERA, Sion Kumari m 1984; Maj, Ind N. b 9 Oct 67. Served in Ind C.

GHULAM, Yousaf (Lahore, 1975); Lt-Col, CS, Pak. b 4 Jan 55; and
YOUSAF, Rebecca (née Charn Masih) (Shantinagar, 1976) m 1976; Lt-Col, TSWM, Pak. b 6 May 56.

GILL, Daniel (Alidullapur, 1980); Maj, Ind N. b 5 Apr 57; and
GILL, Parveen Daniel (Mukerian 1981) m 1981; Maj, Ind N. b 3 Apr 62.

GIUSTI, Rafael (Tucuman, 1991); Maj, S Am E. b 24 Oct 68; and
GIUSTI, Karina (née Acosta) (Tucuman, 1992) m 1993; Maj, S Am E. b 26 Feb 72.

GJERULDSEN, Frank (Brevik, 1981); Maj, Nor. b 21 Jan 58; and
GJERULDSEN, Tone (née Olsen) (Templet, Oslo, 1984) m 1983; Maj, Nor. b 11 Feb 1959.

GLORIES, Pascale (née Alquier) (Ganges, 1981); Maj, TSWM, Frce. b 4 Apr 58; with
GLORIES, Dominique m 1978; Maj, Frce. b 23 Jul 54.

GLUYAS, Miriam (Wauchope, 1981); Lt-Col, Aus E. b 3 Jun 59. Dip Min. Dip Bus.

GNANADASAN, Daniel (Anakotoor, 1981); Maj, Ind SW. b 10 Sep 55; and
D. I. SOSAMMA, Gnanadasan (Kottoor, 1980) m 1982; Maj, Ind SW. b 24 Oct 52.

GOA, Christian (Lae, 1994); Maj, PNG. b 9 Feb 69; with
GOA, Tilitah (née Shong); Maj, PNG. b 6 Apr 69.

GODKIN, David J. (Parramatta, 1986); Maj, Aus E. b 14 Aug 59. Dip Min; with
GODKIN, Sandra F. (née Press) m 1982 Maj, Aus E. b 20 Apr 62. Dip Min.

GONÇALVES, Adão (Pelotas, 1997); Maj, Brz. b 3 Sep 65; and
GONÇALVES, Vilma (née Rosa) (Bosque, 1996) m 1986; Maj, Brz. b 8 Nov 51. BA (SocS).

GONI, Widajati (Bandung 1, 1993); Maj, Indon. b 27 May 69; and
GONI, Banjamin (Palembang, 1993) m 2000; Maj, Indon. b 5 Jul 69.

GONZALEZ, Henry (Orange, TX, 1967); Lt-Col, USA S. b 18 Aug 46. BS (Sociol); and
GONZALEZ, Mary Dorris (née McCollum) (Meridian, MS, 1967) m 1969; Lt-Col, USA S. b 13 Sep 48.

GOWER, Ross R. (Christchurch City, NZ, 1980); Col, IHQ. b 15 Dec 50; with

GOWER, Annette (née Knight) m 1972; Col, IHQ. Served in NZ, UK and Indon (CS/TSWM).

GRAVES, Lee (Tillsonburg, ON, 1983); Lt-Col, Can. b 8 Aug 61. MBA; with
GRAVES, Deborah (née Smith) m 1984; Lt-Col, Can. b 24 Feb 1960. BA (Bible and Theol), BSW.

GREEN, Lynette (née Marion) (Bendigo, Aus S, 1965); Lt-Col, Aus E. b 30 Mar 44. Ww Maj Frederick, pG 1998. Served in Aus S, E Afr and Port (OC).

GRIFFIN, Stanley (St John's, Antigua, 1979); Maj, Carib. b 20 Feb 54; and
GRIFFIN, Hazel (née Whyte) (St John's, Antigua, 1980) m 1981; Maj, Carib. b 23 Sep 57. Served in L Am N.

GRIFFIN, Terry W. (Seattle Temple, WA, USA W, 1970); Col, CS, USA S. b 2 Nov 46. BA (Bib Lit), MA (Relig); with
GRIFFIN, Linda (née Bawden) m 1967; Col, TSWM, USA S. b 28 Aug 46. Served in USA W.

GROVES, Jennifer (Wellington South, NZ, 1990); Lt-Col, IHQ. b 25 Sep 64. Served in NZ and Port.

H

HAGEN, Jan Harald (Templet, Oslo, 1980); Maj, Nor. b 12 Feb 54; with
HAGEN, Eli (née Nodland) m 1976; Maj, Nor. b 25 Mar 57.

HAGGAR, Kerry (née Geers) (Rockdale, 1982); Maj, Aus E, b 30 Nov 59. BComm, MAL; and
HAGGAR, Colin (Rockdale 1983) m 1983; Maj, Aus E. b 16 Mar 59. BE, ATh

HAMILTON, Ian E. (Clayton, Aus E, 1971); Lt-Col, Aus S. b 8 Jun 47. Dip Theol; with
HAMILTON, Marilyn (née Rawiller) m 1968; Lt-Col, Aus S. b 6 Aug 48. Served in Aus E.

HANGOMA, Donald (Munali, 1995); Capt, Zam. b 15 Jan 70; and
HANGOMA, Patricia (née Michelo) (1993); Maj, Zam. b 19 Mar 70.

HANUNKA, Bislon (Chibbuku, 1985); Lt-Col, CS, Zam. b 10 Jun 58; with
HANUNKA, Melody m 1979; Lt-Col, Asst TPWM, Zam. b 15 Dec 62.

HARFOOT, William (Detroit Brightmoor, MI, 1977); Col, CS, USA W. b 6 Sep 48. BS (Ed), MA (Relig); with
HARFOOT, Susan (née Stange) m 1969; Col, TSWM, USA W. b 21 Oct 48. AA. Served in USA E.

HARITA, Naoko (Shibuya, 1968); Maj, Jpn.

b 19 Jul 43. BA (Sociol).

HARMS, Bennie (Johannesburg City, 1974); Lt-Col, S Afr. b 15 Apr 52; with
HARMS, Jennifer (née Hall) m 1972; Lt-Col, S Afr. b 21 Oct 48. Served in Zimb.

HARTVEIT, Jørg Walter (Langesund, 1971); Lt-Col, Nor. b 22 Jun 47. m 1971; Lt-Col Rigmor, ret 2006.

HAUGHTON, Devon (Port Antonio, Jamaica, 1981); Maj, Carib. b 22 Jul 59; and
HAUGHTON, Verona Beverly (née Henry) (Havendale, Jamaica, 1976) m 1982; Maj, Carib. b 15 Apr 54. BA (Guidance and Counselling).

HAUPT, Gary W. (New Orleans, LA, USA S, 1982); Lt-Col, USA Nat. b 27 Nov 53. BS (Bus Adm); with
HAUPT, Suzanne H. (née Hogan); m 1979; Lt-Col, USA Nat. b 3 May 56. BS (Ed). Served in USA S.

HEATWOLE, Merle D. (Milwaukee Citadel, WI, 1984); Lt-Col, USA C. b 7 Jan 60. BS (Maths); with
HEATWOLE, Dawn Idell (née Lewis) m 1981; Lt-Col, USA C. b 26 Nov 62. AA (Pract Min).

HEDGREN, R. Steven (Chicago Mont Clare, IL, USA C, 1978); Comr, TC, USA E. b 7 Mar 50. BS (Bus Adm); with
HEDGREN, Judith Ann (née White) m 1975; Comr, TPWM, USA E. b 14 Feb 49. AS (Bus). Served in USA C, USA S and USA E (CS/TSWM).

HEELEY, William (Rock Ferry, 1974); Lt-Col, UK. b 6 May 48; and
HEELEY, Gillian (née Lacey) (Rock Ferry, 1975) m 1975; Lt-Col, UK. b 18 Apr 52.

HEGGELUND, Brith-Mari (Harstad, 1972); Maj, Nor. b 22 Jul 49.

HENDRICKS, Robert E. (Claremont Temple, 2005); Capt, S Afr. b 25 Mar 54; with
HENDRICKS, Felicia (neé Christian) m 1983; Capt, S Afr. b 11 Jul 57.

HENNE, Ingrid Elisabeth (Bergen 1, 1982); Lt-Col, Nor. b 6 Sep 52.

HENRY, Samuel A. (Atlanta Temple, GA, 1983); Maj, USA S. b 28 Nov 48; with
HENRY, Nancy (née Southwood) m 1969; Maj, USA S. b 13 Apr 47.

HERIVEL, Richard (Dearborn Heights, MI. USA C, 1984); Maj, E Eur. b 4 Oct 51. BS (Bus Adm), MA (Rel); with
HERIVEL, Brenda (née Rhoads) m 1976; Maj, E Eur. b 26 Dec 54. MA (Rel), MSW. Served in USA C.

HERRING, Alistair Chapman (Wellington City, NZ, 1975); Lt-Col, CS, E Eur.

b 4 Mar 51. DipSW; with
HERRING, Verna Astrid (née Weggery) m 1971; Lt-Col, TSWM, E Eur. b 29 Oct 51. Served in NZ

HETTIARACHCHI, Nihal (Colombo, 1985); Maj, Sri Lan. b 20 Jun 64; and
HETTIARACHCHI, Rohini Swarnalatha (née Wettamuni) (Colombo Central, 1994) m 1994; Maj, Sri Lan. b 18 Oct 64.

HIGHTON, Michael (Hinckley, 1985); Maj, UK. b 27 May 53; with
HIGHTON, Lynn (née Edwards) m 1975; Maj, UK. b 10 Mar 53.

HIGUCHI, Kazumitsu (Nagoya, 1976); Maj, Jpn. b 9 Apr 51; and
HIGUCHI, Aiko (née Kutomi) (Shibuya, 1979) m 1982; Maj, Jpn. b 25 Sep 53. BA (Eng Lit).

HILL, Edward (Pasadena Tabernacle, CA 1993); Maj, USA W. b 7 Nov 59. BA (History), MA (Chrstn Ed); with
HILL, Shelley (née Chandler) m 1985; Maj, USA W. b 11 Jul 63.

HILL, Martin (Northampton Central, 1984); Maj, UK. b 3 Jul 55. BA (Hons) (Soc Sci), MTh (Ap Theol).

HINTON, David (Blackheath, 1975); Lt-Col, UK. b 28 Oct 53; and
HINTON, Sylvia (née Brooks) (Bedlington, 1975) m 1977; Lt-Col, UK. b 2 Dec 53.

HIRAMOTO, Naoshi (Ueno, 1971); Lt-Col, CS, Jpn. b 24 Oct 46. BA (Law); and
HIRAMOTO, Seiko (née Kobayashi) (Kyobashi, 1968) m 1973; Lt-Col, TSWM, Jpn. b 7 Oct 43. BA (Eng Lit).

HIRAMOTO, Nobuhiro (Ueno, 1979); Maj, Jpn. b 28 Dec 51. BA (Chinese Lit); and
HIRAMOTO, Yasuko (née Kinoshita) (Ueno, 1979) m 1979; Maj, Jpn. b 7 Dec 51.

HOBGOOD, W. Edward (Greenville, NC, 1983); Lt-Col, USA S. b 6 Apr 58; with
HOBGOOD, M. Kathryn (née Hathaway) m 1978; Lt-Col, USA S. b 12 Jun 54.

HODDER, Kenneth G. (Pasadena Tabernacle, CA, USA W, 1988); Comr, IHQ (IS Int Pers). b 16 Jun 58. BA (Hist), JD (Law); with
HODDER, Jolene (née Lloyd) m 1982; Comr, IHQ (Assoc IS Int Pers). b 30 Jul 61. BA (Home Econ). Served in USA W, USA S, Ken (CS/TLWM) and Ken E (CS/TLWM).

HODGE, John (Wollongong, 1972); Lt-Col, Aus E. b 27 Aug 45. BA (Relig Studies and Ed), Dip Teach, MBA. Ww Lt Marie, pG 1974. Served in PNG; and

HODGE, Pamela (née Henry) (Bankstown, 1972) m 1975; Lt-Col, Aus E. b 29 Oct 49. Served in Carib (CS/TSWO), Phil (TC/TPWO) and NZ.

HOFER, Allan (Sissach Basel, Switz, 1986); Maj, USA S. b 30 Mar 61; and
HOFER, Fiona (née Pressland) (Barking, UK, 1987) m 1987; Maj, USA S, b 15 Apr 64. Served in Switz, Port, UK and Brz.

HOKOM, Eda M. (Caldwell, ID, 1974); Lt-Col, USA W. b 19 Mar 48. BA (Soc Sci), BS (Relig Ed). Served in PNG.

HONSBERG, Frank (Cologne, 1987); Maj, Ger. b 24 Jan 63. Grad Bus Mgmt; with
HONSBERG, Stefanie (née Gossens) m 1985; Maj, Ger. b 17 Dec 65.

HOOD, Sallyann (née Carpenter) (San Diego Citadel, CA, USA W, 1977); Maj, Mex. b 12 Nov 45. BA (Pre-med Zoology), MD (Ob/Gyn); with
HOOD, James m 1971; Maj, Mex. b 27 Oct 46. BS (Agric Eng), MS (Civil Eng), Served in USA W and Ind SE.

HORWOOD, S. Edward (Ted) (Monterey, CA, USA W, 1992); Maj, GS, Ang. b 1 Feb 61. BA (Eng), MA (Intercultural Studies); with
HORWOOD, Deborah (née Haynes) m 1987; Maj, CSWM, Ang. b 22 Mar 66. Served in USA W, Zamb & Mal and at IHQ.

HOWARD, Steven (Hamilton, OH, USA E, 1983); Col, CS, Ken E. b 21 May 57. BS (Architecture), MSc (Bus Adm); with
HOWARD, Janice (née Collopy) m 1979; Col, TLWM, Ken E. b 18 Mar 59. BS (Bus Ed). Served in USA E and at ICO.

HOWELL, Willis (Hyattsville, MD, 1985); Maj, USA S. b 3 Mar 56; with
HOWELL, Barbara (née Leidy) m 1978; Maj, USA S. b 3 Apr 57.

HUDSON, David E. (Portland Tabernacle, OR, 1975); Lt-Col, USA W. b 28 Jun 54. BS (Bus Mgmt); and
HUDSON, Sharon (née Smith) (Santa Ana, CA, 1975) m 1976; Lt-Col, USA W. b 14 Jun 52.

HULSMAN, Everdina (Nijverdal, 1975); Lt-Col, Neth. b 21 Dec 47.

HUNTER, Barbara (née Booth) (Tucson, AZ, USA W, 1967); Lt-Col, USA E. b 17 Mar 47. BS (Org Mgmt). Served in USA W and Rus (CSWO). Ww Lt-Col William, pG 2001.

HWANG, Sun-yup (Ah Hyun, 1985); Maj, Kor. b 28 Dec 55; with
CHOI, Myung-soon m 1982; Maj, Kor. b 9 Sep 59. Served in USA S and UK.

HYNES, Junior (Happy Valley, NL, 1971); Lt-Col, Can. b 6 Jan 51; and

HYNES, Verna (née Downton) (Windsor, NL, 1971) m 1973; Lt-Col, Can. b 27 Aug 50. Served in UK.

I

IGLEHEART, Kelly (Owensboro, KY, 1992); Maj, USA S. b 29 Oct 61; with
IGLEHEART, Donna (née Vincent) m 1981; Maj, USA S. b 30 Apr 62.

IP KAN, Ming-chun Connie (Kwai Chung, 1985); Maj, CSWM, HK. b 16 Jul 62.

ILUNGA, Bidwaya Clément (Salle Centrale, 1987); Maj, DR Con. b 16 Nov 62; with
ILUNGA, Béatrice (née Kalenga Monga) m 1988; Maj, DR Con. b 12 Sep 60.

IMMANUEL, Sam (Thulickal, 1984); Maj, Ind SW. b 27 May 59; with
IMMANUEL, Rachel P. C. m 1982; Maj, Ind SW. b 15 Jun 57.

INDURUWAGE, Malcolm (Colombo Central, Sri Lan, 1977); Comr, TC, Phil. b 24 Sep 50; and
INDURUWAGE, Irene (née Horathalge) (Colombo Central, Sri Lan, 1977) m 1977; Comr, TPWM, Phil. b 29 Nov 55. Served in Sri Lan and Phil (CS/TSWM).

IP KAN, Ming-chun Connie (Kwai Chung, 1985); Maj, CSWM, HK. b 16 Jul 62.

IRVING, Ray (Shiremoor, 1989); Maj, UK. b 20 Apr 51. MVA, MCMI; and
IRVING, Angela (née Richards) (Torquay, 1972) m 1989; Maj, UK. b 12 Feb 51. Served at ITC.

ISRAEL, Betty A. (née Sheinfeldt) (Waltham, MA, USA E, 1971); Maj, USA Nat. b 6 Jan 47. BA (Sociol), MA (Counselling/Human Services), PG Dip (Supervision & Training). Served in USA E and at IHQ. Ww Capt James, pG 1988.

ISRAEL, Mark H. (Warner Robbins, GA, USA S, 1982); Lt-Col, USA Nat. b 8 May 58. BA (Bible), MA (Theol Studies); and
ISRAEL, Carolee J. (née Zarfas) (Des Moines Citadel, IA, USA C, 1981); m 1982; Lt-Col, USA Nat. b 30 Mar 58. BS (Pract Min). Served in USA S.

IUNG, Ricardo (São Paulo Central, 1999); Capt, Brz. b 29 Nov 70. BA (Admin); with
IUNG, Cindy (née Meylan) m 1995; Capt, Brz. b 13 Feb 77. Served in Switz.

J

JACKSON, David (Romford, 1976); Maj, UK. b 10 Nov 52. Served at IHQ.

JADHAV, Bhivsen P. (Evangeline Booth Hospital Corps, 1984); Maj, Ind W.

311

b 21 Aug 53; with
JADHAV, Shoba m 1979; Maj, Ind W.
b 18 Mar 63.

JAMES, M. C. (Monkotta, Ind SW, 1979);
Comr, TC, Ind SE. b 20 Oct 54. MA Soc; and
SUSAMMA, James (Pothencode, Ind SW,
1983) m 1983; Comr, TPWM, Ind SE.
b 1 Mar 61. Served in Ind SW, Ind N and
Ind C (CS/TSWM, TC/TPWM).

JAYARATNASINGHAM, Packianathan
(Jaffna, 1973); Maj, Sri Lan. b 4 Nov 52; and
JAYARATNASINGHAM, Delankage
Chandralatha (née Delankage)
(Siyambalangamua, 1979) m 1980; Maj,
Sri Lan. b 28 Oct 59. Served at IHQ.

JEBAMONY, Jayaseelan (Maharajaduram
1982); Maj, Ind SE. b 20 May 57; and
GNANASELVI, Jayaseelan (Nattalam, 1985)
m 1980; Maj, Ind SE. b 30 Dec 57.

JEYARAJ, Daniel Jebasingh Raj (Booth Tucker
Hall, Nagercoil, 1987); Maj, Ind SE.
b 10 Jun 61. BA (Eng), MA (Social), BTh,
BD, MTh; and
RAJAM, Daniel Jebasingh Raj (Kuzhikalai,
1992) m 1992; Maj, Ind SE. b 12 Mar 64.
BA (Eng), MA (History), BTh PM, MTh PM.
Served in Ind SE and at Ind Nat.

JEYARAJ, Samraj (Booth Tucker Hall,
Nagercoil, 1982); Maj, Ind SE. b 14 Aug 58.
BSc, MA (Sociol), MA (JMC), PGDHM; and
JESSI, Thayammal Samraj (Gnaniahpuram,
1986) m 1986; Maj, Ind SE. b 21 Oct 63.
MusB. Served at Ind Nat.

JEFFREY, David (Morgantown, WV, USA S,
1973); Col, Nat CS, USA Nat. b 2 Aug 51.
BS, MA (Relig); and
JEFFREY, Barbara (née Garris)
(Morgantown, WV, USA S, 1966) m 1969;
Col, NSWM, USA Nat. b 1 Jul 46. Served
in USA S (CS/TSWM).

JERA, Onai (Marowa, 1992); Maj, Zimb.
b 10 Sep 67; and
JERA, Deliwe (née Gasa) (Gunguhwe, 1992)
m 1994; Maj, Zimb. b 18 Jun 68.

JEREMIAH, Edwin (Mupfure, 1990); Maj,
Zimb. b 30 Jun 60; with
JEREMIAH, Tambudzai (née Kabaya)
m 1979; Maj, Zimb. b 10 Feb 62.

JEWETT, Vernon Wayne (Atlanta Temple, GA,
1980); Lt-Col, USA S. b 11 Dec 47. BA,
MA; with
JEWETT, Martha Gaye (née Brewer)
m 1975; Lt-Col, USA S. b 22 Oct 52. BA.

JOB, William (Manalikarai, 1981); Maj, Ind SE.
b 8 Dec 51. BA; and
DAIZY, Bai William (Poottetty, 1982)

m 1982; Maj, Ind SE. b 17 Apr 59.

JOHN, Morris (Rancho Lines, 1975);
Lt-Col, Pak. b 1 Jan 53. Ww Lt-Col Salma,
pG 2007.

JOHN, Rajan K. (Parayankerry, 1979); Maj,
Ind SW. b 26 Mar 52; with
JOHN, Susamma m 1977; Maj, Ind SW.
b 17 Oct 52.

JOHNSON, Kenneth (Charlotte Temple, NC,
USA S, 1984); Col, TC, E Eur. b 10 Aug 56.
BS (Bus Mgmt); with
JOHNSON, Paula (née Salmon) m 1981;
Col, TPWM, E Eur. b 23 Nov 62. Served in
USA S.

JOHNSON, Rex (Auckland Congress Hall, NZ,
1973); Maj, PNG. b 24 May 48; and
JOHNSON, Geraldine (née Stratton)
(Dunedin Fortress, NZ, 1976) m 1976; Maj,
PNG. b 6 Mar 1954. Served in NZ.

JOHNSTONE, Wendy (London South, ON,
Can, 1980); Maj, S Am E. b 31 Oct 57. Served
in Can and at IHQ.

JONAS, Dewhurst (St John's, Antigua, 1982);
Maj, Carib. b 20 May 56; and
JONAS, Vevene (née Gordon) (Rae Town,
Jamaica, 1980) m 1983; Maj, Carib. b 1 Jun 57.

JONES, John Roy, Jr (Gastonia, NC, 1971);
Lt-Col, USA S. b 2 Feb 49; and
JONES, Arduth Eleanor (née Johnson)
(Charlotte Temple, NC, 1971), m 1973;
Lt-Col, USA S. b 1 Jan 50.

JONES, Melvyn (Hoxton, 1976); Maj, UK.
b 21 Nov 51. MA (Nat Sci); with
JONES, Kathleen (née Hall) m 1974; Maj,
UK. b 15 Mar 51. SRN, SCM.

JOSEPH, Roy (Thottamon, 1996); Capt,
Ind SW. b 27 Mar 71. MA; and
JAIMOL, Roy (Niranam, 1998) m 1998;
Capt, Ind SW. b 25 May 75. BSc.

JOSHI, Devadasi (Musunuru, 1981); Maj,
Ind C. b 1 Oct 54; with
JOSHI, Leelamani m 1977; Maj, Ind C.
b 1 Jun 53.

JUNG, Verônica (Cachoeira Paulista, 1984);
Maj, Brz. b 15 Sep 59. BA (Trans and Interp).

K

KADA, Bugave (Kokorogoro, 1994) Maj, PNG.
b 13 Mar 57; with
KADA, Tomuna (née Iobuna) (m 1979;
Maj, PNG. b 5 May 60.

KAKI, Sundara Rao (Denduluru, 1978); Maj,
Ind C. b 9 May 55; with
KAKI, Dasaratna Kumari m 1974; Maj,
Ind C. b 12 Sep 55.

KALAI, Andrew (Koki, 1981); Comr, TC,

Biographical Information

PNG. b 18 Jan 56. BA (Psych). Ww Capt Napa, pG 1994; Ww Col Julie, pG 2006. Served in UK.

KALE, Ratnakar Dinkar (Ahmednagar Central, 1977); Maj, Ind W. b 1 Jul 53; and
KALE, Leela (née Magar) (Byculla, 1981) m 1981; Maj, Ind W. b 1 Mar 60.

KAMAMBO, Clever (Chrome Mine, 1979); Maj, Zimb. b 28 Dec 57; and
KAMAMBO, Daphne (née Mhlanga) (Mufakose, 1981) m 1984; Maj, Zimb. b 16 Dec 59.

KARENGESHA, Annah (née Meda) (Kandeya, 1973); Maj, Zimb. b 1 Jun 50. Ww Maj Micah, pG 1993.

KARTODARSONO, Ribut (Surakarta, 1975); Comr, TC, Indon. b 13 Dec 49. BA (Relig Ed), MA (Relig Ed & Public Societies); and
KARTODARSONO, Marie (née Ticoalu) (Bandung 3, 1975) m 1979; Comr, TPWM, Indon. b 30 Nov 52. Served in Indon (CS/TSWM) and UK.

KASAEDJA, Jones (Kulawi, 1982); Lt-Col, Indon. b 22 Jun 68; and
KASAEDJA, Mariyam (née Barani) (Salupone, 1982) m 1989; Lt-Col, Indon. b 10 Oct 54.

KASBE, Devdan (Ahmednagar Central, 1970); Maj, Ind W. b 9 Feb 49; and
KASBE, Marya B. (née Devhe) (Dapodi, 1972) m 1972; Maj, Ind W. b 16 Oct 52.

KASUSO, Daniel (Pearson, Zimb, 1986); Maj, S Afr. b 15 Jul 65; and
KASUSO, Tracey (née Mashiri) (Torwood, Zimb, 1986); Maj, S Afr. b 19 Oct 64. Served in Zimb.

KATHURI, Gabriel (Mombasa, 1982); Lt-Col, Ken E. b 13 Jan 51; with
KATHURI, Monica (née Minoo) m 1977; Lt-Col, Ken E. b 22 Feb 54.

KATSUCHI, Jiro (Hamamatsu, 1984); Maj, Jpn. b 3 May 49; and
KATSUCHI, Keiko (née Munemori) (Nagoya, 1969) m 1986; Maj, Jpn. b 30 Jun 47.

KELLY, David E. (Cincinnati, OH, 1980); Maj, USA E. b 30 Nov 59. AS (Bus Adm), MA (Ldrshp & Min); and
KELLY, Naomi R. (née Foster) (Tonawanda, NY, 1977) m 1981; Maj, USA E. b 14 Sep 56. BA (Org Mgmt).

KENNEDY, Anthony (Gander, NL, Can, 1998); Capt, E Eur. b 24 Dec 53; with
KENNEDY, Patricia (née Snow) m 1975; Capt, E Eur. b 17 Jul 55. BA, BE, BSc. Served in Can.

KENNEDY, Victor (Fulham, 1974); Maj, UK.

b 3 May 45; with
KENNEDY, Miriam (née Smith) m 1967; Maj, UK. b 30 Nov 46. BD (Hons), DipTh. Served at ITC.

KHAIZADINGA (Bukpui, 1974); Maj, Ind E. b 20 Jan 50; with
RAMTHANMAWII m 1970; Maj, Ind E. b 23 Nov 53.

KHOZA, Jabulani (Mbabane, 1985); Lt-Col, S Afr. b 8 Jun 62; and
KHOZA, Fikile (née Mkhize) (Ezakheni, 1986) m 1986; Lt-Col, S Afr. b 28 Aug 66.

KIM, Byoung-moo (San Kok, 1990); Maj, Kor. b 2 Oct 60; with
LEE, Joo-young m 1987; Maj, Kor. b 10 Mar 61.

KIM, Nam-sun (Ah Hyun, 1983); Maj, Kor. b 11 Sep 54.

KIM, Un-ho (Eum Am, 1979); Lt-Col, Kor. b 31 Jan 52; with
LEE, Ok-kyung m 1977; Lt-Col, Kor. b 9 Jun 53.

KIM, Young-tae (Chin Chook, 1986); Maj, Kor. b 23 Mar 56. BAdm, MBA; with
PYO, Choon-yun m 1977; Maj, Kor. b 30 Aug 53.

KITHOME, Lucas (Mwala, 1986); Maj, Ken E. b 10 Feb 59; with
KITHOME, Agnes (née Nduku) m 1984; Maj, Ken E. b 15 Jan 63.

KIVINDYO, Isaac (Kanzalu, 1982); Maj, Ken W. b 1 Aug 56; with
KIVINDYO, Naomi (née Loko) m 1970; Maj, Ken W. b 1 May 60.

KLARENBEEK, Elsje (Amsterdam Zuid, 1979); Maj, Neth. b 2 Jun 52.

KLEMAN, Johnny (Boras, 1982); Col, CS, Swdn. b 29 Jul 59. BTh; and
KLEMAN, Eva (née Hedberg) (Motala, 1981) m 1982; Col, TSWM, Swdn. b 6 Sep 1960. Served in Fin.

KLEMANSKI, Guy (Lewiston-Auburn, ME, 1970); Lt-Col, USA E. b 21 Nov 50; and
KLEMANSKI, Henrietta (née Wallace) (Cleveland, West Side, OH, 1970) m 1972; Lt-Col, USA E. b 27 Jul 47.

KNAGGS, James (Philadelphia Roxborough, PA, USA E, 1976); Comr, TC, USA W. b 5 Dec 50. MPS (Urban Min); with
KNAGGS, Carolyn (née Lance) m 1972; Comr, TPWM, USA W. b 19 Sep 51. Served in USA E (CS/TSWM) and Aus S (TC/TPWM).

KNAPP, Jocelyn (Camberwell, 1969); Lt-Col, Aus S. b 7 Apr 44. Served in Aus E.

KNEDAL, Jan Øystein (Templet, Oslo, 1974);

Lt-Col, Nor. b 25 Aug 52; and
KNEDAL, Brit (née Kolloen) (Templet, Oslo, 1976) m 1978; Lt-Col, Nor. b 27 Apr 58

KOMBO, Blaise (Makelekele, 1996); Capt, Con (Braz). b 15 Oct 68. MA Psych; with
KOMBO, Evelynne (née Missamon) (Sangolo, 1996) m 1992; Capt, Con (Braz). b 6 Jan 75.

KORNILOW, Petter (Parkano, 1981); Maj, Fin. b 21 Aug 53; and
KORNILOW, Eija Hellevi (née Astikainen) (Tampere Kaleva, 1981) m 1981; Maj, Fin. b 28 Jun 56.

KROMMENHOEK, Dick (Amsterdam Congress Hall, Neth, 1983); Comr, TC, Fin. b 18 Jun 52. MA (Music); with
KROMMENHOEK, Vibeke (née Schou Larsen) m 1978; Comr, TPWM, Fin. b 27 Nov 56. MA (Theol). Served in Neth, Den (TC/TPWM), Frce (TC/TPWM) and at IHQ.

KUMAR BABU, K. Y. Raj (Kahjipalem, 1981); Maj, Ind C. b 11 Jun 55; with
KRUPA, Bai m 1976; Maj, Ind C. b 6 Jan 55.

KUMAR, K. Y. Dhana (Khajipalem, Bapatla, 1980); Maj, Ind C. b 21 Sep 57. BCom; with
KUMAR, Yesamma (née Dasari) m 1978; Maj, Ind C. b 18 May 1961.

KWENDA, Peter (Mutondo, Zimb, 1976); Lt-Col, Nig. b 10 Apr 57; and
KWENDA, Norma (née Nyawo) (Dombwe-Makonde, Zimb, 1977) m 1977; Lt-Col, Nig. b 10 Jul 55. Served in Zimb.

KWON, Sung-dal (Son Chi, 1977); Maj, Kor. b 17 Apr 47; with
KIM, Moon-ok m 1973; Maj, Kor. b 29 Oct 53.

KYEREMEH, Samuel (Nkawkaw, 1991); Maj, Gha. b 18 Feb 60; with
KYEREMEH, Juliana (née Boakye) m 1987; Maj, Gha. b 11 May 63.

L

LAHASE, Kashinath V. (Chapadgaon, Ind W, 1972); Comr, TC, Ind N. b 1 Nov 49; with
LAHASE, Kusum K. m 1970; Comr, TPWM, Ind N. b 7 Jun 49. Served in Ind W, Ind SW and Ind N (CS/TSWM).

LALAC, Valery (Dubossary, Moldova, 1999); Capt, E Eur. b 10 May 59; with
LALAC, Victoria (née Pocotilo) m1986; Capt, E Eur, b 9 May 67.

LALBULLIANA (Darlawn, Ind E, 1987); Lt-Col, Ken E. b 20 Sep 64; and
LALBULLIANA, Lalnunhlui (Thingsulthliah, Ind E, 1990) m 1990; Lt-Col, Ken E. b 12 Dec 65. Served in Ind E.

LALHMINGLIANA (Chaltlang, 1994); Maj, Ind E. b 29 Sep 71. BA (Hons) (Hist); and
LALHLIMPUII (Bethel, 1994) m 1994; Maj, Ind E. b 28 Oct 71. Served at IHQ.

LALKIAMLOVA (Kahrawt, 1971); Comr, IHQ (IS S Asia). b 7 Mar 49. BA; and
LALHLIMPUII (Saitual, 1973) m 1973; Comr, IHQ (ZSWM S Asia). b 25 Sep 53. Served in Ind E, Ind SW (CS/TSWO) and Ind C (TC/TPWM).

LALNGAIHAWMI, Naomi (Aizawl Central, 1978); Col, TC, TPWM, Ind E. b 1 Jan 54. MA. Served at Ind Nat

LALRAMHLUNA (Chaltlang, 1981); Lt-Col, CS, Ind E. b 9 May 51; with
KAWLRAMTHANGI m 1972; Lt-Col, TSWM, Ind E. b 14 Nov 52. Served in Ind W (CS/TSWM).

LALRAMLIANA, Hnamte (Govt Complex, Aizawl, Ind E, 1996); Capt, Ind Nat. b 3 Jan 67. BA, BD; with
C. LALHRIATPUII m 1994; Capt, Ind Nat. b 15 Sep 69. Served in Ind E.

LALZAMLOVA (Tuinu, Ind E, 1986); Col, TC, Sri Lan. b 1 Feb 62. BA; with
NEMKHANCHING (Nu-i) m 1984; Col, TPWM, Sri Lan. b 23 Feb 63. Served in Ind E and Ind N.

LaMARR, William (Yonkers Citadel, NY, 1967); Lt-Col, USA E. b 8 Apr 45; and
LaMARR, Judy (née Lowers) (East Liverpool, OH, 1962) m 1968; Lt-Col, USA E. b 14 Sep 41. LPN (Nursing)

LAMARTINIERE, Lucien (Petit Goave, Haiti, 1992); Maj, Carib. b 13 Jun 57; with
LAMARTINIERE, Marie (née Bonhomme) m 1980; Maj, Carib. b 26 May 57. Served in Can.

LANCE, Donald W. (Philadelphia Roxborough, PA, 1980); Lt-Col, USA E. b 7 Feb 53. BA (Bus), MPA (Non-Profit Mgmt); and
LANCE, Renee (née Hewlett) (Scranton, PA, 2002) m 2003; Lt-Col, USA E. b 3 Jun 53. RN (Nursing).

LANGA, William (Witbank, 1977); Lt-Col, CS, S Afr. b 15 Jul 49; with
LANGA, Thalitha (née Themba) m 1973; Lt-Col, TSWM, S Afr. b 1 Sep 50.

LASUT, Ernie (Bandung 1, 1986); Maj, Indon. b 4 Sep 61.

LAUKKANEN, Arja (Turku 2, 1975); Lt-Col, CS, Fin. b 29 Apr 46.

LAWS, Peter (Wauchope, 1973); Lt-Col, Aus E. b 23 Oct 1950. BAL, MBA; with
LAWS, Jan (née Cook) m 1970; Lt-Col, Aus E. b 18 Jun 50.

LEAVEY, Wendy (Street, UK, 1980); Lt-Col, IHQ. b 17 Feb 53. SRN, SCM. Served in UK and Gha.

LEE, Ki-yong (Chun Yun, Seoul 1982); Maj, Kor. b 9 Aug 52; and
KIM, Sun-ho (Eum Am, 1985); m 1985; Maj, Kor. b 19 Jan 54.

LEE, Kong Chew (Bob) (Balestier, 1983); Lt-Col, CS, Sing. b 8 Oct 57. BDiv; and
LEE, Teoh Gim Leng (Wendy) (Penang, 1983) m 1982; Lt-Col, TSWM, Sing. b 24 Aug 57.

LEMPID, I. Sadia (Polonia, 1989); Maj, Indon. b 13 Dec 64; and
LEMPID, Syastiel (née Haku) (Semarang 3, 1996) m 1996; Maj, Indon. b 9 Oct 72.

LESLIE, Victor A. (Port-of-Spain, Carib, 1980); Lt-Col, USA W. b 5 Nov 56. BA (Mgmt), MA (Relig Studies), CERT (Chem Dpndnce), JD (Law), MBA (Mgmt); and
LESLIE, Rose-Marie (née Campbell) (Lucea, Carib, 1977) m 1980; Lt-Col, USA W. b 15 Aug 57. BS (Soc Wk), AS (Nursing), RN (Nursing), BS (Nursing), CERT (Public Health Nurse). Served in Carib.

LEVIS, Linda (Harrow, UK, 1980); Maj, Tanz. b 2 Nov 49. BA (Hons), PGCE. Served in UK and at ITC.

LIANHLIRA (Ratu, 1979); Maj, Ind E. b 28 Apr 51, with
THANZUALI m 1975; Maj, Ind E. b 20 Jan 57.

LIGT de, Jacoba (née Oosterheerd) (Nieuwegein, Neth, 1987); Maj, Ken W. b 24 Apr 58; and
LIGT de, Cornelis (Nieuwegein, Neth, 1990) m 1988; Maj, Ken W. b 23 Sep 61. Served in Neth, E Afr and Ken.

LIM, Hun-taek (Kunsan, 1979); Lt-Col, Kor. b 24 Aug 50; with
CHUN, Soon-ja m 1977; Lt-Col, Kor. b 9 Mar 50. Served in Aus S.

LINARES, Orestes (Camaguey, 1997); Capt, L Am N. b 13 Aug 60; with
LINARES, Sandra (née Fernández) m 1986; Capt, L Am N. b 26 Jun 63.

LÖFGREN, Kehs David (Norrköping, 1968); Col, Swdn. b 8 Nov 45; and
LÖFGREN, Edith (née Sjöström) (Borlänge, 1974) m 1977; Col, Swdn. b 2 Mar 51. Served in UK and Nor (CS/TSWO).

LOMAX, Denis (Prescot, 1974); Maj, UK. b 26 Jan 53. Dip RS; and
LOMAX, Olive (née Baird) (Prescot, 1974) m 1974; Maj, UK. b 15 Jan 55.

LOSSO, Mesak (Jakarta 2, 1968); Lt-Col, Indon. b 12 Nov 45; and
LOSSO, Mona (née Warani) (Turen, 1971) m 1972; Lt-Col, Indon. b 13 Jun 44.

LOUBACKY, Urbain (Bakongo, 1992); Cap, Con (Braz), b 20 Dec 64; with
LOUBACKY, Judith (née Bikouta) m 1989; Maj, Con (Braz). b 16 Apr 68

LOUZOLO Dieudonnee (Nzoko, 1992); Maj, Con (Braz). b 20 Apr 67. BA Lang; with
LOUZOLO Edith (née Goudzoumou) m 1990; Maj, Con (Braz). b 25 Jul 69.

LUFUMBU, Enock (Londiani, Nakuru, 1982); Maj, Ken E. b 10 Feb 52; with
LUFUMBU, Beatrice (née Kageha) m 1978; Maj, Ken E. b 22 Feb 57.

LUKAU, Joseph (Kimbanseke 1, Con (Kin), 1977); Col, TC, Con (Braz). b 18 Sep 53; with
LUKAU, Angélique (née Makiese) m 1975; Col, TPWM, Con (Braz). b 1 Sep 54. Served in Con (Kin), Frce (CS/TPWM) and at IHQ.

LUTHER, Lise (Harstad, 1992); Maj, Nor. b 20 May 65.

LUYK, Kenneth E. (Columbus, GA, 1985); Maj, USA S. b 2 Oct 55. MA (Relig); with
LUYK, Dawn M. (née Busby) m 1981; Maj, USA S. b 5 Jun 60. BA (Chrstn Min).

M

MABASO, Timothy John (Witbank, S Afr, 1988); Lt-Col, Ken W. b 18 May 60. BA (Bus Adm); with
MABASO, Zakithi (née Zulu) m 1983; Lt-Col, Ken W. b 16 Dec 57. Served in S Afr.

MABUTO, Christopher (Chaanga, Zam, 1979); Lt-Col, CS, Tanz. b 2 Jan 54; with
MABUTO, Anne (née Hamayobe) m 1974; Lt-Col, TSWM, Tanz. b 25 Feb 58. Served in Zam & Mal and Ken W.

MABWIDI, Malonga Philippe (Salle Centrale, 1985); Maj, DR Con. b 25 Jan 53; with
MABWIDI Marie-Thérèse (née Biyela Lukimwena), m 1986; Maj, DR Con. b 13 Mar 63.

MacDONALD, Diana (née Emmanuel) (Karachi, 2000); Capt, Pak. b 20 Sep 60; with
CHANDI, Macdonald m 1998; Capt, Pak. b 10 Aug 64. BA.

MacMILLAN, M. Christine (North York, Can, 1975); Comr, IHQ. b 9 Oct 47. Served in UK, Aus E, PNG (TC, TPWM) and Can (TC, TPWM).

MACWAN, Jashwant Trikam (1986); Maj, Ind W. b 11 Jun 63; and
MACWAN, Sunita J. (1986) m 1986; Maj,

Ind W. b 5 Sep 61.

MACWAN, Paul Vahalji (Palaj, 1982); Maj,
Ind W. b 7 Jul 54; and
MACWAN, Shalomi Paul (Shevgaon, 1986)
m 1991; Maj, Ind W. b 20 Apr 60.

MACWAN, Punjalal Ukabhai (Lingda, 1980);
Maj, Ind W. b 8 Jul 51; with
MACWAN, Margaret m 1975; Maj, Ind W.
b 17 May 55.

McCLIMONT, Graeme, (Brighton, 1977);
Maj, Aus S. b 29 Jan 48. BSW; with
McCLIMONT, Helen (née Clee) m 1969;
Maj, Aus S. b 1 Dec 49. Served in UK and
PNG.

McKENZIE, Sydney (Havendale, Jamaica,
1970); Lt-Col, Carib. b 24 Dec 47; and
McKENZIE, Trypheme (née Forrest)
(Bluefields, Jamaica, 1971) m 1973; Lt-Col,
Carib. b 14 Jan 50.

McLAREN, Phillip (Shortland, 1975); Maj,
Aus E. b 25 Apr 48; with
McLAREN, Nancy (née Bramble) m 1969;
Maj, Aus E. b 27 Aug 49.

McMILLAN, Susan (Montreal Citadel, Can,
1979); Col, S Am E, TC, TPWM. b 20 Oct 54.
BAS, MBA, CGA. Served in Can, Mex &
Cent Am, S Am W (CS) and at IHQ.

MAFUTA, Mavana Denis (Kamina, 1993);
Capt, DR Con. b 18 Oct 54; with
MAFUTA Modestine (née Lumwanga
Ngoy); Maj, DR Con. b 18 Oct 1962.

MAGANLAL, Paul (Vaso, 1979); Maj, Ind W.
b 7 Jan 54; with
MAGANLAL, Febiben m 1973; Maj, Ind W.
b 11 Jun 52.

MAGAR, Bhausaheb J. (Dahiphal, 1977); Maj,
Ind W. b 2 Jun 53; and
MAGAR, Pushpa (née Gajbhiv) (Dahiphal,
1978) m 1979; Maj, Ind W. b 2 Jun 54.

MAGAYA, Jessie (née Milambo) (Chitumbi,
1981); Maj, TSWM, Zam. b 20 Sep 63; with
MAGAYA, Bexter m 1979; Maj, Zam.
b 29 Jan 56.

MAHIDA, Jashwant D. (Vishrampura, 1984);
Maj, Ind W. b 12 Jun 60; and
MAHIDA, Ruth (née Maganlal) (Anand
Central, 1990) m 1990; Maj, Ind W.
b 12 Nov 67.

MAHLANGU, Solomon (Brits, 1983); Maj,
S Afr. b 29 Oct 60; and
MAHLANGU, Mercy (née Razwinani)
(Khubvi, 1983) m 1985; Maj, S Afr.
b 30 Jun 63. BA Soc Studies. Served at IHQ.

MAIN, Gordon (Moonah, 1995); Maj, Aus S.
b 19 Mar 52; with
MAIN, Dianne (née Grice) m 1972; Maj,

Aus S. b 9 May 51.

MAKINA, Amos (Gwelo, Zimb, 1971); Comr,
IHQ (IS Afr). b 28 Jun 47; and
MAKINA, Rosemary (née Chinjiri)
(Mutonda, Zimb, 1973) m 1973; Comr, IHQ
(ZSWM Afr). b 8 Aug 52. Served in Gha and
Zimb (TC/TPWM).

MALABI, Joash (Mulatiwa, Ken, 1984);
Comr, TC, Ken W. b 17 May 55; and
MALABI, Florence (née Mutindi) (Webuye,
Ken, 1988) m 1988; Comr, TLWM, Ken W.
b 26 Jun 64. Served in E Afr, Rw (RC/RPWM)
and S Afr (CS/TSWM).

MAMBO, Tineyi (Seke Materera, 1989); Maj,
Zimb. b 23 Jan 67; and
MAMBO, Rumbidzai (Mungate, 1989)
m 1991; Maj, Zimb. b 29 May 67.

MANGIWA, Indra (Bandung 2, 1976), Maj,
Indon. b 14 Mar 52; and
MANGIWA, Helly (née Salainti) (Surabaya,
1977) m 1982; Maj, Indon. b 16 Jun 56.

MANHARDT, Linda (Pasadena Tabernacle,
USA W, 1978); Maj, Phil. b 11 Apr 52. MA.

MANOHARAN, Yesudian (Nantikuzhy, Ind SE,
1987); Maj, Tanz. b 14 May 64. MCom; and
MANOHARAN, Vethamony (Ettamadai,
Ind SE, 1987) m 1987; Maj, Tanz. b 20 Mar 64.
Served in Ind SE and Ind N.

MARKIEWICZ, Linda V. (Rome, NY,
USA E, 1981); Maj, USA W. b 15 Oct 50.
BA (Arts/ Engl). Served in USA E and at
IHQ and ICO.

MÁRQUEZ, Manuel (La Esperanza, 1995)
Capt, S Am W. b 12 Feb 1971; and
MÁRQUEZ, Paulina (née Condori) (Viacha,
1987) m 1997; Capt, S Am W. b 2 Mar 1964.

MARSEILLE, Gerrit W. J. (Ribe, Den, 1978);
Lt-Col, CS, Con (Braz). b 8 Jun 51. MSc,
MEd; with
MARSEILLE, Eva (née Larsen) m 1976;
Lt-Col, TSWM, Con (Braz). b 18 Jun 52.
Cand Odont. Served in Neth, Zai, Den and
S Afr.

MARSHALL, Norman Stephen (Chicago
Mont Clare, IL, 1978); Lt-Col, USA C.
b 17 Jun 45. BA (Sociol), MS (Org Dev),
MS (Admin & Org Behaviour); with
MARSHALL, Diane Bernice (née
Hedgren) m 1974; Lt-Col, USA C.
b 30 Sep 47. BS (Phys Ed).

MARTI, Paul William (Templet, Oslo, 1980),
Maj, Nor. b 24 Jan 61; and
MARTI, Margaret Saue (née Saue) (Voss,
1980) m 1983, Maj, Nor. b 29 Aug 58. Served
in Switz.

MARTIN, August (Biel, 1977); Maj, Switz.

b 24 Oct 52; with
MARTIN, Ruth (née Beyeler) m 1974; Maj,
Switz. b 22 Oct 51.
MARZAN, Jorge L. (San Juan, PR, 1977);
Maj, USA E. b 3 Nov 56. Cert (Database);
and
MARZAN, Limaris (née Negron) (Ponce, PR,
2002) m 2001; Capt, USA E. b 10 Sep 75.
BA (Soc Wk).
MASANGO, Frederick (Mangula, 1971); Maj,
Zimb. b 24 Jul 49; and
MASANGO, Rosemary (née Handiria)
(Karambazungu, 1981) m 1981; Maj, Zimb.
b 13 Feb 56.
MASIH, Edwin (Bareilly, Ind N, 1979); Maj,
Carib. b 6 Oct 57; and
MASIH, Sumita (Gurdaspur, Ind N, 1983)
m 1983; Maj, Carib. b 9 Oct 63. Served in
Ind N.
MASIH, Gian (Jalalabad, 1972); Maj, Ind N.
b 1 Oct 50; and
MASIH, Salima (Barnala, 1978) m 1978;
Maj, Ind N. b 1 Dec 54.
MASIH, Gurnam (Kaler Kalan, 1991); Maj,
Ind N. b 7 Jan 68; and
MASIH, Razia (Durangla, 1987); m 1992;
Maj, Ind N. b 1 Apr 65.
MASIH, Joginder (Bhoper, 1982); Maj, Ind N.
b 13 Jul 58; with
MASIH, Shanti m 1980; Maj, CSWM, Ban.
b 15 May 59. Served in Ban (GS/CHQ).
MASIH, Lazar (Rampur, 1974); Maj, Ind N.
b 20 May 52; with
MASIH, Sharbati m 1969; Maj, Ind N.
b 15 Jun 53.
MASIH, Makhan (Shahpur Guraya, 1990); Maj,
Ind N. b 30 Mar 68; and
MASIH, Sunila Makhan (City Corps, Amritsar,
1992) m 1992; Maj, Ind N. b 5 May 66.
MASIH, Manga (Bhandal, 1979); Maj, Ind N.
b 1 May 54; and
MASIH, Roseleen (Batala Central, 1980)
m 1980; Maj, Ind N. b 2 Jun 59.
MASIH, Manuel (Amritsar, 1994); Maj, Ind N.
b 1 Apr 64; with
MASIH, Anita m 1991; Maj, Ind N.
b 22 Apr 62.
MASIH, Parkash (Khunda, 1984); Maj, Ind N.
b 10 Mar 58; with
MASIH, Mariam Parkash m 1981; Maj,
Ind N. b 2 Apr 62.
MASIH, Piara (Kathane, 1982); Maj, Ind N.
b 3 Mar 61; with
MASIH, Grace (Babri Jiwanwal, 1984)
m 1985; Maj, Ind N. b 6 Feb 64.
MASIH, Salamat (Chamyari, 1979); Maj,

Ind N. b 2 Jan 59; and
MASIH, Snehalata (Chamyari, 1987)
m 1981; Maj, Ind N. b 18 May 61.
MASIH, Salamat (Shantinagar, 1989); Maj,
Pak. b 12 Aug 64; with
SALAMAT, Grace (née Sardar) m 1987;
Maj, Pak. b 18 Apr 64.
MASIH, Shafqat (Rehimabad, 1981); Maj,
Pak. b 30 Oct 48; with
SHAFQAT, Parveen (née Sardar) m 1979;
Maj, Pak. b 26 Jun 51.
MASON, Winsome (Burnie 1987); Maj, Aus S.
b 2 Feb 1958. Served in UK.
MASSIÉLÉ, Antoine (Yaya, 1982); Maj,
Con (Braz). b 20 Feb 53; with
MASSIÉLÉ, Marianne (née Ngoli) m 1978;
Maj, Con (Braz). b 2 Jan 50.
MATA, Mayisilwa Jean-Baptiste (Kisenso,
DR Con, 1983); Lt-Col, Zam. b 21 Oct 51;
with
MATA, Marie (née Mundele Kisokama)
m 1981; Lt-Col, Zam. b 22 Mar 58. Served
in Con (Kin).
MATEAR, John (Whifflet, 1978); Comr, TC,
UK. b 26 Apr 47; and
MATEAR, Elizabeth (née Kowbus) (Greenock
Citadel, 1977) m 1978; Comr, TPWM, UK.
b 16 Aug 52. Dip Youth, Commun and Soc Wk,
Emp Law. Served in Carib (TC/TPWM).
MATONDO, Gracia Victor (Kimpese, 1985);
Maj, DR Con. b 23 May 60; with
MATONDO, Isabel (née Lydia) m 1982;
Maj, DR Con. b 8 Sep 1962.
MATONDO, Isidore Mayunga (Boma, 1989);
Maj, DR Con. b 6 Jul 56; with
MATONDO, Marthe (née Nlandu Luzoladio)
m 1987; Maj, DR Con. b 7 Dec 62.
MAVOUNA, Nkouka François (Nzoko, 1988);
Maj, Con (Braz). b 15 Mar 60; with
MAVOUNA, Louise (née Matondo) m 1986;
Maj, Con (Braz). b 11 Dec 62.
MAVUNDLA, Hezekiel (Barberton, S Afr,
1970); Col, TC, Tanz. b 19 Jan 47; and
MAVUNDLA, Mirriam (née Maphanga)
(Barberton, S Afr, 1970) m 1970; Col,
TPWM, Tanz. b 2 Aug 52. Served in S Afr
(CS/TSWM).
MAXWELL, Philip (Orange, NSW, Aus E,
1984); Maj, PNG. b 21 Apr 62. B Bus, MBA;
and
MAXWELL, Deslea (née Pethybridge)
(Campsie, NSW, Aus E, 1984) m 1984; Maj,
PNG. b 23 Feb 62. Served in Aus E.
MAXWELL, Wayne (Canberra City Temple,
1984); Col, CS, Aus E. b 31 May 58. DipMin,
BMin, MAL; with

MAXWELL, Robyn (née Alley) m 1980; Col, TSWM, Aus E. b 14 Feb 60. Dip Pastoral Counselling

MAYNOR, Kenneth (Cleveland South, OH, 1980); Lt-Col, USA E. b 1 Feb 59. BS (Org Mgmt); with
MAYNOR, Cheryl Ann (née Staaf) m 1977; Lt-Col, USA E. b 27 Sep 58. BS (Church Mgmt).

MAYORGA, Max (Central, Costa Rica, 1989); Maj, L Am N. b 1 Feb 62; with
MAYORGA, Julia (née Obando); m 1981; Maj, L Am N. b 23 Oct 61.

MBAJA, Tiras Atulo (Kibera, 1986); Maj, Ken W. b 13 Jul 54; with
MBAJA, Mebo (née Mukiza) m 1983; Maj, Ken W. b 25 Mar 60.

MBALA, Lubaki Sébastien (Kifuma, 1987); Maj, DR Con. b 23 Jun 58, and
MBALA, Godette Mboyo (née Moseka) (Kintambo, 1987) m 1988; Maj, DR Con. b 26 Sep 62.

MBAKAYA, Herman (Nairobi Central, 1986), Maj, Ken W. b 11 Jan 57; with
MBAKAYA, Lucia (née Manduu) m 1992; Maj, Ken W. b 13 Oct 67.

MBIZI, Gabin (Ouenze, 1988); Maj, Con (Braz). b 30 Jan 63; with
MBIZI, Philomene (née Nkounkou) m 1986; Maj, Con (Braz). b 22 Aug 67.

MBUNGU, Joyce (Kagumo,1978); Maj, Ken E. b 4 Feb 56.

MBUTHU, Simon (Kilembwa, 1984); Maj, Ken E. b 14 Nov 60; and
MBUTHU, Zipporah (née Mwikali), (Makadara, 1996), m 1996; Capt, Ken E. b 26 Jul 73.

MEITEI, Shamu (Leizhangphai Manipur, 1988); Maj, Ind E. b 1 Jan 61. BCom; with
HOIHNIANG m 1983; Maj, Ind E. b 10 Jun 59.

MENDES, Marcio (Belo Horizonte, 1980); Maj, Brz. b 24 Feb 57. BA (Theol); and
MENDES, Jurema (née Mazzini) (Quarai, 1979) m 1981; Maj, Brz. b 4 Aug 57. BA (Ed).

MENDEZ, Jorge (El Faro, 1988); Maj, L Am N. b 5 Oct 51; with
MENDEZ, Idali (née Jiminez) m 1973; Maj, L Am N. b 24 Aug 52.

MENIA, Virgilio (Asingan, 1990); Lt-Col, Phil. b 2 Jun 61. BSCE (Civil Engr); and
MENIA, Ma Luisa (née Araneta) (Negros Occ, 1984) m 1990; Lt-Col, Phil. b 7 Jan 62.

MERAS, Marja (Turku 2, 1977); Maj, Fin. b 6 Sep 49.

MERRETT, Winsome (née Morris) (Kempsey, 1987) Maj, Aus S. b 21 Sep 58. MA (Theol Studies); and

MERRETT, Kelvin (Renown Pk, 1983) m 1987; Maj, Aus S. b 6 Sep 58. Assoc Theol.

MEYNER, Marianne (née Stettler) (Basle 2, 1983); Maj, Switz. b 14 Apr 57; with
MEYNER, Urs m 1978; Maj, Switz. b 30 Jan 51.

MGBEBUIHE, Benson (Amauzari, 1990); Maj, Nig. b 1 Aug 64; with
MGBEBUIHE, Celine m 1988; Maj, Nig. b 1 Aug 66.

MHASVI, Evan (née Mhizha) (Shirichena, 1977); Lt-Col, Zimb. b 1 Feb 55. Served in Zam. Ww Lt-Col Henry, pG 2006.

MHEMBERE, Isaac (Mukwenya 1989); Maj, Zimb. b 5 May 69; and
MHEMBERE, Charity (née Muchapondwa) (Muchapondwa, 1990) m 1991; Maj, Zimb. b 2 Jan 67.

MILAMBO, Saraphina (née Shikawala) (Kafue, 1989); Maj, TSWM, Zam. b 1 Feb 55. Ww Maj Vincent, pG 2007.

MILLAR, Ronald (Winnipeg Cit, Can, 1978); Maj, Carib. b 22 Oct 50. BA, BEd, MTS, MBA; with
MILLAR, Donna (née Barkwell) m 1973; Maj, Carib. b 12 Dec 51. BA. Served in Can and Aus E.

MKAMI, Samuel Chacha (Kitagutiti, 1988); Maj, Tanz. b 16 Apr 65; with
MKAMI, Mary (née Kibera) m 1985; Maj, Tanz. b 20 Jul 66.

MNYAMPI, Benjamin (Mgulani, Tanz, 1985), Col, CS, Ken W. b 1 Mar 54; with
MNYAMPI, Grace (née Sage) m 1984; Col, TSWM, Ken W. b 3 Jun 63. Served in E Afr, Rwa, Zimb and Tanz (CS/TSWM).

MOCKABEE, William (Anniston, AL, USA S, 1975); Lt-Col, CS, Sri Lan. b 1 Nov 54; and
MOCKABEE, Debra (née Salmon) (Oklahoma City, OK, USA S, 1976) m 1976; Lt-Col, TSWM, Sri Lan. b 9 Sep 54. Served in USA S.

MORAN, Peter (Bradford West Bowling, 1979); Maj, UK. b 11 Feb 51; with
MORAN, Sandra (née Clapham) m 1971; Maj, UK. b 16 Jul 49.

MOTSI, Isiah (Tomlinson, 1989); Maj, Zimb. b 9 Sep 68. Ww Maj Leah, pG 2010.

MOUKOKO, Daniel (Bacongo, Con (Braz), 1990); Maj, S Afr. b 1 Dec 60; with
MOUKOKO, Arschette (née Nguitoukoulou) m 1988; Maj, S Afr. b 30 Oct 62. Served in Con (Braz) and Rwa.

MOYA, Danton (Lo Valledor, 1989); Maj, S Am E. b 17 Jun 58; with

MOYA, Juana (neé Balboa) m 1979, Maj, S Am E. b 24 Jun 60. Served in S Am W.

MPANZU, Manu Emmanuel (Kimbanseke 1, 1979); Maj, DR Con. b 20 Jul 54; with **MPANZU, Albertine** (née Luzayadio Yema) m 1977; Maj, DR Con. b 27 Dec 58.

MSONGWE, Yohana (Ilembo, 1985); Maj, Tanz. b 1 Jan 62; with **MSONGWE, Jesinala** m 1985; Maj, Tanz. b 15 Jun 64.

MUBAIWA, Final (Nyarukunda, 1990); Maj, Zimb. b 29 June 60, with **MUBAIWA, Pfumisai** (née Ngwenya) m 1988; Maj, Zimb. b 12 May 69.

MUDDA, Abraham Lincoln (Nellore Central, Ind C, 1991); Maj, Zim. b 12 Sep 64. MA, MDiv; with **MUDDA, Mercy Manjula** m1988; Maj, Zim. b 22 May 66. BA, BEd, BTS. Served in Ind C.

MUIKKU, Aino (Turku II, Fin, 1985); Lt-Col, CS, Den. b 3 May 56. Served in Fin.

MUKOKO, Mamfweni Pierre (Mbanza-Nsundi, 1979); Maj, DR Con. b 3 Feb 49; with **MUKOKO, Marie-José** (née Sansa Mundele) m 1981; Maj, DR Con. b 25 Feb 59.

MUKONGA, Julius (Kwa Kyambu, 1978); Lt-Col, Ken E. b 10 Mar 53; with **MUKONGA, Phyllis** (née Mumbua) m 1976; Lt-Col, Ken E. b 28 Mar 57.

MÜNCH, Joan (née Nielsen) (Paris, Frce, 1991); Maj, Den. b 12 Nov 65. Served in Frce.

MUNN, Richard (Lexington, KY, USA E, 1987); Lt-Col, IHQ (Principal, ICO). b 16 Jan 56. BA (Ed), MDiv (Theol), DM (Chrstn Ldrshp); with **MUNN, Janet** (née White) m 1980; Lt-Col, IHQ. b 22 Oct 60. BA (Psych/Spanish), MA (Ldrshp & Min). Served in USA E.

MUNYEKHE, Boniface (Kithituni, 1977); Maj, Ken E. b 21 Mar 50; with **MUNYEKHE, Esther** (née Mumbe) m 1973; Maj, Ken E. b 12 May 52.

MUTUNGI, William (Kawaethei, 1990) Maj, Ken W. b 2 Nov 62; with **MUTUNGI, Florence** (née Mbithe) m 1988; Maj Ken W. b 12 Dec 66.

MWALUKANI, Wilson (Maendeleo, 1984); Maj, Tanz. b 1 Aug 59; with **MWALUKANI, Tamali** (née Sanya) m 1983; Maj, Tanz. b 1 Jan 63.

MWANGI, Samson (Maragwa, 1994); Maj, Ken E. b 31 Dec 68; with **MWANGI, Mary** (née Macharia) m 1991; Capt, Ken E. b 14 Aug 70.

MWEEMBA, Richard (Choma, 1989); Maj, Zam. b 24 Feb 54; with

MWEEMBA, Eunice (née Chiyalamanza) m 1975; Maj, Zam. b 15 Apr 60.

N

NALLATHAMBI, Edwin Sathyadhas (Kolvey, 1981); Maj, Ind SE. b 10 Aug 55; with **GNANA, Jessibell Edwin Sathyadhas** m 1980; Maj, Ind SE. b 15 Jun 57

NANGI, Masamba Henri (Kinzadi, 1979); Lt-Col, DR Con. b 21 May 53; with **NANGI, Josephine** (née Nsimba Babinga); Lt-Col, DR Con. b 30 Dec 53.

NANLABI, Priscilla (San Jose, Phil, 1980); Maj, GS, HK. b 15 Nov 58. Served in Phil.

NATO, Joe (Koki, 1979); Maj, PNG. b 30 Mar 57; with **NATO, Areka** (née Kejosefa) m 1976; Maj, PNG. b 17 Aug 58.

NAUD, Daniel (Paris-Montparnasse, Frce, 1979); Lt-Col, OC, It. b 8 Mar 54; and **NAUD Eliane** (née Volet) (Strasbourg, Frce, 1980) m 1980; Lt-Col, CPWM, It. b 3 Apr 60. Served in Frce and Belg.

NAUD, Patrick (Paris Villette, Fra, 1987); Lt-Col, CS, Ger. b 15 Mar 58; and **NAUD, Anne-Dore** (nèe Kaiser) (Hamburg, 1987) m 1987; Lt-Col, TSWM, Ger. b 26 Nov 59. Served in Fra and Belg.

NAYAK, Baldev (Penagoberi, 1990); Maj, Ind N. b 12 Feb 65; and **NAYAK, Chandrika** (Sartaguda, 1994) m 1994; Maj, Ind N. b 5 Jul 74.

NCUBE, Dubayi (Ndola, 1972); Lt-Col, Zimb. b 8 Jun 52; and **NCUBE, Orlipha** (née Ndlovu) (Mpopoma, 1976) m 1976; Lt-Col, Zimb. b 25 Dec 54.

NEEDHAM, John (Atlanta, GA, 1977); Maj, USA S. b 11 Aug 51. BS, MTS; with **NEEDHAM, Marthalynn** (née Ling) m 1973; Maj, USA S. b 5 Jun 52. Served in UK.

NEHAYA, Steven (Aionora, 1979); Maj, PNG. b 30 Dec 58; and **NEHAYA, Eva'aso** (née Abiose) m 1977; Maj, PNG. b 1 Feb 60.

NENEWA, Dinunu (Debadogoro, 1979); Maj, PNG. b 1 Apr 62; and **NENEWA, Ridia** (née Kuriki) (Debadogoro, 1979) m 1981; Maj, PNG. b 25 Dec 65.

NESTERENKO, Alex (Vitarte, 1986); Maj, S Am W. b 13 Dec 63; and **NESTERENKO, Luz** (née Henríquez) (Santiago Central, 1990) m 1991; Capt, S Am W. b 10 May 67. Served in Rus.

NGOY, Wa Mande Hubert (Kamina, 1989); Maj, DR Con. b 5 Jul 60; with

NGOY, Mbayo Célestine (née Mbayokidi) m 1983; Maj, DR Con. b 21 Nov 62. Served in Tanz.

NGWANGA, Kakinanatadiko Madeleine (Matadi, 1979); Comr, TC and TPWM, DR Con. b 25 Nov 55. Served in DR Con (CS and TSWM).

NICOLASA, Pablo (Buenos Aires Central, 1989); Maj, S Am E. b 20 Feb 61; with
NICOLASA, Estela (née Ocampo) m 1984; Maj, S Am E. b 4 Jul 60.

NICOLSON, Clive (Dunedin Fortress, 1990); Maj, NZ. b 31 Jul 47; with
NICOLSON, Lesley (née Ide) m 1970; Maj, NZ. b 20 Mar 52.

NILES, Allie Laura (Pasadena Tabernacle, CA, 1985); Maj, USA W. b 24 Oct 56. BA (Psych), BA (Soc Wk).

NKANU, Bintoma Norbert (Kavwaya, 1981); Maj, DR Con. b 29 Jun 54, with
NKANU, Hèléne (née Makuiza Lutonadio) m 1978; Maj, DR Con. b 18 Nov 61.

NKHOMA, Sammy (Zhombe, 1990); Maj, Zimb. b 7 Jul 61; with
NKHOMA, Ellen (née Mandizvidza) m 1987; Maj, Zimb. b 27 Sep 66.

NOAKES, David (Edendale, 1980); Maj, NZ. b 21 Sep 53. BA, DipTchg, DipGrad, PG DipTh; with
NOAKES, Vyvyenne (née Melhuish) m 1974; Maj, NZ. b 16 Mar 53. DipTchg (ECE).

NORDENBERG, Kenneth (Hisingskåren 1973); Lt-Col, Swdn. b 3 Jan 47; with
NORDENBERG, Ewa (née Landström); Lt-Col, Swdn. b 1 Sep 49.

NSUMBU, Fwadiabana Jean-Jacques (Kavwaya, 1977); Maj, DR Con. b 16 Aug 47; with
NSUMBU, Alice (née Muila Luvengika) m 1970; Maj, DR Con. b 24 Apr 51.

NSUMBU, Mambueni Emmanuel (Kingudi, 1981); Maj, DR Con. b 14 Aug 52; with
NSUMBU, Clémentine (née Mbimbu Bamba) m 1978; Maj, DR Con. b 10 Jun 59.

NTEMBI, Lukombo Esaïe (Mvuila, 1987); Maj, DR Con. b 15 Sep 57; and
NTEMBI, Marie-José (née Yoka Nzakimuena) m 1983; Maj, DR Con. b 6 Oct 60.

NTOYA, Kapela (Kinshasa IV, Con, 1983); Maj, IHQ (Principal, SALT Afr). b 2 Apr 55. BA; and
NTOYA, Rose-Nicole (née Makuena) (Kinshasa IV, Con, 1983); m 1983; Maj, IHQ (SALT Afr). b 21 Nov 60. Served in Con (Kin).

NÜESCH, Néstor R. (New York Temple, NY,

USA E, 1977); Col, CS, USA C. b 1 Dec 49. BA (Bus Adm), MBA; and
NÜESCH, Rebecca (née Brewer) (Ithaca, NY, USA E, 1977) m 1977; Col, TSWM, USA C. b 17 Jan 55. Served in USA E and S Am E (TC/TPWM).

NYAGAH, Henry Njagi (Kagaari, Ken E, 1986); Col, OC, Mal. b 21 Feb 54; with
NYAGAH, Catherine (née Njoki) m 1984; Col, CPWM, Mal. b 3 Sep 59. Served in E Afr and Ken W (CS/TSWM).

NYAMBALO, Francis (Migowi, 1982); Maj, GS, Mal. b 15 Aug 51; with
NYAMBALO, Jamiya (née Khumani) m 1970; Maj, CSWM, Mal. b 14 Aug 56. Served in Zam.

NYBO, Thorgeir (Sandefjord, 1981); Lt-Col, Nor. b 4 Sep 59; and
NYBO, Marianne (née Østensen) (Sandefjord, 1981) m 1981; Lt-Col, Nor. b 19 Jul 59.

NYEREYEMHUKA, Funny (Dombwe, 1973); Maj, Zimb. b 15 Dec 50; and
NYEREYEMHUKA, Ellen (née Mpofu) (Gandiwa Society, 1978) m 1978; Maj, Zimb. b 9 Jul 55.

NZILA, Luyeye Barthélemy (Lemba-Ngaba, 1987); Maj, DR Con. b 16 Mar 61; and
NZILA, Bibisky (née Ntombo Nsosa) m 1985; Maj, DR Con. b 6 Oct 66.

NZINGOULA, Victor (Loussala, 1988); Maj, Con (Braz). b 27 Mar 63; with
NZINGOULA, Emma (née Malonga) m 1986; Maj, Con (Braz). b 27 Apr 68.

NZITA, Jerôme (Bakongo, 1977); Maj, Con (Braz). b 15 Oct 48; with
NZITA, Jeanne (née Nsongala Jeanne) m 1976; Maj, Con (Braz). b 26 Jun 52.

O

OALANG, David (Sta Barbara, 1995); Maj, Phil. b 20 Feb 66. BSc (Bus Adm); and
OALANG, Elsa (née Gallna) (Quezon City 1, 1988) m 1995; Maj, Phil. b 25 May 62. BSc (Mass Comm), MA (Theol).

OBANDO, Javier (Sagrada Familia, Costa Rica, 1991); Maj, L Am N. b 2 Mar 66; with
OBANDO, Maria Eugenia (née Vanegas) m 1988; Maj, L Am N. b 21 Apr 65.

ÖBERG, Leif (Centrumkåren, 1986); Maj, Swdn. b 17 Dec 60; and
ÖBERG, Helena (née Gezelius); Maj, Swdn. b 25 May 61.

O'BRIEN, Douglas G. (San Francisco Citadel, 1976); Lt-Col, USA W. b 1 Aug 49. BA (Speech), MA (Relig); and
O'BRIEN, Diane (née Lillicrap) (Staines, UK,

320

1975) m 1988; Lt-Col, USA W. b 8 Nov 50. FTCL, GTCL. Served in UK.

ODURO, Godfried (Kyekyewere, 1981); Maj, Gha. b 17 Jul 54; with
ODURO, Felicia (née Obeng) m 1978; Maj, Gha. b 25 Jun 60.

ODURO, Rockson (Kwao Nartey, 1993); Maj, Gha. b 29 Jan 63; with
ODURO, Emelia (née Lamtei) m 1991; Maj, Gha. b 12 Mar 64.

ODURO-AMOAH, Peter (Achiase, 1989); Maj, Gha. b 26 Aug 58; with
ODURO-AMOAH, Grace (née Fosua) m 1984; Maj, Gha. b 11 Feb 64.

OGUNDAHUNSI, Raphael (Ogbagi, 1986); Maj, Nig. b 10 Jul 59; with
OGUNDAHUNSI, Esther m 19; Maj, Nig. b 13 Apr 64.

OKLAH, Samuel (Accra Newtown, 1983); Lt-Col, CS, Gha. b 5 Mar 58; and
OKLAH, Philomina (née Addo) (Tema, 1985) m 1985; Lt-Col, TSWM, Gha. b 21 Dec 62. Served in Mal.

OKOROUGO, Edwin Rapurnchukwu (Amesi, 1982); Maj, Nig. b 2 Aug 49. BA (Relig Studies), MA (Eth and Phil); with
OKOROUGO, Agnes (née Nwokekwe) m 1978; Maj, Nig. b 5 Apr 52.

OLAUSSON, Gunilla (née Lind) (Helsingborg, 1986) Maj, Swdn. b 23 Aug 60 and
OLAUSSON, Kjell Edor (Hisingskår, 1978) m 1986; Maj, Swdn. b 12 Nov 56.

OLEWA, John (Mukhombe, 1986); Maj, Ken E. b 12 Nov 54; with
OLEWA, Mary (née Kadzo) m 1982; Maj, Ken E. b 19 Sep 1960.

OLORUNTOBA, Festus (Supare, Nig, 1976); Lt-Col, OC, Lib. b 7 Jul 55. Ww Lt-Col Gloria, pG 2009. Served in Nig (CS).

ONYEKWERE, Paul (Umuogo, 1984); Maj, Nig. b 27 Jul 58; with
ONYEKWERE, Edinah; Maj, Nig. b 29 Oct 61.

ORASIBE, Patrick (Akokwa, 1988); Maj, Nig. b 9 Oct 58; with
ORASIBE, Blessing (née Chituru) Maj, Nig. b 5 Dec 58.

ORD, Norman (Peterborough Citadel, 1992); Maj, UK. b 28 Sep 55. MA (Hons) (French and Music), PGCE, CDRS. Ww Capt Christine, pG 2009.

ØRSNES, Bernt Olaf (Bergen 1, 1983); Maj, Nor. b 22 Apr 59; and
ØRSNES, Hildegard (née Anthun) (Bergen 1, 1984) m 1986; Maj, Nor. b 29 Sep 61. Served in Carib.

OTA, Haruhisa (Hamamatsu, 1973); Maj, Jpn. b 30 Jan 50; and
OTA, Hiromi (née Nakatsugawa) (Hamamatsu, 1973) m 1976; Maj, Jpn. b 21 Jun 48.

OWEN, Graham (Nuneaton, 1977); Lt-Col, UK. b 8 Jul 53; and
OWEN, Kirsten (née Jacobsen) (Copenhagen Temple, Den, 1977) m 1978; Lt-Col, UK. b 2 May 56. Served in Den (CS/THQ).

OYESANYA, Michael (Iperu, 1984); Maj, Nig. b 17 May 61; and
OYESANYA, Roseline (Iperu, 1988) m 1988; Maj, Nig. b 21 Jun 65.

P

PALLANT, Dean (Bromley, UK, 1993); Maj, IHQ. b 23 Nov 64. BSoc Sc, Dip LR, PG Dip (Theol); and
PALLANT, Eirwen (née Lowther) (Leeds Central, UK, 1992) m1993; Maj, IHQ. b 9 May 62. BSc (Hons), MB ChB, DTM&H, MRCGP. Served in UK and Zam.

PANDORANTE, Marthen (Surabaya 4, 1989); Maj, Indon. b 6 Oct 64; and
PANDORANTE, Yulien (née Ganna) (Bandung 2, 1984) m 1981; Maj, Indon. b 22 Jun 61.

PAONE, Massimo (Naples, It, 1977); Col, TC, Frce. b 8 Jun 52; and
PAONE, Elizabeth Jane (née Moir) (Nunhead, UK, 1982) m 1982; Col, TPWM, Frce. b17 Dec 58. BA (Hons). Served in UK, It (OC/CPWM) and Frce (CS/TLWM).

PARDO, Zoilo B. (Hollywood, CA, 1989); Lt-Col, USA W. b 9 Dec 53. BA (Acct); with
PARDO, Magali (née Pacheco) m 1980; Lt-Col, USA W. b 20 Apr 56. BA (Gen Ed), BA (Acct). Served in Mex and L Am N (CS/ TSWM).

PAREDES, Tito E. (La Paz, S Am W, 1976); Col, TC, L Am N. b 14 Aug 54; and
PAREDES, Martha (née Nery) (Cochabamba, S Am W, 1976) m 1977; Col, TPWM, L Am N. b 3 Jun 54. Served in S Am W, USA E and L Am N (CS/TSWM).

PARK, Chong-duk (Pupyung, 1977); Col, CS, Kor. b 22 May 50. ThM, DipMin; with
YOON, Eun-sook m 1975; Col, TSWM, Kor. b 23 Oct 50. Served in Aus S.

PARK, Man-hee (Chung Ju, 1975); Comr, TC, Kor. b 11 Aug 47; with
KIM, Keum-nyeo m 1973; Comr, TPWM, Kor b 13 Jun 51. Served in Kor (CS/TSWM).

PARK, Nai-hoon (Syn Heung, 1978); Maj, Kor. b 23 Oct 46; with

KIL, Soon-boon m 1971; Maj, Kor.
b 26 Nov 49.

PARKER, Michael (Hucknall, 1977); Lt-Col,
UK. b 28 Jul 50; with
PARKER, Joan (née Brailsford) m 1971;
Lt-Col, UK. b 16 Jan 52. Served at ITC.

PARMAR, Kantilal K. (Ode, 1983); Maj,
Ind W. b 1 Jun 53. BA, BEd; and
PARMAR, Eunice K. (née Gaikwad)
(Mohmedwadi, 1977) m 1983; Maj, Ind W.
b 30 Oct 52.

PATRIC, George (Bareilly, 1994); Capt, Ind N.
b 15 Mar 68; with
PATRIC, Veera m 1993; Capt, Ind N.
b 15 Jul 68.

PAWAR, Suresh S. (Ahmednagar Evangeline
Booth Hall, 1981); Maj, Ind W. b 10 Feb 60; and
PAWAR, Martha (née Shirsath) (Ahmednagar
Central, 1981) m 1981; Maj, Ind W. b 17 Nov 63.

PAXTON, Joy (Rosyth, UK, 1976); Maj, Tanz.
b 16 Aug 50. Served in UK. Dip CE (Primary
Ed). Served in UK and at ITC.

PAYNE, Godfrey (Goff) (Tunbridge Wells, UK,
1980); Lt-Col, CS, Nig. b 15 Oct 51; with
PAYNE, Diane (née Harris) m 1975; Lt-Col,
TSWM, Nig. b 28 Dec 52. Served in UK,
E Afr, Zam & Mal, Uga and Mal (OC/CPWM).

PEDDLE, Brian (Dildo/New Harbour, NL,
Can, 1977); Col, CS, UK. b 8 Aug 57; and
PEDDLE, Rosalie (née Rowe) (Carbonear,
NL, Can, 1976) m 1978; Col, TSWM, UK.
b 17 Jan 56. Served in Can and NZ.

PERINBANAYAGAM, Suthananthadhas
(Booth Tucker Hall, Nagercoil, 1986); Maj,
Ind SE. b 14 Oct 56. MA, HACDP; and
ESTER, Evangelin Suthananthadhas
(Attoor, 1986) m 1986; Maj, Ind SE.
b 18 Apr 63. BSc.

PETRUS, I. Made (Den Pasar, Bali, 1983);
Maj, Indon. b 12 Jul 60; and
PETRUS, Margaretha (née Pinontoan)
(Ambon/Bandung 2, 1975) m 1984; Maj,
Indon. b 15 Mar 53.

PETTERSEN, Per Arne (Sarpsborg, 1969);
Maj, Nor. b 20 Mar 47; and
PETTERSEN, Lillian (née Madsø) (Namsos,
1969) m 1971; Maj, Nor. b 5 Jun 45.

PHILIP, P. K. (Thottamon, 1975); Maj, Ind SW.
b 12 Dec 48; and
PHILIP, Rachel (Kottarakara Central, 1980)
m 1979; Maj, Ind SW. b 10 Nov 54.

PHO, Samuel (Altona, Aus S, 1983); Lt-Col,
OC, HK. b 17 Jun 57. BTh; and
PHO, Donni (née Kkuu) (Altona, Aus S, 1985)
m 1985; Lt-Col, CPWM, HK. b 30 May 58.

PILKINGTON, George A. (Lamberhead Green,

1972); Lt-Col, UK. b 11 Apr 50. SRN. Served
at ITC. m 1974; Maj Vera, ret 2007.

PIZZIRUSSO, Hugo (Arroyito, 1989); Maj,
S Am E. b 7 Nov 66; and
PIZZIRUSSO, Elsa (née Coppeto) (Nueva
Chicago, 1989) m 1991; Maj, S Am E.
b 3 Feb 67.

POA, Selly Barak (Jakarta, 1979); Lt-Col,
Indon. b 25 Sep 55; and
POA, Anastasia (née Djoko Slamet)
(Surakarta 2, 1984) m 1985; Lt-Col, Indon.
b 29 Jun 62.

POLSLEY, Randall (Omaha, NE, 1993); Maj,
USA C. b 22 Sep 61; with
POLSLEY, Charlene (née Sniffen) m 1989;
Maj, USA C. b 7 Dec 67.

PONNIAH, Masilamony (Periavilai, Ind SE,
1969); Lt-Col, CS, Ind SW. b 2 Jun 49; and
PONNIAH, Sathiyabama (Layam, Ind SE,
1974) m 1974; Lt-Col, TSWM, Ind SW.
b 14 Apr 56. Served in Ind SE, Ind W and Ind N.

POSADAS, Leopoldo (Dagupan City, Phil,
1981); Maj, GS, Ban. b 18 Aug 58. BSc; and
POSADAS, Evelyn (née Felix) (Hermoza,
Phil, 1982) m 1982; Maj, CSWM, Ban.
b 2 Aug 57. Served in Phil.

POSILLICO, Joseph E. (Los Angeles Lincoln
Heights, CA, 1972); Lt-Col, USA W.
b 29 Dec 50; and
POSILLICO, Shawn L. (née Patrick) (San
Francisco, CA, 1984) m 1988; Lt-Col,
USA W. b 3 Aug 57. BS (Bus Econ).

PRASAD, P. C. (Annavaram, 1981); Maj,
Ind C. b 9 Sep 58; with
PRASAD, Krupamma m 1979; Maj, Ind C.
b 4 Jun 59.

PRITCHETT, Wayne (Deer Lake, NL, 1970);
Lt-Col, Can. b 13 Aug 46. BA, BEd, MTh; and
PRITCHETT, Myra (née Rice) (Roberts
Arm, NL, 1969) m 1972; Lt-Col, Can.
b 19 Jun 50. BA, MTh. Served at IHQ.

PULULU, Celestino Pepe (Makala, DR Con,
1985), Maj, GS, Moz. b 15 Oct 52;
with
PULULU, Veronica Lukombo (née Nkenge)
m 1978; Maj, CSWM, Moz. b 4 Dec 57.
Served in Con (Kin).

PUOTINIEMI, Tella (née Juntunen) (Helsinki IV,
1983); Maj, Fin. b 17 Oct 52; and
PUOTINIEMI, Antero (Oulu, 1981) m 1983;
Maj, Fin. b 15 Oct 48.

R

RAINES, Timothy (Mt Vernon, NY, 1971);
Lt-Col, USA E. b 30 Dec 47. BS (Org Mgmt);
and

RAINES, Lynda Lou (née Swingle)
(Zanesville, OH, 1969) m 1969; Lt-Col,
USA E. b 23 Aug 48. BS (Org Mgmt).

RAJAKUMARI, P. Mary (née Desari)
(New Colony, Bapatla, Ind C, 1978); Comr,
TC, TPWM, Ind W. MA (Engl), MA (Hist).
Served in Ind M & A, at IHQ, at Ind Cent
Off, in Ind W (THLS), Ind N (TPWM) and
Ind SE (TPWM). Ww Comr P. D. Krupa Das,
pG 2007

RAJU, K. Samuel (Kakulapadu, 1980); Maj,
Ind C. b 5 May 58; and
RAJU, K. Raja (née Kumari) (Pedaparapudi,
1980) m 1981; Maj, Ind C. b 3 May 64.

RAJU, M. Daniel (M. R. Nagaram, 1984); Maj,
Ind C. b 20 Jun 54. MA (Econ); with
RAJU, Rachel (née Kondamudi) m 1982;
Maj, Ind C. b 15 Jun 62.

RANGI, Gidion (Kulawi, 1990), Maj, Indon.
b 7 Aug 60; with
RANGI, Lidia (née Norlan) m 1985; Maj,
Indon. b 25 Nov 65.

RAO, S. Jayananda (Madras Central, 1981);
Maj, Ind C. b 29 Oct 52; with
RAO, S. Christiansen m 1976; Maj, Ind C.
b 22 Dec 60.

RASELALOME, Johannes (Seshego, 1982);
Maj, S Afr. b 3 May 60; and
RASELALOME, Veliswa Atalanta (née
Mehu) (Tshoxa, 1982) m 1985; Maj, S Afr.
b 16 Jul 62.

RATHAN, P. Samuel (Mandavalli, 1974); Maj,
Ind C. b 3 May 51; with
KUMARI, P. Ananda m 1976; Maj, Ind C.
b 1 Oct 57.

READ, Alan (Newcastle Byker, 1980); Maj,
UK. b 10 Apr 58. MSc, FCIS. Served at IHQ;
and
READ, Janet (née Rumble) (Redhill, 1977)
m 1982; Maj, UK. b 22 Mar 55. BA (Hons)
(Relig Studies).

REDDISH, Graeme John (Thames, 1974);
Col, CS, NZ. b 28 Aug 49. Ww Maj Nola,
pG 2002; and
REDDISH, Wynne (née Jellyman) (Miramar,
1982) m 2005; Col, TSWM, NZ. b 22 Apr 57.
Dip BRS, BBus, Dip Mgmt (NZIM).
Served at IHQ.

REEL, Robert J. (Wilkes-Barre, PA, 1970); Maj,
USA E. b 28 Dec 44. BA (Org Mgmt);
with
REEL, Lynette M. (née Hufford) m 1964;
Maj, USA E. b 2 Sep 45. BA (Org Mgmt).

REES, David H. (Rockdale, 1976); Lt-Col, Aus
E. b 29 Jun 47; with
REES, Christine F. (née Cairns) m 1969;

Lt-Col, Aus E. b 11 Apr 49. Served in Sri Lan
and at IHQ.

REES, John (Ipswich, 1974); Maj, Aus E.
b 29 Jun 47; with
REES, Narelle (née Lehmann) m 1969; Maj,
Aus E. b 27 Jun 48. Served in PNG and Rus.

REYNOLDS, James (Canton Citadel, OH,
1976); Lt-Col, USA E. b 2 Jun 48. BS (HRM);
with
REYNOLDS, Blanche Louise (née Labus)
m 1972; Lt-Col, USA E. b 16 Dec 49.

RICE, Sandra (Roberts Arm, NL, 1980); Lt-Col,
Can. b 16 Feb 58. BEd, BA, MTS.

RICHARDSON, Alfred (Mount Dennis, ON,
1967); Lt-Col, Can. b 5 Dec 44; with
RICHARDSON, Ethel (née Howell) m 1964;
Lt-Col, Can. b 2 Apr 43.

RICHARDSON, Lonneal (Bloomington, IN,
1983) Maj, USA C. b 3 Mar 59. BA (Bus
Adm); and
RICHARDSON, Patty (née Barton) (Omaha
South, NE, 1979) m 1983; Maj, USA C.
b 30 Jan 57. BA (Bus Adm), MA (Org Ldrshp).

RIGLEY, Graeme (Norwood, 1988); Maj,
Aus S. b 10 Aug 54. BMd, BS; with
RIGLEY, Karyn (née Whitehead) m 1981;
Maj, Aus S. b 8 Apr 59.

RILEY, Douglas F. (Pasadena Tabernacle, CA,
1995); Maj, USA W. b 6 Feb 59. BS (Fin),
MBA (Bus Adm), MA (Theol); with
RILEY, Colleen R. (née Hogan) m. 1991;
Maj, USA W. b 14 Aug. 68.

ROBERTS, Campbell (New Brighton, 1969);
Maj, NZ. b 15 Feb 47. BTh; and
ROBERTS, Gay (née Robertson) (Naenae,
1969) m 1971; Maj, NZ. b 26 Oct 46.

ROBERTS, Jonathan (Leicester Central, UK,
1986); Lt-Col, IHQ. b 20 Feb 62. BA (Theol),
BA (Econ); and
ROBERTS, Jayne (née Melling) (Southend
Citadel, UK, 1985) m 1986; Lt-Col, IHQ.
b 23 Apr 58. BA (Eng Lit) PGCE.
Served in UK.

ROBERTS, William A. (Detroit Citadel, MI,
USA C, 1971); Comr, NC, USA Nat.
b 26 Feb 46; BS, MA; with
ROBERTS, Nancy Louise (née Overly)
m 1968; Comr, NPWM, USA Nat. b 27 Oct 43.
BS, MA. Served in USA C, S Am E (TC/
TPWM), at IHQ (IS Bus Adm/Sec for Staff
Dev) and in Ken W (TC/TPWM).

ROBERTSON, Laurie (Broken Hill, Aus E,
1980); Lt-Col, IHQ. b 26 Sep 55; Dip Min; and
ROBERTSON, Simone (née Riley) (Manly,
Aus E, 1980) m 1980; Lt-Col, IHQ.
b 16 Nov 59. Served in Aus E and Aus S.

RODWELL, Heather (Dunedin South, 1990); Maj, NZ. b 24 Sep 55.

ROTONA, Rabona (Boregaina, 1979); Maj, PNG. b 1 Jan 52; and
ROTONA, Gabi (née Kanau) (Boregaina, 1979) m 1979; Maj, PNG. b 16 May 57.

ROUFFET, Jacques (Regent Hall, UK, 1972) Maj, Frce. b Oct 49; and
ROUFFET, Yvonne (née Chislett) (New Barnet ,UK ,1972) m 1974; Maj, Frce. b 20 Nov 50. Served UK and Belg.

ROWE, Dennis (Norwood, 1971); Maj, Aus S. b 25 Jun 48; and
ROWE, Patricia (née Muir) (Woodville Gardens, 1970) m 1972; Maj, Aus S. b 18 Mar 48. Served in HK and Tai.

ROWE, Lindsay (Chance Cove, NL, Can, 1972); Lt-Col, CS, Carib. b 21 Sep 51. BA (Hons), MDiv; and
ROWE, Lynette (née Hutt) (Winterton, NL, Can, 1971) m 1974; Lt-Col, TSWM, Carib. b 13 Feb 52. Served in Can and S Afr.

S

SAENZ, Jannette (Chihuahua, 1993); Maj, Mex. b 27 Nov 70.

SAKAMESSO, Jean-Aléxis (Ouenze, 1979); Lt-Col, Con (Braz). b 25 May 50; with
SAKAMESSO, Pauline (née Louya) m 1976; Lt-Col, Con (Braz). b 19 Jan 56.

SAMUEL, John (Trivandrum Central, 1984); Maj, Ind SW. b 22 May 53. Ww Maj Annamma, pG 2007.

SAMUEL, M. (Central, Kottarakara, 1974); Maj, Ind SW. b 15 Dec 51; and
SAMUEL, K. Thankamma (Ommanoor, 1977) m 1976; Maj, Ind SW. b 15 Oct 53.

SANCHEZ, Oscar (Lima Central, S Am W, 1982); Comr, TC, Brz. b 21 Nov 56; and
SANCHEZ, Ana Rosa (née Limache) (Huayra K'assa, S Am W, 1985) m 1987; Comr, TPWM, Brz. b 12 Jun 60. Served in Sp, S Am W, USA W and L Am N (TC/TPWM).

SANGCHHUNGA (Ratu, 1974); Maj, Ind E. b 15 Mar 52; and
VANLALAUVI (Ngopa, 1975) m 1975; Maj, Ind E. b 10 Jun 55.

SANGTHANGDULA, S. T. Dula (Diakkawn 1986); Maj, Ind E. b 2 Jul 63. MA, MTh, DD, DMiss, DEvang, DChrstn Counselling;
MALSAWMI m 1984; Maj, Ind E. b 10 Jun 59.

SANTIAGO, José (Guayama, PR, USA E, 1987); Maj, L Am N. b 8 Aug 50; with
SANTIAGO, Hilda (née Amill); m 1975; Maj, L Am N. b 15 Nov 53.

SATHIYASEELAN, D. (Kanacode, 1974);

Maj, Ind SW. b 10 May 51; and
SATHIYASEELAN, Aleyamma (Adoor Central,1975) m 1980; Maj, Ind SW. b 29 Jun 50.

SATTERLEE, Allen (Lakeland, FL, USA S, 1977); Maj, Carib. b 21 Apr 53. BS Psych, MTS; and
SATTERLEE, Esther (née Sands) (Laurel, MS, USA S, 1979) m 1982; Maj, Carib. b 9 Mar 55 BS Bus Adm. Served in USA S, Sing and PNG.

SAYUTI, Yohannes (Surabaya 2, 1975); Lt-Col, Indon. b 28 Jul 51; and
SAYUTI, Asya (née Tonta) (Bandung 3, 1974) m 1979; Lt-Col, Indon. b 5 Jan 51.

SCHMID, Fritz (Adelboden/Thun, 1980); Maj, Switz. b 20 Nov 53; and
SCHMID, Margrit (née Dössegger) (Seon, 1981) m 1981; Maj, Switz. b 4 Dec 52.

SCHOLTENS, Teunis (Zwolle, 1980); Maj, Neth. b 28 Aug 52; with
SCHOLTENS, Hendrika (née Stuurop) m 1977; Maj, Neth. b 28 May 56.

SCHWARTZ, Barry R. (Goodwood, S Afr, 1973); Lt-Col, CS, DR Con. b 17 Apr 48; with
SCHWARTZ, Anja Jacoba (née Kamminga) m 1967; Lt-Col, TSWM, DR Con. b 28 Jul 48. Served in S Afr.

SEILER, Paul R. (Hollywood Tabernacle, CA, USA W, 1981); Comr, TC, USA C. b 23 May 51. MBA, BS (Bus Adm); with
SEILER, Carol (née Sturgess) m 1978; Comr, TPWM, USA C. b 6 Apr 52. RN, BS (Nursing), MPH, MS (Nursing). Served in USA W and USA C (CS/TSWM).

SENARATNE Ranjit (Siyambalangamuwa, 1994) Maj, Sri Lan. b 7 Jan 63; and
SENARATNE Vijayashri (née Kandasamy) (Jaffna, 1994) m 1995; Maj, Sri Lan. b 3 Oct 70.

SERÈM, Alberto (Lisbon Central, Port, 1985), Maj, Brz, b 27 Nov 56; and
SERÈM, Maria José (née Leitão) (Picheleira, Port, 1977) m 1980; Maj, Brz. b 13 Dec 52. Served in UK, It and Port (OC/CPWM).

SEVAK, David Keshav (Sokhada, 1981); Maj, Ind W. b 15 Nov 50; and
SEVAK, Vimalaben (Bharoda, 1983) m 1983; Maj, Ind W. b 5 Jun 63.

SEYMOUR, Geanette (Belmore, Aus E, 1973); Lt-Col, IHQ. b 20 Feb 50. BA (Soc Wk). Served in Aus E (CS)

SHAKESPEARE, David (Catford, UK, 1981); Lt-Col, IHQ. b 8 Oct 59; and

Biographical Information

SHAKESPEARE, Karen (née Grainger) (Catford, UK, 1980) m 1981; Lt-Col, IHQ. b 2 Aug 54. BEd (Hons), MA (Pastoral Theol), MA (Adult Ed with Theol Reflection). Served in UK

SHAROVA, Svetlana (née Blagodirova) (Chisinau Botannica, 1999); Capt, E Eur. b 18 Jun 65; with
SHAROV, Alexander m 1986; Capt, E Eur. b 6 Jul 57.

SHAVANGA, Edward (Matunda, Ken W, 1982); Maj, Zam. b 9 Mar 58; with
SHAVANGA, Florence (née Vulehi) m 1979; Maj, Zam. b 11 Oct 60. Served in E Afr and Ken.

SHAVANGA, Moses (Musudzuu, 1984); Maj, Ken W. b 10 Jun 57; with
SHAVANGA, Gladys (née Sharia) m 1982; Maj, Ken W. b 18 Mar 61. Served in Tanz.

SHEKWA, Albert Zondiwe (Emangweni, 1974); Maj, S Afr. b 12 Mar 51; and
SHEKWA, Peggy (née Maimela) (Louis Trichardt, 1974) m 1974; Maj, S Afr. b 3 Jun 54.

SIAMOYA, Margeret (Loubomba, Zam, 1991) Maj, Zimb. b 15 Jul 65. Ww Maj Siamoya, pG 2010.

SIJUADE, Michael A. (Ife Ife, 1992); Maj, Nig. b 13 Jun 64; with
SIJUADE, Comfort m 1990; Maj, Nig. b 11 Nov 67.

SIMON, T. J. (Perumpetty, 1977); Maj, Ind SW. b 15 Nov 52; and
SIMON, Ammini (Pulickal, 1980) m 1979; Maj, Ind SW. b 1 Feb 60.

SINGH, Dilip (Simultala, 1990); Maj, Ind N. b 4 Nov 68; and
SINGH, Nivedita (née Christian) (Fatapukur, 1992) m 1992; Maj, Ind N. b 14 Sep 71.

SJOGREN, Daniel (St Paul (Temple), MN, 1972); Lt-Col, USA C. b 12 Nov 51; and
SJOGREN, Rebecca (née Nefzger) (Hibbing, MN, 1973) m 1973; Lt-Col, USA C. b 11 Jun 53.

SMITH, Charles (Kansas City (Blue Valley), MO, 1978); Maj, USA C. b 22 Aug 57; with
SMITH, Sharon (née Cockrill) m 1975; Maj, USA C. b 7 Mar 54.

SMITH, Jeffrey (Flint Citadel, MI, 1986); Lt-Col, USA C. b 19 Jan 54. BA (Bible), MRE; with
SMITH, Dorothy R. (née Kumpula) m 1974; Lt-Col, USA C. b 22 Oct 54. BA (Psychol/ Sociol), MSW, MPC (Pastoral Counselling).

SMITH, Judith E. (Monterey Peninsula, CA, 1988); Lt-Col, USA W. b 4 Aug 49. BS (Ed). Served at IHQ.

SMITH, Paul (Lansing Citadel, WI, 1985); Maj, USA C. b 23 Jun 56. BA (Psychol), MA (Theatre), MA (Org Ldrship); and
SMITH, Renea (née Bonifield) (Grand Rapids Centennial Temple, MI, 1984) m 1985; Maj, USA C. b 16 Nov 57. BS (Ed).

SMITH, Stephen C. (Renton, WA, 1988); Maj, USA W. b 12 Jun 58. MA (Music Comp), BA (Music Perf); with
SMITH, Marcia (née Harvey), m 1981, Maj, USA W. b 23 Jan 59. BS (Chrstn Ldrshp).

SONDA, Jean-Pierre (Mahita, 1990); Maj, Con (Braz). b 28 Nov 56; with
SONDA, Jeannette (née Ndoudi) m 1988; Maj, Con (Braz). b 25 Jan 67.

SOUZA, Maruilson (Petrolina, 1987); Maj, Brz. b 6 May 64. BA (Acct), BA (Admin), BA (Theol), MA (Theol), PhD (Theol); with
SOUZA, Francisca (née Rodrigues) m 1982; Maj, Brz. b 15 Oct 66.

STARRETT, Daniel L. (Roswell, NM, USA W, 1973); Lt-Col, USA Nat. b 1 Jun 52. BS (Appl Bus & Mgmt), MBA; and
STARRETT, Helen (née Laverty) (San José, CA, USA W, 1973) m 1974; Lt-Col, USA Nat. b 20 Jul 48. Served in USA W and at IHQ.

STOCKMAN, Mona Valborg (née Ericson) (Uppsala, 1978); Maj, Swdn. b 24 Nov 46. BA (Sociol); and
STOCKMAN, Björn (Kalmar, 1981) m 1984; Maj, Swdn. b 12 Nov 51.

STRASSE, Wilson S. (Rio Grande, 1988); Maj, Brz. b 20 Jul 63; with
STRASSE, Nara (née Charão) m 1985; Maj, Brz. b 12 Feb 68.

STREET, Robert (Stotfold, UK, 1968); Comr, IHQ (IS Eur). b 24 Feb 47; with
STREET, Janet (née Adams) m 1967; Comr, IHQ (ZSWM Eur). b 19 Aug 45. Served in UK, Aus E (CS/TSWM) and at IHQ (IS to CoS/WSWM, IS/ZSWM SPEA).

STRICKLAND, Ron (Santa Barbara, CA, 1978); Lt-Col, USA W. b 7 Aug 45. BS (Bus Mgmt); and
STRICKLAND, Pamela (née Fuss) (Minot, ND, 1969) m 1970; Lt-Col, USA W. b 1 Dec 48.

STRISSEL, Dennis L. (St Louis Northside, MO, USA C, 1974); Col, TC, Gha. b 4 Mar 52; and
STRISSEL, Sharon (née Olson) (Sioux City, IA, USA C, 1974) m 1975; Col, TPWM, Gha. b 7 Oct 51. Served in USA C and S Afr.

SUNDARAM, Motchakan (Aramboly, 1974); Maj, Ind SE. b 17 Mar 50; and
SELVABAI, Motchakan (Kaliancaud, 1974) m 1975; Maj, Ind SE. b 2 May 50.

325

SUPARDI, Immanuel (Magelang, 1975); Maj, Indon. b 7 Nov 52; and
SUPARDI, Sinur - Hariandja (Medan, 1975) m 1977; Maj, Indon. b. 24 Jul 54.

SUSEELKUMAR, John (Pallickal, 1978); Maj, Ind SW. b 11 Oct 51. Ww Maj Aleyamma, pG 2007.

SWANSBURY, Charles (Croydon Citadel, UK, 1983); Maj, GS, Lib. b 7 Dec 52. BA, MBA; with
SWANSBURY, Denise (née Everett) m 1974; Maj, CSWM, Lib. b 9 Nov 53. BA. Served in UK, Zim and at IHQ.

SWANSON, Barry C. (Chicago Mt Greenwood, IL, USA C, 1978); Comr, IHQ (CoS). b 22 Apr 50. BS (Marketing); with
SWANSON, E. Sue (née Miller) m 1975; Comr, IHQ (WSWM). b 13 Aug 50. BA (Soc Work). Served in USA C (CS/TSWM, TC/TPWM), at USA Nat (Nat CS/NSWM) and at IHQ (IS/ZSWM Am and Carib).

T

TADI, Patrick (Bimbouloulou, 1984); Maj, Con (Braz). b 17 Apr 59; with
TADI, Clémentine (née Bassinguinina) m 1982; Maj, Con (Braz). b 4 Apr 58.

TAMPAI, Yusak (Turen, 1993); Maj, Indon. b 25 Mar 66; and
TAMPAI, Widiawati (Anca, 1995) m 1997; Maj, Indon. b 19 Apr 73. Served at ICO.

TAN, Thean Seng (Penang, 1966); Lt-Col, Sing. b 24 Jul 45; and
LOO, Lay Saik (Penang, 1966) m 1969; Lt-Col, Sing. b 12 Jul 47. Served at IHQ and in Sing (OC/CPWM) and HK (OC/CPWM).

TANAKA, Chieko (née Hirose) (Nishinari, 1977); Maj, Jpn. b 22 Apr 48; and
TANAKA, Teiichi (Omori, 1983) m 1984; Maj, Jpn. b 19 Feb 52. MA (Econ).

TANDAYAG, Susana (née Organo) (Santiago Isabela, 1989); Maj, Phil. b 26 Feb 60. BSc (Home Tech), BSSW; and
TANDAYAG, Miguel (Pasig, 1980) m 1982; Capt, Phil. b 30 Sep 58.

TARI, Samuel (Shantinagar, 1970); Maj, Pak. b 7 Sep 49; and
SAMUEL, Victoria (née Khurshid) (Khanewal, 1971) m 1973; Maj, Pak. b 15 Oct 52.

TATY, Daniel (Pointe-Noire, 1982), Maj, Con (Braz). b 14 Feb 54; with
TATY, Angèle (née Louya) m 1980; Maj, Con (Braz). b 6 Dec 56.

TEMINE, David (Lembina, 1992); Maj, PNG. b 12 May 70; and
TEMINE, Doreen (née A'o) (Kamila, 1999)

m 2002; Capt, PNG. b 24 Feb 73.

THAMALAPAKULA, Raj Paul (Rajahmundary, Ind C, 1996); Capt, Ind Nat. b 4 Aug 68; with
JAYA, Santha Kumari m 1993; Capt, Ind Nat. b 28 Jan 73. Served in Ind C.

THANHLIRA (Ratu, 1971); Maj, Ind E. b 15 Feb 49; and
THANTLUANGI (Central, 1975) m 1975; Maj, Ind E. b 5 Jan 50.

THARMAR, Alfred (Arumanai, 1977); Maj, Ind SE. b 23 May 54; and
RAJABAI, Alfred (Pottetty, 1975) m 1977; Maj, Ind SE. b 16 Apr 53.

THEODORE, Sinous (Luly, Haiti, 1981); Maj, Carib. b 20 Oct 52; and
THEODORE, Marie Lourdes (née Doralus) (Port-au-Prince, Haiti, 1981) m 1982; Maj, Carib. b 22 Sep 57.

THEU, Chatonda (Migowi, Mal, 1987); Maj, Zimb. b 3 Mar 59; with
THEU, Joyce (née Banda) m 1986; Maj, Zimb. b 5 Mar 65. Served in Mal.

THOMAS, Darrell (Southend Citadel, UK, 1975); Maj, Sing. b 28 Jun 53; and
THOMAS, Katrina (née Lagunowitsch) (Royston, UK, 1976) m 1976; Maj, Sing. b 27 Sep 51. Served in UK.

THOMSON, Robert E. (Evansville Asplan Citadel, IN, 1971); Maj, USA C. b 20 Nov 50. BS (Soc Wk), MSW; with
THOMSON, Nancy (née Philpot) m 1972; Maj, USA C. b 4 May 50.

THUMATI, Vijayakumar (Denduluru, Ind C, 1970); Lt-Col, CS, Ind SE. b 10 Jun 49; and
THUMATI, Keraham Manikyam Vijayakumar (née Karuhu) (Denduluru, Ind C, 1970) m 1971; Lt-Col, TSWM, Ind SE. b 17 Apr 53. Served in Ind C, Ind SE, Ban (GS/CSWM) and at Ind Nat.

TIDD, Floyd (Sudbury, ON, 1986); Col, CS, Can. b 11 Mar 61. BSc, MTS; with
TIDD, Tracey (née Blacklock) m 1982; Col, TSWM, Can. b 9 Jan 61.

TILLSLEY, Mark W. (East Northport, NY, 1987); Lt-Col, USA E. b 20 Nov 57. BA (Psychol/Sociol), MSW; with
TILLSLEY, Sharon (née Lowman) m 1979; Lt-Col, USA E. b 21 Jun 57. BS (Nursing).

TOKUNAGA, Kojiro (Kanda, 1984); Maj, Jpn. b 27 Apr 57. BSc (Engin); and
TOKUNAGA, Yumi (née Ryugo) (Tsuruhashi, 1977) m 1986; Maj, Jpn. b 28 Dec 55.

TOLLERUD, Douglas (Santa Ana, CA, 1983); Maj, USA W. b 16 Mar 57; with
TOLLERUD, Sheryl (née Smith) m 1978; Maj, USA W. b 12 Jan 59. BS (Org Mngmnt).

TRIM, Kester (Scarborough Citadel, ON, 1983);
Maj, Can. b 16 Jun 53. BA, MDiv; with
TRIM, Kathryn (née Webster) m 1976;
Maj, Can. b 2 Jun 54. BA. Served in Zai and
at IHQ (SALT College).

TURSI, Massimo (Naples, 1983); Maj, GS, It.
b 14 Nov 57; and
TURSI, Anne-Florence (née Cachelin)
(Bern I, Switz, 1983) m 1983; Maj, CSWM,
It. b 25 Mar 59. Served in Switz and Ger.

TVEDT, Terje (Trondheim, Nor, 1974). Maj,
Den. b 8 Jul 48. Served in Nor.

U

UNDERSRUD, Arne (Drammen, 1968); Maj,
Asst CS, Nor. b 15 Mar 44; and
UNDERSRUD, Anne Lise (née Bendiksen)
(Finnsnes, 1969) m 1974; Maj, Nor.
b 12 Feb 48. Served in UK.

URBIEN Elnora (Manila Central, 1980);
Lt-Col, Phil. b 4 Apr 50. BSc (Element Ed).
Served in PNG.

UWAK, Udoh (Ikot Obio Inyang, 1992); Maj,
Nig. b 2 Oct 66; with
UWAK, Esther m 1990; Maj, Nig. b 12 Dec 73.

V

VALDES, Victor (Piedras Negras, 1973); Maj,
Mex. b 28 Oct 53; and
VALDES, Marie (née Clara) (Reynosa
Temple, 1976) m 1977; Maj, Mex.
b 14 Oct 56. Served in USA S.

VAN DUINEN, Susan (née Jewers)
(Mississauga, ON, 1978); Maj, Can.
b 11 Mar 50. BA, MDiv; with
VAN DUINEN, Dirk m 1970; Maj.
b 13 Jun 49. Served Ger and Cze Rep.

VAN VLIET, Johan C. J. (Baarn, 1975);
Comr, TC, Neth. b 17 Jul 52. DSocS Admin;
with
VAN VLIET, Maria (née de Ruiter) m 1971;
Comr, TPWM, Neth. b 9 May 51. Served in
PNG (CS/TSWM).

VANDER WEELE, Richard E. (Kalamazoo,
MI, 1976); Lt-Col, USA C. b 19 May 48.
BS (Soc), MSW, Cert ACSW.

VARGHESE, Davidson (Trivandrum Central,
Ind SW, 1986); Lt-Col, Ind Nat. b 13 Dec 58.
BA; and
DAVIDSON, Mariamma (née Chacko)
(Adoor Central, Ind SW, 1985) m 1988;
Lt-Col, Ind Nat. b 1 May 65. Served in
Ind SW and Zam.

VARUGHESE, Wilfred (Trivandrum Central,
Ind SW, 1985); Col, CS, Zim. b 25 Mar 58.
BSc, BTS; and

WILFRED, Prema (née Prema) (Anayara,
Ind SW, 1987) m 1987; Col, TSWM, Zim.
b 25 May 60. BA, BD. Served in Ind SW and
at Ind Nat.

VELE, David (Hohola, 1997); Capt, PNG .
b 9 May 66; with
VELE, Rita (née Pisin) m 1994; Capt, PNG.
b 26 Sep 73.

VENTER, Alistair (Cape Town Citadel, 1981);
Maj, S Afr. b 19 Aug 58. ThA, BTh; and
VENTER, Marieke (née van Leeuwen)
(Benoni, 1988) m 1987; Maj, S Afr. b 31 Dec
62, BCur (Hons), MTh.

VERA, Facundo (Tampico, 1970); Maj, Mex.
b 27 Nov 48; and
VERA, Bersábe (née Hernández)
(Coatzacoalcos, 1969) m 1971; Maj, Mex.
b 12 Oct 49.

VERU, Zarena (Bhogiwal, 1973); Lt-Col, Pak.
b 1 Jan 52.

VOORHAM, Christina (The Hague South,
1970); Lt-Col, Neth. b 2 Sep 46.

VYLE, Bruce (Hamilton City, 1995); Maj, NZ.
b 5 Jun 46. MA, BA, DipT; with
VYLE, Elaine (née French) m 1968; Maj,
NZ. b 9 Jul 48.

W

WAINWRIGHT, John (Reading Central,
UK, 1979); Col, TC, Zamb. b 13 Mar 51; with
WAINWRIGHT, Dorita (née Willetts)
m 1976; Col, TPWM, Zamb. b 19 Oct 51.
Served in UK, E Afr and Zimb.

WALKER, Peter (Morley, 1982); Col, CS,
Aus S. b 2 Mar 54. BA (Soc); with
WALKER, Jennifer (née Friend) m 1975;
Col, TSWM, Aus S. b 26 Feb 56. BEd.
Served in Mlys.

WALTERS, Rodney (Bundamba, 1983); Maj,
Aus E. b 9 Jan 59. BAL; and
WALTERS, Wendy (née Woodbury)
(Wollongong, 1983) m 1985; Maj, Aus E.
b 15 May 61. Served in Rus.

WALZ, Reinhold (Reutligen, 1975); Maj, Ger.
b 10 Sep 52; and
WALZ, Ruth (née Beckschulte) (Nuremberg,
1987) m 1987; Maj, Ger. b 10 Jul 56.

WANDULU, Moses (Bumbo, 1986); Lt-Col,
OC, Uga. b 5 Aug 60; with
WANDULU, Sarah (née Rwolekya) m 1986;
Lt-Col, CPWM, Uga. b 30 Aug 1964. Served
in E Afr

WANJARE, Sanjay (Vithalwadi, 1994);
Capt, Ind W. b 10 Oct 67. Ww Capt Sunita,
pG 2010.

WANYAMA, Sarah (Wabukhonyi, Ken E, 1978); Lt-Col, Ken W. b 3 Mar 56. Served in Ken E.

WARD, H. Alfred (Atlanta Temple, GA, USA S, 1971); Lt-Col, CS, Brz. b 2 Aug 46. BA (Chem), MBA; with
WARD, Mary M. (née Busby); Lt-Col, TSWM, Brz. b 13 Nov 47. BVA. Served in USA S and Aus E.

WARD, Robert (Brock Avenue, TO, Can, 1970); Col, TC, Pak. b 22 Feb 48. MHSc (Health Mgmt), BA (Adm); and
WARD, Marguerite (née Simon) (Swift Current, SK, Can, 1970) m 1971; Col, TPWM, Pak. b 13 May 48. Served in Can, S Afr, Zimb (CS/TSWM) and USA C.

WATERS, Frederick (Mississauga, ON, 1983); Maj, Can. b 24 Dec 56; with
WATERS, Wendy (née Kitney) m 1979; Maj, Can. b 22 Jul 57.

WATT, Neil (Montreal Citadel, 1977); Lt-Col, Can. b 4 Nov 48. BTh; with
WATT, Lynda (née Westover) m 1968; Lt-Col , Can. b 5 May 46. Served in UK.

WATTERS, Alan (Cape Town Citadel, S Afr/ Brighton East, 1987); Maj, UK. b 2 May 53. BD; with
WATTERS, Linda (née Farrier) m 1980; Maj, UK. b 13 Nov 56. Served in S Afr.

WATTS, Gavin (Carina, 1994); Maj, Aus E. b 30 Oct 69. Dip Min, Dip Bus; with
WATTS, Wendy (née Wallis) m 1990; Maj, Aus E. b 27 Apr 68. DipTeach, DipMin. Served in NZ.

WEBB, Geoff (Ulverstone, 1984); Maj, Aus S. b 18 Jan 59; and
WEBB, Kalie (née Down) (Box Hill, 1997) m 1993; Maj, Aus S. b. 9 Jul 69. Served in Pak.

WEBB, Neil (Nottingham New Basford, UK, 1983); Lt-Col, CS, PNG. b 6 Sep 58; and
WEBB, Christine (née Holdstock) (Bromley, UK, 1983) m 1983; Lt-Col, TSWM, PNG. b 1 Mar 55. BA, Dip RS. Served in UK.

WEBER, Stephan (Nuremberg, 1987); Maj, Ger. b 5 Jul 59; with
WEBER, Andrea (née Mueller) m 1982; Maj, Ger. b 21 Mar 63.

WELANDER, Knud David (Copenhagen Temple, Den/Oslo Temple, Nor, 1984); Lt-Col, Phil. b 20 May 61. BSc (Bus Admin); and
WELANDER, Lisbeth (née Wederhus) (Florø, 1984) m 1984; Lt-Col, Phil. b 29 Nov 63. Served in Nor.

WESTRUPP, Andrew (Dunedin South, 1980); Maj, NZ. b 4 Oct 54; with
WESTRUPP, Yvonne (née Medland) m 1974; Maj, NZ. b 13 Jul 54.

WEYMOUTH, James (Adelaide Congress Hall, Aus S, 1976); Maj, Zam. b 14 Nov 51. BA, BTh; and
WEYMOUTH, Marion (née Campbell) (Adelaide Congress Hall, Aus S, 1977); m 1977; Maj, Zam. b 3 Feb 50. Served in Aus S and HK.

WHITE, Charles (Owensboro, KY, 1967); Lt-Col, USA S. b 7 May 46; with
WHITE, Shirley (née Sanders) m 1962; Lt-Col, USA S. b 24 Apr 43.

WICKINGS, Margaret (Welling, UK, 1976); Maj, IHQ. b 15 Apr 51. BEd, MTh. Served in UK, Zam, E Afr and Gha.

WIDYANOADI, Wayan (Semarang 2, 1990); Maj, Indon. b 2 Jan 68; and
WIDYANOADI, Herlina (née Ayawaila) (Bandung, 1995) m 1995; Maj, Indon. b 30 Jan 65.

WILKINSON, Darrell (Long Bay, Barbados, 1985); Maj, Carib. b 1 Apr 55; and
WILKINSON, Joan (née Marshall) (Carlton, Barbados, 1985) m 1986; Maj, Carib. b 18 Sep 58.

WILLERMARK, Marie (Göteborg 1, 1980); Comr, TC, TPWM, Swdn. b 18 Jun 54. Served in Den and E Eur.

WILLIAMS, John (Murukondapadu, 1991); Maj, Ind C. b 7 May 66. Ww Capt K. Mary Rani; and
WILLIAMS, Ratna Sundari (Murukondapadu, 2000) m 1999; Capt, Ind C. b 22 Nov 67.

WILLIAMS, Michael (Bristol Easton Road, 1967); Lt-Col, UK. b 16 Dec 46. Served at IHQ. m 1969; Lt-Col Ruth, ret 2004.

WITTWER, Bernhard (Brienz, 1988); Maj, Switz. b 1 Feb 61; with
WITTWER, Regina (née Mäder) m 1983; Maj, Switz. b 22 May 63.

WOLTERINK, Theo (Hengelo, 1974); Lt-Col, Neth. b 16 Jun 47; with
WOLTERINK, Albertine (née Riezebos) m 1970; Lt-Col, Neth. b 17 Feb 46. Served at IHQ, in Cz R and Neth (CS/TSWM).

WOODALL, Ann (Croydon Citadel, UK, 1969); Comr, IHQ (IS Bus Adm). b 3 Feb 50. MA, MSc, FCCA, PhD. Served in Con, Zam, Zaï and UK.

WOODWARD, Cecil (Coorparoo, 1969); Maj, Aus E. b 3 Jun 46. BSW (Hons), MSWAP, MBA; and
WOODWARD, Catherine (née Lucas)

(Miranda, 1969) m 1970; Maj, Aus E.
b 20 Jan 48

Y

YANDERAVE, Borley (Lembina, 1991); Maj,
PNG. b 7 Oct 58; with
YANDERAVE, Iveme (née John) m 1985;
Maj, PNG. b 25 Oct 66.
YANG, Tae-soo (Chun Yun, 1978); Lt-Col, Kor.
b 14 Feb 47; with
CHUN, Ok-kyung m 1968; Lt-Col, Kor.
b 14 Jul 47. Served in Sing.
YESUDAS, Kancherla (Pedapalli, 1984); Maj,
Ind C. b 13 Apr 54. BA (Econ); with
YESUDAS, Hemalatha (née Devi) m 1979;
Maj, Ind C. b 16 Jul 58.
YOHANNAN, C. S. (Kaithaparambu, 1975);
Maj, Ind SW. b 8 Jan 54; and
YOHANNAN, L. Rachel (Pathanapuram,
1979) m 1978; Maj, Ind SW. b 31 Jul 55.
YOHANNAN, P. J. (Oollayam Kangazha, 1978);
Maj, Ind SW. b 17 May 49; and
YOHANNAN, Annamma (Oollayam
Kangazha, 1981) m 1981; Maj, Ind SW.
b 31 Aug 55.
YOSHIDA, Makoto (Shibuya, 1969); Comr,
TC, Jap. b 7 Dec 45. BSc (Engin); and

YOSHIDA, Kaoru (née Imamura) (Omori,
1971) m 1974; Comr, TPWM, Jap. b 13 Jan 45.
Served in Jpn (CS/TSWM) and at IHQ (IS/
ZSWM SPEA).
YOSHIDA, Tsukasa (Shibuya, 1982); Maj,
Jpn. b 26 Nov 54; and
YOSHIDA, Kyoko (née Tsuchiya) (Kiyose,
1980) m 1982; Maj, Jpn. b 13 Oct 53.

Z

ZACHARIAH, Juppalli (Hutti, Ind C, 1983);
Maj, Sri Lan. b 6 May 54. BA; with
ZACHARIAH, Usha Rani (née Perumalla)
m 1980; Maj, Sri Lan. b 15 Jun 65. Served in
Ind C.
ZIPINGANI, Langton (Pearson, 1987); Lt-Col,
Zimb. b 22 Nov 61; and
ZIPINGANI, Beauty (née Chimunda)
(Mutonda, 1987) m 1989; Lt-Col, Zimb.
b 2 Aug 66.
ZOLA, Ambroise (Kingudi, DR Con, 1979);
Lt-Col, OC, Ang. b 6 Sep 52; with
ZOLA, Alphonsine Kuzoma (née Nsiesi)
m 1976; Lt-Col, CPWM, Ang. b 2 Jan 57.
Served in Con (Kin) and Con (Braz)
(CS/TSWM)

Retired Generals and Commissioners

The following list contains the names of retired Generals, commissioners and lieut-commissioners, and widows of lieut-commissioners and above, as at 30 November 2010

A

ADIWINOTO, Lilian E. (Malang, Indon, 1954); Comr b 31 Jul 27. Served in UK, Indon (TC) and at IHQ.

ASANO, Hiroshi (Shizuoka, Jpn, 1950); Comr b 5 May 27; and Mrs Comr **Tomoko** (née Ohara) (Kyoto, 1953) m 1955. Served in Jpn (TC/TPWO).

B

BAILLIE, Kenneth (Warren, USA E, 1966); Comr b 3 Nov 42. BA (Soc); with Comr **Joy M.** (née Gabrielsen) m 1962; b 30 May 41. BA (Biochem). Served in Can, USA E, E Eur (OC/CPWO) and USA C (TC/TPWM).

BANKS, Keith (Wokingham, UK, 1963); Comr b 5 Nov 42. Served in UK, PNG (OC), Jpn (CS) and at IHQ (IS Int Per). Ww Comr Pauline, pG 2008.

BASSETT, W. Todd (Syracuse Citadel, NY, USA E, 1965); Comr b 25 Aug 39. BEd; with Comr **Carol A.** (née Easterday) m 1960; b 10 Dec 40. BEd. Served in USA E, at IHQ (IS to CoS/Mission Res Sec) and at USA Nat (NC/NPWM).

BATH, Vida (née McNeill) (Moree, Aus E, 1945); Mrs Comr. Served in Sri Lan, Ind W, Ind NE, Ind SW, at IHQ and in Aus E. Ww Comr Robert, pG 2006.

BAXENDALE, David A. (Pittsburgh, PA, USA E, 1954); Comr b 23 Apr 30. MA (Col), BSc (Sprd); with Mrs Comr **Alice** (née Chamberlain); BMus Ed (Syra). Served in USA A, USA W (CS/THLS), Carib (TC/ TPWO), S Am W (TC/TPWO), at ICO (Principal) and IHQ (IS/SWO Am and Carib).

BIMWALA, Zunga Mbanza Etienne (Kinshasa 1, Zaï, 1959); Comr b 29 Sep 32. Served in Zaï (TC) and Switz. Ww Mrs Comr Alice, pG 2004.

BIRD, Patricia (Fulham, UK, 1958); Comr b 7 Aug 35. Served in Nig, UK, Zam (TC) and at IHQ (IS Fin, IS Afr).

BOVEN van, Johannes (The Hague, Neth, 1955); Comr b 9 Jan 35; and Comr **Klazina** (née Grauwmeijer) (Rotterdam, 1959) m 1960;

b 22 Sep 35. Served in Neth (TC/TPWO).

BRAUN, Françoise (née Volet) (Vevey, Frce, 1968); Comr b 8 Dec 43. Served in Frce and Switz. Ww Comr Edouard, pG 2010.

BROWN, Jean (née Barclay) (Montreal Citadel, Can, 1938); Mrs General. Served at IHQ and in Can. Ww General Arnold Brown, pG 2002.

BUCKINGHAM, Lorraine (née Smith) (Waimate, NZ, 1960); Comr. Served in Aus S, NZ and Aus E. Ww Comr Hillmon, pG 2009.

BURROWS, Eva Evelyn General (1986-93) (see page 25).

BUSBY, John A. (Atlanta Temple, GA, USA S, 1963); Comr b 14 Oct 37. BA (Asbury); with Comr **Elsie Louise** (née Henderson) m 1958; b 11 Jun 36. Served in Can (CS/ TSWO), USA S (TC/TPWO) and USA Nat (NC/NPWM).

C

CACHELIN, Genevieve (née Booth) (Paris Central, Frce, 1947); Mrs Comr. MA. Served in Switz, Belg, Frce, Ger, BT and at IHQ. Ww Comr Francy, pG 2007

CAIRNS, Alistair G. (West End, Aus E, 1942); Comr b 12 Dec 16. AM, Order of Australia (1996). Served in Kor, Aus E (CS), at ITC and in S Afr (TC). Ww Mrs Comr Margery, pG 2006.

CAIRNS, Beulah (née Harris) (Parramatta, Aus E, 1959); Mrs Comr. Served in Aus E and at IHQ. Ww Comr William, pG 2008.

CALVERT, Ruth (Port Hope, ON, 1955); Mrs Comr b 8 Feb 35. Served in Aus E. Ww Comr Roy, pG 1994.

CAMPBELL, Donald (Highgate, Aus S, 1945); Comr b 31 Oct 23. Served in NZ (TC) and Aus S (TC). Ww Comr Crystal, pG 2008.

CHANG, Peter Hei-dong (Seoul Central, Kor, 1960); Comr b 12 May 32. BD, STm (Union, NY), BTh MEd (Columbia, NY); and Comr **Grace Eun-Shik** (née Chung) (Seoul, Kor, 1963) m 1963. BA, BMus (Seoul Nat). Served in UK, Sing, HK, USA E, Kor

(CS/THLS, TC/TPWO), USA W (TC/TPWO) and at IHQ.

CHEVALLY, Simone (née Gindraux) (Lausanne 1, Switz, 1947); Mrs Comr. Served in Switz and at IHQ. Ww Comr Robert, pG 1989.

CHIANGHNUNA (Ngupa, Ind W, 1951); Comr b 10 Jun 29; and Mrs Comr **Barbara** (née Powell) (Ware, UK, 1948) m 1968. Served in Ind N (CS/THLS), Ind E (CS/THLS) and Ind W (TC/TPWO).

CHUN, Kwang-pyo (Duk Am, Kor, 1971); Comr b 15 Sep 41; with Comr **Yoo, Sung-ja** m 1969; b 11 Jan 41. Served in Kor (CS/TSWM) (TC/TPWM).

CLAUSEN, Siegfried (Catford, UK, 1958); Comr b 4 Mar 38; and Comr **Inger-Lise** (née Lydholm) (Valby, 1958) m 1961; b 1 Oct 39. Served in UK, S Am W, Sp (OC/CPWO), L Am N (TC/TPWO), Ger (TC/TPWO) and at IHQ (IS/SWM Am and Carib).

CLINCH, John H. (Fairfield, Aus S, 1956); Comr b 30 Nov 30; with Comr **Beth** (née Barker). Served in Aus S, Aus E (CS/THLS), at IHQ (IS/SWO SPEA) and in Aus S (TC/TPWO).

COLES, Alan C. (Harrow, UK, 1953); Comr b 2 Feb 25. ACIB. Ww Heather, pG 1978; and Mrs Comr **Brenda** (née Deeming) (Tipton, UK, 1959) m 1980. Served in Zimb (TC) and at IHQ.

COLES, Dudley (North Toronto, ON, Can, 1954); Comr b 22 Mar 26; and Mrs Comr **Evangeline** (née Oxbury) (Powell River, BC, Can, 1954) m 1956. Served in Can, Ind Audit, Ind W, Sri Lan (TC/TPWO) and at IHQ (IS/SWO S Asia).

COOPER, Raymond A. (Washington Georgetown, DC, USA S, 1956); Comr b 24 May 37; and Comr **Merlyn S.** (née Wishon) (Winston Salem Southside, NC, USA S, 1957) m 1959; b 2 Sep 36. Served in USA C and USA S (TC/TPWO).

COX, Hilda (née Chevalley) (Geneva, 1949); Mrs Comr. Served in UK, Zam, Zimb, Frce, Neth and at IHQ (WSHL). Ww Comr Ron, pG 1995.

CUTMORE, Ian (Tamworth, Aus E, 1954); Comr b 27 Sep 33; and Comr **Nancy** (née Richardson) (Atherton, Aus E, 1957). Served in Aus E, PNG, UK (CS/TSWO), ICO (Principal) and NZ (TC/TPWO).

D

DAVIS, Douglas E. (Moreland, Aus S, 1960); Comr b 12 Feb 37; with Comr **Beverley J.**

(née Roberts) m 1958; b 23 Feb 38. Served in NZ, UK (CS/TSWO) and Aus S (TC/TPWO).

DELCOURT, France (née Bardiaux) (Lyon 1, Frce, 1943); Mrs Comr. Served in BT and Frce. Ww Comr Raymond A., pG 2010.

DEVAVARAM, Prathipati (New Colony, Ind C, 1964); Comr b 15 Nov 46. MBBS, BSc; and Comr **P. Victoria** (Bapatla Central, Ind C, 1970) m 1974; b 25 Nov 49. BSc, BEd, BLSc. Served in Ind C, at Ind Nat, in Ind E and Ind SE (TC/TPWM).

DIAKANWA, Mbakanu (Poste Francais, Kin, Zaï, 1949); Comr b 1923. Officier de l'Ordre du Leopard (1981). Served in Zaï (TC). Ww Comr Situwa, pG 1998.

DITMER, Anne (née Sharp) (Dayton Central, OH, USA E, 1957) Mrs Comr. Served in USA S, USA C and USA E. Ww Comr Stanley, pG 2003.

DUNSTER, Robin (Dulwich Hill Temple, Aus E, 1970); Comr b 12 Jan 44. SRN, SCM, RPN, RMN, IPPF (Ed). Served in Aus E, Zimb (CS), Con (Kin) (TC, TPWO), Phil (TC, TPWM) and at IHQ (CoS).

DU PLESSIS, Paul (Salt River, S Afr, 1968); Comr b 3 Jul 41. MB ChB, MRCP, DTM&H; with Comr **Margaret** (née Siebrits); m 1964; b 17 Jul 42. BSoc Sc. Served in Zam, Ind C (TC/TPWO), S Afr (TC/TPWO) and at IHQ.

DURMAN, Vera (née Livick) (South Croydon, UK, 1942) Mrs Comr. Served in UK, Ind W and at IHQ. Ww Comr David, pG 2010.

DWYER, June M. (Windsor, NS, Can, 1952); Comr. b 28 Aug 32. Served at USA Nat, in S Afr (CS) and at IHQ (IS Admin).

E

EDWARDS, David (New Market Street, Georgetown, Guyana, Carib, 1962); Comr b 15 May 41; and Comr **Doreen** (née Bartlett) (Wellington St, Barbados, Carib, 1957) m 1966; b 4 Mar 35. Served in USA E, Carib (TC/TPWO), at IHQ (IS/SWO Am and Carib) and in USA W (TC/TPWO).

EGGER, Verena (née Halbenleib) (Solothurn, Switz, 1945); Mrs Comr. Served in Carib and C Am, Zaï, Mex and C Am, S Am E and Switz. Ww Comr Jacques, pG 2001.

ELIASEN, Carl S. (Gartnergade, Den, 1951); Comr b 28 Mar 32. Served in Port (OC), Brz (TC), S Am W (TC) and at IHQ (IS Americas). Ww Comr Maria, pG 2003.

EVANS, Willard S. (Greenville, SC, USA S, 1949), Comr b 2 Sep 24. BA (Bob Jones Univ); with Mrs Comr **Marie** (née Fitton).

Served in USA S, USA E (CS/THLS) and USA W (TC/TPWO).

F

FEWSTER, Lilian (née Hunt) (Hanwell, UK, 1931); Mrs Comr. Served in UK, Can and Zimb. Ww Comr Ernest, pG 1973.

FREI, Werner (Rorbas, Switz, 1965); Comr b 6 Mar 40; and Comr **Paula** (née Berweger) (Heiden, Switz, 1965) m 1967; b 19 Mar 36. Served in Switz (CS/TSWO) and Ger (TC/TPWM).

FULLARTON, Frank (Bromley, UK, 1955); Comr b 3 Mar 31. BSc, DipSoc; and Comr **Rosemarie** (née Steck) (Croydon Citadel, UK, 1958) m 1959. BEd (Hons), MITD. Served at IHQ (CS to CoS, IS/SWO Eur), Soc S (GBI) (Ldr) and in Switz (TC/TPWO).

G

GAITHER, Israel L. (New Castle, PA, USA E, 1964); Comr b 27 Oct 44. Hon LHD, Hon DD; and Comr **Eva D.** (née Shue) (Sidney, OH, USA E, 1964) m 1967; b 9 Sep 43. Served in USA E (CS/TSWO) (TC/TPWM), S Afr (TC/TPWO), at IHQ (CoS/WSWM) and USA Nat (NC/NPWM, USA).

GAUNTLETT, Marjorie (née Markham) (Wood Green, UK, 1952); Mrs Comr. Served at ITC, in Zimb, Frce, Ger, Switz and at IHQ (WSHL). Ww Comr Caughey, pG 2009.

GOODIER, William Robert (Atlanta Temple, GA, USA S, 1941); Comr b 23 May 16; with Mrs Comr **Renee** (née Tilley). Served in USA S (CS/THLS), at USA Nat (CS/NHLS), in Aus S (TC/TPWO) and USA E (TC/TPWO).

GOWANS, John General (1999-2002) (see page 26); and Comr **Gisèle** (née Bonhotal) (Paris Central, Frce, 1955) m 1957. Served in USA W, Frce (TPWO), Aus E (TPWO), UK (TPWO) and at IHQ (WPWM).

GRIFFIN, Joy (née Button) (Tottenham Citadel, UK, 1957); Mrs Lt-Comr. Served in BT. Ww Lt-Comr Frederick, pG 1990.

GRINSTED, Dora (née Bottle) (Sittingbourne, UK, 1950); Mrs Comr. Served in UK, Zam, Zimb, Jpn and at IHQ. Ww Comr David Ramsay, pG 1992.

GULLIKSEN, Thorleif R. (Haugesund, Nor, 1967); Comr b 26 Apr 40; with Comr **Olaug** (née Henriksen) m 1962; b 25 Jan 38. Served in Nor, Neth (TC/TPWO) and at IHQ (IS/SWM Eur).

H

HANNEVIK, Anna (Bergen 2, Nor, 1947); Comr

b 9 Aug 25. Served in Nor, UK (Ldr SocS), Swdn (TC) and at IHQ (IS Eur). Paul Harris Medal (1987), Commander of the Royal Order of the Northern Star (Sweden).

HANNEVIK, Edward (Oslo 3, Nor, 1954); Comr b 6 Dec 32; and Comr **Margaret** (née Moody) (Newfield, UK, 1956) m 1958. Served in UK, Den (TC/TPWO), Nor (TC/TPWO) and at IHQ (IS/SWO Eur).

HARITA, Nozomi (Shibuya, Jap, 1966); Comr b 10 May 39. BA (Mus); and Comr **Kazuko** (née Hasegawa) (Shibuya, Jap, 1966) m 1969; b 19 Dec 37. BA (Ed). Served in Aus E and Jap (TC/TPWM).

HARRIS, Bramwell Wesley (Cardiff Stuart Hall, UK, 1948); Comr b 25 Nov 28; and Mrs Comr **Margaret** (née Sansom) (Barking, UK, 1949), m 1955. Served in UK, at IHQ, in Aus S (CS/THLS), Scot (TC/THLP), NZ (TC/TPWO) and Can (TC/TPWO).

HAWKINS, Mary (née McElroy) (Partick, UK, 1949); Mrs Comr. Served in UK and at IHQ. Ww Comr Peter, pG 2010.

HEDBERG, Lennart (Nykoping, Swdn, 1954); Comr b 12 Oct 32; and Comr **Ingvor** (née Fagerstedt) (Nykoping, Swdn, 1955) m 1956. Served in Den, Swdn (TC/TPWO) and at IHQ (IS/SWO Eur).

HINSON, Harold D. (High Point, NC, USA S, 1955); Comr b 7 Sep 35; and Comr **Betty M.** (née Morris) (New Orleans, LA, USA S, 1955); b 1 Jun 35. Served in USA S (CS/THLS) and USA C (TC/TPWO).

HODDER, Kenneth L. (San Francisco Citadel, CA, USA W, 1958); Comr b 30 Oct 30. BA (Richmond), DSS (Hons) (Richmond), JD (California); and Comr **Marjorie J.** (née Fitton) (San Francisco Citadel, CA, USA W, 1958). Served in USA W, USA C, Aus S (CS), USA S (TC/TPWO) and at USA Nat (NC/NPWM).

HOLLAND, Louise (née Cruickshank) (Invercairn, UK, 1958); Mrs Comr. Served in UK, E Afr, Nig, Gha, Pak and at IHQ. Ww Comr Arthur, pG 1998.

HOOD, H. Kenneth (Denver Citadel, CO, USA W, 1954); Comr b 27 Jan 33; and Comr **Barbara** (née Johnson) (Pasadena, CA, USA W, 1952) m 1957. Served in USA W (CS/THLS), at USA Nat (CS/Asst NPWO) and in USA S (TC/TPWO).

HOUGHTON, Raymond (Woodhouse, UK, 1967); Comr b 12 Apr 44. MCMI; with Comr **Judith** (née Jones) m 1965; b 15 Nov 45. Served in UK (CS/TSWO), at IHQ (IS to CoS/Mission Resources

Sec) and in Carib (TC/TPWM).

HOWE, Norman (Dartford, UK, 1957); Comr b 13 Aug 36; and Comr **Marian** (née Butler) (Boscombe, UK, 1953) m 1959; b 9 Feb 30. Cert Ed. Served in UK, at ITC (Principal), in Aus S (TC/TPWO), Can (TC/TPWO) and at IHQ (IS Prog Res/SWO Eur, General's Travelling Representative).

HUGHES, Alex (Paisley West, UK, 1960); Comr b 29 Jan 42; and Comr **Ingeborg** (née Clausen) (Catford, UK, 1964) m 1971; b 2 Jan 42. Served in L Am N, S Am E (CS/THLS, TC/TPWO), S Am W (TC/TPWO), at IHQ (IS/SWO Am and Carib) and in UK (TC/TPWM).

HUGUENIN, Willy (Le Locle, Switz, 1954); Comr b 22 Sep 31; and Mrs Comr **Miriam** (née Luthi) (La Chaux-de-Fonds, Switz, 1953) m 1955. Served in Zaï (GS), Con (TC/TPWO), Switz (TC/TPWO) and at IHQ (IS/SWO Afr).

I

IRWIN, Ronald G. (Philadelphia, PA, USA E, 1957); Comr b 4 Aug 33. BS (Rutgers), MA (Columbia); and Comr **Pauline** (née Laipply) (Cincinnati, OH, USA E, 1953) m 1967. Served in USA W (CS/THLS) and USA E (TC/TPWO).

ISRAEL, Jillapegu (Peralipadu, Ind N, 1957); Comr b 31 May 32. BA, BEd; with Comr **Rachel** (née Amarthaluri); Served in Ind M & A (CS/THLS), Ind N (TC/TPWO) and Ind SW (TC/TPWO).

K

KANG, Sung-hwan (Noh Mai Sil, Kyung Buk, Kor, 1973); Comr b 15 Dec 39; with Comr **Lee, Jung-ok** m1970; b 10 Nov 49. Served in Aus S and Kor (TC/TPWM).

KELLNER, Paul S. (Miami Citadel, FL, USA S, 1963); Comr b 1 Sep 35. BMus; with Comr **Jajuan** (née Pemberton); b 23 Feb 39. Served in USA S, Carib, Con (Braz) and Zimb (TC/TPWO).

KENDREW, K. Ross (Sydenham, NZ, 1962); Comr b 7 Dec 38; and Comr **M. June** (née Robb) (Wanganui, NZ, 1961) m 1964; b 8 Oct 39. Served in NZ (TC/TPWO) and Aus S (TC/TPWM).

KERR, Donald (Vancouver Temple, BC, Can, 1955); Comr b 25 Oct 33; and Comr **Joyce** (née Knaap) (Mt Dennis, ON, 1955) m 1957; b 12 Jan 35. Served in UK (CS) and Can (TC/TPWO).

KIM, Suk-tai (Choon Chun, Kor, 1957); Comr b 23 Jan 26. ThB, BA, MSoc; and **Lim,**

Jung-sun (Sudaemun, Kor, 1969) m 1975. BMus. Served in Kor (TC/TPWO).

KING, Margaret (née Coull) (Fairview, S Afr, 1936); Mrs Comr. Served in S Afr. Ww Comr Hesketh, pG 1990.

KJELLGREN, Hasse (Östra Kåren, Swdn, 1971); Comr b 1 Nov 45. BSc; and Comr **Christina** (née Forssell) (Hisingskaren, Swdn, 1971) m 1971; b 21 May 47. Served in S Am E (TC/TPWO), Switz (TC/TPWM), Swdn (TC/TPWM) and at IHQ (IS/ZSWM Eur).

L

LALTHANNGURA (Ratu, Ind E, 1963); Comr b 15 Sep 38. BA; with **Kaphliri**; b 9 Sep 43. Served in Ind C (CS/THLS) and Ind E (TC/TPWM).

LANG, Ivan B. (Auburn, Aus S, 1967); Comr b 18 Jul 40. AM, Order of Australia (2007), with Comr **Heather C.** (née Luhrs) m 1961; b 8 Dec 42. Served in Sing (OC/CPWO), Aus E (CS/TSWO), at IHQ (IS/SWM SPEA) and in Aus S (TC/TPWM).

LARSSON, John General (2002-06) (see page 26); and Comr **Freda** (née Turner) (Kingston-upon-Thames, UK, 1964) m 1969. Served in S Am W (THLS), at ITC, in UK (TPWO), NZ (TPWO), Swdn (TPWO) and at IHQ (WSWM, WPWM).

LEE, Sung-duk (Cho Kang, Kor, 1963); Comr b 10 Jun 35; with Comr **Cho, In-sun** (Taejon Central, Kor, 1963) m 1961; b 8 May 40. Served in Kor (TC/TPWM).

LIM, Ah Ang (Balestier Rd, Sing, 1954); Comr b 30 May 32; and Comr **Fong Pui Chan** (Singapore Central, 1954) m 1958. Served in Sing, HK (OC/CPWO), Phil (TC/TPWO) and at IHQ (IS/SWO SPEA).

LINDBERG, Ingrid E. (Norrköping, Swdn, 1951); Comr b 12 Dec 25. Served in Swdn, Zimb, Phil (OC), Den (TC) and Fin (TC).

LINNETT, Merle (née Clinch) (Hindmarsh, Aus S, 1947); Mrs Comr. Served in NZ, at IHQ, ITC, ICO and in Aus S. Ww Comr Arthur, pG 1986.

LOVATT, Olive (née Chapman) (Doncaster, UK, 1949); Mrs Comr. Served in UK, Aus S, Aus E & PNG and at IHQ. Ww Comr Roy, pG 2000.

LUDIAZO, Jean Bakidi (Salle Centrale, Kinshasa, Con (Kin), 1971); Comr b 19 Nov 45; with Comr **Véronique** (née Lusieboko Lutatabio) m 1970; b 26 Sep 53. Served in Con, Can, Con (Kin) (TC/TPWM) and Nig (TC/TPWM).

LUTTRELL, Bill (Greeley, CO, USA W, 1958);

Comr b 4 Jul 38. BA Soc; and Comr **Gwendolyn** (née Shinn) (Long Beach, CA, USA W, 1961) m 1962; b 3 Sep 38. BA Soc. Served at IHQ (IS/SWO Am and Carib) and in Can (TC/TPWM) and USA W (CS/TSWO, TC/TPWM).

LYDHOLM, Carl A. S. (Gartnergade, Den, 1966); Comr b 14 Nov 45; and Comr **Gudrun** (née Arskog) (Odense, Den, 1967) m 1967; b 5 Aug 47. MTh. Served in Den, UK, Rus/CIS (GS/CSWM), Fin (TC/TPWM) and Nor (TC/TPWM).

LYSTER, Ingrid (Valerenga, Nor, 1947); Comr b 7 Apr 22. BA (S Afr). Served in Nig, Zimb, Nor (CS) and at ICO (Principal).

M

MABENA, William (Bloemfontein, S Afr, 1959); Comr b 23 May 40; and Comr **Lydia** (née Lebusho) (Bloemfontein, S Afr, 1959) m 1960; b 25 Jun 39. Served in UK, S Afr (CS/THLS, TC/TPWM), Gha (TC/TPWO) and at IHQ (IS/SWO Afr).

MAILLER, Georges (Neuchatel, Switz, 1961); Comr b 9 Nov 36. BTh; with Comr **Muriel** (née Aeberli) m 1959; b 15 Apr 35. Served at ESFOT, in Frce and Switz (TC/TPWO).

MAKOUMBOU, Antoine (Bacongo, Con (Braz), 1968); Comr b 2 Mar 40; with Comr **Véronique** (née Niangui) m 1967; b 30 Aug 46. Served in Con (Braz) (TC/TPWM).

MANNAM, Samuel (Duggirala, Ind N, 1946); Comr b 3 Jun 21. Ww Mrs M., pG 1974; and Mrs Comr **Ruby** (née Manuel) (Leyton Citadel, UK, 1953) m 1975. Served in Ind M & A (TC/TPWO), Ind W (TC/TPWO), Ind SW (TC/TPWO), Ind E (TC/TPWO) and Ind N (TC/TPWO).

MARSHALL, Marjorie (née Kimball) (New York Temple, USA E, 1944); Mrs Comr. Served in USA C, USA E, at IHQ and at USA Nat. Ww Comr Norman S., pG 1995.

MASIH, Mohan (Khundi, Ind W, 1961); Comr b 29 Sep 39; with Comr **Swarni** m 1958; b 14 Mar 42. Served in Ind N (CS/THLS, Ind C (TC/TPWO), Ind SW (TC/TPWO) and Ind W (TC/TPWM).

MAXWELL, Earle Alexander (Orange, Aus E, 1954); Comr b 8 Jul 34. FCIS, ASA, CPA; and Comr **Wilma** (née Cugley) (Camberwell, Aus S, 1956) m 1957. Served in Aus E, Sing (OC/CPWO), Phil (TC/TPWO), NZ (TC/TPWO) and at IHQ (CoS/WSWO).

McKENZIE, Garth (Wellington City, NZ, 1975); Comr b 19 Feb 44; with Comr **Merilyn**

(née Probert) m 1968; b 20 Jul 46. Served in Aus S and NZ (TC/TPWM).

MILLER, Andrew S. (Newark, NJ, USA E, 1943); Comr b 14 Oct 23. BSc (Akron), Hon LLD (Asbury), Hon LHD (Akron); and Mrs Comr **Joan** (née Hackworth) (Hamilton, OH, USA E, 1945) m 1946. Hon LHD (Wesley Biblical Seminary, MS). Served in USA E, USA C (CS/THLS), USA S (TC/TPWO) and at USA Nat (NC/NPWO).

MORGAN, K. Brian (Bairnsdale, Aus S, 1958); Comr b 5 Oct 37; and Comr **Carolyn** (née Bath) (Melville Park, Aus S, 1958) m 1961; b 5 Mar 38. Served in Rus/CIS (OC/CPWO), Aus S (CS/TSWO) and Aus E (TC/TPWM).

MORETZ, Lawrence R. (Sunbury, PA, USA E, 1964); Comr b 22 Jul 43; and Comr **Nancy A.** (née Burke) (Kingston, NY, USA E, 1964) m 1965; b 29 Nov 44. Served in S Am W (TC/TPWO), USA C (TC/TPWM) and USA E (TC/TPWM).

MORRIS, Louise (née Holmes) (Charleston, W VA, USA S, 1953) Comr. Served in USA S and Jpn. Ww Comr Ted, pG 2004.

MOYO, Gideon (Chikankata, Zam, 1963); Comr b 3 May 33. Served in Zam (GS) and Zimb (TC). Ww Comr Lista, pG 2001.

MOYO, Selina (née Ndhlovu) (Bulayao Central, 1951); Mrs Comr. Served in Zimb. Ww Comr David, pG 2005.

MUNGATE, Stuart (Mabvuku, Zimb, 1970); Comr, b 15 Nov 46. BA, Grad Cert Ed, Dip Bus Admin; and Comr **Hope** (née Musvosvi) (Mucherengi, Zimb, 1974) m 1974; b 23 Mar 53. Dip Journ. Served in Zimb, Con (Kin) (CS/TSWM, TC/TPWM), Nig (TC/TPWM) and DR Con (TC/TPWM).

MUTEWERA, Stanslous (Sinoia, Zimb, 1970); Comr b 25 Dec 47; and Comr **Jannet** (née Zinyemba) (Tsatse, Zimb, 1973) m 1973; b 11 Nov 52. Served in UK and Zimb (TC/TPWM).

N

NEEDHAM, Philip D. (Miami Citadel, USA S, 1969); Comr b 5 Dec 40. BA (Rel), MDiv, ThM, DMin; with Comr **Keitha** (née Holz) m 1963; b 9 Oct 41. BA (Ed). Served at ICO (Principal), in USA W and USA S (TC/TPWM).

NELSON, John (Victoria Citadel, BC, Can, 1952); Comr b 19 Aug 32; and Comr **Elizabeth** (née McLean) (Chatham, Ont, Can, 1953) m 1956. Served in Can, at IHQ (IS/SWO S Asia), in Carib and Pak (TC/TPWO).

NELTING, George L. (Brooklyn, Bushwick, NY, USA E, 1942); Comr b 20 Jun 18. Ww Mrs Kathleen (née McKeag), pG 1976; and Mrs Comr **Juanita** (née Prine) (Cincinnati Cent, OH, USA E, 1962) m 1977. Served in USA E, at USA Nat (CS), Neth (TC/TPWO), at IHQ (IS/SWO Afr and IS Far East) and in USA C (TC/TPWO).

NGUGI, Joshua (Nakuru, 1945); Comr. b 29 Jan 16. Served in E Afr (TC). Ww Comr Bathisheba, pG 2005.

NILSON, Birgitta K. (Boone, IA, USA C, 1964); Comr. b 2 Oct 37. AB (Chicago), MSW (Loyola). Served in USA C, Swdn (TC) and at IHQ (IS Eur).

NILSSON, Sven (Vansbro, Swdn, 1940); Comr b 27 Jul 19. King's Medal (12th size) Sweden (1983). Served in Nor (CS), Den (TC) and Swdn (TC). Ww Mrs Comr Lisbeth, pG 2007.

NOLAND, Joseph J. (Santa Ana, CA, USA W, 1965); Comr b 17 Jul 37. BA, MS; and Comr **Doris** (née Tobin) (Los Angeles Congress Hall, CA, USA W, 1965) m 1966. RN. Served in USA W, Aus E and USA E (TC/TPWO).

NTUK, Patience (née Ekpe) (Ibadan, 1969); Comr. Served in Nig. Ww Comr Joshua, pG 2007.

NUESCH, Ruben D. (Rosario Cent, Brz, 1946); Comr b 28 Feb 21. Served in Brz (TC), S Am W (TC) and S Am E (TC). Ww Mrs Comr Rosario, pG 2010.

O

ØDEGAARD, B. Donald (Oslo 3, Nor, 1966); Comr b 18 Dec 40. Cand Mag; and Comr **Berit** (née Gjersøe) (Tønsberg, Nor, 1964) m 1967; b 27 Sep 44. SRN. Served in Zimb, S Afr, Nig (TC/TPWO), E Afr (TC/TPWO), Nor (TC/TPWM) and at IHQ (IS Prog Resources/'Sally Ann' Coordinator).

OLCKERS, Roy (Uitenhage, S Afr, 1952); Comr b 16 Jul 29; and Mrs Comr **Yvonne** (née Holdstock) (Fairview, S Afr, 1952) m 1955. Served in S Afr (TC/TPWO).

ORD, John (Easington Colliery, UK, 1948); Comr b 7 Sep 29; and Mrs Comr **Lydie** (née Deboeck) (Brussels, Belg, 1951) m1953. Served in Frce, Belg (OC/OPWO), at ITC, at ICO, in UK and Nor (TC/TPWO).

ORSBORN, Amy (née Webb) (Adelaide North, Aus S, 1951); Mrs Comr. Served in Aus S, NZ, UK, Swdn and Aus E. Ww Comr Howard, pG 2008.

OSBORNE, James (Washington 3, DC, USA S, 1947); Comr b 3 Jul 27; with Mrs Comr **Ruth** (née Campbell). Served in USA W (CS), USA S (TC) and at USA Nat (NC).

P

PARKINS, May (née Epplett) (Seattle Citadel, WA, USA W, 1951); Mrs Lt-Comr. Served in USA E, USA S and USA W. Ww Lt-Comr William, pG 1990.

PATTIPEILOHY, Blanche (née Sahanaja) (Djakarta 1, Indon, 1955); Mrs Comr. Served in Indon. Ww Comr Herman G., pG 2000.

PATRAS, Gulzar (Punjgarian, 1973); Comr b 19 Aug 47; and Comr **Sheila** (née John) (Amritnagar, Pak, 1973) m 1973; b 22 Sep 46. Served in Pak (TC/TPWM).

PEARCE, Lynette J. (Parkes, Aus E, 1971); Comr b 13 Jan 45. BA. Served in Aus E, at ICO and IHQ (IS Int Pers, WSWM)

PENDER, Winifred (née Dale) (Godmanchester, UK, 1954); Comr. Served in NZ, S Afr, Scot, at IHQ, in Aus S and UK. Ww Comr Dinsdale, pG 2006.

PINDRED, Gladys (née Dods) (Kitsilano, BC, Can, 1941); Mrs Comr. Served in Can and Carib. Ww Comr Leslie, pG 1990.

PITCHER, Arthur Ralph (St John's, NL, Can, 1939); Comr b 30 Oct 17. Served in S Afr (CS), Carib (TC), USA S (TC) and Can (TC). Ww Mrs Comr Elizabeth, pG 2009.

POBJIE, Barry R. (Paddington, Aus E, 1965); Comr b 25 Jan 45. Served in PNG. Ww Capt Ruth, pG 1978; and Comr **Raemor** (née Wilson) (Port Kembla, Aus E, 1971) m 1980; b 22 Sep 48. Served in NZ, Aus E, Rus (GS/CSWO), E Eur (OC/CPWM, TC/TPWM) and at IHQ (IS/ZSWM SPEA) (IS/ZSWM Eur).

POKE, Victor (Burnie, Aus S, 1968); Comr b 8 Jan 46; and Comr **Roslyn** (née Pengilly) (Maylands, Aus S, 1968) m 1970; b 20 Jun 45. Served in Aus S, UK (CS/ TSWM) and Swdn (TC/TPWM).

PRATT, William (Ilford, UK, 1947); Comr b 8 May 25; and Mrs Comr **Kathleen** (née Lyons) (Harlesden, UK, 1948) m 1949. Served at IHQ, in BT (CS), USA W (TC/TPWO) and Can (TC/TPWO).

R

RADER, Paul A. General (1994-1999) (see page 25); with Comr **Kay F.** (née Fuller) (Cincinnati, OH, USA E, 1995) m 1956. BA (Asbury), Hon DD (Asbury Theol Seminary), Hon LHD (Greenville), Hon DD (Roberts Wesleyan). Served in Kor (THLS), USA E (THLS), USA W (TPWO) and at IHQ (WPWO).

RANGEL, Paulo (Rio Comprido, Brz, 1968); Comr b 19 Nov 41. Hon DD; and Comr **Yoshiko** (née Namba) (São Paulo, Brz, 1967) m 1969; b 1 Sep 44. Served in Brz (TC/TPWM).

READ, Harry (Edinburgh Gorgie, UK, 1948); Comr b 17 May 24. Served in UK, at IHQ, ITC (Principal), in Can (CS), Aus E (TC) and BT (Brit Comr). Ww Mrs Comr Winifred, pG 2007

REFSTIE, Peder R. (Mandal, Nor, 1965); Comr, b 13 Jul 43; and Comr **Janet M.** (née Dex) (Bedford, UK, 1966) m 1969; b 7 Jul 43. Served in UK, S Am W, Port, Nor, Sp (OC/CPWM), at IHQ, in S Am E (TC/TPWM) and Brz (TC/TPWM).

RIGHTMIRE, Robert S. (Cincinnati, OH, USA E, 1946); Comr b 23 Jun 24; and Comr **Katherine** (née Stillwell) (Newark Citadel, USA E, 1942) m 1947. Served in USA E, S Afr (CS), Jpn (TC/TWPWO, Kor (TC/TPWO) and USA C (TC/TPWO).

RIVERS, William (Hadleigh Temple, UK, 1952); Comr b 22 Dec 27; and Mrs Comr **Rose** (née Ross) (Aberdeen Torry, UK, 1956) m 1957. Served in UK and at IHQ (IS Admin).

ROBERTS, William H. (Detroit Brightmoor, MI, USA C, 1943); Comr b 27 May 22; and Mrs Comr **Ivy** (née Anderson) (Marshalltown, IA, USA C, 1943) m 1945. BA (Wayne State). Served in USA C, Aus S (CS) and at IHQ (IS Am and Carib, IS for Dev).

ROOS, Rolf (Uppsala, Swdn, 1962); Comr b 13 Nov 40; and Comr **Majvor** (née Ljunggren) (Uppsala, Swdn, 1964) m 1965; b 15 Sep 38. Served in Fin (TC/TPWO) and Swdn (TC/ TPWM).

RUTH, Fred L. (Shawnee, OK, 1955); Comr b 21 Aug 35. BA (Georgia State), Dip Ed, MA (Counselling and Psychol Studies) (Trinity). Served in Kor, USA W, USA S, at USA Nat and at IHQ (IS SPEA). Ww Mrs Col Sylvia, pG 1990.

S

SAUNDERS, Robert F. (Philadelphia Pioneer, PA, USA E, 1962); Comr b 16 Jan 37. C Th (Fuller); and Comr **Carol J.** (née Rudd) (Seattle Temple, WA, USA E, 1966) m 1967; b 10 Sep 43. Served in Carib, USA E, USA W, Kor (CS/TSWO), Phil (TC/TPWO) and at IHQ (IS/SWO SPEA).

SCHURINK, Reinder J. (Zutphen, Neth, 1947); Comr b 2 Dec 27. Officer Order of Orange Nassau (1987). Ww Mrs Capt Henderika (née Hazeveld), pG 1961. Served

in Ger (CS), Neth (TC) and Rus (Cmndr). Ww Mrs Comr Wietske (née Kloosterman), pG 1997. m Lt-Col Dora Verhagen, 1998.

SCOTT, Albert P. (Lawrence, MA, USA E, 1941); Comr b 15 Oct 18. Ww Mrs Dorothy, pG 1970; and Mrs Comr **Frances O.** (née Clark) (Concord, NH, USA E, 1953) m 1971. Served in USA E (CS) and at IHQ (IS Am and Carib, and IS Development).

SHIPE, Tadeous (Mukakatanwa, Zimb, 1969); Comr b 13 Jul 43. Served in Zimb, Zam & Mal (TC/TPWM) and Zam (TC/TPWM). Ww Comr Nikiwe, pG 2008.

SHOULTS, Harold (St Louis Tower Grove, MO, USA C, 1949); Comr b 6 Mar 29; and Mrs Comr **Pauline** (née Cox) (St Louis Tower Grove, MO, USA C, 1951) m 1952. Served in USA E (CS/TSWO), USA N (CS/Asst NPWO) and USA C (TC/TPWO).

SKINNER, Verna E. (West End, Aus E, 1957); Comr b 5 May 36. Served in Aus E, HK, Sri Lan (TC), Aus S (CS), at IHQ (IS Resources) and in E Afr (TC).

SOLHAUG, Karsten Anker (Sandvika, Nor, 1936); Comr b 9 Nov 14. Kt, St Olav. Served in UK, Den (CS) and Nor (TC). Ww Comr Else, pG 2006.

STRONG, Leslie J. (Kalbar, Aus E, 1965); Comr. b 5 Apr 43. BAL; and Comr **Coral** (née Scholz) (Kalbar, Aus E, 1966) m 1967; b 30 Mar 44. Served in Aus S (CS/TSWM) and Aus E (TC/TPWM).

SUNDARAM, Thota Gnana (Denduluru, Ind SE, 1963); Comr b 1 Oct 35; with Comr **Suseela** m 1955; b 16 Apr 36. Served in Ind C, Ind SE (TC/TPWO) and Ind W (TC/TPWO).

SUTHERLAND, Margaret (Sleaford, UK, 1968); Comr b 22 Jul 43. MA, ARCO. Served in Zam, UK, Zimb (CS), at IHQ (IS Afr) and at ICO (Principal).

SWINFEN, John M. (Penge, UK, 1955); Comr b 24 Jan 31. BA, Cert Ed, Chevalier de l'Ordre du Merite Exceptionnel (Congo); with Comr **Norma** (née Salmon). Served in Zimb, at ITC, in UK, E Afr (CS/THLS), Con (TC/TPWO) and at IHQ (IS/SWO Afr).

SWYERS, B. Gordon (Atlanta Temple, GA, USA S, 1959); Comr b 25 Jul 36. BBA (Georgia State); and Comr **Jacqueline** (née Alexander); b 25 Dec 29. Served in USA S and at IHQ (IS Admin/SWO SPEA).

SWYERS, Philip W. (Dallas Temple, TX, USA S, 1968); Comr b 22 Apr 44. BBA; and Comr **Patricia L.** (née Lowery) (Charlotte, NC, USA S, 1962); b 26 Aug 41. Served in

USA C (CS/TSWM), USA S (CS/TSWM) and USA W (TC/TPWM).

T

TAYLOR, Margaret (née Overton) (Aylsham, UK, 1962); Comr b 13 Feb 40. Served in UK, E Afr, Pak and at IHQ (IS Prog Resources). Ww Comr Brian E., pG 2004.

TAYLOR, Orval (Seattle Citadel, WA, USA W, 1940); Comr b 21 May 19; and Mrs Comr **Muriel** (née Upton) (Long Beach, USA W, 1937) m 1943. Served in USA W, USA S, USA N (CS/TSWO), Carib (TC/TPWO), at IHQ (IS Plan & Dev) and USA E (TC/TPWO).

THOMPSON, Arthur T. (Croydon Citadel, UK, 1961); Comr b 23 Dec 32. BSc, PhD, PGCE, Freeman of City of London; and Comr **Karen** (née Westergaard) (Camberwell, UK, 1961) m 1962. BA, PGCE. Served in Zimb, Zam, UK, NZ (CS/THLS) and at IHQ (IS Admin/IS Resources, SWO Eur).

THOMSON, Robert E. (Racine, WI, USA C, 1951); Comr b 21 Feb 28. BM (St Olaf); with Mrs Comr **Carol** (née Nielsen); BA (St Olaf). Served at USA Nat, in USA C (CS/TSWO), at IHQ (IS/SWO Am and Carib) and in USA E (TC/TPWO).

TILLSLEY, Bramwell Howard General (1993-94) (see page 25); with Mrs General **Maud** (née Pitcher). Served in Can, at ITC, in USA S, Aus S (TPWO) and at IHQ (WSWO, WPWO).

TONDI, Roos (née Mundung) (Sonder, Indon, 1958); Comr. Served in Aus S and Indon. Ww Comr Victor, pG 2002.

TUCK, Trevor M. (Kensington Citadel, S Afr, 1969); Comr b 11 Sep 43; and Comr **Memory** (née Fortune) (Benoni, S Afr, 1965) m 1968; b 28 Apr 45. Served in PNG (TC/TPWM) and S Afr (CS/TSWM, TC/TPWM).

V

VAN DER HARST, Willem (Scheveningen, Neth, 1966); Comr b 13 Mar 44. Ww Capt Suzanne, pG 1985; and Comr **Netty** (née Kruisinga) (Amsterdam Congress Hall, Neth, 1984) m 1985; b 15 Feb 58. Served in Cze R, Neth (TC/TPWM) and E Eur (TC/TPWM).

VERWAAL, Sjoerdje (née Zoethout) (Zaandam, Neth, 1947); Mrs Comr. Served at IHQ and in Neth. Ww Comr Cornelis, pG 2002.

W

WAGHELA, Chimanbhai Somabhai (Ratanpura, Ind W, 1968); Comr b 1 Jun 47; with Comr **Rahelbai** m 1972; b 1 May 52. Served in

Ind W, Ind SE (CS/TSWO), Ind E (CS/TSWO) and Ind SW (TC/TPWM).

WAHLSTRÖM, Maire (née Nyberg) (Helsinki 1, Fin, 1944); Mrs General. Served in Fin (TPWO), Swdn (TPWO), Can (TPWO) and at IHQ (WPWO). Ww General Jarl Wahlström, pG 1999.

WALTER, Alison (née Harewood) (Calgary Citadel, AB, Can, 1955); Mrs Comr. Served in Zimb, E Afr, Can, S Afr and at IHQ. Ww Comr Stanley, pG 2004.

WATERS, Margaret (née Eastland) (Niagara Falls, Can, 1953); Comr b 1 Mar 34. Served in Can and at IHQ. Ww Comr Arthur W., pG 2002.

WATILETE, Johannes G. (Bandung 3, Indon, 1963); Comr b 9 Sep 41. BA, MTh, DTh, DMin (HC); and Comr **Augustina** (née Sarman) (Bandung 3, Indon, 1962) m 1966; b 16 Aug 39. Served in Sing (GS/CHLS), Phil (CS/THLS and TC/TPWO) and Indon (TC/TPWM).

WATSON, Robert A. (Philadelphia Pioneer, PA, USA E, 1955); Comr b 11 Aug 34; and Comr **Alice** (née Irwin) (Philadelphia Pioneer, PA, USA E, 1956) m 1957. Served in USA E (CS/THLS) and at USA Nat (NC/NPWO).

WICKBERG, Eivor (née Lindberg) (Norrköping 1, Swdn, 1946); Mrs General. Ww General Erik Wickberg, pG 1996.

WILLIAMS, Harry William (Wood Green, UK, 1934); Comr b 13 Jul 13. OF, OBE, FRCS (Edin), FICS. Served in Ind W, Ind NE, Ind S (TC), NZ (TC), Aus E (TC) and at IHQ (IS Am, IS Australasia, IS Plan & Dev). Ww Mrs Comr Eileen M., pG 2002.

Y

YOHANNAN, Paulose (Kalayapuram, Ind SW, 1974); Comr b 1 Dec 45. MA (Sociol), DD, PhD; with Comr **Kunjamma** (née Jesaiah) m 1966; b 15 Jun 47. Served in Ind SW, Ind E, Ind SE (TC/TPWM) and Ind N (TC/TPWM).

Retirements from Active Service

AUSTRALIA EASTERN

Lt-Cols Brian and Elaine Hood from Redcliffe
on 10 Jan 2010

Maj Eliana Cristi from Campsie
on 10 Jan 2010

Maj Mervyn Holland from THQ
on 31 Jan 2010

Maj David Brown from Chaplaincy Services,
Dulwich Hill on 7 Feb 2010

Majs Brian and Glenys Holley from Mount
Gravatt/Carina on 7 Feb 2010

Maj Louisa Timmer from Salvo Care Line,
Western Australia on 1 Mar 2010

Capt Jeanne Johnstone from THQ
on 1 Mar 2010

Comr Robin Dunster from IHQ (CoS)
on 30 Apr 2010

Comr Lyn Pearce from IHQ (WSWM)
on 30 Apr 2010

AUSTRALIA SOUTHERN

Majs Allan and Lorraine Daddow from THQ
on 1 Sep 2009

Maj Peter Wright from Northern Territory
Region on 1 Nov 2009

Maj Glenys Ford from THQ on 1 Dec 2009

Maj Merilyn Ingram from Western Australia
DHQ on 1 Feb 2010

Maj Tania McKenna from THQ on
1 Feb 2010

Majs Iain and Dawn Trainor from Western
Australia DHQ on 1 Feb 2010

Maj Kathleen Smith from Southern Australia
DHQ on 1 Feb 2010

Majs Kevin and Lynette Grigsbey from THQ
on 1 Apr 2010

Majs John and Lois Simmonds from
Employment Plus on 1 Apr 2010

Maj Maureen Rawlings from Southern
Australia DHQ on 1 May 2010

Maj Margaret McMillin from Melbourne
DHQ on 1 Jun 2010

Lt-Cols Lyndon and Julie Spiller from THQ
on 1 Jun 2010

Capt Christine Haig from Tasmania DHQ
on 1 Jul 2010

Maj Robert Paterson from THQ
on 1 Jul 2010

BRAZIL TERRITORY

Maj Gelcinete Gonçalves from Porto Alegre
on 1 May 2010

CANADA AND BERMUDA

Maj Audrey Durdle from Saint John, NB,
on 1 Nov 2009.

Maj Judy Bishop from Clarke's Beach, NL,
on 1 Nov 2009.

Maj William Blackman from Vancouver, BC,
on 1 Jan 2010.

Cols Donald and Ann Copple from THQ
(CS/TSWM) on 1 Mar 2010.

Majs Gilles and Armande Gagne from
Trois-Rivieres, QC, on 1 Mar 2010.

CARIBBEAN

Maj Thamsie Ellis from Port Maria, Jamaica,
on 5 Jul 2009

Majs Federico and Dorrit Craig from
St Thomas, Virgin Islands, on 9 Sep 2009

Majs Allan Arthur and Rafleator Richards
from May Pen, Jamaica, on 15 Nov 2009

DENMARK

Capt Jytte Ulriksen from Skagen
on 2 May 2010

EASTERN EUROPE

Maj Maria Kharkova from THQ on 1 Jan 2010

FRANCE AND BELGIUM

Maj Guy Delcourt from Paris Division
on 1 Sep 2009

Maj Jeannine Colasurdo-Tisserand from
Résidence Catherine Booth, Paris.
on 1 Dec 2009

Maj André Vielpeau from Chateau d'Auvilliers
on 1 Mar 2010

Maj Catherine Bösiger-Pouillet from Alès
on 1 Aug 2010

GERMANY AND LITHUANIA

Capt Helga Meinelt from Ulm on 31 Mar 2010

Maj Karin Hagedorn from Stuttgart
on 1 Aug 2010

GHANA

Majs Joseph and Comfort Nkansah from
Abekoase on 19 Oct 2008

Retirements from Active Service

INDIA CENTRAL

Lt-Cols N.J. Karunakara and Vijayalakshmi Rao from National Secretariat on 1 Jun 2008

Maj P. Samuel from Baptala on 10 June 2008

Majs P. Suvarna Pushpa and Kumari from Bapatla on 10 Jun 2008

Maj P. Alice Mathew from Evangeline Booth Hospital, Nidubrolu, on 1 May 2010

Majs P. Yesupadam and Yesupriyam from Alluru on 1 May 2010

Majs B. Abraham and Hema Latha from Vemuru on 1 May 2010

INDIA NORTHERN

Majs Sabita and Samuel Das from Angul on 7 May 2010

Majs Wilson and Issawati from Bareilly on 7 May 2010

INDIA SOUTH EASTERN

Majs Ponniah and Santham Balachandran from Kollencode on 15 Nov 2009.

Majs Suvisesamuthu and Pooranam Chinnappa from Kadaigramam District on 1 Jun 2010

INDIA SOUTH WESTERN

Majs K. P. Chacko and Suseelamma Chacko from THQ on 1 Oct 2009

Maj R. Rajamma from Chettikunnu and Vazhichel Neyattinkara on 1 May 2010

Majs George Philip and Syamalakumari George from Kottarakara Boys' Home on 1 Aug 2010

Majs N. S. George and A. Annamma George from THQ on 1 Aug 2010

Maj R. Sumathy from Villoor on 1 Aug 2010

INDONESIA

Maj Suprijati Handojo from Turen Eventide Home, Java, on 1 Apr 2010

JAPAN

Maj Machiko Yamanaka from Takasaki and Kanto-Tohoku DHQ on 25 Mar 2010

Maj Asako Igarashi from Sendai and Namie on 25 Mar 2010

Maj Masaru Sakuraba from Gifu on 31 Mar 2010

Maj Kiyoshi Namai from Hokkaido DHQ and Sapporo Day Nurseries on 31 Mar 2010

Maj Sachiko Kato from Kobe and Nishi Nihon DHQ on 30 Apr 2010

KENYA EAST

Majs Samuel and Grace Mbindyo Magomere from Makuli on 1 Aug 2010

KENYA WEST

Maj Walker Andolo from Wabukhonyi on 12 Oct 2009

Majs William and Florence Nambale from Bitobo on 1 Oct 2009

Majs Roger and Mary Matodze from Esibembe on 10 Dec 2009

Maj Lenah Ogada from Busiana on 13 Aug 2009

Maj Christopher Mudanya from Sabatia on 10 Dec 2009

Maj Rosbella Odhiambo from Lwanda on 8 Aug 2010

KOREA

Maj Pang, Kie-chang and Maj Park, Keum-ja from Choong Saw DHQ on 30 Oct 2009

Maj Huh, Jin and Maj Kim, Dong-seon from Cho Chi Won on 28 Feb 2010

Maj Suh, Dong-ook and Maj Kwak, Min-ja from Jae Won on 28 Feb 2010

Maj Kim, Shi-byung and Maj Kim, Young-soon from Chin Bo on 30 Jun 2010

Comr Chun, Kwang-pyo and Comr Yoo, Sung-ja from THQ (TC/TPWM) on 30 Sep 2010

THE NETHERLANDS AND CZECH REPUBLIC

Aux-Capts Wil and Ria Muit from Gouda on 22 Aug 2009

Maj Anneke Outhuijse from Enschede on 1 Feb 2010

Comrs Wim and Netty van der Harst from Eastern Europe THQ (TC/TPWM) on 28 Feb 2010

NEW ZEALAND, FIJI AND TONGA

Maj Jan Smithies from THQ on 24 Apr 2009

Maj Adrienne Rive from Pukekohe on 30 Sep 2009

Maj Peter Scadden from THQ, Pakistan, on 31 Oct 2009

Maj Helen Spargo from Wellington Community Ministries on 30 Nov 2009

Majs William and Ailsie Roulston from Dunedin City on 13 Jan 2010

Maj Lindsay Chisholm from Levin on 31 Jan 2010

Maj Heather Kopu from Thames on 31 Mar 2010

Retirements from Active Service

Maj June Sunkel from Waikato Bridge
Programme on 31 Jun 2010
Capt Douglas Rattray from Porirua Community
Ministries on 31 Aug 2010

NORWAY, ICELAND AND THE FÆROES

Maj Jens Petter Krumsvik from the Training
College on 30 Sep 2009
Maj Miriam Óskarsdóttir from Iceland
on 1 Nov 2009
Maj Haldis Kongevold from THQ
on 30 Nov 2009
Maj Berit Olsen from THQ on 30 Apr 2010
Maj Fred Solli from THQ on 30 Apr 2010
Maj Åsta Torgersen from THQ
on 30 Apr 2010
Maj Knut Larsen from THQ on 30 Jun 2010
Comrs Peder and Janet Refstie from Brazil
THQ (TC/TPWM) on 31 Jul 2010
Maj Åsdis K. Molvik from DHQ Midland
on 31 Jul 2010

PAKISTAN

Maj Hanzal Masih from Harbancepura
on 13 Apr 2010
Majs Michael Samuel and Hanaa Michael
from Youhanabad on 13 Apr 2010

THE PHILLIPINES

Maj Fe Campilan from Asingan Educational
Services Northern Luzon on 30 Sep 2009
Maj Herminia Fajardo from Alcala
on 30 May 2010

SINGAPORE, MALAYSIA AND MYANMAR

Maj Zompari from Kalay DHQ, Myanmar,
on 4 Jan 2009

SOUTH AMERICA WEST

Lt-Cols Luis and María Aguilera from
Santiago, Chile, on 30 Jan 2009
Maj Aura Vidal from Santiago, Chile,
on 31 Jan 2009
Maj Noemí Panduro from Tarapoto, Perú,
on 30 Jan 2009
Majs Fabián and Vilma Vargas from
Cochabamba, Bolivia, on 30 Jan 2010

SOUTHERN AFRICA

Maj Vevelyn Tshiyembe from Langa,
Western Cape, on 31 Jan 2009
Maj Agnes Mabena from Mountain Lodge,
Central Division, on 1 Dec 2009
Maj Mary Sithole from Jabavu Creche and
Peart Memorial Corps on 4 Jul 2010

SWEDEN AND LATVIA

Maj Ingelise Linck from THQ on 1 Aug 2009
Maj Torfinn Kurseth from sick furlough
on 4 Oct 2009
Majs Leif and Kerstin Alm from THQ
on 31 Dec 2009
Maj Ann-Margret Ström from THQ
on 31 Jan 2010
Maj Ulf Landin from Sundbyberg
on 10 Jun 2010
Maj Ewa-Maria Wahlström from sick furlough
on 30 Jun 2010

SWITZERLAND, AUSTRIA AND HUNGARY

Maj Stephan Mosimann from ARC Waldkirch
on 31 Jan 2010
Maj Esther Saugy from Ost-Division
on 31 Mar 2010
Maj Ursula Eckert from THQ on 31 Aug 2010
Maj Martha Mosimann from THQ
on 31 Aug 2010
Maj Margrith Müller from Zurich North
on 31 Aug 2010

UNITED KINGDOM WITH THE REPUBLIC OF IRELAND

Maj Yvonne Dare from Newbiggin
on 1 Sep 2009
Maj Alan Leverett from Prison Chaplain,
Yorkshire Division, on 1 Sep 2009
Maj Mary Scott from Catford on 1 Sep 2009
Maj Sheilah Morgan from Stocksbridge
on 1 Oct 2009
Lt-Col Isobel McIntyre from East Scotland
DHQ on 1 Nov 2009
Lt-Col Robert McIntyre from Scotland
Secretariat, THQ and East Scotland DHQ
on 1 Nov 2009
Maj Gwendoline Warner from THQ
on 1 Nov 2009
Maj David Young from Dennistoun
on 1 Nov 2009
Maj Margaret Meldrum from THQ
on 1 Dec 2009
Maj Peter Smith from THQ on 1 Dec 2009
Maj Richard Pears from William Booth
College on 1 Jan 2010
Lt-Col Roland Sewell from THQ on 1 Jan 2010
Maj Susan Collins from Macclesfield
on 1 Apr 2010
Maj Geoffrey Ashdown from Waltham Abbey
on 1 May 2010
Maj Jean Bradbury from South-Western DHQ
on 1 Jul 2010

Maj Clifford Bradbury from South-Western DHQ on 1 Sep 2010

USA CENTRAL

Majs Myron and Nancy Wandling from Midland DHQ on 1 Sep 2009

Majs Robert and Elaine Boone from Lincoln, NE, on 1 Sep 2009

Majs John and Juanite Morrison from THQ on 1 Oct 2009

Maj Eliana Cristi from THQ on 1 Dec 2009

Majs Stanley and Lynda Magoon from Kansas/Western Missouri DHQ on 1 Jan 2010

Maj Deborah Agnew from Fort Dodge, IA, on 1 Feb 2010

Majs Richard and Susan Hartman from Indiana DHQ on 1 Feb 2010

Majs Charles and Janet McCarty from THQ on 1 Feb 2010

Majs David and Jeannette Biggs from Madison, IN, on 1 May 2010

Majs Norman and Margaret Nonnweiler from THQ on 1 Jun 2010

Majs Charles and Janice Hendrickson from Northern DHQ on 1 Jun 2010

Lt-Cols David and Sherry Grindle from Metropolitan DHQ on 1 Jul 2010

Maj Judith Eagle from Indiana DHQ on 1 Jul 2010

Lt-Cols James and Janice Nauta from THQ on 1 Jul 2010

Maj Sally Michael from Marinette, WI, on 1 Jul 2010

Majs George and Violet Windham from Midland DHQ on 1 Jul 2010

Majs David and Debra Dalberg from Metropolitan DHQ on 1 Jul 2010

Majs Jerry and Nancy Curttright from Indiana DHQ on 1 Aug 2010

Majs Robert and Margaret Quinn from Centralia, IL, on 1 Aug 2010

USA EASTERN

Maj Luva Blakely from Buffalo, NY on 1 Nov 2009

Majs David and Rose Cedervall from THQ on 1 Nov 2009

Majs Robert and Donna Green from THQ on 1 Nov 2009

Majs Mark and Sharon Himes from Sharon, MA, 1 Jan 2010

Majs Franklin and Florence Dodridge from Portland, ME, on 1 Feb 2010

Majs Larry and Andrea See from Hempstead, NY, on 1 Mar 2010

Majs Kenneth and Alice Stahl from DHQ, Cleveland, OH, on 1 Apr 2010

Capts Jose and Maria Cruz from Union City, NJ, on 1 May 2010

Majs Sidney and Betty Anderson from THQ on 1 Jul 2010

Majs John and Judith Cheydleur from THQ on 1 Jul 2010

Majs Frank and Sherrie Klemanski from THQ on 1 Jul 2010

Lt-Cols R. Eugene and Edith Pigford from THQ on 1 Jul 2010

Capt Lamont and Maj Beverly Green from ARC on 1 Jul 2010

Comrs Lawrence and Nancy Moretz from THQ (TC/TPWM) on 1 Aug 2010

Capts David and Catherine Stout from Berwick, PA, on 13 Sep 2010

USA SOUTHERN

Maj Rose Wiley from THQ on 1 Sep 2009

Majs Douglas and Wanda Browning from Doraville, GA, on 1 Sep 2009

Maj Carol Clemons from Arlington, VA, on 1 Oct 2009

Majs Newton and Jane Brown from Sumter, SC, on 1 Oct 2009

Majs Marshall and Carolyn Gesner from Houston AC, TX, on 1 Nov 2009

Majs Russell and Johanna Wilt from Winston-Salem, NC, on 1 Nov 2009

Maj John White from THQ on 1 Jan 2010

Majs James and Patricia Witner from ARC Command on 1 Jan 2010

Majs Michael and Betty Jo McDonald from DHQ on 1 Feb 2010

Majs Randall and Barbara Wilson from THQ on 1 May 2010

Majs Terry and Linda Edwards from Easley, NC, on 1 Jun 2010

Majs G. Daniel and Kathleen Whittaker from Washington, NC, on 1 Jun 2010

Majs James Dalton and Wanda Cunningham from DHQ on 10 Jun 2010

Maj Shirley Adams from THQ on 12 Jun 2010

Majs James and Rebecca Smith from ARC, Orlando, on 1 Jul 2010

Majs Jimmy and Janice Bovender from Middlesboro, KY, on 1 Jul 2010

Majs Roy and Mary Dell Tolcher from Fort Worth, TX, on 1 Aug 2010

USA WESTERN

Maj Joyce Stevenson from Long Beach, CA, on 1 Sep 2009

Majs Jerry and Donna Ames from Salem, OR, on 1 Oct 2009

Majs Barry and Arlene Dooley from Seattle, WA, on 1 Oct 2009

Majs Delbert and Victoria Brockelman from Seattle, WA, on 1 Dec 2009

Majs Wesley and Ruth Sundin from Ogden, UT, on 1 Feb 2010

Maj Kyung-Ja Kim from Rancho Palos Verdes, CA, on 1 Mar 2010

Majs Moises and Maria Hernandez from Phoenix, AZ, on 1 Apr 2010

Capt Roberto and Maj Aurora Otero from Bakersfield Temple, CA, on 1 May 2010

Majs Cruz and Linda Rodriguez from Sacramento, CA, on 1 May 2010

Maj Glenda Berko from Medford, OR, on 1 Jul 2010

Majs Douglas and Janice Williams from Reno, NV, on 1 Jul 2010

WORDS OF LIFE

THE Salvation Army's international Bible reading plan, *Words of Life*, is an invaluable aid to daily devotional study. The readings cover a wide selection of Scripture and the comments give opportunity to build a lasting library for further study and reflection. Points for prayer and praise are a further enrichment to personal devotion. Major Beverly Ivany (Canada and Bermuda Territory) begins her term as writer of *Words of Life* with the January–April 2012 edition. Subscriptions are available through Salvationist Publishing and Supplies, UK Territory.

Promotions to Glory

AUSTRALIA EASTERN
Mrs Brig Dawn Jones on 3 Sep 2009
Brig Mrs Muriel Archbold on 17 Sep 2009
Maj Eric Hopkins on 15 Oct 2009
Mrs Maj Grace Ward on 3 Dec 2009
Aux-Capt John Penfold on 9 Jan 2010
Mrs Lt-Col Joy Neimann on 9 Feb 2010
Maj David Mole on 10 Feb 2010
Mrs Maj Madge Fletcher on 26 Feb 2010
Mrs Lt-Col Olive Carpenter on 13 Mar 2010
Mrs Aux-Capt Vera Parker on 14 Mar 2010
Mrs Maj Catherine Ayres on 20 Mar 2010
Mrs Brig Mabel Inmon on 21 May 2010
Maj Brian Holley on 22 May 2010
Capt Christine Davey on 24 May 2010
Mrs Lt-Col Elinore Higgins on 3 Jun 2010
Maj Thelma Ward on 27 Jul 2010
Maj Alan Rushbrook on 27 Jul 2010
Maj Gordon Hosking on 7 Aug 2010
Maj Gordon Fletcher on 19 Aug 2010
Brig Hazel Woodbury on 21Aug 2010
Maj Neville Bedwell on 23 Aug 2010
Capt Les Fuller on 24 Aug 2010

AUSTRALIA SOUTHERN
Maj Florence Badenhop on 2 Apr 2009
Aux-Capt Fred Wells on 18 May 2009
Lt-Col Olive McPherson on 3 Jun 2009
Maj Kenneth Duck on 18 Jun 2009
Brig Stella Bywaters OF, AC on 19 Jun 2009
Maj Pearl Arnott on 24 Sep 2009
Maj John Rasmus on 24 Nov 2009
Maj Vera Hoare on 25 Nov 2009
Aux-Capt Reginald Tolputt on 21 Dec 2009
Brig Norah Yarnold on 17 Apr 2010
Maj Ruby Peeke on 10 May 2010
Maj Jean Bloxham on 20 May 2010
Maj Olive Inglis on 31 May 2010

BRAZIL
Maj Benoni Rodrigues de Campos on
23 Mar 2010

CANADA AND BERMUDA
Maj Sara Wheeler on 27 Oct 2009
Maj Laura Hanson on 3 Nov 2009
Lt-Col Ruth Hawkes on 15 Nov 2009
Maj William McKenzie on 16 Nov 2009
Maj Beryl Harris on 7 Dec 2009
Capt Leaman Eveleigh on 26 Dec 2009
Col Mrs Lenora Church on 3 Jan 2010

Capt Cyril Morey on 3 Feb 2010
Maj Marguerite Belanger on 1 Mar 2010
Maj Phyllis Linder on 15 Mar 2010
Mrs Maj Margaret Rickard on 31 Mar 2010

CARIBBEAN
Lt-Col Lyn Davis on 23 Aug 2009
Maj Percival Benjamin on 11 Jun 2010
Capt Detrice McCartney (A) from Trinidad
and Tobago on 3 Jun 2010
Maj Josephine Raeburn (A) from Belize on
16 Sep 2009

DEMOCRATIC REPUBLIC OF CONGO
Maj Ana Basadila Nswala on 4 Jun 2009
Maj Henriette Mansanga Ntunga on 24 Sep 2009
Maj Pierre Mulomba on 18 Dec 2009
Maj Albert Bainge on 18 Feb 2010
Lt Gédéon Makangu (A) from Kintete on
2 May 2010

DENMARK
Maj Ida Gade on 19 Aug 2009
Lt-Col Gudrun Svendsen on 25 Nov 2009
Maj Gerda Nielsen on 27 Nov 2009
Capt Grethe Sørensen on 5 Jan 2010
Brig Gerda Pedersen on 28 Feb 2010

EASTERN EUROPE
Capt Alexander Onishenko (A) from
Kirovograd, Ukraine on 16 Dec 2009

FINLAND AND ESTONIA
Brig Miriam Leivo on 8 Nov 2009
Maj Terho Tiainen on 20 Nov 2009
Maj Martti Reponen on 1 Feb 2010
Brig Ilma Honkanen on 4 Mar 2010

FRANCE AND BELGIUM
Maj Charles Haldimann on 26 Jun 2009
Maj Claire Hansen-Soulie on 29 Aug 2009
Maj Sonia Euler-Deckheer on 25 Nov 2009

GERMANY AND LITHUANIA
Capt Hildegard Böving on 24 Sep 2009
Maj Ingeborg Rump on 29 Sep 2009
Maj Margret Goldbach on 1 Mar 2010

GHANA
Capt Kwadwo Amoah Bimpong (A) from
CHQ Liberia on 26 May 2010

INDIA CENTRAL

Capt M. Prabhudas (A) fromYaramvaripalem on 24 Jan 2009

Maj M David (A) from New Jojinagar on 15 Jun 2009

Lt-Col P. James on 20 Jun 2009

Maj T Pushpavathi 28 Aug 2009

Lt Jayalakshmi (A) from Machilipatnam on 13 Oct 2009

Maj G.Babu Singh on 5 Nov 2009

Maj D. Samuel Raju (A) from Bhadrachalam on 25 Nov 2009

Capt M. Siva Kumari (A) from Girls' Hostel, Bapatla on 22 Dec 2009

Maj D. Kanthamma on 24 Dec 2009

Maj T. Elia on 10 Jan 2010

Maj K. Neelambaram on 30 Mar 2010

Maj J. Prabhudas on 9 Apr 2010,

Maj M.A. Prabhakar Rao (A) from Gantasalapalem on 11.May 2010

Maj Alice Mathew on 22 Jul 2010

INDIA EASTERN

Brig Ngruauvi on 18 Sep 2009

Maj Hranglianchhunga on 2 Jun 2010

INDIA NORTHERN

Maj Garib Das on 21 Nov 2009

Maj Habiba Feroze Masih on 5 Dec 2009

Maj Elveena Emmanuel (A) from Marar on 31 Dec 2009

Col Garib Das on 13 Mar 2010

INDIA SOUTH EASTERN

Brig S A Paul on 2 Aug 2009.

Maj Packiamony Gray on 14 Aug 2009.

Maj D Abel Raj on 5 Dec 2009.

Brig Inbammal Devadhas on 14 Apr 2010

Maj Y Manoraj (A) from Chaicodu on 3 Sep 2010

INDIA SOUTH WESTERN

Lt. Col K.C. Joseph on 8 Aug 2009

Maj Kunjamma Stephen on 27 Aug 2009

Maj Mariam Yohannan on 29 Oct 2009

Maj S. Kunjamma Jacob on 28 Nov 2009

Maj D. Yesudasan on 31 Dec 2009

Maj S.D. Mary Samuel on 18 Feb 2010

Maj J. Samuel on 22 Feb 2010

Maj C.M. George on 27 Feb 2010

Lt-Col Mariamma Manickavasagar on 7 May 2010

Maj A. David on 8 July 2010

INDIA WESTERN

Maj Kishan Kamble on 18 Aug 2009

Maj Martha K. Pandav on 27 Nov 2009

Maj Dayabai Borde on 2 Nov 2009

Col Shushila J. Makanji on 28 Nov 2009

Maj Agnesh A. Banker on 29 Nov 2009

Maj Prakash Isudas and Maj Saroj Praksh (A) from Emery Hospital, Anand, on 13 Jan 2010

Maj Devdan Y. Gaikwad on 24 Jan 2010

Maj Sunita S. Wanjare (A) on 12 Mar 2010

Maj David N. Pandav on 28 Mar 2010

Maj Sundar J. Bodhak on 23 Apr 2010

Maj Roshanbai D. Padale on 22 May 2010

Maj David Khoda on 28 Jun 2010

INDONESIA

Major Noersiati Wowor on 08 Jul 2009

Major Sri Maryati Ningsih White on 08 Sep 2009

Captain Anatje Poli on 21 Oct 2009

Brigadier Petrus Singkali on 22 Oct 2009

Major Kastuni Utniel on 05 Jan 2010

Brigadier Treesje Ngahu on 10 Mar 2010

ITALY

Maj Orsolina Carpagnano Bianzeno on 13 Feb 2010

JAPAN

Mrs Brig Misao Tarukawa on 24 Nov 2009

Maj Chiyoko Ogawa on 20 Apr 2010

KENYA EAST

Maj Eliakimu Kiduyu on 23 Sep 2009

Maj Philip Ikandi on 9 Dec 2009

KENYA WEST

Lt-Col Rose Ngongo on 22 June 2009

Maj Jason Malabi on 9 Sep 2009

Lt-Col Anna Makhanu on 30 Apr 2009

Maj Peter Wanangata on 26 Jan 2010

Maj Selina Were on 9 May 2010

Maj Rodah Onyango on 22 Apr 2010

KOREA

Maj Cho, In-sook on 17 Jan 2010

Maj Bae, Myong-ok (A) from Sosan on 28 Aug 2010

THE NETHERLANDS AND CZECH REPUBLIC

Maj Iet Staalman on 10 Jun 2009

Brig Johanna Bijleveld on 15 Jul 2009

Brig Riek Aulman on 10 Aug 2009

Maj Alie van Huizen on 21 Sep 2009

Maj Herman van de Wetering on 20 Oct 2009

Maj Christina Gelderman on 24 Oct 2009

Promotions to Glory

Maj Joop van Huizen on 24 Mar 2010
Maj Sjoerd Walma on 14 Jun 2010

NEW ZEALAND, FIJI AND TONGA
Capt Elva Ngaire Williams (A) from Wellington
  Community Ministries on 1 Nov 2009
Maj Margaret McEwen on 14 Feb 2010
Maj Norma Daly on 16 Feb 2010
Maj Richard Prattley on 27 Feb 2010
Maj Vera Watkins on 6 Mar 2010
Maj Olive Jackson on 20 Apr 2010

NIGERIA
Capt Mary Falaiye on 8 Nov 2009
Maj Esther Akpan on 9 Nov 2009
Capt John Ogunde on 7 Jan 2010
Capt Felix Adibeh on 9 Mar 2010
Maj Ayoade Ojo on 14 Jun 2010

NORWAY, ICELAND AND FÆROES
Comr Åse Marti on 9 Aug 2009
Lt-Col Per Raubakken on 15 Nov 2009
Maj Lilly Vevatne on 26 Dec 2009
Maj Alfa Willa on 23 Jan 2010
Lt-Col Alma Rosseland on 21 Mar 2010
Capt Magnhild Andresen on 30 Mar 2010
Maj Arne Bruun on 5 May 2010
Maj Marit Jakobsen on 11 May 2010
Brig Olaf Haug on 21 May 2010
Maj Anne Marie Reinholdtsen (A) from
  Iceland (RO) on 19 Jun 2010

PAKISTAN
Capt Parvaiz Israel (A) from Chak 650/1,
  Jaranwala on 9 Jan 2010
Maj Michael Samuel on 23 Apr 2010
Maj Nazir Taju on 03 May 2010

THE PHILIPPINES
Envoy Josefa Valenzuela (A) from Diffun
  on 19 Sep 2009

SOUTH AMERICA WEST
Maj Martha Magallanes (A) from THQ
  Santiago, Chile on 13 Jul 2009
Maj Mario González (A) from Neptuno,
  Santiago, Chile on 5 Oct 2009
Maj Elsa Carilaf de Salazar on 16 Sep 2009
Brig Sara Kranenburg on 24 Apr 2010

SOUTHERN AFRICA
Capt Alan Gardiner on 22 Jun 2009
Aux-Capt Stella Tucker on 17 Jul 2009
Env Phillip Myburgh on 26 Aug 2009
Brig Olive Campbell on Sep 09, 2009

Maj John Schultz on 24 Oct 2009
Maj Jerry Dlamini on 3 Dec 2009
Maj Zephaniah Mkhize on 18 Jan 2010
Maj Gastar Dlamini on 24 Feb 2010
Maj Sesane Mthombeni on 14 Mar 2010
Aux-Capt John Lang (A) from Thembela
  Eventide Home on 25 Feb 2010
Maj Philip Mvelase on 25 Apr 2010

SRI LANKA
Maj Melder on 18 Aug 2009
Maj Ananda Subasinghe on 22 Aug 2009
Maj T Yesudason on 25 Dec 2009

SWEDEN AND LATVIA
Brig Margit Backlund on 15 Oct 2009
Brig Judit Eklund on 20 Nov 2009
Maj Stig Holmberg on on 4 Dec 2009
Brig Gunborg Lingblom on 13 Dec 2009
Envoy Arvid Enesgård on Feb 2, 2010
Envoy Lili-Ann Lindgren Botvidsson
  on 16 Feb 2010
Capt Anna-Greta Bergebäck on 21 Feb 2010
Brig Gunvor Gustafsson on 27 Mar 2010
Maj Gun Lindström on 5 Apr 2010
Lt-Col Erik Ljungberg on 23 May 2010
Envoy Agnes Persson on 24 Jun 2010
Maj Göta Persson on 22 Aug 2010
Brig Edith Örtberg on 22 Aug 2010
Envoy Alf Wahlström on 27 Aug 2010

SWITZERLAND, AUSTRIA AND HUNGARY
Brig Berta Chevailler-Meier on 27 Jul 2009
Maj Wera Winkler on 16 Aug 2009
Maj Monique Zwahlen-Grobéty on
  28 Oct 2009
Lt-Col Monique Motte-Debouny on
  11 Oct 2009
Maj Paul Stäheli on 9 Nov 2009
Maj Margrit Allenbach on 9 Jan 2010
Maj Hans Rieder on 24 Jan 2010
Maj Ernst Willi Schmid on 24 Mar 2010
Maj Hermine Burger-Studer on 26 May 2010

TANZANIA
Maj Nasson Kituta on 26 Feb 2010

UNITED KINGDOM WITH THE REPUBLIC OF IRELAND
Capt Debra Green (A) from William Booth
  College on 6 Nov 2009
Col Keith Burridge (A) from Singapore, Malaysia
  and Myanmar THQ (TC) on 19 Apr 2009
Aux-Capt Ronald Eaton on 1 Sep 2009

Promotions to Glory

Maj Eric Bentley on 4 Sep 2009
Maj Jean Covey on 6 Sep 2009
Maj Howard Heins on 10 Sep 2009
Col William Clark on 17 Sep 2009
Maj Elizabeth Thorpe on 26 Sep 2009
Comr Caughey Gauntlett on 11 Oct 2009
Col Bramwell Baird on 19 Oct 2009
Brig Hilda Marsh on 23 Oct 2009
Maj Terry Jones on 4 Nov 2009
Maj Kathleen Dolling on 18 Nov 2009
Maj Vivienne Lawson on 24 Nov 2009
Maj Dorothy Rowney on 29 Nov 2009
Mrs Maj Grace Ward on 3 Dec 2009
Mrs Brig Patricia Williams on 3 Dec 2009
Mrs Brig Florence May Horwood on
   16 Dec 2009
Col Stanley Hunt on 29 Dec 2009
Mrs Lt-Col Ivy Sharman on 30 Dec 2009
Maj Robert Waite on 6 Jan 2010
Maj John Bell on 11 Jan 2010
Comr Peter Hawkins on 17 Jan 2010
Maj Elizabeth Jackson on 29 Jan 2010
Mrs Maj Grace Fish on 8 Feb 2010
Maj Margaret Jennings on 8 Feb 2010
Maj Patricia Bassett on 8 Feb 2010
Lt-Col Ray Bowes on 13 Feb 2010
Maj Fredrick Watters on 14 Feb 2010
Maj John Nicholson on 22 Feb2010
Aux-Capt Mary Cowan on 22 Feb 2010
Comr David Durman on 3 Mar 2010
Maj Jean Russell on 3 Mar 2010
Mrs Brig Margaret Moore on 6 Mar 2010
Maj Roy Dickinson on 14 Mar 2010
Lt-Col Ronald Grainger on
   23 Mar 2010
Maj Gordon Thomas on 23 Mar 2010
Mrs Lt-Col Agnes Knapman 26 Mar 2010
Maj Ivy Avis on 2 Apr 2010
Mrs Col Ruth Hunt on 5 Apr 2010
Maj Pauline Fowler on 10 Apr 2010
Mrs Lt-Col Enid Moore on 29 May 2010
Brig Winifred Garner on 7 Jun 2010
Col Phyllis Watts on 15 Jun 2010
Capt Norman Semans on 8 Jun 2010
Brig Doreen Johnstone on 19 Jun 2010
Mrs Maj Margaret Moore on 20 Jun 2010
Maj Muriel Skinner on 25 Jun 2010
Lt-Col George Oakley on 29 Jun 2010
Lt-Col Ruth Gulston on 7 Jul 2010
Maj Trevor Penfold on 9 Jul 2010
Mrs Lt-Col June Smith on 15 Jul 2010
Brig Ella Town on 21 Jul 2010
Maj Shirley Halse on 26 Jul 2010
Mrs Brig Marjorie Grant on 26 Jul 2010

USA CENTRAL

Maj Mary Christine Sonju on 10 Sep 2009
Mrs Maj Eva Coleman on 29 Sep 2009
Mrs Maj Marguerite Hultin on 29 Sep 2009
Mrs Capt Edith Mae Bennett on 19 Oct 2009
Maj John Cunard on 31 Oct 2009
Mrs Maj Rachel Phelps on 8 Nov 2009
Maj Herbert Caldwell on 26 Nov 2009
Mrs Brig Charlotte Quinn on 5 Dec2009
Maj Ruth Legg on 15 Dec 2009
Aux-Capt Mrs Prinzing on 27 Dec 2009
Maj Robert Wilkins on 9 Jan 2010
Mrs Maj Alma Spencer on 11 Feb 2010
Maj Janet Endres on 16 Feb 2010
Mrs Col Mary Miller on 18 Mar 2010
Maj George Watt on 4 Apr 2010
Maj Grace Stephison on 4 Apr 2010
Brig Joseph Vondracek on 7 May 2010
Brig Dorothy Britton on 14 Jun 2010
Mrs Brig Maxine Dye on 22 Jun 2010
Maj Eugene Adney on 4 Jul 2010

USA EASTERN

Maj Judith V. Himes on 24 Aug 2009
Mrs Brig Jessie Sipley on 2 Nov 2009
Mrs Brig Ruth Bittinger on 3 Nov 2009
Maj Ralph R. Leidy on 8 Nov 2009
Maj Theodore Thompson on 13 Nov 2009
Maj Edith A. Copeland on 7 Dec 2009
Maj Gerald Stephens on 17 Jan 2010
Lt-Col Donald Seiler on 11 Feb 2010
Maj Mrs Jean V. Bessant on 25 Feb 2010
Mrs Brig Charlotte R. Geddes on 28 Feb 2010
Maj Mrs Geraldine Knickerbocker on
   18 Mar 2010
Maj Marion L. Goodwin on 24 Mar 2010
Col Henry Gariepy (OF) on 3 Apr 2010
Lt-Col William A. Bamford Jr on 12 Apr 2010
Maj John Connors on 12 Apr 2010
Maj Rose Cedervall on 18 Apr 2010
Maj Mrs Helen Waldron on 23 Apr 2010
Mrs Brig Faith C. Harvey on 10 May 2010
Maj Clark A. Berkhoudt on 20 Jul 2010

USA SOUTHERN

Mrs Maj Mildred Wynn on Sep 2009
Brig Arthur Wesley Ward on 16 Sep 2009
Maj Howard Costner on 1 Oct 2009
Maj Fredrick Russell Smith on 6 Oct 2009
Maj Robert Gordon Butler on 25 Nov 2009
Maj James Trinity Sills (A) from Lubbock, TX
   on 4 Nov 2009
Maj James Richard Worthy on 27 Nov 2009
Maj Dorothy Riggs on 5 December 2009
Brig Lillian Blackburn on 17 Dec 2009

Maj Philip Wise (A) from North Little Rock, AR on 24 Dec 2009

Maj Teresa Tanner (A) from Grayson, GA on 14 Feb 2010

Maj Kenneth Bush on 20 Feb 2010

Maj Carolyn Hudson on 6 Mar 2010

Capt Joe Anderson (A) from Lawrenceville, GA on 13 Mar 2010

Lt-Col Alvin Loy Frierson on 24 Mar 2010

Mrs Brig Kathryn Cranford on Mar 2010

Maj Laura Newsham on 18 Apr 2010

Capt Henry Houston (A) from San Antonio, TX on 10, May 2010

USA WESTERN

Mrs Maj Marian Hanson on 6 Sep 2009

Maj Patricia Jolley on 10 Sep 2009

Mrs Brig Margaret Laverty on 10 Sep 2009

Maj Leticia Saunders (A) from Kauluwela Mission, HI on 14 Dec 2009

Maj Manuela Garza on 17 Dec 2009

Brig Ben Nunes on 17 Dec 2009

Maj Faith Davis on 18 Jan 2010

Lt-Col Luetta Pedersen on 2 Feb 2010

Maj Sheila Bradley (A) from Los Angeles, CA on 10 Mar 2010

Capt Vicki Jackson (A) from Juneau, AK on 25 Jun 2010

Lt-Col Alice Smith on 27 Jun 2010

Lt-Col Rhode Danielson (A) from Phoenix, AZ on 23 Jul 2010

Lt-Col Le Roy Pedersen on 6 Aug 2010

ZAMBIA

Maj David Muleya (A) from Ndola, Copperbelt District on 11 Oct 2009

Maj Last Siamoya (A) from Chiweshe Division (DC) Zimbabwe on 23 Jan 2010

Maj Opper Cheelo (A) from Chikankata Corps and Nurses' Training School on 9 May 2010.

ZIMBABWE

Maj Juliet Mangava on 31 Aug 2009

Maj Samson Munjeri on 26 Sep 2009

Brig Amos Mazindu on 8 Feb 2010

Maj Mary Nyandoro on 14 Aug 2010

PROMOTED TO GLORY

THERE are many descriptions to soften the harshness of the word 'death' but one of the most radical is the Army's descriptive phrase, 'promoted to Glory'. It sounds a triumphant, positive note in support of the Army's belief in eternal life, Heaven and an unending period in Glory with the Father. It declares incontrovertibly that death is not the end, but the beginning of a new and glorious experience for those redeemed by the blood of Jesus Christ.

The term was first used in *The War Cry* of 14 December 1882, at a time when so many other military phrases were being introduced following the advent of the name 'The Salvation Army' four years earlier. It seems to have found ready acceptance and soon entered common usage.

It was also consistent with the Founder's dislike of sombre black clothing as a sign of mourning. He believed that, while Christ sympathises with sorrow, he desires to make personal tragedy a stepping stone to greater faith by seeing death as a victory.

Abbreviations used in *The Year Book*

A

(A) (active officer pG); Acc (Accommodation); Adj (Adjutatnt); Afr (Africa); Am (America); Ang (Angola); AO (Area Officer); Apt (Apartment); Appt (Appointment); ARC (Adult Rehabilitation Centre); Asst (Assistant); Aus (Australia); A/Capt, Aux-Capt (Auxiliary-Captain).

B

b (born); Ban (Bangladesh); Belg (Belgium); B/M (Bandmaster); Braz (Brazzaville); Brig (Brigadier); Brz (Brazil); BT (British Territory).

C

Can (Canada and Bermuda); Capt (Captain); Carib (Caribbean); CIDA (Canadian International Development Agency); CO (Commanding Officer); Col (Colonel); Comr (Commissioner); Con (Congo); CoS (Chief of the Staff); CS (Chief Secretary); C/S (Corps Secretary); CSLD (Centre for Spiritual Life Development); CSM (Corps Sergeant-Major); C/T (Corps Treasurer); CWMO (Command Women's Ministries Officer); Cze R (Czech Republic).

D

DC (Divisional Commander); Den (Denmark); Dis O (District Officer); DO (Divisional Officer); DR Con (Democratic Republic of Congo).

E

E Afr (East Africa); E Eur (Eastern Europe); Ens (Ensign); Env (Envoy); ESFOT (European School for Officers' Training).

F

Fin (Finland and Estonia); Frce (France and Belgium).

G

Ger (Germany and Lithuania); Gha (Ghana); GS (General Secretary).

H

HK (Hong Kong and Macau); HL (Home League); Hun (Hungary).

I

ICO (International College for Officers); IES (International Emergency Services); IHQ (International Headquarters); IHS (International Health Services); Ind C, E, etc (India Central, Eastern, etc); Ind M&A (India Madras and Andhra); Indon (Indonesia); Internl (International); IPDS (International Projects and Development Services); IS (International Secretary); It (Italy); ITC (International Training College).

J

JHLS (Junior Home League Secretary); Jpn (Japan).

K

Ken (Kenya); Kin (Kinshasa); Kor (Korea).

L

L Am N (Latin America North); Lat (Latvia); Lib (Liberia); Lt, Lieut (Lieutenant); Lt-Col, Lieut-Colonel (Lieutenant-Colonel); LOM (League of Mercy).

M

m (married); Maj (Major); Mal (Malawi); Mlys (Malaysia); Mol (Moldova); Moz (Mozambique); My (Myanmar).

N

Nat (National); NC (National Commander); Neth (The Netherlands and Czech Republic); NHQ (National Headquarters); Nor (Norway, Iceland and The Færoes); NZ (New Zealand, Fiji and Tonga).

O

OC (Officer Commanding); ODAS (Order of Distinguished Auxiliary Service); OF (Order of the Founder); O&R (Orders and Regulations).

P

Pak (Pakistan); pG (promoted to Glory); Phil (The Philippines); PINS (Persons in need of supervision); PNG (Papua New Guinea); Port (Portugal); PO (Provincial Officer); Pres (President); PRD (Public Relations Department); PS (Private Secretary).

R

RC (Regional Commander); RDWM (Regional Director of Women's Ministries); ret (retired); RO (Regional Officer); ROS (Retired Officers Secretary); RPWM (Regional President of Women's Ministries); Rtd (Retired); Rus (Russia/CIS); Rwa (Rwanda and Burundi).

S

S/, Snr (Senior); SAAS (Salvation Army

Assurance Society); SABAC (Salvation Army Boys' Adventure Corps); S Afr (Southern Africa); SALT (Salvation Army Leadership Training); S Am E (South America East); SAMF (Salvation Army Medical Fellowship); S Am W (South America West); SAWSO (Salvation Army World Service Office); Scot (Scotland); Sec (Secretary); Sen (Senior); SFOT (School for Officers' Training); Sgt (Sergeant); Sing (Singapore, Malaysia and Myanmar); S/L (Songster Leader); Soc S (Social Services); Sp (Spain); SP&S (Salvationist Publishing and Supplies); Sri Lan (Sri Lanka); Supt (Superintendent); Swdn (Sweden and Latvia); Switz (Switzerland, Austria and Hungary).

T

Tai (Taiwan); Tanz (Tanzania); tba (to be appointed); TC (Territorial Commander); tel (telephone); TCCMS (Territorial Community Care Ministries Secretary); THQ (Territorial Headquarters); TLWM, TPWM, TSWM (Territorial Leader of, President of, Secretary for Women's Ministries); TPWO, TSWO (Territorial President of, Secretary for Women's Ministries); TWMS (Territorial Women's Ministries Secretary).

U

Uga (Uganda); UK (United Kingdom); Uk (Ukraine); USA (United States of America); USA Nat, USA C, etc (USA National, Central, etc).

W

WI (West Indies); WPWM WSWM (World President of, Secretary for Women's Ministries); Ww (Widow).

Z

Zai (Zaïre); Zam (Zambia); Zimb (Zimbabwe).

International Direct Dialling

Telephone country codes to territorial and command headquarters are listed below

In *The Year Book* the international prefix, which varies from country to country, is indicated by [square brackets]. Local codes are indicated by (round brackets)

Angola	[244]	Hong Kong	[852]	Pakistan	[92]
Argentina	[54]	India	[91]	Papua New Guinea	[675]
Australia	[61]	Indonesia	[62]	Philippines (The)	[63]
		Italy	[39]	Portugal	[351]
Bangladesh	[880]				
Belgium	[32]	Jamaica	[1876]	Russia	[7]
Brazil	[55]	Japan	[81]	Rwanda	[250]
				Singapore	[65]
Canada	[1]	Kenya	[254]	South Africa	[27]
Chile	[56]	Korea	[82]	Spain	[34]
Congo (Democratic				Sri Lanka	[94]
Republic)	[243]			Sweden	[46]
Congo (Republic)	[242]	Liberia	[231]	Switzerland	[41]
Costa Rica	[506]				
		Mexico	[525]	Taiwan	[886]
Denmark	[45]	Malawi	[265]	Tanzania	[255]
		Mozambique	[258]		
Finland	[358]			United Kingdom	[44]
France	[33]	Netherlands (The)	[31]	USA	[1]
		New Zealand	[64]		
Germany	[49]	Nigeria	[234]	Zambia	[260]
Ghana	[233]	Norway	[47]	Zimbabwe	[263]

INDEX

Index

Index

Index

Index

Index

NOTES

NOTES

TERRITORIES (T), COMMANDS (C) AND REGIONS (R) WITHIN EACH ZONE

AFRICA
Angola (C)
Congo (Brazzaville) (T)
Democratic Republic of Congo (T)
Ghana (T)
Kenya East (T)
Kenya West (T)
Liberia (C)
Malawi (C)
Mozambique (C)
Nigeria (T)
Rwanda and Burundi (C)
Southern Africa (T)
Tanzania (T)
Uganda (C)
Zambia (T)
Zimbabwe (T)

AMERICAS AND CARIBBEAN
Brazil (T)
Canada and Bermuda (T)
Caribbean (T)
Latin America North (T)
Mexico (T)
South America East (T)
South America West (T)
USA Central (T)
USA Eastern (T)
USA Southern (T)
USA Western (T)

EUROPE
Denmark (T)
Eastern Europe (T)
Finland and Estonia (T)
France and Belgium (T)
Germany and Lithuania (T)
Italy (C)
The Netherlands and Czech
    Republic (T)
Norway, Iceland and The Færoes (T)
Portugal (C)
Spain (C)
Sweden and Latvia (T)
Switzerland, Austria and Hungary (T)
United Kingdom with the Republic
    of Ireland (T)

SOUTH ASIA
Bangladesh (C)
India Central (T)
India Eastern (T)
India Northern (T)
India South Eastern (T)
India South Western (T)
India Western (T)
Pakistan (T)
Sri Lanka (T)

SOUTH PACIFIC AND EAST ASIA
Australia Eastern (T)
Australia Southern (T)
Hong Kong and Macau (C)
Indonesia (T)
Japan (T)
Korea (T)
New Zealand, Fiji and Tonga (T)
Papua New Guinea (T)
The Philippines (T)
Singapore, Malaysia and
    Myanmar (T)
Taiwan (R)